REMEDIES

PUBLIC AND PRIVATE

Sixth Edition

■ ■ ■

Tracy A. Thomas
Seiberling Chair of Constitutional Law
The University of Akron School of Law

David I. Levine
Hon. Raymond L. Sullivan Professor of Law
University of California
Hastings College of the Law

David J. Jung
Hon. Raymond L. Sullivan Professor of Law
University of California
Hastings College of the Law

AMERICAN CASEBOOK SERIES®

For David Schoenbrod and Angus Macbeth, who started it all,

and

For my Remedies students (T.A.T.)

For Arie, Carlo, Liora, Mira and Shoshana (D.I.L.)

For Grady and Brennan (D.J.J.)

PREFACE TO THE SIXTH EDITION

This sixth edition of *Remedies: Public and Private* brings with it new changes in editorship. After fifteen years at the helm, David Levine steps down as lead editor on the book. His work was instrumental in continuing the legacy of this book, and he brought his expertise in integrating the remedial rules of civil procedure. David Jung also takes this time of change to sign off after his years of work focused on damages and restitution. David and David were welcoming in taking on a new junior scholar and providing mentoring in both the substance of the field and the art of casebook authorship.

This book has benefitted much from the work and insights of the editors who started it all, David Schoenbrod and Angus Macbeth. They originated the book with their own teaching materials over thirty years ago to offer a more comprehensive way of thinking about Remedies. The goals of the first edition were to cover all the essential topics of remedies law, including many omitted by traditional case books, organize the material in a coherent transsubstantive way, offer interest and intellectual stimulation beyond the blackletter rules, and teach well by attention to pedagogy. These authors helped distinguish this book from the start, emphasizing that the field of Remedies is not confined to private law, but extends equally into public law. Indeed, as they showed, some of the most advanced thinking about the rules and measures of remedies comes from public law cases.

This sixth edition of the casebook continues that tradition, as we remain convinced that studying the way remedies operate in the public law as well as the private law contexts is critical to a full understanding of the subject. *See* David I. Levine, *Thoughts on Teaching Remedies from A Public Law Perspective*, 39 Brandeis L.J. 557 (2001). The book continues its approach of looking at remedies transsubstantively, appreciating the common core principles that transcend subject matter or cause of action. It updates the cases, particularly those coming from the Supreme Court of the United States. The Teacher's Manual offers a problem-based approach for those who want to partner the doctrinal cases with problem-based learning and formative assessment. We thank all those who contributed ideas and support for this updated edition, including our students and attorney Robert Lehrer.

TAT
DIL
DJJ

September 2016

v

ACKNOWLEDGMENTS

The authors wish to acknowledge the following permissions to reprint copyrighted material:

Abram Chayes, *The Role of the Judge in Public Law Litigation*, 82 Harv.L.Rev. 1281 (1976). Copyright 1976 by the Harvard Law Review Association.

Charles J. Goetz and Robert E. Scott, *Measuring Sellers' Damages: The Lost Profits Puzzle*, 31 Stanford L.Rev. 323 (1979). Copyright 1979 by the Board of Trustees for the Leland Stanford Junior University.

Murray Levine, Charles P. Ewing & David I. Levine, *The Use of Law for Prevention in the Public Interest*, 5 Prevention in Human Services 241 (1987) published by The Haworth Press, Inc., 10 Alice Street, Binghamton, N.Y. 13904.

Michael Lottman, *Enforcement of Judicial Decrees: Now Comes the Hard Part*, 1 Mental Disability Law Reporter 69 (1976).

David Schoenbrod, *The Measure of an Injunction: A Principle to Replace Balancing the Equities and Tailoring the Remedy*, 72 Minn. L.Rev. 627 (1988).

Peter H. Schuck, *The Role of Judges in Settling Complex Cases: The Agent Orange Example*, 53 Univ.Chicago L.Rev 341 (1986). Reprinted by permission of the University of Chicago Law Review.

Restatement of the Law, 2d, Contracts, Copyright 1981 by the American Law Institute; Restatement (Third) of Restitution, Copyright 2011 by the American Law Institute; Restatement of the Law, 2d, Torts, Copyright 1979 by the American Law Institute. All rights reserved. Reprinted with the permission of The American Law Institute.

Special Project—The Remedial Process in Institutional Reform Litigation, 78 Colum.L.Rev. 784 (1978). Copyright 1978 by the Directors of the Columbia Law Review Association, Inc. All Rights Reserved. Reprinted by permission.

SUMMARY OF CONTENTS

PREFACE TO THE SIXTH EDITION.. V

ACKNOWLEDGMENTS VII

TABLE OF CASES XVII

Chapter 1. Introduction to the Law of Remedies 1
A.   A General Approach to Crafting a Remedy 2
B.   Private Law and Public Law 4
C.   "Where There's a Right, There's a Remedy"? 9

Chapter 2. Injunctions 27
A.   The Nature of an Injunction 27
B.   The Plaintiff's Rightful Position as the Measure of an Injunction 33
C.   The Prerequisites for Injunctive Relief 61
D.   Balancing the Equities 79
E.   Specific Performance 128

Chapter 3. Administering and Enforcing the Injunction 141
A.   Obtaining Preliminary Injunctive Relief 141
B.   Formulating and Monitoring the Injunction 170
C.   Modifying and Terminating the Injunction 195
D.   Enforcement of the Decree 233

Chapter 4. Declaratory Judgment 293
A.   The Actual Controversy Requirement 295
B.   Appropriate Discretion 306

Chapter 5. Damages 315
A.   Introduction 315
B.   Elements of Loss 331
C.   Measuring Value 352
D.   Tort Damages 369
E.   Contract Damages 421
F.   Adjustments to the Damage Award 442
G.   Collecting Money Judgments 459

Chapter 6. Punitive Damages 463
A.   The Purpose of Punitive Damages 463
B.   Punitive Damages at Common Law 466
C.   Constitutional Limitations on Punitive Damages 496

Chapter 7. Restitution 517
A.   Introduction 517

B. Liability for Restitution 522
C. Restitution Remedies 539

Chapter 8. Remedial Defenses: Conduct of the Plaintiff 585
A. An Overview of Defenses 586
B. Unclean Hands 588
C. Laches 591
D. Estoppel 595

Chapter 9. Attorney's Fees 605
A. The American Rule 605
B. Fee-Shifting Statutes 610
C. Measuring Fees 617

Appendix: Country Lodge v. Miller 627

INDEX... 637

TABLE OF CONTENTS

PREFACE TO THE SIXTH EDITION V

ACKNOWLEDGMENTS VII

TABLE OF CASES XVII

Chapter 1. Introduction to the Law of Remedies 1
A.   A General Approach to Crafting a Remedy 2
B.   Private Law and Public Law 4
     Abram Chayes, The Role of the Judge in Public Law Litigation 4
     Notes 7
C.   "Where There's a Right, There's a Remedy"? 9
     Bivens v. Six Unknown Named Agents of Federal Bureau of
          Narcotics 13
     Notes 19

Chapter 2. Injunctions 27
A.   The Nature of an Injunction 27
     Hecht Co. v. Bowles 28
     Note 32
B.   The Plaintiff's Rightful Position as the Measure of an Injunction 33
     Mt. Healthy City School District Board of Education v. Doyle 34
     Notes 37
     Note on Rightful Position as Reconsideration or Remand in
          Administrative Law 38
     Problem: Repairing Election Wrongs 40
     Rizzo v. Goode 41
     Notes 47
     Brown v. Plata 48
     Notes 59
     Note on the Microsoft Antitrust Litigation 60
C.   The Prerequisites for Injunctive Relief 61
     1.   Threat of Harm 62
          City of Los Angeles v. Lyons 63
          Notes 69
     2.   Inadequate Remedy at Law 71
          eBay Inc. v. MercExchange, L.L.C. 73
          Notes 77
D.   Balancing the Equities 79
     1.   The Defendant's Undue Hardship: Granting Less than Plaintiff's
          Rightful Position 79
          Smith v. Staso Milling Co. 79
          Notes 82

Note on When Injunctions are Efficient..83
Brown v. Board of Education (*Brown II*) 85
Notes...87
Note on the Practicality of Enforcement...89
Tennessee Valley Authority v. Hill 90
Notes...95
David Schoenbrod, The Measure of an Injunction: A Principle to
    Replace Balancing the Equities and Tailoring the Remedy 96
  2. Prophylaxis: Granting More Than Plaintiff's Rightful Position......97
Madsen v. Women's Health Center, Inc..100
Notes...107
Swann v. Charlotte-Mecklenburg Board of Education 109
Notes...114
Missouri v. Jenkins (*Jenkins III*) 115
Notes...126
E. Specific Performance..128
i.Lan Systems, Inc. v. Netscout Service Level Corp...........................129
Walgreen Co. v. Sara Creek Property Co. 133
Notes 139
Note on Other Remedies 139

Chapter 3. Administering and Enforcing the Injunction 141
A. Obtaining Preliminary Injunctive Relief...141
  1. Procedural Distinctions...141
  2. Standards for Granting Preliminary Relief...............................146
Winter v. Natural Resources Defense Council 147
Notes...159
Occupy Tucson v. City of Tucson..161
Problem: Unauthorized Merchants..164
American Hospital Supply Corp. v. Hospital Products Ltd. 165
Notes...167
Problem 169
B. Formulating and Monitoring the Injunction 170
  1. Drafting the Injunction 170
Portland Feminist Women's Health Center v. Advocates for Life,
    Inc. 170
Notes...172
  2. Implementing the Injunction...175
Special Project—The Remedial Process in Institutional Reform
    Litigation...176
Notes...179
Floyd v. City of New York 180
Note 187
Murray Levine, Charles P. Ewing & David I. Levine, The Use of
    Law for Prevention in the Public Interest 187
Notes...192

Michael S. Lottman, Enforcing Judicial Decrees: Now Comes the
Hard Part 193
C. Modifying and Terminating the Injunction 195
Rufo v. Inmates of Suffolk County Jail 197
Notes 207
Board of Education of Oklahoma City Public Schools v. Dowell 209
Notes 215
Horne v. Flores 217
Notes 228
Note on Modification by Political Successors 229
Note on Legislative Termination and the Prison Litigation Reform
Act 231
D. Enforcement of the Decree 233
1. The Contempt Power 234
Hicks on Behalf of Feiock v. Feiock 235
Notes on In Personam Versus In Rem Enforcement 242
Notes on the Classification of Contempt Proceedings 242
United Mine Workers v. Bagwell 244
Notes 255
Notes on Procedures 258
2. The Collateral Bar Rule 259
In re Providence Journal Co. 259
Notes on the Collateral Bar Rule 266
3. Enforcement Against the Government 269
United States v. City of Yonkers 273
Spallone v. United States 282
Notes 290

Chapter 4. Declaratory Judgment **293**
A. The Actual Controversy Requirement 295
Medimmune, Inc. v. Genentech, Inc. 295
Notes 302
B. Appropriate Discretion 306
Morrison v. Parker 306
Notes 312

Chapter 5. Damages **315**
A. Introduction 315
Charles McCormick, Handbook on the Law of Damages 316
Memphis Community School District v. Stachura 317
Notes 323
Note on Nominal Damages 325
Note on Monetary Relief in Law and Equity 326
Note on the Right to a Jury Trial 329
Note on Election of Remedies 330
B. Elements of Loss 331
Evra Corp. v. Swiss Bank Corp. 335

Notes 342
Dillon v. Evanston Hospital... 342
Note 345
Munn v. Southern Health Plan, Inc. 346
Note 352
C. Measuring Value 352
Barking Hound Village, LLC. v. Monyak 353
Notes 357
Ohio v. Department of the Interior 358
Notes 368
D. Tort Damages 369
1. Elements of Loss... 370
Ayers v. Jackson Township... 370
Notes.. 383
Thorn v. Mercy Memorial Hospital Corp. 386
Notes.. 393
2. Measuring Tort Damages 395
Tullis v. Townley Engineering & Manufacturing Co. 396
Notes.. 399
Arpin v. United States 401
Notes.. 403
Note on Tort Reform and Limitation of Damages 406
Walker v. Ritchie... 407
Notes.. 411
3. Alternative Compensation Systems 414
Peter H. Schuck, The Role of Judges in Settling Complex Cases:
The Agent Orange Example....................................... 415
The 9/11 Victims Compensation Fund 419
E. Contract Damages.. 421
Great American Music Machine, Inc. v. Mid-South Record Pressing
Co... 424
Notes 431
Charles J. Goetz & Robert E. Scott, Measuring Sellers' Damages:
The Lost Profits Puzzle 432
Garden Ridge v. Advance International 433
Note 441
F. Adjustments to the Damage Award 442
1. Prejudgment Interest 442
Kansas v. Colorado 442
Notes.. 448
2. Discounting to Present Value 450
Jones & Laughlin Steel Corporation v. Pfeifer.......... 450
Notes.. 457
Note on Taxation of Damage Awards............................. 458
G. Collecting Money Judgments 459

Chapter 6. Punitive Damages **463**
A. The Purpose of Punitive Damages 463
B. Punitive Damages at Common Law 466
  Grimshaw v. Ford Motor Co. 468
  Notes 477
  Exxon Shipping Co. v. Baker 478
  Notes 492
  Notes on Tort Reform 493
  Note on Economics and Deterrence 495
C. Constitutional Limitations on Punitive Damages 496
  State Farm Mutual Automobile Insurance Co. v. Campbell 497
  Notes 507
  Mathias v. Accor Economy Lodging, Inc. 510
  Notes 515

Chapter 7. Restitution **517**
A. Introduction 517
  Restatement (Third) of Restitution (2011) 518
B. Liability for Restitution 522
  Lewis v. Lewis 522
  Olwell v. Nye & Nissen 533
  Notes 536
C. Restitution Remedies 539
  Montanile v. Board of Trustees of the National Elevator Industry
    Health Benefit Plan 540
  Notes 548
  1. Contract Alternatives 548
    Hutchison v. Pyburn 549
    Notes 551
    EarthInfo, Inc. v. Hydrosphere Resource Consultants, Inc. 553
    Notes 559
  2. Equitable Restitution 561
    Snepp v. United States 563
    Notes 568
    Torres v. Eastlick (In re North American Coin & Currency,
      Ltd.) 570
    Notes 572
    Problem: Moore v. Regents of the University of California 573
  3. Tracing 574
    The Corporation of the President of the Church of Jesus Christ
      of Latter-Day Saints v. Jolley 574
    Note 576
    In re Mushroom Transportation Co. 577
    Notes 582
    A Tracing Problem 584

Chapter 8. Remedial Defenses: Conduct of the Plaintiff............**585**
A. An Overview of Defenses 586
B. Unclean Hands 588
   McKennon v. Nashville Banner Publishing Co. 588
   Note 591
C. Laches 591
   Pro-Football, Inc. v. Harjo 591
   Note 595
D. Estoppel 595
   Petrella v. Metro-Goldwyn-Mayer, Inc. 595
   Note 603

Chapter 9. Attorney's Fees **605**
A. The American Rule... 605
   Boeing Co. v. Van Gemert.. 608
B. Fee-Shifting Statutes 610
   Fogerty v. Fantasy, Inc. 612
   Notes 616
C. Measuring Fees 617
   Perdue v. Kenny A... 617
   Notes 624

Appendix: Country Lodge v. Miller.....................................**627**

INDEX.. 637

TABLE OF CASES

The principal cases are in bold type.

A&M Records, Inc. v. Napster, Inc., 146
A.O. Smith Corp. v. F.T.C., 306
A.V. by Versace, Inc. v. Gianni Versace S.p.A., 256
Abbott Laboratories v. Gardner, 298, 306
Abbott v. Burke, 40
Acuff v. Vinsant, 428
Aetna Life Ins. Co. v. Haworth, 297, 303, 312
African-American Slave Descendants Litigation, In re, 519
Agency Holding Corp. v. Malley-Duff & Associates, Inc., 465
Agent Orange Litigation, In re, 419
Agostini v. Felton, 208, 219
Alcorn County, Mississippi v. U.S. Interstate Supplies, Inc., 552
Alemite Mfg. Corp. v. Staff, 145
Alexander v. Riga, 326
Alexander v. Sandoval, 23
Alexander v. Scheid, 346
Alexis Lichine & Cie. v. Sacha A. Lichine Estate Selections, Ltd., 209
All Funds, United States v., 584
Alliance for the Wild Rockies v. Cottrell, 163
Altvater v. Freeman, 299
Alyeska Pipeline Service Co. v. Wilderness Society, 607, 615
American Airlines, Inc. v. Allied Pilots Association, 256
American Hospital Supply Corp. v. Hospital Products Ltd., 165
American Soc. of Mechanical Engineers, Inc. v. Hydrolevel Corp., 464
American States Insurance Co. v. Bailey, 304, 312
American Tobacco Co., United States v., 180
Amoco Production Co. v. Gambell, 74, 151, 156, 158
Anderson v. Dunn, 257
Anzalone v. Kragness, 357
Arbino v. Johnson & Johnson, 495
Arcambel v. Wiseman, 606
Arlington Central School District Board of Education v. Murphy, 625

Armour & Co., United States v., 196, 203
Armstrong v. Exceptional Child Center, 24
Arpin v. United States, 401
Avitia v. Metropolitan Club of Chicago, Inc., 397
Ayers v. Jackson Township, 370
Bajakajian, United States v., 465
Baker v. Carr, 65, 69
Baker v. General Motors Corp., 90
Baker v. Riverside Church of God, 430
Baker v. State, 273
Banco Cafetero Panama, United States v., 584
Bank of Alex Brown v. Goldberg, 584
Banks, Commissioner v., 458
Barking Hound Village, LLC. v. Monyak, 353
BASF Corp. v. Symington, 310, 312
Bateman Eichler, Hill Richards, Inc. v. Berner, 586, 591
Bayer CropScience LP v. Schafer, 495
Beacon Theatres, Inc. v. Westover, 295
Beatty v. Guggenheim Exploration Co., 562
Belk v. Charlotte-Mecklenburg Board of Education, 114
Bell v. Hood, 13
Bell v. Southwell, 40
Bell v. Wolfish, 199, 202
Bellevue Manor Assoc. v. United States, 209
Benjamin v. Malcolm, 229, 292
Bertero v. National General Corp., 405
Bivens v. Six Unknown Named Agents of Federal Bureau of Narcotics, 13
Blackhorse v. Pro-Football, Inc., 595
Blanchard v. Bergeron, 625
Bloom v. Illinois, 246
Blum v. Stenson, 620, 624
BMW of North America, Inc. v. Gore, 484, 498, 506, 507
Board of Education of Oklahoma City Public Schools v. Dowell, 209
Boeing Co. v. Van Gemert, 608
Boomer v. Atlantic Cement Co., 137
Boomer v. Muir, 560

Bounds v. Smith, 60

Bowen v. Massachusetts, 242

Brabson v. United States, 459

Bradley, In re, 246

Brandau v. Kansas, 326

Bravado Int'l Group Merchand. Servs. Inc. v. Smith, 164

Bray v. Safeway Stores, 89

Bridgestone/Firestone Research, Inc. v. Automobile Club, 594

Brockum International v. Various John Does, 164

Brown v. Board of Education, 87, 200, 204

Brown v. Board of Education (Brown II), 85

Brown v. Plata, 48, 59

Brown v. Unified School District No. 501, 87, 89

Browning-Ferris Industries of Vermont, Inc. v. Kelco Disposal, Inc., 465, 486

Brunswick Corp. v. Jones, 168

Brunswick Corp. v. Pueblo Bowl-O-Mat, Inc., 464

Bryant, People v., 268

Building and Constr. Trades Council v. National Labor Relations Board, 209

Burgess v. Shampooch Pet Industries, Inc., 357

Burlington, City of v. Dague, 625

Bush v. Gore, 41

Bush v. Lucas, 20

Bussell v. DeWalt Products Corp., 459

Cabletron Systems Securities Litigation, In re, 626

Cadell v. Palmer, 487

California Insurance Guarantee Association v. Superior Court, 304

Calva-Cerqueira v. United States, 458

Campbell v. State Farm Mutual Automobile Insurance Co., 507

Capacchione v. Charlotte-Mecklenburg Schools, 114

Carlson v. Green, 20

Caron v. United States, 412

Carr v. Carr, 572

Carroll Towing Co., United States v., 165, 166

Carroll v. President & Commissioners of Princess Anne, 143, 146

Castle Rock, Town of v. Gonzales, 271

Catanzano v. Dowling, 71

Cavel International, Inc. v. Madigan, 168

Cayuga Indian Nation of New York v. Pataki, 448

Center for Food Safety v. Vilsack, 79

Central Railroad & Banking Co. v. Pettus, 609

Chadwick v. Hill, 257

Chambers v. NASCO, Inc., 607

Chandler v. Roudebush, 40

Chappell v. Wallace, 20

Chauffeurs, Teamsters and Helpers, Local No. 391 v. Terry, 28, 329

Cheff v. Schnackenberg, 258

Chesapeake & Ohio R. Co. v. Kelly, 452

Chevron U.S.A., Inc. v. Natural Resources Defense Council, Inc., 359, 364

Chirco v. Crosswinds Communities, Inc., 601, 602

Choctaw Maid Farms, Inc. v. Hailey, 394

Christiansburg Garment Co. v. EEOC, 611, 613

CIGNA Corp. v. Amara, 539

Cisarik v. Palos Community Hospital, 399

Citizens Federal Bank v. Cardian Mortgage Corp., 572

Clark v. Community for Creative Non-Violence, 163

Clausen v. Icicle Seafoods, Inc., 493

CNN, Inc., United States v., 269

Cobbledick v. United States, 262

Cobell v. Norton, 193

Codispoti v. Pennsylvania, 258

Coffin v. Coffin, 284

Coho Resources v. McCarthy, 449

Colorado River Water Conservation District v. United States, 313

Columbus Bd. of Education v. Penick, 289

Commodity Futures Trading Commission v. Frankwell Bullion Ltd., 180

Condemarin v. University Hospital, 407

Connecticut v. Doehr, 461

Consumer Advisory Board v. Glover, 193

Consumer Advisory Board v. Harvey, 193

Continental Paper Bag Co. v. Eastern Paper Bag Co., 75

Cook County v. United States ex rel. Chandler, 464

Cooke v. United States, 246

Cooper Industries, Inc. v. Leatherman Tool Group, Inc., 481, 499, 509

Cooper v. Aaron, 289

Correctional Services Corp. v. Malesko, 21

Cort v. Ash, 22

Cortez v. Trans Union, LLC, 509
Cowan v. Bolivar County Bd. of Educ., 87
Crawford Fitting Co. v. J.T. Gibbons, Inc., 625
Cunningham Bros., Inc. v. Bail, 309
Dahlstrom Metallic Door Co. v. Evatt Constr. Co., 132
Dardinger v. Anthem Blue Cross & Blue Shield, 494
Davis v. Hearst, 471
Davis v. Passman, 20, 22
Delaney v. Cade, 346
Denoyer v. Lamb, 362
Dickinson, United States v., 264
Diet Drugs, In re, 626
Dillon v. Evanston Hospital, 342
Dimick v. Schiedt, 396, 509
Doctor's Associates, Inc. v. Reinert & Duree, P.C., 145
Doe v. Dunbar, 305
Dowell v. Board of Education of Oklahoma City Public Schools, 215
Duffy v. Longo, 290
Dunn v. HOVIC, 468
Dupuy v. Samuels, 173
Duran v. Elrod, 201
Dyer, In re, 258
E.R. Squibb & Sons, Inc. v. Lloyd's & Cos., 304
EarthInfo, Inc. v. Hydrosphere Resource Consultants, Inc., 553
Eastman Kodak Co., United States v., 208
eBay Inc. v. MercExchange, L.L.C., 73
Edelman v. Jordan, 272
Eden Electrical, Ltd. v. Amana Co., 515
Engle v. Liggett Group, Inc., 508
Epperson v. Arkansas, 305
Epping v. Commonwealth Edison Co., 405
Epstein v. Gluckin, 129
Estevez v. United States, 459
Evans v. City of Chicago, 229
Evans v. State, 495
Evans v. Williams, 208, 256, 268
Evergreen Amusement Corp. v. Milstead, 431
Evers v. Dollinger, 381
Evra Corp. v. Swiss Bank Corp., 335
Exxon Shipping Co. v. Baker, 478
Exxon Valdez, In re, 492
F.J. Hanshaw Enterprises, Inc. v. Emerald River Development, Inc., 256
Farrar v. Hobby, 325, 626

Federated Department Stores, Inc. v. Moitie, 195
Feiock, In re, 243
Feltner v. Columbia Pictures Television, Inc., 329
Ferdon ex rel. Petrucelli v. Wisconsin Patients Compensation Fund, 406, 407
Ferguson v. United States, 21
Fischbach & Moore v. Philadelphia Nat. Bank, 580
Fitzgerald v. Barnstable School Committee, 24
Fleischmann Distilling Corp. v. Maier Brewing Co., 606
Fleming v. County of Kane, 397
Flight Attendants v. Zipes, 613, 615
Floyd v. City of New York, 180
Fogerty v. Fantasy, Inc., 612
Fordice, United States v., 88
Fox Film Corp. v. Doyal, 75
Fox v. Vice, 626
Frazar v. Ladd, 230
Freeman v. Pitts, 215
Frew v. Hawkins, 221, 230, 272
Friends for All Children v. Lockheed Aircraft Corp., 378
Frisby v. Schultz, 103, 104
FTC v. National Lead Co., 99
G.D. Searle & Co. v. Superior Court, 472
Garden Ridge v. Advance International, 433
Garratt v. Dailey, 512
Gascho v. Global Fitness Holdings, 626
Gen-Probe Inc. v. Vysis, Inc., 296, 302
Georgia, United States v., 271
Germantown Savings Bank v. City of Philadelphia, 385
Gertz v. Robert Welch, Inc., 466
Giampappa v. American Family Mutual Insurance Co., 467
Gisbrecht v. Barnhart, 620
Gitlitz v. Plankinton Building Properties, Inc., 138
Goldberger v. Integrated Resources, Inc., 626
Goldman v. Simpson, 461
Gompers v. Buck's Stove & Range Co., 238, 239, 246
Gonzaga University v. Doe, 23
Gonzales v. Thomas, 39
Gonzalez, People v., 266
Gore v. Harris, 41
Graham v. Rourke, 408
Grand Trunk Western R.R. Co. v. Consolidated Rail Corp., 308
Granfinanciera S.A. v. Nordberg, 329

Granny Goose Foods, Inc. v.
Teamsters, 152
Gray v. Macklin, 410
**Great American Music Machine,
Inc. v. Mid-South Record
Pressing Co., 424**
Great Lakes Dredge & Dock Co. v.
Huffman, 314
Great-West Life & Annuity Ins.Co. v.
Knudson, 539, 542
Green v. Mansour, 313
Green v. School Board of New Kent
County, 108
Gregg, United States v., 108
Griffin v. County School Board, 278
Grimshaw v. Ford Motor Co., 467, **468**
Griswold v. Connecticut, 305
Groves v. John Wunder Co., 369
Grupo Mexicano de Desarrollo, S.A. v.
Alliance Bond Fund, Inc., 461
Guidance Endodontics, L.L.C. v.
Dentsply Int'l, Inc., 493
Hadley v. Baxendale, 332
Haggart v. Woodley, 626
Hague v. CIO, 44
Hall, United States v., 145
Hallett's Estate, In re [Knatchbull v.
Hallett], 579
Halo Electronics, Inc. v. Pulse
Electronics, 465
Hans v. Louisiana, 271
Harjo v. Pro Football Inc., 592
Harjo v. Pro-Football Inc., 592
Harris v. City of Philadelphia, 255
Hayduk v. City of Johnstown, 493
Hecht Co. v. Bowles, **28**, 86, 94, 111,
158
Helfend v. Southern California Rapid
Transit District, 384
Hendrix, In re, 209
Heninger v. Dunn, 362
Hensley v. Eckerhart, 616, 619
**Hicks on Behalf of Feiock v.
Feiock, 235**, 246
Hilao v. Estate of Marcos, 492
Hill v. Colorado, 107
Hobson v. Wilson, 322
Holton v. Memorial Hospital, 345
Honda Motor Co. v. Oberg, 482, 509
Honeywell International, Inc. v.
E.P.A., 39
Horne v. Flores, 217
Hoskins v. Business Men's Assurance,
494
Hudson v. United States, 465
Hutchison v. Pyburn, 549
Hutto v. Finney, 98, 280, 288, 617
**I.Lan Systems, Inc. v. Netscout
Serv. Level Corp., 129**

Illinois v. Chicago Magnet Wire Corp.,
515
Illinois v. Costle, 270
Indiana Lumbermens Mut. Ins. Co. v.
Reinsurance Results, Inc., 521
Inmates of Suffolk County Jail v.
Rufo, 208
International Brotherhood of
Teamsters v. United States, 40
Irwin v. Degtiarov, 357
Jarrell v. Petoseed Co., 256
Jeff D. v. Kempthorne, 208
Jenkins v. Kansas City Missouri
School District, 126
Joel v. Various John Does, 164
Johnson v. Ford Motor Co., 508
Johnson v. Georgia Highway Express,
Inc., 619
Johnson v. Women's Health Center,
Inc., 107
Joint Anti-Fascist Refugee Committee
v. McGrath, 272
**Jones & Laughlin Steel
Corporation v. Pfeifer, 450**, 459,
487
Jones v. City of Los Angeles, 399
Jones v. Clinton, 257
Joyce v. City and County of San
Francisco, 89
Judd v. Drezga, 407
Jutzi-Johnson v. United States, 402,
404, 405
Kaczkowski v. Bolubasz, 450, 458
Kaiser v. United States, 355
Kansas City Southern Ry. Co. v.
Guardian Trust Co., 607
Kansas Health Care Association, Inc.
v. Kansas Department of Social &
Rehabilitation Services, 71
Kansas v. Colorado, 442, 448
Kasper v. Saint Mary of Nazareth
Hosp., 397
Kelo v. City of New London, 73
Kemp v. American Telephone &
Telegraph Co., 516
Kerr S.S. Co. v. Radio Corp. of
America, 341
Kimel v. Florida Board of Regents, 25
Kinsman Transit Co., Petition of, 342
Kirk v. Denver Publishing Co., 494
Kirtsaeng v. John Wiley & Sons, Inc.,
616
Kolstad v. American Dental
Association, 492
Kondaurov. v. Kerdasha, 358
Koon v. United States, 484
Kovacs v. Commissioner, 459
Laaman v. Warden, New Hampshire
State Prison, 232

Lake Country Estates, Inc. v. Tahoe Regional Planning Agency, 283
Landgraf v. USI Film Products, 324
Lange v. Hoyt, 349
Levine v. Comcoa, Ltd., 146
Lewellen v. Franklin, 495
Lewis v. Casey, 55, 60
Lewis v. Lewis, 522
Lewis v. United States, 258
Lieb v. Topstone Industries, Inc., 616
Liza Danielle, Inc. v. Jamko, Inc., 138
Local No. 93, Int'l Ass'n of Firefighters v. City of Cleveland, 279
Los Angeles, City of v. Lyons, 63, 152
Louisiana ACORN Fair Housing, Inc. v. LeBlanc, 326
Lujan v. Defenders of Wildlife, 298
Madrid v. Marquez, 552
Madsen v. Women's Health Center, Inc., 100, 252
Maggio v. Zeitz, 239
Marbury v. Madison, 15, 94
Marks v. Stinson, 40
Marquardo, United States v., 256
Marsh v. Green, 385
Martin v. Ellandson, 233
Martin v. Industrial Accident Commission, 348
Martinez v. State of California, 414
Maryland Casualty Co. v. Pacific Coal & Oil Co., 297, 303
Massachusetts v. Microsoft Corp., 61
Mathias v. Accor Economy Lodging, Inc., 510
Maxim's Ltd. v. Badonsky, 166
McCahill v. New York Transportation Co., 333
McCarthy v. Tobin, 131
McCullen v. Coakley, 107
McGowan v. Estate of Wright, 394
McKennon v. Nashville Banner Publishing Co., 37, 588
McMillan v. City of New York, 412
Medimmune, Inc. v. Genentech, Inc., 295
Memphis Community School District v. Stachura, 317
Mercer v. Duke University, 625
Mertens v. Hewitt Associates, 327, 539, 542
Metro-North Commuter Railroad Co. v. Buckley, 385
Microsoft Corp., United States v., 60, 61, 144, 175
Miller v. French, 32, 232
Milliken v. Bradley (Milliken I), 116, 117

Milliken v. Bradley (Milliken II), 118, 203, 221, 273, 278
Mills v. Freeman, 217
Milwaukee, City of v. National Gypsum Co., 445
Minneci v. Pollard, 20
Missouri v. Jenkins (Jenkins I), 617, 624
Missouri v. Jenkins (Jenkins II), 117, 204, 254
Missouri v. Jenkins (Jenkins III), 115, 220
Mitchell v. Dunn, 583
Mitchell v. Heinrichs, 358
Mitsui Manufacturers Bank v. Unicom Computer Corp., 573
Monsanto Co. v. Geertson Seed Farms, 78
Montanile v. Board Trus. Nat'l Elevator Indus. Health Benefit Plan, 540
Monterey, City of v. Del Monte Dunes, Ltd., 330
Moore v. Regents of University of California, 574
Morgan v. Foretich, 257
Morrison v. Parker, 306
Moses v. Macferlan, 520
Moss v. Superior Court, 243
Motorola Credit Corp. v. Uzan, 492
Mt. Healthy City School District Board of Education v. Doyle, 34
Munaf v. Geren, 151
Muniz v. Hoffman, 251, 258
Munn v. Algee, 352
Munn v. Southern Health Plan, Inc., 346
Mushroom Transportation Co., In re, 577
Myers v. Central Florida Investments, Inc., 493
Nappe v. Anschelewitz, Barr, Ansell & Bonello, 326
Nashville, C. & St. L.R. Co. v. Wallace, 297
Nelson v. Collins, 203
Nesmith v. Texaco, 458
New Era Publications Int'l v. Henry Holt & Co., 601
New Jersey, United States v., 196
New York State Assn. for Retarded Children, Inc. v. Carey, 201, 206, 320
New York State National Organization of Women v. Terry, 255
New York Times Co. v. Tasini, 75
New York Times Co. v. United States, 73

Newark Coalition for Low Income Housing v. Newark Redevelopment and Housing Authority, 208
Newman v. Piggie Park Enterprises, Inc., 613
Nixon v. Herndon, 321
NLRB v. American Geri-Care Inc., 39
NLRB v. Wyman-Gordon Co., 39
Nordic Village, Inc., United States v., 272
Norfolk & Western R. Co. v. Liepelt, 451, 459
Noriega, United States v., 269
Northern Insurance Co. v. Chatham County, 271
Northern Utilities, Inc. v. Lewiston Radiator Works, Inc., 305
Norton v. Ashcroft, 107
NOW v. Operation Rescue, 256
O'Shea v. Littleton, 65, 152
Oatway, In re (Hertslet v. Oatway), 583
Occupy Sacramento v. City of Sacramento, 163
Occupy Tucson v. City of Tucson, 161
Octane Fitness LLC, v. ICON Health & Fitness, Inc., 616, 617
Oelrichs v. Spain, 606
Ogden v. J.M. Steel Erecting, Inc., 394
Ohio v. Department of the Interior, 358
Olwell v. Nye & Nissen, 533
Pacific Mut. Life Ins. Co. v. Haslip, 482, 503, 508
PacifiCare Health Systems, Inc. v. Book, 464
Palmigiano v. Garrahy, 269
Palsgraf v. Long Island Railroad Co., 333, 341
Parents Involved in Community Schools v. Seattle School District No. 1, 114
Parev Products v. I. Rokeach, 196
Parsons v. Bedford, 329
Pasadena City Board of Education v. Spangler, 203
Patterson v. Newspaper & Mail Deliverers' Union, 209
Peeler v. Village of Kingston Mines, 397, 399
Peevyhouse v. Garland Coal & Mining Company, 368
Penfield Co. v. SEC, 247
Pennsylvania, Commonwealth of v. Porter, 47
People Who Care v. Rockford Board of Education, 97, 217
Perdue v. Kenny A., 617

Perma Life Mufflers, Inc. v. International Parts Corp., 589
Peters, United States v., 289
Petrella v. Metro-Goldwyn-Mayer, Inc., 595, 604
Petriello v. Kalman, 344
Petties ex. rel Martin v. District of Columbia, 229
Philadelphia Welfare Rights Organization v. Shapp, 201
Philip Morris USA v. Williams, 509
Phillips Petroleum Co. v. Shutts, 502
Pierce v. Douglas School District No. 4, 128
Pinter v. Dahl, 591
Plotnik v. Meihaus, 358
Poe v. Ullman, 305
Pollard v. E.I. du Pont de Nemours & Co., 328
Poltorak v. Jackson Chevrolet Co., 132
Portland Feminist Women's Health Center v. Advocates for Life, Inc., 170
Pounders v. Watson, 258
Prasco, LLC v. Medicis Pharmaceutical Corp., 302
Pretre v. United States, 196, 411
Price v. Austin Independent School District, 215
Pro-Football, Inc. v. Harjo, 591
Pro-Football, Inc. v. Harjo (Harjo II), 587, 592
Pro-Football, Inc. v. Harjo (Harjo III), 592
Providence Journal Co., In re, 259
Pyeatte v. Pyeatte, 548
Quern v. Jordan, 272
Railway Employees v. Wright, 199, 202
Rancho Palos Verdes, City of v. Abrams, 24
Real Truth About Obama, Inc. v. Fed. Elec. Comm'n, 159
Reich v. Sea Sprite Boat Co., 256
Rendine v. Pantzer, 625
Republic Supply Co. v. Richfield Oil Co., 583
Rhyne v. K-Mart Corp., 495
Right v. Breen, 325, 396
Rivera v. Horton, 325
Riverside, City of v. Rivera, 625
Rizzo v. Goode, 41, 276
Roberts v. Ohio Permanente Medical Group, 346
Robinson v. Robinson, 548
Roche Products v. Bolar Pharmaceutical Co., 76
RoDa Drilling Co. v. Siegal, 144
Roe v. Operation Rescue, 145

Roe v. Wade, 103

Roginsky v. Richardson-Merrell, Inc., 467

Roland Machinery Co. v. Dresser Industries, Inc., 166

Rosado v. Wyman, 38

Rozpad v. Commissioner, 459

Rufo v. Inmates of Suffolk County Jail, **197**

Rufo v. Simpson, 405

Ruiz v. Estelle, 232

Ruiz v. Johnson, 233

Ruiz v. United States, 232

Salzman v. Bachrach, 532

Samsung Electronics Co. v. ON Semiconductor Corp., 302

Samuels v. Mackell, 313, 314

Sancho v. U.S. Department of Energy, 169

Sasso, United States v., 180

Saunders v. Branch Banking & Trust Co., 516

Schefke v. Reliable Collection Agency, Ltd., 625

Scheiber v. Dolby Laboratories, Inc., 586

Schenck v. Pro-Choice Network of Western NY, 107

Schiavo ex rel. Schindler v. Schiavo, 146

Schmidt v. Lessard, 171

Schweiker v. Chilicky, 20

Scotts Co. v. United Industries Corp., 168

Searles v. Van Bebber, 326

Serawop, United States v., 412

Sereboff v. Mid Atlantic Medical Services, Inc., 27, 539, 542

Serrano v. Priest, 607

Sharon v. Tucker, 294

Shearson/American Express Inc. v. McMahon, 465

Sheldon v. Metro-Goldwyn Pictures Corp., 538

Shera v. N.C. State Univ. Veterinary Teaching Hosp., 355, 356

Sherbert v. Verner, 348

Sherley v. Sebelius, 159

Sheshtawy, In re, 266

Shipp, United States v., 267

Shuttlesworth v. City of Birmingham, 266

Siegel v. Western Union Tel. Co., 338

Sierra Club v. Morton, 83

Simon v. San Paolo U.S. Holding Co., 508

SKS Merch, LLC v. Barry, 164

Slater v. Skyhawk Transportation, Inc., 459

Smith v. Staso Milling Co., **79**

Smith v. Wade, 319

Snepp v. United States, 538, **563**

Snow v. Villacci, 411

Softsolutions, Inc. v. Brigham Young University, 625

Spallone v. United States, 273, **282**

Squire et al. v. Western Union Telegraph Co., 430

Standard Oil Co., United States v., 14

Stanley, United States v., 20

State Farm Mutual Automobile Insurance Co. v. Campbell, 403, 490, 491, **497**, 512

State University of New York v. Denton, 145

Steffel v. Thompson, 157, 298, 313

Stover v. Lakeland Square Owners Association, 459

Strickland v. Medlen, 355, 356

Summers v. Earth Island Institute, 71

Sun Oil Co. v. Transcontinental Gas Pipe Line Corp., 309

Supreme Court of Virginia v. Consumers Union of United States, Inc., 283, 288

Swann v. Charlotte-Mecklenburg Board of Education, 45, 109, 117, 122, 254, 276

Swift & Co., United States v., 196, 197, 199, 200, 211

Tam, In re, 595

Taylor v. Meirick, 537

Taylor v. Superior Court, 472

Tennessee Valley Authority v. Hill, **90**

Tenney v. Brandhove, 283

Terracciano (Guardian ad litem of) v. Etheridge, 410

Terrace v. Thompson, 298

Terry, United States v., 268

The Corporation of the President of the Church of Jesus Christ of Latter-Day Saints v. Jolley, **574**

Thomas v. Collins, 264

Thompson v. KFB Insurance Co., 385

Thompson v. Thompson, 23

Thorn v. Mercy Memorial Hospital Corp., **386**

Tilcon Minerals, Inc. v. Orange & Rockland Utilities, Inc., 313

Time Warner Entertainment v. Six Flags Over Georgia, 492

Timm v. Progressive Steel Treating, Inc., 516

Toilet Goods Association, Inc. v. Gardner, 306

Torres v. Eastlick (In re North American Coin & Currency, Ltd.), 570
Transportation Insurance Co. v. Moriel, 495
Trinity Church v. John Hancock Mut. Life Ins. Co., 364
Triple-A Baseball Club Assocs. v. Northeastern Baseball, Inc., 132
Trustees v. Greenough, 607, 609
Tucker (Public Trustee of) v. Asleson, 410
Tull v. United States, 329
Tullidge v. Wade, 481
Tullis v. Townley Engineering & Manufacturing Co., 396
Turkmen v. Hasty, 21
Twentieth Century Fox Film Corp., United States v., 258
TXO Production Corp. v. Alliance Resources Corp., 483, 491, 508, 515
Union Carbide v. UGI Corp., 62
United Mine Workers of America, United States v., 247, 255, 260, 262, 281
United Mine Workers v. Bagwell, 244
United Shoe Machinery Corp., United States v., 60, 197, 211
United States Catholic Conference v. Abortion Rights Mobilization, 268
US Airways, Inc. v. McCutchen, 539
Vance v. Rumsfeld, 21
Vanguard Outdoor, LLC v. City of Los Angeles, 159
Ventura v. Titan Sports, Inc., 449
Vermont Agency of Natural Resources v. United States ex rel. Stevens, 464
Virginia v. American Booksellers Association, 305
W.L. Gore & Associates, Inc. v. C.R. Bard, Inc., 209
W.R. Grace & Co. v. Waters, 495
W.T. Grant Co., United States v., 62, 212
Walgreen Co. v. Sara Creek Property Co., 133
Walker v. City of Birmingham, 260
Walker v. Farmers Insurance Exchange, 507
Walker v. Ritchie, 407
Ward v. Rock Against Racism, 102
Webster v. Doe, 22
Weinberger v. Romero-Barcelo, 74, 95, 151, 156, 158
Weld County Bd. of Com'rs v. Slovek, 364
West Virginia University Hospitals, Inc. v. Casey, 625

Western Elec. Co., United States v., 209
Wheeler Tarpeh-Doe v. United States, 412
Wilkes v. Wood, 480
Wilkie v. Robbins, 20, 21
Will v. United States, 139
Williams v. Philip Morris, Inc., 510
Willing v. Chicago Auditorium Association, 299
Willy v. Coastal Corp., 607
Wilton v. Seven Falls Co., 308, 312
Winter v. Natural Resources Defense Council, 147, 162
Wisconsin v. Yoder, 348
Women Prisoners v. District of Columbia, 98
Wyatt v. Sawyer, 7
Wyatt v. Stickney, 7
Yonkers, City of, United States v., 273
Young v. United States ex rel. Vuitton et Fils S.A., 235
Young, Ex parte, 272
Younger v. Harris, 313
Youngs v. Old Ben Coal Co., 369
Zazu Designs v. L'Oreal, S.A., 514
Zehner v. Trigg, 21

REMEDIES
PUBLIC AND PRIVATE

Sixth Edition

CHAPTER 1

INTRODUCTION TO THE LAW OF REMEDIES

■ ■ ■

In law school, it is easy to fall into the habit of equating law and liability. Liability—the determination that a defendant is legally responsible for some harm to the plaintiff—is only half the story, however. The other half is the remedy—the action to be taken in response to the harm. For clients, the remedy may be the more important half, because it is with the remedy that the court acts for them or against them.

Perhaps the remedies half of the equation is neglected because it is tempting to think of remedies as mechanically derived from the legal harm and therefore obvious. That is what the Babylonian King Hammurabi suggested 4000 years ago by displaying to his subjects large stone tablets that listed specific remedies for specific wrongs. For example, Rule 206 of the Code of Hammurabi stated, "If a man has struck another in a quarrel, and has wounded him and that man shall swear, 'I did not strike him wittingly,' he shall pay the doctor." Howard L. Oleck, *Damages to Persons and Property* § 2 at 3–4 (1961 rev.ed.).

Remedies, however, cannot be carved in stone. A mechanical approach to determining the appropriate remedy is ultimately impractical because no list can include all harms or take account of the variations in circumstance that could make a given remedy inappropriate. Indeed, Babylonian court records show that courts did not follow the Code of Hammurabi mechanically, but rather took a common law approach to shaping the remedy.

The polar opposite of the mechanical approach is to let each judge select whatever remedy does justice in the case at hand. But this approach also has its problems. A judge with unfettered discretion over the remedy can effectively nullify the provisions of constitutions, statutes, and cases. Thus, neither the purely discretionary nor the mechanical approach explains modern remedies law. Instead, as you will see in this course, the law of remedies provides guiding principles that cabin the courts' discretion, while also allowing flexibility to balance the competing interests of the parties and other public or institutional concerns.

Remedies is often called a capstone course because it provides you with the opportunity to bring together all you have learned in your courses on substantive and procedural law to resolve the intensely practical question, "What can be done about it?" "Remedies, what a winning plaintiff gets, is among the most practice-ready and practical courses in a student's law

1

school experience. A lawyer's client is interested in results, not the procedural and substantive dance to reach those results. Remedies is client-centered and outcome-oriented." Doug Rendleman, *Remedies: A Guide for the Perplexed*, 57 St. Louis Univ. L.J. 567 (2013). Given this practical perspective, Remedies is a good class to teach with the problem method approach, with its focus on applying the doctrinal rules to solve a specific problem for a hypothetical client. Tracy A. Thomas, *Teaching Remedies as Problem-Solving: Keeping it Real*, 57 St. Louis Univ. L.J. 673 (2013). Ultimately, while the subject of Remedies arms you with the tools you will need to accomplish your clients' goals, it also provides the opportunity to reflect on basic questions about the role of law and the role of courts that you have touched on throughout your study of the legal system.

A.   A GENERAL APPROACH TO CRAFTING A REMEDY

Despite its practical importance, the law of remedies has evolved piecemeal. Rather than developing general principles that cut across areas of substantive law—transsubstantive principles, if you will—courts have tended to pair remedies with specific rights: remedies for trespass, remedies for breach of an agreement to sell goods, remedies for violations of civil rights, etc. Thus, while some attention may be paid to remedies in the torts class, the contracts class and so on, transsubstantive principles are ignored.

This cookbook approach sometimes makes it difficult for lawyers to locate or apply the law that they need to help their clients. They may be unable, for instance, to deal with a novel remedies question by drawing appropriate analogies to remedies from other substantive areas of law. One of this casebook's themes is to encourage you to think about remedial principles that reach beyond specific causes of action, empowering you to think creatively about remedies.

As a first step toward transsubstantive remedial principles, here are some critical decisions to identifying the appropriate remedy:

The first critical choice is to identify the remedy's goal. There are many possibilities. One goal might simply be to *declare* the parties' rights, to establish as a matter of principle who was right and who was wrong. Another might be to restore the plaintiff to the *plaintiff's rightful position*, that is, to the position the plaintiff would have occupied if the defendant had never violated the law. Or, its goal might be to restore the defendant to the *defendant's rightful position*, that is, the position that the defendant would have occupied absent the violation. A fourth goal might be to *punish* the defendant for doing wrong.

The second choice in defining an appropriate remedy is the choice between a *specific* and a *substitutionary* remedy. Specific remedies achieve the remedy's goal in kind, by giving the plaintiff the exact thing to which he or she is entitled. For example, if the goal of the remedy in a nuisance case is to restore the plaintiff to his or her rightful position, a specific remedy would order the defendant to stop the nuisance.

Substitutionary remedies operate by giving the plaintiff a substitute—typically, an award of money—equal to the value of the plaintiff's entitlement. Again, for example, in a nuisance case, a substitutionary remedy might be to give the plaintiff the difference between the value of his land before the nuisance occurred and the value of his land after the nuisance began. What principles should guide the choice between a specific and a substitutionary remedy?

The third decision in determining an appropriate remedy addresses how to implement the plaintiff's remedial choice. Implementation of the plaintiff's selected remedy involves questions of both qualification and quantification. First, every remedy has requirements, elements that must be satisfied before a plaintiff qualifies for that remedial option. If that threshold is met, a court must then decide the quantification question—how much relief is appropriate, either in amount of money or scope of injunction relief. There are rules of law guiding the court's decision as to the proper measurement of the remedy.

The fourth decision, sometimes necessary, is how to enforce the remedy. If the defendant does not cooperate, what can and should be done? Here there are additional remedies of contempt and collection that may be utilized to effectuate the relief.

These questions arise when you reach the remedy stage in any substantive area of the law, whether torts or contracts, admiralty or antitrust. Moreover, they are not questions only for courts. Legislatures face the same questions when they craft a statute that creates substantive rights. Although the particular substantive law affects how remedies issues are resolved, the issues themselves are universal. Thus, after a right is declared, whether by legislative enactment or judicial decision, these questions, and the principles that emerge from their study, can be used to craft the remedy.

Accordingly, our focus is transsubstantive. These materials are organized by types of remedies (injunctions, declaratory judgments, compensatory damages, punitive damages, restitution, and attorney's fees), rather than canvassing the remedies for particular harms (remedies for trespass, remedies for conversion, etc.). By studying each remedy across a variety of cases, from administrative law to breach of contract to civil rights, you should be able to see remedies not as a list of responses to specific harms, but as a set of principles exemplified in particular cases and extending beyond them.

B. PRIVATE LAW AND PUBLIC LAW

In a classic law review article, excerpted below, Professor Abram Chayes argued that a new model of civil litigation was emerging. Looking at the challenges that faced courts in enforcing students' rights to attend desegregated schools, prisoners' rights to be free from cruel and unusual punishment, and confined mental patients' right to treatment, Professor Chayes concluded that courts had assumed a new role. Part of what made that role new was the nature of the rights the courts were enforcing. Equally new were the kinds of remedies the courts used.

———

ABRAM CHAYES, THE ROLE OF THE JUDGE IN PUBLIC LAW LITIGATION
89 Harv.L.Rev. 1281, 1282–84, 1292–95, 1298 (1976)

* * * We are witnessing the emergence of a new model of civil litigation and, I believe, our traditional conception of adjudication and the assumptions upon which it is based provide an increasingly unhelpful, indeed misleading framework for assessing either the workability or the legitimacy of the roles of judge and court within this model.

In our received tradition, the lawsuit is a vehicle for settling disputes between private parties about private rights. The defining features of this conception of civil adjudication are:

(1) The lawsuit is *bipolar*. Litigation is organized as a contest between two individuals or at least two unitary interests, diametrically opposed, to be decided on a winner-takes-all basis.

(2) Litigation is *retrospective*. The controversy is about an identified set of completed events: whether they occurred, and if so, with what consequences for the legal relations of the parties.

(3) *Right and remedy are interdependent.* The scope of the relief is derived more or less logically from the substantive violation under the general theory that the plaintiff will get compensation measured by the harm caused by the defendant's breach of duty—in contract by giving plaintiff the money he would have had absent the breach; in tort by paying the value of the damage caused.

(4) The lawsuit is a *self-contained* episode. The impact of the judgment is confined to the parties. If plaintiff prevails there is a simple compensatory transfer, usually of money, but occasionally the return of a thing or the performance of a definite act. If defendant prevails, a loss lies where it has fallen. In either case, entry of judgment ends the court's involvement.

(5) The process is *party-initiated* and *party-controlled*. The case is organized and the issues defined by exchanges between the parties. Responsibility for fact development is theirs. The trial judge is a neutral arbiter of their interactions who decides questions of law only if they are put in issue by an appropriate move of a party.

This capsule description of what I have called the traditional conception of adjudication is no doubt overdrawn. It was not often, if ever, expressed so severely; indeed, because it was so thoroughly taken for granted, there was little occasion to do so. Although I do not contend that the traditional conception ever conformed fully to what judges were doing in fact, I believe it has been central to our understanding and our analysis of the legal system.

Whatever its historical validity, the traditional model is clearly invalid as a description of much current civil litigation in the federal district courts. Perhaps the dominating characteristic of modern federal litigation is that lawsuits do not arise out of disputes between private parties about private rights. Instead, the object of litigation is the vindication of constitutional or statutory policies. The shift in the legal basis of the lawsuit explains many, but not all, facets of what is going on "in fact" in federal trial courts. For this reason, although the label is not wholly satisfactory, I shall call the emerging model "public law litigation."

The characteristic features of the public law model are very different from those of the traditional model. The party structure is sprawling and amorphous, subject to change over the course of the litigation. The traditional adversary relationship is suffused and intermixed with negotiating and mediating processes at every point. The judge is the dominant figure in organizing and guiding the case, and he draws for support not only on the parties and their counsel, but on a wide range of outsiders—masters, experts, and oversight personnel. Most important, the trial judge has increasingly become the creator and manager of complex forms of ongoing relief, which have widespread effects on persons not before the court and require the judge's continuing involvement in administration and implementation. School desegregation, employment discrimination, and prisoners' or inmates' rights cases come readily to mind as avatars of this new form of litigation. But it would be mistaken to suppose that it is confined to these areas. Antitrust, securities fraud and other aspects of the conduct of corporate business, bankruptcy and reorganizations, union governance, consumer fraud, housing discrimination, electoral reapportionment, environmental management—cases in all these fields display in varying degrees the features of public law litigation. * * *

One of the most striking procedural developments of this century is the increasing importance of equitable relief. It is perhaps too soon to reverse the traditional maxim to read that money damages will be awarded only when no suitable form of specific relief can be devised. But surely, the old sense of equitable remedies as "extraordinary" has faded.

I am not concerned here with specific performance—the compelled transfer of a piece of land or a unique thing. This remedy is structurally little different from traditional money-damages. It is a one-time, one-way transfer requiring for its enforcement no continuing involvement of the court. Injunctive relief, however, is different in kind, even when it takes the form of a simple negative order. Such an order is a presently operative prohibition, enforceable by contempt, and it is a much greater constraint on activity than the risk of future liability implicit in the damage remedy. Moreover, the injunction is continuing. Over time, the parties may resort to the court for enforcement or modification of the original order in light of changing circumstances. Finally, by issuing the injunction, the court takes public responsibility for any consequences of its decree that may adversely affect strangers to the action.

Beyond these differences, the prospective character of the relief introduces large elements of contingency and prediction into the proceedings. Instead of a dispute retrospectively oriented toward the consequences of a closed set of events, the court has a controversy about future probabilities. Equitable doctrine, naturally enough, given the intrusiveness of the injunction and the contingent nature of the harm, calls for a balancing of the interests of the parties. And if the immediate parties' interests were to be weighed and evaluated, it was not too difficult to proceed to a consideration of other interests that might be affected by the order.

The comparative evaluation of the competing interests of plaintiff and defendant required by the remedial approach of equity often discloses alternatives to a winner-takes-all decision. An arrangement might be fashioned that could safeguard at least partially the interests of both parties, and perhaps even of others as well. And to the extent such an arrangement is possible, equity seems to require it. Negative orders directed to one of the parties—even though pregnant with affirmative implications—are often not adequate to this end. And so the historic power of equity to order affirmative action gradually freed itself from the encrustation of nineteenth century restraints. The result has often been a decree embodying an affirmative regime to govern the range of activities in litigation and having the force of law for those represented before the court.

At this point, right and remedy are pretty thoroughly disconnected. The form of relief does not flow ineluctably from the liability determination, but is fashioned ad hoc. In the process, moreover, right and remedy have been to some extent transmuted. The liability determination is not simply a pronouncement of the legal consequences of past events, but to some extent a prediction of what is likely to be in the future. And relief is not a terminal, compensatory transfer, but an effort to devise a program to contain future consequences in a way that accommodates the range of interests involved. * * * If a mental patient complains that he has been denied a right to treatment, it will not do to order the superintendent to "cease to deny" it. So with segregation in education, discrimination in hiring, apportionment of legislative districts, environmental management. And the list could be extended. * * *

The centerpiece of the emerging public law model is the decree. It differs in almost every relevant characteristic from relief in the traditional model of adjudication, not the least in that it is the centerpiece. The decree seeks to adjust future behavior, not to compensate for past wrong. It is deliberately fashioned rather than logically deduced from the nature of the legal harm suffered. It provides for a complex, on-going regime of performance rather than a simple, one-shot, one-way transfer. Finally, it prolongs and deepens, rather than terminates, the court's involvement with the dispute. * * *

NOTES

1.   For an example of public law litigation, consider Wyatt v. Stickney, 325 F.Supp. 781 (M.D.Ala.1971), *enforced,* 344 F.Supp. 373, 387 (M.D.Ala.1972), *modified,* 503 F.2d 1305 (5th Cir.1974). *Wyatt* began in 1970 as a class action on behalf of mental patients and employees at a mental hospital against state officials, including the governor, alleging violations of an asserted right of the involuntarily confined to treatment and decent living conditions. The class of plaintiffs grew to include mental patients at other hospitals, geriatric patients, and mentally retarded patients. Judge Frank Johnson issued orders that imposed detailed guidelines on the institutions' operations and tried to prompt the state to provide the funds to implement his orders. Judge Johnson also involved the United States government and established various entities to oversee implementation of his orders. *See, e.g.,* Note, *The* Wyatt *Case: Implementation of a Judicial Decree Ordering Institutional Change,* 84 Yale L.J. 1338 (1975). After thirty years of litigation and judicial supervision, involving more than fifty published opinions, the district court finally dismissed the lawsuit in 2004. Wyatt v. Sawyer, 219 F.R.D. 529 (M.D.Ala.2004). Finding the final settlement and dismissal to be in the class's interest, Judge Myron Thompson wrote:

> [T]his case illustrates why, despite the difficulties inherent in structural reform litigation, such cases are, finally, so important and worthwhile. While this case has followed a "long, winding, and often quite bumpy" road, the enormity of what this case has accomplished cannot be overstated. The principles of humane treatment of people with mental illness and mental retardation embodied in this litigation have become part of the fabric of law in this country and, indeed, international law.

> * * * The *Wyatt* standards have had a reverberating impact on state and national law, and, perhaps even more importantly, on

public consciousness about mental illness. The standards have been incorporated into state and federal mental-health codes and regulations. The concept of treatment in the "least restrictive setting" contained in the *Wyatt* standards was "echoed" in the Americans with Disabilities Act of 1990. The nationwide Protection and Advocacy system is a "direct descendant" of the Human Rights Committees Judge Johnson appointed in the *Wyatt* case. Part of Judge Johnson's March 1972 opinion enumerating rights due the plaintiff class, such as the right to privacy, the right to be treated with dignity, and the right to be free of unnecessary medication and physical restraint, has come to be known among mental-health professionals as a "bill of rights for patients."

* * * Finally, *Wyatt* heightened public awareness of the needs of institutionalized people and people with mental illness and mental retardation. Today, as a result, any judge, legislator, or executive official who would seek to reverse the everyday involvement and oversight of state and local advocacy groups, friends and family members of people with mental disabilities, and self-advocacy by consumers of mental-health care, would face universal condemnation. This legacy of this litigation cannot be terminated by any court.

219 F.R.D. at 533. Litigation over unconstitutional conditions in America's prisons provides another excellent example. *See* Malcolm M. Feeley & Edward L. Rubin, *Judicial Policy Making and the Modern State: How the Courts Reformed America's Prisons* (1998).

2.   While Judge Thompson and some others applaud the role public law litigation played in the evolution of disability law, critics find it troubling that crafting the remedy in a public law case can cast the judge as "a legislator in robes." Thus, public law litigation—or institutional reform litigation—has been a prime focus of calls for courts to abandon what some call "judicial activism." For example, in the area of prison reform litigation, Congress has responded. The Prison Litigation Reform Act (PLRA), 18 U.S.C. § 3626, sharply limits the remedies courts can order in lawsuits over unconstitutional conditions of confinement in American prisons.

3.   Law, of course, is a moving target. There is considerable debate over whether the structural injunction is a relic of the past. For a discussion of the issue, see Margo Schlanger, *Civil Rights Injunctions Over Time: A Case Study of Jail and Prison Court Orders*, 81 N.Y.U.L.Rev. 550 (2006). Professor Schlanger concludes that as far as prison reform is concerned, arguments that institutional reform litigation is "something that is over and done with" are simply wrong. Rather, prison litigation continued at a stable rate up to the passage of the Prison Litigation Reform Act. *See also* Myriam Gilles, *An Autopsy of the Structural Reform Injunction: Oops . . . It's Still Moving!*, 58 U. Miami L. Rev. 143 (2003).

Professor Schlanger suggests, however, that while the rate of litigation did not change, the kind of injunctions courts entered did. Courts moved away from the kind of broad injunctive relief that Chayes saw as characterizing public law litigation, and toward more focused and precise remedies. Similarly, others have argued that public law litigation "has moved away from remedial intervention modeled on command-and-control bureaucracy toward a kind of intervention that can be called 'experimentalist.' " Charles F. Sabel & William Simon, *Destabilization Rights: How Public Law Litigation Succeeds*, 117 Harv.L.Rev. 1015 (2004). The authors claim that this alternative model for public law litigation may answer doctrinal and jurisprudential objections to the Chayes model of public law litigation.

4.   Public law litigation and private law litigation are not separated by a bright line, of course. Remedies in some forms of traditional, private litigation like bankruptcy, probate and trusts have always exhibited many of the characteristics of public law litigation, and the remedial and procedural changes Professor Chayes first observed in public law cases have since migrated to private law. *See* Theodore Eisenberg & Stephen Yeazell, *The Ordinary and the Extraordinary in Institutional Litigation*, 93 Harv.L.Rev. 465, 481–86 (1980); Richard L. Marcus, *Public Law Litigation and Legal Scholarship*, 21 Mich.J.L.Reform 47, 668–82 (1988). Private law litigation and public law litigation are better understood as poles of a continuum. The lessons learned in high profile public law cases about the way judges think about remedies provide critical insights into private law cases as well. That, along with the intrinsic importance of public law, is the reason for this casebook's unique focus on public and private law.

C. "WHERE THERE'S A RIGHT, THERE'S A REMEDY"?

Accusations of judicial activism await courts that interpret the constitution, apply a statute, or construe the common law to recognize a new right. Thus, before judges declare a right, they think carefully not simply about the justice of the party's cause, but also about the limits of a court's power.

Once a right has been established, however, the power of the court to declare a remedy has been much less controversial, and as a result, less scrutinized. Ask where the power to shape a remedy is derived, and the answer is likely to be that it is an inherent power, existing because *ubi ius, ibi remedium*: "Where there's a right, there's a remedy." Professor Tracy Thomas explains the history behind this general principle:

> The principle that rights must have remedies is ancient and venerable. In 1703, the right to a remedy was expressly recognized in Anglo-American law. In *Ashby v. White*, the Chief Justice of the King's Bench stated:

If the plaintiff has a right, he must of necessity have a means to vindicate and maintain it, and a remedy if he is injured in the exercise or enjoyment of it; and indeed it is a vain thing to imagine a right without a remedy; for . . . want of right and want of remedy are reciprocal. . . . Where a man has but one remedy to come at his right, if he loses that he loses his right.

Similarly, the United States Supreme Court from its earliest time has recognized the bedrock principle that deprivations of law require remedies. In *Marbury v. Madison,* Chief Justice Marshall endorsed the common law requirement mandating a remedy for every wrong:

[I]t is a general and indisputable rule, that where there is a legal right, there is also a legal remedy by suit or action at law, whenever that right is invaded. . . . [F]or it is a settled and invariable principle in the laws of England, that every right, when withheld, must have a remedy, and every injury its proper redress.

As the *Marbury* Court acknowledged, the right to a remedy is a core component of ordered liberty:

The very essence of civil liberty certainly consists in the right of every individual to claim the protection of the laws, whenever he receives an injury. One of the first duties of government is to afford that protection. . . . The government of the United States has been emphatically termed a government of laws, and not of men. It will certainly cease to deserve this high appellation, if the laws furnish no remedy for the violation of a vested legal right.

Additional support for the historical presence of the right to a remedy is found in the state constitutions of three-fourths of the states which contain express remedial guarantees. These guarantees requiring the right to a remedy in open court derive from Lord Coke's interpretation of the Magna Carta. First appearing in the late 1700s, the state constitutional rights to a remedy were adopted to ensure the independence of the judiciary against corruption and control by the other political branches. For example, in Ohio, the right to a remedy is a fundamental right guaranteed by the state constitution. The Ohio Constitution provides: "All courts shall be open, and every person, for an injury done him in his land, goods, person, or reputation, shall have remedy by due course of law, and shall have justice administered without denial or delay." Ohio, like other states, has interpreted this provision to require among other things, a "meaningful remedy." * * *

The enforcement power of the remedy is the quality that converts pronouncements of ideals into operational rights. It is this enforceability that makes something a legal rather than moral or natural right. As expressed in the Federalist Papers, the definition of a claim as a "legal" right depends upon the availability of this enforcement:

> It is essential to the idea of a law that it be attended with a sanction; or, in other words, a penalty or punishment for disobedience. If there be no penalty annexed to disobedience, the resolutions of commands which pretend to be laws will, in fact amount to nothing more than advice or recommendation.

> * * * Our judicial system—both federal and state—is premised on the universally-accepted principle that court judgments have meaning and that judicial pronouncements will be backed up by all necessary enforcement actions that may be required to ensure compliance with the law. "The essence of a right is, that it may be exercised contentiously, adversely. *Ubi jus ibi remedium*. Not that it be a mere favor to be granted or withheld by any litigant."

Tracy A. Thomas, *Ubi Jus, Ibi Remedium: The Due Process Right to a Remedy*, 41 San Diego L.Rev. 1633 (2004) (arguing the right to a remedy is a fundamental right guaranteed by the Fourteenth Amendment Due Process Clause).

The danger of disregarding the remedial command is that rights without remedies may no longer be rights at all. Practically, the absence of an effective remedy dilutes the substantive value of the declared right.

> To begin, a right without a remedy is not a legal right; it is merely a hope or a wish. This follows from the definition of a legal right. * * * [By definition], a right entails a correlative duty to act or refrain from acting for the benefit of another person. Unless a duty can be enforced, it is not really a duty; it is only a voluntary obligation that a person can fulfill or not at his whim. In such circumstances, the holder of the correlative "right" can only hope that the act or forbearance will occur. Thus, a right without a remedy is simply not a legal right.

> To understand why it is important for legal claims to be enforceable to be *rights*—rather than mere requests for favors—it is necessary to explore the purposes of rights. Rights define social relations. They serve as means to very important ends. Rights promote well-being in the broadest sense. They secure the dignity and the integrity of human beings. They enable people to grow, to develop, to fulfill their aspirations, and to accumulate necessary material goods. Rights give people control over their lives and are

essential to self-respect. Theories of rights often are considered to conflict with social utility because recognizing rights is sometimes inefficient. Nonetheless, legal rights plainly serve some utilitarian purposes. They assist society in treating people equally. They also promote order and predictability, thus enabling people to act upon reasonable expectations in managing their affairs.

Having described the purposes of rights, it is relatively easy to envision the consequences of their inadequate enforcement. The dignity of the individual is diminished and people are less able to achieve their goals. People feel insecure and lose their self-respect. If the legal system tells a person that it is acceptable for his rights to be violated, the implicit message is that the person lacks worth. And, when the system vindicates another person's rights in similar circumstances, the message is that the other person has greater worth. When denial of rights occurs systematically over time, the result is alienation, isolation, anger, and fear. In extreme cases, the result is totalitarianism or chaos.

Donald H. Zeigler, *Rights Require Remedies: A New Approach to the Enforcement of Rights in the Federal Courts*, 38 Hastings L.J. 665, 678–79 (1987).

Yet, if rights "require" remedies, remedies should be an easy subject. Professor Chayes, however, contends that at least in the context of public law litigation, designing a remedy is far from a mechanical process. Rather, the design of a remedy is an exercise of power independent of the declaration of a right, and so requires its own justification. The remedies course should convince you that public law cases are not unique in this regard. Defining the remedy for any particular wrong is an exercise in judgment and discretion—an exercise of power—no different in kind from the decision to declare a right in the first instance.

Thus, if there is one thing to be learned from a course in remedies, it is that "Where there's a right, there's a remedy" is a singularly unhelpful maxim. Providing a complete remedy for every violation of right is an important, well-accepted goal, but it is not the only goal the law serves. Further, in any particular situation, any number of remedies may be available. In that event, who is to decide which remedy is available to whom, and how is that to be decided?

Questions such as these are rarely discussed plainly in the cases. After all, the nature and source of a court's power are abstract concerns, while adjudication is a pragmatic, concrete business. So, despite its being with the declaration of a remedy that the court's power is truly exercised (or perhaps because this is where the power is truly exercised), the nature of a court's remedial authority goes largely undiscussed.

Sometimes, however, courts cannot veil the exercise of judgment in the design of a remedy. For example, where a right unquestionably exists and the only question is what remedy is appropriate, a court may be forced to explore the whys and wherefores of its remedial power in plain terms. The following case presents such a situation.

BIVENS V. SIX UNKNOWN NAMED AGENTS OF FEDERAL BUREAU OF NARCOTICS

Supreme Court of the United States
403 U.S. 388 (1971)

MR. JUSTICE BRENNAN delivered the opinion of the Court.

The Fourth Amendment provides that:

"The right of the people to be secure in their persons, houses, papers, and effects, against unreasonable searches and seizures, shall not be violated. . . ."

In Bell v. Hood, 327 U.S. 678 (1946), we reserved the question whether violation of that command by a federal agent acting under color of his authority gives rise to a cause of action for damages consequent upon his unconstitutional conduct. Today we hold that it does.

This case has its origin in an arrest and search carried out on the morning of November 26, 1965. Petitioner's complaint alleged that on that day respondents, agents of the Federal Bureau of Narcotics acting under claim of federal authority, entered his apartment and arrested him for alleged narcotics violations. The agents manacled petitioner in front of his wife and children, and threatened to arrest the entire family. They searched the apartment from stem to stern. Thereafter, petitioner was taken to the federal courthouse in Brooklyn, where he was interrogated, booked, and subjected to a visual strip search.

On July 7, 1967, petitioner brought suit in Federal District Court. In addition to the allegations above, his complaint asserted that the arrest and search were effected without a warrant, and that unreasonable force was employed in making the arrest; fairly read, it alleges as well that the arrest was made without probable cause. Petitioner claimed to have suffered great humiliation, embarrassment, and mental suffering as a result of the agents' unlawful conduct, and sought $15,000 damages from each of them. The District Court, on respondents' motion, dismissed the complaint on the ground, *inter alia,* that it failed to state a cause of action. The Court of Appeals, one judge concurring specially, affirmed on that basis. * * * We reverse.

I

Respondents do not argue that petitioner should be entirely without remedy for an unconstitutional invasion of his rights by federal agents. In respondents' view, however, the rights that petitioner asserts—primarily rights of privacy—are creations of state and not of federal law. Accordingly, they argue, petitioner may obtain money damages to redress invasion of these rights only by an action in tort, under state law, in the state courts. In this scheme the Fourth Amendment would serve merely to limit the extent to which the agents could defend the state law tort suit by asserting that their actions were a valid exercise of federal power: if the agents were shown to have violated the Fourth Amendment, such a defense would be lost to them and they would stand before the state law merely as private individuals. * * *

We think that respondents' thesis rests upon an unduly restrictive view of the Fourth Amendment's protection against unreasonable searches and seizures by federal agents, a view that has consistently been rejected by this Court. Respondents seek to treat the relationship between a citizen and a federal agent unconstitutionally exercising his authority as no different from the relationship between two private citizens. In so doing, they ignore the fact that power, once granted, does not disappear like a magic gift when it is wrongfully used. An agent acting—albeit unconstitutionally—in the name of the United States possesses a far greater capacity for harm than an individual trespasser exercising no authority other than his own. Accordingly, as our cases make clear, the Fourth Amendment operates as a limitation upon the exercise of federal power regardless of whether the State in whose jurisdiction that power is exercised would prohibit or penalize the identical act if engaged in by a private citizen. * * *

That damages may be obtained for injuries consequent upon a violation of the Fourth Amendment by federal officials should hardly seem a surprising proposition. Historically, damages have been regarded as the ordinary remedy for an invasion of personal interests in liberty. Of course, the Fourth Amendment does not in so many words provide for its enforcement by an award of money damages for the consequences of its violation. But "it is * * * well settled that where legal rights have been invaded, and a federal statute provides for a general right to sue for such invasion, federal courts may use any available remedy to make good the wrong done." The present case involves no special factors counseling hesitation in the absence of affirmative action by Congress. We are not dealing with a question of "federal fiscal policy," as in United States v. Standard Oil Co., 332 U.S. 301, 311 (1947). In that case we refused to infer from the Government-soldier relationship that the United States could recover damages from one who negligently injured a soldier and thereby caused the Government to pay his medical expenses and lose his services during the course of his hospitalization. Noting that Congress was normally quite solicitous where the federal purse was involved, we pointed out that "the United States [was] the party plaintiff to the suit. And the United States has power at any time to create the liability." Nor are we asked in this case to impose liability upon a congressional employee for actions contrary to no constitutional prohibition, but merely said to be in excess of the authority delegated to him by the Congress. Finally, we cannot accept respondents' formulation of the question as whether the availability of money damages is necessary to enforce the Fourth Amendment. For we have here no explicit congressional declaration that persons injured by a federal officer's violation of the Fourth Amendment may not recover money damages from the agents, but must instead be remitted to another remedy, equally effective in the view of Congress. The question is merely whether petitioner, if he can demonstrate an injury consequent upon the violation by federal agents of his Fourth Amendment rights, is entitled to redress his injury through a particular remedial mechanism normally available in the federal courts. "The very essence of civil liberty certainly consists in the right of every individual to claim the protection of the laws, whenever he receives an injury." Marbury v. Madison, 1 Cranch 137, 163 (1803). Having concluded that petitioner's complaint states a cause of action under the Fourth Amendment, * * * we hold that petitioner is entitled to recover money damages for any injuries he has suffered as a result of the agents' violation of the Amendment.

II

In addition to holding that petitioner's complaint had failed to state facts making out a cause of action, the District Court ruled that in any event respondents were immune from liability by virtue of their official position. This question was not passed upon by the Court of Appeals, and accordingly we do not consider it here. The judgment of the Court of Appeals is reversed and the case is remanded for further proceedings consistent with this opinion.

So ordered.

MR. JUSTICE HARLAN, concurring in the judgment.

* * * For the reasons set forth below, I am of the opinion that federal courts do have the power to award damages for violation of "constitutionally protected interests" and I agree with the Court that a traditional judicial remedy such as damages is appropriate to the vindication of the personal interests protected by the Fourth Amendment.

I

I turn first to the contention that the constitutional power of federal courts to accord Bivens damages for his claim depends on the passage of a statute creating a "federal cause of action." Although the point is not entirely free of ambiguity, I do not understand either the Government or my dissenting Brothers to maintain that Bivens' contention that he is entitled to be free from the type of official conduct prohibited by the Fourth Amendment depends on a decision by the State in which he resides to accord him a remedy. * * * [T]he interest which Bivens claims—to be free from official conduct in contravention of the Fourth Amendment—is a federally protected interest. Therefore, the question of judicial *power* to grant Bivens damages is not a problem of the "source" of the "right"; instead, the question is whether the power to authorize damages as a judicial remedy for the vindication of a federal constitutional right is placed by the Constitution itself exclusively in Congress' hands.

II

The contention that the federal courts are powerless to accord a litigant damages for a claimed invasion of his federal constitutional rights until Congress explicitly authorizes the remedy cannot rest on the notion that the decision to grant compensatory relief involves a resolution of policy considerations not susceptible of judicial discernment. Thus, in suits for damages based on violations of federal statutes lacking any express authorization of a damage remedy, this Court has authorized such relief where, in its view, damages are necessary to effectuate the congressional policy underpinning the substantive provisions of the statute.

If it is not the nature of the remedy which is thought to render a judgment as to the appropriateness of damages inherently "legislative," then it must be the nature of the legal interest offered as an occasion for invoking otherwise appropriate judicial relief. But I do not think that the fact that the interest is protected by the Constitution rather than statute or common law justifies the assertion that federal courts are powerless to grant damages in the absence of explicit congressional action authorizing the remedy. Initially, I note that it would be at least anomalous to conclude that the federal judiciary—while competent to choose among the range of traditional judicial remedies to implement statutory and common-law policies, and even to generate substantive rules governing primary behavior in furtherance of broadly formulated policies articulated by statute or Constitution—is powerless to accord a damages remedy to vindicate social policies which, by virtue of their inclusion in the Constitution, are aimed predominantly at restraining the Government as an instrument of the popular will.

More importantly, the presumed availability of federal equitable relief against threatened invasions of constitutional interests appears entirely to negate the contention that the status of an interest as constitutionally protected divests federal courts of the power to grant damages absent express congressional authorization. * * *

If explicit congressional authorization is an absolute prerequisite to the power of a federal court to accord compensatory relief regardless of the necessity or appropriateness of damages as a remedy simply because of the status of a legal interest as constitutionally protected, then it seems to me that explicit congressional authorization is similarly prerequisite to the exercise of equitable remedial discretion in favor of constitutionally protected interests. Conversely, if a general grant of jurisdiction to the federal courts by Congress is thought adequate to empower a federal court to grant equitable relief for all areas of subject-matter jurisdiction enumerated therein, see 28 U.S.C. § 1331(a), then it seems to me that the same statute is sufficient to empower a federal court to grant a traditional remedy at law. Of course, the special historical traditions governing the federal equity system might still bear on the comparative appropriateness of granting equitable relief as opposed to money damages. That possibility, however, relates, not to whether the federal courts have the power to afford one type of remedy as opposed to the other, but rather to the criteria which should govern the exercise of our power. To that question, I now pass.

III

The major thrust of the Government's position is that, where Congress has not expressly authorized a particular remedy, a federal court should exercise its power to accord a traditional form of judicial relief at the behest of a litigant, who claims a constitutionally protected interest has been invaded, only where the remedy is "essential," or "indispensable for vindicating constitutional rights." * * * It is argued that historically the Court has rarely exercised the power to accord such relief in the absence of an express congressional authorization and that "[i]f Congress had thought that federal officers should be subject to a law different than state law, it would have had no difficulty in saying so, as it did with respect to state officers * * *" 42 U.S.C. § 1983. Although conceding that the standard of determining whether a damage remedy should be utilized to effectuate statutory policies is one of "necessity" or "appropriateness," the Government contends that questions concerning congressional discretion to modify judicial remedies relating to constitutionally protected interests warrant a more stringent constraint on the exercise of judicial power with respect to this class of legally protected interests.

These arguments for a more stringent test to govern the grant of damages in constitutional cases seem to be adequately answered by the point that the judiciary has a particular responsibility to assure the vindication of constitutional interests such as those embraced by the Fourth Amendment. To be sure, "it must be remembered that legislatures are ultimate guardians of the liberties and welfare of the people in quite as great a degree as the courts." But it must also be recognized that the Bill of Rights is particularly intended to vindicate the interests of the individual in the face of the popular will as expressed in legislative majorities; at the very least, it strikes me as no more appropriate to await express congressional authorization of traditional judicial relief with regard to these legal interests than with respect to interests protected by federal statutes.

The question then, is, as I see it, whether compensatory relief is "necessary" or "appropriate" to the vindication of the interest asserted. In resolving that question, it seems to me that the range of policy considerations we may take into account is at least as broad as the range of those a legislature would consider with respect to an express statutory authorization of a traditional remedy. In this regard I agree with the Court that the appropriateness of according Bivens compensatory relief does not turn simply on the deterrent effect liability will have on federal official conduct. Damages as a traditional form of compensation for invasion of a legally protected interest may be entirely appropriate even if no substantial deterrent effects on future official lawlessness might be thought to result. * * *

And I think it is clear that Bivens advances a claim of the sort that, if proved, would be properly compensable in damages. The personal interests protected by the Fourth Amendment are those we attempt to capture by the notion of "privacy"; while the Court today properly points out that the type of harm which officials can inflict when they invade protected zones of an individual's life are different from the types of harm private citizens inflict on one another, the experience of judges in dealing with private trespass and false imprisonment claims supports the conclusion that courts of law are capable of making the types of judgment concerning causation and magnitude of injury necessary to accord meaningful compensation for invasion of Fourth Amendment rights.

* * * [I]t is apparent that some form of damages is the only possible remedy for someone in Bivens' alleged position. It will be a rare case indeed in which an individual in Bivens' position will be able to obviate the harm by securing injunctive relief from any court. However desirable a direct remedy against the Government might be as a substitute for individual official liability, the sovereign still remains immune to suit. Finally, assuming Bivens' innocence of the crime charged, the "exclusionary rule" is simply irrelevant. For people in Bivens' shoes, it is damages or nothing.

The only substantial policy consideration advanced against recognition of a federal cause of action for violation of Fourth Amendment rights by federal officials is the incremental expenditure of judicial resources that will be necessitated by this class of litigation. * * * I simply cannot agree with my Brother Black that the possibility of "frivolous" claims—if defined simply as claims with no legal merit—warrants closing the courthouse doors to people in Bivens' situation. There are other ways, short of that, of coping with frivolous lawsuits.

* * * Judicial resources, I am well aware, are increasingly scarce these days. Nonetheless, when we automatically close the courthouse door solely on this basis, we implicitly express a value judgment on the comparative importance of classes of legally protected interests. And current limitations upon the effective functioning of the courts arising from budgetary inadequacies should not be permitted to stand in the way of the recognition of otherwise sound constitutional principles. * * *

[The dissenting opinions of CHIEF JUSTICE BURGER, JUSTICE BLACK, and JUSTICE BLACKMUN have been omitted.]

NOTES

1.   Did the *Bivens* court usurp a power belonging to Congress? Chief Justice Burger, Justice Blackmun, and Justice Black each dissented in *Bivens*. Although each wrote separately, all agreed that creating a remedy for violations of the Fourth Amendment was a power reserved to Congress under the Constitution:

> Although Congress has created such a federal cause of action against *state* officials acting under color of state law [42 U.S.C. § 1983], it has never created such a cause of action against federal officials. If it wanted to do so, Congress could, of course, create a remedy against federal officials who violate the Fourth Amendment in the performance of their duties. But the point of this case and the fatal weakness in the Court's judgment is that neither Congress nor the State of New York has enacted legislation creating such a right of action. For us to do so is, in my judgment, an exercise of power that the Constitution does not give us.

403 U.S. at 427–28 (Black, J. dissenting).

The dissenters contended that the Court cannot provide a remedy for a violation of some constitutional rights unless the remedy is authorized by Congress or by the Constitution itself. The majority seemed to say that the Court is free to use any traditional remedy to vindicate the plaintiff's rights, unless Congress has withdrawn that authority. Who has the better of the argument?

As Justice Harlan points out, it has always been presumed that the court has the power to issue an injunction at an individual's behest to stop a federal officer from violating the Constitution, even without an express congressional enactment authorizing that remedy. Would the dissenters deny the court the authority to grant an injunction to prevent a threatened violation of the Constitution? What is the difference between enjoining a future violation and awarding damages for a past violation? *See* John C. Jeffries, *The Right-Remedy Gap in Constitutional Law*, 109 Yale L.J. 87, 90 (1999) (arguing that by limiting the damages remedy while affording complete injunctive relief, courts shift the emphasis of constitutional litigation from "reparation toward reform" and thus "facilitate constitutional change by reducing the costs of innovation").

2.   Where does the majority locate the authority it is exercising in *Bivens?* Is it conferred by the text of the Constitution, perhaps by article III, section 2, which extends the judicial power "to all cases * * * arising under this Constitution"? Or is it by the grant of jurisdiction contained in 28 U.S.C. § 1331(a), which provides, "the district courts shall have original jurisdiction of all civil actions arising under the Constitution, laws, or treaties of the United States"? Sometimes it is suggested that a mandate can be found in the due process clause of the Fifth Amendment, see Richard H. Fallon, *Of Legislative*

Courts, Administrative Agencies, and Article III, 101 Harv.L.Rev. 916, 955 n.223 (1988), or that the amendments themselves carry "a self-executing force that not only permits but requires the courts to recognize remedies appropriate for their violation." Walter E. Dellinger, *Of Rights and Remedies: The Constitution as a Sword*, 85 Harv.L.Rev. 1532 (1972).

3.   Once the Supreme Court decided that it did not need express congressional authorization to allow Bivens to sue for damages, it still had to decide whether damages were appropriate. What is it that convinces the Court that an award of damages is an appropriate remedy for a violation of the fourth amendment? After all, Bivens already had a number of remedies at his disposal. He could have sued to enjoin future violations of his rights. If he had been arrested, he could have invoked the exclusionary rule to prevent the use of the evidence in a criminal proceeding. *See* William C. Heffernan, *Foreword: The Fourth Amendment Exclusionary Rule as a Constitutional Remedy*, 88 Geo.L.J. 799 (2000). Bivens could have sued the federal officers in state court for a number of torts, including trespass, assault, battery, false arrest, defamation and intentional infliction of emotional distress. With all of these remedies available, why does the Court allow a suit for damages for violation of Bivens's constitutional rights?

If a damages remedy is appropriate when the Fourth Amendment is violated, does it necessarily follow that a damages remedy is equally appropriate for all constitutional violations? Justice Harlan's concurrence suggests not. After noting that the personal interests the Fourth Amendment protects are very closely analogous to such torts as false imprisonment and trespass, providing judges a background of experience for handling compensation claims, Justice Harlan noted, "The same, of course, may not be true with respect to other types of constitutionally protected interests, and therefore the appropriateness of money damages may well vary with the nature of the personal interest asserted." 403 U.S. at 409 n.9.

4.   The Supreme Court has subsequently limited *Bivens* by holding that there should be no implied remedy where 1) there is "any alternative, existing process for protecting" the plaintiff's interest," or 2) there are "special factors counseling hesitation." Minneci v. Pollard, 565 U.S. ___, 132 S.Ct. 617, 621 (2012); Wilkie v. Robbins, 551 U.S. 537, 550 (2007). Special factors counseling hesitation have included the "the special nature of military life." Chappell v. Wallace, 462 U.S. 296 (1983); United States v. Stanley, 483 U.S. 669 (1987). But most cases ultimately have denied the *Bivens* remedy based on the existence of sufficient alternative available processes like administrative procedures or state tort laws that provide meaningful remedies, even if those remedies are not as comprehensive as a *Bivens* remedy. *Minneci*, 132 S.Ct. at 625–26; Schweiker v. Chilicky, 487 U.S. 412 (1988); Bush v. Lucas, 462 U.S. 367, 368 (1983).

5.   Since *Bivens* itself, the Supreme Court has endorsed a *Bivens* action in only two other cases, Davis v. Passman, 442 U.S. 228 (1979) (Fifth Amendment due process claim based on sexual harassment by member of Congress), and Carlson v. Green, 446 U.S. 14 (1980) (Eighth Amendment claim

for cruel and unusual punishment arising out of prisoner's death from medical malpractice). "[I]n most cases, *Bivens* claims go nowhere." David Zaring, *Three Models of Constitutional Torts*, 2 J.Tort L. 3, 8 (2008).

Justice Scalia made his position clear on why this should be so:

> *Bivens* is a relic of the heady days in which this Court assumed common-law powers to create causes of action—decreeing them to be "implied" by the mere existence of a statutory or constitutional prohibition. As the Court points out, * * * we have abandoned that power to invent "implications" in the statutory field. There is even greater reason to abandon it in the constitutional field, since an "implication" imagined in the Constitution can presumably not even be repudiated by Congress. I would limit *Bivens* and its two follow-on cases [*Davis* and *Carlson*] to the precise circumstances that they involved.

Correctional Services Corp. v. Malesko, 534 U.S. 61, 75 (2001); *accord Wilkie*, 551 U.S. at 568 (Thomas, J., concurring).

Bivens claims, however, are viable in the lower courts. *See* Alexander A. Reinert, *Measuring the Success of* Bivens *Litigation and Its Consequences for the Individual Liability Model*, 62 Stan.L.Rev. 809 (2010) (reporting 38 percent success rate on *Bivens* claims with counsel). Some recent cases have allowed the implied remedy for claims brought by detainees without other clear avenues for relief. Turkmen v. Hasty, 789 F.3d 218 (2d.Cir. 2015) (Eighth Amendment claim by Muslim detainees for punitive conditions of confinement); Ferguson v. United States, ___ F.Supp.3d ___, 2016 WL 1555811 (E.D.Pa. Apr. 18, 2016) (claim by airline passenger detained by security at private hospital); *but see* Vance v. Rumsfeld, 701 F.3d 193 (7th Cir. 2012) (en banc) (denying *Bivens* claim for damages by civilians tor military interrogation and detainment), *cert. denied*, 133 S.Ct. 2796 (2013).

6.   Can Congress prohibit the federal courts from granting a remedy for constitutional violations? In the Prison Litigation Reform Act (PLRA), 18 U.S.C. § 362, Congress prohibited prisoners from bringing a federal civil action for mental or emotional injury suffered while in custody without a showing of prior physical injury. In Zehner v. Trigg, 133 F.3d 459 (7th Cir.1997), the court relied on this section to deny damages for mental distress to prisoners who had been exposed to asbestos, but who had not suffered a physical injury. As for the prisoners' claim that this section of the PLRA was an unconstitutional attempt by Congress to strip the federal courts of their power to remedy constitutional violations, the court said:

> But the legal point remains: the Constitution does not demand an individually effective remedy for every constitutional violation. * * * If other prisoners are currently being exposed to asbestos within the Indiana prison system, they may seek injunctive relief for the violation. If the plaintiffs in this case develop asbestos-related illnesses, they themselves will be able to sue for damages. Because

these remedies remain, Congress' decision to restrict the availability of damages is constitutional as applied in this case.

133 F.3d at 462.

Could Congress eliminate the federal courts' power to grant injunctive relief? The Supreme Court has never directly addressed the issue. In Webster v. Doe, 486 U.S. 592 (1988), however, the Court refused to interpret a statute to preclude all claims for injunctive relief for violations of constitutional rights, because "serious constitutional questions would arise if a federal statute were construed to deny any judicial forum for a colorable constitutional claim." Justice Scalia dissented: "[I]t is simply untenable that there must be a judicial remedy for every constitutional violation." 486 U.S. at 613.

7.   Finally, a note about terminology. In Davis v. Passman, 442 U.S. 228 (1979), Justice Brennan defined some basic terms that are often used incorrectly and synonymously:

> [J]urisdiction is a question of whether a federal court has the power, under the constitution or laws of the United States, to hear a case; standing is a question of whether a plaintiff is sufficiently adversary to a defendant to create an Art. III case or controversy, or at least to overcome prudential limitations on federal court jurisdiction; cause of action is a question of whether a particular plaintiff is a member of the class of litigants that may, as a matter of law, appropriately invoke the power of the court; and relief is a question of the various remedies a federal court may make available.

442 U.S. at 239 n.18. Bivens addressed the last two of these inquiries, asking, does a cause of action for damages exist when the fourth amendment is violated?

Implying Remedies for Statutory Violations

Just as the Constitution often confers rights without mentioning remedies, Congress may enact a statute without expressly indicating whether individuals harmed by a violation of the statute can sue. For example, Congress may pass legislation making conduct a crime, but say nothing about whether injured parties may privately sue for damages, injunctive relief, or any other remedy.

The Supreme Court addressed this issue in Cort v. Ash, 422 U.S. 66 (1975) where, Congress had made it a crime punishable by a fine of $5000 for a corporation to contribute to a Presidential campaign. (The statute was later repealed, although it has been replaced by similar provisions). Cort sued on behalf of a corporation in which he held stock, alleging that the corporation's directors had violated the statute, and seeking damages.

Writing for the majority, Justice Brennan withdrew considerably from the position in Justice Harlan's concurrence in Bivens that a private cause of action will be made available any time a court views it as "necessary or appropriate" to effectuate the statutory scheme. Instead, the Court applied a four-part test looking at whether the plaintiff was an intended beneficiary of the statute, the legislative intent, the legislative scheme, and whether the area of law was traditionally left to state control.

Applying this test, Justice Brennan concluded that the statute was not intended to protect shareholders from the fiscal consequences of campaign contributions, and that therefore it would be inappropriate to allow shareholders a private cause of action for damages.

Subsequently, the Court elevated the second *Cort* factor as the dispositive test, looking exclusively to Congressional intent to decide whether a private cause of action and remedy exist for a statutory violation. Alexander v. Sandoval, 532 U.S. 275 (2001) (inquiry "begins and ends with the text and structure of the statute"); Touche Ross & Co. v. Redington, 442 U.S. 560 (1979) ("[O]ur task is limited solely to determining whether Congress intended to create the private right of action."). Justice Scalia, writing for a divided Court in *Alexander v. Sandoval* explained:

> Implicit in our discussion thus far has been a particular understanding of the genesis of private causes of action. Like substantive federal law itself, private rights of action to enforce federal law must be created by Congress. The judicial task is to interpret the statute Congress has passed to determine whether it displays an intent to create not just a private right but also a private remedy. Statutory intent on this latter point is determinative. Without it, a cause of action does not exist and courts may not create on, not matter how desirable that might be as a policy matter, or how compatible with the statute . . . . Respondents would have us revert in this case to the understanding of private causes of action that held sway 40 years ago . . . . Having sworn of the habit of venturing beyond Congress's intent, we will not accept respondents' invitation to have one last drink.

532 U.S. at 286–87.

Thus, in order to promote certainty in the law, Congress should be on notice that it must speak explicitly if it wishes to create a remedy, and therefore "a flat rule that private rights of action will not be implied in statutes hereafter enacted" should be followed. Thompson v. Thompson, 484 U.S. 174, 192 (1988) (Scalia, J. concurring).

At times the Court seemed to suggest that a plaintiff could avoid the difficulties of implied remedies by pursing a claim under 42 U.S.C. § 1983. Section 1983 is a federal statute providing for civil actions for deprivation of "any rights, privileges, or immunities secured by the Constitution and laws."

In Gonzaga University v. Doe, 536 U.S. 273 (2002), Chief Justice Rehnquist explained the distinction between a claim made under section 1983 and an implied cause of action for violation of a federal law:

> Plaintiffs suing under § 1983 do not have the burden of showing an intent to create a private remedy because § 1983 generally supplies a remedy for the vindication of rights secured by federal statutes. Once

a plaintiff demonstrates that a statute confers an individual right, the right is presumptively enforceable by § 1983.

Not every federal law, however, confers individual rights. Chief Justice Rehnquist continued:

> But the initial inquiry—determining whether a statute confers any right at all—is no different from the initial inquiry in an implied right of action case, the express purpose of which is to determine whether or not a statute "confers rights on a particular class of persons."
>
> * * * Accordingly, where the text and structure of a statute provide no indication that Congress intends to create new individual rights, there is no basis for a private suit, whether under § 1983 or under an implied right of action.

536 U.S. at 284–85. Thus, Chief Justice Rehnquist concluded that a student who was harmed when his school records were wrongly disclosed had no cause of action under the Family Educational Rights and Privacy Act, because Congress did not intend to create individually enforceable rights when it enacted the law. *See also* Armstrong v. Exceptional Child Center, 575 U.S. ___, 135 S.Ct. 1378, 1385 (2015) (no private remedy of injunction available for Medicaid providers to enforce federal reimbursement statute against state). Similarly, no section 1983 cause of action is available if Congress expressly or implicitly indicates that a statute's enforcement scheme is to be the exclusive remedy for a violation. *Compare* Fitzgerald v. Barnstable School Committee, 555 U.S. 246 (2009) (Congress did not intend Title IX to preclude a section 1983 action for unconstitutional gender discrimination in the schools) *with* City of Rancho Palos Verdes v. Abrams, 544 U.S. 113 (2005) (no cause of action under section 1983 for violation of the Telecommunication Act of 1996).

"Where there's a right, there's a remedy"

The idea that there must be a remedy for every violation of a right is a powerful one. It has been used, as in *Bivens,* to justify the creation of a cause of action without express constitutional or statutory warrant. It has also been invoked by state courts to check legislative action that limits the remedies available to injured plaintiffs. *See* Thomas A. Phillips, *The Constitutional Right to a Remedy*, 78 N.Y.U.L.Rev. 1309 (2003) (discussing cases relying on "right to a remedy" or "open courts" guarantees in state constitutions to strike down a variety of tort reform measures). *See also* John C.P. Goldberg, *The Constitutional Status of Tort Law*, 115 Yale L.J. 524 (2005) (providing remedies for private wrongs is a fundamental element of the American legal system that is embodied in the constitution and limits the power of states to enact tort reform legislation).

Yet as this chapter makes clear, the commitment to this principle is hardly total. Not every violation of a law violates an individual's rights; not every violation of a right gives rise to a cause of action in federal or state court. As one scholar has argued, "modern doctrine clearly refutes the notion that there is a constitutional right to a remedy for every constitutional violation." Richard H. Fallon, Jr., *Some Confusions About Due Process, Judicial Review, and Constitutional Remedies*, 93 Colum.L.Rev. 309 (1993). Even in *Bivens,* after all, Justice Brennan made allowance for "special factors counseling hesitation"— concerns, that is, that are allowed to undercut the goal of a complete remedy. Concern for federalism, separation of powers, and a proper accommodation of the interests of the plaintiff and the defendant all factor into the search for the proper remedy.

Questions about the exact nature of the relationship between right and remedy have taken on increased importance as Congress—in the Prison Litigation Reform Act, for example—has attempted to reign in the courts' remedial authority, or as the Supreme Court has attempted to reign in Congress's assertions of its remedial authority under section five of the Fourteenth Amendment. *See, e.g.,* Kimel v. Florida Board of Regents, 528 U.S. 62 (2000) (legislation purporting to abrogate the states' sovereign immunity in age discrimination lawsuits was "so out of proportion to a supposed remedial or preventive object" that it could not be justified as an exercise of Congress's power to remedy violations of the equal protection clause). One result has been a vigorous debate in the law reviews over *whether* "where there's a right, there's a remedy." *See, e.g.,* Judith Resnik, *Constricting Remedies: The Rehnquist Judiciary, Congress and Federal Power*, 78 Ind.L.J. 223 (2003); Tracy A. Thomas, *Congress' Section 5 Power and Remedial Rights*, 34 U.C. Davis L.Rev. 673 (2001).

On balance, it is probably more accurate to say that where there's a right, there may be many remedies, or none. As courts struggle with application on the ground, scholars debate the ultimate goal of remedies. Professor Fallon contends that what is constitutionally indispensable is a "scheme of constitutional remedies sufficient to keep government tolerably within the bounds of law." 93 Colum.L.Rev. at 338. Professor Thomas argues that the proper goal should be plaintiff-focused, so that "an adequate remedy must be one that provides individualized redress to the plaintiff" in a way that is meaningful. *Remedial Rights*, 34 U.C. Davis L.Rev. at 761; Tracy A. Thomas, *Restriction of Tort Remedies and the Constraints of Due Process: The Right to an Adequate Remedy*, 39 Akron L.Rev. 975 (2006). Professor Cover agrees with the goal of a meaningful remedy, grounding that requirement in the First Amendment right of petition. Benjamin Plener Cover, *The First Amendment Right to a Remedy*, 50 U.C.Davis L. Rev. ___ (forthcoming 2017). These are the questions that occupy the remedies course. Whether it is a legislature, a court, or counsel deciding, the key to choosing among remedies lies in understanding the nature and characteristics of each remedy: how it works, how much it costs, when it works well, and what its limits are. To these issues we now turn.

CHAPTER 2

INJUNCTIONS

■ ■ ■

A. THE NATURE OF AN INJUNCTION

An *injunction* is an equitable remedy that is an order directing a person to act or refrain from acting in a specified way. An injunction is a *prospective* remedy meaning that it operates going forward to direct the defendant's future behavior, rather than merely requiring the payment of money. An injunction acts *in personam* because it is personal to the defendant and requires individual compliance by the defendant, enforced by ancillary remedies of contempt. Dan B. Dobbs, *The Law of Remedies* § 2.1(1) (2d ed.1993).

The availability of contempt to enforce the order is a key difference between an injunction and other remedies. Violation of an injunction, as an order of the court, is contempt of court and can be remedied independently by punitive or coercive contempt, as discussed in Chapter 3. The threat of contempt and its additional monetary and prison penalties force the defendant's strict compliance with the injunction and restrains its behavior and operations. For this reason, defendants generally disfavor injunctions and prefer to resolve decisions against them through monetary relief, which avoids this judicial oversight and double sanction.

Injunctions fall within the broad category of equity. "Equity" can mean several things, including the institutional history of courts of equity, the model of judicial decision making emphasizing flexibility and discretion, or simply a general concept of fairness and mercy. In Remedies, we often mean institutional history and judicial discretion when citing equity. Historically, injunctions developed out of English courts of equity, separate tribunals created apart from the courts of common law, in which the petitioner appealed to the discretion of the church or king's chancellor for assistance not otherwise available. F.W. Maitland, *Equity* 1–11 (A.H. Chayton & W.J. Whittaker, eds. 1910). Chancellors had broad discretion to craft remedies specific to the case ordering the defendant to action. Courts of equity had different writs, procedures, and remedies than the courts of common law. Today, virtually all American federal and state courts (except a few states) have merged their courts of law and equity. Equity, however, continues to be a relevant organizing concept for remedies deriving from this historical genesis. For example, many statutes designate the available remedies categorically as either "legal" or "equitable." *E.g.,* Sereboff v. Mid Atlantic Med. Servs., Inc., 547 U.S. 356 (2006) (federal employee retirement act). And the Seventh Amendment right to a trial by jury attaches only to legal relief, and thus judges, not juries, award equitable remedies. Chauffeurs, Teamsters & Helpers v. Terry, 494 U.S. 558, 565 (1990).

Equity conceptually can be thought of as a system comprised of three parts: remedies, enforcement devices, and defenses. Samuel L. Bray, *The System of Equitable Remedies*, 63 U.C.L.A. L. Rev. 530, 533–34 (2016). First, equity includes equitable remedies—predominantly the injunction, and also specific performance and equitable restitution (discussed in Chapter 7). Second, it encompasses equitable managerial devices of contempt, modification, termination, and receivers (discussed in Chapter 3) that assist the court in enforcing the injunction. And third, equity includes equitable defenses like laches, unclean hands, and estoppel (discussed in Chapter 8). *Id.* at 534.

> These three categories of components are logically connected. It is necessary to have remedies that compel action or inaction. And sometimes that compulsion needs to be adverbial or open-ended—requiring not only that something be done but also specifying the manner in which it must be done, or demanding a process of obedience over time. In order to use these remedies well, courts need devices for managing the parties and ensuring compliance (devices that are not needed, for example, for the mere payment of a defined sum of money). But these remedies and managerial devices can be costly, and they are vulnerable to abuse. And because they exist, there need to be constraints. In other words, the equitable remedies need the managerial devices; the equitable remedies and managerial devices need the constraints. This is, roughly speaking, the logic of the system of equitable remedies, i.e., the remedies and the remedy-related rules that are at present called equitable in American law. This logic works in both public and private law.

Id. at 534

We begin our study of equity in this chapter by examining the nature of the equitable remedy of the injunction.

HECHT CO. v. BOWLES

Supreme Court of the United States
321 U.S. 321 (1944)

MR. JUSTICE DOUGLAS delivered the opinion of the Court.

Sec. 205(a) of the Emergency Price Control Act of 1942 provides:

"Whenever in the judgment of the Administrator any person has engaged or is about to engage in any acts or practices which constitute or will constitute a violation of any provision of section 4 of this Act, he may make application to the appropriate court for an order enjoining such acts or practices, or for an order enforcing compliance with such provision, and upon a showing by the Administrator that such person has engaged or is about to engage in any such acts or practices a permanent or temporary injunction, restraining order, or other order shall be granted without bond."

The question in this case is whether the Administrator, having established that a defendant has engaged in acts or practices violative of § 4 of the Act is entitled as of right to an injunction restraining the defendant from engaging in such acts or practices or whether the court has some discretion to grant or withhold such relief.

Sec. 4(a) of the Act makes it unlawful for a person to sell or deliver any commodity in violation of specified orders or regulations of the Administrator. A regulation issued under § 2 of the Act and effective in May, 1942 provided that no person should sell or deliver any commodity at a price higher than the authorized maximum price as fixed and determined by the regulation. Since maximum prices were fixed with reference to earlier base periods, the regulation also provided for the preservation and examination of existing records. And provision was likewise made for the keeping of current records reflecting sales made under the regulation and for the filing of maximum prices with the Administrator.

There is no substantial controversy over the facts. Petitioner operates a large department store in Washington, D.C. and did a business of about $20,000,000 in 1942. There are 107 departments in the store and each sells a separate line of merchandise. In the fall of 1942 the Administrator started an investigation to determine whether petitioner was complying with the Act and the regulation. The investigation was a "spot check," confined to seven departments. In each of the seven departments violations were disclosed. As a result of this suit was brought. The complaint charged violations of the maximum price provisions of the regulation and violations of the regulations governing the keeping of records and reporting to the Administrator. The Administrator prayed for an injunction enjoining petitioner from selling, delivering or offering for sale or delivery any commodity in violation of the regulation and from failing to keep complete and accurate records as required by the regulation. In its answer petitioner pleaded among other things that any failure or neglect to comply with the regulation was involuntary and was corrected as soon as discovered.

Numerous violations both as respects prices and records were discovered. Thus in six of the seven departments investigated there had occurred between May and October, 1942 some 3700 sales in excess of the maximum prices with overcharges of some $4600. The statements filed with the Administrator were deficient, some 400 items of merchandise being omitted. And there were over 300 items with respect to which no records were kept showing how the maximum prices had been determined.

There is no doubt, however, of petitioner's good faith and diligence. The District Court found that the manager of the store had offered it as a laboratory in which the Administrator might experiment with any regulation which might be issued. Prior to the promulgation of the regulation the petitioner had created a new section known as the price control office. That office undertook to bring petitioner into compliance with the requirements of the regulation in advance of its effective date. The head of that office together with seven assistants devoted full time to that endeavor. But the store had about 2,000 employees and over one million two hundred thousand articles of merchandise. In the furniture departments alone there were over fifty-four thousand transactions in the first ten months of 1942. Difficulties were encountered in interpreting the regulation, in determining the exact nature of an article and whether it had been previously sold and at what price, etc. The absence of adequate records made it difficult to ascertain prices during the earlier base-period. Misunderstanding of the regulation, confusion on the part of employees not trained in such problems of interpretation and administration, the complexity of the problem, and the fallibility of humans all combined to produce numerous errors. But the District Court concluded that the "mistakes in pricing and listing were all made in good faith and without intent to violate the regulations."

The District Court also found that the mistakes brought to light "were at once corrected, and vigorous steps were taken by The Hecht Company to prevent recurrence of these mistakes or further mistakes in the future." The company increased its price control office to twenty-eight employees. New methods of internal control were instituted early in November, 1942 with the view of avoiding future violations. That new system of control "greatly improved" the situation. Petitioner undertook to make repayment of all overcharges brought to light by the investigation in case of customers who could be identified. It proposed to contribute the remaining amount of such overcharges to some local charity. The District Court concluded that the issuance of an injunction would have "no effect by way of insuring better compliance in the future" and would be "unjust" to petitioner and not "in the public interest". It accordingly dismissed the complaint. On appeal the Court of Appeals for the District of Columbia reversed that judgment * * * [on the basis that § 205(a) mandated the issuance of an injunction or other order once a violation was found].

Respondent insists that the mandatory character of § 205(a) is clear from its language, history and purpose. He argues that "shall be granted" is not permissive, that since the same section provides that the Administrator "may" apply for an injunction and that, if so, the injunction "shall" be granted, "may" and "shall" are each used in the ordinary sense.

It is pointed out that when the bill (for which the Act in its final form was substituted) passed the House, § 205(a) provided that "upon a proper showing" an injunction or other order "shall be granted without bond." The words "upon a proper showing" were stricken in the Senate and were replaced by the words "upon a showing by the Administrator that such person has engaged or is about to engage in any such acts or practices." * * *

We agree that the cessation of violations, whether before or after the institution of a suit by the Administrator, is no bar to the issuance of an injunction under § 205(a). But we do not think that under all circumstances the court must issue the injunction or other order which the Administrator seeks.

It seems apparent on the face of § 205(a) that there is some room for the exercise of discretion on the part of the court. For the requirement is that a "permanent or temporary injunction, restraining order, or other order" be granted. Though the Administrator asks for an injunction, some "other order" might be more appropriate, or at least so appear to the court. Thus in the present case one judge in the Court of Appeals felt that the District Court should not have dismissed the complaint but should have entered an order retaining the case on the docket with the right of the Administrator, on notice, to renew his application for injunctive relief if violations recurred. It is indeed not difficult to imagine that in some situations that might be the fairest course to follow and one which would be as practically effective as the issuance of an injunction. Such an order, moreover, would seem to be a type of "other order" which a faithful reading of § 205(a) would permit a court to issue in a compliance proceeding. However that may be, it would seem clear that the court might deem some "other order" more appropriate for the evil at hand than the one which was sought. We cannot say that it lacks the power to make that choice. Thus it seems that § 205(a) falls short of making mandatory the issuance of an injunction merely because the Administrator asks it.

There is, moreover, support in the legislative history of § 205(a) for the view that "shall be granted" is less mandatory than a literal reading might suggest. [The Senate Report states that] " * * * courts are given jurisdiction to issue whatever order to enforce compliance is proper in the circumstances of each particular case." A grant of jurisdiction to issue compliance orders hardly suggests an absolute duty to do so under any and all circumstances. We cannot but think that if Congress had intended to make such a drastic departure from the traditions of equity practice, an unequivocal statement of its purpose would have been made.

We do not stop to compare the provisions of § 205(a) with the requirements of other federal statutes governing administrative agencies which, it is said, make it mandatory that those agencies take action when certain facts are shown to exist. We are dealing here with the requirements of equity practice with a background of several hundred years of history. Only the other day we stated that "An appeal to the equity jurisdiction conferred on federal district courts is an appeal to the sound discretion which guides the determinations of courts of equity." The historic injunctive process was designed to deter, not to punish. The essence of equity jurisdiction has been the power of the Chancellor to do equity and to mould each decree to the necessities of the particular case. Flexibility rather than rigidity has distinguished it. The qualities of mercy and practicality have made equity the instrument for nice adjustment and reconciliation between the public interest and private needs as well as between competing private claims. We do not believe that such a major departure from that long tradition as is here proposed should be lightly implied. We do not think the history or language of § 205(a) compel it. It should be noted, moreover, that § 205(a) governs the procedure in both federal and state courts. For § 205(c) gives the state courts concurrent jurisdiction with federal district courts of civil enforcement proceedings. It is therefore even more compelling to conclude that, if Congress desired to make such an abrupt departure from traditional equity practice as is suggested, it would have made its desire plain. Hence we resolve the ambiguities of § 205(a) in favor of that interpretation which affords a full opportunity for equity courts to treat enforcement proceedings under this emergency legislation in accordance with their traditional practices, as conditioned by the necessities of the public interest which Congress has sought to protect.

We do not mean to imply that courts should administer § 205(a) grudgingly. * * * [T]heir discretion under § 205(a) must be exercised in light of the large objectives of the Act. For the standards of the public interest, not the requirements of private litigation measure the propriety and need for injunctive relief in these cases. That discretion should reflect an acute awareness of the Congressional admonition that "of all the consequences of war, except human slaughter, inflation is the most destructive" and that delay or indifference may be fatal. Whether the District Court abused its discretion in dismissing the complaint is a question which we do not reach. The judgment must be reversed and the cause remanded to the Court of Appeals for that determination. * * *

NOTE

Hecht is much cited for its statements that courts have great flexibility in framing injunctions, as you will see in Section D of this chapter. *Hecht* also states an important canon of statutory construction—that courts should not read statutes to limit traditional equity practices unless the legislature clearly states that it intends to do so. *See also* Miller v. French, 530 U.S. 327 (2000) (reiterating canon). *Hecht* applies this canon in refusing to read the Emergency Price Control Act to transfer from the courts to the administrator the power to determine whether an injunction is warranted.

The goal of injunctive relief is to put the plaintiff in her rightful position, that is, the position she would have been in but for the harm. A court cannot aim to give the plaintiff more than her rightful position. But in aiming at the rightful position, it can issue injunctions that achieve more than the plaintiff's rightful position for prophylactic purposes when an injunction precisely targeted at the plaintiff's rightful position would be ineffective.

Section B of this chapter considers problems in determining the plaintiff's rightful position. Section C considers the major prerequisites to qualifying for injunctive relief—threat of harm and no adequate remedy at law. Section D considers the additional parts of the test for qualifying for injunction relief, balancing the equities and public interest, with particular attention to cases of that appear to grant less or more than the plaintiff's rightful position. Section E discusses injunctions in their particular context of specific performance and enforcing the terms of a contract.

B. THE PLAINTIFF'S RIGHTFUL POSITION AS THE MEASURE OF AN INJUNCTION

An injunction's primary aim must be to protect the plaintiff's rightful position. This phrase encompasses preventing future wrongdoing and, if the wrong has already occurred, repairing the harm done to the plaintiff. There are four types of injunctions available that restore plaintiff to her rightful position, though each does so in a different way. *Preventive* injunctions prevent continuing harm by stopping the legal wrong itself. *Reparative* injunctions repair the past wrong and its continuing effects. Professor Owen Fiss in his classic work *The Civil Rights Injunction* (1978) then used the term *structural* to describe injunctions that restructure or change how institutions such as jails or schools or companies work. A fourth category of *prophylactic* injunctions was later identified to describe an injunction that adds precautionary measures to address facilitators of continued harm. Tracy A. Thomas, *The Prophylactic Remedy: Normative Principles and Definitional Parameters of Broad Injunctive Relief*, 52 Buff.L.Rev. 301 (2004). An injunction may contain more than one of these types of measures in crafting an order to redress the threatened harm.

In many cases, what an injunction should do to protect the plaintiff's rightful position is evident from the law of liability. When the defendant fails to make deliveries under a contract, an injunction to protect the plaintiff's rightful position would require the defendant to make the deliveries. Or, when the defendant trespasses, an injunction to protect the plaintiff's rightful position would forbid future trespasses.

Sometimes, however, what an injunction should do to protect the plaintiff's rightful position is not so evident.

MT. HEALTHY CITY SCHOOL DISTRICT BOARD OF EDUCATION V. DOYLE

Supreme Court of the United States
429 U.S. 274 (1977)

MR. JUSTICE REHNQUIST delivered the opinion of the Court.

Respondent Doyle sued petitioner Mt. Healthy Board of Education in the United States District Court for the Southern District of Ohio. Doyle claimed that the Board's refusal to renew his contract in 1971 violated his rights under the First and Fourteenth Amendments to the United States Constitution. After a bench trial the District Court held that Doyle was entitled to reinstatement with backpay. The Court of Appeals for the Sixth Circuit affirmed the judgment, and we granted the Board's petition for certiorari * * * .

Doyle was first employed by the Board in 1966. He worked under one-year contracts for the first three years, and under a two-year contract from 1969 to 1971. In 1969 he was elected president of the Teachers' Association * * * . During Doyle's one-year term as president of the Association, and during the succeeding year when he served on its executive committee, there was apparently some tension in relations between the Board and the Association.

Beginning early in 1970, Doyle was involved in several incidents not directly connected with his role in the Teachers' Association. In one instance, he engaged in an argument with another teacher which culminated in the other teacher's slapping him. Doyle subsequently refused to accept an apology and insisted upon some punishment for the other teacher. His persistence in the matter resulted in the suspension of both teachers for one day, which was followed by a walkout by a number of other teachers, which in turn resulted in the lifting of the suspensions.

On other occasions, Doyle got into an argument with employees of the school cafeteria over the amount of spaghetti which had been served him; referred to students, in connection with a disciplinary complaint, as "sons of bitches"; and made an obscene gesture to two girls in connection with their failure to obey commands made in his capacity as cafeteria supervisor. Chronologically the last in the series of incidents which respondent was involved in during his employment by the Board was a telephone call by him to a local radio station. It was the Board's consideration of this incident which the court below found to be a violation of the First and Fourteenth Amendments.

In February 1971, the principal circulated to various teachers a memorandum relating to teacher dress and appearance, which was apparently prompted by the view of some in the administration that there was a relationship between teacher appearance and public support for bond issues. Doyle's response to the receipt of the memorandum on a subject which he apparently understood was to be settled by joint teacher-administration action was to convey the substance of the memorandum to a disc jockey at WSAI, a Cincinnati radio station, who promptly announced the adoption of the dress code as a news item. Doyle subsequently apologized to the principal, conceding that he should have made some prior communication of his criticism to the school administration.

Approximately one month later the superintendent made his customary annual recommendations to the Board as to the rehiring of nontenured teachers. He recommended that Doyle not be rehired. The same recommendation was made with respect to nine other teachers in the district, and in all instances, including Doyle's, the recommendation was adopted by the Board. Shortly after being notified of this decision, respondent requested a statement of reasons for the Board's actions. He received a statement citing "a notable lack of tact in handling professional matters which leaves much doubt as to your sincerity in establishing good school relationships." That general statement was followed by references to the radio station incident and to the obscene-gesture incident.

[The District Court found that all of these incidents had in fact occurred.]It concluded that respondent Doyle's telephone call to the radio station was "clearly protected by the First Amendment," and that because it had played a "substantial part" in the decision of the Board not to renew Doyle's employment, he was entitled to reinstatement with backpay. * * *

Doyle's claims under the First and Fourteenth Amendments are not defeated by the fact that he did not have tenure. Even though he could have been discharged for no reason whatever, and had no constitutional right to a hearing prior to the decision not to rehire him, he may nonetheless establish a claim to reinstatement if the decision not to rehire him was made by reason of his exercise of constitutionally protected First Amendment freedoms.

* * * We * * * accept the District Court's finding that the communication was protected by the First and Fourteenth Amendments. We are not, however, entirely in agreement with that court's manner of reasoning from this finding to the conclusion that Doyle is entitled to reinstatement with backpay.

The District Court made the following "conclusions" on this aspect of the case:

"1) If a non-permissible reason, e.g., exercise of First Amendment rights, played a substantial part in the decision not to renew even in the face of other permissible grounds—the decision may not stand (citations omitted).

"2) A non-permissible reason did play a substantial part. That is clear from the letter of the Superintendent immediately following the Board's decision, which stated two reasons—the one, the conversation with the radio station, clearly protected by the First Amendment. A court may not engage in any limitation of First Amendment rights based on 'tact'—that is not to say that the 'tactfulness' is irrelevant to other issues in this case."

At the same time, though, it stated that "(i)n fact, as this Court sees it and finds, both the Board and the Superintendent were faced with a situation in which there did exist in fact reason * * * independent of any First Amendment rights or exercise thereof, to not extend tenure."

Since respondent Doyle had no tenure, and there was therefore not even a state-law requirement of "cause" or "reason" before a decision could be made not to renew his employment, it is not clear what the District Court meant by this latter statement. Clearly the Board legally could have dismissed respondent had the radio station incident never come to its attention. One plausible meaning of the court's statement is that the Board and the Superintendent not only could, but in fact would have reached that decision had not the constitutionally protected incident of the telephone call to the radio station occurred. We are thus brought to the issue whether, even if that were the case, the fact that the protected conduct played a "substantial part" in the actual decision not to renew would necessarily amount to a constitutional violation justifying remedial action. We think that it would not.

A rule of causation which focuses solely on whether protected conduct played a part, "substantial" or otherwise, in a decision not to rehire, could place an employee in a better position as a result of the exercise of constitutionally protected conduct than he would have occupied had he done nothing. The difficulty with the rule enunciated by the District Court is that it would require reinstatement in cases where a dramatic and perhaps abrasive incident is inevitably on the minds of those responsible for the decision to rehire, and does indeed play a part in that decision even if the same decision would have been reached had the incident not occurred. The constitutional principle at stake is sufficiently vindicated if such an employee is placed in no worse a position than if he had not engaged in the conduct. A borderline or marginal candidate should not have the employment question resolved against him because of constitutionally protected conduct. But that same candidate ought not to be able, by engaging in such conduct, to prevent his employer from assessing his performance record and reaching a decision not to rehire on the basis of that record, simply because the protected conduct makes the employer more certain of the correctness of its decision.

This is especially true where, as the District Court observed was the case here, the current decision to rehire will accord "tenure." * * *

Initially, in this case, the burden was properly placed upon respondent to show that his conduct was constitutionally protected, and that this conduct was a "substantial factor" * * * in the Board's decision not to rehire him. Respondent having carried that burden, however, the District Court should have gone on to determine whether the Board had shown by a preponderance of the evidence that it would have reached the same decision as to respondent's reemployment even in the absence of the protected conduct.

We cannot tell from the District Court opinion and conclusions, nor from the opinion of the Court of Appeals affirming the judgment of the District Court, what conclusion those courts would have reached had they applied this test. The judgment of the Court of Appeals is therefore vacated, and the case remanded for further proceedings consistent with this opinion.

NOTES

1.   *Plaintiff's rightful position is not necessarily what the plaintiff wants.* On remand in *Mt. Healthy,* the district court determined that the original record established, by a preponderance of the evidence, that Doyle would not have been rehired for reasons quite apart from his constitutionally protected speech, and the Court of Appeals affirmed. Doyle v. Mt. Healthy, 670 F.2d 59 (6th Cir.1982). Should Doyle have gotten his job back anyway? *See Symposium, The Burgeoning* Mt. Healthy *Mixed-Motive Defense to Civil Rights and Employment Discrimination Claims*, 51 Mercer L.Rev. 583 (2000).

2.   *The court cannot always reproduce the plaintiff's rightful position exactly. Mt. Healthy* states that "[t]he constitutional principle at stake is sufficiently vindicated if such an employee is placed in no worse a position than if he had not engaged in the conduct." However, the Court's remedy puts Doyle in a better than rightful position. If Doyle had never contacted the radio station, the school board could have dismissed him without giving any reason; but, having violated his rights, the board must reinstate him unless it can convince the district court that there is good reason not to rehire him. Is there any remedy that would put Doyle in the rightful position exactly? When there is no remedy that will achieve the rightful position exactly, the injunction's *terms* may overreach the rightful position so long as the injunction's *aim* is to achieve no more than the rightful position.

3.   *Multiple grounds for action.* In McKennon v. Nashville Banner Publishing Co., 513 U.S. 352 (1995), Christine McKennon alleged that the company fired her on account of her age in violation of the Age Discrimination in Employment Act of 1967. In discovery, she admitted that she had taken home confidential documents, claiming that she wanted them to defend herself should she be illegally fired. Citing *Mt. Healthy*, the lower courts dismissed McKennon's suit on the theory that this evidence acquired after her supposedly illegal firing provided a supervening legal reason to fire her. A unanimous Supreme Court reversed. It distinguished *Mt. Healthy* because there the employer had two motives at the time of firing, one lawful, the other unlawful. But, McKennon "comes to us on the express assumption that an unlawful motive was the sole basis for the firing," the lawful motive for firing coming to

light only later. Nonetheless, the after-acquired evidence is relevant to the remedy:

> It would be both inequitable and pointless to order the reinstatement of someone the employer would have terminated, and will terminate, in any event and upon lawful grounds. [As to backpay,] [t]he object of compensation is to restore the employee to the position he or she would have been in absent the discrimination, but that principle is difficult to apply with precision where there is after-acquired evidence of wrongdoing that would have led to termination on legitimate grounds had the employer known about it. * * * The beginning point in the trial court's formulation of a remedy should be calculation of backpay from the date of the unlawful discharge to the date the new information was discovered.

513 U.S. at 362. Has the Court put McKennon in her rightful position?

NOTE ON RIGHTFUL POSITION AS RECONSIDERATION OR REMAND IN ADMINISTRATIVE LAW

The most important lesson from *Mt. Healthy* is that the plaintiff's rightful position and therefore the aim of the injunction depend upon a clear understanding of the plaintiff's right. *The framing of an injunction must begin with a careful definition of the plaintiff's right.* In *Mt. Healthy,* Doyle did not have a right to a government job but rather a right not to be fired for his speech. Given this right, Doyle gets consideration of whether he would have kept his job apart from the violation of his free speech rights rather than the job itself.

Mt. Healthy is but one example of a broad range of cases where the plaintiff has no absolute right to an ultimate objective but rather a right not to be denied that objective for the wrong reason or in the wrong way. If Doyle had been fired because of accusations to which he was denied an opportunity to respond in violation of due process or in violation of a civil service statute, the injunction would not restore his job but would give him an appropriate hearing to consider the charges. Or, if Doyle was about to lose his job because the school was to be torn down to make way for a highway whose funding was approved without statutorily required environmental analysis, the injunction would not permanently bar the highway but would bar it unless and until the statutorily required analysis was performed to consider whether to approve or disapprove the highway. Or, if Doyle's school received a state or federal grant one of whose conditions was that teachers be paid more, the injunction would not require that Doyle be paid more but that the school not receive the grant unless the teachers were paid more. The school would then have to consider whether to forego the grant or pay more. Rosado v. Wyman, 397 U.S. 397, 420 (1970).

Reconsideration relief is common in the administrative law context. For example, when an administrative agency denies an application for a permit and in so doing considers a factor that is improper under the governing statute, the court sitting in review of the agency ordinarily will not order the agency to grant the permit. To do so may put the applicant in a better than rightful position because the agency might have denied the permit for a statutorily proper reason.

Quite apart from whether the relief shall be reconsideration is the question of *who* should do the reconsidering. In *Mt. Healthy,* the Supreme Court required the reconsideration to be performed by the district court rather than by the school board. Remanding to the board probably would not have been a reliable way to put Doyle in his rightful position because the board might have continued to punish Doyle for his privileged activities while pretending to fire him for some other reason. Transferring the decision whether to reinstate Doyle from the board to the district court is another instance where the aim of putting the plaintiff in his rightful position resulted in his ending up in a better position.

In judicial review of agency action, a court's determination that the agency has committed an error is like a judgment of liability in a civil suit. The error may be, for instance, consideration of an improper factor, failing to follow the requisite procedures, or arbitrary reasoning. The agency action may be, for example, the issuance of regulations, the grant of a permit, the issuance of a license, or a decision not to take such actions. What the court does in response to that error is a decision about a remedy. The ordinary remedy is a remand to the agency for a proper reconsideration. Gonzales v. Thomas, 547 U.S. 183 (2006). But other remedies are possible. If the court is sure that the agency would, for example, have granted the permit that the petitioner had sought, then the court will reverse the agency, ordering it to grant the permit. NLRB v. Wyman-Gordon Co., 394 U.S. 759, 766 n. 6 (1969). Or, if the agency had granted the permit and the court is sure that it would not have but for the error, the court could reverse the agency and vacate the permit. However, if the court is sure that agency would have reached the same result even if it had not made the error, the court will say there is no reversible error and will affirm the agency action. NLRB v. American Geri-Care Inc., 697 F.2d 56, 64 (2d Cir.1982), *cert. denied,* 461 U.S. 906 (1983). But, when in doubt, the court remands. *See* Honeywell International, Inc. v. E.P.A., 374 F.3d 1363 (D.C.Cir.2004), 393 F.3d 1315 (D.C.Cir.2005) (concurring and dissenting opinions discussing question of propriety of remand or vacatur as proper remedy for agency error); Ronald Mark Levin, *"Vacation" at Sea: Judicial Remedies and Equitable Discretion in Administrative Law,* 53 Duke L.J. 291 (2003) (criticizing the judicial practice of ordering a "remand without vacation," which allows an agency action to remain in place during what might constitute lengthy proceedings on remand).

The remand remedy differs from a simple reversal in two respects. First, as a matter of substance, the successful complainant will not necessarily get what it ultimately wants but rather a reconsideration, theoretically free from error. Second, as a matter of procedure, doubtful cases are to be decided by the governmental entity originally charged with making the decision rather than by the court. Do you see why both these differences are compelled by the rightful position concept?

It may seem bizarre to remand a matter back to the very agency that has reached a flawed result. However, the defendants in these administrative law cases are coordinate branches of government. Courts generally presume that such coordinate branches will act properly once they have a clear understanding of the law, just as appellate courts usually presume that lower courts will act as instructed when a case is remanded. Should the agency repeat its error on remand, the petitioner can once again get the reviewing court to intervene, if petitioner has the money for legal fees and the time to wait and if the agency has not successfully camouflaged its error with pretexts.

In light of *Mt. Healthy,* it should come as no surprise that Congress, in enacting Title VII, the federal statute forbidding employment discrimination, 42 U.S.C. § 2000e et seq., specified that the remedy should be neither reversal of the employer's decision nor a remand to the employer but rather de novo reconsideration by a court. Under this statute, the Supreme Court has specified in some detail how the district court should try to mimic how a non-discriminatory employer would have acted. International Brotherhood of Teamsters v. United States, 431 U.S. 324, 371–72 (1977). When the discriminating employer is a federal agency, the tradition of remand in administrative law could well have resulted in a remand to the agency, but the Supreme Court has read Title VII to require de novo judicial reconsideration. Chandler v. Roudebush, 425 U.S. 840, 862 (1976).

Courts sometimes remand to legislatures to rewrite invalid laws just as they sometimes remand to agencies to reconsider invalid administrative decisions. So, for example, after holding that the state's educational finance statute failed to comply with the state constitution, the New Jersey Supreme Court requested the legislature to rewrite the statute. Abbott v. Burke, 575 A.2d 359 (N.J. 1990).

PROBLEM: REPAIRING ELECTION WRONGS

Where the plaintiff is a losing candidate who proves that the election was flawed because votes were counted that should not have been or votes that should have been counted were not, the court will not usually declare the plaintiff the winner. The court typically will order a new election to repair the harm by re-doing election, but only if the plaintiff proves that more votes were affected than the margin of victory. If that burden cannot be carried, the plaintiff's rightful position is as an electoral loser. *See, e.g.,* Marks v. Stinson, 19 F.3d 873 (3d Cir.1994).

Suppose, rather than fraud, the problem with the election was unconstitutional exclusion of almost all African-American voters in an election between a white and an African-American candidate and that the margin of victory for the white candidate was several times larger than the number of voters excluded. Would the plaintiffs—the African-American candidate and the excluded voters—be in their rightful position if the election is affirmed? On such facts, Bell v. Southwell, 376 F.2d 659 (5th Cir.1967), ordered a new election on the theory that it could not be presumed that the African-American candidate would have lost an election untainted by racial discrimination, which may have created a racially charged atmosphere that dissuaded white voters from voting for her. Given southern politics in the 1960's, does this seem realistic? The court offered an additional argument that "state-imposed racial discrimination cannot be tolerated and to eliminate the practice or the temptation toward it, the law must extinguish the judgment wrought by such a procedure." *Id.* at 663. Does this rationale satisfy the rightful position principle? In connection with another issue in the case, the court stated:

> Mrs. Bell as a former candidate did not seek to be selected over Southwell or any other opponent. What, and all, she and [the other plaintiffs, who were frustrated voters,] sought was an election conducted free of such indefensible, racial distinctions. That being so, it was not the usual case of counting votes and denying relief for want of affirmative proof of a different result.

Id. at 664–65. Does this observation provide a stronger justification for ordering a new election?

In contrast, the courts denied a new election in the dispute arising out of the 2000 U.S. presidential race between George W. Bush and Albert Gore. The Supreme Court of Florida ordered a manual recount for several counties to rectify the failure to count a number of legal votes "sufficient to change or place in doubt the result of the election" in those counties because of defective voting machines and problematic ballots. Gore v. Harris, 772 So.2d 1243 (Fla.2000). The U.S. Supreme Court struck down the state recount remedy, finding that its arbitrary recount standards created unequal treatment of voters in violation of the Equal Protection Clause. Bush v. Gore, 531 U.S. 98 (2000) (per curiam). The Court instead ordered that any recount would need to have additional precautions and safeguards to be constitutionally valid; but that there was insufficient time to actually implement these steps. Gore v. Harris, 773 So.2d 524 (Fla.2000). *See* Tracy A. Thomas, *Understanding Prophylactic Remedies Through the Looking Glass of* Bush v. Gore, 11 Wm. & M. Bill Rts. J. 343 (2002) (suggesting that the Supreme Court overreached its equitable discretion by ordering prophylactic relief that was not designed to remedy the underlying denial of votes). Remedies for election wrongs have been difficult to achieve. *See* Richard L. Hasen, *The Untimely Death of* Bush v. Gore, 60 Stan.L.Rev. 1 (2007) (discussing the courts' failure to create meaningful election reforms); Steven F. Huefner, *Remedying Election Wrongs*, 44 Harv.J.Leg. 265 (2007) (recommending the use of non-judicial forums like administrative or legislative tribunals to issue appropriate remedies for election wrongs).

RIZZO V. GOODE

Supreme Court of the United States
423 U.S. 362 (1976)

MR. JUSTICE REHNQUIST delivered the opinion of the Court.

The District Court for the Eastern District of Pennsylvania, after parallel trials of separate actions filed in 1970, entered an order in 1973 requiring petitioners "to submit to [the District] Court for its approval a comprehensive program for improving the handling of citizen complaints alleging police misconduct" in accordance with a comprehensive opinion filed together with the order. The proposed program, negotiated between petitioners and respondents for the purpose of complying with the order, was incorporated six months later into a final judgment. Petitioner City Police Commissioner was thereby required, inter alia, to put into force a directive governing the manner by which citizens' complaints against police officers should henceforth be handled by the department. The Court of Appeals for the Third Circuit, upholding the District Court's finding that the existing procedures for handling citizen complaints were "inadequate," affirmed the District Court's choice of equitable relief: "The revisions were . . . ordered because they appeared to have the potential for prevention of future police misconduct." We granted certiorari to consider petitioners' claims that the judgment of the District Court represents an unwarranted intrusion by the federal judiciary into the discretionary authority committed to them by state and local law to perform their official functions. [We find ourselves substantially in agreement with these claims, and we therefore reverse the judgment of the Court of Appeals.]

I

The central thrust of respondents' efforts in the two trials was to lay a foundation for equitable intervention, in one degree or another, because of an assertedly pervasive pattern of illegal and unconstitutional mistreatment by police officers. This mistreatment was said to have been directed against minority citizens in particular and against all Philadelphia residents in general. The named individual and group respondents were certified to represent these two classes. The principal petitioners here—the Mayor, the City Managing Director, and the Police Commissioner—were charged with conduct ranging from express authorization or encouragement of this mistreatment to failure to act in a manner so as to assure that it would not recur in the future.

Hearing some 250 witnesses during 21 days of hearings, the District Court was faced with a staggering amount of evidence; each of the 40-odd incidents might alone have been the *piece de resistance* of a short, separate trial. * * *

The District Court made a number of conclusions of law, not all of which are relevant to our analysis. It found that the evidence did not establish the existence of any policy on the part of the named petitioners to violate the legal and constitutional rights of the plaintiff classes, but it did find that evidence of departmental procedure indicated a tendency to discourage the filing of civilian complaints and to minimize the consequences of police misconduct. It found that as to the larger plaintiff class, the residents of Philadelphia, only a small percentage of policemen commit violations of their legal and constitutional rights, but that the frequency with which such violations occur is such that "they cannot be dismissed as rare, isolated instances." * * *

The District Court concluded by directing petitioners to draft, for the court's approval, "a comprehensive program for dealing adequately with civilian complaints", to be formulated along * * * "guidelines" suggested by the court * * * .

While noting that the "guidelines" were consistent with "generally recognized minimum standards" and imposed "no substantial burdens" on the police department, the District Court emphasized that respondents had no constitutional *right* to improved police procedures for handling civilian complaints. But given that violations of constitutional rights of citizens occur in "unacceptably" high numbers, and are likely to continue to occur, the court-mandated revision was a "necessary first step" in attempting to prevent future abuses. * * *

II

These actions were brought, and the affirmative equitable relief fashioned, under the Civil Rights Act of 1871, 42 U.S.C. § 1983. It provides that "[e]very person who, under color of [law] subjects, or causes to be subjected, any . . . person within the jurisdiction [of the United States] to the deprivation of any rights . . . secured by the Constitution and laws, shall be liable to the party injured in an action at law [or] suit in equity. . . ." * * *

The findings of fact made by the District Court at the conclusion of these two parallel trials—in sharp contrast to that which respondents sought to prove with respect to petitioners—disclose a central paradox which permeates that court's legal conclusions. Individual police officers *not named as parties* to the action were found to have violated the constitutional rights of particular individuals, only a few of whom were parties plaintiff. As the facts developed, there was no affirmative link between the occurrence of the various incidents of police misconduct and the adoption of any plan or policy by petitioners—express or otherwise— showing their authorization or approval of such misconduct. Instead, the *sole* causal connection found by the District Court between petitioners and the individual respondents was that in the absence of a change in police disciplinary procedures, the incidents were likely to continue to occur, *not* with respect to them, but as to the members of the classes they represented. In sum, the genesis of this lawsuit—a heated dispute between individual citizens and certain policemen—has evolved into an attempt by the federal judiciary to resolve a "controversy" between the entire citizenry of Philadelphia and the petitioning elected and appointed officials over what steps might, in the Court of Appeals' words, "[appear] to have the potential for prevention of future police misconduct." * * *

B

* * *

Nothing in Hague v. CIO, 307 U.S. 496 (1939), the only decision of this Court cited by the District Court, or any other case from this Court, supports such an open-ended construction of § 1983. In *Hague*, the pattern of police misconduct upon which liability and injunctive relief were grounded was the adoption and enforcement of deliberate policies by the defendants there (including the Mayor and the Chief of Police) of excluding and removing the plaintiff's labor organizers and forbidding peaceful communication of their views to the citizens of Jersey City. These policies were implemented "by force and violence" on the part of individual policemen. There was no mistaking that the defendants proposed to continue their unconstitutional policies against the members of this discrete group. * * *

Respondents stress that the District Court not only found an "unacceptably high" number of incidents but held, as did the Court of Appeals, that "when a *pattern* of frequent police violations of rights is shown, the law is clear that injunctive relief may be granted." However, there was no showing that the behavior of the Philadelphia police was different in kind or degree from that which exists elsewhere; indeed, the District Court found "that the problems disclosed by the record * * * are fairly typical of [those] afflicting police departments in major urban areas." Thus, invocation of the word "pattern" in a case where, unlike *Hague* * * * , the defendants are not causally linked to it, is but a distant echo of the findings in those cases. The focus in *Hague* * * * was not simply on the number of violations which occurred but on the common thread running through them: a "pervasive pattern of intimidation" flowing from a deliberate plan by the *named* defendants to crush the nascent labor organizations. The District Court's unadorned finding of a statistical pattern is quite dissimilar to the factual settings of these two cases.

The theory of liability underlying the District Court's opinion, and urged upon us by respondents, is that even without a showing of direct responsibility for the actions of a small percentage of the police force, petitioners' *failure* to act in the face of a statistical pattern is indistinguishable from the active conduct enjoined in *Hague* * * * . Respondents posit a constitutional "duty" on the part of petitioners (and a corresponding "right" of the citizens of Philadelphia) to "eliminate" future police misconduct; a "default" of that affirmative duty being shown by the statistical pattern, the District Court is empowered to act in petitioners' stead and take whatever preventive measures are necessary, within its discretion, to secure the "right" at issue. Such reasoning, however, blurs accepted usages and meanings in the English language in a way which would be quite inconsistent with the words Congress chose in § 1983. We have never subscribed to these amorphous propositions, and we decline to do so now.

Respondents claim that the theory of liability embodied in the District Court's opinion is supported by desegregation cases such as Swann v. Charlotte-Mecklenburg Board of Education, 402 U.S. 1 (1971). * * *

Respondents, in their effort to bring themselves within the language of *Swann,* ignore a critical factual distinction between their case and the desegregation cases decided by this Court. In the latter, segregation imposed by law had been implemented by state authorities for varying periods of time, whereas in the instant case the District Court found that the responsible authorities had played no affirmative part in depriving any members of the two respondent classes of any constitutional rights. Those against whom injunctive relief was directed in cases such as *Swann* and *Brown* were not administrators and school board members who had in their employ a small number of individuals, which latter on their own deprived Afro-American students of their constitutional rights to a unitary school system. They were administrators and school board members who were found by their *own* conduct in the administration of the school system to have denied those rights. Here, the District Court found that none of the petitioners had deprived the respondent classes of any rights secured under the Constitution. Under the well-established rule that federal "judicial powers may be exercised only on the basis of a constitutional violation," *Swann*, this case presented no occasion for the District Court to grant equitable relief against petitioners.

C

Going beyond considerations concerning the existence of a live controversy and threshold statutory liability, we must address an additional and novel claim advanced by respondent classes. They assert that given the citizenry's "right" to be protected from unconstitutional exercises of police power, and the "need for protection from such abuses," respondents have a right to mandatory equitable relief in some form when those in supervisory positions do not institute steps to reduce the incidence of unconstitutional police misconduct. The scope of federal equity power, it is proposed, should be extended to the fashioning of prophylactic procedures for a state agency designed to minimize this kind of misconduct on the part of a handful of its employees.[However, on the facts of this case, not only is this novel claim quite at odds with the settled rule that in federal equity cases "the nature of the violation determines the scope of the remedy," but important considerations of federalism are additional factors weighing against it.] Where, as here, the exercise of authority by state officials is attacked, federal courts must be constantly mindful of the "special delicacy of the adjustment to be preserved between federal equitable power and State administration of its own law." Section 1983 by its terms confers authority to grant equitable relief as well as damages, but its words "allow a suit in equity only when that is the proper proceeding for redress, and they refer to existing standards to determine what is a proper proceeding." * * * When a plaintiff seeks to enjoin the activity of a government agency, even within a unitary court system, his case must contend with "the well-established rule that the Government has traditionally been granted the widest latitude in the 'dispatch of its own internal affairs.'" The District Court's injunctive order here, significantly revising the internal procedures of the Philadelphia police department, was indisputably a sharp limitation on the department's "latitude in the 'dispatch of its own internal affairs'."

When the frame of reference moves from a unitary court system, governed by the principles just stated, to a system of federal courts representing the Nation, subsisting side by side with 50 state judicial, legislative, and executive branches, appropriate consideration must be given to principles of federalism in determining the availability and scope of equitable relief. * * *

Contrary to the District Court's flat pronouncement that a federal court's legal power to "supervise the functioning of the police department . . . is firmly established," it is the foregoing cases and principles that must govern consideration of the type of injunctive relief granted here. When it injected itself by injunctive decree into the internal disciplinary affairs of this state agency, the District Court departed from these precepts. * * *

MR. JUSTICE STEVENS took no part in the consideration or decision of this case.

MR. JUSTICE BLACKMUN with whom MR. JUSTICE BRENNAN and MR. JUSTICE MARSHALL join, dissenting.

* * * To be sure, federal-court intervention in the daily operation of a large city's police department, as the Court intimates, is undesirable and to be avoided if at all possible. The Court appropriately observes, however, that what the Federal District Court did here was to engage in a careful and conscientious resolution of often sharply conflicting testimony and to make detailed findings of fact, now accepted by both sides, that attack the problem that is the subject of the respondents' complaint. The remedy was one evolved with the defendant officials' assent, reluctant though that assent may have been, and it was one that the police department concededly could live with. Indeed, the District Court * * * stated that "the resolution of all the disputed items was more nearly in accord with the defendants' position than with the plaintiffs' position," and that the relief * * * "did not go beyond what the defendants had always been willing to accept." No one, not even this Court's majority, disputes the apparent efficacy of the relief or the fact that it effectuated a betterment in the system and should serve to lessen the number of instances of deprival of constitutional rights of members of the respondent classes. What is worrisome to the Court is abstract principle, and, of course, the Court has

The primary "worry" of the Supreme Court...

a right to be concerned with abstract principle that, when extended to the limits of logic, may produce untoward results in other circumstances on a future day.

But the District Court here, with detailed, careful, and sympathetic findings, ascertained the existence of violations of citizens' *constitutional* rights, of a *pattern* of that type of activity, of its likely continuance and recurrence, and of an official indifference as to doing anything about it. * * * There must be federal relief available against persistent deprival of federal constitutional rights even by (or, perhaps I should say, particularly by) constituted authority on the state side. * * *

I would regard what was accomplished in this case as one of those rightly rare but nevertheless justified instances * * * of federal-court "intervention" in a state or municipal executive area. The facts, the deprival of constitutional rights, and the pattern are all proved in sufficient degree. And the remedy is carefully delineated, worked out within the administrative structure rather then superimposed by edict upon it, and essentially, and concededly, "livable." In the City of Brotherly Love—or in any other American city—no less should be expected. It is a matter of regret that the Court sees fit to nullify what so meticulously and thoughtfully has been evolved to satisfy an existing need relating to constitutional rights that we cherish and hold dear. * * *

NOTES

1.   What type of injunction did the plaintiffs seek here? What sort of a factual showing would have satisfied the majority that the city and its top officials were liable? The majority's reading of the law of liability itself is controversial; but, because our focus is the law of remedies, the important point is that the majority goes on to argue that the scope of the remedy must be tailored so that it is limited to forcing only those adjudged to have violated the plaintiffs' rights to restore them to their rightful position. In other words, where there is no right against a defendant that has been or will be violated by that defendant, there is no remedy against that defendant.

2.   Why didn't the plaintiffs side-step the majority's argument by seeking damages from the individual police officers who brutalized them instead of an injunction against the city and its top officials?

3.   The *Rizzo* case was but one aspect of an extended controversy over police brutality in Philadelphia going back to 1952. Phillip J. Cooper, *Hard Judicial Choices* 297–327 (1988) (detailing background of case). From mid-1976 to mid-1977, 110 lawsuits seeking compensatory and punitive damages for police brutality were filed. *Roundhouse Punches*, Newsweek, July 4, 1977. After *Rizzo*, a federal investigation brought to light evidence that the City did promote police brutality and an injunction against the chief of police and the mayor was finally granted. Commonwealth of Pennsylvania v. Porter, 659 F.2d 306 (3d Cir.1981). While this litigation was pending, Philadelphia voters

rejected by a 2 to 1 margin a city charter amendment that would have allowed Mayor Rizzo to seek a third term. Both major party candidates for mayor vowed to reform police practices.

BROWN V. PLATA
Supreme Court of the United States
563 U.S. 493 (2011)

JUSTICE KENNEDY delivered the opinion of the Court.

This case arises from serious constitutional violations in California's prison system. The violations have persisted for years. They remain uncorrected. * * *

After years of litigation, it became apparent that a remedy for the constitutional violations would not be effective absent a reduction in the prison system population. The authority to order release of prisoners as a remedy to cure a systemic violation of the Eighth Amendment is a power reserved to a three-judge district court, not a single-judge district court. 18 U.S.C. § 3626(a) (2006). * * *

The appeal presents the question whether the remedial order issued by the three-judge court is consistent with requirements and procedures set forth in . . . the Prison Litigation Reform Act of 1995 (PLRA). 18 U.S.C. § 3626. The order leaves the choice of means to reduce overcrowding to the discretion of state officials. But absent compliance through new construction, out-of-state transfers, or other means [including good-time credits and diversion of low-risk offenders and technical parole violators to community-based programs]—or modification of the order upon a further showing by the State—the State will be required to release some number of prisoners before their full sentences have been served. High recidivism rates must serve as a warning that mistaken or premature release of even one prisoner can cause injury and harm. The release of prisoners in large numbers—assuming the State finds no other way to comply with the order—is a matter of undoubted, grave concern. * * *

Yet so too is the continuing injury and harm resulting from these serious constitutional violations. For years the medical and mental health care provided by California's prisons has fallen short of minimum constitutional requirements and has failed to meet prisoners' basic health needs. Needless suffering and death have been the well-documented result. Over the whole course of years during which this litigation has been pending, no other remedies have been found to be sufficient. * * *

This Court now holds that the PLRA does authorize the relief afforded in this case and that the court-mandated population limit is necessary to remedy the violation of prisoners' constitutional rights. * * *

I

A

The degree of overcrowding in California's prisons is exceptional. * * * The State's prisons had operated at around 200% of design capacity for at least 11 years. Prisoners are crammed into spaces neither designed nor intended to house inmates. As many as 200 prisoners may live in a gymnasium, monitored by as few as two or three correctional officers. As many as 54 prisoners may share a single toilet. * * *

Prisoners in California with serious mental illness do not receive minimal, adequate care. Because of a shortage of treatment beds, suicidal inmates may be held for prolonged periods in telephone-booth sized cages without toilets. * * * Other inmates awaiting care may be held for months in administrative segregation, where they endure harsh and isolated conditions and receive only limited mental health services. Wait times for mental health care range as high as 12 months. In 2006, the suicide rate in California's prisons was nearly 80% higher than the national average for prison populations; and a court-appointed Special Master found that 72.1% of suicides involved "some measure of inadequate assessment, treatment, or intervention, and were therefore most probably foreseeable and/or preventable."

Prisoners suffering from physical illness also receive severely deficient care. California's prisons were designed to meet the medical needs of a population at 100% of design capacity and so have only half the clinical space needed to treat the current population. A correctional officer testified that, in one prison, up to 50 sick inmates may be held together in a 12-by 20-foot cage for up to five hours awaiting treatment. The number of staff is inadequate, and prisoners face significant delays in access to care. A prisoner with severe abdominal pain died after a 5-week delay in referral to a specialist; a prisoner with "constant and extreme" chest pain died after an 8-hour delay in evaluation by a doctor; and a prisoner died of testicular cancer after a "failure of MDs to work up for cancer in a young man with 17 months of testicular pain."[3] Doctor Ronald Shansky [an expert], concluded that extreme departures from the standard of care were "widespread," and that the proportion of "possibly preventable or preventable" deaths was "extremely high." Many more prisoners, suffering from severe but not life-threatening conditions, experience prolonged illness and unnecessary pain.

---

[3] Because plaintiffs do not base their case on deficiencies in care provided on any one occasion, this Court has no occasion to consider whether these instances of delay—or any other particular deficiency in medical care complained of by the plaintiffs—would violate the Constitution under *Estelle v. Gamble,* if considered in isolation. Plaintiffs rely on systemwide deficiencies in the provision of medical and mental health care that, taken as a whole, subject sick and mentally ill prisoners in California to "substantial risk of serious harm" and cause the delivery of care in the prisons to fall below the evolving standards of decency that mark the progress of a maturing society.

B

These conditions are the subject of two federal cases. The first to commence, *Coleman v. Brown,* was filed in 1990. *Coleman* involves the class of seriously mentally ill persons in California prisons. Over 15 years ago, in 1995, after a 39-day trial, the *Coleman* District Court found "overwhelming evidence of the systematic failure to deliver necessary care to mentally ill inmates" in California prisons. * * *

In 2007, 12 years after his appointment, the Special Master in *Coleman* filed a report stating that, after years of slow improvement, the state of mental health care in California's prisons was deteriorating. The Special Master ascribed this change to increased overcrowding. The rise in population had led to greater demand for care, and existing programming space and staffing levels were inadequate to keep pace. * * *

C

The second action, *Plata v. Brown,* involves the class of state prisoners with serious medical conditions. After this action commenced in 2001, the State conceded that deficiencies in prison medical care violated prisoners' Eighth Amendment rights. The State stipulated to a remedial injunction. The State failed to comply with that injunction, and in 2005 the court appointed a Receiver to oversee remedial efforts. The court found that "the California prison medical care system is broken beyond repair," resulting in an "unconscionable degree of suffering and death." The court found: "[I]t is an uncontested fact that, on average, an inmate in one of California's prisons needlessly dies every six to seven days due to constitutional deficiencies in the [California prisons'] medical delivery system." * * *

Prisons were unable to retain sufficient numbers of competent medical staff, and would "hire any doctor who had a license, a pulse and a pair of shoes.'" Medical facilities lacked "necessary medical equipment" and did "not meet basic sanitation standards." "Exam tables and counter tops, where prisoners with . . . communicable diseases are treated, [were] not routinely disinfected."

In 2008, three years after the District Court's decision, the Receiver described continuing deficiencies in the health care provided by California prisons. * * * The Receiver explained that "overcrowding, combined with staffing shortages, has created a culture of cynicism, fear, and despair which makes hiring and retaining competent clinicians extremely difficult." "[O]vercrowding, and the resulting day to day operational chaos of the [prison system], creates regular 'crisis' situations which . . . take time [and] energy . . . away from important remedial programs." Overcrowding had increased the incidence of infectious disease, and had led to rising prison violence and greater reliance by custodial staff on lockdowns, which "inhibit the delivery of medical care and increase the staffing necessary for such care."

D

* * *

The three-judge court heard 14 days of testimony and issued a 184-page opinion, making extensive findings of fact. The court ordered California to reduce its prison population to 137.5% of the prisons' design capacity within two years. Assuming the State does not increase capacity through new construction, the order requires a population reduction of 38,000 to 46,000 persons. Because it appears all but certain that the State cannot complete sufficient construction to comply fully with the order, the prison population will have to be reduced to at least some extent. The court did not order the State to achieve this reduction in any particular manner. Instead, the court ordered the State to formulate a plan for compliance and submit its plan for approval by the court.

II

As a consequence of their own actions, prisoners may be deprived of rights that are fundamental to liberty. Yet the law and the Constitution demand recognition of certain other rights. Prisoners retain the essence of human dignity inherent in all persons. * * * Just as a prisoner may starve if not fed, he or she may suffer or die if not provided adequate medical care. A prison that deprives prisoners of basic sustenance, including adequate medical care, is incompatible with the concept of human dignity and has no place in civilized society.

If government fails to fulfill this obligation, the courts have a responsibility to remedy the resulting Eighth Amendment violation. Courts must be sensitive to the State's interest in punishment, deterrence, and rehabilitation, as well as the need for deference to experienced and expert prison administrators faced with the difficult and dangerous task of housing large numbers of convicted criminals. Courts nevertheless must not shrink from their obligation to "enforce the constitutional rights of all 'persons,' including prisoners." Courts may not allow constitutional violations to continue simply because a remedy would involve intrusion into the realm of prison administration.

Courts faced with the sensitive task of remedying unconstitutional prison conditions must consider a range of available options, including appointment of special masters or receivers and the possibility of consent decrees. When necessary to ensure compliance with a constitutional mandate, courts may enter orders placing limits on a prison's population. * * *

The three-judge court must then find by clear and convincing evidence that "crowding is the primary cause of the violation of a Federal right" and that "no other relief will remedy the violation of the Federal right." As with any award of prospective relief under the PLRA, the relief "shall extend no further than necessary to correct the violation of the Federal right of a particular plaintiff or plaintiffs." The three-judge court must therefore find that the relief is "narrowly drawn, extends no further than necessary . . . , and is the least intrusive means necessary to correct the violation of the Federal right." In making this determination, the three-judge court must give "substantial weight to any adverse impact on public safety or the operation of a criminal justice system caused by the relief." Applying these standards, the three-judge court found a population limit appropriate, necessary, and authorized in this case.

A

The State contends that it was error to convene the three-judge court without affording it more time to comply with the prior orders in *Coleman* and *Plata*. * * *

2

Before a three-judge court may be convened to consider whether to enter a population limit, the PLRA requires that the court have "previously entered an order for less intrusive relief that has failed to remedy the deprivation of the Federal right sought to be remedied." 18 U.S.C. § 3626(a)(3)(A)(i). * * * It is satisfied if the court has entered one order, and this single order has "failed to remedy" the constitutional violation. The defendant must also have had "a reasonable amount of time to comply with the previous court orders." Together, these requirements ensure that the " 'last resort remedy' " of a population limit is not imposed " 'as a first step.' "

The first of these conditions, the previous order requirement, * * * was satisfied in *Coleman* by appointment of a Special Master in 1995, and it was satisfied in *Plata* by approval of a consent decree and stipulated injunction in 2002. * * * When the three-judge court was convened, 12 years had passed since the appointment of the *Coleman* Special Master, and 5 years had passed since the approval of the *Plata* consent decree. The State does not claim that either order achieved a remedy.

Having engaged in remedial efforts for 5 years in *Plata* and 12 in *Coleman,* the District Courts were not required to wait to see whether their more recent efforts would yield equal disappointment. When a court attempts to remedy an entrenched constitutional violation through reform of a complex institution, such as this statewide prison system, it may be necessary in the ordinary course to issue multiple orders directing and adjusting ongoing remedial efforts. Each new order must be given a reasonable time to succeed, but reasonableness must be assessed in light of the entire history of the court's remedial efforts. * * *

The *Coleman* and *Plata* courts acted reasonably when they convened a three-judge court without further delay.

B

Once a three-judge court has been convened, the court must find additional requirements satisfied before it may impose a population limit. The first of these requirements is that "crowding is the primary cause of the violation of a Federal right." 18 U.S.C. § 3626(a)(3)(E)(i). . . . The three-judge court found the primary cause requirement satisfied by the evidence at trial. The court found that overcrowding strains inadequate medical and mental health facilities; overburdens limited clinical and custodial staff; and creates violent, unsanitary, and chaotic conditions that contribute to the constitutional violations and frustrate efforts to fashion a remedy. The three-judge court also found that "until the problem of overcrowding is overcome it will be impossible to provide constitutionally compliant care to California's prison population." * * *

The three-judge court acknowledged that the violations were caused by factors in addition to overcrowding and that reducing crowding in the prisons would not entirely cure the violations. * * * The three-judge court nevertheless found that overcrowding was the primary cause in the sense of being the foremost cause of the violation.

Overcrowding need only be the foremost, chief, or principal cause of the violation. If Congress had intended to require that crowding be the only cause, it would have said so, assuming in its judgment that definition would be consistent with constitutional limitations.

As this case illustrates, constitutional violations in conditions of confinement are rarely susceptible of simple or straightforward solutions. In addition to overcrowding the failure of California's prisons to provide adequate medical and mental health care may be ascribed to chronic and worsening budget shortfalls, a lack of political will in favor of reform, inadequate facilities, and systemic administrative failures. * * * Only a multifaceted approach aimed at many causes, including overcrowding, will yield a solution.

The PLRA should not be interpreted to place undue restrictions on the authority of federal courts to fashion practical remedies when confronted with complex and intractable constitutional violations. Congress limited the availability of limits on prison populations, but it did not forbid these measures altogether. * * * A reading of the PLRA that would render population limits unavailable in practice would raise serious constitutional concerns. A finding that overcrowding is the "primary cause" of a violation is therefore permissible, despite the fact that additional steps will be required to remedy the violation.

C

The three-judge court was also required to find by clear and convincing evidence that "no other relief will remedy the violation of the Federal right." § 3626(a)(3)(E)(ii).

The State argues that the violation could have been remedied through a combination of new construction, transfers of prisoners out of State, hiring of medical personnel, and continued efforts by the *Plata* Receiver and *Coleman* Special Master. The order in fact permits the State to comply with the population limit by transferring prisoners to county facilities or facilities in other States, or by constructing new facilities to raise the prisons' design capacity. And the three-judge court's order does not bar the State from undertaking any other remedial efforts. If the State does find an adequate remedy other than a population limit, it may seek modification or termination of the three-judge court's order on that basis. The evidence at trial, however, supports the three-judge court's conclusion that an order limited to other remedies would not provide effective relief. * * *

The common thread connecting the State's proposed remedial efforts is that they would require the State to expend large amounts of money absent a reduction in overcrowding. The Court cannot ignore the political and fiscal reality behind this case. California's Legislature has not been willing or able to allocate the resources necessary to meet this crisis absent a reduction in overcrowding. There is no reason to believe it will begin to do so now, when the State of California is facing an unprecedented budgetary shortfall. Without a reduction in overcrowding, there will be no efficacious remedy for the unconstitutional care of the sick and mentally ill in California's prisons.

D

The PLRA states that no prospective relief shall issue with respect to prison conditions unless it is narrowly drawn, extends no further than necessary to correct the violation of a federal right, and is the least intrusive means necessary to correct the violation. 18 U.S.C. § 3626(a). When determining whether these requirements are met, courts must "give substantial weight to any adverse impact on public safety or the operation of a criminal justice system."

1

The three-judge court acknowledged that its order "is likely to affect inmates without medical conditions or serious mental illness." This is because reducing California's prison population will require reducing the number of prisoners outside the class through steps such as parole reform, sentencing reform, use of good-time credits, or other means to be determined by the State. Reducing overcrowding will also have positive effects beyond facilitating timely and adequate access to medical care, including reducing the incidence of prison violence and ameliorating unsafe living conditions. According to the State, these collateral consequences are evidence that the order sweeps more broadly than necessary.

The population limit imposed by the three-judge court does not fail narrow tailoring simply because it will have positive effects beyond the plaintiff class. Narrow tailoring requires a "fit between the [remedy's] ends and the means chosen to accomplish those ends." The scope of the remedy must be proportional to the scope of the violation, and the order must extend no further than necessary to remedy the violation. This Court has rejected remedial orders that unnecessarily reach out to improve prison conditions other than those that violate the Constitution. Lewis v. Casey. 518 U.S. 343, 357(1996). But the precedents do not suggest that a narrow and otherwise proper remedy for a constitutional violation is invalid simply because it will have collateral effects.

Nor does anything in the text of the PLRA require that result. The PLRA states that a remedy shall extend no further than necessary to remedy the violation of the rights of a "particular plaintiff or plaintiffs." 18 U.S.C. § 3626(a)(1)(A). This means only that the scope of the order must be determined with reference to the constitutional violations established by the specific plaintiffs before the court.

This case is unlike cases where courts have impermissibly reached out to control the treatment of persons or institutions beyond the scope of the violation. Even prisoners with no present physical or mental illness may become afflicted, and all prisoners in California are at risk so long as the State continues to provide inadequate care. Prisoners in the general population will become sick, and will become members of the plaintiff classes, with routine frequency; and overcrowding may prevent the timely diagnosis and care necessary to provide effective treatment and to prevent further spread of disease. Relief targeted only at present members of the plaintiff classes may therefore fail to adequately protect future class members who will develop serious physical or mental illness. Prisoners who are not sick or mentally ill do not yet have a claim that they have been subjected to care that violates the Eighth Amendment, but in no sense are they remote bystanders in California's medical care system. They are that system's next potential victims.

A release order limited to prisoners within the plaintiff classes would, if anything, unduly limit the ability of State officials to determine which prisoners should be released. As the State acknowledges in its brief, "release of seriously mentally ill inmates [would be] likely to create special dangers because of their recidivism rates." The order of the three-judge court gives the State substantial flexibility to determine who should be released. If the State truly believes that a release order limited to sick and mentally ill inmates would be preferable to the order entered by the three-judge court, the State can move the three-judge court for modification of the order on that basis. The State has not requested this relief from this Court. * * *

2

In reaching its decision, the three-judge court gave "substantial weight" to any potential adverse impact on public safety from its order. The court devoted nearly 10 days of trial to the issue of public safety, and it gave the question extensive attention in its opinion. Ultimately, the court concluded that it would be possible to reduce the prison population "in a manner that preserves public safety and the operation of the criminal justice system."

The PLRA's requirement that a court give "substantial weight" to public safety does not require the court to certify that its order has no possible adverse impact on the public. A contrary reading would depart from the statute's text by replacing the word "substantial" with "conclusive." * * * A court is required to consider the public safety consequences of its order and to structure, and monitor, its ruling in a way that mitigates those consequences while still achieving an effective remedy of the constitutional violation.

This inquiry necessarily involves difficult predictive judgments regarding the likely effects of court orders. Although these judgments are normally made by state officials, they necessarily must be made by courts when those courts fashion injunctive relief to remedy serious constitutional violations in the prisons. These questions are difficult and sensitive, but they are factual questions and should be treated as such. Courts can, and should, rely on relevant and informed expert testimony when making factual findings.

The three-judge court credited substantial evidence that prison populations can be reduced in a manner that does not increase crime to a significant degree. Some evidence indicated that reducing overcrowding in California's prisons could even improve public safety. [By not mistreating prisoners and thus improving recidivism.] Expert witnesses produced statistical evidence that prison populations had been lowered without adversely affecting public safety in a number of jurisdictions.

The court found that various available methods of reducing overcrowding would have little or no impact on public safety. Expansion of good-time credits would allow the State to give early release to only those prisoners who pose the least risk of reoffending. Diverting low-risk offenders to community programs such as drug treatment, day reporting centers, and electronic monitoring would likewise lower the prison population without releasing violent convicts. The State now sends large numbers of persons to prison for violating a technical term or condition of their parole, and it could reduce the prison population by punishing technical parole violations through community-based programs. * * *

III

Establishing the population at which the State could begin to provide constitutionally adequate medical and mental health care, and the appropriate time frame within which to achieve the necessary reduction, requires a degree of judgment. The inquiry involves uncertain predictions regarding the effects of population reductions, as well as difficult determinations regarding the capacity of prison officials to provide adequate care at various population levels. Courts have substantial flexibility when making these judgments. "Once invoked, the scope of a district court's equitable powers . . . is broad, for breadth and flexibility are inherent in equitable remedies." * * *

B

* * *

These observations reflect the fact that the three-judge court's order, like all continuing equitable decrees, must remain open to appropriate modification. They are not intended to cast doubt on the validity of the basic premise of the existing order. The medical and mental health care provided by California's prisons falls below the standard of decency that inheres in the Eighth Amendment. This extensive and ongoing constitutional violation requires a remedy, and a remedy will not be achieved without a reduction in overcrowding. The relief ordered by the three-judge court is required by the Constitution and was authorized by Congress in the PLRA. The State shall implement the order without further delay.

The judgment of the three-judge court is affirmed.

JUSTICE SCALIA, with whom JUSTICE THOMAS joins, dissenting.

Today the Court affirms what is perhaps the most radical injunction issued by a court in our Nation's history: an order requiring California to release the staggering number of 46,000 convicted criminals.

There comes before us, now and then, a case whose proper outcome is so clearly indicated by tradition and common sense, that its decision ought to shape the law, rather than vice versa. One would think that, before allowing the decree of a federal district court to release 46,000 convicted felons, this Court would bend every effort to read the law in such a way as to avoid that outrageous result. Today, quite to the contrary, the Court disregards stringently drawn provisions of the governing statute, and traditional constitutional limitations upon the power of a federal judge, in order to uphold the absurd.

The proceedings that led to this result were a judicial travesty. I dissent because the institutional reform the District Court has undertaken violates the terms of the governing statute, ignores bedrock limitations on the power of Article III judges, and takes federal courts wildly beyond their institutional capacity.

I

* * *

B

Even if I accepted the implausible premise that the plaintiffs have established a systemwide violation of the Eighth Amendment, I would dissent from the Court's endorsement of a decrowding order. That order is an example of what has become known as a "structural injunction." As I have previously explained, structural injunctions are radically different from the injunctions traditionally issued by courts of equity, and presumably part of "the judicial Power" conferred on federal courts by Article III. * * *

Structural injunctions depart from that historical practice [limiting mandatory injunctions to a "single simple act"], turning judges into long-term administrators of complex social institutions such as schools, prisons, and police departments. Indeed, they require judges to play a role essentially indistinguishable from the role ordinarily played by executive officials. Today's decision not only affirms the structural injunction but vastly expands its use, by holding that an entire system is unconstitutional because it *may produce* constitutional violations. * * *

But structural injunctions do not simply invite judges to indulge policy preferences. They invite judges to indulge *incompetent* policy preferences. Three years of law school and familiarity with pertinent Supreme Court precedents give no insight whatsoever into the management of social institutions. Thus, in the proceeding below the District Court determined that constitutionally adequate medical services could be provided if the prison population was 137.5% of design capacity. This was an empirical finding it was utterly unqualified to make. Admittedly, the court did not generate that number entirely on its own; it heard the numbers 130% and 145% bandied about by various witnesses and decided to split the difference. But the ability of judges to spit back or even average-out numbers spoon-fed to them by expert witnesses does not render them competent decisionmakers in areas in which they are otherwise unqualified. * * *

III

I will state my approach briefly: In my view, a court may not order a prisoner's release unless it determines that the prisoner is suffering from a violation of his constitutional rights, and that his release, and no other relief, will remedy that violation. Thus, if the court determines that a particular prisoner is being denied constitutionally required medical treatment, and the release of that prisoner (and no other remedy) would enable him to obtain medical treatment, then the court can order his release; but a court may not order the release of prisoners who have suffered no violations of their constitutional rights, merely to make it less likely that that will happen to them in the future. * * *

JUSTICE ALITO, with whom CHIEF JUSTICE ROBERTS joins, dissenting.

The decree in this case is a perfect example of what the Prison Litigation Reform Act of 1995 (PLRA) was enacted to prevent. * * *

In largely sustaining the decision below, the majority is gambling with the safety of the people of California. Before putting public safety at risk, every reasonable precaution should be taken. * * * I fear that today's decision, like prior prisoner release orders, will lead to a grim roster of victims. I hope that I am wrong.

In a few years, we will see.

NOTES

1. Justice Alito turned out to be wrong. Studies five years after the Supreme Court's decision in *Plata* showed that there was no increase in violent or property crime despite an "astounding" reduction" in the size of the California prison population. Tom Jackman, *Mass Reduction of California Prison Population Didn't Cause Rise in Crime, Two Studies Find*, Wash.Post, May 18, 2016. The state also realized a savings of $453 million.

In order to comply with the mandate to reduce the state prison population to 137.5% of design capacity, California transferred some prisoners to out-of-state facilities and diverted parole violators and non-violent, non-serious offenders to county jails. This "realignment" plan created its own risk of unconstitutional conditions at the county jails as most jails were also overcrowded, underfunded, and under judicial scrutiny. Margo Schlanger, Plata v. Brown *and Realignment: Jails, Prisons, Courts, and Politics*, 48 Harv. Civ.Rgts.Civ.Lib.L.Rev. 165 (2013). Counties responded by accelerating early releases for the least dangerous offenders and by "catch and release" practices of not incarcerating offenders for parole violations, domestic violence, drug use, and driving under the influence. Paige St. John, *Jails With Revolving Doors: Prison Realignment Brings a Surge in Early Releases*, L.A. Times, Aug. 17, 2014. The Supreme Court rejected the state's subsequent appeals of denials of modifications and stays for extension of time. Brown v. Plata, 134 S.Ct. 1 (Aug. 2, 2013); 134 S.Ct. 436 (Oct. 17, 2013). Prison officials reduced the population to 116,000, but were ordered to take further steps to improve the treatment of mentally ill prisoners. Erica Goode, *Federal Judge Approves California Plan to Reduce Isolation of Mentally Ill Inmates*, N.Y. Times, Aug. 29, 2014. The defendants finally achieved compliance with the order in early 2015. Sharon Bernstein, *California Eases Prison Crowding After Years of Trying*, Reuters, Jan. 30, 2015. For the detailed backstory of the *Plata* case, see Jonathan Smith, *Mass Incarceration on Trial: A Remarkable Court Decision and the Future of Prisons in America* (2014).

2. "Notwithstanding Justice Scalia's accusation of radicalism, jail and prison population orders . . . were once commonplace." Schlanger *Realignment*,

at 196. Congress intended to circumscribe this remedial power in the PLRA by limiting what it believed to be the unreasonable judicial management of prisons. *See* Malcolm M. Feeley & Edward L. Rubin, *Judicial Policy Making and the Modern State: How the Courts Reformed America's Prisons* (1998). *Plata*'s endorsement of the overcrowding remedy for systemwide prison deficiencies reaffirms the continued validity of such structural injunctive relief even under the PLRA. Margo Schlanger, *Civil Rights Injunctions Over Time: A Case Study of Jail and Prison Court Orders*, 81 NYUL Rev. 550, 554 (2006).

3.   In Lewis v. Casey, 518 U.S. 343 (1996), the Supreme Court struck down a systemwide structural injunction that all of the Justices agree was overbroad. A class of Arizona prisoners alleged the state denied them their constitutional right to access to the courts by failing to provide adequate law libraries or trained legal assistants. The evidence proved only that a few illiterate inmates were denied access, and thus the Court held that the remedy should be limited to redressing that harm or similar threats of future harm, by for example, providing legal assistants. It invalidated improvements ordered to the general quality of the prison law libraries like enhanced lighting, numbers of books, hours of operation, and provision of Spanish-speaking services, even though similar types of prophylactic measures had been ordered in a prior case, Bounds v. Smith, 430 U.S. 817 (1977). How does *Lewis* square with the Court's decision in *Plata*?

NOTE ON THE MICROSOFT ANTITRUST LITIGATION

The concept of rightful position casts an interesting perspective on the Microsoft antitrust litigation. The United States and many state governments brought civil actions against the huge software company, charging it with violating federal antitrust laws by using unlawful methods to defend its monopoly in the operating systems market and attempting to extend it to the browser market. The district court held for the plaintiffs and ordered, inter alia, that Microsoft submit a plan to separate by divestiture the operating systems business from the applications business, and to establish a compliance committee to be supervised by a newly hired chief compliance officer responsible for development and supervision of Microsoft's internal programs. United States v. Microsoft Corp., 84 F.Supp.2d 9 (D.D.C.1999) (findings of fact); 87 F.Supp.2d 30 (D.D.C.2000) (conclusions of law); 97 F.Supp.2d 59 (D.D.C.2000) (imposing remedy). On appeal, the D.C. Circuit en banc unanimously affirmed the findings of liability in part, reversed them in part, and vacated the remedy. United States v. Microsoft, 253 F.3d 34 (D.C.Cir.), *cert. denied*, 534 U.S. 952 (2001). It vacated the remedy in large measure because the district court had failed to explain the remedy in terms of rightful position. The court of appeals, quoting the Supreme Court's application of the rightful position concept to monopolization cases, United States v. United Shoe Machinery Corp., 391 U.S. 244, 250 (1968), held that the remedy should seek to "terminate the illegal monopoly, deny to the defendant the fruits of its statutory violation, and ensure that there remain no practices likely to result in monopolization in the future." The court of appeals held that "[n]owhere did the District Court discuss the objectives the Supreme Court deems relevant." 253 F.3d at 103.

At the circuit court's direction, the case was reassigned to another district court judge. She ordered the parties to try to settle the matter in light of the circuit's opinion. The United States and several states entered into a consent decree, which the district court approved. After a lengthy hearing and considering competing remedial proposals from the non-settling states, the district court entered an injunction closely paralleling the negotiated consent decree. The district court's injunction contained preventive measures enjoining the exact conduct found to violate the antitrust laws, prophylactic measures to facilitate future software competition, and monitoring to ensure compliance with the order. United States v. Microsoft Corp., 231 F.Supp.2d 144 (D.D.C.2002). Among the original plaintiffs, only Massachusetts appealed the result. In affirming, the circuit court enthusiastically approved of the injunction: "Far from abusing its discretion, therefore, the district court, by remedying the anticompetitive effect of commingling, went to the heart of the problem Microsoft had created, and it did so without intruding itself into the design and engineering of the Windows operating system. We say, Well done!" Massachusetts v. Microsoft Corp., 373 F.3d 1199, 1210 (D.C.Cir. en banc 2004). "The district court certainly did not abuse its discretion by adopting a remedy that denies Microsoft the ability to take the same or similar actions to limit competition in the future rather than a remedy aimed narrowly at redressing the harm suffered by specific competitors in the past. This distinction underlies the difference between a case brought in equity by the Government and a damage action brought by a private plaintiff." *Id.* at 1233.

Despite the broad injunctive remedy, Microsoft still seemed to win the "browser wars." Its primary browser competitor at the time, Netscape, was discontinued. Netscape's technological spinoff, Mozilla's Firefox, initially obtained a small share of the browser market, but Microsoft's Internet Explorer still retained 75 percent of the browser market and more than 90 percent of the desktop operating system market, the market that the district court judge found in 2000 it had illegally monopolized. Andrew I. Gavil and Harry First, *The Challenge of Remedy*, ch. 7 in *The Microsoft Antitrust Cases: Competition Policy for the Twenty-First Century* 235 (2014) (highlighting the problem of remedy in monopolization cases and the need to better evaluate potential remedies, monitor achievement of those remedies, and consider broader remedies such as restructuring and fines)."

C. THE PREREQUISITES FOR INJUNCTIVE RELIEF

Once a plaintiff has chosen the injunction as its preferred remedy to achieve its right position, the court must still determine that the plaintiff satisfies the prerequisites to qualifying for injunctive relief. The plaintiff must show that first there is a *threat of harm* from the defendant. The harm threatened must be legally prohibited, and must be "imminent," that is sufficiently ripe and not moot for the court to take action.

The plaintiff must also, according to black letter law, show that there is *no adequate remedy at law,* such as compensatory damages. Courts often articulate this rule as *irreparable injury*—that the harm is "irreparable" because it cannot be repaired by the legal remedy, which is inadequate to place the plaintiff in the position she would have been without the harm.

The third element that a plaintiff must establish is that the equities of issuing the injunction tip in her favor. Under the rubric of *balancing the equities,* courts grant injunctions that fall short of the plaintiff's rightful position or even deny injunctive relief altogether. For example, a court might conclude that issuing an injunction would impose an undue hardship or impose a burden on the defendant. A court might also deny an injunction if it finds that it would not be practical to enforce the order without unduly burdening the court. Finally, courts will consider whether the injunction is in the *public interest* considering third parties and public policy.

1.   THREAT OF HARM

An injunction to prevent future violations will issue only if the plaintiff faces a threat of being harmed by the defendant. A threat means there is real, imminent facts demonstrated beyond mere subjective, personal fears or hypothetical concerns. The harm must also be of a type prohibited by law, not just disfavored, and it must threaten the individual plaintiff herself. The requirement that the harm be imminent integrates related justiciability doctrines of constitutional ripeness, mootness, and standing as applied to the remedy itself. Richard H. Fallon, Jr., *The Linkage Between Justiciability and Remedies—and Their Connections to Substantive Rights,* 92 Va.L.Rev. 633 (2006). The concept of *remedial ripeness* provides that a threat is not established if it is too early in the dispute for the court to intervene because the facts and events are not yet sufficiently developed or final.

A threat is also not shown if it is *moot,* that is, too late for the court to take action. Mootness, however, is not established simply by promises of the defendant or voluntary cessation of behavior because "the defendant is free to return to his old ways." United States v. W.T. Grant Co., 345 U.S. 629, 632–33 (1953). The case may nevertheless be moot if the defendant can demonstrate that "there is no reasonable expectation that the wrong will be repeated." *Id.*

Past actions are often the best way to show a future threat, as the defendant's propensity can be established or the harm may be continuing. The plaintiff can also show threat of harm if the defendant has made an explicit threat, such as "I'm am building my garage on this property whether you like it or not." But neither past violations nor explicit threats are required. For example, in Union Carbide v. UGI Corp., 731 F.2d 1186,

1191–92 (5th Cir.1984), the court enjoined a former Union Carbide employee who knew the company's trade secrets from working in certain positions at UGI, where the trade secrets would be useful, even in the absence of conclusive proof that the employee had divulged any secrets. The court was influenced by UGI's failure to exclude the employee from situations where disclosure of confidential information would be difficult to avoid.

CITY OF LOS ANGELES V. LYONS

Supreme Court of the United States
461 U.S. 95 (1983)

JUSTICE WHITE delivered the opinion of the Court.

The issue here is whether respondent Lyons satisfied the prerequisites for seeking injunctive relief in the Federal District Court.

I

This case began on February 7, 1977, when respondent, Adolph Lyons, filed a complaint for damages, injunction, and declaratory relief in the United States District Court for the Central District of California. The defendants were the City of Los Angeles and four of its police officers. The complaint alleged that on October 6, 1976, at 2 a.m., Lyons was stopped by the defendant officers for a traffic or vehicle code violation and that although Lyons offered no resistance or threat whatsoever, the officers, without provocation or justification, seized Lyons and applied a "chokehold"—either the "bar arm control" hold or the "carotid-artery control" hold or both—rendering him unconscious and causing damage to his larynx. Counts I through IV of the complaint sought damages against the officers and the City. Count V, with which we are principally concerned here, sought a preliminary and permanent injunction against the City barring the use of the control holds. That count alleged that the city's police officers, "pursuant to the authorization, instruction and encouragement of defendant City of Los Angeles, regularly and routinely apply these chokeholds in innumerable situations where they are not threatened by the use of any deadly force whatsoever," that numerous persons have been injured as the result of the application of the chokeholds, that Lyons and others similarly situated are threatened with irreparable injury in the form of bodily injury and loss of life, and that Lyons "justifiably fears that any contact he has with Los Angeles police officers may result in his being choked and strangled to death without provocation, justification or other legal excuse." Lyons alleged the threatened impairment of rights protected by the First, Fourth, Eighth, and Fourteenth Amendments. Injunctive relief was sought against the use of the control holds "except in situations where the proposed victim of said control reasonably appears to be threatening the immediate use of deadly force." Count VI sought declaratory relief against the City, i.e., a judgment that use of the chokeholds absent the threat of immediate use of deadly force is a *per se* violation of various constitutional rights.

On remand [after appeal on separate issue of standing], Lyons applied for a preliminary injunction. Lyons pressed only the Count V claim at this point. The motion was heard on affidavits, depositions and government records. The District Court found that Lyons had been stopped for a traffic infringement and that without provocation or legal justification the officers involved had applied a "Department-authorized chokehold which resulted in injuries to the plaintiff." The court further found that the department authorizes the use of the holds in situations where no one is threatened by death or grievous bodily harm, that officers are insufficiently trained, that the use of the holds involves a high risk of injury or death as then employed, and that their continued use in situations where neither death nor serious bodily injury is threatened "is unconscionable in a civilized society." The court concluded that such use violated Lyons' substantive due process rights under the Fourteenth Amendment. A preliminary injunction was entered enjoining "the use of both the carotid-artery and bar arm holds under circumstances which do not threaten death or serious bodily injury." An improved training program and regular reporting and recordkeeping were also ordered. The Court of Appeals affirmed * * * . We granted certiorari and now reverse.

II

Since our grant of certiorari, circumstances pertinent to the case have changed. Originally, Lyons' complaint alleged that at least two deaths had occurred as a result of the application of chokeholds by the police. His first amended complaint alleged that 10 chokehold-related deaths had occurred. By May 1982, there had been five more such deaths. On May 6, 1982, the Chief of Police in Los Angeles prohibited the use of the bar-arm chokehold in any circumstances. A few days later, on May 12, 1982, the Board of Police Commissioners imposed a six-month moratorium on the use of the carotid-artery chokehold except under circumstances where deadly force is authorized.

[Lyons contended that these developments mooted the case because he is no longer subject to a threat of injury so that the preliminary injunction should be vacated.] The City, on the other hand, while acknowledging that subsequent events have significantly changed the posture of this case, again asserts that the case is not moot because the moratorium is not permanent and may be lifted at any time.

We agree with the City that the case is not moot, since the moratorium by its terms is not permanent. * * *

III

It goes without saying that those who seek to invoke the jurisdiction of the federal courts must satisfy the threshold requirement imposed by

Art. III of the Constitution by alleging an actual case or controversy. Plaintiffs must demonstrate a "personal stake in the outcome" in order to "assure that concrete adverseness which sharpens the presentation of issues" necessary for the proper resolution of constitutional questions. Baker v. Carr, 369 U.S. 186, 204 (1962). Abstract injury is not enough. The plaintiff must show that he "has sustained or is immediately in danger of sustaining some direct injury" as the result of the challenged official conduct and the injury or threat of injury must be both "real and immediate," not "conjectural" or "hypothetical."

In O'Shea v. Littleton, 414 U.S. 488 (1974), we dealt with a case brought by a class of plaintiffs claiming that they had been subjected to discriminatory enforcement of the criminal law. Among other things, a county magistrate and judge were accused of discriminatory conduct in various respects, such as sentencing members of plaintiff's class more harshly than other defendants. * * *

Although it was claimed in that case that particular members of the plaintiff class had actually suffered from the alleged unconstitutional practices, we observed that "[p]ast exposure to illegal conduct does not in itself show a present case or controversy regarding injunctive relief * * * if unaccompanied by any continuing, present adverse effects." Past wrongs were evidence bearing on "whether there is a real and immediate threat of repeated injury." But the prospect of future injury rested "on the likelihood that [plaintiffs] will again be arrested for and charged with violations of the criminal law and will again be subjected to bond proceedings, trial, or sentencing before petitioners." The most that could be said for plaintiffs' standing was "that *if* [plaintiffs] proceed to violate an unchallenged law and *if* they are charged, held to answer, and tried in any proceedings before petitioners, they will be subjected to the discriminatory practices that petitioners are alleged to have followed." We could not find a case or controversy in those circumstances: the threat to the plaintiffs was not "sufficiently real and immediate to show an existing controversy simply because they anticipate violating lawful criminal statutes and being tried for their offenses * * * ." It was to be assumed "that [plaintiffs] will conduct their activities within the law and so avoid prosecution and conviction as well as exposure to the challenged course of conduct said to be followed by petitioners."

We further observed that case or controversy considerations "obviously shade into those determining whether the complaint states a sound basis for equitable relief," and went on to hold that even if the complaint presented an existing case or controversy, an adequate basis for equitable relief against petitioners had not been demonstrated [because of, inter alia, insufficient threat of harm.]

Another relevant decision for present purposes is *Rizzo v. Goode* * * * . The claim of injury rested upon "what one of a small, unnamed minority of policemen might do to [plaintiffs] in the future because of that unknown policeman's perception of departmental procedures." This hypothesis was "even more attenuated than those allegations of future injury found insufficient in *O'Shea* to warrant [the] invocation of federal jurisdiction."

IV

No extension of *O'Shea* and *Rizzo* is necessary to hold that respondent Lyons has failed to demonstrate a case or controversy with the City that would justify the equitable relief sought. Lyons' standing to seek the injunction requested depended on whether he was likely to suffer future injury from the use of the chokeholds by police officers. * * * That Lyons may have been illegally choked by the police on October 6, 1976, while presumably affording Lyons standing to claim damages against the individual officers and perhaps against the City, does nothing to establish a real and immediate threat that he would again be stopped for a traffic violation, or for any other offense, by an officer or officers who would illegally choke him into unconsciousness without any provocation or resistance on his part. The additional allegation in the complaint that the police in Los Angeles routinely apply chokeholds in situations where they are not threatened by the use of deadly force falls far short of the allegations that would be necessary to establish a case or controversy between these parties.

In order to establish an actual controversy in this case, Lyons would have had not only to allege that he would have another encounter with the police but also to make the incredible assertion either, (1) that *all* police officers in Los Angeles *always* choke any citizen with whom they happen to have an encounter, whether for the purpose of arrest, issuing a citation or for questioning or, (2) that the City ordered or authorized police officers to act in such manner. Although Count V alleged that the City authorized the use of the control holds in situations where deadly force was not threatened, it did not indicate why Lyons might be realistically threatened by police officers who acted within the strictures of the City's policy. If, for example, chokeholds were authorized to be used only to counter resistance to an arrest by a suspect, or to thwart an effort to escape, any future threat to Lyons from the City's policy or from the conduct of police officers would be no more real than the possibility that he would again have an encounter with the police and that either he would illegally resist arrest or detention or the officers would disobey their instructions and again render him unconscious without any provocation.

Under *O'Shea* and *Rizzo,* these allegations were an insufficient basis to provide a federal court with jurisdiction to entertain Count V of the complaint.[8] * * * First, the Court of Appeals thought that Lyons was more

---

8   * * * Lyons alleged that he feared he would be choked in any future encounter with the police. The reasonableness of Lyons' fear is dependent upon the likelihood of a recurrence of the allegedly unlawful conduct. It is the *reality* of the threat of repeated injury that is relevant to the

immediately threatened than the plaintiffs in those cases since, according to the Court of Appeals, Lyons need only be stopped for a minor traffic violation to be subject to the strangleholds. * * * We cannot agree that the "odds" that Lyons would not only again be stopped for a traffic violation but would also be subjected to a chokehold without any provocation whatsoever are sufficient to make out a federal case for equitable relief. We note that five months elapsed between October 6, 1976, and the filing of the complaint, yet there was no allegation of further unfortunate encounters between Lyons and the police.

Of course, it may be that among the countless encounters between the police and the citizens of a great city such as Los Angeles, there will be certain instances in which strangleholds will be illegally applied and injury and death unconstitutionally inflicted on the victim. * * * [I]t is surely no more than speculation to assert either that Lyons himself will again be involved in one of those unfortunate instances, or that he will be arrested in the future and provoke the use of a chokehold by resisting arrest, attempting to escape, or threatening deadly force or serious bodily injury.

Second, the Court of Appeals viewed *O'Shea* and *Rizzo* as cases in which the plaintiffs sought "massive structural" relief against the local law enforcement systems * * * . *O'Shea* and *Rizzo,* however, cannot be so easily confined to their facts. If Lyons has made no showing that he is realistically threatened by a repetition of his experience of October, 1976, then he has not met the requirements for seeking an injunction in a federal court, whether the injunction contemplates intrusive structural relief or the cessation of a discrete practice.

The Court of Appeals also asserted that Lyons "had a live and active claim" against the City "if only for a period of a few seconds" while the stranglehold was being applied to him [so that] the claim had not become moot * * * . [T]he issue here is not whether that claim has become moot but whether Lyons meets the preconditions for asserting an injunctive claim in a federal forum. The equitable doctrine that cessation of the challenged conduct does not bar an injunction is of little help in this respect, for Lyons' lack of standing does not rest on the termination of the police practice but on the speculative nature of his claim that he will again experience injury as the result of that practice even if continued.

* * * The record and findings made on remand do not improve Lyons' position with respect to standing. * * * The City's policy was described as authorizing the use of the strangleholds "under circumstances where no one is threatened with death or grievous bodily harm." That policy was not further described, but the record before the court contained the

---

standing inquiry, not the plaintiff's subjective apprehensions. The emotional consequences of a prior act simply are not a sufficient basis for an injunction absent a real and immediate threat of future injury by the defendant. Of course, emotional upset is a relevant consideration in a damages action.

department's existing policy * * * . [P]olice officers were instructed to use chokeholds only when lesser degrees of force do not suffice and then only "to gain control of a suspect who is violently resisting the officer or trying to escape." * * *

V

* * *

Absent a sufficient likelihood that he will again be wronged in a similar way, Lyons is no more entitled to an injunction than any other citizen of Los Angeles; and a federal court may not entertain a claim by any or all citizens who no more than assert that certain practices of law enforcement officers are unconstitutional. This is not to suggest that such undifferentiated claims should not be taken seriously by local authorities. Indeed, the interest of an alert and interested citizen is an essential element of an effective and fair government, whether on the local, state, or national level. A federal court, however, is not the proper forum to press such claims unless the requirements for entry and the prerequisites for injunctive relief are satisfied.

We decline the invitation to slight the preconditions for equitable relief; for as we have held, recognition of the need for a proper balance between state and federal authority counsels restraint in the issuance of injunctions against state officers engaged in the administration of the states' criminal laws in the absence of irreparable injury which is both great and immediate. As we noted in *O'Shea,* withholding injunctive relief does not mean that the "federal law will exercise no deterrent effect in these circumstances." If Lyons has suffered an injury barred by the Federal Constitution, he has a remedy for damages under § 1983. Furthermore, those who deliberately deprive a citizen of his constitutional rights risk conviction under the federal criminal laws.

JUSTICE MARSHALL, with whom JUSTICE BRENNAN, JUSTICE BLACKMUN and JUSTICE STEVENS join, dissenting.

* * * There is plainly a "case or controversy" concerning the constitutionality of the city's chokehold policy. The constitutionality of that policy is directly implicated by Lyons' claim for damages against the city. The complaint clearly alleges that the officer who choked Lyons was carrying out an official policy, and a municipality is liable under 42 U.S.C. § 1983 for the conduct of its employees only if they acted pursuant to such a policy. . . . Lyons therefore has standing to challenge the city's chokehold policy and to obtain whatever relief a court may ultimately deem appropriate.

* * * In addition to the risk that he will be subjected to a chokehold in the future, Lyons has suffered past injury. Because he has a live claim for damages, he need not rely solely on the threat of future injury to establish his personal stake in the outcome of the controversy. * * *

The Court's decision likewise finds no support in the fundamental policy underlying the Art. III standing requirement—the concern that a federal court not decide a legal issue if the plaintiff lacks a sufficient "personal stake in the outcome of the controversy as to assure that concrete adverseness which sharpens the presentation of issues upon which the court so largely depends for illumination of difficult . . . questions." Baker v. Carr, 369 U.S. 186, 204 (1962).

Because Lyons has a claim for damages against the city, and because he cannot prevail on that claim unless he demonstrates that the city's chokehold policy violates the Constitution, his personal stake in the outcome of the controversy adequately assures an adversary presentation of his challenge to the constitutionality of the policy. Moreover, the resolution of this challenge will be largely dispositive of his requests for declaratory and injunctive relief. No doubt the requests for injunctive relief may raise additional questions. But these questions involve familiar issues relating to the appropriateness of particular forms of relief, and have never been thought to implicate a litigant's standing to sue. The denial of standing separately to seek injunctive relief therefore cannot be justified by the basic concern underlying the Art. III standing requirement. * * *

The Court's decision removes an entire class of constitutional violations from the equitable powers of a federal court. It immunizes from prospective equitable relief any policy that authorizes persistent deprivations of constitutional rights as long as no individual can establish with substantial certainty that he will be injured, or injured again, in the future. [Chief Justice Burger] asked [dissenting] in *Bivens*, "what would be the judicial response to a police order authorizing 'shoot to kill' with respect to every fugitive?" His answer was that it would be "easy to predict our collective wrath and outrage." We now learn that wrath and outrage cannot be translated into an order to cease the unconstitutional practice, but only an award of damages to those who are victimized by the practice and live to sue and to the survivors of those who are not so fortunate. Under the view expressed by the majority today, if the police adopt a policy of "shoot to kill," or a policy of shooting one out of ten suspects, the federal courts will be powerless to enjoin its continuation. The federal judicial power is now limited to levying a toll for such a systematic constitutional violation. * * *

NOTES

1.   What if Justice Marshall's dissenting view had prevailed in *Lyons*? This question was raised when a New York man, Eric Garner, died from a similar use of a police chokehold, and the facts of Lyons's case were revisited:

> An African-American man was stopped by police because he committed a minor offense. Soon, four officers confronted him with their guns drawn. The cops ordered him to stand facing his car, to

spread his legs, and to put his hands on top of his head. Shortly after the man briefly lowered his hands and complained that a key ring he had in his hands was causing him pain, an officer placed him in a chokehold. The man eventually passed out. When he awoke, he was facedown on the ground. His pants were soiled with his own urine and feces. And he was spitting up blood and dirt.

* * * These are the facts of a 1983 Supreme Court case named *City of Los Angeles v. Lyons*. The victim in that case, a black man named Adolph Lyons, was choked out by police in 1976 shortly after he was pulled over for driving with a broken taillight. . . .

Worse, Lyons was just one of many individuals that Los Angeles police targeted with a chokehold, often with fatal results. According to law professor and dean Erwin Chemerinsky's book *The Case Against the Supreme Court*, Lyons discovered that sixteen people died after being choked by an LAPD officer, almost all of whom were black men. When police Chief Daryl Gates was asked why almost all of these fatal chokeholds involved African Americans, Gates replied that the "veins or arteries of blacks do not open up as fast as they do in normal people."

Yet the story of Adolph Lyons and the case that bears his name is also the story of how arcane legal doctrines can reshape decades of police practices. *Lyons* was a 5–4 decision. If just one more justice had sided with Mr. Lyons, it may have enabled the courts to prevent cases like Garner's from ever happening. * * *

Had Marshall's view prevailed, it is possible that Eric Garner would still be alive today. Although the NYPD has had a policy banning chokeholds since 1993, this policy has been wholly ineffective in halting the practice. . . . [A] civilian review board received 219 chokehold complains against NYPD officers in just a single one-year period between 2013 and 2014. "Thousands of NYPD chokeholds" have occurred . . . despite an "outright ban."

The power of an injunction is that it takes the question of how such a ban will be enforced out of the hands of local officials and gives it to a judge who should have no stake in the case other than wanting to see their own injunction enforced. If rampant chokeholds continued even in the presence of an injunction, the judge could have potentially held the NYPD in contempt, or ordered other extraordinary relief to pressure them into compliance.

Ian Millhiser, *How the Supreme Court Helped Make it Possible for Police to Kill by Chokehold*, www.thinkprogress.org, Dec. 4, 2014. In the Garner case, the city settled with the family for $5.9 million. J. David Goodman, *Eric Garner Case is Settled by City for $5.9 Million,* N.Y. Times, July 13, 2015.

2.   The majority in *Lyons* discusses threat of harm in the analogous terms of the standing doctrine. A split Supreme Court reaffirmed this aspect of *Lyons* in denying injunctive relief to group of environmental activists

seeking to enjoin certain practices of the U.S. Forest Service regarding its timber management. Summers v. Earth Island Institute, 555 U.S. 488 (2009). The opinion concisely stated the test for threat of harm: "To seek injunctive relief, a plaintiff must show that he is under threat of suffering 'injury in fact' that is concrete and particularized; the threat must be actual and imminent, not conjectural or hypothetical; it must be fairly traceable to the challenged action of the defendant; and it must be likely that a favorable judicial decision will prevent or redress the injury." *Id.* at 493.

3.   What can a plaintiff in a case like *Lyons* do to satisfy the threat of harm requirement? Possibilities include (a) bringing a class action; (b) alleging racial discrimination and a violation of equal protection; (c) or using statistical data to help demonstrate the possibility of individual future harm. *See* Floyd Weatherspoon, *Ending Racial Profiling of African-Americans in the Selective Enforcement of Laws: In Search of Viable Remedies*, 65 U.Pitt.L.Rev. 721 (2004); Note, *Standing While Black: Distinguishing* Lyons *in Racial Profiling Cases*, 100 Colum.L.Rev. 1815 (2000). Alternatively, plaintiffs will have to rely on large damages actions, where available, and hope that the required payouts create incentives for policy change.

4.   Assuming that Lyons could show sufficient probability of harm to get an injunction, should the injunction limit the use of the chokehold against just him or also against similarly situated persons who are not parties? The question, which arises chiefly in cases against governmental defendants, is answered along two lines: (1) an injunction can protect nonparties where the defendant explicitly or implicitly consents to a decree that protects nonparties, *e.g.,* Catanzano v. Dowling, 847 F.Supp. 1070 (W.D.N.Y.1994); and (2) an injunction can protect only the plaintiffs., *e.g.,* Kansas Health Care Association, Inc. v. Kansas Department of Social & Rehabilitation Services, 31 F.3d 1536 (10th Cir.1994). The group of plaintiffs can, however, be quite large where the court certifies the case as a class action. And even an injunction protecting an individual plaintiff may have the practical effect of protecting others similarly situated.

2.   INADEQUATE REMEDY AT LAW

As discussed, equity developed as a separate court historically under English law. The part of that story relevant here is that the courts of law would hear no suit to prevent an injury to property or to compel performance of a contract. Instead they offered damages after the injury was done. In contrast, the equity courts offered injunctive relief. But, the law courts' jealous protection of their own jurisdiction forced the equity courts to limit access to those who could show that the law courts provided them with no adequate remedy. Thus was born the legal maxim, the guiding rule, that equity will not act unless there is "irreparable injury"— meaning that the plaintiff would suffer an injury that a legal remedy cannot adequately repair.

The eventual merger of law and equity courts in America did away with the jealousy between rival judicial systems, but the merged courts continued to insist on the rule that equitable remedies are available only if the remedy at law is inadequate. With the rule's original jurisdictional purpose gone, additional purposes have been suggested for the modern rule inadequacy rule subordinating injunctions to damages: 1) it preserves the defendant's option in cases at law to have issues of fact heard by a jury; 2) it minimizes the additional problems for the court in drafting and enforcement; and 3) it avoids unnecessary intrusion on the defendant's liberty.

Under the irreparable injury test any one of many different considerations can lead to a finding that the remedy at law is inadequate:

1. the defendant is judgment-proof;

2. the defendant is immune from damages, as may be the case with defendants who are officials or governments;

3. damages arc difficult to estimate because the size of monetary loss is hard to estimate, as in the case of lost profits from a new business, or because the plaintiff is likely to put a money value on the property higher than the market value, as in the case of an heirloom;

4. damages cannot be used to put the plaintiff in its rightful position because what is lost is not available in the market place, as in the cases involving a unique item of property, civil rights, or environmental quality;

5. complete recovery would require a multiplicity of suits, as where the plaintiff seeks an injunction against an ongoing nuisance and the jurisdiction does not allow the recovery of all future damages in one action; or

6. allowing the injury to take place would be morally repugnant even if it can be repaired, as in the case of intentional injury to the plaintiff's property.

See, e.g., Dan B. Dobbs, *Law of Remedies* § 2.5 (2d ed.1993); *Developments in the Law—Injunctions,* 78 Harv.L.Rev. 994, 997–1021 (1965). Courts also presume that there is no adequate remedy at law when real estate is at stake. This presumption is grounded in the historic priority of property rights in the Anglo-American system and arguably justified today by the difficulty in ascertaining the monetary value to the plaintiff of sentimental property or difficulty finding another parcel with exactly the same attributes.

Practically, plaintiffs will seek damages more often than injunctions. Damages is legally easier, money payments can be controlled by the plaintiff, and money will usually suffice to redress the harm. When the plaintiff has a good reason for preferring an injunction to damages, that reason is often sufficient to persuade a court of irreparable injury. Douglas Laycock, *The Death of the Irreparable Injury Rule*, 103 Harv.L.Rev. 687, 722–24 (1990). However, where plaintiffs seek injunctions for mere economic injury, for example in specific performance cases involving fungible goods or patent royalty cases, and/or use injunctions for undue leverage, courts will deny the injunction under the inadequacy rule. *Id.*

Specific laws may adapt the inadequacy requirement for purposes of that particular cause of action. For example, the Fifth Amendment, by permitting the taking of property for a public use through the payment of compensation, effectively denies the property owner injunctive relief. Kelo v. City of New London, 545 U.S. 469 (2005). For another example, the First Amendment's prior restraint doctrine strongly disfavors injunctions, making it much more difficult to enjoin speech than to rectify the harm done after the fact through an action for damages. New York Times Co. v. United States, 403 U.S. 713 (1971). Statutes too sometimes alter the inadequate remedy at law rule. Thus, the Tax Injunction Act provides that "the district courts shall not enjoin, suspend or restrain the assessment, levy or collection of any tax under State law where a plain, speedy and efficient remedy may be had in the courts of such State." 28 U.S.C. § 1341. Where the only state remedy to overassessment of a tax is to pay the tax and seek a refund, the denial of a federal injunction in effect relegates the taxpayer to a remedy at law. *See also, e.g.,* 28 U.S.C. § 1342 (limiting injunctions against administrative decisions affecting utility rates); Norris-LaGuardia Act, 29 U.S.C. §§ 101–115 (barring injunctions against peaceful conduct arising out of labor disputes).

eBAY INC. v. MERCEXCHANGE, L.L.C.
Supreme Court of the United States
547 U.S. 388 (2006)

JUSTICE THOMAS delivered the opinion of the Court.

Ordinarily, a federal court considering whether to award permanent injunctive relief to a prevailing plaintiff applies the four-factor test historically employed by courts of equity. Petitioners eBay Inc. and Half.com, Inc., argue that this traditional test applies to disputes arising under the Patent Act. We agree and, accordingly, vacate the judgment of the Court of Appeals.

I

Petitioner eBay operates a popular Internet Web site that allows private sellers to list goods they wish to sell, either through an auction or at a fixed price. Petitioner Half.com, now a wholly owned subsidiary of eBay, operates a similar Web site. Respondent MercExchange, L.L.C., holds a number of patents, including a business method patent for an electronic market designed to facilitate the sale of goods between private individuals by establishing a central authority to promote trust among participants. *See* U.S. Patent No. 5,845,265. MercExchange sought to license its patent to eBay and Half.com, as it had previously done with other companies, but the parties failed to reach an agreement. MercExchange subsequently filed a patent infringement suit against eBay and Half.com in the United States District Court for the Eastern District of Virginia. A jury found that MercExchange's patent was valid, that eBay and Half.com had infringed that patent, and that an award of damages was appropriate.

Following the jury verdict, the District Court denied MercExchange's motion for permanent injunctive relief. The Court of Appeals for the Federal Circuit reversed, applying its general rule that courts will issue permanent injunctions against patent infringement absent exceptional circumstances. We granted certiorari to determine the appropriateness of this general rule.

II

According to well-established principles of equity, a plaintiff seeking a permanent injunction must satisfy a four-factor test before a court may grant such relief. A plaintiff must demonstrate: (1) that it has suffered an irreparable injury; (2) that remedies available at law, such as monetary damages, are inadequate to compensate for that injury; (3) that, considering the balance of hardships between the plaintiff and defendant, a remedy in equity is warranted; and (4) that the public interest would not be disserved by a permanent injunction. *See, e.g.,* Weinberger v. Romero-Barcelo, 456 U.S. 305, 311–313 (1982); Amoco Production Co. v. Gambell, 480 U.S. 531, 542 (1987). The decision to grant or deny permanent injunctive relief is an act of equitable discretion by the district court, reviewable on appeal for abuse of discretion.

These familiar principles apply with equal force to disputes arising under the Patent Act. As this Court has long recognized, a major departure from the long tradition of equity practice should not be lightly implied. Nothing in the Patent Act indicates that Congress intended such a departure. To the contrary, the Patent Act expressly provides that injunctions may issue in accordance with the principles of equity. 35 U.S.C. § 283.

To be sure, the Patent Act also declares that patents shall have the attributes of personal property, § 261, including the right to exclude others from making, using, offering for sale, or selling the invention, § 154(a)(1). According to the Court of Appeals, this statutory right to exclude alone justifies its general rule in favor of permanent injunctive relief. But the creation of a right is distinct from the provision of remedies for violations of that right. Indeed, the Patent Act itself indicates that patents shall have the attributes of personal property [s]ubject to the provisions of this title,

35 U.S.C. § 261, including, presumably, the provision that injunctive relief may issue only in accordance with the principles of equity, § 283.

This approach is consistent with our treatment of injunctions under the Copyright Act. Like a patent owner, a copyright holder possesses the right to exclude others from using his property. Fox Film Corp. v. Doyal, 286 U.S. 123, 127 (1932); *see also id.*, at 127–128 (A copyright, like a patent, is at once the equivalent given by the public for benefits bestowed by the genius and meditations and skill of individuals, and the incentive to further efforts for the same important objects (internal quotation marks omitted)). Like the Patent Act, the Copyright Act provides that courts may grant injunctive relief on such terms as it may deem reasonable to prevent or restrain infringement of a copyright. 17 U.S.C. § 502(a). And as in our decision today, this Court has consistently rejected invitations to replace traditional equitable considerations with a rule that an injunction automatically follows a determination that a copyright has been infringed. *See, e.g.*, New York Times Co. v. Tasini, 533 U.S. 483, 505 (2001).

Neither the District Court nor the Court of Appeals below fairly applied these traditional equitable principles in deciding respondent's motion for a permanent injunction. Although the District Court recited the traditional four-factor test, it appeared to adopt certain expansive principles suggesting that injunctive relief could not issue in a broad swath of cases. Most notably, it concluded that a plaintiff's willingness to license its patents and its lack of commercial activity in practicing the patents would be sufficient to establish that the patent holder would not suffer irreparable harm if an injunction did not issue. But traditional equitable principles do not permit such broad classifications. For example, some patent holders, such as university researchers or self-made inventors, might reasonably prefer to license their patents, rather than undertake efforts to secure the financing necessary to bring their works to market themselves. Such patent holders may be able to satisfy the traditional four-factor test, and we see no basis for categorically denying them the opportunity to do so. To the extent that the District Court adopted such a categorical rule, then, its analysis cannot be squared with the principles of equity adopted by Congress. The court's categorical rule is also in tension with Continental Paper Bag Co. v. Eastern Paper Bag Co., 210 U.S. 405, 422–430 (1908), which rejected the contention that a court of equity has no jurisdiction to grant injunctive relief to a patent holder who has unreasonably declined to use the patent.

In reversing the District Court, the Court of Appeals departed in the opposite direction from the four-factor test. The court articulated a general rule, unique to patent disputes, that a permanent injunction will issue once infringement and validity have been adjudged. The court further indicated that injunctions should be denied only in the unusual case, under exceptional circumstances and in rare instances . . . to protect the public interest. Just as the District Court erred in its categorical denial of injunctive relief, the Court of Appeals erred in its categorical grant of such relief. Cf. Roche Products v. Bolar Pharmaceutical Co., 733 F.2d 858, 865 (C.A.Fed.1984) (recognizing the considerable discretion district courts have in determining whether the facts of a situation require it to issue an injunction).

Because we conclude that neither court below correctly applied the traditional four-factor framework that governs the award of injunctive relief, we vacate the judgment of the Court of Appeals, so that the District Court may apply that framework in the first instance. In doing so, we take no position on whether permanent injunctive relief should or should not issue in this particular case, or indeed in any number of other disputes arising under the Patent Act. We hold only that the decision whether to grant or deny injunctive relief rests within the equitable discretion of the district courts, and that such discretion must be exercised consistent with traditional principles of equity, in patent disputes no less than in other cases governed by such standards.

Accordingly, we vacate the judgment of the Court of Appeals, and remand for further proceedings consistent with this opinion.

CHIEF JUSTICE ROBERTS, with whom JUSTICE SCALIA and JUSTICE GINSBURG join, concurring.

I agree with the Court's holding that the decision whether to grant or deny injunctive relief rests within the equitable discretion of the district courts, and that such discretion must be exercised consistent with traditional principles of equity, in patent disputes no less than in other cases governed by such standards, and I join the opinion of the Court. That opinion rightly rests on the proposition that a major departure from the long tradition of equity practice should not be lightly implied.

From at least the early 19th century, courts have granted injunctive relief upon a finding of infringement in the vast majority of patent cases. This long tradition of equity practice is not surprising, given the difficulty of protecting a right to *exclude* through monetary remedies that allow an infringer to *use* an invention against the patentee's wishes—a difficulty that often implicates the first two factors of the traditional four-factor test. This historical practice, as the Court holds, does not *entitle* a patentee to a permanent injunction or justify a *general rule* that such injunctions should issue. The Federal Circuit itself so recognized in Roche Products, Inc. v. Bolar Pharmaceutical Co., 733 F.2d 858, 865–867 (1984). At the same time, there is a difference between exercising equitable discretion pursuant to the established four-factor test and writing on an entirely clean slate. Discretion is not whim, and limiting discretion according to legal standards helps promote the basic principle of justice that like cases should be decided alike. When it comes to discerning and applying those standards, in this area as others, a page of history is worth a volume of logic.

JUSTICE KENNEDY, with whom JUSTICE STEVENS, JUSTICE SOUTER, and JUSTICE BREYER join, concurring.

The Court is correct, in my view, to hold that courts should apply the well-established, four-factor test—without resort to categorical rules—in deciding whether to grant injunctive relief in patent cases. The Chief Justice is also correct that history may be instructive in applying this test. The traditional practice of issuing injunctions against patent infringers, however, does not seem to rest on the difficulty of protecting a right to *exclude* through monetary remedies that allow an infringer to *use* an invention against the patentee's wishes. (Roberts, C.J., concurring). Both the terms of the Patent Act and the traditional view of injunctive relief accept that the existence of a right to exclude does not dictate the remedy for a violation of that right. To the extent earlier cases establish a pattern of granting an injunction against patent infringers almost as a matter of course, this pattern simply illustrates the result of the four-factor test in the contexts then prevalent. The lesson of the historical practice, therefore, is most helpful and instructive when the circumstances of a case bear substantial parallels to litigation the courts have confronted before.

In cases now arising trial courts should bear in mind that in many instances the nature of the patent being enforced and the economic function of the patent holder present considerations quite unlike earlier cases. An industry has developed in which firms use patents not as a basis for producing and selling goods but, instead, primarily for obtaining licensing fees. *See* FTC, To Promote Innovation: The Proper Balance of Competition and Patent Law and Policy, ch. 3, pp. 38–39 (Oct.2003). For these firms, an injunction, and the potentially serious sanctions arising from its violation, can be employed as a bargaining tool to charge exorbitant fees to companies that seek to buy licenses to practice the patent. When the patented invention is but a small component of the product the companies seek to produce and the threat of an injunction is employed simply for undue leverage in negotiations, legal damages may well be sufficient to compensate for the infringement and an injunction may not serve the public interest. In addition injunctive relief may have different consequences for the burgeoning number of patents over business methods, which were not of much economic and legal significance in earlier times. The potential vagueness and suspect validity of some of these patents may affect the calculus under the four-factor test. * * *

NOTES

1.   The crux of the problem in *eBay* was the lower courts' use of presumptions, either for or against patent injunctions, to determine relief rather than the flexible considerations of equitable discretion using the traditional test. Tracy A. Thomas, *eBay Rx*, 2 Akron IP L.J.187 (2008). How would the concurring Justices have applied that traditional test of equitable discretion in this case?

2.   On remand in *eBay*, the district court denied the injunction, finding that money damages were adequate, and thus a necessary prerequisite to injunctive relief was not met. 500 F.Supp.2d 556 (E.D.Va.2007). The parties subsequently settled their patent dispute when eBay purchased the patents it was accused of infringing. *EBay Settles Dispute Over "Buy It Now" Feature*, N.Y. Times, C3, Feb. 29, 2008. For some of the voluminous scholarship on the *eBay* case focusing on the remedial issues, see *eBay* Symposium, 2 Akron IP Law J. 1–199 (2008); James M. Fischer, *The "Right" to Injunctive Relief for Patent Infringement*, 24 Santa Clara Comp. & High Tech. L.J. 1 (2007); Doug Rendleman, *The Trial Judge's Discretion After* eBay v. MercExchange, 27 Rev.Lit. 63 (2007). *See also* H. Tomás Gómez-Arostegui, *What History Teaches Us About Copyright Injunctions and the Inadequate-Remedy-at-Law Requirement*, 81 S.Cal.L.Rev. 1197 (2008) (concluding based upon a comprehensive review of Court of Chancery cases from 1660 to 1800 that in *eBay* the Supreme Court incorrectly extended its balancing test to copyright cases because historically the courts did in fact categorically award injunctive relief in these cases).

3.   Note that the *eBay* Court's "traditional" four-part test misstates the first two factors of the qualification rule. It says factor one is "irreparable injury" and factor two is that "remedies available at law are inadequate." However, these are two ways of saying the same thing. The confusion likely stems from the Court's borrowing of precedent from the preliminary injunction context, which is articulated differently. A precise recitation of the first factor would require an "imminent" (rather than irreparable) and "threat of harm" (rather than injury). With this clarification, the factors of *eBay* then resemble the traditional test, but perhaps too late, as now the law has "entered a new world of injunctive relief in which the very particular—and decidedly peculiar—language of *eBay* is king." *See* Mark P. Gergen, John M. Golden & Henry E. Smith, *The Supreme Court's Accidental Revolution? The Test for Permanent Injunctions*, 112 Colum.L.Rev. 203 (2012).

4.   The "public interest" part of the test for injunctive relief allows courts to consider the public policy implications and interests of third parties impacted by the issuance of the injunction. *See* Restatement (Second) of Torts § 942 (defining relevant interests of the public and third parties); *Id.* § 951, cmt. a 8 (1979) (stating that a countervailing public interest may support denial of an otherwise proper award of injunctive relief). Concerns about the practicality of enforcement, such as those involved with personal service contracts, discussed in Section D(2), may also be weighed in here. It is rare, however, that the public interest operates to deny the relief entirely.

5.   The Court reaffirmed *eBay* in Monsanto Co. v. Geertson Seed Farms, 561 U.S. 139 (2010). It criticized the district court for presuming that injunctive relief was appropriate for environmental harm without applying the four-part test. The Court warned that "[n]o such thumb on the scales is warranted." In this highly factual case about the deregulation of genetically engineered alfalfa designed to withstand the weed killer Roundup, the Court invalidated an injunction that enjoined the planting and sale of any new alfalfa

until the agency obtained the statutorily-required environmental impact statement. The plaintiff farmers and environmentalists feared the engineered crop would destroy organic crops through cross-pollenization and create herbicide-resistant superweeds. The Court held that the plaintiffs failed to establish sufficient threat of harm from the agency's delay in obtaining the legally-required environmental report. And it found the injunction overbroad by remedying the lack of report with a nationwide ban on all future alfalfa planting rather than the "less drastic remedy" of vacating the deregulation decision. The agency subsequently conducted the proper environmental review and fully deregulated alfalfa, and the plaintiffs' renewed challenge was denied. Center for Food Safety v. Vilsack, 718 F.3d 839 (9th Cir. 2013).

D. BALANCING THE EQUITIES

Balancing the equities is the next part of the equitable process by which a court weighs the impact of issuing the injunction. The court considers the specific equities of the parties and the injunction's practical effect in deciding whether to issue an injunction and determine its proper scope.

Balancing the equities allows a judge to withhold injunctive relief altogether or to issue an injunction that stops short of fully achieving the plaintiff's rightful position because of undue hardship or unfairness to the defendant, even when the plaintiff's remedies at law are inadequate. This section considers what might justify the court's power to compromise the plaintiff's rightful position, the limits on this power, and whether it undercuts the goals that the common law, constitutions, or statutes seek to achieve.

1. THE DEFENDANT'S UNDUE HARDSHIP: GRANTING LESS THAN PLAINTIFF'S RIGHTFUL POSITION

SMITH V. STASO MILLING CO.

United States Court of Appeals, Second Circuit
18 F.2d 736 (1927)

Appeal from a decree of the District Court of Vermont enjoining the defendant from polluting with slate dust a brook running through the plaintiff's premises, from similarly polluting the air, and from jarring his dwelling house by blasting, and awarding plaintiff judgment in the sum of ten thousand dollars for past damages.

The plaintiff is the owner of a summer residence in the town of Castleton, Vermont, something less than a mile distant from the defendant's crushing mill. This residence he occupied in substantially unchanged form at the time the defendant bought its land and before it put up its mill. The defendant blasts slate rock upon its premises, which it crushes, and makes from the product ground slate roofing material. The grinding creates clouds of dust, part of which, when the wind is in the right direction, is carried over to the plaintiff's premises, which it covers with pulverized dust. This is one grievance.

In the defendant's process of manufacture there are waste products which it puts upon a dump by a belt conveyor. Through the conveyor streams of water are run from driven wells, and the thin, muddy or plastic mass flows out into the first of three settling ponds, the overflow from which passes into a second, and so to a third, the three being together designed to retain all the waste. During heavy rains these ponds become filled with water and carry off through the sluices quantities of the sludge or mud, which the defendant has deposited in them. The last of these empties into a brook which runs through the premises of both parties, and on such occasions quantities of the muddy slate reach the plaintiff's land and leave a sediment upon it. He uses the brook for part of his domestic water supply, and the sludge or silt fills his reservoirs and otherwise interferes with his enjoyment of the premises. This is another and more important grievance.

* * * After the defendant had purchased the land, but before it had put up the plant, the plaintiff wrote, calling attention to the brook which flowed through both premises, advising it that its continued purity was a valuable asset to him, and protesting against any pollution or interference with its flow. The defendant's superintendent called upon him, assured him that there was no danger, because the proposed system of filters and settling basins would prevent any such possibility. The assurance was several times repeated. After the erection of the mill the defendant again assured the plaintiff more than once that the trouble had been in management of the settling ponds.

The defendant has installed dust arresters which are rated to stop 99 per cent of the dust which is produced. It has invested about $1,000,000 altogether in the plant, employs between 125 and 200 men, and its monthly pay roll is between $25,000 and $40,000.

The plaintiff valued his premises at $40,000, though it cost in all less than $30,000 * * * .

The District Judge on conflicting evidence found for the plaintiff on all the questions of fact involved, and absolutely enjoined the activities complained of. * * * The defendant appealed.

LEARNED HAND, Circuit Judge (after stating the facts as above). * * *

The defendant, not arguing that the facts justify no relief, insists that no injunction should go, because of the disastrous effect upon his crushing mill, which must stop its operation if enjoined. We are not satisfied that this must be the consequence, but we are content so to assume. The plaintiff argues that those cases in which such considerations have prevailed, do not represent the law of Vermont, which have never balanced the comparative hardships of the continued wrong and the injunction, when the plaintiff's right is substantial and clear. While we agree that with [a] possible exception [citation omitted], no decision of that state has actually turned upon the doctrine, it appears to us to have had so much recognition in the decisions of its highest court as to be certainly a part of its jurisprudence, at least until we are authoritatively advised to the contrary. * * *

Assuming that the doctrine is not fixed in the law of Vermont, we think that it is as matter of principle a reasonable one. The very right on which the injured party stands in such cases is a quantitative compromise between two conflicting interests. What may be an entirely tolerable adjustment, when the result is only to award damages for the injury done, may become no better than a means of extortion if the result is absolutely to curtail the defendant's enjoyment of his land. Even though the defendant has no power to condemn, at times it may be proper to require of him no more than to make good the whole injury once and for all. If the writ went as of course, we should have no option. Notoriously it * * * is discretionary if any is. To say that whenever an injured party can show that he could recover damages, he has only in addition to prove that the tort will be repeated, appears to us to ignore the substance of the situation in the interest of any apocryphal consistency. Where we are not bound by the local law, we decline to adopt so rigid a canon.

Nevertheless, so far as concerns the pollution of the stream, we think that the injury is so substantial and the wrong so deliberate, that we ought to impose upon the defendant the peril of any failure successfully to avoid it. * * * In the case at bar not only did the defendant have the most explicit warning from the plaintiff, but it gave an equally explicit assurance that it could avoid defiling the brook. It has several times repeated that assurance after occasional overflows. If the plaintiff had filed his bill before the mill was built, the balance of convenience would have been different, and we should not have hesitated to stop what as yet remained only a project. Whether the assurances in fact determined his inaction we need not say; he has shown himself pertinacious, though forbearing, and the chances are that they did. Even if not, these preliminary negotiations seem to us enough absolutely to impose upon the defendant the execution of what it promised. As respects the pollution of the stream, we therefore think that the injunction should remain absolute, and that the defendant must find some way to avoid further injury, or make its peace with the plaintiff as best it can.

As regards the dust the facts are different. True, it is equally a tort so to defile the air. But the injury is less oppressive, and neither the plaintiff's original protest, nor the defendant's promise, covered it. We are not prepared in such a situation to say that, if the defendant cannot by the best known methods arrest all the dust which it emits, it must shut down its mill. The record shows that it has installed arresters which are designed to stop all but one per cent. of the dust, and apparently do so. Yet that which escapes is still enough to affect the plaintiff's enjoyment, and the record does not show beyond question that the defendant cannot prevent it. The best disposition of the case is to affirm the injunction as it stands, but to give leave to the defendant to apply at the foot of the decree for relief upon showing there are no better arresters extant, that it operates those it has at maximum efficiency, that it is theretofore impossible further to reduce the dust, and that if the injunction continues it has no alternative but to stop operation. If that be proved to the satisfaction of the District Judge the injunction should be modified so as merely to limit the dust to that which will escape the arresters now in use. * * *

[The court went on to modify the award of damages.]

NOTES

1.   The holding in *Staso* is consistent with the famous case of Boomer v. Atlantic Cement Co., a favorite of bar examiners. 26 N.Y.2d 219, 309 N.Y.S.2d 312, 257 N.E.2d 870 (1970). In *Boomer*, the court denied an injunction to landowners to stop the pollution nuisance by shutting down the adjacent factory. The court found that the undue, economic hardship to the defendant cement plant weighed against granting the injunction because it had invested $45m in capital costs to build and run the plant, employed over 300 people in the community, built one of the most modern, efficient plants possible, and was unlikely to be able to develop further abatement systems or manufacturing techniques in the next eighteen months to reduce the annoying byproducts since it was already using best practices. The court instead awarded the seven plaintiffs $185,000 in damages based on the diminution in market value of their property. *Boomer*, 55 Misc. 1023, 1026, 287 N.Y.S.2d 112 (N.Y.Sup. 1967).

2.   Professor Chayes, in the article excerpted in Chapter 1, views balancing the equities as giving the trial judge wide-ranging discretion to decree what seems sensible, whether that is more than, less than, or the same as the plaintiff's rightful position. The polar opposite to Professor Chayes' approach would be to deny the judge discretion and require that the decree order the defendant to achieve the plaintiff's rightful position exactly. Professor Schoenbrod has proposed a middle ground in which the judge has discretion, but it is limited by the following principle:

> The injunction should require the defendant to achieve the plaintiff's rightful position unless (a) different relief is consistent with the goals of the violated rule and (b) the case involves a factor justifying departure from the rule that was not reflected in its formulation, but the injunction may never aim to achieve more than the plaintiff's rightful position.

David Schoenbrod, *The Measure of An Injunction: A Principle to Replace Balancing the Equities and Tailoring the Remedy*, 72 Minn.L.Rev. 627, 664 (1988).

3.   Balancing the equities also goes under the names "undue hardship," "the balance of convenience" and "balancing equities and hardships." *Staso* considers hardship/convenience and equities—in other words, efficiency and fairness. Efficiency and fairness are also the chief concerns of the law of nuisance. The gist of the decision on air pollution in *Staso* is that it is efficient to let it continue, should controlling the emissions be impracticable, but unfair to Smith. An award of damages would then provide some recompense for the unfairness. As to the water pollution, the court decides in essence that it would be unfair to take account of the hardship on Staso Milling so that considerations of fairness override considerations of efficiency. In contrast, if the wrong is both unfair and inefficient, the court would readily grant an injunction.

4.   Notice that *Staso* weighs the hardship from an injunction on the defendant and the public (Staso's employees) on one side of the balance and the benefits from an injunction to the plaintiff on the other. So the court considers the detriments to the public but not the benefits. *Boomer,* which also considered the impact on the public in the same one-sided way, offered the following explanation:

> The public concern with air pollution arising from many sources in industry and in transportation is currently accorded ever wider recognition accompanied by a growing sense of responsibility in State and Federal Governments to control it. * * *

> But there is now before the court private litigation in which individual property owners have sought specific relief from a single plant operation. The threshold question raised by the division of view on this appeal is whether the court should resolve the litigation between the parties now before it as equitably as seems possible; or whether, seeking promotion of the general public welfare, it should channel private litigation into broad public objectives.

> A court performs its essential function when it decides the rights of parties before it. Its decision of private controversies may sometimes greatly affect public issues. Large questions of law are often resolved by the manner in which private litigation is decided. But this is normally an incident to the court's main function to settle controversy. It is a rare exercise of judicial power to use a decision in private litigation as a purposeful mechanism to achieve direct public objectives greatly beyond the rights and interests before the court.

26 N.Y.2d at 222–23, 309 N.Y.S.2d at 314–15, 257 N.E.2d at 871. Compare the dictum in Sierra Club v. Morton, 405 U.S. 727, 740 n.15 (1972) ("Once this standing is established, the party may assert the interests of the general public in support of his claims for equitable relief.").

NOTE ON WHEN INJUNCTIONS ARE EFFICIENT

As balancing the equities seeks in part (but only in part) to avoid issuing injunctions that result in inefficiency, it is useful to consider when an injunction will lead to inefficiency. From a law and economics perspective, courts should not impose injunctions that restrain a defendant's behavior by imposing undue burdens and inefficiencies. From an economic perspective, the law wants to allow a defendant to "buy out" the injunction by paying a settlement amount to get out of the injunction. The buyout amount increases with the leverage the plaintiff gains by obtaining an injunction that corresponds with the expectations of the law. But we do not want to trap defendants in inefficient injunctions that they cannot get out of through negotiation.

Inefficiency is not a problem for the court if it can be confident that the parties will bargain to reach an efficient result. Whether the parties can actually strike a deal depends upon what economists call "transaction costs." Transaction costs include the time spent bargaining and attorney fees. If the transaction costs are zero, then by definition the parties will bargain to achieve an efficient outcome regardless of whether the remedy is an injunction or compensatory damages.

Suppose, however, that the transaction costs are sufficiently high that the parties cannot bargain to an outcome different from the one that the court decrees. If the court knows the real stakes for the parties, then it can achieve efficiency by issuing an injunction if and only if the costs of the violation exceeded the costs of its abatement. But, the court will often have trouble determining the true stakes for the parties because the stakes are often subjective or difficult for outsiders to estimate and each party has a reason to exaggerate.

The court has a number of other ways to deal with uncertainty about the stakes to the parties, none of them wholly satisfactory. It could estimate the costs of both violation and abatement, but this course may well lead to inefficiency. Perhaps in part to safeguard plaintiffs from this danger, courts usually require defendants to show that their hardship is not just greater, but much greater than the benefit of granting an injunction.

This final alternative makes it important to consider when transaction costs are likely to be high or low. There is potential for high transaction costs that prohibit the injunction buyout when there is a "bilateral monopoly." Typically this is where each of the parties to the dispute is the only one who can resolve the problem, rather, than for example, the ability to appeal to a third party alternative buyer or actor. The classic cases is of neighbors disputing over a property line. Transaction costs can also be high if there are many potential plaintiffs. Suppose that there are 1000 plaintiffs, each damaged by the harm. Here, transaction costs would prevent bargaining to a more efficient result. (The class action device can sometimes reduce some of these transaction costs.) If any plaintiff can get an injunction as of right, the defendant must make a deal with each or risk wasting its payments. The transaction costs include tracking down and reaching agreement with all the plaintiffs, a time-consuming and expensive undertaking. Some plaintiffs probably could not be found or would refuse to make a deal. Other plaintiffs may insist on more than their fair share of the payment so that disputes among the plaintiffs are likely to arise.

BROWN V. BOARD OF EDUCATION (*BROWN II*)
Supreme Court of the United States
349 U.S. 294 (1955)

MR. CHIEF JUSTICE WARREN delivered the opinion of the Court.

These cases were decided on May 17, 1954. The opinions of that date [*Brown v. Board of Education I* and *Bolling v. Sharpe*] declaring the fundamental principle that racial discrimination in public education is unconstitutional, are incorporated herein by reference. All provisions of federal, state, or local law requiring or permitting such discrimination must yield to this principle. There remains for consideration the manner in which relief is to be accorded.

Because these cases arose under different local conditions and their disposition will involve a variety of local problems, we requested further argument on the question of relief. [Whether a proper decree would permit normal geographic school districting, schools by student choice, gradual adjustment, specific details, and/or a special master.] In view of the nationwide importance of the decision, we invited the Attorney General of the United States and the Attorneys General of all states requiring or permitting racial discrimination in public education to present their views on that question. The parties, the United States, and the States of Florida, North Carolina, Arkansas, Oklahoma, Maryland, and Texas filed briefs and participated in the oral argument.

These presentations were informative and helpful to the Court in its consideration of the complexities arising from the transition to a system of public education freed of racial discrimination. The presentations also demonstrated that substantial steps to eliminate racial discrimination in public schools have already been taken, not only in some of the communities in which these cases arose, but in some of the states appearing as amici curiae, and in other states as well. Substantial progress has been made in the District of Columbia and in the communities in Kansas and Delaware involved in this litigation. The defendants in the cases coming to us from South Carolina and Virginia are awaiting the decision of this Court concerning relief.

Full implementation of these constitutional principles may require solution of varied local school problems. School authorities have the primary responsibility for elucidating, assessing, and solving these problems; courts will have to consider whether the action of school authorities constitutes good faith implementation of the governing constitutional principles. Because of their proximity to local conditions and the possible need for further hearings, the courts which originally heard these cases can best perform this judicial appraisal. Accordingly, we believe it appropriate to remand the cases to those courts.

In fashioning and effectuating the decrees, the courts will be guided by equitable principles. Traditionally, equity has been characterized by a practical flexibility in shaping its remedies and by a facility for adjusting and reconciling public and private needs.[5] These cases call for the exercise of these traditional attributes of equity power. At stake is the personal interest of the plaintiffs in admission to public schools as soon as practicable on a nondiscriminatory basis. To effectuate this interest may call for elimination of a variety of obstacles in making the transition to school systems operated in accordance with the constitutional principles set forth in our May 17, 1954, decision. Courts of equity may properly take into account the public interest in the elimination of such obstacles in a systematic and effective manner. But it should go without saying that the vitality of these constitutional principles cannot be allowed to yield simply because of disagreement with them.

While giving weight to these public and private considerations, the courts will require that the defendants make a prompt and reasonable start toward full compliance with our May 17, 1954, ruling. Once such a start has been made, the courts may find that additional time is necessary to carry out the ruling in an effective manner. The burden rests upon the defendants to establish that such time is necessary in the public interest and is consistent with good faith compliance at the earliest practicable date. To that end, the courts may consider problems related to administration, arising from the physical condition of the school plant, the school transportation system, personnel, revision of school districts and attendance areas into compact units to achieve a system of determining admission to the public schools on a nonracial basis, and revision of local laws and regulations which may be necessary in solving the foregoing problems. They will also consider the adequacy of any plans the defendants may propose to meet these problems and to effectuate a transition to a racially nondiscriminatory school system. During this period of transition, the courts will retain jurisdiction of these cases.

The judgments below, except that in the Delaware case, are accordingly reversed and the cases are remanded to the District Courts to take such proceedings and enter such orders and decrees consistent with this opinion as are necessary and proper to admit to public schools on a racially nondiscriminatory basis with all deliberate speed the parties to these cases. The judgment in the Delaware case—ordering the immediate admission of the plaintiffs to schools previously attended only by white children—is affirmed on the basis of the principles stated in our May 17, 1954, opinion, but the case is remanded to the Supreme Court of Delaware

---

5   *See* Hecht Co. v. Bowles, 321 U.S. 321, 329–330.

for such further proceedings as that Court may deem necessary in light of this opinion.

NOTES

1.   The Topeka schools were not declared unitary until nearly forty-five years later. After the Tenth Circuit ruled that the plaintiffs in *Brown* had yet to be restored fully to their rightful position as of 1992, Brown v. Board of Education, 978 F.2d 585 (10th Cir.1992), *cert. denied*, 503 U.S. 978 (1992), the school district implemented further plans concerning student, staff and faculty assignments. The district court dismissed the case after a period of successful implementation. Brown v. Unified School Dist. No. 501, 56 F.Supp.2d 1212 (D.Kan.1999). Such is "deliberate speed."

In another example, *Brown II's* command still had not achieved a remedy in Cleveland, Mississippi in 2016. A federal judge issued an order to desegregate Cleveland schools fifty-seven years after the case had begun. The school had discontinued racial student assignments, but continued racial policies in faculty assignment and other administration that created a dual system in which the education provided to black students was subpar. The judge dismissed the school's promises to try harder with a magnet school or voluntary choice. Instead, the judge ordered the merger of the two high schools into one integrated school of 1,000 students, and similarly, merger for the middle schools. Cowan v. Bolivar County Bd. of Educ., 2016 WL 2851330 (N.D.Miss. May 13, 2016); NPR, *After 50-Year Legal Struggle, Mississippi School District Ordered to Desegregate*, May 17, 2016.

2.   However the plaintiffs' rightful position is defined, what justification, if any, can there be for failing to grant the plaintiffs their rightful position forthwith in any constitutional case, let alone a case with the importance of *Brown*? Professor Peter Shane writes:

> In some cases, a court may defend remedial delay (rightly or wrongly) as necessary for the maximum vindication of right—because the maximum vindication of right cannot be accomplished without remedial steps that require planning, review, and staged implementation. In some cases, however, such a justification for delay is not available. A pointed example occurs in prisoners' "conditions of confinement" suits. A violation of the constitutional right to freedom from cruel and unusual punishment may be maximally protected by immediate release. While the threat of release is often used to induce state authorities to correct unconstitutional conditions, release is never the remedy of first resort. This can only be because courts recognize a proper place in the remedial process for balancing remedial interests against other legitimate social concerns. Yet, what these concerns comprise and the weight they should enjoy are notably discretionary decisions.

Peter M. Shane, *Rights, Remedies, and Restraint*, 64 Chi.-Kent L.Rev. 531, 557 (1988). Professor Shane builds upon Professor Paul Gewirtz's thoughtful analysis of *Brown II*. Paul Gewirtz, *Remedies and Resistance*, 92 Yale L.J. 585 (1983).

3.   *Brown II* stated that "it should go without saying that the vitality of these constitutional principles cannot be allowed to yield simply because of disagreement with them." Did the Court really mean this or was it just striking an attractive pose because it did not have the power to implement these principles anyway, no matter how it phrased its mandate in *Brown II*? *See* Gerald N. Rosenberg, *Tilting at Windmills:* Brown II *and the Hopeless Quest to Resolve Deep-Seated Social Conflict Through Litigation*, 24 Law & Ineq. 31, 35 (2006) ("Political and social forces (both local and national) did not support desegregation, providing no pressure for compliance.").

4.   Note that the Supreme Court, in remanding to the lower courts, instructs them to give the defendant school boards a substantial role in formulating the remedy. In essence, the matters are remanded to the defendants, although with close judicial supervision. *See* Wendy Parker, *The Decline of Judicial Decisionmaking: School Desegregation and District Court Judges*, 81 N.C.L.Rev. 1623 (2003) (examining pattern of deference from district court judges to defendants in school desegregation cases).

Professor Paul Dimond argues that *Brown II* is a great victory precisely because its strategy of giving the political branches the lead in determining the scope, pace, and design of the remedy left the Supreme Court free to identify the wrong in unstinting terms. He argues that because of the limits on the courts in exercising their countermajoritarian powers:

> We should concede that the more massive and entrenched the wrong of discrimination, the more important it is for the courts to declare the full extent of that wrong. The courts must also permit the ultimate remedy to be worked out in a political process in which those who are aggrieved will at least have a continuing claim that the declared wrong cannot be remedied in the courts alone.

Paul R. Dimond, Brown *and the Transformation of the Constitution: Concluding Remarks*, 61 Fordham L.Rev. 63, 65–66 (1992).

5.   Whether *Brown II* went as far as it should have, make no mistake that it continued to have a huge impact on how schools and other institutions are operated. United States v. Fordice, 505 U.S. 717(1992) (establishing criteria for desegregation in Mississippi's public university system). Moreover, Professor Owen M. Fiss in *The Civil Rights Injunction* (1978) argued that *Brown II* reshaped the law of remedies. Previously, injunctions were the remedies of last resort both because of the inadequate remedy at law rule and the suspicion of injunctions generated by injunctions against strikes in the early days of the union movement. After *Brown II*, the injunction was the remedy of choice for constitutional violations. *See* Doug Rendleman, Brown II's *"All Deliberate Speed" at Fifty: A Golden Anniversary or a Mid-life Crisis for the Constitutional Injunction as a School Desegregation Remedy*? 41 San Diego L.Rev. 1575 (2004).

6. The Supreme Court sometimes decides that courts should deny redress for past violations when the claim for relief rests on new constitutional doctrines. It is then said that the new doctrine has only "prospective" effect, which suggests that the new law of liability applies only to future cases. But Professors Richard H. Fallon, Jr. and Daniel J. Meltzer argue that these decisions are best understood as applications of traditional remedial principles, such as avoiding undue hardship caused by reasonable reliance on the old doctrine. Richard H. Fallon, Jr. & Daniel J. Meltzer, *New Law, Non-Retroactivity, and Constitutional Remedies*, 104 Harv.L.Rev. 1733 (1991).

NOTE ON THE PRACTICALITY OF ENFORCEMENT

"It has long been settled that a court shall not issue an injunction that would be inconvenient or inefficient to administer." Bray v. Safeway Stores, 392 F.Supp. 851, 868 (N.D.Cal.1975). The burden on the court thus factors into the balancing of the equities, though rarely does the modern case deny an injunction on this basis alone.

Concerns about difficulty of enforcement lead to the denial of specific relief of some contracts, particularly personal service or construction contracts where enforcement could involve ongoing monitoring and subjective evaluations of the quality of work. On the other hand, courts often grant injunctions where enforcement will be onerous. Enforcement problems are especially serious in many civil rights and regulatory cases. Indeed, the judicial effort to desegregate the schools of the lead defendant in *Brown v. Board of Education* lasted for nearly 45 years. Brown v. Unified School District No. 501, 56 F.Supp.2d 1212 (D.Kan.1999) (declaring unitary status). Outside of contract cases, injunctions are so rarely denied because of burdens of supervision that the opinions only infrequently even mention the issue. On the other hand, in Joyce v. City and County of San Francisco, 846 F.Supp. 843 (N.D.Cal.1994), the court refused to grant a preliminary injunction barring the police from enforcing the homeless statutes or ordinances prohibiting "life-sustaining" activities in public places. The court was concerned that uncertainty about who is homeless on any particular night and what is a "life-sustaining" activity would create enforcement problems.

The principle does not direct courts to deny specific relief simply because of difficulty of supervision, but only if the "burdens * * * are disproportionate to the advantages to be gained from enforcement and to the harm to be suffered by its denial." Restatement (Second) of Contracts § 366 (1981). Courts generally place a higher value on constitutional, statutory, and common law property rights than they do on enforcement of commercial promises, or at least see compensatory damages as less inadequate in the case of commercial promises.

Practicality of enforcement comprehends not only the burdens of supervising compliance but also impediments to punishing contempt of an order. Courts traditionally hesitate to grant an injunction against out-of-state activity by a non-resident because the defendant might violate the order yet escape punishment. In contrast, judges do not hesitate to issue money judgments against defendants who reside and have their assets outside the geographic limits of the court. The explanation for the difference lies partly in ensuring that court orders are obeyed and partly in the operation of the full faith and credit clause of the United States Constitution. Art. IV, § 1. Although the clause requires the courts of one state to give full faith and credit to "judicial proceedings" of other states, courts have interpreted the clause to require enforcement of money judgments but not injunctions. Restatement (Second) of Conflict of Laws § 102 comment *c* (1971). As matters now stand, a court may enjoin out-of-state activity *(id.* at § 53) and the court of a sister state might choose—but is not obligated—to enforce the injunction as part of its own proceedings. Even if the injunction from the first state is not enforced directly elsewhere, the sister state will give the findings necessary to the original injunction preclusive effect so that the plaintiff might be entitled to obtain a new order from the sister state. *See* Baker v. General Motors Corp., 522 U.S. 222 (1998). It is also possible that the enjoined defendant will comply voluntarily because he or she does not want to risk being found in contempt by the court issuing the injunction, or the defendant's assets might be found in the original jurisdiction. In any event, "the sky will not fall in if the defendant is successful in flouting the decree." Dan B. Dobbs, *Handbook of the Law of Remedies* at 64 (1973).

––––––––

The courts balanced the equities in *Staso,* a common law case, and *Brown II,* a constitutional case. The next question is whether they may balance the equities to allow statutory violations to continue. Professor Zygmunt Plater, who represented the plaintiffs in the following case, later wrote that his clients "made the 'conservative' argument that courts should not be activist but rather should follow the dictates of the words of the statutes before them." Zygmunt Plater, *In the Wake of the Snail Darter: An Environmental Law Paradigm and Its Consequences*, 19 Mich.J.L. Reform 805, 834 (1986).

TENNESSEE VALLEY AUTHORITY V. HILL

Supreme Court of the United States
437 U.S. 153 (1978)

MR. CHIEF JUSTICE BURGER delivered the opinion of the Court.

The question[ ] presented in this case [is] whether the Endangered Species Act of 1973 requires a court to enjoin the operation of a virtually completed federal dam—which had been authorized prior to 1973—when, pursuant to authority vested in him by Congress, the Secretary of the Interior has determined that operation of the dam would eradicate an endangered species.

I

The Little Tennessee River originates in the mountains of northern Georgia and flows through the national forest lands of North Carolina into Tennessee, where it converges with the Big Tennessee River near Knoxville. The lower 33 miles of the Little Tennessee takes the river's clear, free-flowing waters through an area of great natural beauty. * * * Considerable historical importance attaches to the areas immediately adjacent * * * .

In this area of the Little Tennessee River the Tennessee Valley Authority, a wholly owned public corporation of the United States, began constructing the Tellico Dam and Reservoir Project in 1967, shortly after Congress appropriated initial funds for its development. Tellico is a multipurpose regional development project designed principally to stimulate shoreline development, generate sufficient electric current to heat 20,000 homes, and provide flatwater recreation and flood control, as well as improve economic conditions in "an area characterized by underutilization of human resources and outmigration of young people." Of particular relevance to this case is one aspect of the project, a dam which TVA determined to place on the Little Tennessee, a short distance from where the river's waters meet with the Big Tennessee. When fully operational, the dam would impound water covering some 16,500 acres— much of which represents valuable and productive farmland—thereby converting the river's shallow, fast-flowing waters into a deep reservoir over 30 miles in length.

[The Court describes how litigation under statutes other than the Endangered Species Act slowed and sometimes enjoined the dam's completion. After these efforts to halt the dam had failed and just when the dam was about to go into operation,] a discovery was made in the waters of the Little Tennessee which would profoundly affect the Tellico Project. Exploring the area around Coytee Springs, which is about seven miles from the mouth of the river, a University of Tennessee ichthyologist, Dr. David A. Etnier, found a previously unknown species of perch, the snail darter, or Percina (Imostoma) tanasi. This three-inch, tannish-colored fish, whose numbers are estimated to be in the range of 10,000 to 15,000, would soon engage the attention of environmentalists, the TVA, the Department of the Interior, the Congress of the United States, and ultimately the federal courts, as a new and additional basis to halt construction of the dam.

Until recently the finding of a new species of animal life would hardly generate a cause celebre. This is particularly so in the case of darters, of which there are approximately 130 known species, 8 to 10 of these having been identified only in the last five years. The moving force behind the snail darter's sudden fame came some four months after its discovery, when the Congress passed the Endangered Species Act of 1973 (Act), 87 Stat. 884, 16 U.S.C. § 1531 et seq. (1976 ed.). This legislation, among other things, authorizes the Secretary of the Interior to declare species of animal life "endangered" and to identify the "critical habitat" of these creatures.

* * * [T]he Secretary determined that the snail darter apparently lives only in that portion of the Little Tennessee River which would be completely inundated by the reservoir created as a consequence of the Tellico Dam's completion. The Secretary went on to explain the significance of the dam to the habitat of the snail darter: * * * *The proposed impoundment of water behind the proposed Tellico Dam would result in total destruction of the snail darter's habitat.*"

Subsequent to this determination, the Secretary declared the area of the Little Tennessee which would be affected by the Tellico Dam to be the "critical habitat" of the snail darter. Using these determinations as a predicate, and notwithstanding the near completion of the dam, the Secretary declared that pursuant to § 7 of the Act, "all Federal agencies must take such action as is necessary to insure that actions authorized, funded, or carried out by them do not result in the destruction or modification of this critical habitat area." This notice, of course, was pointedly directed at TVA and clearly aimed at halting completion or operation of the dam.

* * * In February 1976, pursuant to § 11(g) of the Endangered Species Act, 16 U.S.C. § 1540(g), respondents filed the case now under review, seeking to enjoin completion of the dam and impoundment of the reservoir on the ground that those actions would violate the Act by directly causing the extinction of the species *Percina (Imostoma) tanasi.*

* * * [T]he court entered its memorandum opinion and order denying respondents their requested relief and dismissing the complaint. The District Court found that closure of the dam and the consequent impoundment of the reservoir would "result in the adverse modification, if not complete destruction, of the snail darter's critical habitat," making it "highly probable" that "the continued existence of the snail darter" would be "jeopardize[d]." Despite these findings, the District Court declined to embrace the plaintiffs' position on the merits: that once a federal project was shown to jeopardize an endangered species, a court of equity is compelled to issue an injunction restraining violation of the Endangered Species Act.

In reaching this result, the District Court stressed that the entire project was then about 80% complete and, based on available evidence, "there [were] no alternatives to impoundment of the reservoir, short of scrapping the entire project." The District Court also found that if the Tellico Project was permanently enjoined, "[s]ome $53 million would be lost in nonrecoverable obligations," meaning that a large portion of the $78 million already expended would be wasted. The court also noted that the Endangered Species Act of 1973 was passed some seven years after construction on the dam commenced and that Congress had continued appropriations for Tellico, with full awareness of the snail darter problem. Assessing these various factors, the District Court concluded:

> "At some point in time a federal project becomes so near completion and so incapable of modification that a court of equity should not apply a statute enacted long after inception of the project to produce an unreasonable result. * * * Where there has been an irreversible and irretrievable commitment of resources by Congress to a project over a span of almost a decade, the Court should proceed with a great deal of circumspection." * * *

Thereafter, in the Court of Appeals, respondents argued that the District Court had abused its discretion by not issuing an injunction in the face of "a blatant statutory violation." The Court of Appeals agreed, and on January 31, 1977, it reversed, remanding "with instructions that a permanent injunction issue halting all activities incident to the Tellico Project which may destroy or modify the critical habitat of the snail darter." * * *

II

* * *

A

It may seem curious to some that the survival of a relatively small number of three-inch fish among all the countless millions of species extant would require the permanent halting of a virtually completed dam for which Congress has expended more than $100 million. The paradox is not minimized by the fact that Congress continued to appropriate large sums of public money for the project, even after congressional Appropriations Committees were apprised of its apparent impact upon the survival of the snail darter. We conclude, however, that the explicit provisions of the Endangered Species Act require precisely that result.

One would be hard pressed to find a statutory provision whose terms were any plainer than those in § 7 of the Endangered Species Act. Its very words affirmatively command all federal agencies "to *insure* that actions *authorized, funded,* or *carried out* by them do not *jeopardize* the continued existence" of an endangered species or "*result* in the destruction or modification of habitat of such species * * * ." 16 U.S.C. § 1536. This language admits of no exception. Nonetheless, petitioner urges, as do the dissenters, that the Act cannot reasonably be interpreted as applying to a federal project which was well under way when Congress passed the Endangered Species Act of 1973. [The Court rejects this argument.] * * *

Concededly, this view of the Act will produce results requiring the sacrifice of the anticipated benefits of the project and of many millions of dollars in public funds. But examination of the language, history, and structure of the legislation under review here indicates beyond doubt that

Congress intended endangered species to be afforded the highest of priorities.

* * * One might * * * [argue] that in this case the burden on the public through the loss of millions of unrecoverable dollars would greatly outweigh the loss of the snail darter. But neither the Endangered Species Act nor Art. III of the Constitution provides federal courts with authority to make such fine utilitarian calculations. On the contrary, the plain language of the Act, buttressed by its legislative history, shows clearly that Congress viewed the value of endangered species as "incalculable." Quite obviously, it would be difficult for a court to balance the loss of a sum certain—even $100 million—against a congressionally declared "incalculable" value, even assuming we had the power to engage in such a weighing process, which we emphatically do not.

B

Having determined that there is an irreconcilable conflict between operation of the Tellico Dam and the explicit provisions of § 7 of the Endangered Species Act, we must now consider what remedy, if any, is appropriate. It is correct, of course, that a federal judge sitting as a chancellor is not mechanically obligated to grant an injunction for every violation of law. This Court made plain in Hecht Co. v. Bowles, 321 U.S. 321, 329 (1944), that "[a] grant of jurisdiction to issue compliance orders hardly suggests an absolute duty to do so under any and all circumstances." As a general matter it may be said that "[s]ince all or almost all equitable remedies are discretionary, the balancing of equities and hardships is appropriate in almost any case as a guide to the chancellor's discretion." D. Dobbs, Remedies 52 (1973). Thus, in *Hecht Co.* the Court refused to grant an injunction when it appeared from the District Court findings that "the issuance of an injunction would have 'no effect by way of insuring better compliance in the future' and would [have been] 'unjust' to [the] petitioner and not 'in the public interest.' "

But these principles take a court only so far. Our system of government is, after all, a tripartite one, with each branch having certain defined functions delegated to it by the Constitution. While "[i]t is emphatically the province and duty of the judicial department to say what the law is," Marbury v. Madison, 1 Cranch 137, 177 (1803), it is equally—and emphatically—the exclusive province of the Congress not only to formulate legislative policies and mandate programs and projects, but also to establish their relative priority for the Nation. Once Congress, exercising its delegated powers, has decided the order of priorities in a given area, it is for the Executive to administer the laws and for the courts to enforce them when enforcement is sought.

Here we are urged to view the Endangered Species Act "reasonably," and hence shape a remedy "that accords with some modicum of common sense and the public weal." But is that our function? We have no expert knowledge on the subject of endangered species, much less do we have a mandate from the people to strike a balance of equities on the side of the Tellico Dam. Congress has spoken in the plainest of words, making it abundantly clear that the balance has been struck in favor of affording endangered species the highest of priorities, thereby adopting a policy which it described as "institutionalized caution."

Our individual appraisal of the wisdom or unwisdom of a particular course consciously selected by the Congress is to be put aside in the process of interpreting a statute. Once the meaning of an enactment is discerned and its constitutionality determined, the judicial process comes to an end. We do not sit as a committee of review, nor are we vested with the power of veto. * * *

We agree with the Court of Appeals that in our constitutional system the commitment to the separation of powers is too fundamental for us to pre-empt congressional action by judicially decreeing what accords with "common sense and the public weal." Our Constitution vests such responsibilities in the political branches.

Affirmed.

NOTES

1.   *After the case was over*. Congress eventually enacted legislation that authorized putting the dam into operation although a cost-benefit analysis concluded that, even not counting the money already spent to build the dam, the additional costs of putting it into operation—such as submerging large amounts of farm land—would outweigh the benefits. Zygmunt J.B. Plater, *Endangered Species Act Lessons Over 30 Years, and the Legacy of the Snail Darter, a Small Fish in a Pork Barrel*, 34 Envt'l L. 289 (2004) (article cites Plater's other writings concerning his experiences with the case). For further information on the environmental and administrative significance of *TVA v. Hill*, see Kenneth M. Murchison, *The Snail Darter Case: TVA Versus the Endangered Species Act* (2007). Snail darters were discovered ultimately in many other habitats. Those who want to develop a listed habitat now hire consultants who will search out unknown habitats of endangered species. *See also* David Schoenbrod, *Saving Our Environment From Washington: How Congress Grabs Power, Shirks Responsibility, and Shortchanges the People* (2005).

2.   Compare *TVA v. Hill* with Weinberger v. Romero-Barcelo, 456 U.S. 305 (1982), where the Court refused to enjoin governmental action to ensure compliance with a statute. The Court reversed an injunction ordering the Navy to cease weapons training in the waters off the Puerto Rico coast while it applied for the permit required under the Federal Water Pollution Control Act, 33 U.S.C. § 1251 (1976). It held that the statute did not alter the traditional equitable discretion of the court to balance the parties' competing interests and factor in the public consequences of the injunction.

DAVID SCHOENBROD, THE MEASURE OF AN INJUNCTION: A PRINCIPLE TO REPLACE BALANCING THE EQUITIES AND TAILORING THE REMEDY

72 Minn.L.Rev. 627, 654–57, 664–66 (1988)

* * * In determining liability, the judge decides only whether the elements of the violation are present, whereas in balancing the equities when fashioning a remedy, the judge also considers whether there are factors that make it unfair to order the defendant to stop the violation immediately. For instance, if the defendant builds a structure that violates the setback requirements of the local zoning ordinance, that is the beginning and end of the question of liability. If the plaintiff wants the violation enjoined, however, the judge will want to know whether the defendant encroached intentionally or recklessly, the cost to defendant of removing the encroachment, whether removing the encroachment will harm innocent third parties, the importance to the plaintiff of having the encroachment removed, and so on. Courts make this broader inquiry at the remedial stage primarily because granting an injunction rather than damages presents a greater threat of gross inefficiency.

Consequently, equity introduces flexibility into the cold enforcement of law to address the inefficiencies associated with injunctive relief. This flexibility is justified because the judicial process in cases that seek remedies at law has sources of flexibility not available in cases that seek equitable relief. In suits for damages, much of what goes into balancing the equities in injunction cases gets reflected in jury nullification, the determination of the amount of compensatory or punitive damages, limits on garnishment and execution designed to avoid severe hardship, and sometimes a kind of balancing of the equities in the damage context itself. Moreover, criminal actions involve flexibility in prosecutorial discretion, jury nullification, and sentencing judgment. Thus, a suit for an injunction without balancing the equities would present a rare instance of the judicial process without a safety valve.

Although Plater claims that judges should not balance the equities in statutory cases and should apply statutory rules strictly, the reasons for balancing in nonstatutory cases apply fully to statutory cases. In nonstatutory cases, courts balance the equities because injunctive enforcement of a rule of liability that is fair and efficient in general may be unfair or inefficient in a particular context. In formulating statutory rules, legislatures can rarely confine statutory definitions of violations to instances in which enjoining them would invariably be fair and efficient. Judges need the kind of flexibility that they have in nonstatutory cases to act as a safety valve to prevent unfair and inefficient application of a statutory rule. Plater argues that legislative relief, not balancing the equities, provides the appropriate safety valve in statutory cases. That safety valve, however, is available only in extraordinary cases that get priority on the legislative agenda, such as *TVA v. Hill,* not in garden variety cases. The proposed principle provides a safety valve for all statutory cases by giving judges the flexibility necessary, but in a way that restrains judges' discretion, forcing them to honor the choices that the legislature did make.

2. PROPHYLAXIS: GRANTING MORE THAN PLAINTIFF'S RIGHTFUL POSITION

Deciding whether to issue an injunction that grants more than the plaintiff's rightful position, like deciding whether to issue an injunction that grants less, involves balancing. *See* Schoenbrod, *Measure of an Injunction, supra.* There are interesting differences and similarities in how the balancing is done. To get an injunction that grants less, the defendant must justify that result through a factor not reflected in the law of liability—a "hardship." To get an injunction that grants more, the plaintiff also must justify the result through a factor not reflected in the law of liability—the difficulty of supervising a resistant defendant or of precisely recreating the plaintiff's rightful position. The defendant must show that the hardship outweighs the plaintiff's interest in getting specific rather than substitutionary relief. The plaintiff must show that the threat to its rightful position from a narrower injunction outweighs the harm to the defendant from an injunction going beyond the plaintiff's rightful position. We have seen that in balancing claims of hardship, the courts take account of the respective faults of the parties and the goals of the law of liability. The same is true in balancing plaintiffs' request for broader relief. The degree of the defendant's culpability in violating either the plaintiff's rights or an earlier injunction counts against the defendant.

The more typical example of courts granting more than rightful position arises in the context of "prophylactic" injunctions. They are called "prophylactic" in reference to prophylactic medicine like vaccinations, drugs, and other steps that are taken as precautions to prevent future harm. In these cases, courts order injunctive relief beyond the rightful position when those additional measures are necessary to ensure that the plaintiff will actually achieve her rightful position. These prophylactic injunctions address ancillary conduct with a sufficient causal nexus to the demonstrated harm that facilitates continued violations of the law. "The discretionary power of a district court to formulate an equitable remedy for an adjudicated violation of law is broad. Where necessary for the elimination of the violation, the decree can properly fence the defendant in by forbidding conduct not unlawful in itself." People Who Care v. Rockford Board of Education, 111 F.3d 528 (7th Cir.1997). Like prophylactic measures in medicine, the additional safeguards are taken to avoid future harm, such as a vaccination given to prevent a more serious disease. *See* Tracy A. Thomas, *The Prophylactic Remedy: Normative Principles and*

Definitional Parameters of Broad Injunctive Relief, 52 Buff.L.Rev. 301 (2004).

A court might order a prophylactic injunction to ensure compliance with an injunction. For example, an injunction whose terms are geared precisely to the plaintiff's rightful position may fail to achieve the plaintiff's rightful position if the defendant can disobey the order without being detected. When the threat of such harm is large enough, courts can hold the defendant to a more readily enforceable standard even though it exceeds the plaintiff's rightful position. The court still *aims* for the plaintiff's rightful position, but the *terms* of the injunction go beyond that position as prophylaxis against falling short of it. Thomas, *Prophylactic Remedy, supra.*

Prophylaxis developed in institutional reform cases involving schools, prisons, and other public institutions. For example, in the case of Women Prisoners v. District of Columbia, 877 F.Supp. 634 (D.D.C.1994), *modified,* 899 F.Supp. 659 (D.D.C.1995), *vacated in part,* 93 F.3d 910 (D.C.Cir.1996) (invalidating the appointment of a special monitor), the district court crafted a detailed prophylactic injunction addressing the proven constitutional and tort violations stemming from sexual harassment and assault of the women inmates by staff members. The defendant's history of similar violations and the egregious nature of the harms weighed in favor of practical alternatives and precautions that could effectively eliminate the opportunity for the behavior to continue. The district court believed further measures were necessary to address the contributing causes of the harm in order to better prevent future incidents. The prophylactic measures ordered included a complaint hotline, a formal grievance system, reporting mechanisms, employee sanctions, expert consultation, and staff training.

Hutto v. Finney, 437 U.S. 678 (1978), is another instance of an injunction that went beyond the plaintiff's rightful position for prophylactic purposes. There, the district court had found that punitive isolation for longer than 30 days was not in itself cruel and unusual punishment but was so in combination with the terrible conditions in Arkansas's punitive isolation cells. The district court enjoined punitive isolation for longer than 30 days and the Supreme Court affirmed:

> In fashioning a remedy, the District Court had ample authority to go beyond earlier orders and to address each element contributing to the violation. The District Court had given the Department repeated opportunities to remedy the cruel and unusual conditions in the isolation cells. If petitioners had fully complied with the court's earlier orders, the present time limit might well have been unnecessary. But taking the long and unhappy history of the litigation into account, the court was

> justified in entering a comprehensive order to insure against the
> risk of inadequate compliance.

437 U.S. at 687. *Hutto* suggests that injunctions that go beyond the
plaintiffs' rightful position require a demonstrated risk that the defendants
would not comply with a narrower order. Such a requirement parallels the
requirement of showing a threat of harm to plaintiff's rightful position as
a prerequisite to the issuance of any injunction.

Prophylactic orders are also common in enforcement of regulatory
statutes. For example, after finding a violation of the securities laws, courts
sometimes not only enjoin future violations but also ensure that they do
not recur by prohibiting the violator from participating as an officer of any
public company, imposing reporting requirements in addition to those in
the securities laws, or appointing an independent majority on the violator's
board of directors, a receiver, or "special professionals" to ensure
compliance. George W. Dent Jr., *Ancillary Relief in Federal Securities Law:
A Study in Federal Remedies*, 67 Minn.L.Rev. 865 (1983). *See also* FTC v.
National Lead Co., 352 U.S. 419, 431 (1957) ("[R]espondents must
remember that those caught violating the Act must expect some fencing
in").

Prophylactic relief, like structural injunctions, has been accused of
constituting judicial activism that improperly extends "beyond the right."
Certainly not all prophylactic injunctions are valid. *Rizzo v. Goode* is an
example where the court failed to aim its injunction at a proven legal
violation, and instead targeted secondary lawful conduct without any
connection to an established wrong by the police department. Professor
Tracy Thomas has argued that even the Supreme Court went too far in its
establishment of "constitutionally required" prophylactic measures in *Bush
v. Gore* that abridged, rather than supported, the voters' legal rights,
thereby threatening the proper use and legitimacy of prophylaxis as a
remedy. *Understanding Prophylactic Remedies Through the Looking Glass
of* Bush v. Gore, 11 Wm. & M. Bill Rts J. 343 (2002).

Courts, however, continue to use broad, prophylactic injunctions as
effective and necessary remediation of complex cases, thus belying the
myth of illegitimacy. *See* Tracy A. Thomas, *The Continued Vitality of
Prophylactic Relief*, 27 Rev.Lit. 99 (2007). For example, an empirical study
of injunctions ordered by the district courts in patent infringement cases
revealed both the prevalence and utility of prophylactic injunctions. John
M. Golden, *Injunctions as More (or Less) Than "Off Switches": Patent-
Infringement Injunctions' Scope*, 90 Texas L.Rev. 1399 (2012). Based on
this study, Professor Golden builds a persuasive argument for expanding
the routine use of specifically tailored prophylactic injunctions and moving
beyond simple "off-switch" injunctions ordering the cessation of
infringement. *See* Tracy A. Thomas, *Switching to Prophylactic Injunctions*,
90 Texas L.Rev. See Also 296 (2012) (response to Golden).

In deciding whether an injunction should grant more than the plaintiff's rightful position, constitutional interests are at stake—liberty or property when the addressee of the injunction is a private person and separation of powers or federalism when the addressee is a governmental institution. When, as in the following case, the injunction allegedly violates First Amendment rights, the constitutional issue gets heightened scrutiny. In reading the case, consider not just how courts should scrutinize injunctions that assertedly violate the First Amendment but also any injunction that intrudes on the liberty or property interests of a private defendant.

MADSEN V. WOMEN'S HEALTH CENTER, INC.

Supreme Court of the United States
512 U.S. 753 (1994)

CHIEF JUSTICE REHNQUIST delivered the opinion of the Court.

Petitioners challenge the constitutionality of an injunction entered by a Florida state court which prohibits antiabortion protestors from demonstrating in certain places and in various ways outside of a health clinic that performs abortions. We hold that the establishment of a 36-foot buffer zone on a public street from which demonstrators are excluded passes muster under the First Amendment, but that several other provisions of the injunction do not.

I

Respondents operate abortion clinics throughout central Florida. Petitioners and other groups and individuals are engaged in activities near the site of one such clinic in Melbourne, Florida. They picketed and demonstrated where the public street gives access to the clinic. In September 1992, a Florida state court permanently enjoined petitioners from blocking or interfering with public access to the clinic, and from physically abusing persons entering or leaving the clinic. Six months later, respondents sought to broaden the injunction, complaining that access to the clinic was still impeded by petitioners' activities and that such activities had also discouraged some potential patients from entering the clinic, and had deleterious physical effects on others. The trial court thereupon issued a broader injunction, which is challenged here.

The court found that, despite the initial injunction, protesters continued to impede access to the clinic by congregating on the paved portion of the street—Dixie Way—leading up to the clinic, and by marching in front of the clinic's driveways. It found that as vehicles heading toward the clinic slowed to allow the protesters to move out of the way, "sidewalk counselors" would approach and attempt to give the vehicle's occupants antiabortion literature. The number of people congregating varied from a handful to 400, and the noise varied from singing and chanting to the use of loudspeakers and bullhorns.

The protests, the court found, took their toll on the clinic's patients. A clinic doctor testified that, as a result of having to run such a gauntlet to enter the clinic, the patients "manifested a higher level of anxiety and hypertension causing those patients to need a higher level of sedation to undergo the surgical procedures, thereby increasing the risk associated with such procedures." The noise produced by the protestors could be heard within the clinic, causing stress in the patients both during surgical procedures and while recuperating in the recovery rooms. And those patients who turned away because of the crowd to return at a later date, the doctor testified, increased their health risks by reason of the delay.

Doctors and clinic workers, in turn, were not immune even in their homes. Petitioners picketed in front of clinic employees' residences; shouted at passersby; rang the doorbells of neighbors and provided literature identifying the particular clinic employee as a "baby killer." Occasionally, the protestors would confront minor children of clinic employees who were home alone.

This and similar testimony led the state court to conclude that its original injunction had proved insufficient "to protect the health, safety and rights of women in Brevard and Seminole County, Florida, and surrounding counties seeking access to [medical and counseling] services." The state court therefore amended its prior order, enjoining a broader array of activities. The amended injunction prohibits petitioners[1] from engaging in the following acts:

(1)   * * * entering the * * * property of the Aware Woman Center for Choice [the Melbourne clinic]. . . .

(2)   * * * obstructing * * * access to * * * the Clinic.

(3)   * * * entering * * * within [36] feet of the property line of the Clinic. . . . [There are exceptions: petitioners may come within 5 feet of the Clinic's east line and owners of property adjacent to the Clinic and their invitees may use their property within the buffer zone.]

(4)   During the hours of 7:30 a.m. through noon, on Mondays through Saturdays, during surgical procedures and recovery periods, from singing, * * * , shouting, * * * , use of bullhorns, * * * or other sounds or images observable to or within earshot of the patients inside the Clinic.

(5)   * * * in an area within [300] feet of the Clinic, from physically approaching any person seeking the services of the

---

[1]   In addition to petitioners, the state court's order was directed at "Operation Rescue * * * and all persons acting in concert or participation with them, or on their behalf."

Clinic unless such person indicates a desire to communicate by approaching or by inquiring of the [petitioners]. . . .

(6) * * * from approaching * * * within [300] feet of the residence of any of the [respondents'] employees * * * or blocking * * * the entrances * * * of [their] residences * * *

(7) * * * from physically abusing, grabbing, intimidating, harassing, touching, pushing, shoving, crowding or assaulting persons entering or leaving, working at or using services at the [respondents'] Clinic or trying to gain access to, or leave, any of the homes of owners, staff or patients of the Clinic.

(8) * * * from harassing, intimidating or physically abusing, assaulting or threatening any present or former * * * employee or volunteer who assists in providing services at the [respondents'] Clinic.

(9) * * * from encouraging, inciting, or securing other persons to commit any of the prohibited acts listed herein.

The Florida Supreme Court upheld the constitutionality of the trial court's amended injunction. * * * [T]he United States Court of Appeals for the Eleventh Circuit heard a separate challenge to the same injunction. [It] struck down the injunction, characterizing the dispute as a clash "between an actual prohibition of speech and a potential hindrance to the free exercise of abortion rights." * * * We granted certiorari to resolve the conflict between the Florida Supreme Court and the Court of Appeals. * * *

III

If this were a content-neutral, generally applicable statute, instead of an injunctive order, its constitutionality would be assessed under the standard set forth in Ward v. Rock Against Racism, 491 U.S. 781 (1989), and similar cases. Given that the forum around the clinic is a traditional public forum, we would determine whether the time, place, and manner regulations were "narrowly tailored to serve a significant governmental interest."

There are obvious differences, however, between an injunction and a generally applicable ordinance. Ordinances represent a legislative choice regarding the promotion of particular societal interests. Injunctions, by contrast, are remedies imposed for violations (or threatened violations) of a legislative or judicial decree. * * * Injunctions also carry greater risks of censorship and discriminatory application than do general ordinances. "[T]here is no more effective practical guaranty against arbitrary and unreasonable government than to require that the principles of law which officials would impose upon a minority must be imposed generally." Injunctions, of course, have some advantages over generally applicable statutes in that they can be tailored by a trial judge to afford more precise relief than a statute where a violation of the law has already occurred.

We believe that these differences require a somewhat more stringent application of general First Amendment principles in this context. In past cases evaluating injunctions restricting speech, * * * we have relied upon such general principles while also seeking to ensure that the injunction was no broader than necessary to achieve its desired goals. * * * Our close attention to the fit between the objectives of an injunction and the restrictions it imposes on speech is consistent with the general rule, quite apart from First Amendment considerations, "that injunctive relief should be no more burdensome to the defendants than necessary to provide complete relief to the plaintiffs." Accordingly, when evaluating a content-neutral injunction, we think that our standard time, place, and manner analysis is not sufficiently rigorous. We must ask instead whether the challenged provisions of the injunction burden no more speech than necessary to serve a significant government interest. * * *

The Florida Supreme Court concluded that numerous significant government interests are protected by the injunction. It noted that the State has a strong interest in protecting a woman's freedom to seek lawful medical or counseling services in connection with her pregnancy. *See* Roe v. Wade, 410 U.S. 113 (1973). The State also has a strong interest in ensuring the public safety and order, in promoting the free flow of traffic on public streets and sidewalks, and in protecting the property rights of all its citizens. In addition, the court believed that the State's strong interest in residential privacy, acknowledged in Frisby v. Schultz, 487 U.S. 474 (1988), applied by analogy to medical privacy. The court observed that while targeted picketing of the home threatens the psychological well-being of the "captive" resident, targeted picketing of a hospital or clinic threatens not only the psychological, but the physical well-being of the patient held "captive" by medical circumstance. We agree with the Supreme Court of Florida that the combination of these governmental interests is quite sufficient to justify an appropriately tailored injunction to protect them. We now examine each contested provision of the injunction to see if it burdens more speech than necessary to accomplish its goal.

A

1

[handwritten: Valid reason for an injunction but is it too much?]

We begin with the 36-foot buffer zone. The state court prohibited petitioners from "congregating, picketing, patrolling, demonstrating or entering" any portion of the public right-of-way or private property within 36 feet of the property line of the clinic as a way of ensuring access to the clinic. This speech-free buffer zone requires that petitioners move to the other side of Dixie Way and away from the driveway of the clinic, where the state court found that they repeatedly had interfered with the free access of patients and staff. * * *

We have noted a distinction between the type of focused picketing banned from the buffer zone and the type of generally disseminated communication that cannot be completely banned in public places, such as handbilling and solicitation. *See Frisby*, 487 U.S. at 486. * * *

The 36-foot buffer zone protecting the entrances to the clinic and the parking lot is a means of protecting unfettered ingress to and egress from the clinic, and ensuring that petitioners do not block traffic on Dixie Way. The state court seems to have had few other options to protect access given the narrow confines around the clinic. As the Florida Supreme Court noted, Dixie Way is only 21 feet wide in the area of the clinic. The state court was convinced that allowing the petitioners to remain on the clinic's sidewalk and driveway was not a viable option in view of the failure of the first injunction to protect access. And allowing the petitioners to stand in the middle of Dixie Way would obviously block vehicular traffic.

The need for a complete buffer zone near the clinic entrances and driveway may be debatable, but some deference must be given to the state court's familiarity with the facts and the background of the dispute between the parties even under our heightened review. Moreover, one of petitioners' witnesses during the evidentiary hearing before the state court conceded that the buffer zone was narrow enough to place petitioners at a distance of no greater than 10 to 12 feet from cars approaching and leaving the clinic. Protesters standing across the narrow street from the clinic can still be seen and heard from the clinic parking lots. We also bear in mind the fact that the state court originally issued a much narrower injunction, providing no buffer zone, and that this order did not succeed in protecting access to the clinic. The failure of the first order to accomplish its purpose may be taken into consideration in evaluating the constitutionality of the broader order. On balance, we hold that the 36-foot buffer zone around the clinic entrances and driveway burdens no more speech than necessary to accomplish the governmental interest at stake. * * *

2

The inclusion of private property on the back and side of the clinic in the 36-foot buffer zone raises different concerns. * * * Patients and staff wishing to reach the clinic do not have to cross the private property abutting the clinic property * * * and nothing in the record indicates that petitioners' activities on the private property have obstructed access to the clinic. * * * We hold that on the record before us the 36-foot buffer zone as applied to the private property to the north and west of the clinic burdens more speech than necessary to protect access to the clinic.

B

In response to high noise levels outside the clinic, the state court restrained the petitioners from "singing, chanting, whistling, shouting, yelling, use of bullhorns, auto horns, sound amplification equipment or other sounds or images observable to or within earshot of the patients inside the [c]linic" during the hours of 7:30 a.m. through noon on Mondays through Saturdays. * * * Noise control is particularly important around hospitals and medical facilities during surgery and recovery periods. * * *

We hold that the limited noise restrictions imposed by the state court order burden no more speech than necessary to ensure the health and well-being of the patients at the clinic. * * *

C

The same, however, cannot be said for the "images observable" provision of the state court's order. Clearly, threats to patients or their families, however communicated, are proscribable under the First Amendment. But rather than prohibiting the display of signs that could be interpreted as threats or veiled threats, the state court issued a blanket ban on all "images observable." This broad prohibition on all "images observable" burdens more speech than necessary to achieve the purpose of limiting threats to clinic patients or their families. Similarly, if the blanket ban on "images observable" was intended to reduce the level of anxiety and hypertension suffered by the patients inside the clinic, it would still fail. * * * [I]t is much easier for the clinic to pull its curtains than for a patient to stop up her ears. * * *

D

The state court ordered that petitioners refrain from physically approaching any person seeking services of the clinic "unless such person indicates a desire to communicate" in an area within 300 feet of the clinic. The state court was attempting to prevent clinic patients and staff from being "stalked" or "shadowed" by the petitioners as they approached the clinic.

But it is difficult, indeed, to justify a prohibition on *all* uninvited approaches of persons seeking the services of the clinic, regardless of how peaceful the contact may be, without burdening more speech than necessary to prevent intimidation and to ensure access to the clinic. Absent evidence that the protesters' speech is independently proscribable (i.e., "fighting words" or threats), or is so infused with violence as to be indistinguishable from a threat of physical harm, this provision cannot stand. "As a general matter, we have indicated that in public debate our own citizens must tolerate insulting, and even outrageous, speech in order to provide adequate breathing space to the freedoms protected by the First Amendment." The "consent" requirement alone invalidates this provision; it burdens more speech than is necessary to prevent intimidation and to ensure access to the clinic.

E

The final substantive regulation challenged by petitioners relates to a prohibition against picketing, demonstrating, or using sound amplification equipment within 300 feet of the residences of clinic staff. The prohibition also covers impeding access to streets that provide the sole access to streets on which those residences are located. The same analysis applies to the use of sound amplification equipment here as that discussed above: the government may simply demand that petitioners turn down the volume if the protests overwhelm the neighborhood.

As for the picketing, our prior decision upholding a law banning targeted residential picketing remarked on the unique nature of the home, as "the last citadel of the tired, the weary, and the sick."

But the 300-foot zone around the residences in this case is much larger than the zone provided for in the ordinance which we approved in *Frisby*. The ordinance at issue there made it "unlawful for any person to engage in picketing before or about the residence or dwelling of any individual." The prohibition was limited to "focused picketing taking place solely in front of a particular residence." By contrast, the 300-foot zone would ban "[g]eneral marching through residential neighborhoods, or even walking a route in front of an entire block of houses." The record before us does not contain sufficient justification for this broad a ban on picketing; it appears that a limitation on the time, duration of picketing, and number of pickets outside a smaller zone could have accomplished the desired result.

JUSTICE STEVENS [concurring in part and dissenting in part, omitted]

JUSTICE SCALIA, with whom JUSTICE KENNEDY and JUSTICE THOMAS join, concurring in the judgment in part and dissenting in part.

The judgment in today's case has an appearance of moderation and Solomonic wisdom, upholding as it does some portions of the injunction while disallowing others. That appearance is deceptive. The entire injunction in this case departs so far from the established course of our jurisprudence that in any other context it would have been regarded as a candidate for summary reversal.

But the context here is abortion. * * *

Because I believe that the judicial creation of a 36-foot zone in which only a particular group, which had broken no law, cannot exercise its rights of speech, assembly, and association, and the judicial enactment of a noise prohibition, applicable to that group and that group alone, are profoundly at odds with our First Amendment precedents and traditions, I dissent.

* * *

[margin, handwritten] Could even achieved by a smaller zone

NOTES

1. After the U.S. Supreme Court remanded the case, the trial court issued a modified injunction in light of *Madsen*. The Florida appellate courts upheld the injunction, as modified. Johnson v. Women's Health Center, Inc., 714 So.2d 580 (Fla.App.), *rev. denied*, 719 So.2d 893 (Fla.1998).

2. The *Madsen* majority relied heavily on the finding that the defendants had violated the previous injunction in upholding the prophylactic injunction. Schenck v. Pro-Choice Network of Western NY, 519 U.S. 357 (1997), made clear that a prophylactic order can be issued even if there was no violation of a narrower order. The abortion clinic had a stronger case in *Schenck* than in *Madsen,* because the defendants had trespassed on clinic property, blockaded the clinic, and assaulted patients. *Schenck* also upheld fixed 15-foot buffer zones around the clinic entrances, but struck floating 15-foot buffer zones that moved with patients as they entered and left the clinic. The floating zones were not narrowly tailored because it would be too difficult for protestors to converse with patients yet avoid trespassing on the zones and the floating zones were not necessary on these facts to serve the purposes of the decree.

3. When prophylaxis has been imposed by legislation, rather than judicial decree, the Court has made a different calculus. In Hill v. Colorado, 530 U.S. 703 (2000), the Supreme Court upheld a state statute that makes it unlawful to knowingly approach within eight feet of a person entering a health facility within 100 feet of its entrance. Justice Stevens distinguished *Schenck* on the basis that it dealt with a judicially created prohibition, which must be reviewed under the *Madsen* test, rather than a statutorily created prohibition, which *Madsen* held must be reviewed under the somewhat milder test of *Ward v. Rock Against Racism*. The Court went on to hold that the statute was a content-neutral, valid time, place and manner regulation because it was narrowly tailored to serve the state's legitimate interest in protecting people entering a health care facility.

However, in a subsequent case, the Supreme Court struck down prophylactic legislation under the *Ward* test, invalidating a 35-foot abortion clinic buffer zone virtually identical to the 36-foot zone upheld in *Madsen* under stricter scrutiny. McCullen v. Coakley, 573 U.S. ___, 134 S.Ct. 2518 (2014). The state claimed it had previously tried other laws and injunctions to control the public demonstrations, but the Court found that the state did not convincingly show "it seriously undertook to address the problem with less intrusive tools readily available to it." The decision thus turned on the availability of less restrictive alternatives, even though the Court reiterated that such alternatives were not mandated by the intermediate scrutiny it applied.

4. Congress has also enacted the Freedom of Access to Clinic Entrances Act (FACE), which makes it a federal crime to block access to a reproductive health facility or use force or threats against people using the facility. The statute has been upheld repeatedly. *See, e.g., McCullen*, 134 S.Ct. at 2537; Norton v. Ashcroft, 298 F.3d 547 (6th Cir.2002), *cert. denied*, 537 U.S. 1172

(2003); United States v. Gregg, 226 F.3d 253 (3d Cir.2000), *cert. denied*, 532 U.S. 971 (2001) (statute valid as exercise of Commerce Clause power and does not violate First Amendment).

The Supreme Court's 1955 order in *Brown II* mandated: (1) the dismantling of dual school systems; and (2) the admission of all children to unitary schools on a racially nondiscriminatory basis. After over a decade of foot dragging by school boards, the Supreme Court finally demanded prompt action: "the burden on a school board today is to come forward with a plan that promises realistically to work, and promises realistically to work *now*." Green v. School Board of New Kent County, 391 U.S. 430 (1968). *Green* struck down a desegregation plan that complied only superficially with *Brown II*'s mandate. The school board in *Green* had adopted a "freedom of choice" plan, under which school children could choose which of the county's two schools (the formerly white school or the formerly African-American school) to attend. All the white children chose to attend the previously white school, and 85% of the African-American children chose the African-American school. A unanimous Court held that the freedom of choice plan perpetuated the racial identification of each school and therefore failed *Brown II*'s first criteria.

Neighborhood-based pupil assignments could achieve racially mixed schools relatively quickly and easily in *Green*. There, half the population was African-American, the other half white, all living in racially integrated neighborhoods. An injunction requiring the school board to assign pupils to the nearest school would integrate the schools with little or no busing.

Subsequent cases presented the courts with tougher logistic and conceptual problems. Where neighborhoods are not racially mixed, a school policy that assigns each child to the nearest school will often produce schools that are not racially mixed. In considering whether the school district has a responsibility to achieve integration, courts distinguish between segregation due to official acts or policies, which is called *de jure* segregation, and segregation due to other factors, which is called *de facto* segregation. In *Green*, the two schools in the County had been segregated due to official acts of the school board, in assigning all African-American children to one school and all white children to the other. However, residential segregation, and therefore the school segregation that results from neighborhood pupil assignment, may have many different causes: (a) past de jure discrimination by the school board; (b) past de jure discrimination by other governments, such as the state or the municipality, that are legally distinct from the school board; (c) private discrimination by real estate agents, landlords, and sellers of real estate; and (d) African-Americans' own preferences and their lower average income. These factors, in turn, have previous causes—some rooted in private actions, some rooted in public actions.

There was a dispute as to whether de facto as well as de jure segregation is unconstitutional and gives rise to liability. If so, the plaintiffs' rightful position is to attend an *integrated* school rather than a school that is *not segregated due to official action*. If not, could a court allow a school that had engaged previously in de jure segregation to adopt a desegregation plan that assigned children to schools on a nondiscriminatory basis, yet still did not produce tangible integration? Or could the court require a desegregation plan that produced integrated schools out of segregated residential patterns, even though the plaintiffs have no right, per se, to integrated schools?

SWANN v. CHARLOTTE-MECKLENBURG BOARD OF EDUCATION

Supreme Court of the United States
402 U.S. 1 (1971)

MR. CHIEF JUSTICE BURGER delivered the opinion of the Court.

* * * This case and those argued with it arose in States having a long history of maintaining two sets of schools in a single school system deliberately operated to carry out a governmental policy to separate pupils in schools solely on the basis of race. That was what *Brown v. Board of Education* was all about. These cases present us with the problem of defining in more precise terms than heretofore the scope of the duty of school authorities and district courts in implementing *Brown I* and the mandate to eliminate dual systems and establish unitary systems at once. * * *

I

The Charlotte-Mecklenburg school system, the 43d largest in the Nation, encompasses the city of Charlotte and surrounding Mecklenburg County, North Carolina. The area is large * * * spanning roughly 22 miles east-west and 36 miles north-south. During the 1968–1969 school year the system served more than 84,000 pupils in 107 schools. Approximately 71% of the pupils were found to be white and 29% Negro. [Most of the] Negro students attended * * * schools which were either totally Negro or more than 99% Negro.

This situation came about under a desegregation plan approved by the District Court at the commencement of the present litigation in 1965, based upon geographic zoning with a free-transfer provision. The present proceedings were initiated in September 1968 by petitioner Swann's motion for further relief based on *Green v. County School Board*. All parties now agree that in 1969 the system fell short of achieving the unitary school system that [*Green* requires].

The District Court * * * found that residential patterns in the city and county resulted in part from federal, state, and local government action other than school board decisions. School board action based on these patterns, for example, by locating schools in Negro residential areas and fixing the size of the schools to accommodate the needs of immediate neighborhoods, resulted in segregated education. These findings were subsequently accepted by the Court of Appeals.

* * * [T]he District Court was presented with two alternative pupil assignment plans—the finalized "board plan" and the "Finger plan."

The Board Plan. * * * The board plan proposed substantial assignment of Negroes to nine of the system's 10 high schools, producing 17% to 36% Negro population in each. The projected Negro attendance at the 10th school, Independence, was 2%. The proposed attendance zones for the high schools were typically shaped like wedges of a pie, extending outward from the center of the city to the suburban and rural areas of the county in order to afford residents of the center city area [which had the largest minority concentration] access to outlying schools.

As for junior high schools, the board plan rezoned the 21 school areas so that in 20 the Negro attendance would range from 0% to 38%. The other school, located in the heart of the Negro residential area, was left with an enrollment of 90% Negro.

The board plan with respect to elementary schools relied entirely upon gerrymandering of geographic zones. More than half of the Negro elementary pupils were left in nine schools that were 86% to 100% Negro; approximately half of the white elementary pupils were assigned to schools 86% to 100% white.

The Finger Plan. The plan submitted by the court-appointed expert, Dr. Finger, adopted the school board zoning plan for senior high schools with one modification: it required that an additional 300 Negro students be transported from the Negro residential area of the city to the nearly all-white Independence High School. [The Finger plan also achieved greater integration of the junior high schools and elementary schools through busing. The District Court adopted the Finger plan.] * * *

On appeal the Court of Appeals affirmed the District Court's order as to * * * the secondary school plans, but vacated the order respecting elementary schools. While agreeing that the District Court properly disapproved the board plan concerning these schools, the Court of Appeals feared that the [busing of elementary school students] would place an unreasonable burden on the board and the system's pupils. * * *

II

* * *

Over the 16 years since *Brown II,* many difficulties were encountered in implementation of the basic constitutional requirement that the State not discriminate between public school children on the basis of their race.

Nothing in our national experience prior to 1955 prepared anyone for dealing with changes and adjustments of the magnitude and complexity encountered since then. Deliberate resistance of some to the Court's mandates has impeded the good-faith efforts of others to bring school systems into compliance. * * *

III

The objective today remains to eliminate from the public schools all vestiges of state-imposed segregation. * * *

If school authorities fail in their affirmative obligations under these holdings, judicial authority may be invoked. Once a right and a violation have been shown, the scope of a district court's equitable powers to remedy past wrongs is broad, for breadth and flexibility are inherent in equitable remedies. * * * Hecht Co. v. Bowles, 321 U.S. 321, 329–330 (1944).

* * * [A] school desegregation case does not differ fundamentally from other cases involving the framing of equitable remedies to repair the denial of a constitutional right. The task is to correct, by a balancing of the individual and collective interests, the condition that offends the Constitution.

In seeking to define even in broad and general terms how far this remedial power extends it is important to remember that judicial powers may be exercised only on the basis of a constitutional violation. Remedial judicial authority does not put judges automatically in the shoes of school authorities whose powers are plenary. Judicial authority enters only when local authority defaults.

School authorities are traditionally charged with broad power to formulate and implement educational policy and might well conclude, for example, that in order to prepare students to live in a pluralistic society each school should have a prescribed ratio of Negro to white students reflecting the proportion for the district as a whole. To do this as an educational policy is within the broad discretionary powers of school authorities; absent a finding of a constitutional violation, however, that would not be within the authority of a federal court. As with any equity case, the nature of the violation determines the scope of the remedy. In default by the school authorities of their obligation to proffer acceptable remedies, a district court has broad power to fashion a remedy that will assure a unitary school system. * * *

IV

* * *

The construction of new schools and the closing of old ones are two of the most important functions of local school authorities and also two of the most complex. * * * The result * * * , when combined with one technique or another of student assignment, will determine the racial composition of the student body in each school in the system. Over the long run, the consequences of the choices will be far reaching. People gravitate toward school facilities, just as schools are located in response to the needs of people. The location of schools may thus influence the patterns of residential development of a metropolitan area and have important impact on composition of inner-city neighborhoods.

In the past, choices in this respect have been used as a potent weapon for creating or maintaining a state-segregated school system. In addition to the classic pattern of building schools specifically intended for Negro or white students, school authorities have sometimes, since *Brown,* closed schools which appeared likely to become racially mixed through changes in neighborhood residential patterns. This was sometimes accompanied by building new schools in the areas of white suburban expansion farthest from Negro population centers in order to maintain the separation of the races with a minimum departure from the formal principles of "neighborhood zoning." Such a policy does more than simply influence the short-run composition of the student body of a new school. It may well promote segregated residential patterns which, when combined with "neighborhood zoning," further lock the school system into the mold of separation of the races. Upon a proper showing a district court may consider this in fashioning a remedy. * * *

V

The central issue in this case is that of student assignment, and there are essentially four problem areas: * * *

(1) *Racial Balances or Racial Quotas.* * * * If we were to read the holding of the District Court to require, as a matter of substantive constitutional right, any particular degree of racial balance or mixing, that approach would be disapproved and we would be obliged to reverse. The constitutional command to desegregate schools does not mean that every school in every community must always reflect the racial composition of the school system as a whole. * * *

(2) *One-race Schools.* The record in this case reveals the familiar phenomenon that in metropolitan areas minority groups are often found concentrated in one part of the city. In some circumstances certain schools may remain all or largely of one race until new schools can be provided or neighborhood patterns change. Schools all or predominantly of one race in a district of mixed population will require close scrutiny to determine that school assignments are not part of state-enforced segregation.

In light of the above, it should be clear that the existence of some small number of one-race, or virtually one-race, schools within a district is not in and of itself the mark of a system that still practices segregation by law. The district judge or school authorities should make every effort to achieve the greatest possible degree of actual desegregation and will thus necessarily be concerned with the elimination of one-race schools. No per se rule can adequately embrace all the difficulties of reconciling the competing interests involved; but in a system with a history of segregation the need for remedial criteria of sufficient specificity to assure a school authority's compliance with its constitutional duty warrants a presumption against schools that are substantially disproportionate in their racial composition. Where the school authority's proposed plan for conversion from a dual to a unitary system contemplates the continued existence of some schools that are all or predominantly of one race, * * * [t]he court should scrutinize such schools, and the burden upon the school authorities will be to satisfy the court that their racial composition is not the result of present or past discriminatory action on their part. * * *

(3) *Remedial Altering of Attendance Zones.* The maps submitted in these cases graphically demonstrate that one of the principal tools employed by school planners and by courts to break up the dual school system has been a frank—and sometimes drastic—gerrymandering of school districts and attendance zones. An additional step was [assigning students to a school not only from its neighborhood but also from a distant neighborhood] to accomplish the transfer of Negro students out of formerly segregated Negro schools and transfer of white students to formerly all-Negro schools. * * * As an interim corrective measure, this cannot be said to be beyond the broad remedial powers of a court.

Busing

Absent a constitutional violation there would be no basis for judicially ordering assignment of students on a racial basis. All things being equal, with no history of discrimination, it might well be desirable to assign pupils to schools nearest their homes. But all things are not equal in a system that has been deliberately constructed and maintained to enforce racial segregation. * * *

In this area, we must of necessity rely to a large extent, as this Court has for more than 16 years, on the informed judgment of the district courts in the first instance and on courts of appeals. * * *

(4) *Transportation of Students.* The scope of permissible transportation of students as an implement of a remedial decree has never been defined by this Court and by the very nature of the problem it cannot be defined with precision. * * * Bus transportation has been an integral part of the public education system for years, and was perhaps the single most important factor in the transition from the one-room schoolhouse to the consolidated school. * * *

[The amount of busing under the District Court's plan] compares favorably with the transportation plan previously operated in Charlotte * * *.

An objection to transportation of students may have validity when the time or distance of travel is so great as to either risk the health of the children or significantly impinge on the educational process. District courts must weigh the soundness of any transportation plan in light of what is said in subdivisions (1), (2), and (3) above. It hardly needs stating that the limits on time of travel will vary with many factors, but probably with none more than the age of the students. The reconciliation of competing values in a desegregation case is, of course, a difficult task with many sensitive facets but fundamentally no more so than remedial measures courts of equity have traditionally employed.

VI

The Court of Appeals, searching for a term to define the equitable remedial power of the district courts, used the term "reasonableness." In *Green,* this Court used the term "feasible" and by implication, "workable," "effective," and "realistic" in the mandate to develop "a plan that promises realistically to work, and . . . to work *now*." On the facts of this case, we are unable to conclude that the order of the District Court is not reasonable, feasible and workable. However, in seeking to define the scope of remedial power or the limits on remedial power of courts in an area as sensitive as we deal with here, words are poor instruments to convey the sense of basic fairness inherent in equity. Substance, not semantics, must govern, and we have sought to suggest the nature of limitations without frustrating the appropriate scope of equity. * * *

The order of the District Court * * * is * * * affirmed. * * *

NOTES

1. For background on *Swann,* see Davison M. Douglas, *Reading, Writing & Race: The Desegregation of the Charlotte Schools* (1995). In 1999, the district court finally terminated its order in *Swann,* finding that the school system had eliminated all vestiges of de jure segregation to the extent practicable. Capacchione v. Charlotte-Mecklenburg Schools, 57 F.Supp.2d 228 (W.D.N.C.1999). The Fourth Circuit en banc affirmed. Belk v. Charlotte-Mecklenburg Board of Education, 269 F.3d 305 (4th Cir. en banc 2001), *cert. denied,* 535 U.S. 986 (2002). The opinions also detail the subsequent history of the lengthy case.

2. The *Swann* Court suggested that school authorities had "broad discretionary powers" to set educational policy, including establishing a "prescribed ratio" of students of different races in each school in the proportion found in the district as a whole. In Parents Involved in Community Schools v. Seattle School District No. 1, 551 U.S. 701 (2007), a plurality of the Supreme Court rejected the attempt of the Seattle and Louisville school districts to use race as an element in student assignments to schools in order to voluntarily promote racial diversity and avoid racial isolation. One key difference from Swann is that these schools used racial quotas as a voluntary program, not as a remedy. That context seemed to make all the difference, as without evidence of a constitutional violation, the school districts could not justify the

assignment plans as remedies. *See* Jonathan Fischbach, Will Rhee & Robert Cacace, *Race at the Pivot Point: The Future of Race-Based Policies to Remedy De Jure Segregation After* Parents Involved in Community Schools, 43 Harv.Civ.Rights–Civ.Lib.L.Rev. 491 (2008); Michael Heise, *Judicial Decision-making, Social Science Evidence, and Equal Educational Opportunity: Uneasy Relations and Uncertain Futures*, 31 Seattle U.L. Rev. 863 (2008); Martha Minow, *After Brown: What Would Martin Luther King Say?* 12 Lewis & Clark L.Rev. 599 (2008).

———

Swann, which was decided during an era of evident resistance to the commands of *Brown*, focused on thwarting that resistance by making clear that the school boards had to take real action. *Missouri v. Jenkins,* decided during an era of concern about the scope of judicial authority, focused on defining the outer limits of the duty to desegregate.

MISSOURI V. JENKINS (*JENKINS III*)
Supreme Court of the United States
515 U.S. 70 (1995)

CHIEF JUSTICE REHNQUIST delivered the opinion of the Court. * * *

I

* * * This case has been before the same United States District Judge since 1977. In that year, the Kansas City, Missouri, School District (KCMSD), the school board, and the children of two school board members brought suit against the State and other defendants. Plaintiffs alleged that the State, the surrounding suburban school districts (SSD's), and various federal agencies had caused and perpetuated a system of racial segregation in the schools of the Kansas City metropolitan area. The District Court realigned the KCMSD as a nominal defendant and certified as a class, present and future KCMSD students. The KCMSD brought a cross-claim against the State for its failure to eliminate the vestiges of its prior dual school system.

After a trial that lasted 7 1/2 months, the District Court dismissed the case against the federal defendants and the SSD's, but determined that the State and the KCMSD were liable for an intradistrict violation, i.e., they had operated a segregated school system within the KCMSD. The District Court determined that prior to 1954 "Missouri mandated segregated schools for black and white children." * * *

The District Court determined that "[s]egregation ha[d] caused a system wide *reduction* in student achievement in the schools of the KCMSD." The District Court made no particularized findings regarding the extent that student achievement had been reduced or what portion of that reduction was attributable to segregation. The District Court also identified 25 schools within the KCMSD that had enrollments of 90% or more black students.

The District Court, pursuant to plans submitted by the KCMSD and the State, ordered a wide range of quality education programs for all students attending the KCMSD. * * * [Under these programs, all schools in the district would get reduced class size, full-day kindergarten, expanded summer school, before- and after-school tutoring, an early childhood development program, and substantial yearly cash grants.] The total cost for these quality education programs has exceeded $220 million.

The District Court also set out to desegregate the KCMSD but believed that "[t]o accomplish desegregation within the boundary lines of a school district whose enrollment remains 68.3% black is a difficult task." Because it had found no interdistrict violation, the District Court could not order mandatory interdistrict redistribution of students between the KCMSD and the surrounding SSD's. * * * Milliken v. Bradley, 418 U.S. 717 (1974) (*Milliken I*). The District Court refused to order additional mandatory student reassignments because they would "increase the instability of the KCMSD and reduce the potential for desegregation." * * *

In November 1986, the District Court approved a comprehensive magnet school and capital improvements plan and held the State and the KCMSD jointly and severally liable for its funding. Under the District Court's plan, every senior high school, every middle school, and one-half of the elementary schools were converted into magnet schools. The District Court adopted the magnet-school program to "provide a greater educational opportunity to *all* KCMSD students," and because it believed "that the proposed magnet plan [was] so attractive that it would draw non-minority students from the private schools who have abandoned or avoided the KCMSD, and draw in additional non-minority students from the suburbs." * * * Since its inception, the magnet school program has operated at a cost, including magnet transportation, in excess of $448 million. In April 1993, the District Court considered, but ultimately rejected, the plaintiffs' and the KCMSD's proposal seeking approval of a long-range magnet renewal program that included a 10-year budget of well over $500 million, funded by the State and the KCMSD on a joint-and-several basis.

In June 1985, the District Court ordered substantial capital improvements to combat the deterioration of the KCMSD's facilities. In formulating its capital-improvements plan, the District Court dismissed as "irrelevant" the "State's argument that the present condition of the facilities [was] not traceable to unlawful segregation." Instead, the District Court focused on its responsibility to "remed[y] the vestiges of segregation" and to "implemen[t] a desegregation plan which w[ould] maintain and attract non-minority members." [The total cost of the program was over $540 million.]

As part of its desegregation plan, the District Court has ordered salary assistance to the KCMSD. * * * [T]he District Court has ordered salary assistance to all but three of the approximately 5,000 KCMSD employees. The total cost of this component of the desegregation remedy since 1987 is over $200 million.

The District Court's desegregation plan has been described as the most ambitious and expensive remedial program in the history of school desegregation. The annual cost per pupil at the KCMSD far exceeds that of the neighboring SSD's or of any school district in Missouri. * * * These massive expenditures have financed

> high schools in which every classroom will have air conditioning, an alarm system, and 15 microcomputers; a 2,000-square-foot planetarium; green houses and vivariums; a 25-acre farm with an air-conditioned meeting room for 104 people; a Model United Nations wired for language translation; broadcast capable radio and television studios with an editing and animation lab; a temperature controlled art gallery; movie editing and screening rooms; a 3,500-square-foot dust-free diesel mechanics room; 1,875-square-foot elementary school animal rooms for use in a zoo project; swimming pools; and numerous other facilities.

Missouri v. Jenkins (*Jenkins II*), 495 U.S. 33, 77(1990) (Kennedy, J., concurrence). Not surprisingly, the cost of this remedial plan has "far exceeded KCMSD's budget, or for that matter, its authority to tax." The State, through the operation of joint-and-several liability, has borne the brunt of these costs. The District Court candidly has acknowledged that it has "allowed the District planners to dream" and "provided the mechanism for th[ose] dreams to be realized." * * *

III

* * * An analysis of the permissible scope of the District Court's remedial authority is necessary for a proper determination of whether the order of salary increases is beyond the District Court's remedial authority, and thus, it is an issue subsidiary to our ultimate inquiry. * * *

Almost 25 years ago, in Swann v. Charlotte-Mecklenburg Bd. of Ed., 402 U.S. 1 (1971), * * * [a]lthough recognizing the discretion that must necessarily adhere in a district court in fashioning a remedy [in a school desegregation case], we also recognized the limits on such remedial power. * * *

Three years later, in [Milliken v. Bradley, 418 U.S. 717 (1974) (*Milliken I*)], we held that a District Court had exceeded its authority in fashioning interdistrict relief where the surrounding school districts had not themselves been guilty of any constitutional violation. We said that a desegregation remedy "is necessarily designed, as all remedies are, to restore the victims of discriminatory conduct to the position they would have occupied in the absence of such conduct." "[W]ithout an interdistrict violation and interdistrict effect, there is no constitutional wrong calling for an interdistrict remedy." We also rejected "[t]he suggestion . . . that schools which have a majority of Negro students are not 'desegregated,' whatever the makeup of the school district's population and however neutrally the district lines have been drawn and administered."

Three years later, in Milliken v. Bradley, 433 U.S. 267 (1977) (*Milliken II*), we articulated a three-part framework derived from our prior cases to guide district courts in the exercise of their remedial authority.

> In the first place, like other equitable remedies, the nature of the desegregation remedy is to be determined by the nature and scope of the constitutional violation. *Swann.* The remedy must therefore be related to 'the condition alleged to offend the Constitution. . . .' *Milliken I.* Second, the decree must indeed be *remedial* in nature, that is, it must be designed as nearly as possible 'to restore the victims of discriminatory conduct to the position they would have occupied in the absence of such conduct.' *Milliken I.* Third, the federal courts in devising a remedy must take into account the interests of state and local authorities in managing their own affairs, consistent with the Constitution.

We added that the "principle that the nature and scope of the remedy are to be determined by the violation means simply that federal-court decrees must directly address and relate to the constitutional violation itself." * * *

Proper analysis of the District Court's orders challenged here, then, must rest upon their serving as proper means to the end of restoring the victims of discriminatory conduct to the position they would have occupied in the absence of that conduct and their eventual restoration of "state and local authorities to the control of a school system that is operating in compliance with the Constitution." We turn to that analysis.

The State argues that the order approving salary increases is beyond the District Court's authority because it was crafted to serve an "interdistrict goal," in spite of the fact that the constitutional violation in this case is "intradistrict" in nature. * * *

Here, the District Court has found, and the Court of Appeals has affirmed, that this case involved no interdistrict constitutional violation that would support interdistrict relief. Thus, the proper response by the District Court should have been to eliminate to the extent practicable the vestiges of prior de jure segregation within the KCMSD: a system-wide reduction in student achievement and the existence of 25 racially identifiable schools with a population of over 90% black students.

The District Court and Court of Appeals, however, have felt that because the KCMSD's enrollment remained 68.3% black, a purely intra district remedy would be insufficient. * * *

Instead of seeking to remove the racial identity of the various schools within the KCMSD, the District Court has set out on a program to create a school district that was equal to or superior to the surrounding SSD's. * * * The District Court's remedial order has all but made the KCMSD itself into a magnet district.

We previously have approved of intradistrict desegregation remedies involving magnet schools. *Milliken II.* * * *

The District Court's remedial plan in this case * * * [seeks] to attract nonminority students from outside the KCMSD schools. But this *inter*district goal is beyond the scope of the *intra*district violation identified by the District Court. In effect, the District Court has devised a remedy to accomplish indirectly what it admittedly lacks the remedial authority to mandate directly: the interdistrict transfer of students. * * *

[In *Milliken I*, Justice Stewart, who provided the Court's fifth vote,] wrote separately to underscore his understanding of that decision. In describing the requirements for imposing an "interdistrict" remedy, Justice Stewart stated: "Were it to be shown, for example, that state officials had contributed to the separation of the races by drawing or redrawing school district lines; by transfer of school units between districts; or by purposeful, racially discriminatory use of state housing or zoning laws, then a decree calling for the transfer of pupils across district lines or for restructuring of district lines might well be appropriate. In this case, however, no such interdistrict violation was shown." Justice Stewart concluded that the Court properly rejected the District Court's interdistrict remedy because "[t]here were no findings that the differing racial composition between schools in the city and in the outlying suburbs was caused by official activity of any sort."

* * * Nothing in *Milliken I* suggests that the District Court in that case could have circumvented the limits on its remedial authority by requiring the State of Michigan, a constitutional violator, to implement a magnet program designed to achieve the same interdistrict transfer of students that we held was beyond its remedial authority. Here, the District Court has done just that. * * *

Respondents argue that the District Court's reliance upon desegregative attractiveness is justified in light of the District Court's statement that segregation has "led to white flight from the KCMSD to suburban districts." The lower courts' "findings" as to "white flight" are both inconsistent internally, and inconsistent with the typical supposition, bolstered here by the record evidence, that "white flight" may result from desegregation, not *de jure* segregation. * * *

In *Freeman*, we stated that "[t]he vestiges of segregation that are the concern of the law in a school case may be subtle and intangible but nonetheless they must be so real that they have a causal link to the *de jure* violation being remedied.'] The record here does not support the District Court's reliance on "white flight" as a justification for a permissible expansion of its intradistrict remedial authority through its pursuit of desegregative attractiveness. * * *

The District Court's pursuit of "desegregative attractiveness" cannot be reconciled with our cases placing limitations on a district court's remedial authority. It is certainly theoretically possible that the greater the expenditure per pupil within the KCMSD, the more likely it is that some unknowable number of nonminority students not presently attending schools in the KCMSD will choose to enroll in those schools. Under this reasoning, however, every increased expenditure, whether it be for teachers, noninstructional employees, books, or buildings, will make the KCMSD in some way more attractive, and thereby perhaps induce nonminority students to enroll in its schools. But this rationale is not susceptible to any objective limitation. This case provides numerous examples demonstrating the limitless authority of the District Court operating under this rationale. In short, desegregative attractiveness has been used "as the hook on which to hang numerous policy choices about improving the quality of education in general within the KCMSD."

Nor are there limits to the duration of the District Court's involvement. The expenditures per pupil in the KCMSD currently far exceed those in the neighboring SSD's. Sixteen years after this litigation began, the District Court recognized that the KCMSD has yet to offer a viable method of financing the "wonderful school system being built." Each additional program ordered by the District Court—and financed by the State—to increase the "desegregative attractiveness" of the school district makes the KCMSD more and more dependent on additional funding from the State; in turn, the greater the KCMSD's dependence on state funding, the greater its reliance on continued supervision by the District Court. But our cases recognize that local autonomy of school districts is a vital national tradition, and that a district court must strive to restore state and local authorities to the control of a school system operating in compliance with the Constitution. * * *

The District Court's pursuit of the goal of "desegregative attractiveness" results in so many imponderables and is so far removed from the task of eliminating the racial identifiability of the schools within the KCMSD that we believe it is beyond the admittedly broad discretion of the District Court. In this posture, we conclude that the District Court's order of salary increases, which was "grounded in remedying the vestiges of segregation by improving the desegregative attractiveness of the KCMSD," is simply too far removed from an acceptable implementation of a permissible means to remedy previous legally mandated segregation.]

Similar considerations lead us to conclude that the District Court's order requiring the State to continue to fund the quality education programs because student achievement levels were still "at or below national norms at many grade levels" cannot be sustained. The State does not seek from this Court a declaration of partial unitary status with respect to the quality education programs. It challenges the requirement of indefinite funding of a quality education program until national norms are met, based on the assumption that while a mandate for significant educational improvement, both in teaching and in facilities, may have been justified originally, its indefinite extension is not. * * *

[T]his clearly is not the appropriate test to be applied in deciding whether a previously segregated district has achieved partially unitary status. The basic task of the District Court is to decide whether the reduction in achievement by minority students attributable to prior de jure segregation has been remedied to the extent practicable. Under our precedents, the State and the KCMSD are "entitled to a rather precise statement of [their] obligations under a desegregation decree." Although the District Court has determined that "[s]egregation has caused a system wide *reduction* in achievement in the schools of the KCMSD," it never has identified the incremental effect that segregation has had on minority student achievement or the specific goals of the quality education programs. Cf. *Dayton I.*

In reconsidering this order, the District Court should * * * consider that the State's role with respect to the quality education programs has been limited to the funding, not the implementation, of those programs. As all the parties agree that improved achievement on test scores is not necessarily required for the State to achieve partial unitary status as to the quality education programs, the District Court should sharply limit, if not dispense with, its reliance on this factor. * * * Insistence upon academic goals unrelated to the effects of legal segregation unwarrantably postpones the day when the KCMSD will be able to operate on its own.

The District Court also should consider that many goals of its quality education plan already have been attained: the KCMSD now is equipped with "facilities and opportunities not available anywhere else in the country." KCMSD schools received AAA rating [the state's highest rating] eight years ago, and the present remedial programs have been in place for seven years. It may be that in education, just as it may be in economics, a "rising tide lifts all boats," but the remedial quality education program should be tailored to remedy the injuries suffered by the victims of prior *de jure* segregation. Minority students in kindergarten through grade 7 in the KCMSD always have attended AAA-rated schools; minority students in the KCMSD that previously attended schools rated below AAA have since received remedial education programs for a period of up to seven years.

On remand, the District Court must bear in mind that its end purpose is not only "to remedy the violation" to the extent practicable, but also "to restore state and local authorities to the control of a school system that is operating in compliance with the Constitution." *Freeman.*

The judgment of the Court of Appeals is reversed.

JUSTICE O'CONNOR, concurring. * * *

What the District Court did in this case, * * * and how it transgressed the constitutional bounds of its remedial powers, is to make desegregative attractiveness the underlying goal of its remedy for the specific purpose of reversing the trend of white flight. However troubling that trend may be, remedying it is within the District Court's authority only if it is "directly caused by the constitutional violation." The Court and the dissent attempt to reconcile the different statements by the lower courts as to whether white flight was caused by segregation or desegregation. One fact, however, is uncontroverted. When the District Court found that KCMSD was racially segregated, the constitutional violation from which all remedies flow in this case, it also found that there was neither an interdistrict violation nor significant interdistrict segregative effects. Whether the white exodus that has resulted in a school district that is 68% black was caused by the District Court's remedial orders or by natural, if unfortunate, demographic forces, we have it directly from the District Court that the segregative effects of KCMSD's constitutional violation did not transcend its geographical boundaries. In light of that finding, the District Court cannot order remedies seeking to rectify regional demographic trends that go beyond the nature and scope of the constitutional violation.

This case, like other school desegregation litigation, is concerned with "the elimination of the discrimination inherent in the dual school systems, not with myriad factors of human existence which can cause discrimination in a multitude of ways on racial, religious, or ethnic grounds." Swann v. Charlotte-Mecklenburg Bd. of Ed., 402 U.S. 1, 22 (1971). Those myriad factors are not readily corrected by judicial intervention, but are best addressed by the representative branches; time and again, we have recognized the ample authority legislatures possess to combat racial injustice. * * *

JUSTICE THOMAS, concurring.

It never ceases to amaze me that the courts are so willing to assume that anything that is predominantly black must be inferior. Instead of focusing on remedying the harm done to those black schoolchildren injured by segregation, the District Court here sought to convert the Kansas City, Missouri, School District (KCMSD) into a "magnet district" that would reverse the "white flight" caused by de segregation. * * *

"Racial isolation" itself is not a harm; only state-enforced segregation is. After all, if separation itself is a harm, and if integration therefore is the only way that blacks can receive a proper education, then there must be something inferior about blacks. Under this theory, segregation injures blacks because blacks, when left on their own, cannot achieve. To my way of thinking, that conclusion is the result of a jurisprudence based upon a theory of black inferiority. * * *

II

* * *

A

* * *

Our impatience with the pace of desegregation and with the lack of a good-faith effort on the part of school boards led us to approve * * * extraordinary remedial measures. But such powers should have been temporary and used only to overcome the widespread resistance to the dictates of the Constitution. The judicial overreaching we see before us today perhaps is the price we now pay for our approval of such extraordinary remedies in the past. * * *

Our willingness to unleash the federal equitable power has reached areas beyond school desegregation * * * [to include] the reconstruction of entire institutions and bureaucracies. * * *

B

* * *

Anticipating the growth of our modern doctrine, the Anti-Federalists criticized the Constitution because it might be read to grant broad equitable powers to the federal courts. In response, the defenders of the Constitution "sold" the new framework of government to the public by espousing a narrower interpretation of the equity power. * * * [T]he appropriate conclusion is that the drafters and ratifiers of the Constitution approved the more limited construction offered in response. * * *

In light of this historical evidence, it should come as no surprise that there is no early record of the exercise of broad remedial powers. * * *

D

* * *

Contrary to the dissent's conclusion, the District Court's remedial orders are in tension with two common-sense principles. First, the District Court retained jurisdiction over the implementation and modification of the remedial decree, instead of terminating its involvement after issuing its remedy. Although briefly mentioned in *Brown II* as a temporary measure to overcome local resistance to desegregation, 349 U.S., at 301 ("[d]uring this period of transition, the courts will retain jurisdiction"), this concept of continuing judicial involvement has permitted the District Courts to revise their remedies constantly in order to reach some broad, abstract, and often elusive goal. Not only does this approach deprive the parties of finality and a clear understanding of their responsibilities, but it also tends to inject the judiciary into the day-to-day management of institutions and local policies-a function that lies outside of our Article III competence. * * *

Second, the District Court failed to target its equitable remedies in this case specifically to cure the harm suffered by the victims of segregation. Of course, the initial and most important aspect of any remedy will be to eliminate any invidious racial distinctions in matters such as student assignments, transportation, staff, resource allocation, and activities. This element of most desegregation decrees is fairly straightforward and has not produced many examples of overreaching by the district courts. It is the "compensatory" ingredient in many desegregation plans that has produced many of the difficulties in the case before us.

* * * In the absence of special circumstances, the remedy for de jure segregation ordinarily should not include educational programs for students who were not in school (or were even alive) during the period of segregation. * * *

JUSTICE SOUTER, with whom JUSTICE STEVENS, JUSTICE GINSBURG, and JUSTICE BREYER join, dissenting.

* * *

I

[T]he District Court entered a series of remedial orders aimed at eliminating the vestiges of segregation. Since the District Court found that segregation had caused, among other things, "a system wide reduction in student achievement in the schools of the KCMSD," it ordered the adoption, starting in 1985, of a series of remedial programs to raise educational performance. . . .

II

A

* * * In the development of a proper unitary status record, test scores will undoubtedly play a role. It is true, as the Court recognizes, that all parties to this case agree that it would be error to require that the students in a school district attain the national average test score as a prerequisite to a finding of partial unitary status, if only because all sorts of causes independent of the vestiges of past school segregation might stand in the way of the goal. That said, test scores will clearly be relevant in determining whether the improvement programs have cured a deficiency in student achievement to the practicable extent. * * *

B

The other question properly before us has to do with the propriety of the District Court's recent salary orders. While the Court suggests otherwise, the District Court did not ground its orders of salary increases solely on the goal of attracting students back to the KCMSD. From the start, the District Court has consistently treated salary increases as an important element in remedying the systemwide reduction in student achievement resulting from segregation in the KCSMD. * * *

III

* * *

[T]he District Court did not mean by an "intradistrict violation" what the Court apparently means by it today. The District Court meant that the violation within the KCMSD had not led to segregation outside of it, and that no other school districts had played a part in the violation. * * *

[The District Court's finding that segregation caused white flight is not contradicted, as the majority asserts, by the Court of Appeals's conclusion that the District Court " 'made specific findings that negate current significant interdistrict effects. . . .' " because the Court of Appeals meant interdistrict *segregative* effects.]

Without the contradiction, the Court has nothing to justify its rejection of the District Court's finding that segregation caused white flight but its supposition that flight results from integration, not segregation. The supposition, and the distinction on which it rests, are untenable. At the more obvious level, there is in fact no break in the chain of causation linking the effects of desegregation with those of segregation. There would be no desegregation orders and no remedial plans without prior unconstitutional segregation as the occasion for issuing and adopting them, and an adverse reaction to a desegregation order is traceable in fact to the segregation that is subject to the remedy. When the Court quotes the District Court's reference to abundant evidence that integration caused flight to the suburbs, then, it quotes nothing inconsistent with the District Court's other findings that segregation had caused the flight. The only difference between the statements lies in the point to which the District Court happened to trace the causal sequence.

* * * [For example, property tax-paying] parents of white children, seeing the handwriting on the wall in 1985, could well have decided that the inevitable cost of clean-up would produce an intolerable tax rate and could have moved to escape it. The District Court's remedial orders had not yet been put in place. Was the white flight caused by segregation or desegregation? The distinction has no significance. * * *

JUSTICE GINSBURG, dissenting.

The Court stresses that the present remedial programs have been in place for seven years. But compared to more than two centuries of firmly entrenched official discrimination, the experience with the desegregation remedies ordered by the District Court has been evanescent. . . .

NOTES

1. *An update on Jenkins.* After the remand in *Jenkins III*, the court agreed to a settlement in which the state would be dismissed from the litigation after paying an additional $320 million. Jenkins v. Missouri, 959 F.Supp. 1151 (W.D.Mo.1997). The court, however, retained jurisdiction over the KCMSD, finding its violations were responsible for 26% of the performance gap between students of different races. Whether the decree has done much good for the plaintiffs is another question. "Billions of dollars in desegregation money had built the most expensive magnet school system in history. * * * The money had resulted in better buildings and better pay for the teachers, but hadn't brought improvement in the academic performance of students." Barbara Shelly, *Schools Still a Tangled Mess,* Kansas City Star (Nov. 18, 1999). The Missouri State Board of Education revoked the KCMSD's accreditation because of poor teaching and inadequate educational results. *See* Catherine Gewertz, *Hard Lesson For Kansas City's Troubled Schools,* Education Week, Apr. 26, 2000. District Judge Dean Whipple subsequently ruled that test scores showed the school district had met the constitutional threshold for closing the achievement gap, but cautioned the district still had a "long distance to travel" even as he dismissed the case and dissolved the long-standing injunction.

The plaintiffs dropped their appeal from this decision, bringing the case to a close after 26 years of litigation. Deann Smith, *Plaintiff Drops Appeal in Federal School Desegregation Case*, Kansas City Star, Sept. 27, 2003; *see* Preston C. Green, III & Bruce D. Baker, *Urban Legends, Desegregation and School Finance: Did Kansas City Really Prove that Money Doesn't Matter?*, 12 Mich.J. Race & Law 57 (2006) (using empirical study to refute claims of critics that *Jenkins* proves that exorbitant school funding has no correlation to learning outcomes). A related new action filed by the school district and school children in 2006 challenged part of the order requiring property tax money to be paid to charter schools. The Eighth Circuit upheld the court's "ancillary jurisdiction" to enforce the remedial provisions of the prior desegregation order and struck down the funding of the charter schools. Jenkins v. Kansas City Missouri School District, 516 F.3d 1074 (8th Cir. 2008). The ruling noted the fact that the court of appeals "has heard over thirty appeals in the case." *Id.* at 1077 n.3.

2. In *Complex Justice: The Case of* Missouri v. Jenkins (2008), political science professor Joshua Dunn carefully traces the underlying social history of the case. Professor Dunn sees the behind-the-scenes story as one of well-meaning but paternalistic white lawyers, sometimes incompetent school administrators, and increasingly hostile black community leaders. The book provides fascinating detail of how black parents, community leaders and activists resisted what they saw as misguided reforms, which were improperly aimed at attracting white families to the KCMSD rather than addressing the real educational needs of black students. Ultimately, some of the activists took over the school board and worked to end both judicial oversight and the magnet school ideals.

3. *Jenkins III* seems to require more precision in justifying the remedy than did *Madsen* and *Swann*. Justice Thomas argues that such precision is harder to achieve with reparative than preventive remedies. It is easier to be precise in justifying a remedy to repair the damage done by an individual defendant to an individual plaintiff than a remedy to repair the damage done by society to a group. Does the difficulty of achieving much precision mean that society should let bygones be bygones, or that judgments about when and how to repair such damage are so steeped in policy that courts should leave them to legislatures? An article written years before Clarence Thomas became a Supreme Court Justice perhaps helps to understand why he favors letting bygones be:

> Thomas told me a story from his boyhood to illustrate what fairness means to him. He was on the back porch, playing blackjack for pennies with other boys. As the game went on, one boy kept winning. Thomas finally saw how: the cards were marked. The game was stopped. There were angry words. * * * From all sides fast fists snatched back lost money. There could be no equitable redistribution of the pot. The strongest, fastest hands, including those of the boy who had been cheating, got most of the pile of pennies. * * * But no one really wanted to fight—they wanted to keep playing cards. So a different deck was brought out and shuffled, and the game resumed with a simple promise of no more cheating.

> That story, Thomas said, is a lot like the story of race relations in America. Whites had an unfair advantage. But in 1964, with the passage of the Civil Rights Act, the government stopped the cheating. The question now is, Should the government return the ill-gotten gains to the losers? * * *

> Thomas believes that government simply cannot make amends, and therefore should not try. The best it can do is deal a clean deck and let the game resume, enforcing the rules as they have now come to be understood. * * * Thomas said, " * * * Use what was used to get others into the economy. Show us the precedent for all this experimentation on our race."

> * * * "I would be lying to you if I said that I didn't want sometimes to be able to cheat in favor of those of us who were cheated. But you have to ask yourself, in doing that, you do violence to the safe harbor, and that is the Constitution, which says you are to protect an individual's rights no matter what."

Juan Williams, *A Question of Fairness*, Atlantic Monthly 70, 78–79 (Feb. 1987).

4. Consider the following from Judge Frank H. Easterbrook, *Civil Rights and Remedies*, 14 Harv.J.L. & Pub.Pol'y 103, 103–04 (1991):

> When we hear an objection to the remedy, it is almost always a disguised objection to the definition of what is due, and not to the methods used to apply the balm. * * *

Because this point is *so* obvious that almost everyone will deny it, I will proceed by example through some contemporary remedial questions. In thinking about each subject, it will help to consider three questions. First, who holds the "rights": individual persons or groups of persons? Second, what does "equality" mean: equal treatment or equal outcomes? Third, what do we expect the government to teach us: the importance of disregarding the characteristics that often are chosen as a basis of private discrimination, or the worth of a society in which persons of diverse backgrounds appear side by side? * * *

There are systematic differences in emphasis between those who think on the one hand that rights are personal, that the government should assure equal treatment, and that it should teach people the irrelevance of race (for example), and, on the other, those who believe that rights belong to groups, that equality of outcomes is most important, and that the government should assure diversity in many walks of life. * * * [T]he conclusions we reach on these questions govern the choice of remedy.

E. SPECIFIC PERFORMANCE

The contract remedy of specific performance is an order to perform as required by the terms of a contract. Like an injunction, specific performance is a personal, coercive, equitable remedy, enforced through the contempt power. In essence, specific performance is simply an injunction enforcing the terms of the contract. The same balancing test for injunctive relief applies for specific performance, requiring damages to be inadequate and factoring in the undue hardship to the defendant, the difficulty of enforcement, and the public interest. Restatement (Second) of Contracts §§ 360, 364–66.

In addition, specific performance has some special requirements. The Restatement (Second) of Contracts § 362 states that "specific performance or an injunction will not be granted unless the terms of the contract are sufficiently certain to provide a basis for an appropriate order." Under this *certainty* requirement, a court could find that the parties had an understanding that was certain enough to be a contract and to lead to damages, but not certain enough to lead to specific performance. Although courts often recite this rule, certainty that is sufficient for liability is usually sufficient for specific performance so long as the court is certain enough of the bargain to formulate a workable decree.

Courts will not direct specific performance of *personal service* contracts. *E.g.,* Pierce v. Douglas School District No. 4, 686 P.2d 332, 337 (Or. 1984) (teacher may not be compelled to perform employment contract). Specific enforcement of such contracts would impose difficult burdens of supervision on the court and raise issues of involuntary servitude. Courts sometimes avoid these problems by forbidding the employee to work for others rather than compelling performance. *E.g.,* Lumley v. Wagner, 42 Eng.Rep. 687 (1852) (forbidding opera singer to perform at theaters other than the one where she had contracted to perform). Professor Oman rejects the claim that specific performance of personal service contracts constitutes involuntary servitude and argues against the per se rule against enforcement, suggesting that specific performance should be available on the same basis as other contracts. Nathan Oman, *Specific Performance and the Thirteenth Amendment*, 93 Minn.L.Rev. 2020 (2009).

The doctrine of *mutuality of remedy* requires that one party be denied specific performance of a contract if the other party would be barred from that remedy. Some jurisdictions have explicitly revoked the rule. Other jurisdictions consider mutuality a relevant, but not controlling, factor in granting specific relief. Still others continue to cite the rule while recognizing broad exceptions to it. As Judge Cardozo put it:

> If there ever was a rule [of] mutuality of remedy * * * , it has been so qualified by exceptions that, viewed as a precept of general validity, it has ceased to be a rule to-day. What equity exacts today as a condition of relief is the assurance that the decree, if rendered, will operate without injustice or oppression either to plaintiff or to defendant.

Epstein v. Gluckin, 135 N.E. 861, 862 (N.Y. 1922). So, for instance, if there is a substantial risk that a plaintiff seeking specific performance might not perform later duties under the contract, a court might deny specific performance or condition it in such a way that the plaintiff would have to perform.

I.LAN SYSTEMS, INC. V. NETSCOUT SERVICE LEVEL CORP.

United States District Court
183 F.Supp.2d 328 (D.Mass. 2002)

YOUNG, CHIEF JUDGE.

Has this happened to you? You plunk down a pretty penny for the latest and greatest software, speed back to your computer, tear open the box, shove the CD-ROM into the computer, click on "install" and, after scrolling past a license agreement which would take at least fifteen minutes to read, find yourself staring at the following dialog box: "I agree." Do you click on the box? You probably do not agree in your heart of hearts, but you click anyway, not about to let some pesky legalese delay the moment for which you've been waiting. Is that "clickwrap" license agreement enforceable? Yes, at least in the case described below.

I. INTRODUCTION

The plaintiff, i.LAN Systems, Inc. ("i.LAN"), helps companies monitor their computer networks. The defendant, NetScout Service Level Corp., formerly known as NextPoint Networks, Inc. ("NextPoint"), sells sophisticated software that monitors networks. In 1998, i.LAN and NextPoint signed a detailed Value Added Reseller ("VAR") agreement whereby i.LAN agreed to resell NextPoint's software to customers. This dispute concerns a transaction that took place in 1999.

i.LAN claims that for $85,231.42 it purchased the unlimited right to use NextPoint's software, replete with perpetual upgrades and support, whereby it effectively could rent, rather than sell, NextPoint's software to customers. In support of its argument, i.LAN points to the purchase order associated with the transaction. NextPoint, in response, points to the 1998 VAR agreement and the clickwrap license agreement contained in the software itself to reach a different conclusion.

The parties continued their relationship for several months without confronting their conflicting interpretations of the 1999 purchase order, but eventually the disagreement erupted into litigation. i.LAN filed a complaint that alleges, among other things, breach of contract and violation of Massachusetts General Laws Chapter 93A. * * *

i.LAN quickly took the offensive and brought a motion for summary judgment, Fed.R.Civ.P. 56(a). i.LAN argued that it should be awarded specific performance—in particular, perpetual upgrades of NextPoint's software and unlimited support. * * * NextPoint argued that even if i.LAN's allegations were true, the clickwrap license agreement limits NextPoint's liability to the price paid for the software, in this case $85,231.42. The Court * * * ruled in favor of NextPoint. This memorandum explains why.

II. DISCUSSION

Before turning to NextPoint's clickwrap license agreement, the stage must be set. First, the Court will identify the set of rules by which to judge this dispute. [The court concludes that the clickwrap license agreement governs and the Uniform Commercial Code applies to the software license though it is not strictly a "good."] Next, the Court will examine what is at stake, in particular i.LAN's claim for specific performance and NextPoint's limitation-of-liability defense. * * * .

B. What Is at Stake?

1. Specific Performance

More than anything else, i.LAN wants specific performance—in particular, perpetual upgrades of NextPoint's software and unlimited support. Assuming the clickwrap license agreement is enforceable, NextPoint argues that the agreement prohibits specific performance as a remedy. In the alternative, NextPoint argues that specific performance is inappropriate under the UCC.

Section 4 of the clickwrap license agreement states, "NEXTPOINT'S LIABILITY FOR DAMAGES TO LICENSEE FOR ANY CAUSE WHATSOEVER, REGARDLESS OF THE FORM OF ANY CLAIM OR ACTION, SHALL BE LIMITED TO THE LICENSE FEES PAID FOR THE LICENSED PRODUCT." From this provision, NextPoint concludes that money damages are the only possible remedy. An equally plausible reading of the provision, however, is that the limitation only applies to "damages," not equitable remedies. Indeed, section 6 of the agreement states, "[E]ach party shall have the right to institute judicial proceedings against the other party . . . in order to enforce the instituting party's rights hereunder through reformation of contract, specific performance, injunction or similar equitable relief." On balance, sections 4 and 6 cut against NextPoint's argument that the clickwrap license agreement prohibits specific performance as a remedy.

That being said, the law does not permit specific performance simply because a contract does not prohibit it. The UCC provides, in relevant part:

§ 2–716. Buyer's Right to Specific Performance or Replevin.

(1) Specific performance *may* be decreed *where the goods are unique* or in other proper circumstances.

(2) The decree for specific performance may include such terms and conditions as to payment of the price, damages, or other relief as the court may deem just.

UCC § 2–716, Mass. Gen. Laws ch. 106, § 2–716 (emphasis added). Although the UCC also allows specific performance in "other proper circumstances," i.LAN has not argued that the circumstances here are proper. Instead, i.LAN has argued that NextPoint's software is unique, a determination left to the discretion of the Court. *See* UCC § 2–716 cmt. 1; cf., e.g., McCarthy v. Tobin, 429 Mass. 84, 89, 706 N.E.2d 629 (1999) (applying common law).

The UCC commentary states that the UCC "seeks to further a more liberal attitude than some courts have shown in connection with the specific performance of contracts of sale." UCC § 2–716 cmt. 1. "Specific performance is no longer limited to goods which are already specific or ascertained at the time of contracting. The test of uniqueness under this section must be made in terms of the total situation which characterizes the contract." *Id.* cmt. 2. One court has restated the test for specific performance as follows: "Basically courts now determine whether goods are replaceable as a practical matter—for example, whether it would be difficult to obtain similar goods on the open market." * * *

Before turning to the facts of this case, the Court considers the facts of other cases, which are instructive. No published decision in Massachusetts has applied UCC section 2–716, but three decisions are notable. In the first and most recent case, the First Circuit, applying Maine common law but looking to UCC section 2–716 for guidance, awarded specific performance in a case involving a minor-league baseball team. Triple-A Baseball Club Assocs. v. Northeastern Baseball, Inc., 832 F.2d 214 (1st Cir.1987). The First Circuit reasoned that "the Triple-A franchise has no readily ascertainable market value, it cannot be easily obtained from other sources, and it is of special interest to [the appellee]." In short, "There can be no doubt that what [the appellee] sought, a Triple-A franchise, was unique." In another instructive case, the Massachusetts Supreme Judicial Court many years ago refused to award specific performance in a case involving an automobile whose delivery was delayed by World War II. Poltorak v. Jackson Chevrolet Co., 322 Mass. 699, 79 N.E.2d 285 (1948). The court reasoned:

> The scarcity of automobiles, which went no farther than to occasion considerable delay in delivery, is not sufficient basis for a decree of specific performance in favor of one who sought the completion of a contract for the sale of an ordinary passenger vehicle, and who showed no substantial harm of a kind of character which could not be adequately compensated by an award of damages in an action at law.

Id. at 702. In a third helpful case, the Supreme Judicial Court did allow specific performance in a case involving doors custom-made for an elevator. Dahlstrom Metallic Door Co. v. Evatt Constr. Co., 256 Mass. 404, 152 N.E. 715 (1926). The court reasoned:

> The materials were designed and made for use in the chamber of commerce building; they were limited in number and could not readily be used in any other building; they could not have been purchased in the open market. To have had them manufactured elsewhere would have caused serious delay in the construction of the building to the great damage of the contractor as well as of the owners. The contractor would not have an adequate remedy at law.

Id. at 414–15. Although Poltorak and Dahlstrom predate the UCC, they are significant because the Massachusetts comment to UCC section 2–716 states that the two cases are consistent with the UCC's vision of when specific performance should be allowed. Mass. Gen. Laws ch. 106 § 2–716, cmt.

Turning to the facts of this case, i.LAN makes three arguments why NextPoint's software is unique. First, i.LAN argues that the software is copyrighted and took years to design. The same could be said of any mass-produced item, however, and certainly a mass-produced item is the antithesis of the word "unique." More importantly, NextPoint's software is one of several competing software packages in the market; all run on ordinary computers and perform substantially the same functions. Although these software packages may be copyrighted and the product of intense labor, they are interchangeable as a practical matter and thus none is unique. Second, i.LAN argues that *it* has tailored its business around NextPoint's software, thus making the software unique to *it*. The UCC is sensitive to this consideration, but at the same time this Court will not conflate reliance with uniqueness. Much as i.LAN may not want to, it certainly *could* purchase comparable software on the open market and reconfigure its systems to run that software, just as any person could buy such software and run it. Finally, i.LAN argues that it does not know the number of software licenses it will need in the future to provide its rental services, so money damages would not adequately compensate it. This argument is not that NextPoint's goods are unique, but that i.LAN had struck what it thought to be a unique contract: for a mere $85,231.42 it would have unlimited copies of all of NextPoint's software forever. The UCC, however, looks to the uniqueness of the goods, not the contract.

In sum, even if the clickwrap license agreement permits specific performance, and even if the Court were to enter judgment in favor of i.LAN, NextPoint's software is not unique or irreplaceable as a practical matter, so the Court would not award specific performance.

2.   Limitation of Liability

If i.LAN's only remedy is money damages, the limitation of liability found in the clickwrap license agreement becomes very important. * * * [The court concludes the clickwrap is an enforceable contract and limits plaintiffs' damages in accordance with the liquidated damages clause.]

WALGREEN CO. v. SARA CREEK PROPERTY CO.

United States Court of Appeals
966 F.2d 273 (7th Cir. 1992)

POSNER, CIRCUIT JUDGE.

This appeal from the grant of a permanent injunction raises fundamental issues concerning the propriety of injunctive relief. The essential facts are simple. Walgreen has operated a pharmacy in the Southgate Mall in Milwaukee since its opening in 1951. Its current lease, signed in 1971 and carrying a 30-year, 6-month term, contains, as had the only previous lease, a clause in which the landlord, Sara Creek, promises not to lease space in the mall to anyone else who wants to operate a pharmacy or a store containing a pharmacy. * * *

In 1990, fearful that its largest tenant—what in real estate parlance is called the "anchor tenant"—having gone broke was about to close its store, Sara Creek informed Walgreen that it intended to buy out the anchor tenant and install in its place a discount store operated by Phar-Mor Corporation, a "deep discount" chain, rather than, like Walgreen, just a "discount" chain. Phar-Mor's store would occupy 100,000 square feet, of which 12,000 would be occupied by a pharmacy the same size as Walgreen's. The entrances to the two stores would be within a couple of hundred feet of each other.

Walgreen filed this diversity suit for breach of contract against Sara Creek and Phar-Mor and asked for an injunction against Sara Creek's letting the anchor premises to Phar-Mor. After an evidentiary hearing, the judge found a breach of Walgreen's lease and entered a permanent injunction against Sara Creek's letting the anchor tenant premises to Phar-Mor until the expiration of Walgreen's lease. He did this over the defendants' objection that Walgreen had failed to show that its remedy at law—damages—for the breach of the exclusivity clause was inadequate. Sara Creek had put on an expert witness who testified that Walgreen's damages could be readily estimated, and Walgreen had countered with evidence from its employees that its damages would be very difficult to compute, among other reasons because they included intangibles such as loss of goodwill.

Sara Creek reminds us that damages are the norm in breach of contract as in other cases. Many breaches, it points out, are "efficient" in the sense that they allow resources to be moved into a more valuable use. * * * Perhaps this is one—the value of Phar-Mor's occupancy of the anchor premises may exceed the cost to Walgreen of facing increased competition. If so, society will be better off if Walgreen is paid its damages, equal to that cost, and Phar-Mor is allowed to move in rather than being kept out by an injunction. That is why injunctions are not granted as a matter of course, but only when the plaintiff's damages remedy is inadequate. * * * Walgreen's is not, Sara Creek argues; the projection of business losses due to increased competition is a routine exercise in calculation. Damages representing either the present value of lost future profits or (what should be the equivalent) diminution in the value of the leasehold have either been awarded or deemed the proper remedy in a number of reported cases for breach of an exclusivity clause in a shopping-center lease. * * * Why, Sara Creek asks, should they not be adequate here?

Sara Creek makes a beguiling argument that contains much truth, but we do not think it should carry the day. For if, as just noted, damages have been awarded in some cases of breach of an exclusivity clause in a shopping-center lease, injunctions have been issued in others. * * * The choice between remedies requires a balancing of the costs and benefits of the alternatives. *Hecht Co.* * * *

The plaintiff who seeks an injunction has the burden of persuasion—damages are the norm, so the plaintiff must show why his case is abnormal. But when, as in this case, the issue is whether to grant a permanent injunction, not whether to grant a temporary one, the burden is to show that damages are inadequate, not that the denial of the injunction will work irreparable harm. "Irreparable" in the injunction context means not rectifiable by the entry of a final judgment. * * * It has nothing to do with whether to grant a permanent injunction, which, in the usual case anyway, *is* the final judgment. The use of "irreparable harm" or "irreparable injury" as synonyms for inadequate remedy at law is a confusing usage. It should be avoided. Owen M. Fiss & Doug Rendleman, *Injunctions* 59 (2d ed. 1984).

The benefits of substituting an injunction for damages are twofold. First, it shifts the burden of determining the cost of the defendant's conduct from the court to the parties. If it is true that Walgreen's damages are smaller than the gain to Sara Creek from allowing a second pharmacy into the shopping mall, then there must be a price for dissolving the injunction that will make both parties better off. Thus, the effect of upholding the injunction would be to substitute for the costly processes of forensic fact determination the less costly processes of private negotiation. Second, a premise of our free-market system, and the lesson of experience here and abroad as well, is that prices and costs are more accurately determined by the market than by government. A battle of experts is a less reliable method of determining the actual cost to Walgreen of facing new competition than negotiations between Walgreen and Sara Creek over the price at which Walgreen would feel adequately compensated for having to face that competition.

That is the benefit side of injunctive relief but there is a cost side as well. Many injunctions require continuing supervision by the court, and that is costly. * * * Some injunctions are problematic because they impose costs on third parties. * * * . A more subtle cost of injunctive relief arises from the situation that economists call "bilateral monopoly," in which two parties can deal only with each other: the situation that an injunction creates. * * * The sole seller of widgets selling to the sole buyer of that product would be an example. But so will be the situation confronting Walgreen and Sara Creek if the injunction is upheld. Walgreen can "sell" its injunctive right only to Sara Creek, and Sara Creek can "buy" Walgreen's surrender of its right to enjoin the leasing of the anchor tenant's space to Phar-Mor only from Walgreen. The lack of alternatives in bilateral monopoly creates a bargaining range, and the costs of negotiating to a point within that range may be high. Suppose the cost to Walgreen of facing the competition of Phar-Mor at the Southgate Mall would be $1 million, and the benefit to Sara Creek of leasing to Phar-Mor would be $2 million. Then at any price between those figures for a waiver of Walgreen's injunctive right both parties would be better off, and we expect parties to bargain around a judicial assignment of legal rights if the assignment is inefficient. R.H. Coase, "The Problem of Social Cost," 3 J. Law & Econ. 1 (1960). But each of the parties would like to engross as much of the bargaining range as possible—Walgreen to press the price toward $2 million, Sara Creek to depress it toward $1 million. With so much at stake, both parties will have an incentive to devote substantial resources of time and money to the negotiation process. The process may even break down, if one or both parties want to create for future use a reputation as a hard bargainer; and if it does break down, the injunction will have brought about an inefficient result. All these are in one form or another costs of the injunctive process that can be avoided by substituting damages.

The costs and benefits of the damages remedy are the mirror of those of the injunctive remedy. The damages remedy avoids the cost of continuing supervision and third-party effects, and the cost of bilateral monopoly as well. It imposes costs of its own, however, in the form of diminished accuracy in the determination of value, on the one hand, and of the parties' expenditures on preparing and presenting evidence of damages, and the time of the court in evaluating the evidence, on the other.

The weighing up of all these costs and benefits is the analytical procedure that is or at least should be employed by a judge asked to enter a permanent injunction, with the understanding that if the balance is even the injunction should be withheld. The judge is not required to explicate every detail of the analysis and he did not do so here, but as long we are satisfied that his approach is broadly consistent with a proper analysis we shall affirm; and we are satisfied here. The determination of Walgreen's damages would have been costly in forensic resources and inescapably inaccurate. * * * The lease had ten years to run. So Walgreen would have had to project its sales revenues and costs over the next ten years, and then project the impact on those figures of Phar-Mor's competition, and then discount that impact to present value. All but the last step would have been fraught with uncertainty.

* * * It is difficult to forecast the profitability of a retail store over a decade, let alone to assess the impact of a particular competitor on that profitability over that period. Of course one can hire an expert to make such predictions, * * * and if injunctive relief is infeasible the expert's testimony may provide a tolerable basis for an award of damages. We cited cases in which damages have been awarded for the breach of an exclusivity clause in a shopping-center lease. But they are awarded in such circumstances not because anyone thinks them a clairvoyant forecast but because it is better to give a wronged person a crude remedy than none at all. It is the same theory on which damages are awarded for a disfiguring injury. No one thinks such injuries readily monetizable, * * * but a crude estimate is better than letting the wrongdoer get off scot-free (which, not incidentally, would encourage more such injuries). * * *Sara Creek presented evidence of what happened (very little) to Walgreen when Phar-Mor moved into other shopping malls in which Walgreen has a pharmacy, and it was on the right track in putting in comparative evidence. But there was a serious question whether the other malls were actually comparable to the

Southgate Mall, so we cannot conclude, in the face of the district judge's contrary conclusion, that the existence of comparative evidence dissolved the difficulties of computing damages in this case. Sara Creek complains that the judge refused to compel Walgreen to produce all the data that Sara Creek needed to demonstrate the feasibility of forecasting Walgreen's damages. Walgreen resisted, on grounds of the confidentiality of the data and the cost of producing the massive data that Sara Creek sought. Those are legitimate grounds; and the cost (broadly conceived) they expose of pretrial discovery, in turn presaging complexity at trial, is itself a cost of the damages remedy that injunctive relief saves.

Damages are not always costly to compute, or difficult to compute accurately. In the standard case of a seller's breach of a contract for the sale of goods where the buyer covers by purchasing the same product in the market, damages are readily calculable by subtracting the contract price from the market price and multiplying by the quantity specified in the contract. But this is not such a case and here damages would be a costly and inaccurate remedy; and on the other side of the balance some of the costs of an injunction are absent and the cost that is present seems low. The injunction here, like one enforcing a covenant not to compete (standardly enforced by injunction* * *) is a simple negative injunction—Sara Creek is not to lease space in the Southgate Mall to Phar-Mor during the term of Walgreen's lease—and the costs of judicial supervision and enforcement should be negligible. There is no contention that the injunction will harm an *unrepresented* third party. It may harm Phar-Mor but that harm will be reflected in Sara Creek's offer to Walgreen to dissolve the injunction. (Anyway Phar-Mor *is* a party.) The injunction may also, it is true, harm potential customers of Phar-Mor—people who would prefer to shop at a deep-discount store than an ordinary discount store—but their preferences, too, are registered indirectly. The more business Phar-Mor would have, the more rent it will be willing to pay Sara Creek, and therefore the more Sara Creek will be willing to pay Walgreen to dissolve the injunction.

The only substantial cost of the injunction in this case is that it may set off a round of negotiations between the parties. In some cases, illustrated by Boomer v. Atlantic Cement Co., 26 N.Y.2d 219, 309 N.Y.S.2d 312, 257 N.E.2d 870 (1970), this consideration alone would be enough to warrant the denial of injunctive relief. The defendant's factory was emitting cement dust that caused the plaintiffs harm monetized at less than $200,000, and the only way to abate the harm would have been to close down the factory, which had cost $45 million to build. An injunction against the nuisance could therefore have created a huge bargaining range (could, not would, because it is unclear what the current value of the factory was), and the costs of negotiating to a point within it might have been immense. If the market value of the factory was actually $45 million, the plaintiffs would be tempted to hold out for a price to dissolve the injunction in the tens of millions and the factory would be tempted to refuse to pay anything more than a few hundred thousand dollars. Negotiations would be unlikely to break down completely, given such a bargaining range, but they might well be protracted and costly. There is nothing so dramatic here. Sara Creek does not argue that it will have to close the mall if enjoined from leasing to Phar-Mor. Phar-Mor is not the only potential anchor tenant. Liza Danielle, Inc. v. Jamko, Inc., 408 So.2d 735, 740 (Fla.App.1982), on which Sara Creek relies, presented the converse case where the grant of the injunction would have forced an existing tenant to close its store. The size of the bargaining range was also a factor in the denial of injunctive relief in Gitlitz v. Plankinton Building Properties, Inc., 228 Wis. 334, 339–40, 280 N.W. 415, 418 (1938).

To summarize, the judge did not exceed the bounds of reasonable judgment in concluding that the costs (including forgone benefits) of the damages remedy would exceed the costs (including forgone benefits) of an injunction. We need not consider whether, as intimated by Walgreen, exclusivity clauses in shopping-center leases should be considered presumptively enforceable by injunctions. Although we have described the choice between legal and equitable remedies as one for case-by-case determination, the courts have sometimes picked out categories of case in which injunctive relief is made the norm. The best-known example is specific performance of contracts for the sale of real property. * * * The rule that specific performance will be ordered in such cases as a matter of course is a generalization of the considerations discussed above. Because of the absence of a fully liquid market in real property and the frequent presence of subjective values (many a homeowner, for example, would not sell his house for its market value), the calculation of damages is difficult; and since an order of specific performance to convey a piece of property does not create a continuing relation between the parties, the costs of supervision and enforcement if specific performance is ordered are slight. The exclusivity clause in Walgreen's lease relates to real estate, but we hesitate to suggest that every contract involving real estate should be enforceable as a matter of course by injunctions. Suppose Sara Creek had covenanted to keep the entrance to Walgreen's store free of ice and snow, and breached the covenant. An injunction would require continuing supervision, and it would be easy enough if the injunction were denied for Walgreen to hire its own ice and snow remover and charge the cost to Sara Creek. * * * On the other hand, injunctions to enforce exclusivity clauses are quite likely to be justifiable by just the considerations present here—damages are difficult to estimate with any accuracy and the injunction is a one-shot remedy requiring no continuing judicial involvement. So there is an argument for making injunctive relief presumptively appropriate in such cases, but we need not decide in this case how strong an argument.

NOTES

1.   In *Walgreen*, Judge Posner offers both equitable and economic analyses supporting the issuance of an injunction. How does he explain how this injunction is efficient?

2.   Judge Posner cites the established common-law rule that injuries to real property are irreparable. But he cautions against automatically applying it. When does he think we should *not* apply the general rule?

NOTE ON OTHER REMEDIES

Other types of writs that resemble injunctive relief include writs of mandamus, prohibition, and habeas corpus. A writ of mandamus is an order to a public or corporate officer to perform a ministerial duty. A writ of prohibition is an order to a judge to refrain from unwarranted conduct. Will v. United States, 389 U.S. 90, 95 (1967). This writ of prohibition often operates like an interlocutory appeal, and thus has procedural limitations under the final judgment rule. A writ of habeas corpus is an order to someone who detains another person in custody to bring that person to court and justify the detention or relinquish it. Habeas corpus derives from the Sixth Amendment because it prevents imprisonment without judicial process. Habeas corpus also provides review of criminal convictions in the judicial process supplemental to ordinary appeals and can sometimes be used in military service, immigration, and child custody cases. Like injunctions, these writs are specific and coercive remedies, enforced through the contempt power.

Nonetheless, the courts usually do not see these writs as the equivalent of injunctions. The most obvious but least important difference is that, unlike injunctions, they are classified as legal remedies because they were originally issued from the courts of law rather than the courts of equity. This might suggest that the writs are free from the requirement that there be no adequate remedy at law. Yet, mandamus and prohibition, but not habeas corpus, are said to be available only where there is no other adequate remedy at law. In addition, courts view mandamus and prohibition as extraordinary and accordingly set up other prerequisites to limit their availability. These prerequisites vary with both the writ and the jurisdiction, and result from both historical anachronisms and modern needs so that it is difficult to generalize about each one's availability and how it may affect the availability of other writs or an injunction to accomplish the same objective.

CHAPTER 3

ADMINISTERING AND ENFORCING THE INJUNCTION

■ ■ ■

A. OBTAINING PRELIMINARY INJUNCTIVE RELIEF

The normal process for seeking a remedy from a court is to file a complaint which includes a prayer for relief specifying the remedies the plaintiff is requesting after prevailing in the action. The remedies requested may include one or more of the types of relief studied in this course, including damages or the specific relief a court may afford through an injunction. Sometimes, however, the plaintiff cannot wait for the wheels of justice to turn completely. The plaintiff may need some additional relief immediately.

Such an order is called "temporary" or "preliminary" because it lasts only long enough to give the court time to deliberate further on the merits. A temporary injunction typically lasts only for one to two weeks. A preliminary injunction may last during the entire pendency of a trial. In contrast, an injunction issued after a final determination is called a "permanent injunction." The word "permanent" signifies not the injunction's duration but rather that it is not contingent upon some further finding on the merits. A permanent injunction continues to apply unless it expires by its own terms or is later modified or dissolved by a court of competent jurisdiction.

1. PROCEDURAL DISTINCTIONS

Federal Rule of Civil Procedure 65, for example, distinguishes among temporary restraining orders ("TRO"), preliminary injunctions, and permanent injunctions, but not because their purposes differ. All three command that a defendant do or not do some act. Instead they are distinguished by their different procedures and durations.

Rule 65.   Injunctions and Restraining Orders

(a) Preliminary Injunction.

(1) *Notice.* The court may issue a preliminary injunction only on notice to the adverse party.

(2) *Consolidating the Hearing with the Trial on the Merits.* Before or after beginning the hearing on a motion for a

preliminary injunction, the court may advance the trial on the merits and consolidate it with the hearing. Even when consolidation is not ordered, evidence that is received on the motion and that would be admissible at trial be-comes part of the trial record and need not be repeated at trial. But the court must preserve any party's right to a jury trial.

(b) Temporary Restraining Order.

(1) *Issuing Without Notice.* The court may issue a temporary restraining order without written or oral notice to the adverse party or its attorney only if:

    (A) specific facts in an affidavit or a verified complaint clearly show that immediate and irreparable injury, loss, or damage will result to the movant before the adverse party can be heard in opposition; and

    (B) the movant's attorney certifies in writing any efforts made to give notice and the reasons why it should not be required.

(2) *Contents; Expiration.* Every temporary restraining order issued without notice must state the date and hour it was issued; describe the injury and state why it is irreparable; state why the order was is-sued without notice; and be promptly filed in the clerk's office and entered in the record. The order expires at the time after entry—not to exceed 10 days—that the court sets, unless before that time the court, for good cause, extends it for a like period or the adverse party consents to a longer extension. The reasons for an extension must be entered in the record.

(3) *Expediting the Preliminary-Injunction Hearing.* If the order is issued without notice, the motion for a preliminary injunction must be set for hearing at the earliest possible time, taking precedence over all other matters except hearings on older matters of the same character. At the hearing, the party who obtained the order must proceed with the motion; if the party does not, the court must dissolve the order.

(4) *Motion to Dissolve.* On 2 days' notice to the party who obtained the order without notice—or on shorter notice set by the court—the adverse party may appear and move to dissolve or modify the order. The court must then hear and decide the motion as promptly as justice requires.

(c) Security. The court may issue a preliminary injunction or a temporary restraining order only if the movant gives security in an amount that the court considers proper to pay the costs and damages sustained by any party found to have been wrongfully enjoined or restrained. The United States, its officers, and its agencies are not required to give security * * * .

A TRO is an emergency order, which can be granted if, but only if, immediate and irreparable harm will result before a hearing can be held; as a result, it can be granted *ex parte* (i.e., without any notice to the defendant). Usually, the judge issues the TRO on the basis of affidavits or a verified complaint rather than on the basis of live testimony. Because this drastic emergency procedure is subject to abuse, especially when it is used without notice to the adverse party, there are several built-in safeguards. For example, Federal Rule of Civil Procedure 65(b) requires that a TRO may be granted without notice to the adverse party only if specific facts set forth in an affidavit or verified complaint clearly show that there will be immediate and irreparable injury to the requesting party before the adverse party can be heard. In addition, the attorney of the party seeking the TRO must certify in writing what efforts were made to give notice (formal or informal, such as by telephone or email) to the adverse party and must provide the reasons supporting the claim that notice should not be required. (If, for example, there were a specific concern that the defendant might take some destructive action between the time notice would be given and the TRO was issued and served.) A TRO issued without notice is valid for a very limited time—the fourteen-day limit (which can be extended once) established in Rule 65(b)(2) is a common pattern. The enjoined party may move for the dissolution of the TRO on two-days' notice or even less with leave of court.

The Supreme Court has acknowledged that: "There is a place in our jurisprudence for *ex parte* issuance, without notice, of temporary restraining orders of short duration." Carroll v. President & Commissioners of Princess Anne, 393 U.S. 175, 180 (1968). However, the Court also observed that "there is no place within the area of basic freedoms guaranteed by the First Amendment for such orders where no showing is made that it is impossible to serve or notify the opposing parties and to give them an opportunity to participate." *Id.* Accordingly, it found unconstitutional a ten-day TRO that a state trial court issued prohibiting a public rally by Nazis because the order was granted ex parte and without any attempt to provide notice.

One variation on the attempted notice requirement for TROs is for civil domestic violence orders. Most state processes eliminate any requirement of notice efforts to the defendant at the temporary stage, due to the nature of the personal harm threatened. For example in Ohio, the court "shall hold an ex parte hearing on the same day that the petition is filed" and issue a temporary order where "[i]mmediate and present danger of domestic violence to the family or household member" is shown. Ohio Rev.Code § 3113.31(D)(1). However, domestic violence ex parte orders, like all temporary injunctions, last only a short time and must be followed shortly by a hearing at which the defendant is provided notice and an opportunity to appear. *E.g.*, Ohio Rev. Code § 3113.31(D)(2) (full hearing must be scheduled within seven days). The order at this second stage is effectively a final order on the matter and can be quite extensive, including orders to stay away from the home and victim; parental rights; counseling; eviction and possession of the family home; removal of firearms; and financial support. *Id.* § 3113.31(E). *See* David H. Taylora, et.al., *Ex Parte Domestic Violence Orders of Protection: How Easing Access To Judicial Process Has Eased The Possibility for Abuse of The Process*, 18 Kan.J.L.& Pub.Pol'cy 83 (2008) (noting that ex parte orders are awarded routinely and tracing the laws of the various states).

A preliminary injunction is another mechanism for granting provisional relief before the court can conduct a full hearing on the merits; often, the preliminary injunction is granted after the TRO has expired. In contrast to the TRO, there must be both proper notice to the defendant (*see, e.g.*, F.R.Civ.P. 65(a)(1)) and a hearing (however informal) on the motion for a preliminary injunction. *See* United States v. Microsoft Corp., 147 F.3d 935 (D.C.Cir.1998) (defendant did not have adequate notice that it might be the subject of a preliminary injunction). A permanent injunction cannot issue until there has been a full opportunity to hear from both sides, at a hearing or on a motion for summary judgment.

Even if the trial court is convinced that the plaintiff is entitled to preliminary or temporary injunctive relief, it must decide to what degree the defendant deserves protection in the event that the initial decision proves to be incorrect. In particular, the court must decide the amount of *security* to be imposed on the plaintiff as a prerequisite to obtaining a TRO or a preliminary injunction. Fed.R.Civ.P. 65(c). Although Rule 65 is phrased n mandatory terms, stating that the injunction may issue "only if the movant gives security," the remaining portion of the rule provides that the security required shall be "in an amount that the court considers proper to pay the costs and damages sustained by any party found to have been wrongfully enjoined or restrained." This language has led some courts to conclude that the decision is discretionary, so long as the district court actually considers the question. *See, e.g.*, RoDa Drilling Co. v. Siegal, 552 F.3d 1203, 1215 (10th Cir. 2009). The issue then becomes whether the court in exercising its discretion can waive the security requirement altogether or set the amount of the bond at a level below the estimated costs and damages that the enjoined party may actually suffer if the order is granted improperly. *See also* Note, *Recovery for Wrongful Interlocutory Injunctions Under Rule 65(c)*, 99 Harv.L.Rev. 828 (1986).

The defendant in both temporary and preliminary injunctions is not bound by the restraining order until receiving actual notice that it exists and what its terms are. Fed.R.Civ.P. 65(d)(2). An injunction can only bind the parties, the "parties' officers, agents, servants, employees, and attorneys," and "other person who are in active concert or participation." *Id.* The rationale is due process. *E.g.,* Doctor's Associates, Inc. v. Reinert & Duree, P.C., 191 F.3d 297, 305 (2d Cir.1999); Richard A. Bales & Ryan A. Allison, *Enjoining Nonparties*, 26 Am. J. Trial Advoc. 79 (2002). The frequently cited opinion of Judge Learned Hand in Alemite Mfg. Corp. v. Staff, 42 F.2d 832 (2d Cir.1930) explains:

> [N]o court can make a decree which will bind any one but a party; a court of equity is as much so limited as a court of law; it cannot lawfully enjoin the world at large, no matter how broadly it words its decree. If it assumes to do so, the decree is *pro tanto brutum fulmen* [to that extent, harmless thunder], and the persons enjoined are free to ignore it. It is not vested with sovereign powers to declare conduct unlawful; its jurisdiction is limited to those over whom it gets personal service, and who therefore can have their day in court. Thus, the only occasion when a person not a party may be punished, is when he has helped to bring about, not merely what the decree has forbidden, because it may have gone too far, but what it has power to forbid, an act of a party. This means that the respondent must either abet the defendant, or must be legally identified with him.

Thus in the case, an ex-employee of the defendant, acting on his own, was not in contempt of the prior injunction against patent infringement. In another example, forty-five faculty who staged a sit-in in the university president's office were not bound by and thus not in contempt of an injunction barring students and all persons acting in concert with them from disrupting behavior on campus. State University of New York v. Denton, 35 A.D.2d 176, 316 N.Y.S.2d 297 (N.Y.App.1970). In *Denton,* the court noted that merely posting the injunctive order around campus, without personal service or reading aloud was likely insufficient notice. *Id.* There are, however, exceptions where courts have found non-parties bound by an order and found them in contempt. *See* United States v. Hall, 472 F.2d 261 (5th Cir. 1972) (upholding conviction for contempt against non-party adult protestor for violating desegregation injunction restraining all high school students from interfering with high school operations); *see also* Roe v. Operation Rescue, 54 F.3d 133 (3d Cir.1995) (leader of abortion protest organization held in contempt for urging others to commit acts from which he was enjoined). Rule 65(d) establishes a special rule for successors to public office and provides that the successor is "automatically substituted as a party."

A final and important safeguard is appellate review. Despite the final judgment rule, federal and state law permit an exception for interlocutory appeal from the trial court's decision on the motion to issue a permanent or a preliminary injunction. *E.g.,* 28 U.S.C. § 1292(a)(1); Mass.Gen.L.

ch.231 § 118. Generally, courts hold that there is no interlocutory appeal from decisions regarding a TRO, because of its extremely short duration. However there are exceptions. *See Carroll*, 393 U.S. at 180; Schiavo ex rel. Schindler v. Schiavo, 403 F.3d 1223, 1229 (11th Cir.) ("when a grant or denial of a TRO might have a serious, perhaps irreparable, consequence, and can be effectually challenged only by immediate appeal, we may exercise appellate jurisdiction"), *stay denied*, 544 U.S. 945 (2005); Levine v. Comcoa, Ltd., 70 F.3d 1191 (11th Cir.1995), *cert. denied*, 519 U.S. 809 (1996) (discussing circumstances of when an extension of time can convert a TRO into a valid, and appealable, preliminary injunction). In some jurisdictions, the appeal will act as an automatic stay of the injunction until the appeal is resolved. In others, a stay must be obtained from the trial or appellate court. If there is no stay, the injunction must be obeyed pending the outcome of the appeal. *See* John Y. Gotanda, *The Emerging Standards for Issuing Appellate Stays*, 45 Baylor L.Rev. 809 (1993). The standard of review is abuse of discretion, which usually means, "[a]s long as the district court got the law right, 'it will not be reversed simply because the appellate court would have arrived at a different result if it had applied the law to the facts of the case.'" A&M Records, Inc. v. Napster, Inc., 239 F.3d 1004, 1013 (9th Cir.2001).

2. STANDARDS FOR GRANTING PRELIMINARY RELIEF

Appellate courts typically state that the granting of a preliminary injunction or a TRO is within the discretion of the trial court; they also note that such preliminary relief is an extraordinary and drastic remedy that should issue only if the plaintiff makes a proper showing. *See* 11A Charles Alan Wright, Arthur R. Miller & Mary Kay Kane, *Federal Practice and Procedure* § 2948 at 429 (3d ed.) (Supp. 2016) (noting "the courts' general reluctance to impose an interim restraint on defendant before the parties' rights have been adjudicated" as well as the need to make "a sound evaluation of the factors relevant to granting relief"). For example, courts will sometimes state that a preliminary injunction may issue only if necessary to preserve the court's power to decide the merits or only to preserve the status quo. *See, e.g.,* Morton Denlow, *The Motion for a Preliminary Injunction: Time for a Uniform Federal Standard*, 22 Rev.Litig. 495 (2003) (U.S. magistrate judge reviews varying standards in the circuit courts). A good summary of the historical origins and modern standards of preliminary relief is provided in Andrew Muscato, *The Preliminary Injunction in Business Litigation,* 3 N.Y.U.J.L. & Bus. 649 (2007). Despite this blackletter rule, preliminary injunctions are quite common.

As the following materials discuss, the courts apply a four-part test for granting preliminary and temporary injunctions that is a variation on the usual four-part test for permanent injunctive relief.

WINTER V. NATURAL RESOURCES DEFENSE COUNCIL
Supreme Court of the United States
555 U.S. 7 (2008)

CHIEF JUSTICE ROBERTS delivered the opinion of the Court.

"To be prepared for war is one of the most effectual means of preserving peace." 1 Messages and Papers of the Presidents 57 (J. Richardson comp. 1897). So said George Washington in his first Annual Address to Congress, 218 years ago. One of the most important ways the Navy prepares for war is through integrated training exercises at sea. These exercises include training in the use of modern sonar to detect and track enemy submarines, something the Navy has done for the past 40 years. The plaintiffs complained that the Navy's sonar training program harmed marine mammals, and that the Navy should have prepared an environmental impact statement before commencing its latest round of training exercises. The Court of Appeals upheld a preliminary injunction imposing restrictions on the Navy's sonar training, even though that court acknowledged that "the record contains no evidence that marine mammals have been harmed" by the Navy's exercises.

The Court of Appeals was wrong, and its decision is reversed.

I

* * *

Antisubmarine warfare is currently the Pacific Fleet's top war-fighting priority. Modern diesel-electric submarines pose a significant threat to Navy vessels because they can operate almost silently, making them extremely difficult to detect and track. Potential adversaries of the United States possess at least 300 of these submarines.

The most effective technology for identifying submerged diesel-electric submarines within their torpedo range is active sonar, which involves emitting pulses of sound underwater and then receiving the acoustic waves that echo off the target. Active sonar is a particularly useful tool because it provides both the bearing and the distance of target submarines; it is also sensitive enough to allow the Navy to track enemy submarines that are quieter than the surrounding marine environment. This case concerns the Navy's use of "mid-frequency active" (MFA) sonar, which transmits sound waves at frequencies between 1 kHz and 10 kHz.

Not surprisingly, MFA sonar is a complex technology, and sonar operators must undergo extensive training to become proficient in its use. * * * The Navy conducts regular training exercises under realistic conditions to ensure that sonar operators are thoroughly skilled in its use in a variety of situations.

The waters off the coast of southern California (SOCAL) are an ideal location for conducting integrated training exercises, as this is the only area on the west coast that is relatively close to land, air, and sea bases, as well as amphibious landing areas. At issue in this case are the Composite Training Unit Exercises and the Joint Tactical Force Exercises, in which individual naval units (ships, submarines, and aircraft) train together as members of a strike group. A strike group cannot be certified for deployment until it has successfully completed the integrated training exercises, including a demonstration of its ability to operate under simulated hostile conditions. * * * The use of MFA sonar during these exercises is "mission-critical," given that MFA sonar is the only proven method of identifying submerged diesel-electric submarines operating on battery power.

Sharing the waters in the SOCAL operating area are at least 37 species of marine mammals, including dolphins, whales, and sea lions. The parties strongly dispute the extent to which the Navy's training activities will harm those animals or disrupt their behavioral patterns. The Navy emphasizes that it has used MFA sonar during training exercises in SOCAL for 40 years, without a single documented sonar-related injury to any marine mammal. The Navy asserts that, at most, MFA sonar may cause temporary hearing loss or brief disruptions of marine mammals' behavioral patterns.

The plaintiffs are the Natural Resources Defense Council, Jean-Michael Cousteau (an environmental enthusiast and filmmaker), and several other groups devoted to the protection of marine mammals and ocean habitats. They contend that MFA sonar can cause much more serious injuries to marine mammals than the Navy acknowledges, including permanent hearing loss, decompression sickness, and major behavioral disruptions. According to the plaintiffs, several mass strandings of marine mammals (outside of SOCAL) have been "associated" with the use of active sonar. They argue that certain species of marine mammals—such as beaked whales—are uniquely susceptible to injury from active sonar; these injuries would not necessarily be detected by the Navy, given that beaked whales are "very deep divers" that spend little time at the surface.

II

The procedural history of this case is rather complicated. The Marine Mammal Protection Act of 1972 (MMPA), 86 Stat. 1027, generally prohibits any individual from "taking" a marine mammal, defined as harassing, hunting, capturing, or killing it. 16 U.S.C. §§ 1362(13), 1372(a). The Secretary of Defense may "exempt any action or category of actions" from the MMPA if such actions are "necessary for national defense." § 1371(f)(1). In January 2007, the Deputy Secretary of Defense—acting for the Secretary—granted the Navy a 2-year exemption from the MMPA for the training exercises at issue in this case. The exemption was conditioned on the Navy adopting several mitigation procedures * * * [including shutting down MFA sonar in order to protect any marine mammals detected within 200 yards of a vessel during the exercises].

The National Environmental Policy Act of 1969 (NEPA) requires federal agencies "to the fullest extent possible" to prepare an environmental impact statement (EIS) for "every . . . major Federal actio[n] significantly affecting the quality of the human environment." 42 U.S.C. § 4332(2)(C). An agency is not required to prepare a full EIS if it determines—based on a shorter environmental assessment (EA)—that the proposed action will not have a significant impact on the environment.

In February 2007, the Navy issued an EA concluding that the 14 SOCAL training exercises scheduled through January 2009 would not have a significant impact on the environment. The EA divided potential injury to marine mammals into two categories: Level A harassment, defined as the potential destruction or loss of biological tissue (i.e., physical injury), and Level B harassment, defined as temporary injury or disruption of behavioral patterns such as migration, feeding, surfacing, and breeding.

The Navy's computer models predicted that the SOCAL training exercises would cause only eight Level A harassments of common dolphins each year, and that even these injuries could be avoided through the Navy's voluntary mitigation measures, given that dolphins travel in large pods easily located by Navy lookouts. The EA also predicted 274 Level B harassments of beaked whales per year, none of which would result in permanent injury. * * * In light of its conclusion that the SOCAL training exercises would not have a significant impact on the environment, the Navy determined that it was unnecessary to prepare a full EIS.

Shortly after the Navy released its EA, the plaintiffs sued the Navy, seeking declaratory and injunctive relief on the grounds that the Navy's SOCAL training exercises violated NEPA, the Endangered Species Act of 1973 (ESA), and the Coastal Zone Management Act of 1972 (CZMA).[2] The District Court granted plaintiffs' motion for a preliminary injunction and prohibited the Navy from using MFA sonar during its remaining training exercises. The court held that plaintiffs had "demonstrated a probability of success" on their claims under NEPA and the CZMA. * * * Based on scientific studies, declarations from experts, and other evidence in the record, the District Court concluded that there was in fact a "near certainty" of irreparable injury to the environment, and that this injury outweighed any possible harm to the Navy.

* * * After hearing oral argument, the Court of Appeals agreed with the District Court that preliminary injunctive relief was appropriate. The appellate court concluded, however, that a blanket injunction prohibiting

---

[2]   The CZMA states that federal agencies taking actions "that affec[t] any land or water use or natural resources of the coastal zone" shall carry out these activities "in a manner which is consistent to the maximum extent practicable with the enforceable policies of approved State management programs." 16 U.S.C. § 1456(c)(1)(A).

the Navy from using MFA sonar in SOCAL was overbroad, and remanded the case to the District Court "to narrow its injunction so as to provide mitigation conditions under which the Navy may conduct its training exercises."

On remand, the District Court entered a new preliminary injunction allowing the Navy to use MFA sonar only as long as it implemented the following mitigation measures (in addition to the measures the Navy had adopted pursuant to its MMPA exemption): (1) imposing a 12-mile "exclusion zone" from the coastline; (2) using lookouts to conduct additional monitoring for marine mammals; (3) restricting the use of "helicopter-dipping" sonar; (4) limiting the use of MFA sonar in geographic "choke points"; (5) shutting down MFA sonar when a marine mammal is spotted within 2,200 yards of a vessel; and (6) powering down MFA sonar by 6 dB during significant surface ducting conditions, in which sound travels further than it otherwise would due to temperature differences in adjacent layers of water. The Navy filed a notice of appeal, challenging only the last two restrictions.

The Navy then sought relief from the Executive Branch. The President * * * granted the Navy an exemption from the CZMA. Section 1456(c)(1)(B) permits such exemptions if the activity in question is in the paramount interest of the United States. * * *

Simultaneously, the Council on Environmental Quality (CEQ) authorized the Navy to implement "alternative arrangements" to NEPA compliance in light of "emergency circumstances." * * * Under the alternative arrangements, the Navy would be permitted to conduct its training exercises under the mitigation procedures adopted in conjunction with the exemption from the MMPA. * * *

In light of these actions, the Navy then moved to vacate the District Court's injunction with respect to the 2,200-yard shutdown zone and the restrictions on training in surface ducting conditions. The District Court refused to do so and the Court of Appeals affirmed. The Ninth Circuit held that there was a serious question regarding whether the CEQ's interpretation of the "emergency circumstances" regulation was lawful. Specifically, the court questioned whether there was a true "emergency" in this case, given that the Navy has been on notice of its obligation to comply with NEPA from the moment it first planned the SOCAL training exercises. The Court of Appeals concluded that the preliminary injunction was entirely predictable in light of the parties' litigation history. * * * The Ninth Circuit agreed with the District Court's holding that the Navy's EA—which resulted in a finding of no significant environmental impact— was "cursory, unsupported by cited evidence, or unconvincing."

The Court of Appeals further determined that plaintiffs had carried their burden of establishing a "possibility" of irreparable injury. Even under the Navy's own figures, the court concluded, the training exercises would cause 564 physical injuries to marine mammals, as well as 170,000 disturbances of marine mammals' behavior. Lastly, the Court of Appeals held that the balance of hardships and consideration of the public interest weighed in favor of the plaintiffs. The court emphasized that the negative impact on the Navy's training exercises was "speculative," since the Navy has never before operated under the procedures required by the District Court. * * * The Ninth Circuit concluded that the District Court's preliminary injunction struck a proper balance between the competing interests at stake.

* * *

III

A

A plaintiff seeking a preliminary injunction must establish that he is likely to succeed on the merits, that he is likely to suffer irreparable harm in the absence of preliminary relief, that the balance of equities tips in his favor, and that an injunction is in the public interest. *See* Munaf v. Geren, 553 U.S. ___, ___, 128 S.Ct. 2207, 2218–2219 (2008); Amoco Production Co. v. Gambell, 480 U.S. 531, 542 (1987); Weinberger v. Romero-Barcelo, 456 U.S. 305, 311–312 (1982).

The District Court and the Ninth Circuit concluded that plaintiffs have shown a likelihood of success on the merits of their NEPA claim. The Navy strongly disputes this determination, arguing that plaintiffs' likelihood of success is low because the CEQ reasonably concluded that "emergency circumstances" justified alternative arrangements to NEPA compliance. * * *

The District Court and the Ninth Circuit also held that when a plaintiff demonstrates a strong likelihood of prevailing on the merits, a preliminary injunction may be entered based only on a "possibility" of irreparable harm. The lower courts held that plaintiffs had met this standard because the scientific studies, declarations, and other evidence in the record established to "a near certainty" that the Navy's training exercises would cause irreparable harm to the environment.

The Navy challenges these holdings, arguing that plaintiffs must demonstrate a likelihood of irreparable injury—not just a possibility—in order to obtain preliminary relief. On the facts of this case, the Navy contends that plaintiffs' alleged injuries are too speculative to give rise to irreparable injury, given that ever since the Navy's training program began 40 years ago, there has been no documented case of sonar-related injury to marine mammals in SOCAL. And even if MFA sonar does cause a limited number of injuries to individual *marine mammals,* the Navy asserts that plaintiffs have failed to offer evidence of species-level harm that would adversely affect *their* scientific, recreational, and ecological interests. For their part, plaintiffs assert that they would prevail under any formulation of the irreparable injury standard, because the District Court found that they had established a "near certainty" of irreparable harm.

We agree with the Navy that the Ninth Circuit's "possibility" standard is too lenient. Our frequently reiterated standard requires plaintiffs seeking preliminary relief to demonstrate that irreparable injury is *likely* in the absence of an injunction. Los Angeles v. Lyons, 461 U.S. 95, 103 (1983); Granny Goose Foods, Inc. v. Teamsters, 415 U.S. 423, 441 (1974); O'Shea v. Littleton, 414 U.S. 488, 502 (1974); *see also* 11A C. Wright, A. Miller, & M. Kane, *Federal Practice and Procedure* § 2948 (applicant must demonstrate that in the absence of a preliminary injunction, "the applicant is likely to suffer irreparable harm before a decision on the merits can be rendered"); *id.*, at 155 ("a preliminary injunction will not be issued simply to prevent the possibility of some remote future injury"). Issuing a preliminary injunction based only on a possibility of irreparable harm is inconsistent with our characterization of injunctive relief as an extraordinary remedy that may only be awarded upon a clear showing that the plaintiff is entitled to such relief.

It is not clear that articulating the incorrect standard affected the Ninth Circuit's analysis of irreparable harm. Although the court referred to the "possibility" standard, and cited Circuit precedent along the same lines, it affirmed the District Court's conclusion that plaintiffs had established a " 'near certainty' " of irreparable harm. At the same time, however, the nature of the District Court's conclusion is itself unclear. The District Court originally found irreparable harm from sonar-training exercises generally. But by the time of the District Court's final decision, the Navy challenged only two of six restrictions imposed by the court. The District Court did not reconsider the likelihood of irreparable harm in light of the four restrictions not challenged by the Navy. * * *

We also find it pertinent that this is not a case in which the defendant is conducting a new type of activity with completely unknown effects on the environment. * * * Part of the harm NEPA attempts to prevent in requiring an EIS is that, without one, there may be little if any information about prospective environmental harms and potential mitigating measures. Here, in contrast, the plaintiffs are seeking to enjoin—or substantially restrict—training exercises that have been taking place in SOCAL for the last 40 years. And the latest series of exercises were not approved until after the defendant took a "hard look at environmental consequences," as evidenced by the issuance of a detailed, 293-page EA.

As explained in the next section, even if plaintiffs have shown irreparable injury from the Navy's training exercises, any such injury is outweighed by the public interest and the Navy's interest in effective, realistic training of its sailors. A proper consideration of these factors alone requires denial of the requested injunctive relief. For the same reason, we do not address the lower courts' holding that plaintiffs have also established a likelihood of success on the merits.

B

A preliminary injunction is an extraordinary remedy never awarded as of right. In each case, courts "must balance the competing claims of injury and must consider the effect on each party of the granting or withholding of the requested relief." *Amoco.* "In exercising their sound discretion, courts of equity should pay particular regard for the public consequences in employing the extraordinary remedy of injunction." *Romero-Barcelo.* In this case, the District Court and the Ninth Circuit significantly understated the burden the preliminary injunction would impose on the Navy's ability to conduct realistic training exercises, and the injunction's consequent adverse impact on the public interest in national defense.

This case involves "complex, subtle, and professional decisions as to the composition, training, equipping, and control of a military force," which are "essentially professional military judgments." * * *

Here, the record contains declarations from some of the Navy's most senior officers, all of whom underscored the threat posed by enemy submarines and the need for extensive sonar training to counter this threat. Admiral Gary Roughead—the Chief of Naval Operations—stated that during training exercises:

> "It is important to stress the ship crews in all dimensions of warfare simultaneously. If one of these training elements were impacted—for example, if effective sonar training were not possible—the training value of the other elements would also be degraded. . . ."

Captain Martin May—the Third Fleet's Assistant Chief of Staff for Training and Readiness—emphasized that the use of MFA sonar is "mission-critical." He described the ability to operate MFA sonar as a "highly perishable skill" that must be repeatedly practiced under realistic conditions. * * * Several Navy officers emphasized that realistic training cannot be accomplished under the two challenged restrictions imposed by the District Court—the 2,200-yard shutdown zone and the requirement that the Navy power down its sonar systems during significant surface ducting conditions. * * * We accept these officers' assertions that the use of MFA sonar under realistic conditions during training exercises is of the utmost importance to the Navy and the Nation.

These interests must be weighed against the possible harm to the ecological, scientific, and recreational interests that are legitimately before this Court. Plaintiffs have submitted declarations asserting that they take whale watching trips, observe marine mammals underwater, conduct scientific research on marine mammals, and photograph these animals in their natural habitats. Plaintiffs contend that the Navy's use of MFA sonar will injure marine mammals or alter their behavioral patterns, impairing plaintiffs' ability to study and observe the animals.

While we do not question the seriousness of these interests, we conclude that the balance of equities and consideration of the overall public interest in this case tip strongly in favor of the Navy. For the plaintiffs, the most serious possible injury would be harm to an unknown number of the marine mammals that they study and observe. In contrast, forcing the Navy to deploy an inadequately trained antisubmarine force jeopardizes the safety of the fleet. Active sonar is the only reliable technology for detecting and tracking enemy diesel-electric submarines, and the President—the Commander in Chief—has determined that training with active sonar is "essential to national security."

The public interest in conducting training exercises with active sonar under realistic conditions plainly outweighs the interests advanced by the plaintiffs. Of course, military interests do not always trump other considerations, and we have not held that they do. In this case, however, the proper determination of where the public interest lies does not strike us as a close question.

C

1. Despite the importance of assessing the balance of equities and the public interest in determining whether to grant a preliminary injunction, the District Court addressed these considerations in only a cursory fashion. The court's entire discussion of these factors consisted of one (albeit lengthy) sentence: "The Court is also satisfied that the balance of hardships tips in favor of granting an injunction, as the harm to the environment, Plaintiffs, and public interest outweighs the harm that Defendants would incur if prevented from using MFA sonar, absent the use of effective mitigation measures, during a subset of their regular activities in one part of one state for a limited period." * * *

The Court of Appeals held that the balance of equities and the public interest favored the plaintiffs, largely based on its view that the preliminary injunction would not in fact impose a significant burden on the Navy's ability to conduct its training exercises and certify its strike groups. The court deemed the Navy's concerns about the preliminary injunction "speculative" because the Navy had not operated under similar procedures before. But this is almost always the case when a plaintiff seeks injunctive relief to alter a defendant's conduct. The lower courts failed properly to defer to senior Navy officers' specific, predictive judgments about how the preliminary injunction would reduce the effectiveness of the Navy's SOCAL training exercises. * * *

2. The preliminary injunction requires the Navy to shut down its MFA sonar if a marine mammal is detected within 2,200 yards of a sonar-emitting vessel. The Ninth Circuit stated that the 2,200-yard shutdown zone would not be overly burdensome because sightings of marine mammals during training exercises are relatively rare. But regardless of the frequency of marine mammal sightings, the injunction will greatly increase the size of the shutdown zone. * * * Increasing the radius of the shutdown zone from 200 to 2,200 yards would * * * expand the surface area of the shutdown zone by a factor of over 100 (from 125,664 square yards to 15,205,308 square yards).

The lower courts did not give sufficient weight to the views of several top Navy officers, who emphasized that because training scenarios can take several days to develop, each additional shutdown can result in the loss of several days' worth of training. Limiting the number of sonar shutdowns is particularly important during the Joint Tactical Force Exercises, which usually last for less than two weeks. Admiral Bird explained that the 2,200-yard shutdown zone would cause operational commanders to "lose awareness of the tactical situation through the constant stopping and starting of MFA [sonar]." * * * Even if there is a low likelihood of a marine mammal sighting, the preliminary injunction would clearly increase the number of disruptive sonar shutdowns the Navy is forced to perform during its SOCAL training exercises.

* * *

3.   The Court of Appeals also concluded that the Navy's training exercises would not be significantly affected by the requirement that it power down MFA sonar by 6 dB during significant surface ducting conditions. Again, we think the Ninth Circuit understated the burden this requirement would impose on the Navy's ability to conduct realistic training exercises.

Surface ducting is a phenomenon in which relatively little sound energy penetrates beyond a narrow layer near the surface of the water. When surface ducting occurs, active sonar becomes more useful near the surface but less useful at greater depths. Diesel-electric submariners are trained to take advantage of these distortions to avoid being detected by sonar.

The Ninth Circuit determined that the power-down requirement during surface ducting conditions was unlikely to affect certification of the Navy's strike groups because surface ducting occurs relatively rarely, and the Navy has previously certified strike groups that did not train under such conditions. This reasoning is backwards. Given that surface ducting is both rare and unpredictable, it is especially important for the Navy to be able to train under these conditions when they occur. Admiral Bird explained that the 6 dB power-down requirement makes the training less valuable because it "exposes [sonar operators] to unrealistically lower levels of mutual interference caused by multiple sonar systems operating together by the ships within the Strike Group." Although a 6 dB reduction may not seem terribly significant, decibels are measured on a logarithmic scale, so a 6 dB decrease in power equates to a 75% reduction.

4.   The District Court acknowledged that " 'the imposition of these mitigation measures will require the Navy to alter and adapt the way it conducts antisubmarine warfare training—a substantial challenge. Nevertheless, evidence presented to the Court reflects that the Navy has employed mitigation measures in the past, without sacrificing training objectives.' " Apparently no good deed goes unpunished. The fact that the Navy has taken measures in the past to address concerns about marine mammals—or, for that matter, has elected not to challenge four additional restrictions imposed by the District Court in this case hardly means that other, more intrusive restrictions pose no threat to preparedness for war.

The Court of Appeals concluded its opinion by stating that "the Navy may return to the district court to request relief on an emergency basis" if the preliminary injunction "actually result[s] in an inability to train and certify sufficient naval forces to provide for the national defense." This is cold comfort to the Navy. The Navy contends that the injunction will hinder efforts to train sonar operators under realistic conditions, ultimately leaving strike groups more vulnerable to enemy submarines. Unlike the Ninth Circuit, we do not think the Navy is required to wait until the injunction "actually result[s] in an inability to train . . . sufficient naval forces for the national defense" before seeking its dissolution. By then it may be too late.

IV

As noted above, we do not address the underlying merits of plaintiffs' claims. While we have authority to proceed to such a decision at this point, doing so is not necessary here. * * *

At the same time, what we have said makes clear that it would be an abuse of discretion to enter a permanent injunction, after final decision on the merits, along the same lines as the preliminary injunction. An injunction is a matter of equitable discretion; it does not follow from success on the merits as a matter of course. *Romero-Barcelo,* 456 U.S. at 313 ("a federal judge sitting as chancellor is not mechanically obligated to grant an injunction for every violation of law").

The factors examined above—the balance of equities and consideration of the public interest—are pertinent in assessing the propriety of any injunctive relief, preliminary or permanent. *See Amoco Production Co.,* 480 U.S. at 546 n.12 ("The standard for a preliminary injunction is essentially the same as for a permanent injunction with the exception that the plaintiff must show a likelihood of success on the merits rather than actual success"). Given that the ultimate legal claim is that the Navy must prepare an EIS, not that it must cease sonar training, there is no basis for enjoining such training in a manner credibly alleged to pose a serious threat to national security. This is particularly true in light of the fact that the training has been going on for 40 years with no documented episode of harm to a marine mammal. A court concluding that the Navy is required to prepare an EIS has many remedial tools at its disposal, including declaratory relief or an injunction tailored to the preparation of an EIS rather than the Navy's training in the interim. *See, e.g.,* Steffel v. Thompson, 415 U.S. 452, 466 (1974) ("Congress plainly intended declaratory relief to act as an alternative to the strong medicine of the injunction"). In the meantime, we see no basis for jeopardizing national security, as the present injunction does.

* * *

President Theodore Roosevelt explained that "the only way in which a navy can ever be made efficient is by practice at sea, under all the conditions which would have to be met if war existed." President's Annual Message, 42 Cong.Rec. 67, 81 (1907). We do not discount the importance of plaintiffs' ecological, scientific, and recreational interests in marine mammals. Those interests, however, are plainly outweighed by the Navy's need to conduct realistic training exercises to ensure that it is able to neutralize the threat posed by enemy submarines. The District Court abused its discretion by imposing a 2,200-yard shutdown zone and by requiring the Navy to power down its MFA sonar during significant surface ducting conditions. The judgment of the Court of Appeals is reversed, and the preliminary injunction is vacated to the extent it has been challenged by the Navy.

* * *

JUSTICE BREYER, with whom JUSTICE STEVENS joins, concurring in part and dissenting in part.

* * *

While a District Court is often free simply to state its conclusion in summary fashion, in this instance neither that conclusion, nor anything else I have found in the District Court's opinion, answers the Navy's documented claims that the two extra conditions the District Court imposed will, in effect, seriously interfere with its ability to carry out necessary training exercises.

* * *

JUSTICE GINSBURG, with whom JUSTICE SOUTER joins, dissenting.

The central question in this action under the National Environmental Policy Act of 1969 (NEPA) was whether the Navy must prepare an environmental impact statement (EIS). The Navy does not challenge its obligation to do so, and it represents that the EIS will be complete in

January 2009—one month after the instant exercises conclude. If the Navy had completed the EIS before taking action, as NEPA instructs, the parties and the public could have benefited from the environmental analysis—and the Navy's training could have proceeded without interruption. Instead, the Navy acted first, and thus thwarted the very purpose an EIS is intended to serve.

* * *

III

A

Flexibility is a hallmark of equity jurisdiction. "The essence of equity jurisdiction has been the power of the Chancellor to do equity and to mould each decree to the necessities of the particular case. Flexibility rather than rigidity has distinguished it." Weinberger v. Romero-Barcelo, 456 U.S. 305, 312 (1982) (quoting Hecht Co. v. Bowles, 321 U.S. 321, 329 (1944)). Consistent with equity's character, courts do not insist that litigants uniformly show a particular, predetermined quantum of probable success or injury before awarding equitable relief. Instead, courts have evaluated claims for equitable relief on a "sliding scale," sometimes awarding relief based on a lower likelihood of harm when the likelihood of success is very high. This Court has never rejected that formulation, and I do not believe it does so today.

Equity's flexibility is important in the NEPA context. Because an EIS is the tool for *uncovering* environmental harm, environmental plaintiffs may often rely more heavily on their probability of success than the likelihood of harm. The Court is correct that relief is not warranted "simply to prevent the possibility of some remote future injury." "However, the injury need not have been inflicted when application is made or be certain to occur; a strong threat of irreparable injury before trial is an adequate basis." I agree with the District Court that NRDC made the required showing here.

B

The Navy's own EA predicted substantial and irreparable harm to marine mammals. Sonar is linked to mass strandings of marine mammals, hemorrhaging around the brain and ears, acute spongiotic changes in the central nervous system, and lesions in vital organs. * * *

In light of the likely, substantial harm to the environment, NRDC's almost inevitable success on the merits of its claim that NEPA required the Navy to prepare an EIS, the history of this litigation, and the public interest, I cannot agree that the mitigation measures the District Court imposed signal an abuse of discretion. Cf. Amoco Production Co. v. Gambell, 480 U.S. 531, 545 (1987) ("Environmental injury, by its nature, can seldom be adequately remedied by money damages and is often permanent or at least of long duration, *i.e.,* irreparable. If such injury is sufficiently likely, therefore, the balance of harms will usually favor the issuance of an injunction to protect the environment."). * * *

NOTES

1.   Courts often state that the goal of a preliminary injunction is to maintain the "status quo." But what does that mean in *Winter*? Does it mean just prior to the training exercises at issue here have commenced or the fact that the Navy has engaged in periodic training exercises in the SOCAL region for the previous 40 years? In an ordinary case, should "status quo" refer to the situation immediately prior to the filing of the suit? Before the filing of the motion for preliminary injunction? Or does the court mean by status quo the plaintiffs' rightful position? If so, how does the court know what that is in advance of deciding the case on the merits? *See* Thomas R. Lee, *Preliminary Injunctions and the Status Quo,* 58 Wash. & Lee L.Rev. 109 (2001).

2.   Justice Ginsburg in her dissent emphasizes that the majority opinion does not reject the "sliding scale" test of preliminary relief. The sliding scale is a flexible test previously adopted by most courts of appeals in which "the elements of the preliminary injunction test are balanced, so that a stronger showing of one element may offset a weaker showing of another." Vanguard Outdoor, LLC v. City of Los Angeles, 648 F.3d 737 (9th Cir. 2011). Practically this means that plaintiffs do not have to establish likelihood of success on the merits with a 51% certainty, but need only to raise "serious questions going to the merits" balanced with strong showings on the other factors. Citigroup Global Markets, Inc. v. VCG Special Opport. Master Fund, 598 F.3d 30, 35–38 (2d Cir. 2010). Dicta in the *Winter* majority opinion seems to call into doubt the sliding scale test, at least with respect to the irreparable injury prong, when it says that low "possibility" of irreparable harm cannot suffice nor be overcome by a balance of other factors. The Fourth Circuit read *Winter* this way and abandoned its sliding scale test. Real Truth About Obama, Inc. v. Fed. Elec. Comm'n, 575 F.3d 342, 346 (4th Cir. 2009), *vacated on other grounds,* 559 U.S. 1089 (2010), *decision reinstated,* 607 F.3d 355 (2010); *see also* Sherley v. Sebelius, 644 F.3d 388 (D.C. Cir. 2011) (suggesting without deciding that *Winter* may preclude the sliding scale test). Other circuits, however, have reaffirmed their sliding scale tests after *Winter. Vanguard* (9th); Judge v. Quinn, 612 F.3d 537, 546 (7th Cir. 2010); *Citigroup* (2d). One study confirmed that *Winter* has had minimal impact on the approach of the appellate courts in granting preliminary relief, finding that the number of preliminary injunctions granted in environmental cases after the case has stayed the same. Sarah J. Morath, *A Mild* Winter: *The Status of Environmental Preliminary Injunctions,* 37 Seattle U.L.Rev. 111 (2013).

3.   As Chief Justice Roberts noted in *Winter*, the test for deciding a motion for a preliminary injunction includes consideration of whether the injunction would be adverse to the public interest. But, how do courts determine what the "public interest" is? How does the court determine what public policies and which third-party interests are relevant? In *Winter*, the

Court found that the sworn statements of senior Navy personnel regarding the need for training in order to keep the Navy and the country safe from enemy submarines easily outweighed the plaintiffs' interests in whale watching trips, photography, and scientific research. But what about the public interest represented by enforcement of three federal statutes: the Marine Mammals Act, the National Environmental Policy Act and the Coastal Zone Management Act? What about harm to the marine mammals? *See* Laura W. Stein, *The Court and Community: Why Non-Party Interests Should Count in Preliminary Injunction Actions*, 16 Rev.Litig. 27 (1997); Note, *"The Wild Card that is the Public Interest": Putting a New Face on the Fourth Preliminary Injunction Factor*, 72 Tex.L.Rev. 849 (1994) (contending that courts should use the factor to weigh particular non-party harm which will be suffered as a direct consequence of the granting or denying of a particular preliminary injunction).

Professor John Leubsdorf addressed the question of whose interests should be weighed when applying the preliminary injunction test:

> In recent years, federal courts have given increasing attention to the effect of preliminary relief on the public interest. No doubt this reflects the flowering of broad injunctive relief which affects many persons and the judicial recognition of public interest plaintiffs. On a deeper level, it shows increasing judicial concern with the impact of legal decisions on society, as opposed to their adequacy as remedies for past misconduct.
>
> It does not follow, however, that the interests of everyone affected by the grant or denial of preliminary relief should figure in the interlocutory hearing. The court must determine whose interests it should consider by reference to the substantive law that will apply when the case goes to trial on the merits. An interlocutory decision about specific performance of a contract to make parts for a power plant should turn on the applicable contract law, not the plant's environmental impact. To consider interests irrelevant to the final decision at the preliminary stage will only increase the cost of the litigation and undermine the substantive law. Those whom the law excludes from protection at the final hearing have no greater claim to be taken into account earlier. This is implicit in the basic perception that preliminary relief guards against irreparable loss of rights, not against *damnum absque injuria*.
>
> The substantive law does not always specify the objects of its protection. So long as a party with standing is present, courts granting final relief can limit their inquiry to what the law forbids. The balancing test for preliminary relief, by contrast, calls for difficult judgments about who—parties, neighbors, future generations, and so forth—have interests deserving consideration. These judgments have to be made quickly, and the law of standing provides only a partial guide. Not surprisingly, some courts avoid the problem by invoking generalizations about the public interest.

The Standard for Preliminary Injunctions, 91 Harv.L.Rev. 525, 549–50 (1978).

Occupy Tucson v. City of Tucson

United States District Court, District of Arizona
2011 WL 6747860 (D.Ariz.2011)

Cindy K. Jorgenson, District Judge.

Currently pending before the Court is Plaintiffs' Renewed Motion for Temporary Restraining Order and Preliminary Injunction. In their motion Plaintiffs request the Court to "issue * * * a temporary restraining order that will prevent the City of Tucson from forcing them out of Viente de Agosto Park for a brief period until a hearing can be held, or until Plaintiffs' Counsel has time to file a Memorandum in Support of their Renewed Request for Temporary Restraining Order."

I.   Background

Plaintiffs are participants in a local movement known as "Occupy Tucson." This movement is loosely affiliated with the "Occupy Wall Street" movement and "is opposed to excessive corporate power and influence in the American political system." The Occupy Tucson movement began on October 15, 2011 in Armory Park located in downtown Tucson, Arizona. From the inception of Occupy Tucson, the City of Tucson has issued citations for violations of Section of the Tucson Code. On November 3, 2011, the Occupy Tucson movement moved from Armory Park to Veinte De Agosto Park, also in downtown Tucson.

On November 7, 2011, Plaintiffs filed the instant case alleging *inter alia* a First Amendment violation pursuant to 42 U.S.C. § 1983. Plaintiffs allege that Section 21, Tucson Code, is unconstitutional on its face and as applied by Defendants. Plaintiffs also allege a violation of Article 2 § 5 of the Arizona Constitution including infringement upon their rights to freedom of speech, freedom of assembly, freedom of association and freedom to petition the government for redress of grievances. Plaintiffs also filed a Motion for Temporary Restraining Order and Preliminary Injunction. On November 8, 2011, this Court entered its Order denying Plaintiffs request for TRO. * * * On December 21, 2011, Plaintiffs filed their Renewed Motion for Temporary Restraining Order and Preliminary Injunction.

II.   Standard of Review

Whether to grant or deny a motion for a temporary restraining order is within the Court's discretion. * * * "The standard for issuing a temporary restraining order is identical to the standard for issuing a preliminary injunction." * * * A preliminary injunction is an extraordinary and drastic remedy and will not be granted absent a clear showing of likely success in the underlying claim and likely irreparable injury. * * * Fed.R.Civ.P. 65. To obtain a preliminary injunction, the moving party must show "that he is likely to succeed on the merits, that he is likely to suffer irreparable harm in the absence of preliminary relief, that the balance of equities tips in his favor, and that an injunction is in the public interest." Winter v. Natural Resources Defense Council, Inc., 555 U.S. 7, 20 (2008). * * * The moving party has the burden of proof on each element of the test. * * *

Additionally, the function of a preliminary injunction is to preserve the status quo pending a determination on the merits. * * * As such, there is heightened scrutiny where the movant seeks to alter rather than maintain the status quo. * * * There is also heightened scrutiny where the injunction would provide substantially all the relief the movant may recover after a full trial on the merits. * * *

III. ANALYSIS

"The court may issue a temporary restraining order without written or oral notice to the adverse party or its attorney only if . . . specific facts in an affidavit or a verified complaint clearly show that immediate and irreparable injury, loss, or damage will result to the movant before the adverse party can be heard in opposition; and . . . the movant's attorney certifies in writing any efforts made to give notice and the reasons why it should not be required." Fed.R.Civ.P. 65(b)(1). Plaintiffs previous motion for TRO did not assert any change in circumstances or policies surrounding the Occupy Tucson movement. Plaintiffs now aver that "a permit has been requested for the use of Viente de Agosto Park for December 28th." In light of the permit, "a staff person for City Council Member Regina Romero called a member of Occupy Tucson with information that the Park was going to be cleared by the police tonight." Plaintiffs counsel avers that "he has attempted to contact City Attorney Michael Rankin regarding this renewed request [for TRO]." Additionally, counsel notes that "the Motion to Dismiss/For Summary Judgment that Defendant City of Tucson filed contains all of their arguments as to why a TRO should not be granted."

In light of the changed circumstances of this case, the Court will consider the merits of Plaintiffs' TRO request.

A.   Preserving the Status Quo

Section 21, Tucson Code provides [it shall be unlawful to disfigure parks, erect structures like tents in parks, camp or remain overnight in a park, or utilize any park property for any political purpose, except by permit.] * * * Tucson Code, § 21–3. This section of the Tucson Code was adopted on January 10, 1977.

"A temporary restraining order is designed to preserve the status quo until there is an opportunity to hold a hearing on the application for a preliminary injunction." * * * Here, the status quo is that Tucson Code § 21–3 has been in effect since 1977, and since the inception of the Occupy Tucson movement, the City has indicated its intention to enforce the Code by issuing citations to violators. As such, the status quo is that there is currently a thirty-four year old ordinance which is being enforced by the government.

Plaintiffs request seeks to alter the status quo by precluding the City from enforcing § 21–3. There is no allegation that the City was not enforcing § 21–3 previously. Although enforcement since October 15, 2003 has primarily consisted of the issuance of citations, Occupy Tucson members were previously removed from Armory Park. Thus, any argument that the status quo is Plaintiffs' constitutional right to free speech which is abridged by enforcement of § 21–3, presumes that § 21–3 is facially unconstitutional. Every regulation of speech, however, is not unconstitutional. The Court cannot conclude that the enforcement of § 21–3 results in a disturbance of the status quo thereby justifying the issuance of a TRO.

B.   Likelihood of Success on the Merits

At this juncture, Plaintiffs have not provided any authority or argument to suggest that Tucson Code § 21–3 is not a valid time, manner, place restriction on speech. To obtain a preliminary injunction, the moving party must show "that he is likely to succeed on the merits, that he is likely to suffer irreparable harm in the absence of preliminary relief, that the balance of equities tips in his favor, and that an injunction is in the public interest." *Winter*. The Ninth Circuit has also recognized a "sliding scale" approach, under which "the elements of the preliminary injunction test are balanced, so that a stronger showing of one element may offset a weaker showing of another." Alliance for the Wild Rockies v. Cottrell, 632 F.3d 1127, 1131 (9th Cir.2011).

"Expression, whether oral or written or symbolized by conduct, is subject to reasonable time, place, or manner restrictions." Clark v. Community for Creative Non-Violence, 468 U.S. 288, 293 (1984). Moreover, "a content-neutral time, place and manner regulation can be applied in such a manner as to stifle free expression[; however, it] thus must contain adequate standards to guide an official's decision and render that decision subject to effective judicial review." * * * On its face, Section 21–3 appears to "(1) be content neutral; (2) be narrowly-tailored; (3) support a substantial government purpose; (4) provide the Director with constitutionally sufficient discretion; and (5) be constitutionally sufficient." Occupy Sacramento v. City of Sacramento, 2011 WL 5374748 (E.D.Cal.). Indeed, the Supreme Court's decision in *Clark* would appear to compel a decision contrary to Plaintiffs' position. In *Clark,* the Court stated:

No one contends that aside from its impact on speech a rule against camping or overnight sleep in public parks is beyond the constitutional power of the Government to enforce. And for the reasons we have discussed above, there is a substantial Government interest in conserving park property, an interest that is plainly served by, and requires for its implementation, measures such as the proscription of sleeping that are designed to limit the wear and tear on park properties.

* * *

Currently, a valid permit holder will be using Veinte De Agosto Park on December 28, 2011. It appears that since the inception of this lawsuit, none of the Plaintiffs have sought a permit from the City for use of the park. The regulation that Plaintiffs seek to enjoin enforcement of is content-neutral. It regulates the hours during which any individual may use the park. Plaintiffs have not put forth any arguments to indicate that there is a content-based component to the regulation. Indeed, Plaintiffs have not put forth any legal arguments as to why the City's ordinance is invalid. As such, Plaintiffs have failed to meet their burden to demonstrate a likelihood of success on the merits. * * *

Accordingly, IT IS HEREBY ORDERED that Plaintiffs' Renewed Motion for Temporary Restraining Order and Preliminary Injunction is DENIED.

PROBLEM: UNAUTHORIZED MERCHANTS

Many recording artists feel plagued by entrepreneurs who show up at their live concerts and sell merchandise, especially T-shirts, to fans outside of the hall. The unauthorized merchants cut into the revenues that would be generated through the sale of souvenirs by authorized vendors inside the hall. Typically, no one connected with the recording artists knows the identities of the unauthorized merchants. Assume your clients are the group "Law Students Rock," starring Eric Sarmiento and Chelsea Price, who are about to go out on tour to promote their new CD. They have their first big stadium concert of the tour scheduled just a few days hence. Can a TRO banning unauthorized souvenir sales be granted? Compare Billy Joel v. Various John Does, 499 F.Supp. 791 (E.D.Wis.1980) (granted) with Plant v. Doe, 19 F.Supp.2d 1316 (S.D.Fla.1998) (denied). Could the recording artists keep legal expenses down by seeking a single TRO that prohibits such unauthorized selling in all cities to be visited on a national tour? The same court that had given Billy Joel an injunction denied The Who a TRO that would apply nationally. Brockum International v. Various John Does, 551 F.Supp. 1054 (E.D.Wis.1982). Is this just a matter of the court's taste in music? SKS Merch, LLC v. Barry, 233 F.Supp.2d 841 (E.D.Ky.2002) (country music singer Toby Keith granted permanent injunction within the district and a preliminary injunction nationwide effective against any persons served); Shae Yatta Harvey, *National, Multi-District Preliminary Tour Injunctions: Why The Hesitation?,* 40 IDEA: J.L. & Tech. 195 (2000). Courts are also concerned that concert promoters manufacture emergencies for a TRO by waiting until a week before the concert date to seek relief, to try and get around the problem of unknown defendants. Bravado Int'l Group Merchand. Servs. Inc. v. Smith, 2012 WL 1155858 (M.D.Fla. 2012) (denying TRO for Red Hot Chili Peppers concert).

AMERICAN HOSPITAL SUPPLY CORP. V. HOSPITAL PRODUCTS LTD.

United States Court of Appeals, Seventh Circuit
780 F.2d 589 (7th Cir. 1986)

POSNER, CIRCUIT JUDGE.

* * * A district judge asked to decide whether to grant or deny a preliminary injunction must choose the course of action that will minimize the costs of being mistaken. Because he is forced to act on an incomplete record, the danger of a mistake is substantial. And a mistake can be costly. If the judge grants the preliminary injunction to a plaintiff who it later turns out is not entitled to any judicial relief—whose legal rights have not been violated—the judge commits a mistake whose gravity is measured by the irreparable harm, if any, that the injunction causes to the defendant while it is in effect. If the judge denies the preliminary injunction to a plaintiff who it later turns out is entitled to judicial relief, the judge commits a mistake whose gravity is measured by the irreparable harm, if any, that the denial of the preliminary injunction does to the plaintiff.

These mistakes can be compared, and the one likely to be less costly can be selected, with the help of a simple formula: grant the preliminary injunction if but only if $P \times Hp > (1-P) \times Hd$, or, in words, only if the harm to the plaintiff if the injunction is denied, multiplied by the probability that the denial would be an error (that the plaintiff, in other words, will win at trial), exceeds the harm to the defendant if the injunction is granted, multiplied by the probability that granting the injunction would be an error. That probability is simply one minus the probability that the plaintiff will win at trial; for if the plaintiff has, say, a 40 percent chance of winning, the defendant must have a 60 percent chance of winning (1.00–.40 = .60). The left-hand side of the formula is simply the probability of an erroneous denial weighted by the cost of denial to the plaintiff, and the right-hand side simply the probability of an erroneous grant weighted by the cost of grant to the defendant.

This formula, a procedural counterpart to Judge Learned Hand's famous negligence formula, see United States v. Carroll Towing Co., 159 F.2d 169, 173 (2d Cir.1947), is not offered as a new legal standard; it is intended not to force analysis into a quantitative straitjacket but to assist analysis by presenting succinctly the factors that the court must consider in making its decision and by articulating the relationship among the factors. It is actually just a distillation of the familiar four (sometimes five) factor test that courts use in deciding whether to grant a preliminary injunction. The court asks whether the plaintiff will be irreparably harmed if the preliminary injunction is denied (sometimes also whether the plaintiff has an adequate remedy at law), whether the harm to the plaintiff if the preliminary injunction is denied will exceed the harm to the defendant if it is granted, whether the plaintiff is reasonably likely to prevail at trial, and whether the public interest will be affected by granting or denying the injunction (i.e., whether third parties will be harmed—and these harms can then be added to Hp or Hd as the case may be). The court undertakes these inquiries to help it figure out whether granting the injunction would be the error-minimizing course of action, which depends on the probability that the plaintiff is in the right and on the costs to the plaintiff, the defendant, or others of granting or denying the injunction. All this is explained at length in Roland Machinery Co. v. Dresser Industries, Inc., 749 F.2d 380, 382–88 (7th Cir.1984), where a panel of this court applied the verbal counterpart to our algebraic formula, as did a different panel in Maxim's Ltd. v. Badonsky, 772 F.2d 388, 391 (7th Cir.1985). *See also* Leubsdorf, The Standard for Preliminary Injunctions, 91 Harv.L.Rev. 525 (1978). The formula is new; the analysis it capsulizes is standard. * * *

SWYGERT, SENIOR CIRCUIT JUDGE, dissenting.

The court today continues what it began in Roland Machinery v. Dresser Industries, 749 F.2d 380 (7th Cir.1984): a wholesale revision of the law of preliminary injunctions. * * *

I would have preferred to avoid commenting on the majority's attempt to reduce the well-developed and complex law of preliminary injunctions to a "simple" mathematical formula. But because of the potentially far-reaching and baneful consequences of today's decision, I must regretfully voice my concerns.

Henceforth, the district courts of this circuit should grant a preliminary injunction if, "but only if," $P \times Hp > (1-P) \times Hd$ * * * .

The majority describes its formula as a procedural counterpart to Judge Hand's negligence formula first appearing in United States v. Carroll Towing, 159 F.2d 169, 173 (2d Cir.1947). *Carroll Towing* was an admiralty case in which a shipowner's duty to provide against injuries resulting from the breaking of a vessel's moorings was expressed in algebraic terms. In Hand's formula the liability of the shipowner depends on whether $B < PL$, where P is the probability that the ship will break away; where L is the gravity of the resulting injury if she does; and where B is the burden of adequate precautions. Various attempts have been made to apply the Hand formula, or some derivation of it, to areas other than negligence. * * * Most courts, however, have continued to view the *Carroll Towing* opinion as a negligence formula. * * * My quarrel, however, is not with *Carroll Towing* but rather with the majority's attempt today to create its equitable analogue. A quantitative approach may be an appropriate and useful heuristic device in determining negligence in tort cases, but it has limited value in determining whether a preliminary injunction should issue. Proceedings in equity and cases sounding in tort demand entirely different responses of a district judge. The judgment of the district judge in a tort case must be definite; the judgment of the district judge in an injunction proceeding cannot, by its very nature, be as definite. The judgment of a district judge in an injunction proceeding must be flexible and discretionary—within the bounds of the now settled four-prong test.

I question the necessity and the wisdom of the court's adoption of a mathematical formula as the governing law of preliminary injunctions. The majority claims that its formula is merely a distillation of the traditional four-prong test. But if nothing is added to the substantive law, why bother? The standard four-prong test for determining whether a preliminary injunction should issue has survived for so many years because it has proven to be a workable summation of the myriad factors a district court must consider in deciding whether to grant an injunction. The test * * * may not exhibit the "precision" the majority seems to demand, but such "precision" is antithetical to the underlying principles of injunctive relief. Equity, as the majority concedes, involves the assessment of factors that cannot be quantified. A district court faced with the task of deciding whether to issue a preliminary injunction must to some extent, the majority concedes, rely on the "feel" of the case. The majority's formula will not assist the district courts in their assessment of this aspect of the decision to grant a preliminary injunction. The traditional element of discretion residing in the decision of a trial court to grant a preliminary injunction has been all but eliminated by today's decision.

Ironically, the majority never attempts to assign a numerical value to the variables of its own formula. We are never told how to measure P or Hp or Hd. I believe, and the majority appears to concede, that a numerical value could never be assigned to these variables. Who can say, for instance, what *exactly* the probability is that the granting of the injunction was an error? How then will the majority's formula ease in a meaningful way the responsibilities of the district courts? Judges asked to issue a preliminary injunction must, in large part, rely on their own judgment, not on mathematical quanta.

We must, of course, be mindful not to vest too much imprecision in the preliminary injunction standard, for law implies a system of known and generally applicable rules. The existing four-prong test, however, represents the historical balance struck by the courts between the rigidity of law and the flexibility of equity. * * *

NOTES

1.   Does Judge Posner's approach change the traditional test as applied in *Winter*? If so, is the formula an improvement? If not, is it useful nevertheless? *Compare, e.g.,* Douglas Lichtman, *Uncertainty and the Standard for Preliminary Relief*, 70 U.Chi.L.Rev. 197 (2003) (exploring the implications of the fact that the court will be just as uncertain about its estimates of the harms inflicted by a wrongfully-issued preliminary injunction as it is about its prediction as to the outcome of the case) and Linda J. Silberman, *Injunctions by the Numbers: Less Than the Sum of Its Parts*, 63 Chi-Kent L.Rev. 279, 282

(1987) (the formula "does not clarify the standard and emerges as a disguised effort to extend the heavy hand of appellate review") with Linz Audain, *Of Posner, and Newton, and Twenty-First Century Law: An Economic and Statistical Analysis of the Posner Rule for Granting Preliminary Injunctions*, 23 Loy.L.A.L.Rev. 1215, 1218 (1990) (comparing Judge Posner's insight favorably with Sir Isaac Newton's scientific contributions). Citations to other commentators on the *American Hospital* formula are collected in Robert J.C. Deane, *Varying the Plaintiff's Burden: An Efficient Approach to Interlocutory Injunctions to Preserve Future Money Judgements*, 49 U. Toronto L.J. 1, 22 (1999). Judge Posner has discussed the formula a bit more in Richard A. Posner, *Economic Analysis of Law* § 22.3 at 776–78 (9th ed.2014).

2.   There may be less to the formula than meets the eye. In another Seventh Circuit case decided soon after *American Hospital,* Judge Eschbach (who was not a member of that panel) wrote:

> *American Hospital* does not set forth a new standard for granting preliminary injunctions. * * *

> As a distillation, the formula admirably reflects the balancing of irreparable harms inherent in the traditional test. However, a formula, of necessity cannot incorporate all of the elements of the traditional test. We note, therefore, that before the district court balances the irreparable harms suffered by the parties, the plaintiff still must establish the other prerequisites to the issuance of a preliminary injunction—namely, that the plaintiff has no adequate remedy at law; that it has a reasonable likelihood of prevailing on the merits; and that an injunction would not harm the public interest.

Brunswick Corp. v. Jones, 784 F.2d 271, 274 n. 1 (7th Cir.1986). With this "clarification," is the test in the Seventh Circuit any different from the traditional test? However, one commentator believes that *the American Hospital* test has emerged as the "triumphant, dominant theory of preliminary injunctions" because courts now overwhelmingly believe that it is proper to employ a sliding scale in which a stronger showing of irreparable harm can compensate for a smaller likelihood of success on the merits. Thomas R. Lee, *Preliminary Injunctions and the Status Quo*, 58 Wash. & Lee L.Rev. 110, 154 (2001). *See, e.g.,* Scotts Co. v. United Industries Corp., 315 F.3d 264 (4th Cir.2002) (quoting and applying *American Hospital*).

Judge Posner and Judge Easterbrook have disagreed over the application of the sliding scale test in the context of a request for an injunction pending appeal. In Cavel International, Inc. v. Madigan, 500 F.3d 544 (7th Cir.2007), Judge Posner stayed enforcement of an Illinois statute making it unlawful for any person to slaughter a horse for human consumption (a delicacy in Europe). He found that the strong showing of irreparable harm (enforcement of the statute would have completely shut down Cavel International) compensated for the limited chance of success on the merits. Judge Easterbrook disagreed, believing that the sliding scale test of preliminary injunctions did not apply to a stay or injunction pending appeal, because a higher standard was required after the movant has lost at the trial level. He would have denied the injunction because of the absence of a strong showing of potential success on the merits. The same panel subsequently upheld the validity of the statute. 500 F.3d 551 (7th Cir.2007), *cert. denied,* 554 U.S. 902(2008).

3.   In developing the formula in *American Hospital,* the court was influenced strongly by a law review article, John Leubsdorf, *The Standard for Preliminary Injunctions,* 91 Harv.L.Rev. 525 (1978. Scholars agree with the need for a court to account for the probability of error in making the preliminary injunction decision. *See* Joshua P. Davis, *Taking Uncertainty Seriously: Revising Injunction Doctrine,* 34 Rutgers L.J. 363, 369 (2003) (arguing to consider adjudicative error in both preliminary and final injunction decisions). Professor Leubsdorf defends the traditional approach of accounting for this within the evaluation of the merits and the irreparability of plaintiff's claim. Others criticize the conventional approach and suggest alternative approaches, though not that offered by Judge Posner in *American Hospital. See* Richard R.W. Brooks & Warren F. Schwartz, *Legal Uncertainty, Economic Efficiency, and the Preliminary Injunction Doctrine,* 58 Stan.L.Rev. 381 (2005) (proposing to grant preliminary injunctions to all plaintiffs who post a bond covering the defendant's potential damages from the injunction in order to reallocate the economic incentives by giving the plaintiff leverage to counter the defendant's likely refusal to perform where legal rights are uncertain); Douglas Lichtman, *Irreparable Benefits,* 116 Yale. L.J. 1284 (2007) (highlighting the inability of the conventional approach to account for irreparable benefits gained by the temporary winner from the erroneous grant or denial of a preliminary injunction).

PROBLEM

How would the following case come out under *American Hospital?* What if a court was asked to prevent the Earth from being sucked into a black hole? Certain individuals brought suit under the National Environmental Policy Act to enjoin the operation of the Large Hadron Collider, a new 17-mile long subatomic particle accelerator located underground near Geneva, Switzerland, until the Collider was proven "reasonably safe." The Collider, the most expensive scientific instrument and the most powerful subatomic particle smasher ever built, was developed in hopes of resolving some fundamental questions about the universe. The plaintiffs' fear, supported by some scientists, was that the Collider might implode, creating mini-black holes, which could eventually swallow and destroy the Earth. The defendants, the consortium of international scientific organizations involved in the project, claimed that the plaintiffs had little to no chance of succeeding on their legal claims under either U.S. or European Union law. Sancho v. U.S. Department of Energy, 578 F.Supp.2d 1258 (D. Hawaii 2008).

B. FORMULATING AND MONITORING THE INJUNCTION

1. DRAFTING THE INJUNCTION

PORTLAND FEMINIST WOMEN'S HEALTH CENTER v. ADVOCATES FOR LIFE, INC.

United States Court of Appeals
859 F.2d 681 (9th Cir. 1988)

HUG, CIRCUIT JUDGE.

* * *

FACTS

* * * The clinic brought an action against [Advocates for Life, Inc and certain individuals] that was based on several spirited demonstrations in front of the clinic's building. * * * The clinic moved for a preliminary injunction, and the motion was brought before a magistrate for an evidentiary hearing.

The magistrate recommended to the district court that a preliminary injunction be issued based on his findings of fact. * * *

The district court adopted the findings in their entirety and issued the following injunction:

IT IS HEREBY ORDERED that defendants, their agents, servants, employees, and all persons, groups, and organizations acting in concert with one or more of the defendants are enjoined from committing any of the following acts:

1.   obstructing the free and direct passage of any person in or out of the Portland Feminist Women's Health Center (the Center);

2.   demonstrating or distributing literature on the Foster Road sidewalk in front of the Center in a rectangular zone that extends from the Center's front door to the curb and twelve and one-half feet on either side of a line from the middle of the Center's door to the curb;

3.   shouting, screaming, chanting, or yelling during on-site demonstrations;

4.   producing noise by any other means which substantially interferes with the provision of medical services within the Center, including counseling;

5.   trespassing on Center property;

6. damaging the property of the Center, its employees or clients; and

7. interfering with the Center's receipt of public utility services.

This Order shall remain in effect until further order of the court.

After the injunction was issued, the demonstrations continued, and at a hearing the district court found several of the individual advocates in contempt. We are asked to determine the validity of both the injunction and the contempt citations.

ANALYSIS

* * * Appellants do not seriously challenge the magistrate's findings of fact or his determination under the preliminary injunction standard. He explicitly found that the defendants engaged in the offending conduct. We proceed in our analysis on the basis that the findings of fact are not clearly erroneous, and the preliminary injunction standard was satisfied.

Appellants challenge the injunction's content with arguments asserting impermissible vagueness for failure to set forth an objective decibel level for prohibited shouting, yelling, chanting, and noise making. They argue that this purported vagueness has a chilling effect on protected activities and places demonstrators at the mercy of the appellees' subjective standards. Because we are dealing with an injunction, the vagueness issue is controlled by Fed.R.Civ.P. 65(d).

Rule 65(d) requires that injunctions "shall be specific in terms; [and] shall describe in reasonable detail . . . the act or acts sought to be restrained." The Supreme Court has indicated that the policy behind the rule is "to prevent uncertainty and confusion on the part of those faced with injunctive orders, and to avoid the possible founding of a contempt citation on a decree too vague to be understood." Schmidt v. Lessard, 414 U.S. 473, 476 (1974). We have interpreted the rule and its policy to require that "the language of injunctions . . . be reasonably clear so that ordinary persons will know precisely what action is proscribed." While ambiguities in an injunction are construed in favor of the enjoined party, nonetheless "[i]njunctions are not set aside under Rule 65(d) . . . unless they are so vague that they have no reasonably specific meaning."

We do not find the injunction here in dispute impermissibly vague under the applicable standards. The language that the advocates attack enjoins "shouting, screaming, chanting, or yelling during on-site demonstrations; [and] . . . [p]roducing noise by any other means which substantially interferes with the provision of medical services within the Center, including counseling. . . ." They argue that without a specific decibel level or other objective standard they cannot know whether their conduct violates the injunction. They argue further that without such a standard, the imposition of contempt sanctions under the injunction will be based on the biased and subjective interpretation of the clinic. While an enumerated decibel level certainly would provide a more specific definition of the enjoined conduct than the injunction now provides, we do not believe that such specificity is required. The terms of the injunction place the enjoined parties on fair notice of the actions that are prohibited in language that is reasonably understandable. Greater particularity, while it may be desirable, is not required under Rule 65(d). * * *

The advocates' strongest challenge to the preliminary injunction is against the third and fourth paragraphs, which prohibit shouting, screaming, chanting, yelling, and producing noise. Whether these provisions are tailored narrowly enough is a close question. The district court found that chanting, shouting, and screaming during demonstrations were audible on the second floor, where medical procedures are performed. Chanting, shouting, screaming, or yelling may be an expressive, albeit unpleasant, form of behavior. If it causes no disruption of clinic operations, such expression would not materially affect the interest at stake here. On the other hand, if the conduct rises to a volume that obstructs the provision of services in the Center, it may be enjoined. Accordingly, we modify the injunction by combining its paragraphs numbered 3 and 4 in the following fashion:

> 3.   shouting, screaming, chanting, yelling, or producing noise by any other means, in a volume that substantially interferes with the provision of medical services within the Center, including counseling; . . . .

The remainder of the preliminary injunction is not contested. We see no problem with the prohibition against trespassing, damaging property, and interfering with utility services. * * *

Appellants also challenge the injunction as constitutionally void for vagueness. However, that doctrine does not affect our decision. The vagueness doctrine is based on due process principles that require fair notice and warning. It also incorporates a requirement that specificity be sufficient to avoid arbitrary and discriminatory enforcement. The doctrine's goal is to avoid "allow[ing] policemen, prosecutors, and juries to pursue their personal predilection," by requiring legislators to promulgate specific standards in criminal statutes. These concerns arise in a different context here, where enforcement lies entirely in judicial hands. So viewed, the injunction is not unconstitutionally vague, for reasons we have already set forth. * * *

NOTES

1.   One of the other important ways in which Rule 65 protects enjoined parties is the requirement that the order "describe in reasonable detail—and

not by referring to the complaint or other document—the act or acts restrained or required." F.R.Civ.P. 65(d)(1)(C). Usually the court can accommodate this requirement without difficulty. However, the requirement can pose some problems and is sometimes overlooked. For example, Dupuy v. Samuels, 465 F.3d 757 (7th Cir.2006), chastised the parties and lower court for failing to enforce the commands of Rule 65(d). The plaintiff parents sought review of a preliminary injunction requiring the state department of children's services to provide informal administrative review of "safety plans" when children were taken into temporary custody; the parents contended that the injunction provided too little relief. Writing for the court, Judge Posner objected to enforcing an injunction that improperly referenced other documents:

> The injunction of which the plaintiffs complain violates Rule 65(d) of the civil rules (though that is not the plaintiffs' complaint about it), which requires that an injunction be a self-contained document rather than incorporate by reference materials in other documents. The purpose is to minimize disputes over what has been enjoined. * * * . The Ninth Circuit allows incorporation by reference if the material thus incorporated is physically attached, as by stapling, to the injunction order. There is no reason to complicate the administration of the rule by such an interpretation. There are times when literal interpretation is best; this is one of them. The Ninth Circuit's approach would encourage just the kind of mistake that the rule aims to prevent—the thoughtless attachment of separately composed documents when if the judge had integrated their contents into the injunction order he might have realized that they would not cohere with the rest of the order without changes.

> Rule 65(d) is simple, clear, sensible, easily complied with, and not even new; we are distressed by the failure of the parties and the district judge to have complied with it in this case—a case that underscores the good sense of the rule.

Nevertheless, the court went on to affirm the injunction because the defendants had failed to challenge it on cross-appeal. *Id.* at 763.

2.   In the run-of-the-mill case, where the requested relief is fairly apparent, the plaintiff drafts a proposed order and the defendant gets to approve it as to form before the trial court signs it. In many courts, the plaintiff is required to submit a proposed order with the moving papers. *E.g.,* McKinney's New York Rules of Court, Rules of the United States District Court for the Northern District of New York, General Rule 10(d). This simple procedure forces the plaintiff to draft an order that is fairly specific (and therefore enforceable) and is not overreaching in scope. *See, e.g., Developments in the Law—Injunctions*, 78 Harv.L.Rev. 994, 1064 (1967) ("Specificity has long been the hallmark of a well-drafted injunctive decree."). If the proposed order would impose broader relief than the plaintiff is entitled to on the basis of the moving papers, the defendant can object before it is signed and entered by the court.

3.   There are cases, however, where the task of drafting the injunction is not so simple and the appropriate scope of injunctive relief is not so clear cut. In those cases, who gets to decide exactly what burdens the decree will impose on the defendants? For one answer, see *Special Project—The Remedial Process in Institutional Reform Litigation*, 78 Colum.L.Rev. 784 (1978). That Special Project concludes:

> The court supervising an institutional reform case must organize remedy formulation to attain two primary goals. The formulation process must produce a viable plan, and the plan must be chosen and implemented as rapidly as possible. Speedy production of an adequate and viable plan is most likely when the court maximizes the parties' participation in devising the remedy. Of course, the greater the parties' participation, the larger the amount of factual and interpretive information the court obtains from them.
>
> Although increasing party participation might be thought to slow the remedy formulation process, it frequently has the opposite effect. By provoking simultaneously the efforts of several participants a court protects itself against the failure of any one participant to produce an adequate remedy, and may goad one or more of the others to an at least minimally acceptable effort. Indeed, delay may be avoided by simultaneous, rather than sequential, adoption of a variety of formulation techniques.
>
> The infinite variety of factual circumstances in which federal district courts take responsibility for fashioning institutional relief precludes the academic prescription of any one technique of remedy formulation, or even a comparative evaluation of the alternatives. Different situations will, of course, require different approaches. Observation suggests, however, that there are two important procedural steps courts should consider when formulating remedies. One is to involve all the parties in remedy development. The other is to obtain by the appointment of a special master a neutral source of expert information and a knowledgeable delegate who will push for a prompt and adequate remedial decree.

78 Colum. L. Rev. at 812–13.

The Columbia Special Project strongly advocated the use of a special master to aid the court in the formulation of an injunction (or decree) in complex cases. Special masters have undertaken the task in many cases, and have taken on many different roles. For a review of the roles played by masters in several different school desegregation cases, see, e.g., David L. Kirp & Gary Babcock, *Judge and Company: Court–Appointed Masters, School Desegregation, and Institutional Reform*, 32 Ala.L.Rev. 313 (1981). Rule 53 was revised in 2003, in part to recognize expressly and regulate such appointments. *See* Advisory Committee Notes to F.R.Civ.P. 53, 215 F.R.D. 158, 197–200 (2003). The court has to be careful, however, not to abdicate too much authority to an appointed special master. For example, in the Microsoft antitrust case, the Court of Appeals reversed the nonconsensual appointment of a special master where "the parties' rights must be determined, not merely enforced." United States v. Microsoft Corp., 147 F.3d 935, 954 (D.C.Cir.1998).

4.   Should nonparties and members of the public have an opportunity to comment on proposed decrees that may affect them? *See, e.g.,* Tunney Act, 15 U.S.C. § 16(b)(1981); and Consent Judgments in Actions to Enjoin Discharges of Pollutants, 28 C.F.R. § 50.7(b) (requiring, respectively, time for public comment on antitrust and pollution discharge consent decrees). *Cf.* F.R.Civ.P. 23(e) (class action may not be dismissed or compromised without prior notification of the class members and court approval).

5.   How active a role may the judge play? In United States v. Microsoft Corp., 56 F.3d 1448 (D.C.Cir.1995), the court of appeals found that the district court had exceeded its authority under the Tunney Act in refusing to enter a proposed antitrust consent decree the Department of Justice had negotiated with the computer software behemoth. The district court concluded that the decree was not in the public interest because the decree did not address certain anticompetitive practices beyond those violations alleged in the original complaint. (The judge happened to have read a book putting Microsoft's practices in a very unfavorable light.) The court of appeals saw the district court as usurping the role of the Attorney General rather than reviewing the decree itself. The appellate court even took the rare step of ordering the case remanded to a different judge, who then approved the settlement. 1995–2 Trade Cases ¶ 71,096 (D.D.C.1995). *See* Symposium, *Pyrrhic Victories? Reexamining the Effectiveness of Antitrust Remedies in Restoring Competition and Deterring Misconduct*, 69 Geo.Wash.L.Rev. 693 (2001); Lloyd C. Anderson, *United States v. Microsoft, Antitrust Consent Decrees, and the Need for a Proper Scope of Judicial Review*, 65 Antitrust L.J. 1 (1996).

2.   IMPLEMENTING THE INJUNCTION

With the average "plain vanilla" injunction, it is the plaintiff's responsibility to monitor the defendant's compliance with the terms of the injunction. If the plaintiff detects a violation, she should file for an Order to Show Cause with the court—an order directing the defendant to show cause why he should not be held in contempt of court for violating the injunction. In most cases, this monitoring system works reasonably well. It does not work so well whenever it is difficult to determine whether the defendant—be it a public entity or private corporation—is in compliance with the injunction. Other than relying entirely upon the defendant's good faith, the court needs some mechanism to help it determine whether its orders are being obeyed.

It is usually impractical for the injunction to describe precisely all that must happen to cure the violation. All of the activities of a major government department or enterprise cannot be described in any one document. Moreover, the method of administering the injunction cannot simply funnel all the conceivably relevant bits of information to the court nor should it be permitted to consume overwhelming amounts of time of the parties and counsel. If it does, the substantive progress that the court intends to achieve through the injunction will be thwarted. However, the injunction must be clear enough so that it is evident when the defendants violate its terms. Thus, the court must simultaneously avoid the twin evils of issuing an injunction that is so open ended that it is nothing more than aspirational platitudes on the one hand and so detailed as to tie everyone up in nothing but counterproductive paper work on the other. *See* Michael G. Starr, *Accommodation and Accountability: A Strategy for Judicial Enforcement of Institutional Reform Decrees*, 32 Ala.L.Rev. 399 (1981); James A. Henderson, Jr. & Richard A. Pearson, *Implementing Federal Environmental Policies: The Limits of Aspirational Commands*, 78 Colum.L.Rev. 1429, 143–36 (1978).

SPECIAL PROJECT—THE REMEDIAL PROCESS IN INSTITUTIONAL REFORM LITIGATION
78 Colum.L.Rev. 784, 821–836 (1978)

Implementation of the decree involves more than judicial retention of jurisdiction and the revision of the substantive aspects of the decree that retention of jurisdiction makes possible. Additionally, there remain problems of resolving disputes, monitoring compliance, and supervising the defendant's actions. The court's response to these problems requires the choice, and sometimes the modification, of a technique of administration. Retention of jurisdiction acknowledges the necessity for judicial involvement during implementation of the remedy but does not in itself constitute a choice of administrative technique.

A wide variety of techniques are available. Traditionally, administration is party oriented, depending on adversarial interplay. However, some judges supplement this by court oriented administration, in which the court acts on its own initiative. A court acting in this latter mode may delegate to court-appointed officers some or most of the necessary functions of administration. The available techniques of judicial administration fall along a continuum between party oriented and court oriented views of implementation. * * *

1. *Party-Centered Administration.* When courts rely on the parties, implementation occurs in the traditional adversarial mode. The court assumes a passive role, playing no part in implementation unless solicited by one of the parties. This judicial passivity places a considerable burden on the plaintiff, particularly when relief is gradual or implementation is drawn out. Overseeing implementation requires a cohesive plaintiff with considerable resources, and courts sometimes act to strengthen a weak plaintiff. As a variant of this practice, with a similar effect, courts sometimes request the participation of the United States as amicus curiae.

The common requirement that the defendant submit compliance reports eases the plaintiff's burden only slightly. Since defendants are unlikely to report noncompliance frankly, the plaintiff's monitoring task remains both crucial and burdensome.

* * *

2. *Administrative Techniques with Reduced Reliance on Parties.*

* * *

a. *Direct Judicial Initiative as an Administrative Technique.* When courts give themselves a supervisory role, in which they will act without further stimulus by the parties, they have taken a step beyond their traditional passivity. On their own initiative, courts frequently set hearing dates to consider compliance reports and take any necessary action. In addition, a vigorous judge may resort to various informal methods to further implementation.

Yet such court-ordered hearings, once begun, will remain adversarial in nature, with the customary reliance on the parties, and active judicial involvement in remedy administration will be constrained by the limited expertise and time of federal judges. Direct judicial initiative can only provide a limited supplement to party-centered administration. When the latter proves inadequate, the court must often not merely assume a more active role in implementation but also delegate administrative functions to an individual or group whose duties are primarily to the court, rather than to the parties.

b. *Use of Court Appointed Agents to Administer the Remedy.* These court appointed agents are identified by a confusing plethora of titles.

* * *

In this discussion, the terms used by the courts will be replaced by terms based on the officer's principal function. The terms that will be used are master, monitor, mediator, administrator, and receiver. This function-based vocabulary provides a consistent basis for discussing the various court-appointed agents.

Masters. The master's role is to gather information and make recommendations. He reports to the court and, if required, makes findings of facts and conclusions of law. In the remedial phase of litigation, the master's principal role is to assist the court in formulating the substantive remedy, rather than in implementing it. However, masters sometimes continue to participate in the litigation, assuming implementation functions without change of title. Furthermore, because the remedy formulation and implementation phases of the lawsuit are often simultaneous, an administrator with extensive supervisory power over the defendant's activities may at the same time act as a master and be charged with developing a further plan.

Monitors. The monitor's role is to report on the defendant's compliance with the decree and on the achievement of the decree's goals. * * *

Monitors are appropriate if the remedy is complex, if compliance is difficult to measure, or if observation of the defendant's conduct is restricted. If the remedy is complex or covers many institutions, measuring compliance may be a task beyond the plaintiff's resources. If standards of compliance are not evident from the decree, a monitor can help formulate them. When the defendant is a closed institution, such as a prison or mental hospital, observing compliance may be difficult, and then monitors will be appropriate. * * *

Mediators. While the monitor's task is only to measure compliance, other court appointees play a more direct role in implementation. A mediator is a delegate whose primary responsibility is handling disputes over the decree's meaning, compliance standards, and the pace of compliance. In addition, a mediator must resolve individual grievances that arise during the remedial regime. Although retention of jurisdiction facilitates bringing such problems into court, doing so is time consuming, expensive, and strains judicial resources, even if the judicial role is informal and the procedural safeguards of a full dress evidentiary hearing are not invoked. * * *

Administrators. The administrator is the most innovative and unusual of the devices utilized by the courts for remedy implementation. The administrator's role extends beyond that of the master, monitor, or mediator but, unlike a receiver, the administrator supplements, and does not replace, the normal management of the institutional defendant. The administrator acts at his own instance to implement the remedy and has an executive role.

The authority to appoint an administrator is best grounded in the inherent power of courts "to provide themselves with appropriate instruments required for the performance of their duties" and the Supreme Court's directive that the courts make full use of their equitable powers in civil rights cases. * * *

Appointment of an administrator is most appropriate if implementation is complex and difficult to supervise. In title VII pattern and practice suits, for instance, compliance requires nondiscriminatory handling of hundreds or thousands of individual cases, a task that no judge can supervise. The complex actions required to implement comprehensive prison and mental hospital decrees are also appropriate occasions for the appointment of an administrator. An administrator may also be called for as a reaction to noncompliance with the court's orders.

The reluctance of the courts to use administrators in areas where they would be effective is probably due to considerations of equity and federalism, as the appointment of an administrator is an intrusive technique of remedy implementation. * * *

An administrator's powers normally include monitoring and mediation, but are more extensive. The variety of its functions is often obscured by the variety in terminology used, the variety of tasks a single agency sometimes performs, and the casualness with which the reported opinions describe these tasks. However, the administrator normally is given powers to supervise, coordinate, approve, or even command actions of the defendant to implement the remedy. This involves a substantial delegation of power, either with consent of the parties or imposed by the court.

The scope of this delegation varies. Some administrators are given very specific tasks, while others are granted broad and undefined power to secure implementation. * * *

Receivers. While an administrator's power derogates from the authority of the defendant's officers, these officers retain their posts. Administrators, like masters, monitors, and mediators, can only be effective if some cooperation is forthcoming from the defendant. When this is not forthcoming, a receivership may be appropriate. In a receivership, a court-appointed officer replaces the defendant's officers either completely or temporarily and for limited purposes. Imposition of a receivership is consequently a more drastic means of implementation than the appointment of an administrator or any lesser administrative agent. It is the most dramatic assertion of federal equitable power possible and courts have so regarded it. Obviously, removing state political officials from authority is more drastic than merely forcing them to act constitutionally. Receivership remains a device of last resort, used only when less intrusive devices have failed to achieve compliance, although the traditional strict restrictions on its use have been shed.

* * *

NOTES

1. For a time, there was some doubt whether courts had the authority to appoint agents to oversee the implementation of judicial injunctions. *See* David I. Levine, *The Authority for the Appointment of Remedial Special Masters in Federal Institutional Reform Litigation: The History Reconsidered*, 17 U.C.Davis L.Rev. 753 (1984); Vincent M. Nathan, *The Use of Masters in Institutional Reform Litigation*, 10 U.Tol.L.Rev. 419 (1979) (for different reasons, both articles contended that despite the doubts expressed about the then-fairly narrow language of Fed.R.Civ.P. 53, there was sufficient authority to make such appointments). In 2003, Fed.R.Civ.P. 53 was revised to expressly authorize judicial appointment of special masters to handle post-trial matters. *See* Fed.R.Civ.P. 53(a)(1)(C) Advisory Committee Notes to Fed.R.Civ.P. 53, 215 F.R.D. 158, 197–200 (2003). As an alternative approach to the use of *ad hoc*

agents, Joanna Kudisch Weinberg, *The Judicial Adjunct and Public Law Remedies*, 1 Yale L. & Pol'y Rev. 367 (1983), suggests that courts set up permanent offices of judicial adjuncts to handle such assignments. *See also* T. Willging et al., Special Masters' Incidence and Activity (Federal Judicial Center 2000).

2.   For a discussion of the payment of special masters and other court appointed agents, see David I. Levine, *Calculating Fees of Special Masters*, 37 Hastings L.J. 141 (1985). No governmental entity—even the United States—is immune from paying for the cost of a remedial special master, as it is part of the costs of the litigation. *See* Fed.R.Civ.P. 53(g); Commodity Futures Trading Commission v. Frankwell Bullion Ltd., 99 F.3d 299 (9th Cir.1996) (costs of master or receiver may be assessed against United States).

3.   As the Special Project mentions, another equitable tool, *receivership*, is available if the conditions precedent are established. Most commonly, a court will appoint a receiver to manage the defendant's property (such as a business in economic distress) on a temporary basis only if there is a danger that the defendant is or will become insolvent or the property at issue will be removed from the jurisdiction of the court, injured or destroyed before the merits of the dispute are decided. Fed.R.Civ.P. 66; 12 Charles Alan Wright, Arthur R. Miller & Richard L. Marcus, *Federal Practice and Procedure*: Civil §§ 2981–86 (2d ed. 1997). Sometimes, courts have used receivers to enforce compliance with the law. *E.g.,* United States v. American Tobacco Co., 221 U.S. 106 (1911) (indicating that receiver might take charge of a company to enforce compliance with antitrust laws); United States v. Sasso, 215 F.3d 283 (2d Cir.2000) (noting use of monitors and trustees to eliminate corruption in labor unions).*See generally* Carolyn Hoecker Luedtke, *Innovation or Illegitmacy: Remedial Receivership in Tinsley v. Kemp Public Housing Litigation*, 65 Mo.L.Rev. 655 (2000); Comment, *The Case for Imposing Equitable Receiverships Upon Recalcitrant Polluters*, 12 U.C.L.A.J. Envt'l L. & Pol'y 207 (1993) (reviewing traditional and modern uses of receivers).

FLOYD V. CITY OF NEW YORK

United States District Court
959 F.Supp.2d 668 (S.D.N.Y. 2013)

SHIRA A. SCHEINDLIN, DISTRICT JUDGE.

I.   INTRODUCTION

In an Opinion issued today I found the City of New York liable in the *Floyd* case for violating the Fourth and Fourteenth Amendment rights of the plaintiff class because of the way the New York City Police Department ("NYPD") has conducted stops and frisks over the past decade (the "Liability Opinion"). * * *

The purpose of this Opinion (the "Remedies Opinion") is to determine what remedies are appropriate in these cases. [The Liability Opinion] requires that the NYPD reform practices and policies related to stop and frisk to conform with the requirements of the United States Constitution. I stress, at the outset, that the remedies imposed in this Opinion are as narrow and targeted as possible. To be very clear: I am *not* ordering an end to the practice of stop and frisk. The purpose of the remedies addressed in this Opinion is to ensure that the practice is carried out in a manner that protects the rights and liberties of all New Yorkers, while still providing much needed police protection.

II. REMEDIES IN FLOYD

A. *The Court Has the Power to Order Broad Equitable Relief*

1. *Plaintiffs Satisfied the Requirements for a Permanent Injunction*

* * * The evidence discussed in the Liability Opinion shows that plaintiffs have suffered violations of their Fourth and Fourteenth Amendment rights, and that the prevalence of the practices leading to those violations creates a likelihood of future injury. Thus, plaintiffs have satisfied the first two requirements for obtaining permanent injunctive relief.

[T]he burden on the plaintiff class of continued unconstitutional stops and frisks far outweighs the administrative hardships that the NYPD will face in correcting its unconstitutional practices. * * *

Ensuring that people are not seized and searched by the police on the streets of New York City without a legal basis is an important interest meriting judicial protection.

Eliminating the threat that blacks and Hispanics will be targeted for stops and frisks is also an important interest. In addition to the significant intrusion on liberty that results from any stop, increased contact with the police leads to increased opportunities for arrest, even when the reason for the arrest was not the reason for the stop. As a result, targeting racially defined groups for stops—even when there is reasonable suspicion—perpetuates the stubborn racial disparities in our criminal justice system. Although the costs of complying with the permanent injunction in *Floyd* will be significant, they are clearly outweighed by the urgent need to curb the constitutional abuses described in the Liability Opinion. * * *

2. *The Court's Broad Authority to Enter Injunctive Relief*

"[T]he scope of a district court's equitable powers to remedy past wrongs is broad, for breadth and flexibility are inherent in equitable remedies." At the same time, it is " 'the essence of equity jurisdiction' that a court is only empowered 'to grant relief no broader than necessary to cure the effects of the harm caused by the violation.' " "Discretion to frame equitable relief is limited by considerations of federalism, and remedies that intrude unnecessarily on a state's governance of its own affairs should be avoided." * * *

I have always recognized the need for caution in ordering remedies that affect the internal operations of the NYPD, the nation's largest municipal police force and an organization with over 35,000 members. I would have preferred that the City cooperate in a joint undertaking to develop some of the remedies ordered in this Opinion. Instead, the City declined to participate, and argued that "the NYPD systems already in place"—perhaps with unspecified "minor adjustments"—would suffice to address any constitutional wrongs that might be found. I note that the City's refusal to engage in a joint attempt to craft remedies contrasts with the many municipalities that have reached settlement agreements or consent decrees when confronted with evidence of police misconduct.

B.   Equitable Relief

Federal Rule of Civil Procedure 65(d) requires that "[e]very order granting an injunction . . . must: (A) state the reasons why it issued; (B) state its terms specifically; and (C) describe in reasonable detail—and not by referring to the complaint or other document—the act or acts restrained or required." These specificity provisions are " 'no mere technical requirements,' " but were " 'designed to prevent uncertainty and confusion on the part of those faced with injunctive orders, and to avoid the possible founding of a contempt citation on a decree too vague to be understood.' " The specificity provisions also ensure " 'that the appellate court knows precisely what it is reviewing.' " * * *

1.   Appointment of a Monitor to Oversee Reforms

Because of the complexity of the reforms that will be required to bring the NYPD's stop and frisk practices into compliance with the Constitution, it would be impractical for this Court to engage in direct oversight of the reforms. As a more effective and flexible alternative, I am appointing an independent monitor (the "Monitor") to oversee the reform process. I have chosen Peter L. Zimroth to serve as Monitor.

Mr. Zimroth, a partner in the New York office of Arnold & Porter, LLP, is a former Corporation Counsel of the City of New York, and the former Chief Assistant District Attorney of New York County. * * *

It is within the power of a district court to order the appointment of a monitor to oversee judicially ordered reforms. The DOJ recommended the appointment of a monitor in this case, in the event that the Court found the City liable. Based on "decades of police reform efforts across the country," the DOJ concluded that "the appointment of a monitor to guide implementation of . . . injunctive relief may provide substantial assistance to the Court and the parties and can reduce unnecessary delays and litigation over disputes regarding compliance." In addition, the DOJ noted:

[T]he experience of the United States in enforcing police reform injunctions teaches that the appointment of an independent monitor is a critically important asset to the court, the parties, and the community in cases involving patterns or practices of unlawful conduct by law enforcement officials. A court-appointed monitor in this case would help the Court ensure that . . . any pattern or practice . . . is effectively and sustainably remedied.

The appointment of a monitor will serve the interests of all stakeholders, including the City, by facilitating the early and unbiased detection of non-compliance or barriers to compliance. By identifying problems promptly, the Monitor will save the City time and resources.

I also note that the Monitor will have a distinct function from the other oversight entities identified by the City, such as the NYPD's Internal Affairs Bureau, federal prosecutors, the Civilian Complaint Review Board, and "the public electorate." The Monitor will be specifically and narrowly focused on the City's compliance with reforming the NYPD's use of stop and frisk—although this will inevitably touch on issues of training, supervision, monitoring, and discipline. Finally, the Monitor will operate in close coordination with this Court, which retains jurisdiction to issue orders as necessary to remedy the constitutional violations described in the Liability Opinion.

I now specify the Monitor's role and functions:

1.   The Monitor will be subject to the supervision and orders of the Court.

2.   The Monitor will not, and is not intended to, replace or assume the role or duties of any City or NYPD staff or officials, including the Commissioner. The Monitor's duties, responsibilities, and authority will be no broader than necessary to end the constitutional violations in the NYPD's stop and frisk practices described in the Liability Opinion.

3.   The Monitor's initial responsibility will be to develop, based on consultation with the parties, a set of reforms of the NYPD's policies, training, supervision, monitoring, and discipline regarding stop and frisk. These reforms (the "Immediate Reforms") are outlined below * * * . They will be developed as soon as practicable and implemented when they are approved by the Court.

4.   After the completion of the Joint Remedial Process, described below * * * , the Monitor will work with the Facilitator and the parties to develop any further reforms necessary to ending the constitutional violations described in the Liability Opinion. These reforms ("Joint Process Reforms") will be implemented upon approval by the Court.

5.   The Monitor will inform the City of the milestones the City must achieve in order to demonstrate compliance and bring the monitoring process to an end.

6.   The Monitor will regularly conduct compliance and progress reviews to assess the extent to which the NYPD has implemented and complied with the Immediate and Joint Process Reforms.

7.   The Monitor will issue public reports every six months detailing the NYPD's compliance with the Immediate and Joint Process Reforms. The Monitor will also file these reports with the Court.

8.   The Monitor will work with the parties to address any barriers to compliance. To the extent possible, the Monitor should strive to develop a collaborative rather than adversarial relationship with the City.

9.   The Monitor may request the Court to modify the Immediate and Joint Process Reforms, if evidence shows that such modifications are warranted.

10.   The Monitor may request technical assistance from outside experts. He may also employ staff assistance as he finds reasonable and necessary.

11.   The City will be responsible for the reasonable costs and fees of the Monitor, his staff, and any experts he retains.

12.   The Monitor's position will come to an end when the City has achieved compliance with the Immediate and Joint Process Reforms.

2.   *Immediate Reforms Regarding Stop and Frisk*

Ending the constitutional violations inherent in the NYPD's current use of stop and frisk will require reforms to a number of NYPD policies and practices. It would be unwise and impractical for this Court to impose such reforms at this time, prior to input from the Monitor and the participants in the Joint Remedial Process ordered below. Instead, as noted above, the development of reforms will take place in two stages. *First,* the Monitor will develop, in consultation with the parties, an initial set of reforms to the NYPD's policies, training, supervision, monitoring, and discipline regarding stop and frisk (the "Immediate Reforms"). These reforms will be developed and submitted to the Court as soon as practicable, and implemented when they are approved. *Second,* the Facilitator will work with the parties and other stakeholders to develop, through the Joint Remedial Process, a more thorough set of reforms (the "Joint Process Reforms") to supplement, as necessary, the Immediate Reforms. * * *

Based on the liability and remedies evidence presented at trial, the Immediate Reforms must include the following elements: [Revisions to policies and training materials; detailed changes to documentation and record keeping; and changes to officer supervision, monitoring, and discipline.]

3. Body-Worn Cameras

The subject of police officers wearing "body-worn cameras" was inadvertently raised during the testimony of the City's policing expert. * * *

Because body-worn cameras are uniquely suited to addressing the constitutional harms at issue in this case, I am ordering the NYPD to institute a pilot project in which body-worn cameras will be worn for a one-year period by officers on patrol in one precinct per borough—specifically the precinct with the highest number of stops during 2012. The Monitor will establish procedures for the review of stop recordings by supervisors and, as appropriate, more senior managers. The Monitor will also establish procedures for the preservation of stop recordings for use in verifying complaints in a manner that protects the privacy of those stopped. Finally, the Monitor will establish procedures for measuring the effectiveness of body-worn cameras in reducing unconstitutional stops and frisks. At the end of the year, the Monitor will work with the parties to determine whether the benefits of the cameras outweigh their financial, administrative, and other costs, and whether the program should be terminated or expanded. The City will be responsible for the costs of the pilot project.

It would have been preferable for this remedy to have originated with the NYPD, which has been a leader and innovator in the application of technology to policing, as Compstat illustrates. Nevertheless, there is reason to hope that not only civilians but also officers will benefit from the use of cameras.

4. Joint Remedial Process for Developing Supplemental Reforms

A community input component is increasingly common in consent decrees and settlements directed at police reform. * * *

Although the remedies in this Opinion are not issued on consent and do not arise from a settlement, community input is perhaps an even more vital part of a sustainable remedy in this case. The communities most affected by the NYPD's use of stop and frisk have a distinct perspective that is highly relevant to crafting effective reforms. No amount of legal or policing expertise can replace a community's understanding of the likely practical consequences of reforms in terms of both liberty and safety.

It is important that a wide array of stakeholders be offered the opportunity to be heard in the reform process: members of the communities where stops most often take place; representatives of religious, advocacy, and grassroots organizations; NYPD personnel and representatives of police organizations; the District Attorneys' offices; the CCRB; representatives of groups concerned with public schooling, public housing, and other local institutions; local elected officials and community leaders; representatives of the parties, such as the Mayor's office, the NYPD, and the lawyers in this case; and the non-parties that submitted briefs: the

Civil Rights Division of the DOJ, Communities United for Police Reform, and the Black, Latino, and Asian Caucus of the New York City Council.

If the reforms to stop and frisk are not perceived as legitimate by those most affected, the reforms are unlikely to be successful. Neither an independent Monitor, nor a municipal administration, nor this Court can speak for those who have been and will be most affected by the NYPD's use of stop and frisk. * * * It is surely in everyone's interest to prevent another round of protests, litigation, and divisive public conflicts over stop and frisk.

Drawing on this Court's broad equitable powers to remedy the wrongs in this case, I am ordering that all parties participate in a joint remedial process, under the guidance of a Facilitator to be named by the Court. I hereby order the following specific relief:

1.   All parties shall participate in the Joint Remedial Process for a period of six to nine months to develop proposed remedial measures (the "Joint Process Reforms") that will supplement the Immediate Reforms discussed above. The Joint Process Reforms must be no broader than necessary to bring the NYPD's use of stop and frisk into compliance with the Fourth and Fourteenth Amendments.

2.   The Joint Remedial Process will be guided by the Facilitator, with such assistance as the Facilitator deems necessary and in consultation with the Monitor.

3.   The initial responsibility of the Facilitator will be to work with the parties to develop a time line, ground rules, and concrete milestones for the Joint Remedial Process. The Cincinnati Collaborative Procedure and subsequent DOJ consent decrees and letters of intent may be used as models.

4.   At the center of the Joint Remedial Process will be input from those who are most affected by the NYPD's use of stop and frisk, including but not limited to the people and organizations noted above. Input from academic and other experts in police practices may also be requested.

5.   The Facilitator will convene "town hall" type meetings in each of the five boroughs in order to provide a forum in which all stakeholders may be heard. It may be necessary to hold multiple meetings in the larger boroughs in order to ensure that everyone will have an opportunity to participate. The Facilitator will endeavor to prepare an agenda for such meetings, through consultation with the various interested groups prior to the meeting. The Monitor will also attend these meetings to the extent possible.

6.   The NYPD will appoint a representative or representatives to serve as a liaison to the Facilitator during the Joint Remedial Process.

7.   The Facilitator may receive anonymous information from NYPD officers or officials, subject to procedures to be determined by the parties.

8.   When the parties and the Facilitator have finished drafting the Joint Process Reforms, they will be submitted to the Court and the Monitor. The Monitor will recommend that the Court consider those Reforms he deems appropriate, and will then oversee their implementation once approved by the Court.

9.   In the event that the parties are unable to agree on Joint Process Reforms, the Facilitator will prepare a report stating the Facilitator's findings and recommendations based on the Joint Remedial Process, to be submitted to the parties, the Monitor, and the Court. The parties will have the opportunity to comment on the report and recommendations.

10. The City will be responsible for the reasonable costs and fees of the Facilitator and the Joint Remedial Process.

NOTE

The trial judge in *Floyd* was subsequently removed from the case due to the appearance of impartiality based on her encouragement of a new, related lawsuit and media appearances in which she seemed opposed to the city's stop and frisk practices. Ligon v. New York, 736 F.3d 118 (2d.Cir. 2013).After the election of a new mayor, the city dismissed its appeals and agreed to comply with the remedial order. *Floyd*, 302 F.R.D. 69 (S.D.N.Y. 2014). It requested only one modification: that the monitor's term be limited to three years if the city demonstrated substantial compliance with the order. The police officers' motion to intervene to challenge the order was denied. For more on the case and the remedial orders, see William A. Margeson, Note, *Bringing the Gavel Down on Stops and Frisks: The Equitable Regulation of Police Power*, 51 Am. Crim. L.Rev. 739 (2014).

————

The following article discusses an example of a fairly successful judicial intervention. What factors led to this success?

MURRAY LEVINE, CHARLES P. EWING & DAVID I. LEVINE, THE USE OF LAW FOR PREVENTION IN THE PUBLIC INTEREST
5 Prevention in Human Services 241, 265–271 (1987)

* * *

WUORI V. ZITNAY: SUCCESSFUL IMPLEMENTATION OF A CONSENT DECREE.

Wuori v. Zitnay (No. 75–80, D.Me.1975) is one of the most successful of the institutional reform cases. The case is unusual because the court gave up active supervision within a relatively few years. The defendants achieved substantial, if not full, compliance with an extensive consent decree which committed the state to improve an institution for the retarded and to create new community facilities as well.

The case was brought in 1975 by Neville Woodruff, an attorney who headed the Legal Services Corporation office in Portland, Maine. In the course of visiting the Pineland Center, an institution that at its peak had housed nearly 1500 mentally retarded individuals, Woodruff received information and documents from some employees who were frustrated by their inability to provide decent care. The institution was overcrowded and in poor condition. The residents had inadequate clothing. Their personal hygiene was poor. Residents were in restraints for unconscionable periods and were overmedicated. There was a lack of both programming and professional services. Dentists were pulling teeth from some residents to prevent self-abuse or harm to others. Moreover, many who had been released to the community as part of an earlier deinstitutionalization thrust were living in inadequate homes and were not receiving adequate habilitation services.

The suit, alleging violations of the Eighth Amendment right to be free of cruel and unusual punishment, or to be free from harm at the hands of the state, was brought in 1975 on behalf of a class of all residents in the institution and all residents who had been conditionally discharged but were still under the supervision of Pineland Center. Shortly after the suit was initiated, George Zitnay was hired by the state of Maine to become Director of Pineland Center. Zitnay, an experienced and gifted institutional administrator, immediately recognized the opportunity the suit presented to gain resources and leverage to improve Pineland. When he was deposed * * * he told the full truth about the institution. Zitnay's testimony, along with the plaintiffs' fully documented case, convinced the state that it could not win. Moreover, state officials would be subject to highly adverse publicity as long as the case was in court. The state agreed to settle out of court.

For the next two years, the plaintiffs' attorney negotiated with the state to develop a satisfactory plan for correcting deficiencies. Meanwhile, Zitnay was promoted from Superintendent of Pineland to State Commissioner of Mental Health and Corrections. The then Governor, the late James B. Longley, under whom Zitnay served, sincerely supported substantial improvement in the care of the mentally retarded. Zitnay was also very able in winning support from parents' groups as well as influential private citizens throughout the state of Maine. Despite such support, progress was slow in arriving at a satisfactory plan to remedy Pineland's deficiencies.

In 1978, the plaintiff's attorney called for assistance from the Mental Health Law Project, a Washington, D.C. public interest law firm with a great deal of experience in this type of litigation. The Mental Health Law Project assisted in developing an extensive, highly detailed plan for institutional reform covering both the Pineland Center and especially community residences and programs. The plan called for the appointment of a special master to oversee implementation. Zitnay and Kevin Concannon, then Director of the Bureau of Mental Retardation, recommended that the State of Maine accept the settlement, for both men understood it could be used as a blueprint and as leverage for modernizing and improving the entire system of care for the mentally retarded throughout Maine. The State's Attorney General, Joseph Brennan, who was later to succeed Longley as governor, accepted their recommendation.

Implementation Under a Special Master

In July, 1978, United States District Court Judge Edward T. Gignoux, a highly respected jurist, entered the consent decree, based on the plan developed by the parties with the assistance of the Mental Health Law Project, as the judgment of the court. After a search, the judge appointed David Gregory, a University of Maine law professor, as special master for a period of two years. The participants believed the decree would be fully implemented by that time.

The special master began with two assumptions. The first was that the state would not have agreed to anything it did not intend to do. The second was that the limit of what he had to know was what was in the court order. He believed at the time that the total job was one of looking at what the decree required, looking at what was going on in the institution, and then reporting on the differences. As he became aware of institutional dynamics and of the organizational and political complexities of introducing change in public agencies, he soon realized that both assumptions were incorrect.

After the first six months of educating himself about the problems of mental retardation, the culture of the institution, and interagency issues, Gregory took a more active role. He not only gathered information about the state of compliance with the decree, but he began educating the heads of other agencies as to how their actions were affecting implementation of the decree. In effect, he became an advocate for the decree. He worked closely with Zitnay, who was the named defendant, and with Concannon on the task of implementation. He came to understand that although Zitnay was commissioner, he had little direct control over Pineland Center itself and no power over state agencies on the same organizational level as his department (e.g., the state personnel department, the Commissioner of Finance, and the Commissioner of Human Services, basically responsible for Medicaid and other welfare programs). As a consequence of that decision, he tended to confront some department heads vigorously, strongly intimating that he expected their cooperation. For instance, he once had a difficult confrontation with Governor Brennan (Governor Longley's successor) who, as Attorney General, had consented to the decree. Governor

Brennan objected strongly to the critical tone of Gregory's reports. Gregory also worked with operators of group homes around the state to encourage them to organize politically to obtain changes in state regulations that limited their ability to program effectively. That activity, too, led to friction between Gregory and some state officials.

During this period, Zitnay and Concannon worked through the state's governmental structure to gain resources to modernize services for the retarded. They kept Gregory fully informed about barriers to implementation and other institutional problems. Gregory conducted his own investigations as to the state of compliance with the decree. He continued to receive information from some employees about deficiencies in programming or about abuses. (Other employees viewed his activities less benignly.) His reports to the court depicted the shortcomings and remaining problems in the institutions. Zitnay and Concannon could make bold requests for resources to correct deficiencies and point to the special master's reports to bolster their requests. In effect, the "blame" for the necessary large budget increases and other legislative changes could be placed on the special master. * * *

As the two year period of court supervision ended, Gregory's reports were still highly critical of the limited progress. He recommended extending the period of the court's supervision until compliance had been achieved. The plaintiffs and defendants resumed negotiations arriving at a stipulation * * * as to what further needed to be done to satisfy the terms of the decree. The state defendants agreed to the continuation of the special master's office, but in view of the friction between Gregory and the defendants, they insisted that Gregory be replaced. The change may have been at the insistence of the Governor.

In retrospect, all parties agreed that Gregory had done a superb job as special master. Although some questioned whether his reports too greatly emphasized the negatives of the defendant's actions, all agreed that had he not adopted an aggressive stance, there would have been much less progress in implementing the decree. * * *

The Next Phase

The new master was Lincoln Clark, the head of the state court mediation service. An experienced executive and a highly skilled mediator, Clark was a close friend of Judge Gignoux. He knew the major figures in state government and in the legislature. All of the major actors agreed to his appointment. Judge Gignoux appointed Clark to replace Gregory.

With a new governor taking office, Zitnay resigned as commissioner, returned to Pineland Center as superintendent, and was replaced by Kevin Concannon. Clark decided to focus first on Pineland rather than the community facilities, because it had moved far along the road to compliance under Zitnay. The most difficult part of the task was to establish criteria for deciding when the defendant had finally brought Pineland into compliance with the consent decree. Issues such as the number of beds in a room were easy to decide. Issues such as "adequate programming" required a great deal of subjective judgment.

Clark held a great many negotiating sessions among Zitnay, Concannon, and the plaintiffs' attorneys to agree to standards for compliance. Once the parties agreed, Clark brought in an outside consultant to review Pineland against the standards that had been agreed to, and to offer an opinion as to whether its programs met the standards. On the basis of an extensive review, the consultant concluded that Pineland Center was in substantial compliance with the institutional provisions of the consent decree. Clark therefore recommended that Pineland be discharged from the court's active supervision. In September, 1981, Judge Gignoux formally discharged the center from the court's direct supervision through Clark's office. Although this was an important milestone, Clark still faced correcting the remaining deficiencies in the community based treatment system, such as substandard housing, poor programming, and an insufficient number of community residences. Concannon, as Director of the Bureau of Mental Retardation, and later as Commissioner, had made progress in opening new group homes. However, persons seeking to develop group homes were faced with conflicting regulations and fiscal controls that led to great delays in opening new facilities.

In a spirit of negotiation and cooperation, Clark and the plaintiff's attorneys were willing to accept as substantial compliance the establishment of organizational means of accomplishing solutions, even if the precise program for each class member had not yet been achieved. While Clark effectively employed the skills of a mediator, he was well aware that his effectiveness depended upon the coercive power of the court. Clark also used the threat of adverse publicity, as did Gregory before him, to move matters along when progress seemed to be blocked.

Clark's reports to the court assisted the defendants' attempts to augment their budgets. Clark mailed his reports to all of the state legislators, to state officials, and to advocacy organizations. He also spoke informally with the chairman of the health committee of the state legislature, a person he knew well. Commissioner Concannon worked skillfully with the legislature as well to gain new resources and other legislation to assist the development of programs in the community.

Two years after Judge Gignoux had discharged Pineland Center from the court's active supervision, Clark believed that sufficient progress had been made in implementing the community portion of the decree. In the summer of 1983, Clark contracted with outside consultants to determine whether the defendants' claims of progress were warranted. One consultant concluded that not all of the requirements of the consent decree had been met, but that enough had been put into place that the defendants would be able to come into full compliance. Another consultant studied the lives of those class members who left Pineland Center and were living in the community. On the basis of interviews with a randomly selected sample of clients and staff, she concluded that the living, working, and learning experiences of the class members substantially adhered to the standards involved in the two major themes of the consent decree—normalization and habilitation.

An obvious concern was whether the improvements and the progress would survive if the court were to give up jurisdiction and cease supervising the programs. Two methods were developed to continue to monitor the system. A Consumer Advisory Board, created earlier as part of the consent decree, was now given greater monitoring responsibilities. The Board began developing a network of "correspondents"—people to act as next friends to those who have no families or have been abandoned by their families and to help in monitoring conditions in the many group homes scattered throughout the state. The defendants also agreed to undertake an annual, independent and public review of compliance with standards for institutional and community care incorporated into the consent decree and to publish a plan to remedy any identified deficiencies.

Clark's report, finding compliance with the terms of the consent decree as interpreted through the various stipulations, was submitted to the court in October, 1983. Shortly afterwards Judge Gignoux accepted the findings, discharged the special master, and relinquished active supervision of the case. It was one of the first cases of its kind to come to this degree of successful completion. In August, 1985, M. Levine visited Pineland Center and conducted interviews with important participants. Maine has developed a very good system of care for class members and has improved the system of care for all. Undoubtedly, one could find gaps in the provision of care, and some problems are relatively intractable, but the worst abuses have certainly been curbed, and for most, humane care at the state of the art is being provided. The state continues to identify problems in the system of care, and officials are making efforts to plan for the future. The goal of prevention is being met. * * *

NOTES

1.   After a long period of quiescence, there was further litigation regarding the matters addressed in *Wuori*. In October 1991, the Consumer Advisory Board that had been established in the consent decree brought an action seeking enforcement of the rights established in the 1978 consent decree. The Board's primary concerns were that the defendants had stopped making appropriate annual assessments of the medical, educational and training needs of the Pineland Center residents and outpatients, that the defendants had failed to create sufficient new community placements for residents and that basic safety at Pineland had been neglected. After some

skirmishing over whether Judge Gignoux (who died in the interim) had intended to terminate jurisdiction over the case by 1986, Consumer Advisory Board v. Glover, 989 F.2d 65 (1st Cir.1993) (no such intent expressed), the district court denied the defendants' motions to dissolve the injunction and terminate the decree, 151 F.R.D. 496 (D.Me.1993), and to dismiss the Board's complaint, 151 F.R.D. 490 (D.Me.1993). The case continued to be active. *see* Consumer Advisory Board v. Harvey, 2008 WL 4594353 (D.Me.2008) (accepting special master's report on defendants' non-compliance) until the court finally found the defendants' in compliance with the decree and granted them relief from judgment. Consumer Advisory Board v. Harvey, 697 F. Supp. 2d 131 (D. Me. 2010).

2. For a more detailed description of the implementation of the injunction in *Wuori,* see Murray Levine, *The Role of Special Master in Institutional Reform Litigation: A Case Study,* 8 Law & Policy 275 (1986). For another example of successful implementation of a detailed decree, see Judy Scales-Trent, *A Judge Shapes and Manages Institutional Reform: School Desegregation in Buffalo,* 17 N.Y.U.Rev.L. & Soc. Change 119 (1989–90) (showing how district court skillfully used decree implementation process to turn the Buffalo, N.Y. public schools into a "national model of integration"). But for a considerably more skeptical analysis of the use of court-appointed monitors, see Cobell v. Norton, 334 F.3d 1128 (D.C.Cir.2003) (reversing appointment). On remand, a monitor was re-appointed, but in light of the guidance from the circuit court. Cobell v. Norton, 283 F.Supp.2d 66, 214–19 (D.D.C.2003).

———

One attorney with extensive experience litigating institutional reform cases has specified the elements he believes are needed for any effective compliance mechanism. Considering what we have examined so far in this course, what would constrain a judge from doing all that the author recommends?

MICHAEL S. LOTTMAN, ENFORCING JUDICIAL DECREES: NOW COMES THE HARD PART

Mental Disability L.Rep. 69, 74–75 (July–August 1976)

a. An effective compliance mechanism must be established, first of all, in the context of an order, based upon a factual record, which binds the necessary officials and fixes specific responsibility on one or more of such officials for implementation of particular standards or requirements.

b. The order should be as precise and quantitative as possible, and should set forth clearly measurable, objective standards (including deadlines), so that compliance can be monitored accurately and, as far as possible, by clerical or mechanical means.

c.   The order should provide for financing of required staff, physical plant improvements, development of community facilities, and other such items, and fix the responsibility for obtaining the necessary funds on the proper defendants.

d.   The court should retain jurisdiction over the action.

e.   If reporting requirements are included, they should serve as a starting point for compliance activity, not as an exclusive fact-gathering device. The court order, or the monitoring body, should prescribe with great specificity the format, contents, and timing of any required reports, and should structure such reports to elicit factual information rather than opinions. The reporting document should be directly related to specific provisions of the order. If feasible, such reports should be required to be verified under oath or otherwise designated as admissible in evidence, without more, in any proceeding for enforcement or contempt.

f.   The monitoring body, whatever its specific form, must be on the premises of the defendant institution or otherwise in contact with the defendants on a full-time, daily basis, and must have access to all relevant records or documents and to residents or patients, defendants' employees, and other persons affected by or involved in the implementation of the order. The monitoring body must be independent of the person or agency whose conduct it is monitoring, and must owe its first allegiance to the court.

g.   The monitoring body must be provided with sufficient full-time staff to monitor the defendants' operations on a daily basis, develop required plans or reports, respond to inquiries and complaints, and carry out other functions as assigned by the court. The monitoring body must also have access to professional and legal experts, either on a full-time or consulting basis.

h.   While enforcement of court orders should not be made to depend solely on the efforts of attorneys for the plaintiffs, no enforcement mechanism should operate so as to interfere in any way with such attorneys' continuing duty to represent their clients. Counsel for all parties should be served with copies of any communication between the monitoring body and the court.

i.   To the extent possible, monitoring bodies should not also be charged with responsibility for developing the plans and designing the requirements whose implementation they must then oversee. This "legislative-executive" role mixture is likely to dilute the effectiveness of the monitoring body.

j.   Monitoring bodies should be empowered to do more than merely mediate disputes or make reports to the court; they should, at least, have the authority to make recommendations in regard to implementation of the order which must be followed unless an objection thereto is upheld by the court. The order should spell out in detail the procedure to be followed when the monitoring body identifies a violation of the order or a related problem, and the procedure for making, objecting to, and enforcing the monitoring body's recommendations—in other words, an implementation structure. The monitoring body should be given the procedural and technical weapons necessary to enable it to investigate violations and formulate recommendations.

k.   Finally, the court should make it clear from the start that noncompliance with its order will be dealt with by measures of whatever severity is necessary, up to and including proceedings for contempt of court.
* * *

C. MODIFYING AND TERMINATING THE INJUNCTION

Federal Rule of Civil Procedure 60(b)(5) specifically grants a court power to relieve a party from a final judgment if "it has been satisfied, released or discharged," or if "applying it prospectively is no longer equitable." Thus if a defendant has completed the order, for example, returning the ordered property, then it has satisfied the injunction and it can be terminated.

A typical defendant will want to be released as promptly as possible from the court's jurisdiction for several reasons. Once released, the defendant will once again have the ability to take action (and in more complex private and public law cases, make policy decisions) without judicial scrutiny or fear of judicial sanctions. Moreover, the defendant will not have to comply with monitoring rules, such as the necessity to file regular reports. Unless the conduct is independently prohibited by law (such as a statute), the defendant will be under no obligation to continue to avoid the conduct which had been proscribed by the injunction. *See* David I. Levine, *The Latter Stages of Enforcement of Equitable Decrees: The Course of Institutional Reform Cases After* Dowell, Rufo *and* Freeman, 20 Hastings Const.L.Q. 579, 629–32 (1993).

The question becomes whether injunctions can be terminated or modified at some point prior to full satisfaction of the order. As prospective orders, injunctions are practically subject to the reality of changed circumstances.

Generally speaking, the law strongly values the finality of judgments. Thus, it is fairly difficult to modify a final judgment of a court as to liability. *See* Fed.R.Civ.P. 60(b) (relief may be granted only upon a showing of limited conditions, such as mistake or fraud, and generally only within a limited period of time, usually one year). Similarly, the doctrine of res judicata applies even where the law which a court relied upon to render the original judgment is later changed by a higher court. *E.g.,* Federated

Department Stores, Inc. v. Moitie, 452 U.S. 394 (1981). The law also values finality in private negotiations. Thus, you probably read cases in contracts that required a party to continue to perform under long-term or indefinite contracts even though economic conditions had changed and the contract was no longer economically advantageous to one party. *E.g.,* Parev Products v. I. Rokeach, 124 F.2d 147 (2d Cir.1941) (court refused to modify a 25-year contract after 15 years of performance). Tort law also has a strong element of finality. A judgment rendered in a tort case is designed to compensate for all injury—past, present and future. A later change of circumstance (for example, after judgment, the plaintiff actually lives longer than the life expectancy assumed at trial) is not permitted to be the basis for reopening the litigation or for a modification of the judgment to change the amount awarded originally at trial. *See, e.g.,* Pretre v. United States, 531 F.Supp. 931 (E.D.Mo.1981). As the materials in this section demonstrate, however, at times the finality of an injunction (and its close cousin, the consent decree), has been treated somewhat differently.

Sometimes the court can assist the parties and avoid modification by simply interpreting the injunction or consent decree. "To interpret is to explain and elucidate, not to add or subtract from the text." 2 Milton Handler, *Twenty-Five Years of Antitrust* 952 (1973). As the Supreme Court has explained:

> Consent decrees are entered into by parties to a case after careful negotiation has produced agreement on their precise terms. The parties waive their right to litigate the issues involved in the case and thus save themselves the time, expense, and inevitable risk of litigation. Naturally, the agreement reached normally embodies a compromise; in exchange for the saving of cost and elimination of risk, the parties each give up something they might have won had they proceeded with the litigation. Thus the decree itself cannot be said to have a purpose; rather the parties have purposes, generally opposed to each other, and the resultant decree embodies as much of those opposing purposes as the respective parties have the bargaining power and skill to achieve. For these reasons, the scope of a consent decree must be discerned within its four corners, and not by reference to what might satisfy the purposes of one of the parties to it.

United States v. Armour & Co., 402 U.S. 673, 681–82 (1971). *See also* United States v. New Jersey, 194 F.3d 426, 430 (3d Cir.1999) ("focus remains on the contractual language itself, rather than on the parties' subjective understanding of the language").

If interpretation will not suffice and modification is necessary, then the question becomes whether modification should be easy or exceptional. The Supreme Court's apparent stated position for many years was that it should be difficult to obtain a modification. In United States v. Swift & Co.,

286 U.S. 106 (1932), the Supreme Court reversed a lower court's modification of a consent decree entered over ten years earlier in an antitrust case against the five largest meat packers in the country. Although the trial court had the power to modify consent decrees because they were judicial acts, and not private contracts, Justice Cardozo's opinion seemed to demand that the power to modify was to be used rarely. "Nothing less than a clear showing of grievous wrong evoked by new and unforeseen conditions should lead us to change what was decreed after years of litigation with the consent of all concerned." 286 U.S. at 119. In another famous phrase from the opinion, Justice Cardozo said that there should be no modification from changed conditions unless the original dangers that were the reason for the decree originally, "once substantial, have become attenuated to a shadow." *Id.* The meat packer decree was not finally dissolved until 1981. United States v. Swift & Co., 1982–1 Trade Cases (CCH) ¶ 64,464 (N.D.Ill.1981).

However, in 1968, the Court relaxed *Swift's* "grievous wrong" standard. In United States v. United Shoe Machinery Corp., 391 U.S. 244 (1968), the trial court had entered a permanent injunction designed to restore competition to the market of the manufacture of shoe machinery. Several years later, the government petitioned the trial court for further relief on the grounds that the defendant continued to dominate the market. The district court refused to grant the requested relief on the strength of *Swift.* The Supreme Court reversed, holding that the "grievous wrong" standard applied only to modifications requested by defendants seeking to avoid the responsibilities imposed by an order.

This standard for modification was further loosened in the following case, which has become the prevailing standard for modifying injunctive relief.

RUFO v. INMATES OF SUFFOLK COUNTY JAIL

Supreme Court of the United States
502 U.S. 367 (1992)

JUSTICE WHITE delivered the opinion of the Court.

* * *

I

This litigation began in 1971 when inmates sued * * * claiming that inmates not yet convicted of the crimes charged against them were being held under unconstitutional conditions at what was then the Suffolk County Jail. The facility, known as the Charles Street Jail, had been constructed in 1848 with large tiers of barred cells. * * * The court held that conditions at the jail were constitutionally deficient. * * *

The Court permanently enjoined the government defendants: "(a) from housing at the Charles Street Jail after November 30, 1973 in a cell with another inmate, any inmate who is awaiting trial and (b) from housing at the Charles Street Jail after June 30, 1976 any inmate who is awaiting trial." The defendants did not appeal.

In 1977, with the problems of the Charles Street Jail still unresolved, the District Court ordered defendants, including the Boston City Council, to take such steps and expend the funds reasonably necessary to renovate another existing facility as a substitute detention center. * * * The Court of Appeals [subsequently] ordered that the Charles Street Jail be closed on October 2, 1978, unless a plan was presented to create a constitutionally adequate facility for pretrial detainees in Suffolk County.

Four days before the deadline, the plan that formed the basis for the consent decree now before this Court was submitted to the District Court. * * *

Seven months later, the Court entered a formal consent decree in which the government defendants expressed their "desire . . . to provide, maintain and operate as applicable a suitable and constitutional jail for Suffolk County pretrial detainees." The decree specifically incorporated the provisions of the Suffolk County Detention Center, Charles Street Facility, Architectural Program, which—in the words of the consent decree—"sets forth a program which is both constitutionally adequate and constitutionally required."

Under the terms of the Architectural Program, the new jail was designed to include a total of 309 "[s]ingle occupancy rooms" of 70 square feet arranged in modular units that included a kitchenette and recreation area, inmate laundry room, education units, and indoor and outdoor exercise areas. The size of the jail was based on a projected decline in inmate population, from 245 male prisoners in 1979 to 226 at present.

Although the Architectural Program projected that construction of the new jail would be completed by 1983, work on the new facility had not been started by 1984. During the intervening years, the inmate population outpaced population projections. Litigation in the state courts ensued, and defendants were ordered to build a larger jail. Thereupon, plaintiff prisoners, with the support of the sheriff, moved the District Court to modify the decree to provide a facility with 435 cells. Citing "the unanticipated increase in jail population and the delay in completing the jail," the District Court modified the decree to permit the capacity of the new jail to be increased in any amount, provided that: "(a) single-cell occupancy is maintained under the design for the facility;" * * * The number of cells was later increased to 453. Construction started in 1987.

In July 1989, while the new jail was still under construction, the sheriff moved to modify the consent decree to allow the double bunking of male detainees in 197 cells, thereby raising the capacity of the new jail to 610 male detainees. The sheriff argued that changes in law and in fact required the modification. The asserted change in law was this Court's 1979 decision in Bell v. Wolfish, 441 U.S. 520 (1979), handed down one week after the consent decree was approved by the District Court. The asserted change in fact was the increase in the population of pretrial detainees.

The District Court refused to grant the requested modification, holding that the sheriff had failed to meet the standard of United States v. Swift & Co., 286 U.S. 106, 119 (1932):

> "Nothing less than a clear showing of grievous wrong evoked by new and unforeseen conditions should lead us to change what was decreed after years of litigation with the consent of all concerned."

The court rejected the argument that *Bell* required modification of the decree because the decision "did not directly overrule any legal interpretation on which the 1979 consent decree was based, and in these circumstances it is inappropriate to invoke Rule 60(b)(5) to modify a consent decree." The court refused to order modification because of the increased pretrial detainee population, finding that the problem was "neither new nor unforeseen."

The District Court briefly stated that, even under the flexible modification standard adopted by other Courts of Appeals, the sheriff would not be entitled to relief because "[a] separate cell for each detainee has always been an important element of the relief sought in this litigation-perhaps even the most important element." Finally, the court rejected the argument that the decree should be modified because the proposal complied with constitutional standards, reasoning that such a rule "would undermine and discourage settlement efforts in institutional cases." The District Court never decided whether the sheriff's proposal for double celling at the new jail would be constitutionally permissible.

The new Suffolk County Jail opened shortly thereafter.

The Court of Appeals affirmed * * * . We granted certiorari.

II

In moving for modification of the decree, the sheriff relied on Federal Rule of Civil Procedure 60(b)[(5) & (6)] * * * .

There is no suggestion in these cases that a consent decree is not subject to Rule 60(b). A consent decree no doubt embodies an agreement of the parties and thus in some respects is contractual in nature. But it is an agreement that the parties desire and expect will be reflected in and be enforceable as a judicial decree that is subject to the rules generally applicable to other judgments and decrees. Railway Employees v. Wright, 364 U.S. 642, 650–651 (1961). The District Court recognized as much but held that Rule 60(b)(5) codified the "grievous wrong" standard of United States v. Swift, that a case for modification under this standard had not been made, and that resort to Rule 60(b)(6) was also unavailing. This construction of Rule 60(b) was error. * * *

Our decisions since *Swift* reinforce the conclusion that the "grievous wrong" language of *Swift* was not intended to take on a talismanic quality, warding off virtually all efforts to modify consent decrees. *Railway Employees* emphasized the need for flexibility in administering consent decrees, stating: "There is . . . no dispute but that a sound judicial discretion may call for the modification of the terms of an injunctive decree if the circumstances, whether of law or fact, obtaining at the time of its issuance have changed, or new ones have since arisen." * * *

There is thus little basis for concluding that Rule 60(b) misread the *Swift* opinion and intended that modifications of consent decrees in all cases were to be governed by the standard actually applied in *Swift*. That Rule, in providing that, on such terms as are just, a party may be relieved from a final judgement or decree where it is no longer equitable that the judgment have prospective application, permits a less stringent, more flexible standard.

The upsurge in institutional reform litigation since Brown v. Board of Education, 347 U.S. 483 (1954), has made the ability of a district court to modify a decree in response to changed circumstances all the more important. Because such decrees often remain in place for extended periods of time, the likelihood of significant changes occurring during the life of the decree is increased. * * *

It is urged that any rule other than the *Swift* "grievous wrong" standard would deter parties to litigation such as this from negotiating settlements and hence destroy the utility of consent decrees. Obviously that would not be the case insofar as the state or local government officials are concerned. As for the plaintiffs in such cases, they know that if they litigate to conclusion and win, the resulting judgment or decree will give them what is constitutionally adequate at that time but perhaps less than they hoped for. They also know that the prospective effect of such a judgment or decree will be open to modification where deemed equitable under Rule 60(b). Whether or not they bargain for more than what they might get after trial, they will be in no worse position if they settle and have the consent decree entered. At least they will avoid further litigation and perhaps will negotiate a decree providing more than what would have been ordered without the local government's consent. And, of course, if they litigate, they may lose.

III

Although we hold that a district court should exercise flexibility in considering requests for modification of an institutional reform consent decree, it does not follow that a modification will be warranted in all circumstances. Rule 60(b)(5) provides that a party may obtain relief from a court order when "it is no longer equitable that the judgment should have prospective application," not when it is no longer convenient to live with the terms of a consent decree. Accordingly, a party seeking modification of a consent decree bears the burden of establishing that a significant change in circumstances warrants revision of the decree. If the moving party meets this standard, the court should consider whether the proposed modification is suitably tailored to the changed circumstance.[7]

A

A party seeking modification of a consent decree may meet its initial burden by showing either a significant change in factual conditions or in law.

1

Modification of a consent decree may be warranted when changed factual conditions make compliance with the decree substantially more onerous. Such a modification was approved by the District Court in this litigation in 1985 when it became apparent that plans for the new jail did not provide sufficient cell space. Modification is also appropriate when a decree proves to be unworkable because of unforeseen obstacles, New York State Assn. for Retarded Children, Inc. v. Carey, 706 F.2d at 969 (modification allowed where State could not find appropriate housing facilities for transfer patients); Philadelphia Welfare Rights Organization v. Shapp, 602 F.2d at 1120–1121 (modification allowed where State could not find sufficient clients to meet decree targets); or when enforcement of the decree without modification would be detrimental to the public interest, Duran v. Elrod, 760 F.2d 756, 759–761 (C.A.7 1985) (modification allowed to avoid pretrial release of accused violent felons).

Respondents urge that modification should be allowed only when a change in facts is both "unforeseen and unforeseeable." Such a standard would provide even less flexibility than the exacting *Swift* test; we decline to adopt it. Litigants are not required to anticipate every exigency that could conceivably arise during the life of a consent decree.

---

    [7]   The standard we set forth applies when a party seeks modification of a term of a consent decree that arguably relates to the vindication of a constitutional right. Such a showing is not necessary to implement minor changes in extraneous details that may have been included in a decree (*e.g.*, paint color or design of a building's facade) but are unrelated to remedying the underlying constitutional violation. Ordinarily, the parties should consent to modifying a decree to allow such changes. If a party refuses to consent and the moving party has a reasonable basis for its request, the court should modify the decree. In this case the entire architectural plan became part of the decree binding on the local authorities. Hence, any change in the plan technically required a change in the decree, absent a provision in the plan exempting certain changes. Such a provision was furnished by the 1985 modification of the decree. Of course, the necessity of changing a decree to allow insignificant changes could be avoided by not entering an overly detailed decree.

Ordinarily, however, modification should not be granted where a party relies upon events that actually were anticipated at the time it entered into a decree. If it is clear that a party anticipated changing conditions that would make performance of the decree more onerous but nevertheless agreed to the decree, that party would have to satisfy a heavy burden to convince a court that it agreed to the decree in good faith, made a reasonable effort to comply with the decree, and should be relieved of the undertaking under Rule 60(b).

Accordingly, on remand the District Court should consider whether the upsurge in the Suffolk County inmate population was foreseen by the petitioners. * * *

Even if the decree is construed as an undertaking by petitioners to provide single cells for pretrial detainees, to relieve petitioners from that promise based on changed conditions does not necessarily violate the basic purpose of the decree. That purpose was to provide a remedy for what had been found, based on a variety of factors, including double celling, to be unconstitutional conditions obtaining in the Charles Street Jail. If modification of one term of a consent decree defeats the purpose of the decree, obviously modification would be all but impossible. That cannot be the rule. The District Court was thus in error in holding that even under a more flexible standard than its version of *Swift* required, modification of the single cell requirement was necessarily forbidden.

2

A consent decree must of course be modified if, as it later turns out, one or more of the obligations placed upon the parties has become impermissible under federal law. But modification of a consent decree may be warranted when the statutory or decisional law has changed to make legal what the decree was designed to prevent.

This was the case in Railway Employees v. Wright, 364 U.S. 642 (1961). A railroad and its unions were sued for violating the Railway Labor Act, 45 U.S.C. § 151 et seq., which banned discrimination against nonunion employees, and the parties entered a consent decree that prohibited such discrimination. Later, the Railway Labor Act was amended to allow union shops, and the union sought a modification of the decree. Although the amendment did not require but purposely permitted union shops, this Court held that the union was entitled to the modification because the parties had recognized correctly that what the consent decree prohibited was illegal under the Railway Act as it then read and because a "court must be free to continue to further the objectives of th[e] Act when its provisions are amended."

Petitioner Rapone urges that, without more, our 1979 decision in Bell v. Wolfish, 441 U.S. 520 (1979), was a change in law requiring modification of the decree governing construction of the Suffolk County Jail. We disagree. *Bell* made clear what the Court had not before announced: that double celling is not in all cases unconstitutional. But it surely did not cast doubt on the legality of single celling, and petitioners were undoubtedly aware that *Bell* was pending when they signed the decree. Thus, the case must be judged on the basis that it was immaterial to petitioners that double celling might be ruled constitutional, i.e., they preferred even in that event to agree to a decree which called for providing only single cells in the jail to be built.

Neither *Bell* nor the Federal Constitution forbade this course of conduct. Federal courts may not order States or local governments, over their objection, to undertake a course of conduct not tailored to curing a constitutional violation that has been adjudicated. *See* Milliken v. Bradley (*Milliken II*), 433 U.S. 267, 281 (1977). But we have no doubt that, to "save themselves the time, expense, and inevitable risk of litigation," United States v. Armour & Co., 402 U.S. 673, 681 (1971), petitioners could settle the dispute over the proper remedy for the constitutional violations that had been found by undertaking to do more than the Constitution itself requires (almost any affirmative decree beyond a directive to obey the Constitution necessarily does that), but also more than what a court would have ordered absent the settlement. Accordingly, the District Court did not abuse its discretion in entering the agreed upon decree, which clearly was related to the conditions found to offend the Constitution.[12]

To hold that a clarification in the law automatically opens the door for relitigation of the merits of every affected consent decree would undermine the finality of such agreements and could serve as a disincentive to negotiation of settlements in institutional reform litigation. * * *

While a decision that clarifies the law will not, in and of itself, provide a basis for modifying a decree, it could constitute a change in circumstances that would support modification if the parties had based their agreement on a misunderstanding of the governing law. For instance, in Pasadena City Board of Education v. Spangler, 427 U.S. 424, 437–438 (1976), we held that a modification should have been ordered when the parties had interpreted an ambiguous equitable decree in a manner contrary to the District Court's ultimate interpretation and the District Court's interpretation was contrary to intervening decisional law. And in Nelson v. Collins, 659 F.2d 420, 428–429 (C.A.4 1981) (en banc), the Fourth Circuit

---

[12] Petitioner Rapone contends that the District Court was required to modify the consent decree because "the constitutional violation underlying the decree has disappeared and will not recur" and that "no constitutional violation [is] even alleged" at the new jail, "so there is no constitutional violation to serve as a predicate for the federal court's continued exercise of its equitable power." His argument is not well taken. The District Court did not make findings on these issues, and even if it had ruled that double celling at the new jail is constitutional and that the modification should be granted, we do not have before us the question whether the entire decree should be vacated.

vacated an equitable order that was based on the assumption that double bunking of prisoners was *per se* unconstitutional.

Thus, if the Sheriff and Commissioner could establish on remand that the parties to the consent decree believed that single celling of pretrial detainees was mandated by the Constitution, this misunderstanding of the law could form a basis for modification. In this connection, we note again that the decree itself recited that it "sets forth a program which is both constitutionally adequate and constitutionally *required*." (Emphasis added).

B

Once a moving party has met its burden of establishing either a change in fact or in law warranting modification of a consent decree, the District Court should determine whether the proposed modification is suitably tailored to the changed circumstance. In evaluating a proposed modification, three matters should be clear.

Of course, a modification must not create or perpetuate a constitutional violation. Petitioners contend that double celling inmates at the Suffolk County Jail would be constitutional under *Bell*. Respondents counter that *Bell* is factually distinguishable and that double celling at the new jail would violate the constitutional rights of pretrial detainees. If this is the case—the District Court did not decide this issue—modification should not be granted.

A proposed modification should not strive to rewrite a consent decree so that it conforms to the constitutional floor. Once a court has determined that changed circumstances warrant a modification in a consent decree, the focus should be on whether the proposed modification is tailored to resolve the problems created by the change in circumstances. A court should do no more, for a consent decree is a final judgment that may be reopened only to the extent that equity requires. The court should not "turn aside to inquire whether some of [the provisions of the decree] upon separate as distinguished from joint action could have been opposed with success if the defendants had offered opposition." *Swift*.

Within these constraints, the public interest and "[c]onsiderations based on the allocation of powers within our federal system," *Dowell*, require that the district court defer to local government administrators, who have the "primary responsibility for elucidating, assessing, and solving" the problems of institutional reform, to resolve the intricacies of implementing a decree modification. Brown v. Board of Education, 349 U.S. at 299. *See also* Missouri v. Jenkins, 495 U.S. 33 (1990); *Milliken II*.[14]

---

[14] The concurrence mischaracterizes the nature of the deference that we would accord local government administrators. As we have stated, the moving party bears the burden of establishing that a significant change in circumstances warrants modification of a consent decree. No deference is involved in this threshold inquiry. However, once a court has determined that a modification is warranted, we think that principles of federalism and simple common sense require the court to

Although state and local officers in charge of institutional litigation may agree to do more than that which is minimally required by the Constitution to settle a case and avoid further litigation, a court should surely keep the public interest in mind in ruling on a request to modify based on a change in conditions making it substantially more onerous to abide by the decree. To refuse modification of a decree is to bind all future officers of the State, regardless of their view of the necessity of relief from one or more provisions of a decree that might not have been entered had the matter been litigated to its conclusion. The District Court seemed to be of the view that the problems of the fiscal officers of the State were only marginally relevant to the request for modification in this case. Financial constraints may not be used to justify the creation or perpetuation of constitutional violations, but they are a legitimate concern of government defendants in institutional reform litigation and therefore are appropriately considered in tailoring a consent decree modification.

IV

To conclude, we hold that the *Swift* "grievous wrong" standard does not apply to requests to modify consent decrees stemming from institutional reform litigation. Under the flexible standard we adopt today, a party seeking modification of a consent decree must establish that a significant change in facts or law warrants revision of the decree and that the proposed modification is suitably tailored to the changed circumstance. * * *

JUSTICE THOMAS took no part in the consideration or decision of this case.

JUSTICE O'CONNOR, concurring in the judgment.

* * * I would emphasize that we find fault only with the *method* by which the District Court reached its conclusion. The District Court may well have been justified, for the reasons suggested by Justice Stevens, in refusing to modify the decree, and the court is free, when fully exercising its discretion, to reach the same result on remand. This is a case with no satisfactory outcome. The new jail is simply too small. Someone has to suffer, and it is not likely to be the government officials responsible for underestimating the inmate population and delaying the construction of the jail. Instead, it is likely to be either the inmates of Suffolk County, who will be double celled in an institution designed for single celling; the inmates in counties not yet subject to court supervision, who will be double celled with the inmates transferred from Suffolk County; or members of the public, who may be the victims of crimes committed by the inmates the county is forced to release in order to comply with the consent decree. The District Court has an extraordinarily difficult decision to make. We should

---

give significant weight to the views of the local government officials who must implement any modification.

not be inclined to second-guess the court's sound judgment in deciding who will bear this burden. * * *

JUSTICE STEVENS, with whom JUSTICE BLACKMUN joins, dissenting.

Today the Court endorses the standard for modification of consent decrees articulated by Judge Friendly in New York State Association for Retarded Children, Inc. v. Carey, 706 F.2d 956 (CA2), *cert. denied,* 464 U.S. 915 (1983). I agree with that endorsement, but under that standard I believe the findings of the District Court in this action require affirmance of its order refusing to modify this consent decree.

* * *

III

* * * The remedy is constrained by the requirement that it not perpetuate a constitutional violation, and in this sense the Constitution does provide a "floor." Beyond that constraint, however, the remedy's attempt to give expression to the underlying constitutional value does not lend itself to quantitative evaluation. In view of the complexity of the institutions involved and the necessity of affording effective relief, the remedial decree will often contain many, highly detailed commands. It might well be that the failure to fulfill any one of these specific requirements would not have constituted an independent constitutional violation, nor would the absence of any one element render the decree necessarily ineffective. The duty of the District Court is not to formulate the decree with the fewest provisions, but to consider the various interests involved and, in the sound exercise of its discretion, to fashion the remedy that it believes to be best.[2] Similarly, a consent decree reflects the parties' understanding of the best remedy, and, subject to judicial approval, the parties to a consent decree enjoy at least as broad discretion as the District Court in formulating the remedial decree. * * *

---

[2]   It is the difficulty in determining prospectively which remedy is best that justifies a flexible standard of modification. This relationship between the characteristics of a remedial decree in structural reform litigation and the flexible standard of modification is explained in the passage that Judge Friendly found to be the best statement of the applicable legal standard:

> The judge must search for the "best" remedy, but since his judgment must incorporate such open-ended considerations as effectiveness and fairness, and since the threat and constitutional value that occasions the intervention can never be defined with great precision, the intervention can never be defended with any certitude. It must always be open to revisions, even without the strong showing traditionally required for modification of a decree, namely, that the first choice is causing grievous hardship. A revision is justified if the remedy is not working effectively or is unnecessarily burdensome.

New York State Association for Retarded Children, Inc. v. Carey, 706 F.2d 956, 970 (C.A.2 1983) (quoting Fiss, The Supreme Court—1978 Term—Foreword: The Forms of Justice, 93 Harv.L.Rev. 1, 49 (1979)). The justification for modifying a consent decree is not that the decree did "too much," but that in light of later circumstances, a modified remedy would better achieve the decree's original goals.

IV

* * * The increase in the average number of pretrial detainees is, of course, a change of fact. Because the size of that increase had not been anticipated in 1979, it was appropriate to modify the decree in 1985. But in 1985, the steady progression in the detainee population surely made it foreseeable that this growth would continue. The District Court's finding that "the overcrowding problem faced by the Sheriff is neither new nor unforeseen," is amply supported by the record.

Even if the continuing increase in inmate population had not actually been foreseen, it was reasonably foreseeable. Mere foreseeability in the sense that it was an event that "could conceivably arise" during the life of the consent decree should not, of course, disqualify an unanticipated development from justifying a modification. But the parties should be charged with notice of those events that reasonably prudent litigants would contemplate when negotiating a settlement. Given the realities of today's society, it is not surprising that the District Court found a continued growth in inmate population to be within petitioners' contemplation.

Other important concerns counsel against modification of this consent decree. Petitioners' history of noncompliance after the 1973 injunction provides an added reason for insisting that they honor their most recent commitments. Petitioners' current claims of fiscal limitation are hardly new. These pleas reflect a continuation of petitioners' previous reluctance to budget funds adequate to avoid the initial constitutional violation or to avoid prolonged noncompliance with the terms of the original decree. The continued claims of financial constraint should not provide support for petitioners' modification requests.

The strong public interest in protecting the finality of court decrees always counsels against modifications. In the context of a consent decree, this interest is reinforced by the policy favoring the settlement of protracted litigation. To the extent that litigants are allowed to avoid their solemn commitments, the motivation for particular settlements will be compromised, and the reliability of the entire process will suffer.

NOTES

1.   On remand, the district court found that although some increase was reasonably foreseeable, the specific and sustained rise in the inmate population was not actually foreseen by the parties either when the decree was originally entered in 1979 or was modified in 1985. However, the court also found that single-bunking was "at the least among the most significant objectives of the consent decree" and that the plaintiffs would not have consented to the decree without the provision for single-bunking. Moreover, double-bunking would increase the risk of violence and the risk of transmission of tuberculosis among the inmates. As a result, although the increased inmate population qualified as a change of factual circumstances, the court found that

the Sheriff's proposed solution—double-bunking in 197 of the 322 cells in the jail—was not narrowly tailored to those circumstances. The court invited the Sheriff to submit a new proposal that met the objectives of the decree. The district court also denied a motion brought by the Commissioner of Corrections for the Commonwealth to entirely vacate the decree. Inmates of Suffolk County Jail v. Rufo, 148 F.R.D. 14 (D.Mass.1993). The First Circuit turned away an appeal by the Commissioner. 12 F.3d 286 (1st Cir.1993). On the Sheriff's revised motion to modify, the district court granted permission to alter up to 100 cells to permit double-bunking, and stated its intent to close the case after an additional five-year monitoring period. 844 F.Supp. 31 (D.Mass.1994). The district court partially granted the Sheriff's subsequent motion to terminate jurisdiction over the jail pursuant to the Prison Litigation Reform Act. 129 F.3d 649 (1st Cir.1997), *cert. denied*, 524 U.S. 951 (1998).

The Charles Street Jail was finally closed and then sold and converted into a luxury hotel in Boston called The Liberty Hotel with rates of $325 to $4,000 per night. The jail-themed hotel invites guests to "be captivated" and includes such amenities as Do-Not-Disturb signs reading "Solitary," the "Clink" restaurant, and the "Alibi" bar. *See* The Liberty Hotel, http://www. libertyhotel.com (last visited Sept. 8, 2016); Beth Greenfield, *Check In/Check Out*, N.Y.Travel at 4, Dec. 23, 2007.

2.   *Rufo* has encouraged defendants to seek re-examination of many consent decrees for a variety of reasons. For examples of changes in fact, see, e.g., United States v. Eastman Kodak Co., 63 F.3d 95 (2d Cir.1995) (lifting antitrust decrees entered in 1921 and 1954); Newark Coalition for Low Income Housing v. Newark Redevelopment and Housing Authority, 524 F.Supp.2d 559 (D.N.J.2007) (terminating most of settlement agreement for low-income housing due to changed factual circumstances and inappropriateness of indefinite court monitoring of competently managed governmental agency); Evans v. Williams, 206 F.3d 1292 (D.C.Cir.2000) (requiring modification of consent decree, which obligated the District of Columbia to pay vendors of goods and services within 30 days, because the court saw a distinction between the local government's "generic inability or refusal to pay the vendors," which was well-known at the time the decree was entered, and the District's later severe and unforeseen fiscal crisis and near-bankruptcy, making it impossible to pay bills). In addition, the Supreme Court, by a 5–4 vote, allowed Rule 60(b)(5) to be used as a vehicle to seek modification of an injunction on the basis that the underlying law had been "undermined" by subsequent developments, even if it had not yet been explicitly changed by the Court. Agostini v. Felton, 521 U.S. 203 (1997) (rule not limited to recognizing changes in law; may be used to effect changes). *See* Note, *Putting the Cart Before the Horse:* Agostini v. Felton *Blurs the Line Between Res Judicata and Equitable Relief*, 49 Case W.Res.L.Rev. 407 (1999). For an example of state defendants trying unsuccessfully to use *Rufo* as the basis for modification or termination of consent decrees, see Jeff D. v. Kempthorne, 365 F.3d 844 (9th Cir.2004).

3.   Most courts have applied Rufo's modification standard to all types of injunctive relief under Rule 60(b)(5). They have not confined it to consent

decrees or institutional reform cases or governmental defendants. *See* Bellevue Manor Assoc. v. United States, 165 F.3d 1249 (9th Cir. 1999); Building and Constr. Trades Council v. National Labor Relations Board, 64 F.3d 880, 887–88 (3d Cir.1995); United States v. Western Elec. Co., 46 F.3d 1198, 1203 (D.C.Cir.1995); Alexis Lichine & Cie. v. Sacha A. Lichine Estate Selections, Ltd., 45 F.3d 582, 586 (1st Cir.1995); In re Hendrix, 986 F.2d 195, 198 (7th Cir.1993); Patterson v. Newspaper & Mail Deliverers' Union, 13 F.3d 33, 38 (2d Cir.1993); *but see* W.L. Gore & Associates, Inc. v. C.R. Bard, Inc., 977 F.2d 558 (Fed.Cir.1992) (refusing to apply *Rufo* to commercial patent case). Courts have also applied the same standard to both plaintiffs and defendants, though plaintiffs sometimes seek a more relaxed standard. *See* Hook v. Arizona, 120 F.3d 932 (9th Cir. 1997).

————

There are also cases in which the defendants seek to terminate the order, rather than modify. In these cases, the defendants may not have fully complied with all of the terms of the injunction or consent decree, but nevertheless seek relief from futher compliance.

BOARD OF EDUCATION OF OKLAHOMA CITY PUBLIC SCHOOLS V. DOWELL

Supreme Court of the United States
498 U.S. 237 (1991)

CHIEF JUSTICE REHNQUIST delivered the opinion of the Court.

* * *

I

This school desegregation litigation began almost 30 years ago. [The Court reviewed the prolonged history of the case from its inception in 1961.] * * * In 1972, finding that previous efforts had not been successful at eliminating state-imposed segregation, the District Court ordered the Board [of Education of Oklahoma City, Oklahoma] to adopt the "Finger Plan," under which kindergartners would be assigned to neighborhood schools unless their parents opted otherwise; children in grades 1–4 would attend formerly all white schools, and thus black children would be bused to those schools; children in grade 5 would attend formerly all black schools, and thus white children would be bused to those schools; students in the upper grades would be bused to various areas in order to maintain integrated schools; and in integrated neighborhoods there would be stand-alone schools for all grades.

In 1977, after complying with the desegregation decree for five years, the Board made a "Motion to Close Case." The District Court held in its "Order Terminating Case":

"The Court has concluded that [the Finger Plan] worked and that substantial compliance with the constitutional requirements has been achieved. * * *

" . . . The School Board, as now constituted, has manifested the desire and intent to follow the law. The court believes that the present members and their successors on the Board will now and in the future continue to follow the constitutional desegregation requirements. * * *

" . . . Jurisdiction in this case is terminated ipso facto subject only to final disposition of any case now pending on appeal."

This unpublished order was not appealed.

In 1984, the School Board faced demographic changes that led to greater burdens on young black children. As more and more neighborhoods became integrated, more stand-alone schools were established, and young black students had to be bused farther from their inner-city homes to outlying white areas. In an effort to alleviate this burden and to increase parental involvement, the Board adopted the Student Reassignment Plan (SRP), which relied on neighborhood assignments for students in grades K–4 beginning in the 1985–1986 school year. Busing continued for students in grades 5–12. Any student could transfer from a school where he or she was in the majority to a school where he or she would be in the minority. Faculty and staff integration was retained, and an "equity officer" was appointed.

In 1985, respondents filed a "Motion to Reopen the Case," contending that the School District had not achieved "unitary" status and that the SRP was a return to segregation. Under the SRP, 11 of 64 elementary schools would be greater than 90% black, 22 would be greater than 90% white plus other minorities, and 31 would be racially mixed. The District Court refused to reopen the case, holding that its 1977 finding of unitariness was res judicata as to those who were then parties to the action, and that the district remained unitary. * * * Because unitariness had been achieved, the District Court concluded that court-ordered desegregation must end.

The Court of Appeals for the Tenth Circuit reversed. It held that, while the 1977 order finding the district unitary was binding on the parties, nothing in that order indicated that the 1972 injunction itself was terminated. The court reasoned that the finding that the system was unitary merely ended the District Court's active supervision of the case, and because the school district was still subject to the desegregation decree, respondents could challenge the SRP. The case was remanded to determine whether the decree should be lifted or modified.

On remand, the District Court found that demographic changes made the Finger Plan unworkable, that the Board had done nothing for 25 years to promote residential segregation, and that the school district had bused students for more than a decade in good-faith compliance with the court's orders. The District Court found that present residential segregation was the result of private decisionmaking and economics, and that it was too attenuated to be a vestige of former school segregation. It also found that the district had maintained its unitary status, and that the neighborhood assignment plan was not designed with discriminatory intent. The court concluded that the previous injunctive decree should be vacated and the school district returned to local control.

The Court of Appeals again reversed, holding that " 'an injunction takes on a life of its own and becomes an edict quite independent of the law it is meant to effectuate.' " That court approached the case "not so much as one dealing with desegregation, but as one dealing with the proper application of the federal law on injunctive remedies." Relying on United States v. Swift & Co., 286 U.S. 106 (1932), it held that a desegregation decree remains in effect until a school district can show "grievous wrong evoked by new and unforeseen conditions," and "dramatic changes in conditions unforeseen at the time of the decree that . . . impose extreme and unexpectedly oppressive hardships on the obligor," (quoting Jost, *From Swift to Stotts and Beyond: Modification of Injunctions in the Federal Courts*, 64 Tex.L.Rev. 1101, 1110 (1986)). Given that a number of schools would return to being primarily one-race schools under the SRP, circumstances in Oklahoma City had not changed enough to justify modification of the decree. * * *

We now reverse the Court of Appeals. * * *

III

The Court of Appeals relied upon language from this Court's decision in *United States v. Swift and Co.* * * * . We hold that its reliance was mistaken. * * *

United States v. United Shoe Machinery Corp., 391 U.S. 244 (1968), explained that the language used in *Swift* must be read in the context of the continuing danger of unlawful restraints on trade which the Court had found still existed. * * * In the present case, a finding by the District Court that the Oklahoma City School District was being operated in compliance with the commands of the Equal Protection Clause of the Fourteenth Amendment, and that it was unlikely that the school board would return to its former ways, would be a finding that the purposes of the desegregation litigation had been fully achieved. No additional showing of "grievous wrong evoked by new and unforeseen conditions" is required of the Board. * * *

Considerations based on the allocation of powers within our federal system, we think, support our view that * * * *Swift* does not provide the proper standard to apply to injunctions entered in school desegregation cases. Such decrees, unlike the one in *Swift*, are not intended to operate in perpetuity. * * * The legal justification for displacement of local authority by an injunctive decree in a school desegregation case is a violation of the Constitution by the local authorities. Dissolving a desegregation decree after the local authorities have operated in compliance with it for a reasonable period of time properly recognizes that "necessary concern for the important values of local control of public school systems dictates that a federal court's regulatory control of such systems not extend beyond the time required to remedy the effects of past intentional discrimination."

The Court of Appeals * * * relied for its statement that "compliance alone cannot become the basis for modifying or dissolving an injunction" on our decision in United States v. W.T. Grant Co., 345 U.S. at 633. That case, however, did not involve the dissolution of an injunction, but the question of whether an injunction should be issued in the first place. This Court observed that a promise to comply with the law on the part of a wrongdoer did not divest a district court of its power to enjoin the wrongful conduct in which the defendant had previously engaged.

A district court need not accept at face value the profession of a school board which has intentionally discriminated that it will cease to do so in the future. But in deciding whether to modify or dissolve a desegregation decree, a school board's compliance with previous court orders is obviously relevant. * * * The test espoused by the Court of Appeals would condemn a school district, once governed by a board which intentionally discriminated, to judicial tutelage for the indefinite future. Neither the principles governing the entry and dissolution of injunctive decrees, nor the commands of the Equal Protection Clause of the Fourteenth Amendment, require any such Draconian result.

Petitioner urges that we reinstate the decision of the District Court terminating the injunction, but we think that the preferable course is to remand the case to that court so that it may decide, in accordance with this opinion, whether the Board made a sufficient showing of constitutional compliance as of 1985, when the SRP was adopted, to allow the injunction to be dissolved. The District Court should address itself to whether the Board had complied in good faith with the desegregation decree since it was entered, and whether the vestiges of past discrimination had been eliminated to the extent practicable.

In considering whether the vestiges of *de jure* segregation had been eliminated to the extent practicable, the District Court should look not only at student assignments, but "to every facet of school operations—faculty, staff, transportation, extra-curricular activities and facilities." *Green.* * * *

After the District Court decides whether the Board was entitled to have the decree terminated, it should proceed to decide respondent's challenge to the SRP. A school district which has been released from an injunction imposing a desegregation plan no longer requires court authorization for the promulgation of policies and rules regulating matters such as assignment of students and the like, but it of course remains subject to the mandate of the Equal Protection Clause of the Fourteenth Amendment. If the Board was entitled to have the decree terminated as of 1985, the District Court should then evaluate the Board's decision to implement the SRP under appropriate equal protection principles. * * *

JUSTICE MARSHALL, with whom JUSTICE BLACKMUN and JUSTICE STEVENS join, dissenting.

* * * [Justice Marshall began by reviewing Oklahoma's record of segregation since the state's admission to the Union in 1907. Turning to the *Dowell* litigation, Justice Marshall found that its] history reveals nearly unflagging resistance by the Board to judicial efforts to dismantle the city's dual education system. * * *

II

I agree with the majority that the proper standard for determining whether a school desegregation decree should be dissolved is whether the purposes of the desegregation litigation, as incorporated in the decree, have been fully achieved. * * * I strongly disagree with the majority, however, on what must be shown to demonstrate that a decree's purposes have been fully realized. In my view, a standard for dissolution of a desegregation decree must take into account the unique harm associated with a system of racially identifiable schools and must expressly demand the elimination of such schools.

A

Our pointed focus in *Brown I* upon the stigmatic injury caused by segregated schools explains our unflagging insistence that formerly *de jure* segregated school districts extinguish all vestiges of school segregation. The concept of stigma also gives us guidance as to what conditions must be eliminated before a decree can be deemed to have served its purpose. * * *

Just as it is central to the standard for evaluating the formation of a desegregation decree, so should the stigmatic injury associated with segregated schools be central to the standard for dissolving a decree. The Court has indicated that "the ultimate end to be brought about" by a desegregation remedy is "a unitary, nonracial system of public education." *Green.* * * * Although the Court has never explicitly defined what constitutes a "vestige" of state-enforced segregation, the function that this concept has performed in our jurisprudence suggests that it extends to any condition that is likely to convey the message of inferiority implicit in a policy of segregation. So long as such conditions persist, the purposes of the decree cannot be deemed to have been achieved.

B

The majority suggests a more vague and, I fear, milder standard. * * *

By focusing heavily on present and future compliance with the Equal Protection Clause, the majority's standard ignores how the stigmatic harm identified in *Brown I* can persist even after the State ceases actively to enforce segregation.[6] * * * [O]ur school-desegregation jurisprudence establishes that the *effects* of past discrimination remain chargeable to the school district regardless of its lack of continued enforcement of segregation, and the remedial decree is required until those effects have been finally eliminated.

III

Applying the standard I have outlined, I would affirm the Court of Appeals' decision ordering the District Court to restore the desegregation decree. For it is clear on this record that removal of the decree will result in a significant number of racially identifiable schools that could be eliminated. * * *

It is undisputed that replacing the Finger Plan with a system of neighborhood school assignments for grades K–4 resulted in a system of racially identifiable schools. * * * Because this principal vestige of *de jure* segregation persists, lifting the decree would clearly be premature at this point. * * *

In its concern to spare local school boards the "Draconian" fate of "indefinite" "judicial tutelage," the majority risks subordination of the constitutional rights of Afro-American children to the interest of school board autonomy. The courts must consider the value of local control, but that factor primarily relates to the feasibility of a remedial measure, see *Milliken II*, not whether the constitutional violation has been remedied. *Swann* establishes that if further desegregation is "reasonable, feasible, and workable," then it must be undertaken. * * * The School Board does not argue that further desegregation of the one-race schools in its system is unworkable * * * .

We should keep in mind that the court's active supervision of the desegregation process ceased in 1977. Retaining the decree does not require a return to active supervision. It may be that a modification of the decree which will improve its effectiveness and give the school district more flexibility in minimizing busing is appropriate in this case. But retaining the decree seems a slight burden on the school district compared with the risk of not delivering a full remedy to the Afro-American children in the school system. * * *

---

[6] Faithful compliance with the decree admittedly is relevant to the standard for dissolution. The standard for dissolution should require that the school district have exhibited faithful compliance with the decree for a period sufficient to assure the District Court that the school district is committed to the ideal of integrated system. * * *

NOTES

1.   The majority noted that on remand the district court first needed to decide "whether the Board made a sufficient showing of constitutional compliance as of 1985, when the SRP was adopted, to allow the injunction to be dissolved." The Supreme Court then instructed the district court that if it decided that the decree should have been terminated by 1985, the lower court "should then evaluate the Board's decision to implement the SRP under appropriate equal protection principles." What is the legal standard to be used in this portion of the proceeding? Who bears the burden of proof? For example, must the school board show that its decision to implement the SRP will not have a segregative effect? Must the plaintiffs demonstrate that the Board's decision was made with intent to re-segregate the Oklahoma City schools? *See* Dowell v. Board of Education of Oklahoma City Public Schools, 8 F.3d 1501 (10th Cir.1993) (affirming district court's decisions in the defendants' favor on remand).

In this second portion of the proceeding on remand, may the plaintiffs rely on the history of segregation in Oklahoma that Justice Marshall reviewed and the prior "unflagging resistance by the Board to judicial efforts to dismantle the City's dual education system"? *See* Price v. Austin Independent School District, 945 F.2d 1307 (5th Cir.1991).

2.   Suppose on remand in *Dowell* that the district court finds that there are no vestiges of de jure segregation with respect to student assignments to schools (because any variation is due to changes in the housing patterns), but there are some vestiges with respect to other facets of school operations, such as faculty or staff assignments, transportation, extra-curricular activities or facilities. What should the district court do?

In Freeman v. Pitts, 503 U.S. 467, 490–96 (1992), Justice Kennedy explained for the Supreme Court:

> We hold that, in the course of supervising desegregation plans, federal courts have the authority to relinquish supervision and control of school districts in incremental stages, before full compliance has been achieved in every area of school operations. While retaining jurisdiction over the case, the court may determine that it will not order further remedies in areas where the school district is in compliance with the decree. That is to say, upon a finding that a school system subject to a court-supervised desegregation plan is in compliance in some but not all areas, the court in appropriate cases may return control to the school system in those areas where compliance has been achieved, limiting further judicial supervision to operations that are not yet in full compliance with the court decree. In particular, the district court may determine that it will not order further remedies in the area of student assignments where racial imbalance is not traceable, in a proximate way, to constitutional violations.

* * *

That there was racial imbalance in student attendance zones was not tantamount to a showing that the school district was in noncompliance with the decree or with its duties under the law. Racial balance is not to be achieved for its own sake. It is to be pursued when racial imbalance has been caused by a constitutional violation. Once the racial imbalance due to the *de jure* violation has been remedied, the school district is under no duty to remedy imbalance that is caused by demographic factors. * * * If the unlawful *de jure* policy of a school system has been the cause of the racial imbalance in student attendance, that condition must be remedied. The school district bears the burden of showing that any current imbalance is not traceable, in a proximate way, to the prior violation. * * *

In one sense of the term, vestiges of past segregation by state decree do remain in our society and in our schools. Past wrongs to the black race, wrongs committed by the State and in its name, are a stubborn fact of history. And stubborn facts of history linger and persist. But though we cannot escape our history, neither must we overstate its consequences in fixing legal responsibilities. The vestiges of segregation that are the concern of the law in a school case may be subtle and intangible but nonetheless they must be so real that they have a causal link to the *de jure* violation being remedied. It is simply not always the case that demographic forces causing population change bear any real and substantial relation to a *de jure* violation. And the law need not proceed on that premise.

* * *

Justice Scalia, in a concurring opinion, urged the Court to:

acknowledge that it has become absurd to assume, without any further proof, that violations of the Constitution dating from the days when Lyndon Johnson was President, or earlier, continue to have an appreciable effect upon current operation of schools. * * * We must soon revert to the ordinary principles of our law, of our democratic heritage, and of our educational tradition: that plaintiffs alleging equal protection violations must prove intent and causation and not merely the existence of racial disparity; that public schooling, even in the South, should be controlled by locally elected authorities acting in conjunction with parents; and that it is "desirable" to permit pupils to attend "schools nearest their homes."

Id. at 506–07.

Justice Souter took a very different approach in his concurring opinion. He noted that judicial control over student assignments (or some other facet of school operations) might be required in a number of situations. For example, judicial control might be needed: (a) "to remedy persisting vestiges of the unconstitutional dual system, such as remaining imbalance in faculty assignments;" (b) the dual school system were a cause of the demographic shifts; or (c) a "*Green*-type factor other than student assignments [were] a possible cause of imbalanced student assignment patterns in the future." Justice Souter would allow the district courts to reassert control over student assignments in any of these circumstances. *Id.* at 507–08.

Justices Blackmun, Stevens and O'Connor, concurring in the judgment, stated: "It is not enough, however, for [the school district] to establish that demographics exacerbated the problem; it must prove that its own policies did not contribute. Such contribution can occur in at least two ways: DCSS may have contributed to the demographic changes themselves, or it may have contributed directly to the racial imbalance in the schools." *Id.* at 512–13.

After taking further evidence, the district court subsequently concluded that the school district's constitutional violations had been fully remedied to the extent practicable and granted final dismissal from the court's supervision. Mills v. Freeman, 942 F.Supp. 1449, 1464 (N.D.Ga.1996).

3.   Many courts and scholars have taken *Dowell* and *Freeman* as strong signals from the Supreme Court to end supervision over school desegregation decrees. *E.g.,* People Who Care v. Rockford Board of Education, 246 F.3d 1073, 1074 (7th Cir.2001) ("heed the admonition of the Supreme Court * * * to bend every effort to winding up school litigation and returning the operation of the schools to the local school authorities"); Bradley W. Joondeph, *Skepticism and School Desegregation*, 76 Wash.U.L.Q. 161 (1998) ("curtain falls on court-ordered desegregation nationwide"). Empirical work demonstrates that although several cases have been terminated, "the vast majority of school desegregation litigation continues, with no hint of impending termination." Wendy Parker, *The Future of School Desegregation*, 94 Nw.U.L.Rev. 1157, 1160 (2000). "The clear majority of school districts appear content with their outstanding court orders. Not seeking termination imposes only known costs, while dismissal proceedings would require additional resources and, more importantly, an examination of how the district treats minority school children." *Id. Accord,* David I. Levine, *The Chinese American Challenge to Court-Mandated Quotas in San Francisco's Public Schools: Notes from a (Partisan) Participant-Observer*, 16 Harv. Blackletter L.J. 39, 124–29 (2000) (desire of school districts to return to local control is a myth).

After several decades, the Supreme Court took up the question of modification and termination of injunctions again. It returned to the core of the procedural rule providing a flexible standard towards deciding when applying an injunction "prospectively is no longer equitable."

HORNE V. FLORES

Supreme Court of the United States
557 U.S. 433 (2009)

JUSTICE ALITO delivered the opinion of the Court.

These consolidated cases arise from litigation that began in Arizona in 1992 when a group of English Language-Learner (ELL) students in the

Nogales Unified School District and their parents filed a class action, alleging that the State was violating the Equal Educational Opportunities Act of 1974 (EEOA), 20 U.S.C. § 1703(f), which requires a State "to take appropriate action to overcome language barriers that impede equal participation by its students in its instructional programs." [The District Court concluded that defendants were violating the EEOA because the amount of funding the State allocated for the special needs of ELL students was arbitrary and not related to the actual funding needed to cover the costs of ELL instruction.] The District Court entered a declaratory judgment with respect to Nogales, and in 2001, the court extended the order [and granted injunctive relief] to apply to the entire State. Over the next eight years, petitioners repeatedly sought relief from the District Court's orders, but to no avail. [The court imposed contempt fines for failure to comply with the order that escalated from $500,000 to $2 million per day.] We granted certiorari after the Court of Appeals for the Ninth Circuit affirmed the denial of petitioners' motion for relief under Federal Rule of Civil Procedure 60(b)(5), and we now reverse the judgment of the Court of Appeals and remand for further proceedings.

As we explain, the District Court and the Court of Appeals misunderstood both the obligation that the EEOA imposes on States and the nature of the inquiry that is required when parties such as petitioners seek relief under Rule 60(b)(5) on the ground that enforcement of a judgment is "no longer equitable." Both of the lower courts focused excessively on the narrow question of the adequacy of the State's incremental funding for ELL instruction instead of fairly considering the broader question whether, as a result of important changes during the intervening years, the State was fulfilling its obligation under the EEOA by other means. The question at issue in these cases is not whether Arizona must take "appropriate action" to overcome the language barriers that impede ELL students. Of course it must. But petitioners argue that Arizona is now fulfilling its statutory obligation by new means that reflect new policy insights and other changed circumstances. Rule 60(b)(5) provides the vehicle for petitioners to bring such an argument.

I

* * *

C

The defendants did not appeal any of the District Court's orders, and the record suggests that some state officials supported their continued enforcement. In June 2001, the state attorney general acquiesced in the statewide extension of the declaratory judgment order, a step that the State has explained by reference to the Arizona constitutional requirement of uniform statewide school funding. * * *

In March 2006, after accruing over $20 million in fines, the state legislature passed HB 2064, which was designed to implement a permanent funding solution to the problems identified by the District Court in 2000. Among other things, HB 2064 increased ELL incremental funding (with a 2-year per-student limit on such funding) and created two new funds-a structured English immersion fund and a compensatory instruction fund-to cover additional costs of ELL programming. Moneys in both newly created funds were to be offset by available federal moneys. HB 2064 also instituted several programming and structural changes. * * *

With the principal defendants in the action siding with the plaintiffs, the Speaker of the State House of Representatives and the President of the State Senate filed a motion to intervene as representatives of their respective legislative bodies. In support of their motion, they stated that although the attorney general had a "legal duty" to defend HB 2064, the attorney general had shown "little enthusiasm" for advancing the legislature's interests. Among other things, the Legislators noted that the attorney general "failed to take an appeal of the judgment entered in this case in 2000 and has failed to appeal any of the injunctions and other orders issued in aid of the judgment." The District Court granted the Legislators' motion for permissive intervention, and the Legislators and superintendent moved to purge the District Court's contempt order in light of HB 2064. Alternatively, they moved for relief under Federal Rule of Civil Procedure 60(b)(5) based on changed circumstances. * * *

[T]he District Court denied petitioners' Rule 60(b)(5) motion. * * * The Court of Appeals affirmed. * * * We granted certiorari, and now reverse.

III

A

Federal Rule of Civil Procedure 60(b)(5) permits a party to obtain relief from a judgment or order if, among other things, "applying [the judgment or order] prospectively is no longer equitable." Rule 60(b)(5) may not be used to challenge the legal conclusions on which a prior judgment or order rests, but the Rule provides a means by which a party can ask a court to modify or vacate a judgment or order if "a significant change either in factual conditions or in law" renders continued enforcement "detrimental to the public interest." *Rufo.* The party seeking relief bears the burden of establishing that changed circumstances warrant relief, but once a party carries this burden, a court abuses its discretion "when it refuses to modify an injunction or consent decree in light of such changes." Agostini v. Felton, 521 U.S. 203, 215 (1997).

Rule 60(b)(5) serves a particularly important function in what we have termed "institutional reform litigation."[3] *Rufo.* For one thing, injunctions

---

[3]   The dissent is quite wrong in contending that these are not institutional reform cases because they involve a statutory, rather than a constitutional claim, and because the orders of the

issued in such cases often remain in force for many years, and the passage of time frequently brings about changed circumstances-changes in the nature of the underlying problem, changes in governing law or its interpretation by the courts, and new policy insights-that warrant reexamination of the original judgment.

Second, institutional reform injunctions often raise sensitive federalism concerns. Such litigation commonly involves areas of core state responsibility, such as public education. See Missouri v. Jenkins, 515 U.S. 70, 99 (1995) ("[O]ur cases recognize that local autonomy of school districts is a vital national tradition, and that a district court must strive to restore state and local authorities to the control of a school system operating in compliance with the Constitution") (KENNEDY, J., concurring).

Federalism concerns are heightened when, as in these cases, a federal court decree has the effect of dictating state or local budget priorities. States and local governments have limited funds. When a federal court orders that money be appropriated for one program, the effect is often to take funds away from other important programs. See *Jenkins* ("A structural reform decree eviscerates a State's discretionary authority over its own program and budgets and forces state officials to reallocate state resources and funds").

Finally, the dynamics of institutional reform litigation differ from those of other cases. Scholars have noted that public officials sometimes consent to, or refrain from vigorously opposing, decrees that go well beyond what is required by federal law. *See, e.g.,* McConnell, *Why Hold Elections? Using Consent Decrees to Insulate Policies from Political Change*, 1987 U. Chi. Legal Forum 295, 317 (noting that government officials may try to use consent decrees to "block ordinary avenues of political change" or to "sidestep political constraints"); Horowitz, *Decreeing Organizational Change: Judicial Supervision of Public Institutions*, 1983 Duke L.J. 1265, 1294–1295 ("Nominal defendants [in institutional reform cases] are sometimes happy to be sued and happier still to lose"); R. Sandler & D. Schoenbrod, Democracy by Decree: What Happens When Courts Run Government 170 (2003) ("Government officials, who always operate under fiscal and political constraints, 'frequently win by losing' " in institutional reform litigation).

Injunctions of this sort bind state and local officials to the policy preferences of their predecessors and may thereby "improperly deprive

---

District Court do not micromanage the day-to-day operation of the schools. For nearly a decade, the orders of a federal district court have substantially restricted the ability of the State of Arizona to make basic decisions regarding educational policy, appropriations, and budget priorities. The record strongly suggests that some state officials have welcomed the involvement of the federal court as a means of achieving appropriations objectives that could not be achieved through the ordinary democratic process. Because of these features, these cases implicate all of the unique features and risks of institutional reform litigation future officials of their designated legislative and executive powers." Frew v. Hawkins, 540 U.S. 431, 441 (2004). * * *

States and localities "depen[d] upon successor officials, both appointed and elected, to bring new insights and solutions to problems of allocating revenues and resources." *Frew*. Where "state and local officials . . . inherit overbroad or outdated consent decrees that limit their ability to respond to the priorities and concerns of their constituents," they are constrained in their ability to fulfill their duties as democratically-elected officials. American Legislative Exchange Council, Resolution on the Federal Consent Decree Fairness Act (2006).

It goes without saying that federal courts must vigilantly enforce federal law and must not hesitate in awarding necessary relief. But in recognition of the features of institutional reform decrees, we have held that courts must take a "flexible approach" to Rule 60(b)(5) motions addressing such decrees. *Rufo*. A flexible approach allows courts to ensure that "responsibility for discharging the State's obligations is returned promptly to the State and its officials" when the circumstances warrant. *Frew*. In applying this flexible approach, courts must remain attentive to the fact that "federal-court decrees exceed appropriate limits if they are aimed at eliminating a condition that does not violate [federal law] or does not flow from such a violation." Milliken v. Bradley, 433 U.S. 267, 282 (1977). "If [a federal consent decree is] not limited to reasonable and necessary implementations of federal law," it may "improperly deprive future officials of their designated legislative and executive powers." *Frew*.

For these reasons, a critical question in this Rule 60(b)(5) inquiry is whether the objective of the District Court's 2000 declaratory judgment order-*i.e.,* satisfaction of the EEOA's "appropriate action" standard-has been achieved. If a durable remedy has been implemented, continued enforcement of the order is not only unnecessary, but improper. See *Milliken*. We note that the EEOA itself limits court-ordered remedies to those that "are *essential* to correct particular denials of equal educational opportunity or equal protection of the laws."

B

The Court of Appeals did not engage in the Rule 60(b)(5) analysis just described. Rather than applying a flexible standard that seeks to return control to state and local officials as soon as a violation of federal law has been remedied, the Court of Appeals used a heightened standard that paid insufficient attention to federalism concerns. And rather than inquiring broadly into whether changed conditions in Nogales provided evidence of an ELL program that complied with the EEOA, the Court of Appeals concerned itself only with determining whether increased ELL funding complied with the original declaratory judgment order. The court erred on both counts.

1

The Court of Appeals began its Rule 60(b)(5) discussion by citing the correct legal standard, but it quickly strayed. It referred to the situations in which changed circumstances warrant Rule 60(b)(5) relief as "likely rare," and explained that, to succeed on these grounds, petitioners would have to make a showing that conditions in Nogales had so changed as to "sweep away" the District Court's incremental funding determination. The Court of Appeals concluded that the District Court had not erred in determining that "the landscape was not so *radically* changed as to justify relief from judgment without compliance."

Moreover, after recognizing that review of the denial of Rule 60(b)(5) relief should generally be "somewhat closer in the context of institutional injunctions against states 'due to federalism concerns,'" the Court of Appeals incorrectly reasoned that "federalism concerns are substantially lessened here, as the state of Arizona and the state Board of Education wish the injunction to remain in place." This statement is flatly incorrect, as even respondents acknowledge. Precisely because different state actors have taken contrary positions in this litigation, federalism concerns are elevated. And precisely because federalism concerns are heightened, a flexible approach to Rule 60(b)(5) relief is critical. "[W]hen the objects of the decree have been attained"—namely, when EEOA compliance has been achieved—"responsibility for discharging the State's obligations [must be] returned promptly to the State and its officials." *Frew.*

2

In addition to applying a Rule 60(b)(5) standard that was too strict, the Court of Appeals framed a Rule 60(b)(5) inquiry that was too narrow—one that focused almost exclusively on the sufficiency of incremental funding. In large part, this was driven by the significance the Court of Appeals attributed to petitioners' failure to appeal the District Court's original order. The Court of Appeals explained that "the central idea" of that order was that without sufficient ELL incremental funds, "ELL programs would necessarily be inadequate." It felt bound by this conclusion, lest it allow petitioners to "reopen matters made final when the Declaratory Judgment was not appealed." It repeated this refrain throughout its opinion, emphasizing that the "interest in finality must be given great weight," and explaining that petitioners could not now ask for relief "on grounds that could have been raised on appeal from the Declaratory Judgment and from earlier injunctive orders but were not," "If [petitioners] believed that the district court erred and should have looked at all funding sources differently in its EEOA inquiry," the court wrote, "they should have appealed the Declaratory Judgment."

In attributing such significance to the defendants' failure to appeal the District Court's original order, the Court of Appeals turned the risks of institutional reform litigation into reality. By confining the scope of its analysis to that of the original order, it insulated the policies embedded in the order—specifically, its incremental funding requirement—from challenge and amendment.[5] But those policies were supported by the very officials who could have appealed them—the state defendants—and, as a result, were never subject to true challenge.

Instead of focusing on the failure to appeal, the Court of Appeals should have conducted the type of Rule 60(b)(5) inquiry prescribed in *Rufo*. This inquiry makes no reference to the presence or absence of a timely appeal. It takes the original judgment as a given and asks only whether "a significant change either in factual conditions or in law" renders continued enforcement of the judgment "detrimental to the public interest. It allows a court to recognize that the longer an injunction or consent decree stays in place, the greater the risk that it will improperly interfere with a State's democratic processes.

The Court of Appeals purported to engage in a "changed circumstances" inquiry, but it asked only whether changed circumstances affected ELL funding and, more specifically, ELL incremental funding. Relief was appropriate, in the court's view, only if petitioners "demonstrate[d] either that there [we]re no longer incremental costs associated with ELL programs in Arizona or that Arizona's 'base plus incremental costs' educational funding model was so altered that focusing on ELL-specific incremental costs funding has become irrelevant and inequitable."

This was a Rule 60(b)(5) "changed circumstances" inquiry in name only. In reality, it was an inquiry into whether the deficiency in ELL incremental funding that the District Court identified in 2000 had been remedied. And this, effectively, was an inquiry into whether the original order had been satisfied. Satisfaction of an earlier judgment is *one* of the enumerated bases for Rule 60(b)(5) relief—but it is not the only basis for such relief.

Rule 60(b)(5) permits relief from a judgment where "[i] the judgment has been satisfied, released or discharged; [ii] it is based on an earlier judgment that has been reversed or vacated; *or* [iii] applying it prospectively is no longer equitable." Use of the disjunctive "or" makes it clear that each of the provision's three grounds for relief is independently sufficient and therefore that relief may be warranted even if petitioners have not "satisfied" the original order. As petitioners argue, they may

---

[5]   This does not mean, as the dissent misleadingly suggests, that we are faulting the Court of Appeals for declining to decide whether the District Court's original order was correct in the first place. On the contrary, as we state explicitly in the paragraph following this statement, our criticism is that the Court of Appeals did not engage in the changed-circumstances inquiry prescribed by *Rufo*. By focusing excessively on the issue of incremental funding, the Court of Appeals was not true to the *Rufo* standard.

obtain relief if prospective enforcement of that order "is no longer equitable."

To determine the merits of this claim, the Court of Appeals needed to ascertain whether ongoing enforcement of the original order was supported by an ongoing violation of federal law (here, the EEOA). See *Milliken*. It failed to do so.

As previously noted, the EEOA, while requiring a State to take "appropriate action to overcome language barriers," "leave[s] state and local educational authorities a substantial amount of latitude in choosing" how this obligation is met. Of course, any educational program, including the "appropriate action" mandated by the EEOA, requires funding, but funding is simply a means, not the end. By focusing so intensively on Arizona's incremental ELL funding, the Court of Appeals misapprehended the EEOA's mandate. And by requiring petitioners to demonstrate "appropriate action" through a particular funding mechanism, the Court of Appeals improperly substituted its own educational and budgetary policy judgments for those of the state and local officials to whom such decisions are properly entrusted. Cf. *Jenkins* (Federal courts do not possess the capabilities of state and local governments in addressing difficult educational problems"). * * *

E

Because the lower courts—like the dissent—misperceived both the nature of the obligation imposed by the EEOA and the breadth of the inquiry called for under Rule 60(b)(5), these cases must be remanded for a proper examination of at least four important factual and legal changes that may warrant the granting of relief from the judgment: the State's adoption of a new ELL instructional methodology, Congress' enactment of NCLB, structural and management reforms in Nogales, and increased overall education funding. * * *

Because the lower courts engaged in an inadequate Rule 60(b)(5) analysis, and because the District Court failed to make up-to-date factual findings, the analysis of the lower courts was incomplete and inadequate with respect to all of the changed circumstances just noted. These changes are critical to a proper Rule 60(b)(5) analysis, however, as they may establish that Nogales is no longer in violation of the EEOA and, to the contrary, is taking "appropriate action" to remove language barriers in its schools. If this is the case, continued enforcement of the District Court's original order is inequitable within the meaning of Rule 60(b)(5), and relief is warranted.

* * *

We reverse the judgment of the Court of Appeals and remand the cases for the District Court to determine whether, in accordance with the standards set out in this opinion, petitioners should be granted relief from the judgment. * * *

JUSTICE BREYER, with whom JUSTICE STEVENS, JUSTICE SOUTER, and JUSTICE GINSBURG join, dissenting.

* * *The Court reaches its ultimate conclusion—that the lower courts did not "*fairly consider*" the changed circumstances—in a complicated way. It begins by placing this case in a category it calls "institutional reform litigation." It then sets forth special "institutional reform litigation" standards applicable when courts are asked to modify judgments and decrees entered in such cases. It applies those standards, and finds that the lower courts committed error.

I disagree with the Court for several reasons. For one thing, the "institutional reform" label does not easily fit this case. For another, the review standards the Court enunciates for "institutional reform" cases are incomplete and, insofar as the Court applies those standards here, they effectively distort Rule 60(b)(5)'s objectives. Finally, my own review of the record convinces me that the Court is wrong regardless. *The lower courts did "fairly consider" every change in circumstances that the parties called to their attention.* The record more than adequately supports this conclusion. In a word, I fear that the Court misapplies an inappropriate procedural framework, reaching a result that neither the record nor the law adequately supports. In doing so, it risks denying schoolchildren the English-learning instruction necessary "to overcome language barriers that impede" their "equal participation."

* * *

II

* * *

To understand my concern about the Court's discussion of standards, it is important to keep in mind the well-known standards that ordinarily govern the evaluation of Rule 60(b)(5) motions. The Rule by its terms permits modification of a judgment or order (1) when "the judgment has been satisfied," (2) "released," or (3) "discharged;" when the judgment or order (4) "is based on an earlier judgment that has been reversed or vacated;" or (5) "applying [the judgment] prospectively is no longer equitable." No one can claim that the second, third, or fourth grounds are applicable here. The relevant judgment and orders have not been released or discharged; nor is there any relevant earlier judgment that has been reversed or vacated. Thus the only Rule 60(b)(5) questions are whether the judgment and orders have been satisfied, or, if not, whether their continued application is "equitable." And, as I have explained, in context these come down to the same question: Is continued enforcement inequitable because the defendants have satisfied the 2000 declaratory judgment or at least have come close to doing so, and, given that degree of satisfaction, would it work unnecessary harm to continue the judgment in effect?

To show sufficient inequity to warrant Rule 60(b)(5) relief, a party must show that "a significant change either in factual conditions or in law" renders continued enforcement of the judgment or order "detrimental to the public interest." *Rufo*. The party can claim that "the statutory or decisional law has changed to make legal what the decree was designed to prevent." Or the party can claim that relevant facts have changed to the point where continued enforcement of the judgment, order, or decree as written would work, say, disproportionately serious harm. See *Rufo*. (modification may be appropriate when changed circumstances make enforcement "substantially more onerous" or "unworkable because of unforeseen obstacles").

The Court acknowledges, as do I, as did the lower courts, that *Rufo*'s "flexible standard" for relief applies. The Court also acknowledges, as do I, as did the lower courts, that this "flexible standard" does not itself define the inquiry a court passing on a Rule 60(b)(5) motion must make. To give content to this standard, the Court refers to *Milliken v. Bradley*, in which this Court said that a decree cannot seek to "eliminat[e] a condition that does not violate" federal law or "flow from such a violation," and to *Frew v. Hawkins*, in which this Court said that a "*consent decree*" must be "limited to reasonable and necessary implementations of federal law". The Court adds that in an "institutional reform litigation" case, a court must also take account of the need not to maintain decrees in effect for too long a time, the need to take account of "sensitive federalism concerns," and the need to take care lest "consent decrees" reflect collusion between private plaintiffs and state defendants at the expense of the legislative process.

Taking these cases and considerations together, the majority says the critical question for the lower courts is "whether ongoing enforcement of the original order was supported by an ongoing violation of federal law." If not—*i.e.,* if a current violation of federal law cannot be detected—then " 'responsibility for discharging the State's obligations [must be] returned promptly to the State.' " * * *

Nor is the decree at issue here a "consent decree" as that term is normally understood in the institutional litigation context. The State did consent to a few peripheral matters that have nothing to do with the present appeal. But the State vigorously contested the plaintiffs' basic original claim, namely, that the State failed to take resource-related "appropriate action" within the terms of subsection (f).

Regardless, the Court's discussion of standards raises a far more serious problem. In addition to the standards I have discussed, our precedents recognize *other,* here outcome-determinative, hornbook principles that apply when a court evaluates a Rule 60(b)(5) motion. * * * As a result, I am uncertain, and perhaps others will be uncertain, whether the Court has set forth a correct and workable method for analyzing a Rule 60(b)(5) motion.

* * *

[First, the Court considers issues the parties did not raise, and second, does not require the party seeking relief to bear the burden of establishing changed circumstances.]

Third, the Court ignores the well-established distinction between a Rule 60(b)(5) request to *modify* an order and a request to set an unsatisfied judgment entirely aside—a distinction that this Court has previously emphasized. Cf. *Rufo* (emphasizing that "we do not have before us the question whether the entire decree should be vacated"). Courts normally do the latter only if the "party" seeking "to have" the "decree set aside entirely" shows "that the decree has served its purpose, and there is no longer any need for the injunction." Instead of applying the distinction, the majority says that the Court of Appeals "strayed" when it referred to situations in which changes justified setting an unsatisfied judgment entirely aside as " 'likely rare.' "

Fourth, the Court says nothing about the well-established principle that a party moving under Rule 60(b)(5) for relief that amounts to having a "decree set aside entirely" must show *both* (1) that the decree's objects have been "attained," *Frew, and* (2) that it is unlikely, in the absence of the decree, that the unlawful acts it prohibited will again occur. This Court so held in *Dowell,* a case in which state defendants sought relief from a school desegregation decree on the ground that the district was presently operating in compliance with the Equal Protection Clause. The Court agreed with the defendants that "a finding by the District Court that the Oklahoma City School District was being operated in compliance with . . . the Equal Protection Clause" was indeed relevant to the question whether relief was appropriate. But the Court added that, to show entitlement to relief, the defendants must *also* show that "it was unlikely that the [school board] would return to its former ways." Only then would the "purposes of the desegregation litigation ha[ve] been fully achieved." The principle, as applicable here, simply underscores petitioners' failure to show that the "changes" to which they pointed were sufficient to warrant entirely setting aside the original court judgment. [Fifth, the Court fails to apply the basic Rule 60(b)(5) principle that a party cannot use the motion as a substitute for appeal and reconsideration of the original decision, and sixth, it fails to apply the proper standard of abuse of discretion.] * * *

The Court now applies a new set of new rules that are *not* faithful to our cases and which will create the dangerous possibility that orders, judgments, and decrees long final or acquiesced in, will be unwarrantedly subject to perpetual challenge, offering defendants unjustifiable opportunities endlessly to relitigate underlying violations with the burden of proof imposed once again upon the plaintiffs.

I recognize that the Court's decision, to a degree, reflects one side of a scholarly debate about how courts should properly handle decrees in "institutional reform litigation." Compare, in general, R. Sandler & D. Schoenbrod, *Democracy by Decree: What Happens When Courts Run Government* (2003), with, *e.g.,* Chayes, *The Role of the Judge in Public Law Litigation*, 89 Harv. L.Rev. 1281, 1307–1309 (1976). But whatever the merits of that debate, this case does not involve the kind of "institutional litigation" that most commonly lies at its heart. *See, e.g.,* M. Feeley & E. Rubin, *Judicial Policy Making and the Modern State: How the Courts Reformed America's Prisons* (1998).

The case does not involve schools, prisons, or mental hospitals that have failed to meet basic constitutional standards. It does not involve a comprehensive judicial decree that governs the running of a major institution. It does not involve a highly detailed set of orders. It does not involve a special master charged with the task of supervising a complex decree that will gradually bring a large institution into compliance with the law. Rather, it involves the more common complaint that a state or local government has failed to meet a federal statutory requirement. It involves a court imposition of a fine upon the State due to its lengthy failure to take steps to comply. And it involves court orders that leave the State free to pursue the English-learning program of its choice while insisting only that the State come up with a funding plan that is rationally related to the program it chooses. * * *

As I have said, the framework that I have just described, filling in those principles the Court neglects, is precisely the framework that the lower courts applied. In the opinions below, I can find no misapplication of the legal standards relevant to this case. To the contrary, the Court of Appeals' opinion is true to the record and fair to the decision of the District Court. And the majority is wrong to conclude otherwise.

NOTES

1.   On remand, the district court evaluated the changed circumstances and the merits of the alternative program under *Horne*'s "flexible approach," and terminated the case as requested by defendants. It found alternatively that the state had made a good faith effort to remedy the problem, and that the court order "previously entered in this case has been satisfied, or at the very least, that prospective application of the judgment is no longer equitable in light of the changed factual and legal circumstances." Flores v. Arizona, No. 92-CV-596 (D. Ariz. May 29, 2013). The U.S. Department of Education and Office of Civil Rights investigated Arizona for its ELL practices and the state's failure to identify students qualified for services. Press Release, U.S. Departments of Education and Justice Reach Settlement, Mar. 25, 2011.

2.   *Horne* brings the inquiry for terminating or modifying injunctive relief back to the broad equitable parameters of Rule 60(b)(5) and it's provision allowing a party to obtain relief from a court order when "it is no longer equitable that the judgment should have prospective application." Rather than limiting the rule to the *Rufo* modification setting or the *Dowell* substantial compliance situation, *Horne* applies the rule to a different context to permit relief where the defendants argue that the original purposes of the law are satisfied by means other than those required by the injunction. Petties ex. rel Martin v. District of Columbia, 662 F.3d 564 (D.C. Cir. 2011) (remanding for district court to conduct *Horne* inquiry on government's motion to vacate order requiring special education payments).

3.   The majority and dissent in *Horne* disagree on whether this case is an example of "institutional reform litigation." How does each define this category of litigation? What are they concerned about? The problems with such litigation were perhaps complicated in this case, where, as the Court notes, the government defendants were strangely aligned when the board of education and attorney general sided with the plaintiffs and failed to appeal the order, and the legislature intervened to assert the government's defense.

4.   In an omitted part of the option, the Court holds that the statewide scope of the original injunction was inappropriate for a violation found in a single district. Nogales was one of 239 school districts, yet the injunction extended to all schools in the state though the record contained "no factual findings of evidence that any school districts other than Nogales failed * * * to provide equal educational opportunities to ELL students." *Horne.* Yet the defendant attorney general had requested a statewide remedy to avoid any violations of the state constitutional requirement of a uniform public school system. The proper way to do this, the Court held, would be to use the attorney general's usual political, and democratically accountable powers, rather than an injunction.

NOTE ON MODIFICATION BY POLITICAL SUCCESSORS

The defendant's resistance to compliance in both *Rufo* and *Horne* derived from the subsequent election of political successors with differing policy views. Sheriff Rufo never personally agreed to the consent decree at issue in the case which bears his name; his predecessor, Sheriff Kearney, did. Successor governments, however, are generally bound to follow the initial injunction despite political changes. *See, e.g.,* Benjamin v. Malcolm, 156 F.R.D. 561 (S.D.N.Y.1994); *but see* Evans v. City of Chicago, 10 F.3d 474, 478–79 (7th Cir.en banc 1993), *cert. denied,* 511 U.S. 1082 (1994) (releasing city from consent decree where provisions extended beyond the contours of the law and policymakers had changed after a decade).

Political successors, however, can use modification to challenge the continuing binding effect of prior injunctions. As the Court emphasized in *Horne,* modification should be a flexible standard, and governmental accountability to the voters and the political process is a relevant concern in evaluating whether it is equitable to continue prospective relief.

The Court foreshadowed this governmental interest in modification and termination in an earlier case, Frew v. Hawkins, 540 U.S. 431, 441–42 (2004). *See* Ross Sandler & David Schoenbrod, *The Supreme Court, Democracy and Institutional Reform Litigation*, 49 N.Y.L.Sch.L.Rev. 915 (2005) (discussing impact of *Frew* on the law of modification). In *Frew*, a unanimous Court stated:

> *Rufo* rejected the idea that the institutional concerns of government officials were "only marginally relevant" when officials moved to amend a consent decree, and noted that "principles of federalism and simple common sense require the [district] court to give significant weight" to the views of government officials. * * *

> The federal court must exercise its equitable powers to ensure that when the objects of the decree have been attained, responsibility for discharging the State's obligations is returned promptly to the State and its officials. As public servants, the officials of the State must be presumed to have a high degree of competence in deciding how best to discharge their governmental responsibilities. A State, in the ordinary course, depends upon successor officials, both appointed and elected, to bring new insights and solutions to problems of allocating revenues and resources. The basic obligations of federal law may remain the same, but the precise manner of their discharge may not. If the State establishes reason to modify the decree, the court should make the necessary changes; where it has not done so, however, the decree should be enforced according to its terms.

However, on remand, the court in *Frew* refused to terminate the consent decree requiring the provision of adequate medical and dental care to indigent children in Texas. Frazar v. Ladd, 457 F.3d 432 (5th Cir. 2006), *cert denied* 549 U.S. 1118 (2007). In contrast to *Horne*, the *Frew* court held that the state had not shown sufficient change in facts to warrant modification, and that the state's alleged compliance with federal law was not, by itself, adequate ground for dissolving the consent decree. Does it matter than *Horne* was an injunction, rather than a consent decree as in *Frew*?

Professors Ross Sandler and David Schoenbrod argue that consent decrees should be aimed at putting plaintiffs in their rightful position when initially entered and that defendants should be able to modify and terminate them so long as that objective is achieved. Building upon work in their book, *Democracy by Decree: What Happens When Courts Run Government* (2003), they argue that public officials frequently agree to relief that goes beyond putting plaintiffs in their rightful position and courts then enforce the decree to rigidly, inappropriately treating the plaintiffs as owners of contractual rights rather than more limited constitutional or statutory rights. The result is that successor officials are locked into politics agree to by their predecessors regardless of their motives and whether the policies have worked as planned. Ross Sandler & David Schoenbrod, *From Status to Contract and Back Again: Consent Decrees in Institutional Reform Litigation*, 27 Rev.Lit. 115 (2007); Ross Sandler & David Schoenbrod, *The Supreme Court, Democracy and Institutional Reform Litigation*, 49 N.Y.L.Sch.L.Rev. 915 (2005). Their work has been the basis of proposed legislation, the Federal Consent Decree Fairness Act, which would have limited the duration of federal consent decrees to which state and local governments are parties to the earlier of four years or the expiration of the term of office of the official who consented to the order.

NOTE ON LEGISLATIVE TERMINATION AND THE PRISON LITIGATION REFORM ACT

In addition to guidance from the Supreme Court of the United States regarding when lower courts are obligated to withdraw supervision over an institutional defendant, the Congress of the United States has also provided specific direction for prisoner cases through the Prison Litigation Reform Act (PLRA). Pub. L. No. 104–134, 110 Stat. 1321–66 (April 26, 1996). The two primary purposes of the PLRA were: (i) to end what congressional sponsors perceived to be judicial micromanagement of correctional facilities across the country; and (ii) to discourage prisoners from filing what sponsors of the legislation charged was a flood of frivolous lawsuits. *See* Note, *Peanut Butter and Politics: An Evaluation of the Separation-of-Powers Issues in Section 802 of the Prison Litigation Reform Act*, 73 Ind. L.J. 329 (1997) (noting congressional indignation at prisoner's suit complaining of being served the wrong type of peanut butter).

In order to stop what Congress considered unreasonable judicial supervision of prisons and jails nationwide, the PLRA limits the prospective relief (i.e., other than compensatory damages, 18 U.S.C. § 3626(g)(7)) that a federal district court can order in a suit concerning prison conditions in federal, state or local incarceration facilities, § 3626(g)(2)(5). The PLRA does not merely apply to suits filed after its passage into law. Because facilities in over two-thirds of the states and territories were then under federal court order, National Prison Project, Status Report: State Prisons and the Courts 1 (Jan. 1, 1996), Congress also provided that the PLRA would reach prospective relief awarded in cases even where the court had entered judgment prior to its enactment. Under 18 U.S.C. § 3626(b)(2), prospective relief in pending cases is subject to "immediate termination" unless the court approving or granting the relief had found that the relief was narrowly drawn, extended no further than necessary to correct the violation of a federal right, and was the least intrusive way to remedy this violation.

Congress did recognize that consent decrees issued prior to the existence of the PLRA would be unlikely to have the requisite judicial findings. Indeed, as Professor Branham (from whose article this summary of the PLRA was adapted) has noted, correctional officials would typically demand that consent decrees provide that their existence did not constitute an admission that conditions in the correctional facility were unconstitutional; otherwise, the officials would have been "deluged by a wave of suits for damages filed by prisoners riding on the coattails of the consent decrees awarding injunctive relief to the plaintiffs." Lynn S. Branham, *Keeping the "Wolf Out of the Fold": Separation of Powers and Congressional Termination of Equitable Relief*, 26 J.Legis. 185, 191 (2000). Under § 3626(b)(3), a federal district court must grant a motion to terminate jurisdiction over a correctional facility unless the court makes written findings that: (1) the prospective relief is still needed to correct a "current and ongoing" violation of a federal right; (2) the relief extends no further than necessary to correct the violation; (3) the relief is "narrowly drawn"; and (4) the relief is the "least intrusive means" of rectifying the violation. Defendants or intervenors can renew the motion to terminate on an annual basis and the court must renew its findings that the prospective relief still meets all these conditions. 18 U.S.C. § 3626(b)(1)(ii). In response, plaintiffs need an opportunity to demonstrate "current and ongoing" violations of constitutional rights that would justify a court in refusing to terminate a consent decree pursuant to § 3626(b)(3). Laaman v. Warden, New Hampshire State Prison, 238 F.3d 14 (1st Cir.2001).

The PLRA also includes an automatic stay provision that mandates that the ordered relief shall be stayed 30 days upon the filing of a motion to terminate under the law. 18 U.S.C. § 3626(e)(2). The Supreme Court in Miller v. French, 530 U.S. 327 (2000), interpreted this provision as removing the equitable discretion from a court to decide not to stay relief pending consideration of a motion to terminate. It then upheld the automatic stay provision against a separation of powers challenge, finding that the legislation did not improperly suspend a final judgment, but instead, merely provided changed legal standards for the enforcement of prospective relief.

Following these principles, nine circuit courts have found the termination provisions of the PLRA to be constitutional. Ruiz v. United States, 243 F.3d 941, 945 n.6 (5th Cir.2001) (citing cases). For example, the Fifth Circuit reasoned:

> When a court enters prospective injunctive relief and retains jurisdiction over the case, the judgment is not final. As long as the court retains the power to terminate or modify prospective injunctive relief in a particular case, Congress has the power to change the law and require that the change be applied with respect to the relief over which the court has retained power.

Id. at 948.

The PLRA also attempted to address the concern that the defendants in certain prison conditions cases, like their counterparts in some school desegregation cases may not want to seek termination of the decree. The PLRA grants the right to intervene to seek termination or to oppose the imposition or continuation of prospective relief to "any state or local official including a legislator or unit of government whose jurisdiction or function includes the appropriation of funds for . . . prison facilities." 18 U.S.C. § 3626(a)(3)(F). *See, e.g.,* Ruiz v. Estelle, 161 F.3d 814 (5th Cir.1998) (ordering intervention of individual state legislators in prison litigation even though "appropriation of funds" requires action of legislature as a unit or whole). Should this concept be extended to other types of institutional reform litigation? *See* David I. Levine, *The Chinese American Challenge to Court-Mandated Quotas in San Francisco's Public Schools: Notes from a (Partisan) Participant-Observer,* 16 Harv.

Blackletter L.J. 39, 127 (2000) (creation of a comparable right to intervene in school desegregation cases "would encourage another source of interested parties to call problems to the attention of a court that might otherwise be tempted to look the other way in the name of doing good").

Some critics feared (and some proponents may have hoped) that the PLRA would lead to the end of all existing prison decrees. *See, e.g.,* Ira Bloom, *Prisons, Prisoners, and Pine Forests: Congress Breaches the Wall Separating Legislative from Judicial Power,* 40 Ariz.L.Rev. 389, 410 (1998) (contending that the PLRA violates *Klein* because it "virtually compel[s] a decision favorable to the governmental entity involved"). A decade of experience under the PLRA shows that the actual results are more mixed. Some courts have terminated supervision over prison consent decrees. *E.g.,* Martin v. Ellandson, 122 F.Supp.2d 1017 (S.D.Iowa 2000). Other district courts have reviewed decrees and have narrowed their scope, but have not terminated jurisdiction entirely. *E.g.,* Ruiz v. Johnson, 154 F.Supp.2d 975 (S.D.Tex.2001) (finding persisting violations in the Texas prisons in the areas of: the conditions of confinement in administrative segregation, the failure to provide reasonable safety to inmates against assault and abuse, and the excessive use of force by correctional officers). For a careful examination of the effect of the PLRA on litigation in correctional settings, see Margo Schlanger, *Civil Rights Injunctions Over Time: A Case Study of Jail and Prison Court Orders,* 81 N.Y.U.L.Rev. 550 (2006) (documenting the reduction in the volume of existing and new court orders regulating jails and prisons).

D. ENFORCEMENT OF THE DECREE

The contempt power is the court's ultimate weapon to deter, overcome, or punish disobedience of an injunction. Because contempt is a powerful weapon, it may harm the defendant more than it helps the plaintiff and can require a heavy expenditure of judicial time and credibility. So, when a plaintiff complains that a defendant has violated an injunction, courts will often explore less intrusive techniques to prompt compliance, such as "clarifying" the original injunction or issuing a more prophylactic one, instead of initiating contempt proceedings. Such techniques, although nonpunitive in theory, can be quite painful to the defendant.

Just as the likelihood that the defendant will violate the plaintiff's rights helps determine whether a court will issue an injunction and its scope, so the likelihood that the defendant will continue to resist compliance with an injunction helps determine how a court will respond to allegations that the defendant has violated it in the past. Professor Robert Goldstein suggests one possible "scenario of escalating intrusiveness" in an institutional reform case:

1. Declaratory judgment with or without guidelines for compliance;

2. Time for good faith compliance;

3.   A hearing on the reasons for failure to comply;

4.   Plaintiff request for supplemental relief;

5.   An order for defendant to submit a detailed remedial plan;

6.   An order to plaintiff to submit a plan or to plaintiff and defendant to negotiate a plan;

7.   Hearings on a court-ordered plan and/or the appointment of a master to formulate a plan;

8.   The remedial order;

9.   Appointment of a master or oversight committee with power to gather data and review and guide decree implementation;

10.   Time for good faith compliance;

11.   Receivership, annulment of state laws slowing relief, closing of institutions, replacement of state officials, reordering of governmental budgets, and other intrusive actions;

12.   Contempt.

Robert Goldstein, *A Swann Song for Remedies: Equitable Relief in the Burger Court*, 13 Harv.C.R.-C.L.L.Rev. 1, 65–68 (1978).

This section will look first at contempt's elements, sanctions, and procedures. It will then turn to the issues of when parties are bound, the limits on enforcing decrees against persons who are not parties, and the special problems in enforcing decrees against governmental defendants.

1.   THE CONTEMPT POWER

The contempt power used to deal with violations of injunctions and other court orders is the same power used to deal with disruptive conduct in the court room, the intimidation of jurors, and other obstructions of the judicial process. A prima facie case of contempt is made out by showing a court order, of which the defendant had notice, and which the defendant violated. There is an additional element for criminal contempt— willfulness. Punishment and deterrence, which are the purposes of criminal contempt, are inappropriate when the contempt was not willful.

The judicial contempt power takes three forms: criminal contempt, coercive civil contempt, and compensatory civil contempt. *Criminal contempt* ordered to punish the defendant for failure to comply with the injunction. It is retrospective, punitive, and can include either fines or jail time. *Coercive civil contempt* is forward looking as it seeks to force the defendant into compliance through escalating fines or jail time. *Compensatory civil contempt* is remedial; it looks back to try and compensate the plaintiff with money for the losses stemming from a violation of the injunction.

Contempt proceedings are usually triggered by the plaintiff bringing the violation of the order to the court's attention. Because criminal contempt is brought in the name of the public, the judge and not the plaintiff gets to decide whether to initiate a prosecution for criminal contempt. Indeed the court may initiate such a prosecution without any prompting from the plaintiff or continue it even if the plaintiff beseeches the court to stop the prosecution. If the court does decide to commence criminal contempt proceedings, it will generally ask the prosecutor of the jurisdiction to press the charges. The Supreme Court has invoked its supervisory powers over federal courts to forbid judges from appointing a special prosecutor unless the United States Attorney has declined the case or from appointing the plaintiff's attorney as the special prosecutor because of conflicts of interest. Young v. United States ex rel. Vuitton et Fils S.A., 481 U.S. 787 (1987). In contrast to criminal contempt, where the prosecutor normally presses the charges, with compensatory or coercive civil contempt, the plaintiff usually does so.

HICKS ON BEHALF OF FEIOCK V. FEIOCK
Supreme Court of the United States
485 U.S. 624 (1988)

JUSTICE WHITE delivered the opinion of the Court.

* * *

I

On January 19, 1976, a California state court entered an order requiring respondent, Phillip Feiock, to begin making monthly payments to his ex-wife for the support of their three children. Over the next six years, respondent only sporadically complied with the order, and by December 1982 he had discontinued paying child support altogether. His ex-wife sought to enforce the support orders. On June 22, 1984, a hearing was held in California state court on her petition for ongoing support payments and for payment of the arrearage due her. The court examined respondent's financial situation and ordered him to begin paying $150 per month commencing on July 1, 1984. The court reserved jurisdiction over the matter for the purpose of determining the arrearages and reviewing respondent's financial condition.

Respondent apparently made two monthly payments but paid nothing for the next nine months. He was then served with an order to show cause why he should not be held in contempt on nine counts of failure to make the monthly payments ordered by the court. At a hearing on August 9, 1985, petitioner made out a prima facie case of contempt against respondent by establishing the existence of a valid court order, respondent's knowledge of the order, and respondent's failure to comply with the order. Respondent defended by arguing that he was unable to pay support during the months in question. This argument was partially successful, but respondent was adjudged to be in contempt on five of the nine counts. He was sentenced to five days in jail on each count, to be served consecutively, for a total of 25 days. This sentence was suspended, however, and respondent was placed on probation for three years. As one of the conditions of his probation, he was ordered once again to make support payments of $150 per month. As another condition of his probation, he was ordered, starting the following month, to begin repaying $50 per month on his accumulated arrearage, which was determined to total $1650.

At the hearing, respondent had objected to the application of Cal.Civ.Proc.Code Ann. § 1209.5 (1982) against him, claiming that it was unconstitutional under the Due Process Clause of the Federal Constitution because it shifts to the defendant the burden of proving inability to comply with the order, which is an element of the crime of contempt.[1] This objection was rejected, and he renewed it on appeal. The intermediate state appellate court agreed with respondent and annulled the contempt order, ruling that the state statute purports to impose "a mandatory presumption compelling a conclusion of guilt without independent proof of an ability to pay," and is therefore unconstitutional because "the mandatory nature of the presumption lessens the prosecution's burden of proof." In light of its holding that the statute as previously interpreted was unconstitutional, the court went on to adopt a different interpretation of that statute to govern future proceedings: "For future guidance, however, we determine the statute in question should be construed as authorizing a permissive inference, but not a mandatory presumption." The court explicitly considered this reinterpretation of the statute to be an exercise of its "obligation to interpret the statute to preserve its constitutionality whenever possible." The California Supreme Court denied review, but we granted certiorari.

II

Three issues must be decided to resolve this case. First is whether the ability to comply with a court order constitutes an element of the offense of contempt or, instead, inability to comply is an affirmative defense to that charge. Second is whether § 1209.5 requires the alleged contemnor to shoulder the burden of persuasion or merely the burden of production in attempting to establish his inability to comply with the order. Third is whether this contempt proceeding was a criminal proceeding or a civil proceeding, i.e., whether the relief imposed upon respondent was criminal or civil in nature.

---

[1]   California Civ.Proc.Code Ann. § 1209.5 (1982) states that "[w]hen a court of competent jurisdiction makes an order compelling a parent to furnish support . . . for his child, proof that . . . the parent was present in court at the time the order was pronounced and proof of noncompliance therewith shall be prima facie evidence of a contempt of court."

Petitioner argues that the state appellate court erred in its determinations on the first two points of state law. The court ruled that whether the individual is able to comply with a court order is an element of the offense of contempt rather than an affirmative defense to the charge, and that § 1209.5 shifts to the alleged contemnor the burden of persuasion rather than simply the burden of production in showing inability to comply. We are not at liberty to depart from the state appellate court's resolution of these issues of state law. * * *

The third issue, however, is a different matter: the argument is not merely that the state court misapplied state law, but that the characterization of this proceeding and the relief given as civil or criminal in nature, for purposes of determining the proper applicability of federal constitutional protections, raises a question of federal law rather than state law. This proposition is correct as stated. The fact that this proceeding and the resultant relief were judged to be criminal in nature as a matter of state law is thus not determinative of this issue, and the state appellate court erred insofar as it sustained respondent's challenge to the statute under the Due Process Clause simply because it concluded that this contempt proceeding is "quasi-criminal" as a matter of California law.

III

A

The question of how a court determines whether to classify the relief imposed in a given proceeding as civil or criminal in nature, for the purposes of applying the Due Process Clause and other provisions of the Constitution, is one of long standing, and its principles have been settled at least in their broad outlines for many decades. When a State's proceedings are involved, state law provides strong guidance about whether or not the State is exercising its authority "in a non-punitive, non-criminal manner," and one who challenges the State's classification of the relief imposed as "civil" or "criminal" may be required to show "the clearest proof" that it is not correct as a matter of federal law. Nonetheless, if such a challenge is substantiated, then the labels affixed either to the proceeding or to the relief imposed under state law are not controlling and will not be allowed to defeat the applicable protections of federal constitutional law. This is particularly so in the codified laws of contempt, where the "civil" and "criminal" labels of the law have become increasingly blurred.[4]

Instead, the critical features are the substance of the proceeding and the character of the relief that the proceeding will afford. "If it is for civil contempt the punishment is remedial, and for the benefit of the complainant. But if it is for criminal contempt the sentence is punitive, to

---

[4] California is a good example of this modern development, for although it defines civil and criminal contempts in separate statutes, compare Cal.Civ.Proc.Code Ann. § 1209 (Supp.1988) with Cal.Penal Code Ann. § 166 (1970), it has merged the two kinds of proceedings under the same procedural rules. See Cal.Civ.Proc.Code Ann. §§ 1209–1222 (1982 and Supp.1988).

vindicate the authority of the court." Gompers v. Buck's Stove & Range Co., 221 U.S. 418, 441 (1911). The character of the relief imposed is thus ascertainable by applying a few straightforward rules. If the relief provided is a sentence of imprisonment, it is remedial if "the defendant stands committed unless and until he performs the affirmative act required by the court's order," and is punitive if "the sentence is limited to imprisonment for a definite period." If the relief provided is a fine, it is remedial when it is paid to the complainant, and punitive when it is paid to the court, though a fine that would be payable to the court is also remedial when the defendant can avoid paying the fine simply by performing the affirmative act required by the court's order. These distinctions lead up to the fundamental proposition that criminal penalties may not be imposed on someone who has not been afforded the protections that the Constitution requires of such criminal proceedings, including the requirement that the offense be proved beyond a reasonable doubt.[5]

The Court has consistently applied these principles. In *Gompers*, decided early in this century, three men were found guilty of contempt and were sentenced to serve 6, 9, and 12 months respectively. The Court found this relief to be criminal in nature because the sentence was determinate and unconditional. "The distinction between refusing to do an act commanded,—remedied by imprisonment until the party performs the required act; and doing an act forbidden,—punished by imprisonment for a definite term; is sound in principle, and generally, if not universally, affords a test by which to determine the character of the punishment." In the former instance, the conditional nature of the punishment renders the relief civil in nature because the contemnor "can end the sentence and discharge himself at any moment by doing what he had previously refused to do." In the latter instance, the unconditional nature of the punishment renders the relief criminal in nature because the relief "cannot undo or remedy what has been done nor afford any compensation" and the contemnor "cannot shorten the term by promising not to repeat the offense." * * *

B

In repeatedly stating and following the rules set out above, the Court has eschewed any alternative formulation that would make the classification of the relief imposed in a State's proceedings turn simply on what their underlying purposes are perceived to be. Although the purposes that lie behind particular kinds of relief are germane to understanding their character, this Court has never undertaken to psychoanalyze the subjective intent of a State's laws and its courts, not only because that effort would be unseemly and improper, but also because it would be

---

[5] We have recognized that certain specific constitutional protections, such as the right to trial by jury, are not applicable to those criminal contempts that can be classified as petty offenses, as is true of other petty crimes as well. This is not true, however, of the proposition that guilt must be proved beyond a reasonable doubt.

misguided. In contempt cases, both civil and criminal relief have aspects that can be seen as either remedial or punitive or both. * * * As was noted in *Gompers*:

> It is true that either form of [punishment] has also an incidental effect. For if the case is civil and the punishment is purely remedial, there is also a vindication of the court's authority. On the other hand, if the proceeding is for criminal contempt and the [punishment] is solely punitive, to vindicate the authority of the law, the complainant may also derive some incidental benefit from the fact that such punishment tends to prevent a repetition of the disobedience. But such indirect consequences will not change [punishment] which is merely coercive and remedial, into that which is solely punitive in character, or *vice versa*. * * *

IV

The proper classification of the relief imposed in respondent's contempt proceeding is dispositive of this case. As interpreted by the state court here, § 1209.5 requires respondent to carry the burden of persuasion on an element of the offense, by showing his inability to comply with the court's order to make the required payments. If applied in a criminal proceeding, such a statute would violate the Due Process Clause because it would undercut the State's burden to prove guilt beyond a reasonable doubt. If applied in a civil proceeding, however, this particular statute would be constitutionally valid, Maggio v. Zeitz, 333 U.S. 56, 75–76 (1948) * * *.[9]

The state court found the contempt proceeding to be "quasi-criminal" in nature without discussing the point. There were strong indications that the proceeding was intended to be criminal in nature, such as the notice sent to respondent, which clearly labeled the proceeding as "criminal in nature," and the participation of the District Attorney in the case. Though significant, these facts are not dispositive of the issue before us, for if the trial court had imposed only civil coercive remedies, as surely it was authorized to do, then it would be improper to invalidate that result merely because the Due Process Clause, as applied in criminal proceedings, was not satisfied.[10] It also bears emphasis that the purposes underlying this proceeding were wholly ambiguous. Respondent was charged with violating nine discrete prior court orders, and the proceeding may have

---

[9] Our precedents are clear, however, that punishment may not be imposed in a civil contempt proceeding when it is clearly established that the alleged contemnor is unable to comply with the terms of the order.

[10] This can also be seen by considering the notice given to the alleged contemnor. This Court has stated that one who is charged with a crime is "entitled to be informed of the nature of the charge against him but to know that it is a charge and not a suit." Gompers v. Buck's Stove & Range Co., 221 U.S. 418, 446 (1911). Yet if the relief ultimately given in such a proceeding is wholly civil in nature, then this requirement would not be applicable. It is also true, of course, that if *both* civil and criminal relief are imposed in the same proceeding, then the " 'criminal feature of the order is dominant and fixes its character for purposes of review.' "

been intended primarily to vindicate the court's authority in the face of his defiance. On the other hand, as often is true when court orders are violated, these charges were part of an ongoing battle to force respondent to conform his conduct to the terms of those orders, and of future orders as well.

Applying the traditional rules for classifying the relief imposed in a given proceeding requires the further resolution of one factual question about the nature of the relief in this case. Respondent * * * was sentenced to five days in jail on each of the five counts, for a total of 25 days, but his jail sentence was suspended and he was placed on probation for three years. If this were all, then the relief afforded would be criminal in nature.[11] But this is not all. One of the conditions of respondent's probation was that he begin making payments on his accumulated arrearage, and that he continue making these payments at the rate of $50 per month. At that rate, all of the arrearage would be paid before respondent completed his probation period. Not only did the order therefore contemplate that respondent would be required to purge himself of his past violations, but it expressly states that "[i]f any two payments are missed, whether consecutive or not, the entire balance shall become due and payable." What is unclear is whether the ultimate satisfaction of these accumulated prior payments would have purged the determinate sentence imposed on respondent. * * * [N]either party was able to offer a satisfactory explanation of this point at argument.[12] If the relief imposed here is in fact a determinate sentence with a purge clause, then it is civil in nature.

* * * [T]he Due Process Clause does not necessarily prohibit the State from employing this presumption [of ability to pay] as it was construed by the state court, if respondent would purge his contempt judgment by paying off his arrearage. In these circumstances, the proper course for this Court is to vacate the judgment below and remand for further consideration of § 1209.5 free from the compulsion of an erroneous view of federal law. If on remand it is found that respondent would purge his sentence by paying his arrearage, then this proceeding is civil in nature

---

[11] That a determinate sentence is suspended and the contemnor put on probation does not make the remedy civil in nature, for a suspended sentence, without more, remains a determinate sentence, and a fixed term of probation is itself a punishment that is criminal in nature. A suspended sentence with a term of probation is not equivalent to a conditional sentence that would allow the contemnor to avoid or purge these sanctions. A determinate term of probation puts the contemnor under numerous disabilities that he cannot escape by complying with the dictates of the prior orders, such as: any conditions of probation that the court judges to be reasonable and necessary may be imposed; the term of probation may be revoked and the original sentence (including incarceration) may be reimposed at any time for a variety of reasons without all the safeguards that are ordinarily afforded in criminal proceedings; and the contemnor's probationary status could affect other proceedings against him that may arise in the future (for example, this fact might influence the sentencing determination made in a criminal prosecution for some wholly independent offense).

[12] It is also perhaps of some significance, though not binding upon us, that the parties reinforce the ambiguity on this point by entitling this contempt order, in the Joint Appendix, as "Order of the Superior Court of the State of California, County of Orange, to Purge Arrearage and Judgment of Contempt."

and there was no need for the state court to reinterpret its statute to avoid conflict with the Due Process Clause. * * *

JUSTICE O'CONNOR, with whom CHIEF JUSTICE [REHNQUIST] and JUSTICE SCALIA join, dissenting. * * *

" * * * In 1983, only half of custodial parents received the full amount of child support ordered; approximately 26% received some lesser amount, and 24% received nothing at all." Brief for Women's Legal Defense Fund et al. as Amici Curiae 26. * * *

Contempt proceedings often will be useless if the parent seeking enforcement of valid support orders must prove that the obligor can comply with the court order. The custodial parent will typically lack access to the financial and employment records needed to sustain the burden imposed by the decision below, especially where the noncustodial parent is self-employed, as is the case here. Serious consequences follow from the California Court of Appeal's decision to invalidate California's statutory presumption that a parent continues to be able to pay the child support previously determined to be within his or her means.

* * * [T]he substance of the proceeding below and the conditions on which the sentence was suspended reveal that the proceeding was civil in nature. Mrs. Feiock initiated the underlying action in order to obtain enforcement of the child support order for the benefit of the Feiock children. The California District Attorney conducted the case under a provision of the [Uniform Reciprocal Enforcement of Support Act (URESA)] that authorizes him to act on Mrs. Feiock's behalf. As the very caption of the case in this Court indicates, the District Attorney is acting on behalf of Mrs. Feiock, not as the representative of the State of California in a criminal prosecution. Both of the provisions of California's enactment of the URESA that authorize contempt proceedings appear in a chapter of the Code of Civil Procedure entitled "Civil Enforcement." It appears that most States enforce child and spousal support orders through civil proceedings like this one, in which the burden of persuasion is shifted to the defendant to show inability to comply. * * *

It is true that the order imposing the sentence does not expressly provide that, if respondent is someday incarcerated and if he subsequently complies, he will be released immediately. The parties disagree about what will happen if this contingency arises, and there is no need to address today the question of whether the failure to grant immediate release would render the sanction criminal. In the case before us respondent carries something even better than the "keys to the prison" in his own pocket: as long as he meets the conditions of his informal probation, he will never enter the jail.

It is critical that the only conditions placed on respondent's probation, apart from the requirement that he conduct himself generally in accordance with the law, are that he cure his past failures to comply with the support order and that he continue to comply in the future.* The sanction imposed on respondent is unlike ordinary criminal probation because it is collateral to a civil proceeding initiated by a private party, and respondent's sentence is suspended on the condition that he comply with a court order entered for the benefit of that party. This distinguishes respondent's sentence from suspended criminal sentences imposed outside the contempt context.

This Court traditionally has inquired into the substance of contempt proceedings to determine whether they are civil or criminal, paying particular attention to whether the sanction imposed will benefit another party to the proceeding. In this case, the California Superior Court suspended respondent's sentence on the condition that he bring himself into compliance with a court order providing support for his children, represented in the proceeding by petitioner. I conclude that the proceeding in this case should be characterized as one for civil contempt, and I would reverse the judgment below.

NOTES ON IN PERSONAM VERSUS IN REM ENFORCEMENT

1. Enforcing money judgments differs fundamentally from enforcing court orders. A money judgment is not an order of the court and therefore failure to satisfy it does not constitute disobedience of the court. Rather, unless satisfied, the judgment authorizes the sheriff to seize the defendant's property, sell it, and pay the plaintiff from the proceeds. So a money judgment is directed against the defendant's property rather than the defendant's person. It is in rem rather than in personam. In contrast, injunctions and other court orders are generally orders to the defendant personally. This is the origin of the maxim that "equity acts in personam."

2. Although most awards of money are by money judgments, courts do sometimes directly order the payment of money. *E.g.,* Bowen v. Massachusetts, 487 U.S. 879 (1988). But an order to pay money is enforced as a money judgment because society does not want to jail debtors. An exception is made for failure to pay alimony or child support, as in *Hicks.* A child support order requires the parent to support his child in the future, and thus is an in personam injunction rather than a mere money judgment.

NOTES ON THE CLASSIFICATION OF CONTEMPT PROCEEDINGS

1. *Hicks* holds that a jail sentence for contempt, suspended upon condition of future compliance with a court order in a civil case, is criminal

---

* Unlike the Court, I find no ambiguity in the court's sentencing order that hints that respondent can purge his jail sentence by paying off the arrearage alone. The sentencing order suspends execution of the jail sentence and places respondent on probation on the conditions that he *both* make future support payments at $150 per month *and* pay $50 per month on the arrearage. If respondent pays off the arrearage before the end of his probation period, but then fails to make a current support payment, the suspension will be revoked and he will go to jail.

unless the contemnor can purge the contempt. The dissent disagrees. Which side has the better argument?

2.   *Hicks* also holds that a suspended jail sentence for contempt is civil if it can be purged. The majority remands for a determination of whether paying off the $1650 of arrearages would effect a purge. One way he might pay off the arrearages is to make the required payments of $50 a month. But that would take 33 months of the 36 months of his probation. Another way he might purge is if he fails to make 2 payments, which would result in his being jailed and the entire balance being due immediately, and then pays off the balance. But, it seems implausible that he could come up with that much money when in jail if he could not come up with the smaller sums needed to avoid jail. No wonder the trial court did not bother to explain in advance whether paying the arrearages would purge the contempt. On the other hand, can you think of another blackletter test to determine whether the suspended sentence was imposed to punish past violations or to coerce future compliance?

3.   After *Hicks*, can states use civil contempt to coerce the payment of alimony and child support? On remand, the state appellate court held that the California statute at issue in *Hicks* was "unmistakably criminal in nature." However, the court also held that the statute made ability to pay an affirmative defense in contempt proceedings. In re Feiock, 215 Cal.App.3d 141, 263 Cal.Rptr. 437 (1989). The majority opinion explained that once the alleged contemnor raises the affirmative defense by making a prima facie showing of inability to pay, the party seeking criminal contempt has the burden of proving all elements beyond a reasonable doubt, including ability to pay. The dissent charged that the majority had abandoned its original position that the possibility of compliance was an element of the offense and was, by subterfuge, putting on the alleged contemnor the burden to disprove an element of the offense.

In a later case, the state's high court embraced *In re Feoick's* holding that impossibility is an affirmative defense and not an element of the offense under the child support statute, but disagreed on the burden of proof, holding that the alleged contemnor bears the burden of persuasion. Moss v. Superior Court, 17 Cal.4th 396, 71 Cal.Rptr.2d 215, 950 P.2d 59 (1998). Finding that child support orders are obeyed in only seventeen percent of cases in California, the state legislature subsequently enacted a statute that replaced district attorneys with administrative officials in the collection process. Cal.Fam.Code § 17404.

4.   Coercive civil contempt usually requires three steps: (1) the issuance of an injunction; (2) a determination of contempt and the imposition of sanctions subject to the condition that the defendant can purge; and (3) a finding as to whether the defendant has purged. *Hicks* decided that the second step can be taken civilly. Can the third step also be taken civilly? For example, suppose that Mr. Feiock receives a purgeable suspended sentence, fails to pay, is jailed, and then claims he has no money with which to purge. Should that claim be decided criminally or civilly?

UNITED MINE WORKERS V. BAGWELL

Supreme Court of the United States
512 U.S. 821 (1994)

JUSTICE BLACKMUN delivered the opinion of the Court.

We are called upon once again to consider the distinction between civil and criminal contempt. Specifically, we address whether contempt fines levied against a union for violations of a labor injunction are coercive civil fines, or are criminal fines that constitutionally could be imposed only through a jury trial. We conclude that the fines are criminal and, accordingly, we reverse the judgment of the Supreme Court of Virginia.

I

Petitioners, the International Union, United Mine Workers of America and United Mine Workers of America, District 28 (collectively, the union) engaged in a protracted labor dispute with the Clinchfield Coal Company and Sea "B" Mining Company (collectively, the companies) over alleged unfair labor practices. In April 1989, the companies filed suit in the Circuit Court of Russell County, Virginia, to enjoin the union from conducting unlawful strike-related activities. The trial court entered an injunction which, as later amended, prohibited the union and its members from, among other things, obstructing ingress and egress to company facilities, throwing objects at and physically threatening company employees, placing tire-damaging "jackrocks" on roads used by company vehicles, and picketing with more than a specified number of people at designated sites. The court additionally ordered the union to take all steps necessary to ensure compliance with the injunction, to place supervisors at picket sites, and to report all violations to the court.

On May 16, 1989, the trial court held a contempt hearing and found that petitioners had committed 72 violations of the injunction. After fining the union $642,000 for its disobedience,[1] the court announced that it would fine the union $100,000 for any future violent breach of the injunction and $20,000 for any future nonviolent infraction, "such as exceeding picket numbers, [or] blocking entrances or exits." The Court early stated that its purpose was to "impos[e] prospective civil fines[,] the payment of which would only be required if it were shown the defendants disobeyed the Court's orders."

In seven subsequent contempt hearings held between June and December 1989, the court found the union in contempt for more than 400 separate violations of the injunction, many of them violent. Based on the court's stated "intention that these fines are civil and coercive," each contempt hearing was conducted as a civil proceeding before the trial judge, in which the parties conducted discovery, introduced evidence, and called

---

[1] A portion of these fines was suspended conditioned on the union's future compliance. The court later vacated these fines, concluding that they were "criminal in nature."

and cross-examined witnesses. The trial court required that contumacious acts be proved beyond a reasonable doubt, but did not afford the union a right to jury trial.

As a result of these contempt proceedings, the court levied over $64,000,000 in fines against the union, approximately $12,000,000 of which was ordered payable to the companies. Because the union objected to payment of any fines to the companies and in light of the law enforcement burdens posed by the strike, the court ordered that the remaining roughly $52,000,000 in fines be paid to the Commonwealth of Virginia and Russell and Dickenson Counties, "the two counties most heavily affected by the unlawful activity."

While appeals from the contempt orders were pending, the union and the companies settled the underlying labor dispute, agreed to vacate the contempt fines, and jointly moved to dismiss the case. A special mediator representing the Secretary of Labor, and the governments of Russell and Dickenson Counties, supported the parties' motion to vacate the outstanding fines. The trial court granted the motion to dismiss, dissolved the injunction, and vacated the $12,000,000 in fines payable to the companies. After reiterating its belief that the remaining $52,000,000 owed to the counties and the Commonwealth were coercive, civil fines, the trial court refused to vacate these fines, concluding they were "payable in effect to the public."

The companies withdrew as parties in light of the settlement and declined to seek further enforcement of the outstanding contempt fines. Because the Commonwealth Attorneys of Russell and Dickenson Counties also had asked to be disqualified from the case, the court appointed respondent John L. Bagwell to act as Special Commissioner to collect the unpaid contempt fines on behalf of the counties and the Commonwealth.

The Court of Appeals of Virginia reversed and ordered that the contempt fines be vacated pursuant to the settlement agreement. Assuming for the purposes of argument that the fines were civil, the court concluded "that civil contempt fines imposed during or as a part of a civil proceeding between private parties are settled when the underlying litigation is settled by the parties and the court is without discretion to refuse to vacate such fines."

On consolidated appeals, the Supreme Court of Virginia reversed. The court held that whether coercive, civil contempt sanctions could be settled by private parties was a question of state law, and that Virginia public policy disfavored such a rule, "if the dignity of the law and public respect for the judiciary are to be maintained." The court also rejected petitioners' contention that the outstanding fines were criminal and could not be imposed absent a criminal trial. Because the trial court's prospective fine schedule was intended to coerce compliance with the injunction and the union could avoid the fines through obedience, the court reasoned, the fines were civil and coercive and properly imposed in civil proceedings. * * *

II

A

"Criminal contempt is a crime in the ordinary sense," Bloom v. Illinois, 391 U.S. 194, 201 (1968), and "criminal penalties may not be imposed on someone who has not been afforded the protections that the Constitution requires of such criminal proceedings." Hicks v. Feiock, 485 U.S. 624, 632 (1988). See In re Bradley, 318 U.S. 50 (1943) (double jeopardy); Cooke v. United States, 267 U.S. 517, 537 (1925) (rights to notice of charges, assistance of counsel, summary process, and to present a defense); Gompers v. Bucks Stove & Range Co., 221 U.S. 418, 444 (1911) (privilege against self-incrimination, right to proof beyond a reasonable doubt). For "serious" criminal contempts involving imprisonment of more than six months, these protections include the right to jury trial. *Bloom*. In contrast, civil contempt sanctions, or those penalties designed to compel future compliance with a court order, are considered to be coercive and avoidable through obedience, and thus may be imposed in an ordinary civil proceeding upon notice and an opportunity to be heard. Neither a jury trial nor proof beyond a reasonable doubt is required.[2]

Although the procedural contours of the two forms of contempt are well established, the distinguishing characteristics of civil versus criminal contempts are somewhat less clear.[3] In the leading early case addressing this issue in the context of imprisonment, *Gompers v. Bucks Stove & Range Co.,* the Court emphasized that whether a contempt is civil or criminal turns on the "character and purpose" of the sanction involved. * * *

The paradigmatic coercive, civil contempt sanction, as set forth in *Gompers*, involves confining a contemnor indefinitely until he complies with an affirmative command such as an order "to pay alimony, or to surrender property ordered to be turned over to a receiver, or to make a conveyance." Imprisonment for a fixed term similarly is coercive when the contemnor is given the option of earlier release if he complies. In these circumstances, the contemnor is able to purge the contempt and obtain his release by committing an affirmative act, and thus "carries the keys of his prison in his own pocket." *Gompers*.

---

[2]   We address only the procedures required for adjudication of indirect contempts, i.e., those occurring out of court. Direct contempts that occur in the court's presence may be immediately adjudged and sanctioned summarily, and, except for serious criminal contempts in which a jury trial is required, the traditional distinction between civil and criminal contempt proceedings does not pertain.

[3]   Numerous scholars have criticized as unworkable the traditional distinction between civil and criminal contempt. *See, e.g.,* Dudley, Getting Beyond the Civil/Criminal Distinction: A New Approach to Regulation of Indirect Contempts, 79 Va. L. Rev. 1025, 1033 (1993) (describing the distinction between civil and criminal contempt as "conceptually unclear and exceedingly difficult to apply").

By contrast, a fixed sentence of imprisonment is punitive and criminal if it is imposed retrospectively for a "completed act of disobedience," *Gompers*, such that the contemnor cannot avoid or abbreviate the confinement through later compliance. * * * When a contempt involves the prior conduct of an isolated, prohibited act, the resulting sanction has no coercive effect. "[T]he defendant is furnished no key, and he cannot shorten the term by promising not to repeat the offense."

This dichotomy between coercive and punitive imprisonment has been extended to the fine context. A contempt fine accordingly is considered civil and remedial if it either "coerce[s] the defendant into compliance with the court's order, [or] . . . compensate[s] the complainant for losses sustained." United States v. United Mine Workers of America, 330 U.S. 258, 303–304 (1947). Where a fine is not compensatory, it is civil only if the contemnor is afforded an opportunity to purge. See Penfield Co. v. SEC, 330 U.S. 585, 590 (1947). Thus, a "flat, unconditional fine" totalling even as little as $50 announced after a finding of contempt is criminal if the contemnor has no subsequent opportunity to reduce or avoid the fine through compliance.

A close analogy to coercive imprisonment is a per diem fine imposed for each day a contemnor fails to comply with an affirmative court order. Like civil imprisonment, such fines exert a constant coercive pressure, and once the jural command is obeyed, the future, indefinite, daily fines are purged. Less comfortable is the analogy between coercive imprisonment and suspended, determinate fines. In this Court's sole prior decision squarely addressing the judicial power to impose coercive civil contempt fines, *United Mine Workers*, it held that fixed fines also may be considered purgeable and civil when imposed and suspended pending future compliance. See also *Penfield* ("One who is fined, unless by a day certain he [complies] . . ., has it in his power to avoid any penalty"); but see *Hicks* (suspended or probationary sentence is criminal). *United Mine Workers* involved a $3,500,000 fine imposed against the union for nationwide post-World War II strike activities. Finding that the determinate fine was both criminal and excessive, the Court reduced the sanction to a flat criminal fine of $700,000. The Court then imposed and suspended the remaining $2,800,000 as a coercive civil fine, conditioned on the union's ability to purge the fine through full, timely compliance with the trial court's order.[4] The Court concluded, in light of this purge clause, that the civil fine operated as "a coercive imposition upon the defendant union to compel obedience with the court's outstanding order."

This Court has not revisited the issue of coercive civil contempt fines addressed in *United Mine Workers*. Since that decision, the Court has

---

[4] Although the size of the fine was substantial, the conduct required of the union to purge the suspended fine was relatively discrete. According to the Court, purgation consisted of (1) withdrawal of the union's notice terminating the Krug-Lewis labor agreement; (2) notifying the union members of this withdrawal; and (3) withdrawing and notifying the union members of the withdrawal of any other notice questioning the ongoing effectiveness of the Krug-Lewis agreement.

erected substantial procedural protections in other areas of contempt law, such as criminal contempts and summary contempts. Lower federal courts and state courts such as the trial court here nevertheless have relied on *United Mine Workers* to authorize a relatively unlimited judicial power to impose noncompensatory civil contempt fines.

B

Underlying the somewhat elusive distinction between civil and criminal contempt fines, and the ultimate question posed in this case, is what procedural protections are due before any particular contempt penalty may be imposed. Because civil contempt sanctions are viewed as nonpunitive and avoidable, fewer procedural protections for such sanctions have been required. To the extent that such contempts take on a punitive character, however, and are not justified by other considerations central to the contempt power, criminal procedural protections may be in order.

The traditional justification for the relative breadth of the contempt power has been necessity: Courts independently must be vested with "power to impose silence, respect, and decorum, in their presence, and submission to their lawful mandates, and . . . to preserve themselves and their officers from the approach and insults of pollution." Courts thus have embraced an inherent contempt authority, as a power "necessary to the exercise of all others."

But the contempt power also uniquely is "liable to abuse." Unlike most areas of law, where a legislature defines both the sanctionable conduct and the penalty to be imposed, civil contempt proceedings leave the offended judge solely responsible for identifying, prosecuting, adjudicating, and sanctioning the contumacious conduct. Contumacy "often strikes at the most vulnerable and human qualities of a judge's temperament," and its fusion of legislative, executive, and judicial powers "summons forth . . . the prospect of 'the most tyrannical licentiousness.' " Accordingly, "in [criminal] contempt cases an even more compelling argument can be made [than in ordinary criminal cases] for providing a right to jury trial as a protection against the arbitrary exercise of official power."

Our jurisprudence in the contempt area has attempted to balance the competing concerns of necessity and potential arbitrariness by allowing a relatively unencumbered contempt power when its exercise is most essential, and requiring progressively greater procedural protections when other considerations come into play. The necessity justification for the contempt authority is at its pinnacle, of course, where contumacious conduct threatens a court's immediate ability to conduct its proceedings, such as where a witness refuses to testify, or a party disrupts the court. Thus, petty, direct contempts in the presence of the court traditionally have been subject to summary adjudication, "to maintain order in the courtroom and the integrity of the trial process in the face of an 'actual obstruction of justice.' " In light of the court's substantial interest in rapidly coercing compliance and restoring order, and because the contempt's occurrence before the court reduces the need for extensive factfinding and the likelihood of an erroneous deprivation, summary proceedings have been tolerated.

Summary adjudication becomes less justifiable once a court leaves the realm of immediately sanctioned, petty direct contempts. If a court delays punishing a direct contempt until the completion of trial, for example, due process requires that the contemnor's rights to notice and a hearing be respected. There "it is much more difficult to argue that action without notice or hearing of any kind is necessary to preserve order and enable [the court] to proceed with its business." Direct contempts also cannot be punished with serious criminal penalties absent the full protections of a criminal jury trial. * * *

Still further procedural protections are afforded for contempts occurring out of court, where the considerations justifying expedited procedures do not pertain. Summary adjudication of indirect contempts is prohibited, and criminal contempt sanctions are entitled to full criminal process. Certain indirect contempts nevertheless are appropriate for imposition through civil proceedings. Contempts such as failure to comply with document discovery, for example, while occurring outside the court's presence, impede the court's ability to adjudicate the proceedings before it and thus touch upon the core justification for the contempt power. Courts traditionally have broad authority through means other than contempt— such as by striking pleadings, assessing costs, excluding evidence, and entering default judgment-to penalize a party's failure to comply with the rules of conduct governing the litigation process. *See, e.g.,* Fed. Rule Civ. Proc. 11, 37. Such judicial sanctions never have been considered criminal, and the imposition of civil, coercive fines to police the litigation process appears consistent with this authority. Similarly, indirect contempts involving discrete, readily ascertainable acts, such as turning over a key or payment of a judgment, properly may be adjudicated through civil proceedings since the need for extensive, impartial factfinding is less pressing.

For a discrete category of indirect contempts, however, civil procedural protections may be insufficient. Contempts involving out-of-court disobedience to complex injunctions often require elaborate and reliable factfinding. Such contempts do not obstruct the court's ability to adjudicate the proceedings before it, and the risk of erroneous deprivation from the lack of a neutral factfinder may be substantial. Under these circumstances, criminal procedural protections such as the rights to counsel and proof beyond a reasonable doubt are both necessary and appropriate to protect the due process rights of parties and prevent the arbitrary exercise of judicial power.

C

In the instant case, neither any party nor any court of the Commonwealth has suggested that the challenged fines are compensatory. * * * The issue before us accordingly is limited to whether these fines, despite their noncompensatory character, are coercive civil or criminal sanctions.

The parties propose two independent tests for determining whether the fines are civil or criminal. Petitioners argue that because the injunction primarily prohibited certain conduct rather than mandated affirmative acts, the sanctions are criminal. Respondent in turn urges that because the trial court established a prospective fine schedule that the union could avoid through compliance, the fines are civil in character.

Neither theory satisfactorily identifies those contempt fines that are criminal and thus must be imposed through the criminal process. Petitioners correctly note that *Gompers* suggests a possible dichotomy "between refusing to do an act commanded,—remedied by imprisonment until the party performs the required act; and doing an act forbidden,—punished by imprisonment for a definite term." The distinction between mandatory and prohibitory orders is easily applied in the classic contempt scenario, where contempt sanctions are used to enforce orders compelling or forbidding a single, discrete act. In such cases, orders commanding an affirmative act simply designate those actions that are capable of being coerced.

But the distinction between coercion of affirmative acts and punishment of prohibited conduct is difficult to apply when conduct that can recur is involved, or when an injunction contains both mandatory and prohibitory provisions. Moreover, in borderline cases injunctive provisions containing essentially the same command can be phrased either in mandatory or prohibitory terms. Under a literal application of petitioners' theory, an injunction ordering the union: "Do not strike," would appear to be prohibitory and criminal, while an injunction ordering the union: "Continue working," would be mandatory and civil. In enforcing the present injunction, the trial court imposed fines without regard to the mandatory or prohibitory nature of the clause violated. Accordingly, even though a parsing of the injunction's various provisions might support the classification of contempts such as rock-throwing and placing tire-damaging "jackrocks" on roads as criminal and the refusal to place supervisors at picket sites as civil, the parties have not asked us to review the order in that manner. In a case like this involving an injunction that prescribes a detailed code of conduct, it is more appropriate to identify the character of the entire decree.

Despite respondent's urging, we also are not persuaded that dispositive significance should be accorded to the fact that the trial court prospectively announced the sanctions it would impose. Had the trial court simply levied the fines after finding the union guilty of contempt, the resulting "determinate and unconditional" fines would be considered "solely and exclusively punitive." Respondent nevertheless contends that the trial court's announcement of a prospective fine schedule allowed the union to "avoid paying the fine[s] simply by performing the . . . act required by the court's order," *Hicks*, and thus transformed these fines into coercive, civil ones. Respondent maintains here, as the Virginia Supreme Court held below, that the trial court could have imposed a daily civil fine to coerce the union into compliance, and that a prospective fine schedule is indistinguishable from such a sanction.

Respondent's argument highlights the difficulties encountered in parsing coercive civil and criminal contempt fines. The fines imposed here concededly are difficult to distinguish either from determinate, punitive fines or from initially suspended, civil fines. Ultimately, however, the fact that the trial court announced the fines before the contumacy, rather than after the fact, does not in itself justify respondent's conclusion that the fines are civil or meaningfully distinguish these penalties from the ordinary criminal law. Due process traditionally requires that criminal laws provide prior notice both of the conduct to be prohibited and of the sanction to be imposed. The trial court here simply announced the penalty—determinate fines of $20,000 or $100,000 per violation—that would be imposed for future contempts. The union's ability to avoid the contempt fines was indistinguishable from the ability of any ordinary citizen to avoid a criminal sanction by conforming his behavior to the law. The fines are not coercive day fines, or even suspended fines, but are more closely analogous to fixed, determinate, retrospective criminal fines which petitioners had no opportunity to purge once imposed. We therefore decline to conclude that the mere fact that the sanctions were announced in advance rendered them coercive and civil as a matter of constitutional law.

Other considerations convince us that the fines challenged here are criminal. The union's sanctionable conduct did not occur in the court's presence or otherwise implicate the court's ability to maintain order and adjudicate the proceedings before it. Nor did the union's contumacy involve simple, affirmative acts, such as the paradigmatic civil contempts examined in *Gompers*. Instead, the Virginia trial court levied contempt fines for widespread, ongoing, out-of-court violations of a complex injunction. In so doing, the court effectively policed petitioners' compliance with an entire code of conduct that the court itself had imposed. The union's contumacy lasted many months and spanned a substantial portion of the State. The fines assessed were serious, totalling over $52,000,000.[5] Under

---

[5] "Petty contempt like other petty criminal offenses may be tried without a jury," and the imposition only of serious criminal contempt fines triggers the right to jury trial. *Bloom*. The Court to date has not specified what magnitude of contempt fine may constitute a serious criminal sanction, although it has held that a fine of $10,000 imposed on a union was insufficient to trigger the Sixth Amendment right to jury trial. See Muniz v. Hoffman, 422 U.S. 454, 477 (1975); see also 18 U.S.C. § 1(3) (defining petty offenses as crimes "the penalty for which . . . does not exceed

such circumstances, disinterested factfinding and even-handed adjudication were essential, and petitioners were entitled to a criminal jury trial.

In reaching this conclusion, we recognize that this Court generally has deferred to a legislature's determination whether a sanction is civil or criminal, and that "[w]hen a State's proceedings are involved, state law provides strong guidance about whether or not the State is exercising its authority 'in a nonpunitive, noncriminal manner.'" *Hicks*. We do not deviate from either tradition today. Where a single judge, rather than a legislature, declares a particular sanction to be civil or criminal, such deference is less appropriate. Cf. Madsen v. Women's Health Center, Inc., 512 U.S. 1277 (1994). Moreover, this Court has recognized that even for state proceedings, the label affixed to a contempt ultimately "will not be allowed to defeat the applicable protections of federal constitutional law." *Hicks*. We conclude that the serious contempt fines imposed here were criminal and constitutionally could not be imposed absent a jury trial.

III

Our decision concededly imposes some procedural burdens on courts' ability to sanction widespread, indirect contempts of complex injunctions through noncompensatory fines. Our holding, however, leaves unaltered the longstanding authority of judges to adjudicate direct contempts summarily, and to enter broad compensatory awards for all contempts through civil proceedings. Because the right to trial by jury applies only to serious criminal sanctions, courts still may impose noncompensatory, petty fines for contempts such as the present ones without conducting a jury trial. We also do not disturb a court's ability to levy, albeit through the criminal contempt process, serious fines like those in this case.

Ultimately, whatever slight burden our holding may impose on the judicial contempt power cannot be controlling. The Court recognized more than a quarter-century ago:

> "We cannot say that the need to further respect for judges and courts is entitled to more consideration than the interest of the individual not be subjected to serious criminal punishment without the benefit of all the procedural protections worked out carefully over the years and deemed fundamental to our system of justice. Genuine respect, which alone can lend true dignity to our judicial establishment, will be engendered, not by the fear of unlimited authority, but by the firm administration of the law through those institutionalized procedures which have been worked out over the centuries." *Bloom*. Where, as here, "a serious

___

imprisonment for a period of six months or a fine of not more than $5,000 for an individual and $10,000 for a person other than an individual, or both"). We need not answer today the difficult question where the line between petty and serious contempt fines should be drawn, since a $52,000,000 fine unquestionably is a serious contempt sanction.

contempt is at issue, considerations of efficiency must give way to the more fundamental interest of ensuring the even-handed exercise of judicial power."

* * *

JUSTICE SCALIA, concurring.

I join the Court's opinion classifying the $52,000,000 in contempt fines levied against petitioners as criminal. As the Court's opinion demonstrates, our cases have employed a variety of not easily reconcilable tests for differentiating between civil and criminal contempts. Since all of those tests would yield the same result here, there is no need to decide which is the correct one—and a case so extreme on its facts is not the best case in which to make that decision. I wish to suggest, however, that when we come to making it, a careful examination of historical practice will ultimately yield the answer. * * *

[At common law,] incarceration until compliance was a distinctive sanction, and sheds light upon the nature of the decrees enforced by civil contempt. That sanction makes sense only if the order requires performance of an identifiable act (or perhaps cessation of continuing performance of an identifiable act). A general prohibition for the future does not lend itself to enforcement through conditional incarceration, since no single act (or the cessation of no single act) can demonstrate compliance and justify release. * * *

As one would expect from this, the orders that underlay civil contempt fines or incarceration were usually mandatory rather than prohibitory, directing litigants to perform acts that would further the litigation (for example, turning over a document), or give effect to the court's judgment (for example, executing a deed of conveyance). * * * The mandatory injunctions issued upon termination of litigation usually required "a single simple act." H. McClintock, *Principles of Equity* § 15, pp. 32–33 (2d ed.1948). * * * And where specific performance of contracts was sought, it was the categorical rule that no decree would issue that required ongoing supervision. Compliance with these "single act" mandates could, in addition to being simple, be quick; and once it was achieved the contemnor's relationship with the court came to an end, at least insofar as the subject of the order was concerned. * * *

Even equitable decrees that were prohibitory rather than mandatory were, in earlier times, much less sweeping than their modern counterparts. Prior to the labor injunctions of the late 1800's, injunctions were issued primarily in relatively narrow disputes over property.

Contemporary courts have abandoned these earlier limitations upon the scope of their mandatory and injunctive decrees. They routinely issue complex decrees which involve them in extended disputes and place them in continuing supervisory roles over parties and institutions. *See, e.g.,*

Missouri v. Jenkins, 495 U.S. 33, 56–58 (1990); Swann v. Charlotte-Mecklenburg Bd. of Ed., 402 U.S. 1, 16 (1971). Professor Chayes has described the extent of the transformation:

> [The modern decree] differs in almost every relevant characteristic from relief in the traditional model of adjudication, not the least in that it is the centerpiece. . . . It provides for a complex, on-going regime of performance rather than a simple, one-shot, one-way transfer. Finally, it prolongs and deepens, rather than terminates, the court's involvement with the dispute.

Chayes, *The Role of the Judge in Public Law Litigation*, 89 Harv. L. Rev. 1281, 1298 (1976).

The consequences of this change for the point under discussion here are obvious: When an order governs many aspects of a litigant's activities, rather than just a discrete act, determining compliance becomes much more difficult. Credibility issues arise, for which the factfinding protections of the criminal law (including jury trial) become much more important. And when continuing prohibitions or obligations are imposed, the order cannot be complied with (and the contempt "purged") in a single act; it continues to govern the party's behavior, on pain of punishment-not unlike the criminal law.

The order at issue here provides a relatively tame example of the modern, complex decree. The amended injunction prohibited, inter alia, rock-throwing, the puncturing of tires, threatening, following or interfering with respondents' employees, placing pickets in other than specified locations, and roving picketing; and it required, inter alia, that petitioners provide a list of names of designated supervisors. Although it would seem quite in accord with historical practice to enforce, by conditional incarceration or per diem fines, compliance with the last provision—a discrete command, observance of which is readily ascertained-using that same means to enforce the remainder of the order would be a novelty. * * *

As the scope of injunctions has expanded, they have lost some of the distinctive features that made enforcement through civil process acceptable. It is not that the times, or our perceptions of fairness, have changed (that is in my view no basis for either tightening or relaxing the traditional demands of due process); but rather that the modern judicial order is in its relevant essentials not the same device that in former times could always be enforced by civil contempt. So adjustments will have to be made. We will have to decide at some point which modern injunctions sufficiently resemble their historical namesakes to warrant the same extraordinary means of enforcement. We need not draw that line in the present case, and so I am content to join the opinion of the Court.

JUSTICE GINSBURG, with whom CHIEF JUSTICE [REHNQUIST] joins, concurring in part and concurring in the judgment.

* * *

Two considerations persuade me that the contempt proceedings in this case should be classified as "criminal" rather than "civil." First, were we to accept the logic of Bagwell's argument that the fines here were civil, because "conditional" and "coercive," no fine would elude that categorization. The fines in this case were "conditional," Bagwell says, because they would not have been imposed if the unions had complied with the injunction. The fines would have been "conditional" in this sense, however, even if the court had not supplemented the injunction with its fines schedule; indeed, any fine is "conditional" upon compliance or noncompliance before its imposition.†

Second, the Virginia courts' refusal to vacate the fines, despite the parties' settlement and joint motion is characteristic of criminal, not civil proceedings. In explaining why the fines outlived the underlying civil dispute, the Supreme Court of Virginia stated: "Courts of the Commonwealth must have the authority to enforce their orders by employing coercive, civil sanctions if the dignity of the law and public respect for the judiciary are to be maintained." The Virginia court's references to upholding public authority and maintaining "the dignity of the law" reflect the very purposes *Gompers* ranked on the criminal contempt side. * * *

Concluding that the fines at issue "are more closely analogous to . . . criminal fines" than to civil fines, I join the Court's judgment and all but Part II-B of its opinion.

NOTES

1. Has the *Hicks* test for distinguishing coercive civil contempt from criminal contempt been overruled? If so, what is the new test? In New York State National Organization of Women v. Terry, 159 F.3d 86 (2d Cir.1998), *cert. denied*, 527 U.S. 1003 (1999), the district court levied contempt fines against Terry for violating an injunction while protesting the operation of an abortion clinic. Terry argued that the fine was criminal, and therefore unconstitutional under *Bagwell*. The court of appeals upheld the fines because the district court included in the sanction a clause that allowed Terry to purge the fine by filing and publishing in a newspaper his affirmative intention to obey the permanent injunction. *See also* Harris v. City of Philadelphia, 47 F.3d 1311 (3d Cir.1995) (contempt fine not criminal if the contemnor can purge through an affirmative act).

---

†   Bagwell further likens the prospective fines schedule to the civil contempt fine imposed in United States v. Mine Workers, 330 U.S. 258 (1947). In that case, however, the contemnor union was given an opportunity, after the fine was imposed, to avoid the fine by "effect[ing] full compliance" with the injunction. As the Court explains, for purposes of allowing the union to avoid the fine, "full compliance" with the broad no-strike injunction, was reduced to the performance of three affirmative acts. This opportunity to purge, consistent with the civil contempt scenario described in *Gompers*, was unavailable to the unions in this case.

If the fine cannot be purged, what is the test? In NOW v. Operation Rescue, 37 F.3d 646, 659 (D.C.Cir.1994), the court read *Bagwell* to hold that the classification of prospective fixed fines as criminal or civil turns on "what procedural protections are due before any particular contempt penalty may be imposed, in light of the 'competing concerns' of protecting the judicial process and preventing arbitrary exercises of the contempt power." In striking that balance, courts should consider such factors as (1) whether the contempts go to the core justification of protecting the court's ability to adjudicate the proceedings before it; (2) whether the contempts consist of discrete, readily ascertainable acts so that the factfinding is less troublesome; and, (3) the characterization by the district court; however, the appeals court is not bound by the district court's characterization of the prospective nature of the fine. Reich v. Sea Sprite Boat Co., 50 F.3d 413 (7th Cir.1995), cited *Bagwell* for the proposition that sanctions for completed acts are presumptively criminal sanctions. The First Circuit, in United States v. Marquardo, 149 F.3d 36 (1st Cir.1998), cited *Bagwell* for the proposition that a "frequent scenario for civil contempt situations arises as a result of the exercise of the courts' equity jurisdiction, in which the coercive tool is often periodic monetary fines, tailored to compensate the party aggrieved for the damages suffered as a result of the contumacious conduct of the noncomplying party." *Id.* at 40. In a later case, the D.C. Circuit carefully emphasized another point—whether the fines imposed were non-petty. Evans v. Williams, 206 F.3d 1292 (D.C.Cir.2000). The Ninth Circuit, in a discussion of "serious" fines, noted that the "Supreme Court has not decided where the line between serious and petty fines should be drawn." F.J. Hanshaw Enterprises, Inc. v. Emerald River Development, Inc., 244 F.3d 1128, 1139 (9th Cir.2001).

2. *Compensatory civil contempt.* The measure of the fine in compensatory contempt is ordinarily the plaintiff's rightful position—the measure of compensatory damages. *See, e.g.*, American Airlines, Inc. v. Allied Pilots Association, 228 F.3d 574 (5th Cir.2000), *cert. denied*, 531 U.S. 1191 (2001) (affirming award to airline of $45.5 million dollars for compensatory civil contempt after finding that union failed to carry out a temporary restraining order mandating that it call off a "sick out" by pilots).

But what if the defendant's gain is greater than the plaintiff's loss? Restitution—which will be covered in Chapter 7—sometimes makes the measure of relief the defendant's rightful position in order to deprive the defendant of its "unjust enrichment." Because the court, in granting an injunction, denies the defendant the option of violating the plaintiff's rights for the payment of compensatory damages, isn't the excess of the defendant's gain over the plaintiff's loss unjust enrichment, especially if the defendant's violation of the injunction was willful? Some courts allow a fine pegged to unjust enrichment, some do not. Compare, e.g., A.V. by Versace, Inc. v. Gianni Versace S.p.A., 87 F.Supp.2d 281 (S.D.N.Y.2000) (fine based on profits earned by the defendant) with Jarrell v. Petoseed Co., 331 S.C. 207, 500 S.E.2d 793 (App.1998) (goal is to return injured party to status quo). *See* Dan B. Dobbs, *Law of Remedies* § 2.8(2) n.23 (2d ed.1993).

Other responses to violations include requiring the contemnor to pay the attorney's fees and expenses caused by the violation. *E.g.,* Jones v. Clinton, 57 F.Supp.2d 719 (E.D.Ark.1999) (ordering President Clinton to pay in excess of $90,000 in fees and expenses to compensate court and attorneys for failure to obey discovery orders in deposition).

3.   *Coercive civil contempt.* The basic rule is that the court may never apply more than "the least possible power adequate to the end proposed." Anderson v. Dunn, 19 U.S. (6 Wheat.) 204, 231 (1821). In other words, the sanction must be for coercive rather than punitive purposes. Sometimes, however, what it takes to coerce determined opposition can be awesome or even infinite, as where witnesses subpoenaed to testify against organized crime fear for their lives. There are occasionally statutory limits on coercive civil contempt sanctions. For instance, in federal court, a witness who disobeys an order to testify cannot be held for longer than the life of the proceeding, up to a maximum of eighteen months. 28 U.S.C. § 1826.

In the absence of statutory limits, coercive civil contempt sanctions can substantially exceed sanctions for the same conduct punished as criminal contempt or as an ordinary crime. For an extreme example, when a husband refused to obey an Israeli rabbinical court's order to grant his wife a divorce by saying, as is necessary under Jewish law, "I am willing," the court ordered him held in jail until he obeyed. He died in jail 32 years later without saying the words. Married to Principles, San Francisco Chronicle, Dec. 6, 1994 at A7. See also Chadwick v. Hill, 2008 WL 1886128 (E.D.Pa.2008) (rejecting husband's petition for federal habeas corpus relief from incarceration since 1995 for civil contempt for refusal to comply with state court order to return funds from offshore accounts in matrimonial proceeding).

The case of Dr. Elizabeth Morgan also illustrates the potential severity of coercive civil sanctions. Dr. Morgan, then a prominent Washington, D.C. surgeon, sought to deny her former husband, Dr. Eric Foretich, an oral surgeon, unsupervised visits with their then-six-year-old daughter. Dr. Morgan believed that Dr. Foretich had sexually abused the child. After extensive hearings that produced sharply clashing testimony, the trial court ordered Dr. Morgan to produce the child for unsupervised visits with Dr. Foretich. Dr. Morgan instead hid their daughter. The trial court held Dr. Morgan in civil contempt and, in August, 1987, incarcerated her until she produced the child. In the summer of 1989, Dr. Morgan, who by then had the most seniority among the inmates of the D.C. House of Detention, testified that she would stay in jail until the child turned 18 and would be free of the court's directives. At that point, should the trial court have freed her from incarceration for civil contempt? *See, e.g.,* Morgan v. Foretich, 564 A.2d 1 (D.C.App. en banc 1989) (appellate court directs Dr. Morgan be freed because incarceration no longer serves coercive purpose). Before the court could act, Charles Colson (the convicted Watergate-conspirator and Prison Fellowship founder), the National Organization for Women, Ross Perot, and others successfully lobbied Congress for legislation that would forbid District of Columbia courts from incarcerating anyone for civil contempt longer than one year in a custody case. The contemnor could be held longer only after being convicted of criminal contempt before a different judge, with the right to a jury and bail. District of Columbia Civil Contempt Imprisonment Limitation Act of 1989, P.L. 101–97. Is this legislation appropriate? For a detailed account of the Morgan case, see June Carbone & Leslie J. Harris, *Family Law Armageddon: The Story of* Morgan v. Foretich, in *Family Law Stories* (2007). See also Margaret M. Mahoney, *The Enforcement of Child Custody Orders by Contempt Remedies*, 68 U.Pitt.L.Rev. 835 (2007).

How should courts handle confrontations with such stubborn contemnors? See Doug Rendleman, *Disobedience and Coercive Contempt Confinement: The Terminally Stubborn Contemnor,* 48 Wash. & Lee L.Rev. 185 (1991); Linda S. Beres, *Games Civil Contemnors Play*, 18 Harv. J.L. & Pub. Pol'y 795 (1995).

NOTES ON PROCEDURES

1.   *Criminal contempt.* As pointed out in *Hicks* and *Bagwell*, criminal contempt requires many of the same procedural safeguards as an ordinary criminal prosecution. In particular, the United States Constitution requires that alleged contemnors in state or federal court are entitled to a jury trial unless the offense is petty. The offense is serious if the contumacious behavior is a crime that carries a maximum sentence of six months or more. Nor is it petty if the contumacious behavior is not otherwise a crime, but the actual sentence imposed is of six months or more. Codispoti v. Pennsylvania, 418 U.S. 506 1974). Nonetheless, in a subsequent case, the Court held that an aggregate sentence exceeding six months is still petty if each count tried individually is a petty crime. Lewis v. United States, 518 U.S. 322 (1996).

A sufficiently large fine also can make a contempt serious, but how large depends on the nature and means of the defendant. In 1966, the Supreme Court said that the rule of thumb is that a $500 fine against an individual is not petty, Cheff v. Schnackenberg, 384 U.S. 373, 375 (1966), but the thumb may have swollen along with inflation. See In re Dyer, 322 F.3d 1178, 1193 (9th Cir.2003) (suggesting that any fine above $5,000, "at least in 1998 dollars," would be serious). As to organizational defendants, Muniz v. Hoffman, 422 U.S. 454 (1975), held that a fine of $10,000 was petty in light of a defendant union's ability to collect dues from 13,000 members. The Second Circuit has held that a $100,000 fine against a large corporation was serious, even though it represented less than one percent of its net earnings in one year. United States v. Twentieth Century Fox Film Corp., 882 F.2d 656 (2d Cir.1989), *cert. denied*, 493 U.S. 1021 (1990).

As *Bagwell* points out, a person who disrupts a trial can summarily be held in contempt, without notice or a hearing. Pounders v. Watson, 521 U.S. 982 (1997), a 7–2 per curiam decision, held that summary contempt can be used not only to ward off future disruptions, but also to punish past ones. *See* Note, *Why Contempt is Different: Agency Costs and "Petty Crime" in Summary Contempt Proceedings*, 112 Yale L.J. 1223 (2003) (comprehensive analysis of the evolution of contempt, the role of the jury, and the use of summary adjudication procedures).

2.   *Compensatory Civil contempt.* A small number of states, including North Carolina and California, do not allow compensatory civil contempt, apparently on the theory that compensation is really "damages" so that "the defendant ought to have a trial 'at law' with a jury * * * . On the other hand, that equity took the case in the first place is an indication that the jury trial was a secondary value in the case * * * ." Dan B. Dobbs, *Handbook on the Law of Remedies* 100 (1973). *See* Doug Rendleman, *Compensatory Contempt: Plaintiff's Remedy When a Defendant Violates an Injunction*, 1980 U.Ill.L.F. 971, 982–83. In any event, the plaintiff may well prefer to seek compensation in an action for damages rather than in contempt in order to have a jury and to avoid the clear and convincing evidence standard.

2.   THE COLLATERAL BAR RULE

The collateral bar rule provides that a defendant may not challenge the validity of the underlying injunction during a contempt proceeding. The case and following notes help explain why.

IN RE PROVIDENCE JOURNAL CO.

United States Court ofAppeals, First Circuit
820 F.2d 1342, 820 F.2d 1354 (1987), *cert. dismissed*, 485 U.S. 693[c]

WISDOM, CIRCUIT JUDGE.

This appeal presents an apparent conflict between two fundamental legal principles: the hallowed First Amendment principle that the press shall not be subjected to prior restraints; the other, the sine qua non of orderly government, that, until modified or vacated, a court order must be obeyed. The district court adjudged the defendants/appellants, the Providence Journal Company and its executive editor, Charles M. Hauser, (collectively referred to as the "Journal") guilty of criminal contempt. The Journal admits that it violated the order but argues that the order was a prior restraint and that the unconstitutionality of the order is a defense in the contempt proceeding. We agree. A party subject to an order that constitutes a transparently invalid prior restraint on pure speech may challenge the order by violating it.

FACTS

From 1962 to 1965, the Federal Bureau of Investigation conducted electronic surveillance of Raymond L.S. Patriarca, reputedly a prominent figure in organized crime. The FBI conducted this surveillance without a warrant in violation of his Fourth Amendment rights. The FBI later destroyed all tape recordings relating to this surveillance but retained the logs and memoranda compiled from the recordings. In 1976, the Journal

---

[c]   Certiorari was dismissed because it was filed by a special prosecutor appointed by the district court while 28 U.S.C. § 518(a) provides that only the Attorney General or the Solicitor General can conduct or argue suits "in which the United States is interested" in the Supreme Court. It was such a suit because it involved a crime against the United States, criminal contempt.

requested the logs and memoranda from the FBI under the Freedom of Information Act ("FOIA"). The FBI refused this request on the ground that disclosure would be an unwarranted invasion of personal privacy. * * *

In the spring of 1985, after the death of Raymond L.S. Patriarca, the Journal renewed its FOIA request to the FBI for the logs and memoranda. The FBI assented to this request and furnished the materials not only to the Journal, but also to WJAR Television Ten and other news media. On November 8, 1985, Raymond J. Patriarca ("Patriarca"), Raymond L.S. Patriarca's son, filed a summons and complaint against the FBI, WJAR, and the Journal * * * [for an injunction preventing the defendants from publishing the released material.]

On November 12, 1985, the summons, complaint, and motion were served on the Journal. One day later, the district court held a conference concerning the request for a temporary restraining order. Counsel for the Journal argued that any restraining order would constitute a prior restraint forbidden by the First Amendment. Over the objections of counsel for the Journal and the government, the court entered a temporary restraining order barring publication of the logs and memoranda by the Journal and WJAR. The district court set a hearing for November 15, 1985, at which time it would decide whether to vacate the order. The district court later vacated the order and denied preliminary injunctive relief against the Journal and WJAR.

On November 14, 1985, the day after the district court issued the order, and while that order was still in effect, the Journal published an article on the deceased Patriarca that included information taken from the logs and memoranda. The son filed a motion to judge the Journal in contempt. When he declined to prosecute the criminal contempt motion, the district court invoked Fed.R.Crim.P. 42(b) and appointed a special prosecutor. Following a hearing, the district court found the Journal guilty of criminal contempt. Subsequent to a sentencing hearing, the court imposed an 18-month jail term on Hauser, which was suspended, ordered Hauser to perform 200 hours of public service, and fined the Journal $100,000. The Journal appealed.

DISCUSSION

This appeal propounds a question that admits of no easy answer. Each party stands on what each regards as an unassailable legal principle. The special prosecutor relies on the bedrock principle that court orders, even those that are later ruled unconstitutional, must be complied with until amended or vacated.[9] This principle is often referred to as the "collateral bar" rule. The Journal relies on the bedrock principle that prior restraints against speech are prohibited by the First Amendment. In this opinion we

---

[9]   *See* Walker v. City of Birmingham, 388 U.S. 307 (1967); United States v. United Mine Workers, 330 U.S. 258 (1947).

endeavor to avoid deciding which principle should take precedence by reaching a result consistent with both principles. * * *

If a publisher is to print a libelous, defamatory, or injurious story, an appropriate remedy, though not always totally effective, lies not in an injunction against that publication but in a damages or criminal action after publication. Although the threat of damages or criminal action may chill speech, a prior restraint "freezes" speech before the audience has the opportunity to hear the message. Additionally, a court asked to issue a prior restraint must judge the challenged speech in the abstract. And, as was true in the instant case, a court may issue a prior restraint in the form of a temporary restraining order or preliminary injunction without a full hearing; a judgment for damages or a criminal sanction may be imposed only after a full hearing with all the attendant procedural protections.

Equally well-established is the requirement of any civilized government that a party subject to a court order must abide by its terms or face criminal contempt. Even if the order is later declared improper or unconstitutional, it must be followed until vacated or modified. As a general rule, a party may not violate an order and raise the issue of its unconstitutionality collaterally as a defense in the criminal contempt proceeding. Rather, the appropriate method to challenge a court order is to petition to have the order vacated or amended.

In *Walker v. City of Birmingham*, the Supreme Court upheld contempt citations against Dr. Martin Luther King, Jr. and other civil rights protestors enjoined from parading without a permit. The protestors argued that the order and the ordinance upon which it was based were unconstitutional because they constituted impermissible prior restraints upon the right to free speech and assembly. The Court noted that the ordinance "unquestionably raise[d] substantial constitutional issues" and that "[t]he breadth and vagueness of the injunction itself would also unquestionably be subject to substantial constitutional question". Nonetheless, the Court ruled that the protestors could not raise those constitutional issues collaterally in the contempt proceedings. As the Supreme Court noted in *United States v. United Mine Workers*, so long as the court has jurisdiction over the parties and the subject matter of the controversy, an order it issues must be obeyed.

The *Walker* Court found it significant that the contemnors had not sought to appeal the order they violated. The Court declared: "This case would arise in quite a different constitutional posture if the petitioners, before disobeying the injunction, had challenged it in the Alabama courts, and had been met with delay or frustration of their constitutional claims." The *Walker* Court concluded by noting that "no man can be judge in his own case, however exalted his station, however righteous his motives, and irrespective of his race, color, politics, or religion".

At first glance, *Walker* would appear to control the instant case. There, as here, a party chose to violate an arguably unconstitutional prior restraint rather than to comply with the orderly process of law by seeking relief from an appellate court. *Walker* declares that the contemnors are collaterally barred from challenging the constitutionality of the order forming the basis of the contempt citation. The *Walker* Court was, however, careful to point out that the order issued by the Alabama court was not "transparently invalid". The Court specifically noted that "this is not a case where the injunction was *transparently invalid* or had only a frivolous pretense to validity". The unmistakable import of this language is that a transparently invalid order cannot form the basis for a contempt citation.

Court orders are accorded a special status in American jurisprudence. While one may violate a statute and raise as a defense the statute's unconstitutionality, such is not generally the case with a court order. Nonetheless, court orders are not sacrosanct.[28] An order entered by a court clearly without jurisdiction over the contemnors or the subject matter is not protected by the collateral bar rule.[29] Were this not the case, a court could wield power over parties or matters obviously not within its authority—a concept inconsistent with the notion that the judiciary may exercise only those powers entrusted to it by law.

The same principle supports an exception to the collateral bar rule for transparently invalid court orders. Requiring a party subject to such an order to obey or face contempt would give the courts powers far in excess of any authorized by the Constitution or Congress. Recognizing an exception to the collateral bar rule for transparently invalid orders does not violate the principle that "no man can be judge in his own case" anymore than does recognizing such an exception for jurisdictional defects. The key to both exceptions is the notion that although a court order—even an arguably incorrect court order—demands respect, so does the right of the citizen to be free of clearly improper exercises of judicial authority.

Although an exception to the collateral bar rule is appropriate for transparently void orders, it is inappropriate for arguably proper orders. This distinction is necessary both to protect the authority of the courts when they address close questions and to create a strong incentive for parties to follow the orderly process of law. No such protection or incentive is needed when the order is transparently invalid because in that instance the court is acting so far in excess of its authority that it has no right to expect compliance and no interest is protected by requiring compliance.

---

[28] *See* Cobbledick v. United States, 309 U.S. 323 (1940). In *Cobbledick,* the Supreme Court ruled that when a motion to quash a subpoena is denied, the movant may either obey its commands or violate them, and, if cited for contempt, properly contest its validity in the contempt proceeding. * * *

[29] *United Mine Workers*, 330 U.S. at 293.

The line between a transparently invalid order and one that is merely invalid is, of course, not always distinct. As a general rule, if the court reviewing the order finds the order to have had any pretense to validity at the time it was issued, the reviewing court should enforce the collateral bar rule. Such a heavy presumption in favor of validity is necessary to protect the rightful power of the courts. Nonetheless, there are instances where an order will be so patently unconstitutional that it will be excepted from the collateral bar rule. We now turn to consider whether the order issued by the district court on November 13, 1985, was, as the Journal contends, transparently invalid.

[The court concludes that the Supreme Court has never upheld a prior restraint on publication of news, but that it has implied that such a restraint might be appropriate in certain extreme cases.]

The special prosecutor argues, however, that the order was to last only a short period and merely preserved the status quo while allowing the court a full opportunity to assess the issues. We are sympathetic with the district court on this score. This matter came before the district court on an emergency basis. The court was forced to drop its other duties and immediately address this issue. Counsel for the Journal had received the papers less than 24 hours before they presented their arguments to the district court. Based on counsel's hastily prepared authority and without the opportunity for cool reflection, the district court was forced to make a decision. The court's natural instinct was to delay the matter temporarily so that a careful, thoughtful answer could be crafted. This approach is proper in most instances, and indeed to follow any other course of action would often be irresponsible. But, absent the most compelling circumstances, when that approach results in a prior restraint on pure speech by the press it is not allowed.

It must be said, it is misleading in the context of daily newspaper publishing to argue that a temporary restraining order merely preserves the status quo. The status quo of daily newspapers is to publish news promptly that editors decide to publish. A restraining order disturbs the status quo and impinges on the exercise of editorial discretion. News is a constantly changing and dynamic quantity. Today's news will often be tomorrow's history. This is especially true in the case of news concerning an imminent event such as an election. A restraining order lasting only hours can effectively prevent publication of news that will have an impact on that event and on those that the event affects.

Although there is no question that the Patriarca story was not news concerning an imminent event, extraneous factors required its reasonably prompt publication. The Journal had promised its readers that the Patriarca story would be forthcoming. Moreover, other media not subject to the court order had the same logs and memoranda. Were they to disseminate this information while the Journal remained silent, some readers of the Journal might lose confidence in that paper's editorial competence.[65] * * *

Although the Journal arguably had avenues of appellate relief immediately available to it,[70] we decline to invoke the collateral bar rule because of the Journal's failure to avail itself of these opportunities. When, as here, the court order is a transparently invalid prior restraint on pure speech, the delay and expense of an appeal is unnecessary. Indeed, the delay caused by an appellate review requirement could, in the case of a prior restraint involving news concerning an imminent event, cause the restrained information to lose its value. The absence of such a requirement will not, however, lead to wide-spread disregard of court orders. Rarely will a party be subject to a transparently invalid court order. Prior restraints on pure speech represent an unusual class of orders because they are presumptively unconstitutional. And even when a party believes it is subject to a transparently invalid order, seeking review in an appellate court is a far safer means of testing the order. For if the party chooses to violate the order and the order turns out not to be transparently invalid, the party must suffer the consequences of a contempt citation.

CONCLUSION

We conclude that the district court's order of November 13, 1985, was transparently invalid. * * *

Because the order was transparently invalid, the appellants should have been allowed to challenge its constitutionality at the contempt proceedings.[74] A fortiori, the order cannot serve as the basis for a contempt citation. The order of the district court finding the Providence Journal

---

[65] In United States v. Dickinson, 465 F.2d 496 (5th Cir.1972), the Court of Appeals for the Fifth Circuit applied the collateral bar rule in a contempt proceeding involving a gag order against a newspaper. We decline to follow *Dickinson* for two reasons. First, *Dickinson* involved an order issued to protect a defendant's Sixth Amendment right to a fair trial, while the order in the instant matter was issued merely to protect an individual's interest in privacy. Second, *Dickinson* was decided before [the Supreme Court handed down a case that announced a particularly strict test for prior restraints].

[70] Arguably, the Journal could have immediately appealed the order to this Court under 28 U.S.C. § 1292(a)(1). And, although difficult to obtain, the Journal might have sought a writ of mandamus. 28 U.S.C. § 1651(a).

[74] [In Thomas v. Collins, 323 U.S. 516 (1945)], a labor organization was enjoined from soliciting union memberships. The organizer violated the order and subsequently challenged its constitutionality arguing that the temporary restraining order constituted a prior restraint on pure speech. The Supreme Court allowed this challenge and reversed the contempt citation.

The Journal argues that *Thomas* stands for the proposition that the collateral bar rule does not apply to prior restraints on pure speech. Because the order of November 13, 1985, was transparently invalid, however, we need not address this issue. We note, however, that *Thomas* does provide support for our holding. *Thomas* held that any prior restraint on pure speech was invalid absent clear and present danger of immediate and irreparable injury to the public welfare. Moreover, *Thomas* establishes that the collateral bar rule is not impregnable in cases involving prior restraints on pure speech.

Company and its executive editor, Charles M. Hauser, in criminal contempt is therefore reversed.[75]

ORDER

We hereby grant petitioner's suggestion for rehearing en banc. We do not, however, vacate the panel's opinion and order. Rather, we issue the attached en banc opinion as an addendum to, and modification of, said panel opinion; and as so modified said panel opinion and order may stand as reflecting the opinion of the en banc court. * * *

OPINION ON REHEARING

PER CURIAM.

In reflecting en banc upon the conflicting principles of "collateral bar" and "no prior restraint against pure speech," the court recognizes, with the panel, the difficulties of imposing upon a publisher the requirement of pursuing the normal appeal process. Not only would such entail time and expense, but the right sought to be vindicated could be forfeited or the value of the embargoed information considerably cheapened. Nevertheless, it seems to us that some finer tuning is available to minimize the disharmony between respect for court orders and respect for free speech.

It is not asking much, beyond some additional expense and time, to require a publisher, even when it thinks it is the subject of a transparently unconstitutional order of prior restraint, to make a good faith effort to seek emergency relief from the appellate court. If timely access to the appellate court is not available or if timely decision is not forthcoming, the publisher may then proceed to publish and challenge the constitutionality of the order in the contempt proceedings. In such event whatever added expense and time are involved, such a price does not seem disproportionate to the respect owing court processes; and there is no prolongation of any prior restraint. On the other hand, should the appellate court grant the requested relief, the conflict between principles has been resolved and the expense and time involved have vastly been offset by aborting any contempt proceedings.

We realize that our ruling means that a publisher seeking to challenge an order it deems transparently unconstitutional must concern itself with establishing a record of its good faith effort. But that is a price we should pay for the preference of court over party determination of invalidity. In the instant case, assertions have been made that some eight-and-one-half hours elapsed between the issuance of the order by the district court and

---

[75] In reversing the contempt citation against the Journal and its executive editor, we in no way condone their conduct. From all appearances, the Journal used the presence of the court order to bolster the importance of the Patriarca story. On November 14, 1985, the day before the scheduled hearing on whether to vacate the Court order of November 13, the Journal's front page headline read: "Court restricts media use of FBI tapes on Patriarca; Journal decides to print". * * * [I]t appears to this court that the Journal published the story concerning the court order more for its publicity value than for its news value. * * *

the deadline for publication. Not only are we left without a clear conviction that timely emergency relief was available within the restraints governing the publisher's decision making, but we would deem it unfair to subject the publisher to the very substantial sanctions imposed by the district court because of its failure to follow the procedure we have just announced. We recognize that our announcement is technically dictum, but are confident that its stature as a deliberate position taken by us in this en banc consideration will serve its purpose.

NOTES ON THE COLLATERAL BAR RULE

1.   *The collateral bar rule is not mandatory. Walker* merely held that it was permissible for states to enforce the collateral bar rule. For example, Texas recognizes an exception when the trial court's injunction unconstitutionally restrains speech. In re Sheshtawy, 154 S.W.3d 114, 126 (2004). Accord, People v. Gonzalez, 12 Cal.4th 804, 50 Cal.Rptr.2d 74, 910 P.2d 1366 (1996) (citing cases from other jurisdictions declining to follow the rule). *See* Comment, *The Collateral Bar Rule and Rule 26 Protective Orders: Overprotection of Judicial Discretion*, 35 Ariz.L.Rev. 1029 (2003) (overview of collateral bar rule; comment contends that collateral bar rule should not be applied to Fed.R.Civ.P. 26 protective orders).

2.   *Does the rule make sense? Providence Journal* develops an exception to the collateral bar rule, but does not question the rule itself. Unless one of the exceptions to the rule applies—more about them below—someone who violates an injunction is barred from defending a prosecution for criminal contempt by asserting that the order was invalid. In other words, one may attack the order's validity by direct appeal, but not collaterally in a criminal contempt proceeding. For example, in *Walker v. City of Birmingham,* Dr. King and others were barred from collaterally attacking the validity of an injunction enforcing a constitutionally suspect anti-parade ordinance. In contrast, other participants in the march, who were charged only with violating the ordinance because they were not named in the injunction, were not collaterally barred from making an ultimately successful attack upon the ordinance's invalidity. Shuttlesworth v. City of Birmingham, 394 U.S. 147 (1969). So, on account of an invalid order based upon an invalid ordinance issued by a judge who was part of a segregationist system, Dr. King and his enjoined colleagues were forced to choose. If the long-planned march were delayed until after lawyers got the order overturned or stayed on appeal, the dramatic moment for the march over the Easter weekend would have passed. Dr. King and the others chose to march and go to jail. (There he wrote the famous "Letter from Birmingham Jail." See David Benjamin Oppenheimer, Martin Luther King, and the Letter from Birmingham Jail, 26 U.C.Davis L.Rev. 791 (1993); and David Benjamin Oppenheimer, Kennedy, King, Shuttlesworth and Walker: The Events Leading to the Introduction of the Civil Rights Act of 1964, 29 U.S.F.L.Rev. 645 (1995).)

Walker v. City of Birmingham shows the harm that can result from the collateral bar rule. Yet, harm could also ensue from getting rid of it. Consider the fate of Ed Johnson. Mr. Johnson, an African-American, was convicted by an all-white jury of raping a white woman and sentenced to death. The conviction was appealed to the United States Supreme Court, which took the case on March 19, 1906. This was the first time it had ever agreed to review a state court criminal trial. Pending appeal, the Court immediately stayed the execution and telegraphed an order to Sheriff Joseph Shipp to protect Johnson. On the night of March 19, with the connivance of Sheriff Shipp, and with full knowledge of the Court's orders, a mob took Johnson out of jail and lynched him. The Supreme Court ordered the Attorney General of the United States to prosecute Sheriff Shipp for criminal contempt and he was convicted. United States v. Shipp, 214 U.S. 386 (1909). See Mark Curriden & Leroy Phillips, Jr., *Contempt of Court: The Turn-of-the-Century Lynching That Launched 100 Years of Federalism* (1999). Without a collateral bar rule, Sheriff Shipp would not be guilty of contempt if the order to protect Johnson had been issued in error. The abolition of the collateral bar rule would tempt some defendants to defy a court order in the belief that later it will be found invalid. If they are wrong, however, irreparable injury will have been done to the plaintiff. The collateral bar rule reflects the judgment of appellate judges that trial court judges are generally more trustworthy than defendants in deciding whether to subject plaintiffs to such irreparable harm.

3. *Exceptions to the collateral bar rule.*

(a) *No direct appeal available.* Footnote 28 in *Providence Journal* shows that the collateral bar rule does not apply to certain discovery orders for which no direct appeal is available. The court also notes a passage in *Walker* indicating that the collateral bar rule would not apply if the demonstrators had appealed but had been given the run around. As the court acknowledges, it is difficult to appeal temporary restraining orders. Should the collateral bar rule apply to such orders? Professor Rendleman argues that the collateral bar rule should not apply to ex parte orders. Doug Rendleman, *More on Void Orders*, 7 Ga.L.Rev. 246 (1973).

(b) *The court lacks jurisdiction.* The collateral bar rule, in effect, puts the burden on the defendant of either obeying the order or going to the trouble of getting it overturned on appeal. The justification for this burden is that the order did not come from just anyone but rather from a judge. However, if the judge is from a low level tribunal that lacks subject matter jurisdiction to issue the injunction—say traffic court or small claims court—then putting the burden on the defendant loses plausibility. This is the rationale for the lack of jurisdiction exception. However, the most powerful trial courts sometimes may lack jurisdiction for reasons that are quite complex and difficult to evaluate. For instance, the Supreme Court in *United Mine Workers* split 5–4 in holding that the federal district court had jurisdiction to enjoin a strike against the government. Moreover, there is an exception to the no-jurisdiction-exception. Five justices in *United Mine Workers* held that even if the district court ultimately lacked jurisdiction, it had jurisdiction to issue a temporary restraining order to gain the time to determine whether it had jurisdiction. What result if the court failed to consider the jurisdictional issue at all but rather issued the temporary restraining order without mentioning it? See United States Catholic Conference v. Abortion Rights Mobilization, 487 U.S. 72, 79–80 (1988).

(c) *Transparent invalidity. Walker* suggested transparent invalidity as an exception, but not until *Providence Journal* did a federal court base a holding on this theory. Why hadn't a case gone off on transparent invalidity in the two decades since *Walker*? Should there be a transparent invalidity exception? Should it require, as the en banc decision says, an effort to appeal? The Second Circuit Court of Appeals, in United States v. Terry, 17 F.3d 575, 579 (2d Cir.), *cert. denied*, 513 U.S. 946 (1994), joined the First Circuit in finding that a party seeking to invoke the transparent invalidity exception must make a "good faith effort to seek emergency relief from the appellate court."

(d) *Prior restraints. Thomas*, discussed in footnote 74, involved a union official found in contempt of an order not to violate a statute that forbade soliciting union membership. The Court struck down the statute on the grounds of prior restraint and freed the official without mention of the collateral bar rule. So *Thomas* is not square support for an exception to the collateral bar rule for prior restraints. Courts in a few states have considered whether there should be such an exception, with mixed results. *See* Richard E. Labunski, *A First Amendment Exception to the "Collateral Bar" Rule: Protecting Freedom of Expression and the Legitimacy of Courts*, 22 Pepp.L.Rev. 405 (1995). Should there be such an exception? *See* Christina E. Wells, *Bringing Structure to the Law of Injunctions Against Expression*, 51 Case W.Res.L.Rev. 1 (2000). *See also* McGraw-Hill Cos. v. Procter & Gamble Co., 515 U.S.1309 (1995) (Memorandum of Justice Stevens) (refusing to lift a prior restraint because McGraw-Hill did not seek trial court review before seeking an appeal); People v. Bryant, 94 P.3d 624 (Colo.2004) (upholding an injunction constituting a prior restraint; injunction forbid publication of a transcript of an in camera rape shield hearing in the Kobe Bryant case where the transcript was inadvertently released to the media by trial court personnel).

(e) *Inability to Comply Pending Modification.* The D.C. Circuit has held that the collateral bar rule cannot justify subjecting a defendant to liability where the party is faced with an injunction with which it is unable to comply (in this case for inability to pay). Nor can the rule justify subjecting the defendant to liability for the period in which the district court was considering the defendant's motion for modification based on inability to comply. Thus, the district court, which had granted the motion to modify on a prospective basis only, abused its discretion when it did not also make the modification retroactive. Evans v. Williams, 206 F.3d 1292 (D.C.Cir.2000).

4. *A cautionary tale.* When Cable News Network got recordings made by prison officials of conversations between General Manuel Noriega and the attorneys defending him against drug charges, the criminal trial court issued a preliminary injunction barring CNN from broadcasting the tapes for ten days or such lesser time as needed for the court to review the tapes and determine whether a restraint was warranted. To that end, the court also ordered CNN

to turn over copies of the tapes. United States v. Noriega, 752 F.Supp. 1032 (S.D.Fla.1990). CNN appealed, but also broadcast portions of the tapes. The order was upheld on appeal. 917 F.2d 1543 (11th Cir.), *cert. denied*, 498 U.S. 976 (1990). After CNN finally gave the trial court copies of the tapes, the judge ruled that their contents did not justify the restraint, but that it was correct to restrain CNN because of its initial refusal to supply the tapes. 752 F.Supp. 1045 (S.D.Fla.1990). Four years later, CNN was found guilty of criminal contempt and directed to pay a fine covering the government's legal fees incurred during the contempt prosecution and to broadcast an apology or, in alternative, pay an additional punitive fine. United States v. CNN, Inc., 865 F.Supp. 1549 (S.D.Fla.1994). CNN apologized.

5. *The attorney's liability.* The ABA Model Code of Professional Responsibility EC 7–22 (1980) states that "[r]espect for judicial rulings is essential to the proper administration of justice; however, a litigant or his lawyer may, in good faith and within the framework of the law, take steps to test the correctness of a ruling of a tribunal." If one of the exceptions to the collateral bar rule is not available, "then counsel may give his opinion that an order is no good, or he may outline to his client the boundaries of that order and what conduct is and is not included. Except for these limited situations, it is otherwise the duty of the attorney to urge his client to comply with all orders * * * ." Denise A. Lier, *Liability of the Attorney Who Advises Disobedience*, 6 J.Legal Prof. 333, 345 (1981).

3. ENFORCEMENT AGAINST THE GOVERNMENT

This section considers problems that are special to enforcing injunctions against governmental defendants. One such problem is that sanctions against the government may harm innocent citizens. A fine would come out of the pockets of taxpayers rather than the responsible public officials. The court could theoretically jail the officials for criminal contempt, but on scholar reported that there was "no federal case decided within the past twenty-five years in which a public official has been imprisoned for civil or criminal contempt for violating an injunction." James M. Hirshhorn, *Where the Money Is: Remedies to Finance Compliance With Strict Structural Injunctions*, 82 Mich.L.Rev. 1815, 1841 (1984). *Spallone v. United States* is a subsequent example that underlines judicial reluctance to jail officials. Jailing officials is rare partly because the conflict over the jailing could well divert energies and attention from complying with the injunction. In Palmigiano v. Garrahy, 448 F.Supp. 659 (D.R.I.1978), the court responded to contempt by threatening coercive civil fines against the state rather than punishing the officials through criminal contempt. The court emphasized that the violations arose from mismanagement and that the officials could avoid wasting the taxpayers' money on fines by obeying promptly. In this way, the judge used the threat of coercive sanctions against the state to apply political pressure on the officials; punishing the officials could have created political, practical and separation of powers problems for the judge.

Judicial Reluctance: Another problem special to enforcement against government is judicial reluctance to exercise powers assigned to other branches or levels of government. A narrow preventive injunction, by doing no more than stopping a governmental defendant from interfering with the plaintiff's rightful position, does not exercise the power of another branch of government but rather keeps that defendant from exceeding its powers. But, reparative injunctions as well as many of the devices for dealing with the difficulties in enforcing injunctions—such as prophylactic orders, monitors, and receivers—go beyond simply preventing future violations. Such devices, by intruding on a governmental defendant's power, raise separation of powers or federalism issues. *See* Gerald E. Frug, *The Judicial Power of the Purse*, 126 U.Pa.L.Rev. 715 (1978). If the case involves a federal court and a federal agency or a state court and a state agency, the case would raise separation of powers issues. If it involves a federal court and a state agency, it would raise federalism issues. Robert F. Nagel, *Separation of Powers and the Scope of Federal Equitable Remedies*, 30 Stan.L.Rev. 661 (1978).

Judges worry about separation of powers and federalism for diverse reasons. Judicial intrusion on the powers of governmental defendants shifts power from politically accountable to unaccountable hands. Moreover, a judge who strays from public expectations of the judicial role endangers the presumptive legitimacy that public opinion gives to court orders. *See* Colin S. Diver, *The Judge as Political Powerbroker: Superintending Structural Change in Public Institutions*, 65 Va.L.Rev. 43 (1979). Furthermore, the judge may not feel competent to make the necessary administrative or political decisions, either because of limited expertise or because the court lacks the fact-finding or outreach capacity of a legislature or an agency.

Political Motivations: Moreover, when dealing with enforcement against government defendants, the injunction must overcome the political motives or bureaucratic inertia that led the governmental defendants to violate the plaintiff's rights in the first place. The injunction in Illinois v. Costle, 9 Envt.L.Rep. 20243 (D.D.C. 1979) is a classic example of a judge trying to motivate the defendants by changing the political and bureaucratic milieu. EPA failed to meet the statutory deadlines for promulgating regulations for hazardous and solid waste because of a lack of resources and bureaucratic inertia. To grapple with these root sources of the violation, Judge Gesell took what steps he could. He required the agency to report any further slippage to the court and he required that such reports, as well as the regular reports to the court, be signed by the EPA Administrator. He also required that all such reports be sent to the congressional oversight committees. Since the EPA Administrator would be reluctant to report bad news to Congress and more reluctant still to have to testify before Congress or the court about such failures, the decree changed the course of least resistance at EPA from letting the regulations come out when they will to getting them out on the schedule in the decree. Also, by putting the congressional committees on notice, the decree might prompt them to pressure EPA to act more quickly. Finally, by blaming Congress for some of the delay, Judge Gesell was trying to prompt the plaintiffs to get Congress to give the agency resources commensurate with the deadlines that it had imposed upon it.

More troublesome are cases when enough voters positively oppose compliance that the legislators or other politically accountable officials refuse to take necessary action. For example, the state legislature might refuse to grant a local government the authority to promulgate regulations required by an injunction or refuse to grant state officials the authority needed to raise and spend money needed to comply. The legislature might be tempted to retaliate against the court system by challenging its independence. See Michele Demary, *Legislative-Judicial Relations on Contested Issues: Taxes and Same-Sex Marriage*, 89 Judicature 202 (2006).

Governmental Immunity: Resistance by governmental defendants is also complicated by the immunity of some governments to suit. Sovereign immunity bars suits against a state in its own courts, or suits against the federal government in a federal or a state court. The Eleventh Amendment has been read to bar suits by private persons against states in federal courts. Hans v. Louisiana, 134 U.S. 1 (1890). *See generally Symposium, Shifting the Balance of Power? The Supreme Court, Federalism, and State Sovereign Immunity*, 53 Stan. L. Rev. 1115 (2001). Further complications on the resistance of governmental defendants are added by the government's practical immunity for failing to enforce injunctive relief for citizens. In Town of Castle Rock v. Gonzales, 545 U.S. 748 (2005), the plaintiff was held not to have a cognizable property interest in a civil restraining order obtained against her husband. Although the plaintiff theoretically had a right to protection via the injunction, the Court held that no remedy for damages applied for the police's failure to enforce the order, resulting in the horrific murder of the plaintiff's three children.

Given sovereign immunity, how is it that governmental actions can get challenged in court? For starters, the Eleventh Amendment does not bar suits brought by the United States or other states. Second, local governments are not generally considered sovereigns under the Eleventh Amendment and so are amenable to suit in federal court, which explains *Brown v. Board of Education*, for example. *E.g.,* Northern Insurance Co. v. Chatham County, 547 U.S. 189 (2006) (county not immune from federal suit unless acting as "arm of the State"). However, the courts of some states treat local governments as sovereigns. Third, Congress has circumscribed power under Section 5 of the Fourteenth Amendment to abrogate the states' Eleventh Amendment immunity. *E.g.,* United States v. Georgia, 546 U.S. 151 (2006); Marcia L. McCormick, *Federalism Re-Constructed: The Eleventh Amendment's Illogical Impact on Congress' Power*, 37 Ind.L.Rev.

345 (2004). Fourth, sovereigns can waive their immunity, although statutes that allegedly waive immunity in categories of cases are strictly construed. *See, e.g.,* United States v. Nordic Village, Inc., 503 U.S. 30, 34 (1992). Governments are more likely to consent to suit over contracts, accidents, or specified types of administrative actions than over broader policy choices.

Fifth, and finally, the plaintiff can sometimes dispense with suing an immune government by suing governmental officials instead. Officials themselves often have some sort of immunity against suits in damages on the theory that the prospect of personal financial liability for official acts would dissuade them from taking office, or, once in office, acting decisively. But, official immunity generally does not stop suits for injunctive relief. In the landmark case of Ex parte Young, 209 U.S. 123 (1908), the Court allowed a private plaintiff to seek an injunction against the enforcement of an allegedly unconstitutional state statute. Although the suit challenged a state statute, the Court offered as an explanation the argument that the suit was not against the state because an state official who enforces an unconstitutional statute acts ultra vires. See Joint Anti-Fascist Refugee Committee v. McGrath, 341 U.S. 123 (1951) (applying *Ex Parte Young's* reasoning in a suit against a federal official). *Compare* James Leonard, *Ubi Remedium Ibi Jus, or, Where There's a Remedy, There's a Right: a Skeptic's Critique of* Ex Parte Young, 54 Syracuse L.Rev. 215 (2004) (criticizing the *Ex parte Young* fiction as enabling a judicially-created federal forum for private claims against nonconsenting states, a result expressly rejected in 1787) and John Harrison, Ex Parte Young, 60 Stan.L.Rev. 989 (2008) (not an exceptional case because the plaintiff requested a traditional tool of equity, an anti-suit injunction, to restrain proceedings at law and thus it does not support a broad claim that all prospective injunctive relief is consistent with sovereign immunity) with Pratik A. Shah, *Saving Section 5: Lessons Learned from Consent Decrees and* Ex Parte Young, 62 Wash.& Lee L.Rev. 1001 (2005) (Congress should get same judicial deference when acting against states under Section 5 of the Fourteenth Amendment as when litigants enter into consent decrees with state officials under the *Ex Parte Young* fiction).

The key question under *Ex parte Young* is whether the relief sought is against the state and so barred by the Eleventh Amendment even though the state is not the defendant. In Edelman v. Jordan, 415 U.S. 651 (1974), and Quern v. Jordan, 440 U.S. 332 (1979), the Court decided that prospective relief, such as an injunction concerning future behavior, is permitted, while retrospective relief, such as an order that effectively awards compensation for past wrongdoing, is not because the money would come from the state treasury. Nonetheless, subsequent cases have allowed prospective relief that imposes large costs on the state. *See, e.g.,* Frew v. Hawkins, 540 U.S. 431 (2004) (enforcement of consent decree obligations as a federal court order did not violate *Ex parte Young* or the Eleventh

Amendment, even though the decree obliged Texas to provide medical services not required under federal Medicaid legislation to over one million children); Milliken v. Bradley, 433 U.S. 267 (1977) (*Milliken II*) (affirming injunction requiring state officers to provide remedial education as part of reparative injunctive relief in Detroit school segregation case).

This thumbnail sketch of blackletter immunity law (which is a core topic in the federal courts course) makes it evident that immunity law influences remedies. Immunity often makes it harder to attack government action through damages than through injunctive relief. Moreover, immunity can complicate successful injunctive relief against state action.

This then is the ultimate problem: putting the plaintiff in the rightful position requires action that state law does not empower the defendant officials to take and the legislature refuses to grant them the necessary power. A court could defer to the political powers for example, by simply striking down the existing illegal law or directing the legislature to help develop a remedy. *See* Baker v. State, 170 Vt. 194, 744 A.2d 864 (Vt.1999) (directing state legislature to develop a statutory remedy to ensure that same-sex couples would receive the same benefits and protections afforded married couples as required by state constitution); Barry Friedman, *When Rights Encounter Reality: Enforcing Federal Remedies*, 65 S.Cal.L.Rev. 735 (1992) (arguing that courts often intentionally give the political branches a voice in not only how, but also the extent to which constitutional wrongs are remedied).

But is the court limited to these actions? A key question is whether and how a court could hold punish or coerce government officials through contempt. It is a difficult task, at best. The Yonkers housing saga discussed in the next two cases exemplifies the problems.

UNITED STATES V. CITY OF YONKERS

United States Court of Appeals
856 F.2d 444 (2d. Cir. 1988), *cert. denied in part,* 489 U.S. 1065 (1989), *and rev'd in part,*
sub nom. Spallone v. United States, 493 U.S. 265 (1990)

JON O. NEWMAN, CIRCUIT JUDGE.

This appeal presents important issues concerning the enforcement of orders of a United States District Court requiring action by a municipality to remedy violations of the Constitution and statutes of the United States. The principal issues are whether members of the Yonkers City Council may be required to vote to implement remedies contained in a consent judgment agreed to by the City and approved by the City Council, and whether the City, in addition to the council members, may be subjected to the coercive sanctions of civil contempt when the agreed upon legislative action has not been taken. The issues arise on appeals by the City of Yonkers and four members of the Yonkers City Council from orders of the District Court for the Southern District of New York (Leonard B. Sand, Judge) adjudicating the City and the council members in civil contempt and imposing coercive sanctions. We conclude that under the circumstances of this case the recalcitrant council members may be required to vote to implement the consent judgment and that the City, in addition to the council members, may be adjudicated in contempt and subjected to coercive sanctions for failure to abide by the consent judgment and subsequent implementing orders of the District Court. We also conclude that the amount of the monetary sanctions imposed on the City, though properly substantial, should be somewhat reduced. We therefore affirm the order adjudicating the council members in contempt and affirm, as modified, the order adjudicating the City in contempt.

BACKGROUND

1. The Underlying Lawsuit

The United States filed the underlying lawsuit on December 1, 1980, against the City of Yonkers * * * . The complaint [alleges] that the City * * * had "intentionally . . . perpetuated and seriously aggravated residential racial segregation" in violation of the Constitution and Title VIII of the Civil Rights Act of 1968, 42 U.S.C. §§ 3601–3619 (1982) * * * .

The District Court found the City * * * liable * * * .

The Housing Remedy Order [entered on May 28, 1986] included provisions for the construction of 200 units of public housing and for the planning of additional units of subsidized housing. The City had previously agreed to provide acceptable sites for the 200 units of public housing as a condition of receiving its 1983 Community Development Block Grant from the United States Department of Housing and Urban Development (HUD). * * * The City was required to propose sites for 140 units within thirty days and sites for the remaining 60 units within ninety days.

[The Housing Remedy Order also required the City to present a plan for the subsidized housing by November 15, 1986]. * * *

2. Attempts to Implement the Housing Remedy Order

* * * [The City violated the Housing Remedy Order.] The United States and the NAACP [which had intervened] then moved for an adjudication of civil contempt and the imposition of coercive sanctions. Rather than proceed immediately to consideration of contempt sanctions, the District Court patiently endeavored to secure voluntary compliance. * * *

A consent decree was agreed to by the parties [on January 25, 1988], approved by the City Council on January 27, and entered as a consent judgment of the District Court on January 28 ("the Consent Judgment").

With respect to the 200 units of public housing, the Consent Judgment renewed the City's commitment to build the units and identified seven specific sites. * * *

[The Consent Judgment also set 800 units of subsidized housing as "an appropriate target in fulfilling its obligations" under the Housing Remedy Order, required the City to make good-faith efforts to achieve 600 of the units in annual installments of 200 units within each of the next three years. After citizens protested vehemently, the City promptly violated the Consent Decree. The City moved to modify the Consent Decree, offering to return the $30 million federal housing grant. That motion was denied and, on June 13, 1988 after prolonged consultation with the City and other parties, the District Court entered a Long Term Plan Order that specified the terms of the legislation that the City must adopt pursuant to the Consent Decree.]

On June 28 the City Council voted against a resolution "indicating [the Council's] commitment to the implementation of" the Housing Remedy Order, the Consent Judgment, and the Long Term Plan Order.

The following day the District Court directed the plaintiffs to submit an order requiring the City to take "specific implementing action" under a prescribed timetable, violation of which would subject the City to contempt sanctions. In response to the plaintiffs' proposed order setting forth such a timetable, the City argued that the defeat of the resolution on June 28 indicated that the City would not voluntarily adopt legislation contemplated by the Long Term Plan Order and suggested that the Court itself should enter an order adopting the necessary legislation. At a hearing on the proposed timetable on July 12, the District Court invited the parties' comments on the possible creation by the Court of an Affordable Housing Commission to exercise the City Council's functions concerning implementation of the housing remedy orders. The City opposed creation of the Commission because it would divest the Council of its "core legislative as well as executive functions."

3. *The Prospect of Contempt* * * *

[On July 26 the District Court issued an order that gave the City until August 1 to enact the required legislation called the Affordable Housing Ordinance. If that did not occur, the July 26 Order provided that] the City and the council members were to show cause at 10:00 a.m., August 2, why they should not be adjudged in contempt. If such cause was not shown, each council member failing to vote for such legislation would be fined $500 per day, and, if the legislation was not passed by August 10, such council member would be imprisoned on August 11. The contempt sanction against the City would be daily fines starting at $100 on August 2 and doubling in amount each day of continued noncompliance. The cumulative total of the fines against the City would exceed $10,000 by day 7, exceed $1 million by day 14, exceed $200 million by day 21, and exceed $26 billion by day 28.

The order provided that a council member could be purged of contempt by voting in favor of the legislation or by enactment of the legislation. The City could be purged of contempt by enactment of the legislation. The order further provided that all fines would be paid into the Treasury of the United States and would not be refundable, that the Council would meet at least once a week to vote on the legislative package, and that any incarcerated council member would be released to attend such meetings. * * *

[On August 1, the City Council voted four to three not to comply with the July 26 Order.]

4.   The Contempt Adjudications * * *

The Court held the City in contempt, imposed the coercive sanctions set forth in the July 26 order, and entered written findings of fact. * * *

[The District Court also held in contempt the four council members who had voted against compliance: Nicholas Longo, Edward Fagan, Peter Chema, and Henry Spallone.]

The District Court denied requests for stays by the City and the four council members. On August 9, after fines for seven days had become due, this Court stayed the contempt sanctions and ordered an expedited appeal. * * *

DISCUSSION

A.   The Council Members

* * *

2.   Abuse of Discretion

* * * [T]he council members contend that the District Court exceeded its discretion in adjudicating them in contempt * * * [because] a less confrontational resolution of the matter could have been achieved had the District Court selected the alternatives of either appointing a commission to exercise the Council's housing and related powers or ordering the Affordable Housing Ordinance into effect.

These arguments blend two somewhat different propositions of law, but in the end, both are unavailing. In challenging the District Court's decision to require the Council to enact the Affordable Housing Ordinance, the contemnors are alleging an abuse of discretion in the Court's choice of remedies for the constitutional violations adjudicated in 1986. As the contemnors point out, a District Court, though endowed with broad discretion in fashioning remedies for constitutional violations, see Swann v. Charlotte-Mecklenburg Board of Education, 402 U.S. 1 (1971), must exercise restraint in determining what actions ought to be required of state and local governmental officials. See Rizzo v. Goode, 423 U.S. 362, 380 (1976). In challenging the District Court's decision to impose coercive contempt sanctions, the contemnors are alleging an abuse of discretion in the Court's method of enforcing the remedy that had been selected. Though there is no question that courts have authority to enforce their lawful orders through civil contempt, the contemnors properly point out that in selecting contempt sanctions, a court is obliged to use the " 'least possible power adequate to the end proposed.' "

In this case, however, there is a fundamental reason why the choice of implementing legislation as a remedy and the choice of coercive contempt sanctions to enforce compliance with that remedy cannot possibly be an abuse of the District Court's discretion. That reason is the blunt fact that the City agreed in the Consent Judgment to comply with the Housing Remedy Order by the adoption of necessary implementing legislation, specifically including tax abatements and zoning changes. By its approval of the Consent Judgment the City Council itself selected the remedy of implementing legislation and cannot complain that the District Court approved the agreement. Moreover, once committed by its own agreement to adopting implementing legislation, the Council cannot complain that its obligation is enforced by the coercive sanctions of civil contempt. Consent judgments are important devices for resolving difficult controversies. Their effectiveness depends on the ability of all concerned to rely on the enforcement of their terms. In the context of a consent judgment, use of civil contempt sanctions is the "least possible power *adequate* to the end proposed" because faithful performance of the agreement is precisely the end proposed.

To the extent that the council members are contending that the District Court exceeded its discretion in ordering them to adopt the precise terms of the Affordable Housing Ordinance, this argument also is unavailing. * * * The Court proceeded cautiously, according the City a full opportunity to draft the plan and ultimately accepting nearly everything that the City proposed. Similarly, with the specifics of the Affordable Housing Ordinance, the District Court afforded the City the opportunity to have its consultants draft the ordinance and accepted the draft they produced. By ordering passage of the Affordable Housing Ordinance, the District Court was carrying out the terms of the Consent Judgment under which the City agreed to adopt implementing legislation on tax abatements and zoning changes and doing so with details supplied by the City itself. The order of July 26 was well within the discretion of the District Court, as was its decision to enforce that order by civil contempt sanctions. * * *

4. *Legislative Immunity*

The major defense asserted by the council members is that they are entitled to legislative immunity and that such immunity prohibits a district court from compelling them to vote in favor of a particular ordinance. There is no doubt that state legislators enjoy immunity when engaged "in the sphere of legitimate legislative activity." * * *

Even if we assume for purposes of this appeal that city council members enjoy the same immunity available to state legislators, we would seriously doubt that such immunity insulates them from district court orders requiring them to comply with remedial decrees redressing constitutional violations. The Supreme Court has instructed a district court that, if necessary to secure compliance with a prior federal court remedial decree, it could order county legislators "to exercise the power that is theirs to levy taxes" to reopen the public schools of Prince Edward County, Virginia. Griffin v. County School Board, 377 U.S. 218, 233 (1964). Though appellants minimize the force of this instruction by calling it dictum, since the need to issue such an order had not then arisen, it is especially forceful dictum when the Supreme Court specifically informs a district court what action it may take in the course of significant litigation. If it had become necessary to order the county legislators to levy taxes, there can be no doubt that the Supreme Court expected the district court to make sure that its order was enforced.

The Supreme Court has also upheld a district court's remedial order that required state and local officials to provide necessary public funds to implement a school desegregation plan. Milliken v. Bradley, 433 U.S. 267, (1977). In *Milliken* the Court expressly rejected an immunity defense based on Eleventh Amendment sovereign immunity a claim at least as substantial as the immunity defense now asserted by the four council members. The Court pointed out that though a state enjoyed immunity from damage actions, its immunity did not insulate it from a district court judgment requiring prospective action to comply with constitutional requirements, even when compliance would have "a direct and substantial impact on the state treasury." * * *

On this appeal, however, we need not definitively decide whether as a general matter a district court may order city council members to vote in favor of a particular ordinance, even to implement remedies for constitutional violations. This appeal presents the more narrow issue whether such an order may be entered and enforced by contempt sanctions after a city has agreed to entry of a consent judgment committing itself to enact implementing ordinances and a city's legislative body has voted in favor of such a consent decree. On that narrow issue, we have no doubt that federal court authority must prevail. No litigant, least of all public officials sworn to uphold the Constitution of the United States, may be permitted to avoid compliance with solemn commitments they have made in a consent judgment entered by a federal district court to remedy constitutional violations. Without intending to cast doubt on a district court's authority to order legislative action in contested litigation concerning the appropriate choice of remedies for constitutional violations, we note that the Supreme Court has recently observed that consent judgments may contain enforceable obligations that might have been beyond the authority of a district court to enter in contested litigation. See Local No. 93, Int'l Ass'n of Firefighters v. City of Cleveland, 478 U.S. 501 (1986).

Nor is there any merit in appellant Spallone's suggestion that he may not be required to implement the Consent Judgment because he voted against its approval as a member of the City Council. A federal court must be able to rely upon the assurances given by municipalities and their legislative bodies, without regard to the dissenting votes of individual local officials. Once the Yonkers City Council approved the terms of the Consent Judgment, the Council became obligated to carry out its commitments. If a member of the Council is unwilling to abide by such commitments, his option is to decline to serve on the body that is bound, not to act in defiant disregard of the commitments and the federal court judgment that memorializes them.

Whatever the scope of local legislators' immunity, it does not insulate them from compliance with a consent judgment to which their city has agreed and which has been approved by their legislative body.

5.   *First Amendment*

The council members' assertion of a First Amendment defense to the July 26 order and its enforcement requires no extended discussion. Even if we acknowledge that the act of voting has sufficient expressive content to be accorded some First Amendment protection as symbolic speech, the public interest in obtaining compliance with federal court judgments that remedy constitutional violations unquestionably justifies whatever burden on expression has occurred. The council members remain free to express their views on all aspects of housing in Yonkers. But just as the First Amendment would not permit them to incite violation of federal law, it does not permit them to take action in violation of such law.

B.   The City

To the extent that the City advances the same objections as the council members, particularly the contention that the District Court should have chosen to adopt the Affordable Housing Ordinance itself or to appoint a commission to exercise the City's housing functions, we need not repeat our reasons for rejecting those objections. [Some] contentions, however, require further discussion.

1.   *Defense of Impossibility*

The claim most vigorously pressed by the City is the defense of impossibility. The City contends that enactment of the Affordable Housing Ordinance requires an affirmative vote of a majority of the City Council and that the City, as a corporate entity, is powerless to compel the council members to act. We recognize that civil contempt sanctions may not be imposed upon a person or entity unable to comply with a court's orders.

Nevertheless, we conclude that the City's defense of impossibility is unavailing.

Preliminarily, we have some doubt whether the City has done everything it can, apart from securing the favorable votes of a Council majority, to obtain compliance with the orders of the District Court. The City has not requested the Governor of New York to use whatever authority he may have to remove local officials for misconduct, nor has the City requested the New York Emergency Financial Control Board for the City of Yonkers to take whatever action its broad authorizing statute permits it to take under the current circumstances, 1984 N.Y. Laws ch. 103.

More fundamentally, we agree with the position urged by the United States that the City cannot view itself as an entity separate from the City Council for purposes of complying with the Consent Judgment. The City bound itself to take necessary legislative action when it agreed to the Consent Judgment, which explicitly calls for implementing legislation. Having made that commitment, the City may properly be subjected to the coercive force of civil contempt sanctions until compliance with its commitment occurs. The suggestion that the administrative officials of the City are willing to comply but cannot take legislative action conjures up a scheme of separated powers that does not obtain in Yonkers. For purposes of taking official governmental action, the City of Yonkers is the City Council and vice versa. The Council sets municipal policy, it appoints and can replace the city manager, and it is the principal agency of governance for the City. There is not even a separately elected executive authority. The mayor is a council member elected to the Council in a citywide election; the other council members are elected from districts. Under the circumstances of this case, the Council's defiance of the Consent Judgment and the implementing orders of the District Court is the defiance of the City, and the City, along with the defiant council members, may be subject to civil contempt sanctions. As the Supreme Court has observed, "If a state agency refuses to adhere to a court order, a financial penalty may be the most effective means of insuring compliance." Hutto v. Finney, 437 U.S. 678, 691 (1978). The same may be said of a city.

The City further contends that even if it can legally be held in civil contempt because of the violation of the July 26 order, it was an abuse of discretion to do so under the circumstances here presented, especially since the District Court had available the alternative of ordering the Affordable Housing Ordinance into effect. We conclude, however, that the District Court neither erred as a matter of law nor exceeded its permissible discretion by using contempt sanctions to coerce the City to fulfill commitments that it had undertaken in the Consent Judgment or by determining that such sanctions were necessary to achieve enactment of the Ordinance. * * *

3. *The Amount of the Monetary Sanctions*

The City contends that the amount of the coercive fines imposed as a remedial sanction for civil contempt is excessive and a violation of the Due Process Clause of the Fifth Amendment and the Excessive Fines Clause of the Eighth Amendment. [The court concludes that neither the Excessive Fines Clause nor the Cruel and Unusual Punishment Clause of the Eighth Amendment apply to coercive contempt sanctions.]

* * * In any event, the law of contempt itself exerts some outer limits on the normally "wide discretion" of a district court to fashion appropriate remedies to secure compliance with its lawful orders.

The fact that a coercive monetary sanction requires payment of a large daily fine does not necessarily render that sanction beyond the discretion of a district court. The Supreme Court has itself selected as an appropriate sanction a coercive fine of $2,800,000 (in 1947 dollars) to be imposed upon a union if it should fail to comply with a district court order within five days. United States v. United Mine Workers, 330 U.S. 258, 305 (1947). * * *

The City of Yonkers has an annual budget of $337 million. The need for a substantial daily fine to coerce compliance is demonstrated by the City's announcement to the District Court of its willingness to pay $30 million to be relieved of its commitment to build the 200 units of public housing. Obviously, the City believes that there is a price it is willing to pay to avoid compliance with the orders of the District Court. The District Court was entitled to establish a schedule of fines that would secure compliance with its orders, and under the circumstances of this case that schedule would have to reach, without undue delay, a cumulative fine significantly above the price the City was willing to pay for noncompliance. * * * At some point, however, the doubling reaches unreasonable proportions. Under the current schedule the fine for day 25 is more than $1 billion; the fine for day 30 is more than $50 billion.

We believe that the doubling exceeds the bounds of the District Court's discretion when the level of each day's fine exceeds $1 million. The present schedule calls for a fine of more than $800,000 on day 14. We will therefore modify the contempt sanction against the City to provide that the fine shall be $1 million per day on day 15 and $1 million per day for every subsequent day of noncompliance.

CONCLUSION

* * * Unless a stay is granted by the Supreme Court or a Justice thereof, our mandate shall issue seven days from the date of this decision and our prior stay of the contempt sanctions shall at that time be vacated. On the date our mandate issues, the fines against each of the four council members shall resume at the level of $500 per day and, if noncompliance continues, each shall be imprisoned, pursuant to paragraph 5 of the Order of July 26, two days after the date our mandate issues. * * *

SPALLONE V. UNITED STATES
Supreme Court of the United States
493 U.S. 265 (1990)

CHIEF JUSTICE REHNQUIST delivered the opinion of the Court.

* * * Both the city and the councilmembers [who were held in contempt] requested this Court to stay imposition of sanctions pending filing and disposition of petitions for certiorari. We granted a stay as to [the councilmembers (petitioners)], but denied the city's request. 487 U.S. 1251 (1988) [Justices Brennan and Marshall dissenting from the grant of the stay]. With the city's daily contempt sanction approaching $1 million per day, the city council finally enacted the Affordable Housing Ordinance on September 9, 1988, by a vote of 5 to 2, petitioners Spallone and Fagan voting no. Because the contempt orders raise important issues about the appropriate exercise of the federal judicial power against individual legislators, we granted certiorari [to the councilmembers but not the city], and now reverse.

II

* * *

Petitioners contend that the District Court's orders violate their rights to freedom of speech under the First Amendment, and they also contend that they are entitled as legislators to absolute immunity for actions taken in discharge of their legislative responsibilities. We find it unnecessary to reach either of these questions, because we conclude that the portion of the District Court's order of July 26 imposing contempt sanctions against the petitioners if they failed to vote in favor of the court-proposed ordinance was an abuse of discretion under traditional equitable principles.

* * * [A]s the Court of Appeals recognized, "in selecting contempt sanctions, a court is obliged to use the 'least possible power adequate to the end proposed.' "

Given that the city had entered a consent judgment committing itself to enact legislation implementing the long-term plan, we certainly cannot say it was an abuse of discretion for the District Court to have chosen contempt sanctions against the city, as opposed to petitioners, as a means of ensuring compliance. The city * * * was a party to the action from the beginning, had been found liable for numerous statutory and constitutional violations, and had been subjected to various elaborate remedial decrees which had been upheld on appeal. Petitioners, the individual city councilmen, on the other hand, were not parties to the action, and they had not been found individually liable for any of the violations upon which the remedial decree was based. * * *

It was the city, in fact, which capitulated. * * * While the District Court could not have been sure in late July that this would be the result, the city's arguments against imposing sanctions on it pointed out the sort of pressure that such sanctions would place on the city. * * *

Only eight months earlier, the District Court had secured compliance with an important remedial order through the threat of bankrupting fines against the city alone. After the city had delayed for several months the adoption of a 1987–1988 Housing Assistance Plan (HAP) vital to the public housing required by * * * the remedial order, the court ordered the city to carry out its obligation within two days. The court set a schedule of contempt fines equal to that assessed for violation of the orders in this case, and recognized that the consequence would be imminent bankruptcy for the city. Later the same day, the city council agreed to support a resolution putting in place an effective HAP and reaffirming the commitment of Yonkers to accept funds to build the 200 units of public housing mandated by * * * the remedial order.[4]

The nub of the matter, then, is whether in the light of the reasonable probability that sanctions against the city would accomplish the desired result, it was within the court's discretion to impose sanctions on the petitioners as well under the circumstances of this case.

In Tenney v. Brandhove, 341 U.S. 367 (1951), we held that state legislators were absolutely privileged in their legislative acts in an action against them for damages. We applied this same doctrine of legislative immunity to regional legislatures in Lake Country Estates, Inc. v. Tahoe Regional Planning Agency, 440 U.S. 391, 404–405 (1979), and to actions for both damages and injunctive relief in Supreme Court of Virginia v. Consumers Union of United States, Inc., 446 U.S. 719, 731–734 (1980). The holdings in these cases do not control the question whether local legislators such as practitioners should be immune from contempt sanctions imposed for failure to vote in favor of a particular legislative bill. But some of the same considerations on which the immunity doctrine is based must inform the District Court's exercise of its discretion in a case such as this. "Freedom of speech and action in the legislature," we observed, "was taken as a matter of course by those who severed the Colonies from the Crown and founded our Nation."

In perhaps the earliest American case to consider the import of the legislative privilege, the Supreme Judicial Court of Massachusetts, interpreting a provision of the Massachusetts Constitution granting the rights of freedom of speech and debate to state legislators, recognized that

---

4 The Solicitor General distinguishes the instant sanctions from those threatened in January 1988, because in this case the city and the city council had indicated by the defeat of a resolution proposed by the court that it "Would not 'voluntarily adopt the legislation contemplated by the [court's orders].' " Before the court threatened sanctions for refusal to adopt the 1987–1988 HAP, however, the city council had twice tabled an initiative to enact the HAP and the court previously had been forced to "deem" HAPs to have been submitted for two previous years. Suffice it to say that the council's conduct with regard to the HAP hardly suggested a willingness to comply "voluntarily."

"the privilege secured by it is not so much the privilege of the house as an organized body, *as of each individual member composing it, who is entitled to this privilege, even against the declared will of the house.* For he does not hold this privilege at the pleasure of the house; but derives it from the will of the people. . . ." Coffin v. Coffin, 4 Mass. 1, 27 (1808). This theme underlies our cases interpreting the Speech or Debate Clause and the federal common law of legislative immunity, where we have emphasized that any restriction on a legislator's freedom undermines the "public good" by interfering with the rights of the people to representation in the democratic process. *Lake Country Estates*; * * * Sanctions directed against the city for failure to take actions such as required by the consent decree coerce the city legislators and, of course, restrict the freedom of those legislators to act in accordance with their current view of the city's best interests. But we believe there are significant differences between the two types of fines. The imposition of sanctions on individual legislators is designed to cause them to vote, not with a view to the interest of their constituents or of the city, but with a view solely to their own personal interests. Even though an individual legislator took the extreme position or felt that his constituents took the extreme position that even a huge fine against the city was preferable to enacting the Affordable Housing Ordinance, monetary sanctions against him individually would motivate him to vote to enact the ordinance simply because he did not want to be out of pocket financially. Such fines thus encourage legislators, in effect, to declare that they favor an ordinance not in order to avoid bankrupting the city for which they legislate, but in order to avoid bankrupting themselves.

This sort of individual sanction effects a much greater perversion of the normal legislative process than does the imposition of sanctions on the city for the failure of these same legislators to enact an ordinance. In that case, the legislator is only encouraged to vote in favor of an ordinance that he would not otherwise favor by reason of the adverse sanctions imposed on the city. A councilman who felt that his constituents would rather have the city enact the Affordable Housing Ordinance than pay a "bankrupting fine" would be motivated to vote in favor of such an ordinance because the sanctions were a threat to the fiscal solvency of the city for whose welfare he was in part responsible. This is the sort of calculus in which legislators engage regularly.

We hold that the District Court, in view of the "extraordinary" nature of the imposition of sanctions against the individual councilmen, should have proceeded with such contempt sanctions first against the city alone in order to secure compliance with the remedial orders. Only if that approach failed to produce compliance within a reasonable time should the question of imposing contempt sanctions against petitioners even have been considered. * * *

JUSTICE BRENNAN, with whom JUSTICE MARSHALL, JUSTICE BLACKMUN, and JUSTICE STEVENS join, dissenting.

I understand and appreciate the Court's concern about the District Court's decision to impose contempt sanctions against local officials acting in a legislative capacity. We must all hope that no court will ever again face the open and sustained official defiance of established constitutional values and valid judicial orders that prompted Judge Sand's invocation of the contempt power in this manner. But I firmly believe that its availability for such use, in extreme circumstances, is essential. As the District Court was aware: "The issues transcend Yonkers. They go to the very foundation of the system of constitutional government. If Yonkers can defy the orders of a federal court in any case, but especially a civil rights case, because compliance is unpopular, and if that situation is tolerated, then our constitutional system of government fails. The issues before the court this morning are no less significant than that." * * *[3]

II

* * *

The Court's disfavor of personal sanctions rests on two premises: (1) Judge Sand should have known when he issued the Contempt Order that there was a "reasonable probability that sanctions against the city [alone] would accomplish the desired result,"; and (2) imposing personal fines "effects a much greater perversion of the normal legislative process than does the imposition of sanctions on the city." Because personal fines were both completely superfluous to and more intrusive than sanctions against the city alone, the Court reasons, the personal fines constituted an abuse of discretion. Each of these premises is mistaken.

A

While acknowledging that Judge Sand "could not have been sure in late July that this would be the result," the Court confidently concludes that Judge Sand should have been sure enough that fining the city would eventually coerce compliance that he should not have personally fined the councilmembers as well. In light of the information available to Judge Sand in July, the Court's confidence is chimerical. Although the escalating city fines eventually would have seriously disrupted many public services and

---

[3] While [the vote enacting the Housing Ordinance] terminated the contempt sanctions, it by no means heralded a lasting commitment on the part of the city council actually to follow through on the remedial obligations imposed by the Housing Ordinance. Since this date, no new public housing has been built in Yonkers. During the local city council election last November, petitioner Spallone "campaigned [for Mayor] on a pledge to continue the city's resistance to a Federal desegregation order requiring it to build low-income housing in white neighborhoods," N.Y. Times, Nov. 8, 1989, p. 31, col. 5, and Spallone was elected in a "race [that] was widely seen as a referendum on the housing desegregation plan." Petitioners Chema and Fagan were reelected to the council, and the new member filling Spallone's vacated seat also opposes compliance; thus "candidates opposed to the housing plan appea[r] to hold a majority." Whether Yonkers officials will *ever* comply with Judge Sand's orders attempting to remedy Yonkers' longstanding racial segregation remains an open question.

employment, the Court's failure even to consider the possibility that the councilmembers would maintain their defiant posture despite the threat of fiscal insolvency bespeaks an ignorance of Yonkers' history of entrenched discrimination and an indifference to Yonkers' political reality.

The Court first fails to adhere today to our longstanding recognition that the "district court has firsthand experience with the parties and is best qualified to deal with the 'flinty, intractable realities of day-to-day implementation of constitutional commands.'" Deference to the court's exercise of discretion is particularly appropriate where, as here, the record clearly reveals that the court employed extreme caution before taking the final step of holding the councilmembers personally in contempt. Judge Sand patiently weathered a whirlwind of evasive maneuvers and misrepresentations; considered and rejected alternative means of securing compliance other than contempt sanctions; and carefully considered the ramifications of personal fines. * * *

[T]he Court compounds its error by committing two more. First, the Court turns a blind eye to most of the evidence available to Judge Sand suggesting that, because of the councilmembers' continuing intransigence, sanctions against the city alone might not coerce compliance and that personal sanctions would significantly increase the chance of success. Second, the Court fails to acknowledge that supplementing city sanctions with personal ones likely would secure compliance more promptly, minimizing the overall disruptive effect of the city sanctions on city services generally and long-term compliance with the Consent Decree in particular.

As the events leading up to the Contempt Order make clear, the recalcitrant councilmembers were extremely responsive to the strong segments of their constituencies that were vociferously opposed to racial residential integration. Councilmember Fagan, for example, explained that his vote against the Housing Ordinance required by the Consent Decree "was an act of defiance. The people clearly wanted me to say no to the judge." Councilmember Spallone declared openly that "I will be taking on the judge all the way down the line. I made a commitment to my people and that commitment remains." Moreover, once Yonkers had gained national attention over its refusal to integrate, many residents made it clear to their representatives on the council that they preferred bankrupt martyrdom to integration. As a contemporaneous article observed, "[t]he defiant Councilmen are riding a wave of resentment among their white constituents that is so intense that many insist they are willing to see the city bankrupted. . . ." N.Y.Times, Aug.5, 1988, p.B2, col.4. It thus was not evident that petitioners opposed bankrupting the city; at the very least, capitulation by any individual councilmember was widely perceived as political suicide. As a result, even assuming that each recalcitrant member sought to avoid city bankruptcy, each still had a very strong incentive to play "chicken" with his colleagues by continuing to defy the Contempt Order while secretly hoping that at least one colleague would change his position and suffer the wrath of the electorate. As Judge Sand observed, "[w]hat we have here is competition to see who can attract the greatest notoriety, who will be the political martyr . . . *without regard to what is in the best interests of the city of Yonkers.*" (Emphasis added).

Moreover, acutely aware of these political conditions, the city attorney repeatedly warned Judge Sand *not* to assume that the threat of bankruptcy would compel compliance. * * *

The Court's opinion ignores this political reality surrounding the events of July 1988 and instead focuses exclusively on the fact that, eight months earlier, Judge Sand had secured compliance with another remedial order through the threat of city sanctions alone. But this remedial order had required only that the city council adopt a 1987–1988 Housing Assistance Plan, a prerequisite to the city's qualification for federal housing subsidies. In essence, Judge Sand had to threaten the city with contempt fines just to convince the Council to *accept* over $10 million in federal funds. Moreover, the city council capitulated by promising merely to accept the funds any implied suggestion that it ever intended to *use* the money for housing was, of course, proven false by subsequent events. * * *

Moreover, any confidence that city sanctions alone would ever work again was eroded even further by the public outcry against the council's approval of the Consent Decree, which magnified the councilmembers' determination to defy future judicial orders. * * *

The Court, in addition to ignoring all of this evidence before concluding that city sanctions alone would eventually coerce compliance, also inexplicably ignores the fact that imposing personal fines in addition to sanctions against the city would not only help ensure but actually *hasten* compliance. * * * Judge Sand knew that each day the councilmembers remained in contempt, the city would suffer an ever-growing financial drain that threatened not only to disrupt many critical city services but also to frustrate the long-term success of the underlying remedial scheme. * * *

B

The Court purports to bolster its judgment by contending that personal sanctions against city councilmembers effect a greater interference than city sanctions with the " 'interests of . . . local authorities in managing their own affairs, consistent with the Constitution.' "

* * * [T]he Court seems to suggest that personal sanctions constitute a "greater perversion of the normal legislative process" merely because they do not replicate that process' familiar mode of decisionmaking.

But the Court has never evinced an overriding concern for replicating the "normal" decisionmaking process when designing coercive sanctions for state and local executive officials who, like legislators, presumably are guided by their sense of public duty rather than private benefit. While recognizing that injunctions against such executive officials occasionally must be enforced by criminal or civil contempt sanctions of fines or imprisonment, *see, e.g.,* Hutto v. Finney, 437 U.S. 678, 690–691 (1978), we have never held that fining or even jailing these officials for contempt is categorically more intrusive than fining their governmental entity in order to coerce compliance indirectly. * * * But the Court cannot fairly derive this premise from the principle underlying the doctrine of legislative immunity.

The doctrine of legislative immunity recognizes that, when acting collectively to pursue a vision of the public good through legislation, legislators must be free to represent their constituents "without fear of outside interference" that would result from private lawsuits. Supreme Court of Virginia v. Consumers Union of United States, Inc., 446 U.S. 719, 731. Of course, legislators are bound to respect the limits placed on their discretion by the Federal Constitution; they are duty-bound not to enact laws they believe to be unconstitutional, and their laws will have no effect to the extent that courts believe them to be unconstitutional. But when acting "in the sphere of legitimate legislative activity," i.e., formulating and expressing their vision of the public good within self-defined constitutional boundaries legislators are to be "immune from deterrents to the uninhibited discharge of their legislative duty." Private lawsuits threaten to chill robust representation by encouraging legislators to avoid controversial issues or stances in order to protect themselves "not only from the consequences of litigation's results but also from the burden of defending themselves." To encourage legislators best to represent their constituents' interests, legislators must be afforded immunity from private suit.

But once a federal court has issued a valid order to remedy the effects of a prior, specific constitutional violation, the representatives are no longer "acting in a field where legislators traditionally have power to act."[9] At this point, the Constitution itself imposes an overriding definition of the "public good," and a court's valid command to obey constitutional dictates is not subject to override by any countervailing preferences of the polity, no matter how widely and ardently shared. Local legislators, for example, may not frustrate valid remedial decrees merely because they or their constituents would rather allocate public funds for other uses. More to the point here, legislators certainly may not defy court-ordered remedies for

---

[9]   I do not mean to suggest that public policy concerns may play no role in designing the scope or content of the underlying remedial order. When each of a variety of different remedial programs would fully remedy the constitutional violation, for example, a district court should take into account relevant and important policy concerns voiced by government defendants in choosing among such remedies. * * *

racial discrimination merely because their constituents prefer to maintain segregation: * * * Defiance at this stage results, in essence, in a perpetuation of the very constitutional violation at which the remedy is aimed.[11] Hence, once Judge Sand found that the city (through acts of its council) had engaged in a pattern and practice of racial discrimination in housing and had issued a valid remedial order, the city councilmembers became obliged to respect the limits thereby placed on their legislative independence.

* * * Moreover, even if the Court's characterization of personal fines against legislators as "perverse" were persuasive, it would still represent a myopic view of the relevant remedial inquiry. To the extent that equitable limits on federal courts' remedial power are designed to protect against unnecessary judicial intrusion into state or local affairs, it was obviously appropriate for Judge Sand to have considered the fact that the city's accrual of fines would have quickly disrupted every aspect of the daily operation of local government. Particularly when these broader effects are considered, the Court's pronouncement that fining the city is categorically less intrusive than fining the legislators personally is untenable. * * *

III

The Court's decision today that Judge Sand abused his remedial discretion by imposing personal fines simultaneously with city fines creates no new principle of law; indeed, it invokes no principle of any sort. * * * I worry that the Court's message will have the unintended effect of emboldening recalcitrant officials continually to test the ultimate reach of the remedial authority of the federal courts, thereby postponing the day when all public officers finally accept that "the responsibility of those who exercise power in a democratic government is not to reflect inflamed public feeling but to help form its understanding." Cooper v. Aaron, 358 U.S. 1, 26 (1958) (Frankfurter, J., concurring).

---

[11] *See* Columbus Bd. of Education v. Penick, 443 U.S. 449, 459 (1979) (once court orders desegregation remedy, "[e]ach instance of a failure or refusal to fulfill this affirmative duty continues the violation of the Fourteenth Amendment"). Put another way, remedial defiance by the legislature circumvents the structural protections afforded the citizenry from unconstitutional government behavior by a multi-branch review process, by allowing the legislature de facto to override the court's ruling in a particular case that its behavior violates the Fourteenth Amendment. *Cf.* Cooper v. Aaron, 358 U.S. 1, 18 (1958) ("If the legislatures of the several states may, at will, annul the judgments of the courts of the United States, and destroy the rights acquired under those judgments, the constitution itself becomes a solemn mockery") (quoting United States v. Peters, 5 Cranch 115, 136 (1809)).

Indeed, even were the councilmembers to maintain that the Housing Ordinance they were required to enact itself violated the Constitution, for example, by mandating unjustified racial preferences, the members would nevertheless be bound by a court order considering yet rejecting their constitutional objection. *See Cooper, supra*, at 18 ("[F]ederal judiciary is supreme in the exposition of the law of the Constitution" in case adjudication). But in any event, the councilmembers raised no serious substantive objections, constitutional or otherwise, to the Ordinance (which after all was based on the city council-approved Consent Decree).

NOTES

1. *Update on the Yonkers case.* In December 1990, a state trial judge ruled that the four council members who voted to defy Judge Sand were liable to the City under a state statute that makes government officials liable for illegal acts that waste public assets. New York's Appellate Division, however, held that the actions taken by the defendant council members "lack[ed] the necessary element of collusion, fraud, or personal gain," necessary for the attachment of personal liability on the Council members. Duffy v. Longo, 207 A.D.2d 860, 616 N.Y.S.2d 760 (1994), *appeal dismissed*, 86 N.Y.2d 779, 655 N.E.2d 708, 631 N.Y.S.2d 611 (1995).

After the Council backed down, Judge Sand changed the composition of those who would occupy the 200 units of public housing in a direction favoring existing residents of the neighborhoods by giving some preference to current occupants of public housing who had been model tenants. Occupancy began without more high drama, but with some tension. N.Y. Times, June 27, 1993, at A25.

Mayor Nicholas Wasicsko, elected in 1987 at the age of 28 and a former student of one of the casebook's original authors, was defeated in his bid for reelection in 1989 by Spallone because Wasicsko favored obeying the injunction. In 1991, a candidate supported by Wasicsko defeated Spallone, and Wasicsko was elected to the City Council. In 1993, he ran for City Council President and lost, which meant he would be out of office again. The following month Wasicsko committed suicide. N.Y. Times, Oct. 31, 1993.

The parties finally settled the housing segregation dispute 27 years after the initiation of the case. The consent plan Judge Sand approved in 2007 guaranteed that 425 owner-occupied homes, 315 private rental dwellings and 200 public housing units in Yonkers will remain affordable for at least 30 years. The city had previously settled the related school segregation claims in 2002. In reflecting on the case, Judge Sand stated: "Any efforts not to comply with the law are counterproductive to the image of the community and its well-being. The millions and millions of dollars that the City of Yonkers has spent . . . could have gone to better things for the community." One of the most vocal community opponents of the integration effort commented more recently: "In a sense, the desegregation plan did work. It didn't spoil our neighborhoods; we had a lot of nice people who lived there. It wasn't the horror that we all thought it was going to be." Fernanda Santos, *After 27 Years, Yonkers Housing Desegregation Battle Ends Quietly in Manhattan Court*, N.Y.Times B5, May 2, 2007; Fernanda Santos, *Yonkers Settles 27-Year Battle Over Desegregation*, N.Y.Times A22, April 20, 2007.

The documentary Brick by Brick details the story of the Yonkers litigation. http://www.brick-by-brick.com. "Coming back out of the courtroom into the community, the story describes the bitter local confrontation about race and the very concept of community that follows." The video tells the story from "a first person perspective," where "characters weave a tale of years of work attempting to achieve justice, with a labyrinth of successes and setbacks that the struggle entails." Ultimately, "it also illustrates the difference housing opportunity can make in a single family's life." For a journalist's account of the events surrounding the public housing case, see Lisa Belkin, *Show Me a Hero* (1999), and Jonathan L. Entin, *Learning from Yonkers: On Race, Class, Housing, and Courts,* 44 How.L.J. 375 (2001) (review of Belkin's book).

2.   *Yonkers* and *Spallone* illustrate a number of tactics to get unwilling governments or government officials to act and their legal and practical limitations. For a survey of others, see Daryl J. Levinson, *Collective Sanctions,* 56 Stan.L.Rev. 345 (2003). But ultimately it was the contempt sanction that provided leverage, even if it was uncertain how it could be enforced.

Then-Mayor of Yonkers Nicholas Wasicsko said, before the Supreme Court stayed the contempt sanctions against the Councilmen, that "if anything forces compliance, it will be the Councilmen in the cooler," rather than the fines against the City. N.Y. Times, Aug. 27, 1988 at A1, 28. "As contempt fines against Yonkers passed $1 million and one-fourth of the city work force faced lay-offs in two days, even steadfast opponents of a court-ordered housing desegregation plan seemed jolted today, and pressure grew for city officials to resolve the crisis." N.Y. Times, Sept. 9, 1988 at A1.

Some citizens will blame hardships not on the recalcitrant officials but on the judge or the plaintiffs. As one Yonkers councilman who resisted compliance said, "[c]learly the blood is on the judge's hands."

Early in the morning of September 9—although the court was willing to view it as late in the day on September 8 for the purpose of computing contempt fines—Councilmen Chema and Longo changed their votes so that the required legislation was enacted by a vote of 5 to 2. N.Y. Times, Sept. 10, 1988, at A1; N.Y. Times, Sept. 11, 1988, at A1. The vote took place after the Supreme Court had stayed the contempt sanctions against the councilmembers. In response to the Supreme Court's decision, Mr. Spallone, who had been elected mayor while the case was pending, said that he and his allies on the city council would try to use the decision as a means of opposing implementation of Judge Sand's orders. N.Y. Times, Jan. 11, 1990, at B9. Subsequently, the Spallone-led City Council fired the City's outside law firm, which said the City had no grounds left upon which to fight compliance, and hired new lawyers. N.Y. Times, Mar. 9, 1990.

Still another Yonkers councilman who resisted compliance said, "I say to [Judge Sand] 'if you want the money, come and get it.'" N.Y. Times, Sept. 10, 1988, at A1. The Yonkers corporation counsel responded that he assumed that the judge "would direct that the check be issued without the Council's OK, or that he could suspend the law making it illegal to transfer funds without the Council's vote—or he could move against the assets of the city."

In contrast to the fierce resistance to the 200 units of housing, Yonkers complied without great fanfare with extensive orders from Judge Sand to desegregate its 20,000 student school system. One explanation for the difference is that the schools are run by officials appointed for five-year terms, while action on the housing had to be taken by council members elected for two-year terms. Some council members made careers by feeding the flames of resistance, but then found that they could not back down without destroying their political careers. Note, *Implementing Structural Injunctions: Getting a Remedy When Local Officials Resist*, 80 Geo.L.J. 2227 (1992), concludes that judges should take direct action. It argues that the alternative of ordering the legislators to act is fraught with First Amendment and immunity problems and that the other alternative of sanctioning the government often hurts those who should benefit from the injunction.

3.   *Appointing a receiver to take the action.* In *Yonkers*, Judge Sand considered appointing an Affordable Housing Commission, which would, in essence, have been a receiver. Why did the city resist this option while wanting the judge to take the action himself? Why did the judge resist this option? After the City Council backed down, Judge Sand did appoint a Fair Housing Opportunity Commission to administer parts of the decree.

4.   While cases like *Spallone* are fascinating and useful for exploring the outer limits of the remedial power, they are not typical of injunction cases against governments. According to Ross Sandler and David Schoenbrod, *Democracy by Decree* (2003), New York City is the target of many structural injunctions and consent decrees (as are many other municipalities). Most of the injunctions enforce state or federal statutory rights rather than constitutional rights. The cost of implementing the more important injunctions is equal to a quarter of the city's tax revenues. The impact on New York's truly discretionary spending is even larger because the bulk of the city's budget is made up of such necessities as paying interest on the city's debt and the salaries of essential employees. Although New York City does not resist compliance in the sense that neighboring Yonkers did, it rarely succeeds in fully complying with the decrees. One reason is that the statutes being enforced cumulatively require the city to do more than its resources allow. A question that such injunctions raise is who gets to make city policy and to whom are they accountable. The statutes are typically unfunded mandates, in which state and federal legislators have made large promises to be fulfilled by local government. The policy choices about the extent to which these promises will be kept, and how, are typically made in consent decrees. Frequently, elected officials consent to decrees under which the big expenses come after they are out of office. As discussed earlier, it can be difficult for the next official to modify the decree. *E.g.,* Benjamin v. Malcolm, 156 F.R.D. 561 (S.D.N.Y.1994) (refusing to allow the new mayor of New York City to alter his predecessor's agreement concerning where meals for pre-trial detainees would be cooked). *See also* Ross Sandler & David Schoenbrod, *The Supreme Court, Democracy and Institutional Reform Litigation*, 49 N.Y.L.Sch.L.Rev. 915, 929 (2005) (applauding a shift in the "judicial balance toward democratic values and away from contractual rigidity" in the enforcement of consent decrees).

CHAPTER 4

DECLARATORY JUDGMENT

■ ■ ■

A declaratory judgment settles disputed issues by declaring the parties' legal rights, status and relationship without imposing any other court-ordered relief. Declaratory judgment is not a coercive remedy; it does not result in a court order requiring either party to act. The court's judgment nonetheless binds the parties because traditional rules of issue preclusion apply to prevent the parties from relitigating the issues the declaratory judgment resolves.

The declaratory judgment is an important remedy in many areas of law. In civil rights litigation, declaratory relief offers an efficient way to define constitutional norms and secure governmental compliance. Many of the cases you read in Chapters 2 and 3 on injunctive relief in fact combined a claim for declaratory relief with the claim for injunctive relief. *E.g., Brown v. Board of Education*; *City of Los Angeles v. Lyons*. In intellectual property law, declaratory relief can be used to define the scope of intellectual property rights without waiting for costly infringement actions to be filed. Similarly, in insurance litigation and across a range of contract disputes declaratory relief allows legal obligations to be defined in the early stages of a dispute, perhaps making further litigation unnecessary.

The declaratory judgment's value is in resolving uncertainty. What makes it a powerful remedy is its timing. It offers parties the opportunity to determine how the law will operate on the facts of a specific case *before* they act in a way that might violate the law. Samuel L. Bray, *The Myth of the Mild Declaratory Judgment*, 63 Duke L.J. 1091 (2014) (arguing the differences between the declaratory judgment and the injunction are best seen in terms of ease of judicial management and early timing). This ability to make legal norms particular and concrete, and thus to guide people in obeying the law, provides an essential element of fairness to the legal system. *See* Lawrence Slocum, *Procedural Justice*, 78 S.Cal.L.Rev. 181, 188–189, 219–220 (2004).

Declaratory judgments also make the legal system more efficient, allowing parties to resolve their liability without incurring the cost of litigating all aspects of a dispute, or perhaps even without waiting for the other party to sue. Suppose a creditor claims a debtor has defaulted on a debt, and has informed a credit rating company. By seeking a declaratory judgment, the alleged debtor can establish whether anything is owed, and clear her credit record without waiting for the creditor to sue. For the same reason, insurers frequently rely on the declaratory judgment to resolve coverage issues, hoping to exonerate themselves or to avoid punitive damage awards, without waiting for the underlying liability issues to be resolved. *See* Itzhak Zamir & Jeremy Woolf, *The Declaratory Judgment* (3d ed.2001).

The declaratory judgment is a statutory creation.[a] The first effective state declaratory judgment act was passed by New Jersey in 1915. Beginning in 1917, Professors Edwin M. Borchard and Edson R. Sunderland, in a series of articles and books, advocated the passage of declaratory judgment statutes. Their efforts culminated in the Uniform Declaratory Judgment Act, promulgated in 1922 and since adopted in 41 states.

The Uniform Act provides:

§ 1 Courts of record * * * shall have power to declare rights, status, and other legal relations whether or not further relief is or could be claimed. No action or proceeding shall be open to objection on the ground that a declaratory judgment or decree is prayed for. The declaration may be either affirmative or negative in form and effect; and such declarations shall have the force and effect of a final judgment or decree.

The federal Declaratory Judgment Act was not enacted until 1934, apparently because of congressional concern as to its constitutionality. The Act, as amended, is codified at 28 U.S.C. §§ 2201 & 2202. Its effective language echoes the Uniform Act:

In a case of actual controversy within its jurisdiction, [subject to certain exceptions[b]] any court of the United States, upon the filing of an appropriate pleading, may declare the rights and other legal relations of any interested party seeking such declaration, whether or not further relief is or could be sought. Any such declaration shall have the force and effect of a final judgment or decree and shall be reviewable as such.

28 U.S.C. § 2201. Both the Uniform Act and the federal act allow the court to grant further relief based on a declaratory judgment after the adverse

---

[a] Before the advent of the modern declaratory judgment, similar relief was sometimes available through specific forms of action like bills to quiet or remove a cloud from title. There were a variety of forms of relief, each with its own prerequisites, resulting in considerable complexity. Sharon v. Tucker, 144 U.S. 533 (1892), in which the Court had to wade through the distinctions between three archaic forms of action before clearing the plaintiffs' title to their property, provides a nice example. In many instances, particularized forms for resolving such questions remain, though they have frequently been simplified and modernized. In the main, however, the declaratory judgment has replaced the old forms of action.

[b] The Act does not authorize declaratory relief with respect to federal income taxes (for which 26 U.S.C. § 7428 provides limited declaratory relief), some anti-dumping laws and duty proceedings, and several specific provisions of the tax code.

party has been given notice and an opportunity to be heard. 28 U.S.C. § 2202; U.D.J.A. § 8.

Declaratory judgment is not inherently an equitable or a legal form of action. It can be used to adjudicate both legal and equitable claims. As a consequence, the right to a jury trial will depend on whether the parallel coercive claim would be legal or equitable, which it may not be easy to ascertain, particularly when counterclaims are involved. The Supreme Court has put emphasis on preserving the right to jury trial, so competing characterizations of the issues in the suit are likely to be resolved in favor of affording a jury trial. Beacon Theatres, Inc. v. Westover, 359 U.S. 500 (1959).

Ironically, the qualities that make declaratory relief valuable—the fact that it is available in a dispute's early stages, that it can be used to anticipate litigation that has not yet been filed, that it can define legal obligations without waiting for the law to be violated—also define the critical issues concerning the remedy's availability. If the dispute is embryonic, is there truly a case or controversy? Is it ripe? Is it appropriate for the courts to become involved at such an early stage in the dispute rather than waiting for a party who could seek coercive relief to act?

Under both the federal and the uniform acts, declaratory relief is discretionary. As you read through the following cases, try to identify the factors that will determine whether a court will grant a declaratory judgment.

A. THE ACTUAL CONTROVERSY REQUIREMENT

MEDIMMUNE, INC. V. GENENTECH, INC.
Supreme Court of the United States
549 U.S. 118 (2007)

JUSTICE SCALIA delivered the opinion of the Court.

We must decide whether Article III's limitation of federal courts' jurisdiction to "Cases" and "Controversies," reflected in the "actual controversy" requirement of the Declaratory Judgment Act, 28 U.S.C. § 2201(a), requires a patent licensee to terminate or be in breach of its license agreement before it can seek a declaratory judgment that the underlying patent is invalid, unenforceable, or not infringed.

I

Because the declaratory-judgment claims in this case were disposed of at the motion-to-dismiss stage, we take the following facts from the allegations in petitioner's amended complaint and the unopposed declarations that petitioner submitted in response to the motion to dismiss. Petitioner MedImmune, Inc., manufactures Synagis, a drug used to prevent respiratory tract disease in infants and young children. In 1997, petitioner entered into a patent license agreement with respondent Genentech, Inc. (which acted on behalf of itself as patent assignee and on behalf of the coassignee, respondent City of Hope). The license covered an existing patent relating to the production of "chimeric antibodies" and a then-pending patent application relating to "the coexpression of immunoglobulin chains in recombinant host cells." Petitioner agreed to pay royalties on sales of "Licensed Products," and respondents granted petitioner the right to make, use, and sell them. The agreement defined "Licensed Products" as a specified antibody, "the manufacture, use or sale of which . . . would, if not licensed under th[e] Agreement, infringe one or more claims of either or both of [the covered patents,] which have neither expired nor been held invalid by a court or other body of competent jurisdiction from which no appeal has been or may be taken." The license agreement gave petitioner the right to terminate upon six months' written notice.

In December 2001, the "coexpression" application covered by the 1997 license agreement matured into the "Cabilly II" patent. Soon thereafter, respondent Genentech delivered petitioner a letter expressing its belief that Synagis was covered by the Cabilly II patent and its expectation that petitioner would pay royalties beginning March 1, 2002. Petitioner did not think royalties were owing, believing that the Cabilly II patent was invalid and unenforceable, and that its claims were in any event not infringed by Synagis. Nevertheless, petitioner considered the letter to be a clear threat to enforce the Cabilly II patent, terminate the 1997 license agreement, and sue for patent infringement if petitioner did not make royalty payments as demanded. If respondents were to prevail in a patent infringement action, petitioner could be ordered to pay treble damages and attorney's fees, and could be enjoined from selling Synagis, a product that has accounted for more than 80 percent of its revenue from sales since 1999. Unwilling to risk such serious consequences, petitioner paid the demanded royalties "under protest and with reservation of all of [its] rights." This declaratory judgment action followed.

Petitioner sought the declaratory relief discussed * * * below. Petitioner also requested damages and an injunction with respect to other federal and state claims not relevant here. The District Court granted respondents' motion to dismiss the declaratory-judgment claims for lack of subject-matter jurisdiction, relying on the decision of the United States Court of Appeals for the Federal Circuit in Gen-Probe Inc. v. Vysis, Inc., 359 F.3d 1376 (2004). Gen-Probe had held that a patent licensee in good standing cannot establish an Article III case or controversy with regard to validity, enforceability, or scope of the patent because the license agreement "obliterate[s] any reasonable apprehension" that the licensee will be sued for infringement. The Federal Circuit affirmed the District Court * * * .

* * *

III

The Declaratory Judgment Act provides that, "[i]n a case of actual controversy within its jurisdiction . . . any court of the United States . . . may declare the rights and other legal relations of any interested party seeking such declaration, whether or not further relief is or could be sought." 28 U.S.C. § 2201(a). There was a time when this Court harbored doubts about the compatibility of declaratory-judgment actions with Article III's case-or-controversy requirement. We dispelled those doubts, however, in Nashville, C. & St. L.R. Co. v. Wallace, 288 U.S. 249 (1933), holding (in a case involving a declaratory judgment rendered in state court) that an appropriate action for declaratory relief *can* be a case or controversy under Article III. The federal Declaratory Judgment Act was signed into law the following year, and we upheld its constitutionality in Aetna Life Ins. Co. v. Haworth, 300 U.S. 227 (1937). Our opinion explained that the phrase "case of actual controversy" in the Act refers to the type of "Cases" and "Controversies" that are justiciable under Article III.

Aetna and the cases following it do not draw the brightest of lines between those declaratory-judgment actions that satisfy the case-or-controversy requirement and those that do not. Our decisions have required that the dispute be "definite and concrete, touching the legal relations of parties having adverse legal interests"; and that it be "real and substantial" and "admi[t] of specific relief through a decree of a conclusive character, as distinguished from an opinion advising what the law would be upon a hypothetical state of facts." In Maryland Casualty Co. v. Pacific Coal & Oil Co., 312 U.S. 270, 273 (1941), we summarized as follows: "Basically, the question in each case is whether the facts alleged, under all the circumstances, show that there is a substantial controversy, between parties having adverse legal interests, of sufficient immediacy and reality to warrant the issuance of a declaratory judgment."

There is no dispute that these standards would have been satisfied if petitioner had taken the final step of refusing to make royalty payments under the 1997 license agreement. Respondents claim a right to royalties under the licensing agreement. Petitioner asserts that no royalties are owing because the Cabilly II patent is invalid and not infringed; and alleges (without contradiction) a threat by respondents to enjoin sales if royalties are not forthcoming. The factual and legal dimensions of the dispute are well defined and, but for petitioner's continuing to make royalty payments, nothing about the dispute would render it unfit for judicial resolution. Assuming (without deciding) that respondents here could not claim an anticipatory breach and repudiate the license, the continuation of royalty payments makes what would otherwise be an imminent threat at least remote, if not nonexistent. As long as those payments are made, there is no risk that respondents will seek to enjoin petitioner's sales. Petitioner's own acts, in other words, eliminate the imminent threat of harm.[8] The question before us is whether this causes the dispute no longer to be a case or controversy within the meaning of Article III.

Our analysis must begin with the recognition that, where threatened action by *government* is concerned, we do not require a plaintiff to expose himself to liability before bringing suit to challenge the basis for the threat—for example, the constitutionality of a law threatened to be enforced. The plaintiff's own action (or inaction) in failing to violate the law eliminates the imminent threat of prosecution, but nonetheless does not eliminate Article III jurisdiction. For example, in Terrace v. Thompson, 263 U.S. 197 (1923), the State threatened the plaintiff with forfeiture of his farm, fines, and penalties if he entered into a lease with an alien in violation of the State's anti-alien land law. Given this genuine threat of enforcement, we did not require, as a prerequisite to testing the validity of the law in a suit for injunction, that the plaintiff bet the farm, so to speak, by taking the violative action. Likewise, in Steffel v. Thompson, 415 U.S. 452 (1974), we did not require the plaintiff to proceed to distribute handbills and risk actual prosecution before he could seek a declaratory judgment regarding the constitutionality of a state statute prohibiting such distribution. As then-Justice Rehnquist put it in his concurrence, "the declaratory judgment procedure is an alternative to pursuit of the arguably illegal activity." In each of these cases, the plaintiff had eliminated the imminent threat of harm by simply not doing what he claimed the right to do (enter into a lease, or distribute handbills at the shopping center). That did not preclude subject-matter jurisdiction because the threat-eliminating behavior was effectively coerced. The dilemma posed by that coercion— putting the challenger to the choice between abandoning his rights or risking prosecution—is "a dilemma that it was the very purpose of the Declaratory Judgment Act to ameliorate." Abbott Laboratories v. Gardner, 387 U.S. 136, 152 (1967).

Supreme Court jurisprudence is more rare regarding application of the Declaratory Judgment Act to situations in which the plaintiff's self-avoidance of imminent injury is coerced by threatened enforcement action of *a private party* rather than the government. Lower federal courts, however (and state courts interpreting declaratory judgment Acts requiring "actual controversy"), have long accepted jurisdiction in such cases.

---

[8] The justiciability problem that arises, when the party seeking declaratory relief is himself preventing the complained-of injury from occurring, can be described in terms of standing (whether plaintiff is threatened with "imminent" injury in fact " 'fairly . . . trace[able] to the challenged action of the defendant,' " Lujan v. Defenders of Wildlife, 504 U.S. 555, 560 (1992)), or in terms of ripeness (whether there is sufficient "hardship to the parties [in] withholding court consideration" until there is enforcement action, Abbott Laboratories v. Gardner, 387 U.S. 136, 149 (1967)). As respondents acknowledge, standing and ripeness boil down to the same question in this case.

The only Supreme Court decision in point is, fortuitously, close on its facts to the case before us. Altvater v. Freeman, 319 U.S. 359 (1943), held that a licensee's failure to cease its payment of royalties did not render nonjusticiable a dispute over the validity of the patent. In that litigation, several patentees had sued their licensees to enforce territorial restrictions in the license. The licensees filed a counterclaim for declaratory judgment that the underlying patents were invalid, in the meantime paying "under protest" royalties required by an injunction the patentees had obtained in an earlier case. The patentees argued that "so long as [licensees] continue to pay royalties, there is only an academic, not a real controversy, between the parties." We rejected that argument and held that the declaratory-judgment claim presented a justiciable case or controversy: "The fact that royalties were being paid did not make this a 'difference or dispute of a hypothetical or abstract character.'" The royalties "were being paid under protest and under the compulsion of an injunction decree," and "[u]nless the injunction decree were modified, the only other course [of action] was to defy it, and to risk not only actual but treble damages in infringement suits." We concluded that "the requirements of [a] case or controversy are met where payment of a claim is demanded as of right and where payment is made, but where the involuntary or coercive nature of the exaction preserves the right to recover the sums paid or to challenge the legality of the claim."

The Federal Circuit's *Gen-Probe* decision distinguished *Altvater* on the ground that it involved the compulsion of an injunction. But *Altvater* cannot be so readily dismissed. Never mind that the injunction had been privately obtained and was ultimately within the control of the patentees, who could permit its modification. More fundamentally, and contrary to the Federal Circuit's conclusion, *Altvater* did not say that the coercion dispositive of the case was governmental, but suggested just the opposite. The opinion acknowledged that the licensees had the option of stopping payments in defiance of the injunction, but explained that the *consequence* of doing so would be to risk "actual [and] treble damages in infringement suits" by the patentees. It significantly did not mention the threat of prosecution for contempt, or any other sort of governmental sanction. Moreover, it cited approvingly a treatise which said that an "actual or threatened serious injury to business or employment" by a private party can be as coercive as other forms of coercion supporting restitution actions at common law; and that "[t]o imperil a man's livelihood, his business enterprises, or his solvency, [was] ordinarily quite as coercive" as, for example, "detaining his property." F. Woodward, *The Law of Quasi Contracts* § 218 (1913), cited in *Altvater*.

Jurisdiction over the present case is not contradicted by Willing v. Chicago Auditorium Association, 277 U.S. 274 (1928). There a ground lessee wanted to demolish an antiquated auditorium and replace it with a modern commercial building. The lessee believed it had the right to do this without the lessors' consent, but was unwilling to drop the wrecking ball first and test its belief later. Because there was no declaratory judgment act at the time under federal or applicable state law, the lessee filed an action to remove a "cloud" on its lease. This Court held that an Article III case or controversy had not arisen because "[n]o defendant ha[d] wronged the plaintiff or ha[d] threatened to do so." It was true that one of the co-lessors had disagreed with the lessee's interpretation of the lease, but that happened in an "informal, friendly, private conversation" a year before the lawsuit was filed; and the lessee never even bothered to approach the other co-lessors. The Court went on to remark that "[w]hat the plaintiff seeks is simply a declaratory judgment," and "[t]o grant that relief is beyond the power conferred upon the federal judiciary." Had *Willing* been decided after the enactment (and our upholding) of the Declaratory Judgment Act, and had the legal disagreement between the parties been as lively as this one, we are confident a different result would have obtained. The rule that a plaintiff must destroy a large building, bet the farm, or (as here) risk treble damages and the loss of 80 percent of its business, before seeking a declaration of its actively contested legal rights finds no support in Article III.

Respondents assert that the parties in effect settled this dispute when they entered into the 1997 license agreement. When a licensee enters such an agreement, they contend, it essentially purchases an insurance policy, immunizing it from suits for infringement so long as it continues to pay royalties and does not challenge the covered patents. Permitting it to challenge the validity of the patent without terminating or breaking the agreement alters the deal, allowing the licensee to continue enjoying its immunity while bringing a suit, the elimination of which was part of the patentee's *quid pro quo*. Of course even if it were valid, this argument would have no force with regard to petitioner's claim that the agreement does not call for royalties because their product does not infringe the patent. But even as to the patent invalidity claim, the point seems to us mistaken. To begin with, it is not clear where the prohibition against challenging the validity of the patents is to be found. It can hardly be implied from the mere promise to pay royalties on patents "which have neither expired nor been held invalid by a court or other body of competent jurisdiction from which no appeal has been or may be taken." Promising to pay royalties on patents that have not been held invalid does not amount to a promise *not to seek* a holding of their invalidity.

* * *

Lastly, respondents urge us to affirm the dismissal of the declaratory-judgment claims on discretionary grounds. The Declaratory Judgment Act provides that a court "*may* declare the rights and other legal relations of any interested party," 28 U.S.C. § 2201(a) (emphasis added), not that it *must* do so. This text has long been understood "to confer on federal courts unique and substantial discretion in deciding whether to declare the rights of litigants." We have found it "more consistent with the statute," however, "to vest district courts with discretion in the first instance, because facts bearing on the usefulness of the declaratory judgment remedy, and the fitness of the case for resolution, are peculiarly within their grasp." The District Court here gave no consideration to discretionary dismissal, since, despite its "serious misgivings" about the Federal Circuit's rule, it considered itself bound to dismiss by *Gen-Probe*. Discretionary dismissal was irrelevant to the Federal Circuit for the same reason. Respondents have raised the issue for the first time before this Court, exchanging competing accusations of inequitable conduct with petitioner. Under these circumstances, it would be imprudent for us to decide whether the District Court should, or must, decline to issue the requested declaratory relief. We leave the equitable, prudential, and policy arguments in favor of such a discretionary dismissal for the lower courts' consideration on remand. Similarly available for consideration on remand are any merits-based arguments for denial of declaratory relief.

* * *

We <u>hold</u> that petitioner was not required, insofar as Article III is concerned, to break or terminate its 1997 license agreement before seeking a declaratory judgment in federal court that the underlying patent is invalid, unenforceable, or not infringed. The Court of Appeals erred in affirming the dismissal of this action for lack of subject-matter jurisdiction.

* * *

JUSTICE THOMAS, dissenting.

* * * To reach today's result, the Court misreads our precedent and expands the concept of coercion from *Steffel* to reach voluntarily accepted contractual obligations between private parties. * * *

No court has ever taken such a broad view of *Steffel*.

In *Steffel,* the Court held that in certain limited circumstances, a party's anticipatory cause of action qualified as a case or controversy under Article III. Based expressly on the coercive nature of governmental power, the Court found that "it is not necessary that petitioner first expose himself to *actual arrest* or *prosecution* to be entitled to challenge a *statute* that he claims deters the exercise of his constitutional rights" (emphasis added). Limited, as it is, to governmental power, particularly the power of arrest and prosecution, *Steffel* says nothing about coercion in the context of private contractual obligations. It is therefore not surprising that, until today, this Court has never applied *Steffel* and its theory of coercion to private contractual obligations; indeed, no court has ever done so.

The majority not only extends *Steffel* to cases that do not involve governmental coercion, but also extends *Steffel's* rationale. If "coercion" were understood as the Court used that term in *Steffel,* it would apply only if Genentech had threatened MedImmune with a patent infringement suit *in the absence of a license agreement.* At that point, MedImmune would have had a choice, as did the declaratory plaintiff in *Steffel,* either to cease the otherwise protected activity (here, selling Synagis) or to continue in that activity and face the threat of a lawsuit. But MedImmune faced no such choice. Here, MedImmune could continue selling its product without threat of suit because it had eliminated any risk of suit by entering into a license agreement. By holding that the voluntary choice to enter an agreement to avoid some other coerced choice is itself coerced, the Court goes far beyond *Steffel.*

The majority explains that the "coercive nature of the exaction preserves the right . . . to challenge the legality of the claim." The coercive nature of what "exaction"? The answer has to be the voluntarily made license payments because there was no threat of suit here. By holding that contractual obligations are sufficiently coercive to allow a party to bring a declaratory judgment action, the majority has given every patent licensee a cause of action and a free pass around Article III's requirements for challenging the validity of licensed patents. But the reasoning of today's opinion applies not just to patent validity suits. Indeed, today's opinion contains no limiting principle whatsoever, casting aside Justice Stewart's understanding that *Steffel's* use would "be exceedingly rare."

For the foregoing reasons, I respectfully dissent.

NOTES

1.   Until *MedImmune,* the Federal Circuit applied a "reasonable apprehension" test to determine whether declaratory relief was available to test a patent's validity. David I. Levine & Charles E. Belle, *Declaratory Relief After* Medimmune, 14 Lewis & Clark L.Rev. 491 (2010). As applied, the test required that the declaratory judgment plaintiff have undertaken steps that would lead to infringement and that the patentee explicitly or implicitly threaten to sue. Gen-Probe Inc. v. Vysis, Inc., 359 F.3d 1376, 1380 (Fed.Cir.2004). *MedImmune* abrogates this standard. Samsung Electronics Co. v. ON Semiconductor Corp., 541 F.Supp.2d 645 (D.Del.2008).

Does this mean that there are no limits on the availability of declaratory relief in patent cases? In Prasco, LLC v. Medicis Pharmaceutical Corp. 537 F.3d 1329 (Fed.Cir.2008), a manufacturer sought a declaratory judgment that its medication did not infringe several patents the defendant held. The defendant, Medicis Pharmaceutical, marketed a similar product marked with its patents, and had sued to enforce its patent against the manufacturer of a different generic product, but did not know that the plaintiff's product existed until Prasco filed suit. On these facts, the court found there was no Article III case or controversy:

> Where Prasco has suffered no actual present injury traceable to the defendants, and the defendants have not asserted any rights against Prasco related to the patents nor taken any affirmative actions concerning Prasco's current product, one prior suit concerning unrelated patents and products and the defendants' failure to sign a covenant not to sue are simply not sufficient to establish that Prasco is at risk of imminent harm from the defendants and that there is an actual controversy between the parties. * * *

537 F.3d at 1341. According to the court, a purely subjective fear, not grounded in the defendant's actions, does not establish a case or controversy.

Setting the threshold for declaratory relief is not a procedural formality. In the patent context, making it easier to litigate the validity of patents will spur competition, but it may undercut innovation, because fending off more frequent challenges will make patents less valuable. *See* Amy Kapczynski, *The Access to Knowledge Mobilization and the New Politics of Intellectual Property*, 117 Yale L.J. 804 (2008) (describing *MedIummune* as one example of the Supreme Court stepping "decisively" into the debate over patent reform).

The notes that follow introduce the use of declaratory judgments in other common contexts—disputes over insurance coverage, challenges to statutes, and challenges to agency action. As each is introduced, think about the values that are in play in adjusting the interests of those who would seek declaratory relief and the interests of those who would argue declaratory relief is not proper.

2.   *Insurance.* As in *MedImmune,* the Court often relies on two insurance cases, Aetna Life Insurance Co. v. Haworth, 300 U.S. 227 (1937), and Maryland Casualty Co. v. Pacific Coal & Oil Co., 312 U.S. 270 (1941), to articulate the basic standard for establishing that a case or controversy exists. In *Aetna Life,* an insured stopped paying premiums on several Aetna life insurance policies and claimed the disability benefits the policies provided included a waiver of premiums. Aetna denied his claim. The insured took no further action, but Aetna sued under the Declaratory Judgment Act to have the policies declared void. The insured had given no indication that he planned to sue over the policies; nonetheless, the Court found that the dispute presented a concrete case or controversy:

> Prior to this suit, the parties had taken adverse positions with respect to their existing obligations. * * * On the one side, the insured claimed that he had become totally and permanently disabled and hence was relieved of the obligation to continue the payment of premiums * * * .On the other side, the company made an equally definite claim that the alleged basic fact did not exist * * * and that the company was thus freed of its obligation either to pay disability benefits or to continue the insurance in force. Such a dispute is manifestly susceptible of judicial determination. It calls, not for an advisory opinion upon a hypothetical basis, but for an adjudication of present right upon established facts.

300 U.S. at 242. Aetna's injury in fact was established by the need to maintain a reserve adequate to cover the insured's claim until it was resolved. *Id.* at 239.

Maryland Casualty Co. is important because it resolved another major issue concerning the use of declaratory judgment actions in insurance disputes. *Maryland Casualty Co.* permitted a liability insurance company to seek a declaration that its policy did not cover a claim made against its insured, although the insured had not yet been held liable to anyone. Despite the insured's (and the injured party's) claim that they had no controversy with the insurance company until the insured's liability had been adjudicated, the court allowed the declaratory judgment action to proceed.

Following the decisions in *Aetna Life* and *Maryland Casualty Co.*, the use of declaratory judgment to resolve a wide range of disputes between insurance companies and insureds has become common. One court has described litigation seeking declaratory relief over insurance coverage as "the paradigm for asserting jurisdiction despite future contingencies that will determine whether a controversy ever becomes real." E.R. Squibb & Sons, Inc. v. Lloyd's & Cos., 241 F.3d 154 (2d Cir.2001). Insurance companies have used declaratory judgments to determine whether they have a duty to defend under the policy (*see, e.g.,* American States Insurance Co. v. Bailey, 133 F.3d 363 (5th Cir.1998) (no duty to defend ministers charged with sexual abuse)), to settle coverage disputes, as in *Aetna Life*, and to resolve a wide range of other disputes. Prompt resolution of these issues through declaratory judgment is of great benefit because insurers avoid the risk of subsequent punitive damage awards for failing to meet their obligations to insured parties.

The declaratory judgment action is particularly important in states that bar liability insurers who undertake the defense of an insured without a non-waiver agreement from later asserting defenses under the policy such as breach of condition, scope of coverage or continuance of coverage. In such states, a declaratory judgment action that precedes the liability action allows the insurer to have fair knowledge of its responsibilities under the policy before the liability action itself is tried. In some states, declaratory judgment actions are given preference on trial calendars and the preference is usually of greatest importance in the insurance context. *See, e.g.,* Cal.Code Civ.Pro. § 1062.3; California Insurance Guarantee Association v. Superior Court, 231 Cal.App.3d 1617 (1991).

3.   Note how the declaratory judgment remedy reverses the usual positions of the parties. In *Aetna Life*, the insured—who would usually be the plaintiff in an action to collect on the policy—becomes the defendant. In the patent context, such as in *MedImmune*, the patent holder can be the defendant in the declaratory judgment action, while in an enforcement action, the patent holder would be the plaintiff.

4.   *Challenges to statutes*: As the *MedImmune* Court notes, declaratory judgments are frequently used to challenge government conduct or to avoid the risk of criminal prosecution. For a time, there was some uncertainty about how the case or controversy requirement applied to lawsuits challenging the

constitutionality of statutes that had yet to be enforced. In Poe v. Ullman, 367 U.S. 497 (1961), a married couple sued the State of Connecticut, seeking a declaration that a statute prohibiting the use of contraceptives or giving medical advice about them was unconstitutional. The statute had been on the books since 1879 and had never been enforced. Skeptical of the plaintiffs' claim that the statute motivated their doctor's refusal to prescribe contraceptives, the Court denied declaratory relief:

> [W]e cannot accept, as the basis of constitutional adjudication, other than as chimerical the fear of enforcement of provisions that have during so many years gone uniformly and without exception unenforced.

367 U.S. at 508. Is this the same sort of purely subjective fear the *Prasco* court found insufficient to establish a case or controversy in note 1, above?

Following the Court's decision in *Poe,* the plaintiffs' physician, Dr. Buxton, served as Medical Director at a center run by the Planned Parenthood League of Connecticut, where he provided information and medical advice to married persons about contraception. Dr. Buxton and the Executive Director of the League were found guilty as accessories of violating the Connecticut statute that was the subject of *Poe*. Each was fined $100 and appealed. In Griswold v. Connecticut, 381 U.S. 479 (1965), the Supreme Court found the statute unconstitutional. For a detailed historical account of the development of *Poe* and *Griswold*, including the reactions of the individual justices to the cases, see David J. Garrow, *Liberty and Sexuality* (1994).

These days, *Poe* is rarely invoked to turn back constitutional challenges to statutes; indeed, actions seeking a declaratory and injunctive relief are often filed as soon as legislation is signed into law, well before anyone has been charged with a violation. With regard to one pre-enforcement action, the Supreme Court commented:

> We are not troubled by the pre-enforcement nature of this suit. The State has not suggested that the newly enacted law will not be enforced, and we see no reason to assume otherwise. We conclude that plaintiffs have alleged an actual and well-founded fear that the law will be enforced against them. Further, the alleged danger of this statute is, in large measure, one of self-censorship; a harm that can be realized even without an actual prosecution.

Virginia v. American Booksellers Association, 484 U.S. 383 (1988). *See also* Epperson v. Arkansas, 393 U.S. 97 (1968) (striking down a statute with no record of enforcement); Doe v. Dunbar, 320 F.Supp. 1297 (D.Colo.1970) (*Poe* does not preclude relief unless there is "a clear finding of non-enforcement").

That is not to say that *Poe* is a dead letter. *See* Northern Utilities, Inc. v. Lewiston Radiator Works, Inc., 2005 WL 758466 (D.Me. Feb. 3, 2005) (relying on *Poe* to find no jurisdiction over constitutional challenge to Maine's punitive damages law when declaratory judgment plaintiff had not yet been held liable for punitive damages).

5.   *Ripeness and administrative rule-making.* Three 1967 Supreme Court decisions known as the *Abbott Laboratories* trilogy set out the ground rules for pre-enforcement challenges to agency rules. Abbott Laboratories v. Gardner, 387 U.S. 136 (1967) (cited in *MedImmune*); Toilet Goods Association, Inc. v. Gardner, 387 U.S. 167 (1967); Toilet Goods Association, Inc. v. Gardner, 387 U.S. 158 (1967). The test for ripeness has two prongs: (a) the issues presented must be fit for judicial resolution; and (b) withholding judicial consideration would result in hardship to the parties. The Court described the basic rationale of the test as being "to prevent the courts, through avoidance of premature adjudication, from entangling themselves in abstract disagreement over administrative policies, and also to protect the agencies from judicial interference until an administrative decision has been formalized and its effects felt in a concrete way by the challenging parties." *Abbott Laboratories*, 387 U.S. at 148–149.

The Third Circuit has summarized this result in A.O. Smith Corp. v. F.T.C., 530 F.2d 515, 524 (3d Cir.1976):

> [I]t appears from the *Abbott Laboratories* trilogy that one seeking discretionary relief may not obtain pre-enforcement judicial review of agency action if there is no immediate threat of sanctions for noncompliance, or if the potential sanction is de minimis. Conversely, the court should find agency action ripe for judicial review if the action is final and clear-cut, and if it puts the complaining party on the horns of a dilemma: if he complies and awaits ultimate judicial determination of the action's validity, he must change his course of day-to-day conduct, for example, by undertaking substantial preliminary paper work, scientific testing and record-keeping, or by destroying stock; alternatively, if he does not comply, he risks sanctions or injuries including, for example, civil and criminal penalties, or loss of public confidence.

B. APPROPRIATE DISCRETION

Even if a case or controversy is established, relief under the Declaratory Judgment Act is discretionary. On remand in *MedImmune*, what factors should guide the district court's discretion? The following case may be helpful.

MORRISON V. PARKER
United States District Court
90 F.Supp.2d 876 (W.D.Mich. 2000)

McKEAGUE, DISTRICT JUDGE.

This case presents a claim for declaratory judgment relief under 28 U.S.C. § 2201. On March 6, 2000, after having received briefing on the issue, United States Magistrate Judge Joseph G. Scoville issued a report and recommendation recommending that this Court, in the exercise of its discretion, decline to entertain the action. * * *

[T]he report and recommendation will be adopted as the opinion of the Court. The Court, in the exercise of its discretion, declines to exercise jurisdiction over this matter. An order of dismissal shall issue forthwith.

REPORT AND RECOMMENDATION

SCOVILLE, UNITED STATES MAGISTRATE JUDGE.

* * *

Factual Background

This declaratory judgment action arises from a motor vehicle accident that occurred in Muskegon County on December 5, 1998. One motor vehicle was owned by plaintiff Hertz Corporation and operated by its lessee, Thelma Morrison. The other motor vehicle was operated by Brian Edgerton, Jr., then fifteen years old. Allegedly, Brian Edgerton, Jr. did not have a driver's license or a permit, and the vehicle that he was operating was not titled or insured. Also occupying the vehicle was defendant Gerald R. Parker, Jr., the apparent owner of the car, and members of his family. Brian Edgerton, Jr. and Gerald Parker, Jr. suffered serious injuries as a result of the accident.

In April of 1999, Gerald R. Parker, Jr. filed a negligence action in the Muskegon County Circuit Court. That action * * * alleges that Thelma Morrison was negligent in that she disregarded a stop sign and struck the vehicle occupied by Edgerton and Parker. Liability is asserted against Hertz Corporation on the basis of the Michigan owner's statute.

Brian Edgerton, Jr. is not a party to the Muskegon County Circuit Court action.[1] Brian Edgerton, Jr. has, however, made a demand against Hertz in the amount of $100,000, arising from his closed-head injury, collapsed right lung, and other injuries sustained in the accident. The demand was contained in a letter dated October 7, 1999, sent by attorney Paul Ladas on behalf of the minor. Brian Edgerton, Jr. has not, however, instituted a lawsuit.

Plaintiffs initiated the present declaratory judgment action by complaint filed December 8, 2000. In this action, plaintiffs seek a declaration of non-liability, based solely upon principles of Michigan law. Count 1 seeks a declaration that plaintiffs are not liable to Gerald R. Parker, Jr., because of his failure to insure his motor vehicle at the time of the accident. Alternatively, plaintiffs assert that Parker forfeited his right to recovery by allowing an unlicensed minor, Brian Edgerton, Jr., to operate his motor vehicle in violation of Mich.Comp.Laws § 257.904(1).

---

[1]   It is undisputed that Brian Edgerton, Jr. is under the legal disability of infancy, as he was under the age of eighteen when his claim accrued. Michigan law therefore allows him to file suit up to one year after reaching the age of majority.

Plaintiffs seek a declaration that Brian Edgerton, Jr., a minor, is foreclosed from recovery because of his alleged operation of a motor vehicle without a license, in violation of Mich.Comp.Laws § 257.301.

The question presently before the court is whether the court should exercise its discretion in favor of entertaining this declaratory judgment action.

Discussion

The Judicial Code empowers the federal district courts to entertain civil actions for declaratory judgment in a case of actual controversy otherwise within the court's jurisdiction. 28 U.S.C. § 2201. The Supreme Court has long held that the exercise of the jurisdiction created by section 2201 is discretionary in the district court. The Court has recently reaffirmed the breadth of discretion granted the district courts by the Declaratory Judgment Act. In Wilton v. Seven Falls Co., 515 U.S. 277 (1995), the Court made the following observations:

> By the Declaratory Judgment Act, Congress sought to place a remedial arrow in the district court's quiver; it created an opportunity, rather than a duty, to grant a new form of relief to qualifying litigants. Consistent with the nonobligatory nature of the remedy, a district court is authorized, in the sound exercise of its discretion, to stay or to dismiss an action seeking a declaratory judgment before trial or after all arguments have drawn to a close. In the declaratory judgment context, the normal principle that federal courts should adjudicate claims within their jurisdiction yields to considerations of practicality and wise judicial administration.

The United States Court of Appeals for the Sixth Circuit has provided substantial guidance concerning the principles that should guide the court's exercise of its broad discretion. The Sixth Circuit has stated that the district court should exercise its discretion in favor of a declaratory judgment action (1) when the judgment will serve a useful purpose in clarifying and settling the legal relations in issue, and (2) when it will terminate and afford relief from the uncertainty, insecurity, and controversy giving rise to the proceeding. Grand Trunk Western R.R. Co. v. Consolidated Rail Corp., 746 F.2d 323, 326 (6th Cir.1984). In applying these criteria, the appellate court requires consideration by the district court of the following factors: (1) whether the declaratory action would settle the controversy; (2) whether the declaratory action would serve a useful purpose in clarifying the legal relations in issue; (3) whether the declaratory remedy is being used merely for the purpose of "procedural fencing" or "to provide an arena for a race for res judicata;" (4) whether the use of a declaratory action would increase friction between our federal and state courts and improperly encroach upon state jurisdiction; and (5) whether there is an alternative remedy which is better or more effective.

In applying the same criteria and evaluating the same factors, the federal courts have isolated two circumstances, both present in the instant case, that militate strongly against entertaining a declaratory judgment action. The first circumstance arises where, as here, a putative tortfeasor sues the victims of his negligence in an effort to force an adjudication on the tortfeasor's terms. Second is the circumstance where a coercive state-court action is already pending. * * *

In the present action, the putative tortfeasors have sued the injured parties, seeking a declaration that the injured parties cannot recover by reason of certain state-law affirmative defenses. The federal courts have long resisted such declaratory judgment actions as a perversion of the Declaratory Judgment Act. The seminal case is Cunningham Bros., Inc. v. Bail, 407 F.2d 1165 (7th Cir.1969). *Cunningham* was an action by an alleged tortfeasor against injured employees of a subcontractor, in which the tortfeasor sought a declaration that it did not have charge of the work being performed by the employees at the time of their injuries. The district court dismissed the complaint, on the ground that the case was not appropriate for the exercise of federal court discretion under the Declaratory Judgment Act. On appeal, the tortfeasor made the same argument now advanced by Hertz: instead of having to wait to be sued in different state and federal forums by the various injured parties, the tortfeasors should be allowed to bring them together in one action, and thereby adjudicate the rights of all parties in one case. The Seventh Circuit disagreed. "Regarding the individual defendants, we are of the opinion that to compel potential personal injury plaintiffs to litigate their claims at a time and in a forum chosen by the alleged tortfeasor would be a perversion of the Declaratory Judgment Act." Relying upon earlier authority, the court noted that it was not one of the purposes of the Declaratory Judgment Act "to enable a prospective negligence action defendant to obtain a declaration of non-liability." *Id.* at 1168 (quoting Sun Oil Co. v. Transcontinental Gas Pipe Line Corp., 108 F.Supp. 280, 282 (E.D.Pa.1952)). The Seventh Circuit acknowledged that the existence of another remedy does not automatically preclude a declaratory judgment action, but determined that the traditional personal injury action was preferable, because it would afford more effective relief. The court then made an observation that applies equally to the present case.

> Since the sustaining of plaintiff's suit in the instant case would force an injured party to litigate a claim which he may not have wanted to litigate at a time which might be inconvenient to him or which might precede his determination of the full extent of his damages, and in a forum chosen by the alleged tortfeasor, we hold the action was inappropriate for declaratory relief and was therefore properly dismissed against the individual defendants.

407 F.2d at 1169.

Following *Cunningham,* the uniform approach of the federal courts is that declaratory relief is generally inappropriate when a putative tortfeasor sues the injured party for a declaration of nonliability. The recent comments of the Eighth Circuit are instructive:

> It is our view that where a declaratory plaintiff raises chiefly an affirmative defense, and it appears that granting relief could effectively deny an allegedly injured party its otherwise legitimate choice of the forum and time for suit, no declaratory judgment should issue.

BASF Corp. v. Symington, 50 F.3d 555, 559 (8th Cir.1995); accord 10B Charles Alan Wright, Arthur R. Miller & Mary Kay Kane, Federal Practice & Procedure § 2765 at 638–39 (2d ed.1998) ("The courts have also held that it is not one of the purposes of the declaratory judgments act to enable a prospective negligence action defendant to obtain a declaration of nonliability. They have felt that even though a declaratory judgment action might reduce multiple litigation with a number of injured persons, this result should not outweigh the right of a personal-injury plaintiff to choose the forum and the time, if at all, to assert his claim.").

Viewed from the perspective of the five *Grand Trunk* standards, an action by a putative tortfeasor fares poorly as a declaratory judgment action. First, the action would not necessarily settle the controversy. In their complaint, plaintiffs do not assert that Thelma Morrison was not at fault in causing defendants' injuries. Rather, they seek to raise only two state-law affirmative defenses which allegedly bar recovery as a matter of law. If plaintiffs are correct in their legal assertions, the controversy may well end. If, however, plaintiffs are incorrect, then the issues of negligence, proximate cause, and damages must still be litigated in some forum. At best, maintenance of the present case raises only the possibility of settling the controversy.

Second, this action would not serve a useful purpose in clarifying the legal relations in issue. Traditionally, affirmative defenses such as those now advanced by plaintiffs are litigated in the context of a personal injury action. I fail to see what useful purpose is served by divorcing affirmative defenses from the facts of the case and seeking an adjudication of those defenses in a vacuum.

Third, the conclusion is virtually inescapable that Hertz is using this federal court action for the purpose of procedural fencing. Plaintiffs have never explained to this court why their affirmative defenses could not be raised in response to a traditional personal injury action. In the case of Mr. Parker, such an action has been pending in the Muskegon County Circuit Court for a period of months. If plaintiffs believe that their defense is meritorious, there is nothing preventing them from raising it in a dispositive motion before the state circuit court. With regard to defendant Edgerton, a minor, the aspects of procedural fencing are even more apparent. As a minor, Mr. Edgerton is privileged under state law to wait until his nineteenth birthday before initiating a lawsuit. By bringing this action, plaintiffs would effectively force an unwilling minor to litigate his personal injury claim prematurely, perhaps before all effects of the accident become manifest. Plaintiffs have not advanced any reason why this court should be a party to depriving an injured minor of a benefit bestowed upon him by state statute.

[Fourth,] the maintenance of a declaratory judgment action would indeed increase friction between the federal and state courts and improperly encroach upon state jurisdiction, at least with regard to defendant Parker. As noted above, Parker presently has pending a traditional personal injury action in the state courts. The Supreme Court has long held that "ordinarily it would be uneconomical as well as vexatious for a federal court to proceed in a declaratory judgment suit where another suit is pending in a state court presenting the same issues, not governed by federal law, between the same parties." In its recent decision in *Wilton,* the Supreme Court reiterated this concept and underscored the discretion of the district court to dismiss or stay proceedings where parallel state proceedings are already pending. Presumably, plaintiffs wish to receive a declaration of nonliability from this court and then to present it to the Muskegon County Circuit Court as a bar to that court's further consideration of Parker's personal injury action. I cannot imagine the circumstances in which a federal court would choose to exercise its discretion to lecture the state courts on an issue of state law central to the resolution of a claim properly pending before those courts.

Finally, there is an alternate remedy that is better and more effective, namely, a traditional personal injury action. The Supreme Court has taught that the crucial issue is not whether the state-court action was commenced first, but whether it will most fully serve the interests of the parties and provide a comprehensive resolution of their dispute. In a personal injury action, all issues between the parties may be resolved in a comprehensive proceeding. This is certainly preferable to a federal declaratory judgment action, in which certain affirmative defenses are the only matters at issue. It is difficult to see how justice would be better served by the maintenance of this federal declaratory judgment action.

* * *

Recommended Disposition

The unanimous attitude of the federal courts is to decline to exercise declaratory judgment jurisdiction where a putative tortfeasor attempts to choose the time and forum to litigate the claims of the injured party. In these circumstances, all five of the relevant Sixth Circuit factors weigh against entertaining the action. I therefore recommend that this declaratory judgment action be dismissed without prejudice. * * *

NOTES

1.   The Declaratory Judgment Act does not say that the remedy is forbidden in tort actions. *Cunningham Brothers*, which the *Morrison* court calls the seminal case, cites no authority for its conclusion that declaratory judgments are generally unavailable in tort actions. In tort, however, there is less likelihood of the ability of the declaratory judgment to avert future harm, as in many cases of tort, the harm has already occurred. The purpose of declaratory judgments therefore is not typically seen in many torts, where the question is merely to resolve past liability.

2.   The Supreme Court has emphasized that the Declaratory Judgment Act gives the district courts discretion to declare the parties' rights; federal courts are never required to hear an action under the statute. Wilton v. Seven Falls Co., 515 U.S. 277(1995). So long as there is a case or controversy under Article III, the district court's decision to hear or not to hear an action under the Declaratory Judgment Act will be reversed only on a showing of an abuse of discretion. *Wilton*, 515 U.S. at 289–90.

What factors does the *Morrison* court consider important to its decision? The Fifth Circuit has articulated a six factor test to determine whether a declaratory judgment claim should be entertained:

> The relevant factors which the district court must consider include, but are not limited to, 1) whether there is a pending state action in which all of the matters in controversy may be fully litigated, 2) whether the plaintiff filed suit in anticipation of a lawsuit filed by the defendant, 3) whether the plaintiff engaged in forum shopping in bringing the suit, 4) whether possible inequities in allowing the declaratory plaintiff to gain precedence in time or to change forums exist, 5) whether the federal court is a convenient forum for the parties and witnesses, and 6) whether retaining the lawsuit in federal court would serve the purposes of judicial economy.

American States Insurance Co. v. Bailey, 133 F.3d 363 (5th Cir. 1998).

3.   Among these factors, how much weight should be attached to who commences a lawsuit? In the *Aetna Life* case, the court of appeals had found that: (a) the only advantage to be derived from a declaratory judgment was the adjudication of Aetna's right of cancellation; and (b) the only value of such adjudication was that it settled a defense to a lawsuit that might be filed in the future, such as after the death of the insured. Aetna Life Insurance Co. v. Haworth, 84 F.2d 695 (8th Cir.1936), *rev'd,* 300 U.S. 227 (1937). Of course, it is usual and unremarkable that the party who would be a defendant in a suit seeking a coercive remedy will be the plaintiff in a declaratory judgment action—it is frequently the only avenue by which the traditional defendant can initiate resolution of the legal dispute. As a result, by using declaratory judgment, the traditional defendant is also able to choose the forum. Is there any reason to disparage this result? *See* BASF Corp. v. Symington, 50 F.3d 555 (8th Cir.1995) (courts normally dismiss declaratory judgment actions "aimed solely at wresting the choice of forum from the 'natural' plaintiff").

4.　Should it change the outcome if the declaratory judgment defendant has already filed an action in state court, or if he files one while the federal declaratory judgment action is pending? If a state has begun a *criminal* prosecution while a challenge to the state statute in federal court is in its embryonic stages, the federal courts will not enjoin the state court proceedings, Younger v. Harris, 401 U.S. 37 (1971), or grant declaratory judgment, Samuels v. Mackell, 401 U.S. 66 (1971), except in the most exceptional circumstances.

Civil actions are different, however. When faced with competing state litigation, a federal district court can exercise its discretion to hear the case, or it can choose to defer to the state courts. *See, e.g.,* Colorado River Water Conservation District v. United States, 424 U.S. 800 (1976) (actions for declaratory relief brought under 28 U.S.C. § 1345 should not be stayed in deference to state court actions unless exceptional circumstances are present, because the statute evinced a clear congressional intent to have the issues decided in federal court).

5.　Is it relevant that other remedies might be available to the declaratory judgment plaintiff? While the availability of other remedies can be a factor that would lead a court to exercise its discretion not to hear the case, *see, e.g.,* Tilcon Minerals, Inc. v. Orange & Rockland Utilities, Inc., 851 F.Supp. 529 (S.D.N.Y.1994) (neither injunctive nor declaratory relief would be granted in a dispute where monetary damages were an adequate remedy), the existence of alternative remedies is not dispositive:

> [E]ngrafting upon the Declaratory Judgment Act a requirement that all of the traditional equitable prerequisites to the issuance of an injunction be satisfied before the issuance of a declaratory judgment is considered would defy Congress' intent to make declaratory relief available in cases where an injunction would be inappropriate. . . . Thus, the Court of Appeals was in error when it ruled that a failure to demonstrate irreparable injury—a traditional prerequisite to injunctive relief, having no equivalent in the law of declaratory judgments—precluded the granting of declaratory relief. The only occasions where this Court has disregarded these "different considerations" and found that preclusion of injunctive relief inevitably led to a denial of declaratory relief have been cases in which principles of federalism militated altogether against federal intervention in a class of adjudications.

Steffel v. Thompson, 415 U.S. 452, 471–72 (1974).

The reference to "principles of federalism" in *Steffel* encompasses a series of cases in which the Court has held declaratory relief is not available if its effect would be to end-run federalism-based limitations on damages or injunctive relief. Thus, a declaratory judgment is not available where the judgment's res judicata effect would make the federal court's decision tantamount to an award of damages against the state, which the Eleventh Amendment would otherwise prohibit. Green v. Mansour, 474 U.S. 64(1985). Neither is declaratory relief available if its effect would be to end run the Anti-

Tax Injunction Act's prohibition on enjoining tax collections (Great Lakes Dredge & Dock Co. v. Huffman, 319 U.S. 293(1943)), or the prohibition on enjoining ongoing criminal prosecutions (Samuels v. Mackell, 401 U.S. 66, 73(1971)).

CHAPTER 5

DAMAGES

■ ■ ■

A. INTRODUCTION

Compensatory damages are the default remedy in most civil lawsuits. This preference comes from both the history of American law as well as the fact that money often provides the best option for clients given their objectives and the facts, which is to simply resolve a past harm.

THE NATURE OF THE SUBJECT

The law of damages consists of the rules, standards, and methods used by the courts for measuring in money the compensation given for losses and injuries. It plays an unusually large part in Anglo-American law because of two distinctive features of the English judicial machinery. First is the presence of the jury, who award the damages under the judge's supervision and control. The rules and formulas used in the exercise of that control make up a substantial part of the law of damages. Second, in dividing jurisdiction between courts of law and courts of equity, the tradition was established that resort must be had to compensation by money damages in preference to specific relief, unless such damages are affirmatively shown to be inadequate for the just protection of the plaintiff's interest. It results from this traditional rule that a judgment for money damages is the normal and preferred remedy in our courts.

Charles McCormick, *Handbook on the Law of Damages* 1 (1935).

The goal of compensatory damages, like that of injunctive relief, is to return the plaintiff to her rightful position. As we previously saw, the legal basis of the plaintiff's cause of action is the starting point for determining what damages are available, as the rightful position is defined by the substantive law.

The viewpoint for assessing rightful position varies a bit depending on whether the case sounds in tort or contract. In tort cases, the rightful position is looks backwards, pre-harm, to restore the plaintiff to the position he occupied before the tort. In contract cases, the rightful position looks forward, defining the rightful position as the "the benefit of the bargain," to award the plaintiff the advantageous position he would have occupied had the contract been performed. Both place the plaintiff in the position they would have occupied in the absence of a legal violation.

Once the rightful position is identified, a lawyer must then must analytically address questions of qualification and quantification for compensatory damages. Professor McCormick provides the classic framework for thinking through issues of damages.

CHARLES MCCORMICK, HANDBOOK ON THE LAW OF DAMAGES
2–3 (1935)

What is included in the subject of Damages? * * * First, the lawyer to whom is presented such a claim will consider whether the claim is enforceable at all, or, in legal parlance, whether there is a "cause of action." * * * Similar in effect are all the questions relating to whether a good defense is available to the whole claim, such as the questions of release, accord and satisfaction, and contributory negligence. * * *

A second inquiry which the lawyer investigating his client's claim for damages would frequently make, is this: What are the *elements* or items of the client's loss, injury, or grievance which will be recognized by the court as grounds of compensation? Will allowance be made, for example, in a contract case for disappointment due to the failure of the bargain; or, in an action for personal injury, can expense of nursing be recovered? Third, and closely allied to the last, is the inquiry: What formula of *measurement* is to be used in fixing compensation for the element or elements of loss which are recognized? The choice here may be between standards of value, e.g., whether the value of some property wrongfully appropriated shall be the market value or the value in use, or the value at the time of taking or the time of trial. Again, the standard may be one of reasonable and necessary expenditure, or the measure may be fixed, as in case of liquidated damages, by agreement of the parties. A fourth avenue of inquiry is the ascertainment of the general rules, standards, and doctrines which place *limits* upon the application of the formulas of compensation to the recognized elements. Chief among these are the requirements of certainty, and of foreseeability either at the time of the making of a contract, or as of the time of the commission of a wrong. Fifth, in examining the claim, the lawyer must inquire into the procedural rules which regulate the manner in which he can best plead and prove the elements of loss or injury, the fashion in which the judge should state the problem of compensation to the jury, and the standards to be used by the trial and appellate judges in reviewing the jury's award.

The case that follows introduces compensatory damages and contrasts them with the other two types of damages, nominal damages and punitive damages. Punitive damages will be discussed in Chapter 6.

MEMPHIS COMMUNITY SCHOOL DISTRICT V. STACHURA

Supreme Court of the United States
477 U.S. 299 (1986)

JUSTICE POWELL delivered the opinion of the Court.

This case requires us to decide whether 42 U.S.C. § 1983 authorizes an award of compensatory damages based on the factfinder's assessment of the value or importance of a substantive constitutional right.

I

Respondent Edward Stachura is a tenured teacher in the Memphis, Michigan, public schools. When the events that led to this case occurred, respondent taught seventh-grade life science, using a textbook that had been approved by the school board. The textbook included a chapter on human reproduction. During the 1978–1979 school year, respondent spent six weeks on this chapter. As part of their instruction, students were shown pictures of respondent's wife during her pregnancy. Respondent also showed the students two films concerning human growth and sexuality. These films were provided by the County Health Department, and the Principal of respondent's school had approved their use. Both films had been shown in past school years without incident.

After the showing of the pictures and the films, a number of parents complained to school officials about respondent's teaching methods. These complaints, which appear to have been based largely on inaccurate rumors about the allegedly sexually explicit nature of the pictures and films, were discussed at an open School Board meeting held on April 23, 1979. Following the advice of the School Superintendent, respondent did not attend the meeting, during which a number of parents expressed the view that respondent should not be allowed to teach in the Memphis school system. The day after the meeting, respondent was suspended with pay. The School Board later confirmed the suspension, and notified respondent that an "administration evaluation" of his teaching methods was underway. No such evaluation was ever made. Respondent was reinstated the next fall, after filing this lawsuit.

Respondent sued the School District, the Board of Education, various Board members and school administrators, and two parents who had participated in the April 23 School Board meeting. The complaint alleged that respondent's suspension deprived him of both liberty and property without due process of law and violated his First Amendment right to academic freedom. Respondent sought compensatory and punitive damages under 42 U.S.C. § 1983 for these constitutional violations.

At the close of trial on these claims, the District Court instructed the jury as to the law governing the asserted bases for liability. Turning to damages, the court instructed the jury that on finding liability it should award a sufficient amount to compensate respondent for the injury caused by petitioners' unlawful actions:

> You should consider in this regard any lost earnings; loss of earning capacity; out-of-pocket expenses; and any mental anguish or emotional distress that you find the Plaintiff to have suffered as a result of conduct by the Defendants depriving him of his civil rights.

In addition to this instruction on the standard elements of compensatory damages, the court explained that punitive damages could be awarded, and described the standards governing punitive awards. Finally, at respondent's request and over petitioners' objection, the court charged that damages also could be awarded based on the value or importance of the constitutional rights that were violated:

> If you find that the Plaintiff has been deprived of a Constitutional right, you may award damages to compensate him for the deprivation. Damages for this type of injury are more difficult to measure than damages for a physical injury or injury to one's property. There are no medical bills or other expenses by which you can judge how much compensation is appropriate. In one sense, no monetary value we place upon Constitutional rights can measure their importance in our society or compensate a citizen adequately for their deprivation. However, just because these rights are not capable of precise evaluation does not mean that an appropriate monetary amount should not be awarded. The precise value you place upon any Constitutional right which you find was denied to Plaintiff is within your discretion. You may wish to consider the importance of the right in our system of government, the role which this right has played in the history of our republic, [and] the significance of the right in the context of the activities which the Plaintiff was engaged in at the time of the violation of the right.

The jury found petitioners liable, and awarded a total of $275,000 in compensatory damages and $46,000 in punitive damages. * * *

In an opinion devoted primarily to liability issues, the Court of Appeals for the Sixth Circuit affirmed. * * *

We granted certiorari limited to the question whether the Court of Appeals erred in affirming the damages award in light of the District Court's instructions that authorized not only compensatory and punitive damages, but also damages for the deprivation of "any constitutional right" * * * .

III

A

We have repeatedly noted that 42 U.S.C. § 1983 creates " 'a species of tort liability' in favor of persons who are deprived of 'rights, privileges, or immunities secured' to them by the Constitution." Accordingly, when § 1983 plaintiffs seek damages for violations of constitutional rights, the level of damages is ordinarily determined according to principles derived from the common law of torts.

Punitive damages aside,[9] damages in tort cases are designed to provide "*compensation* for the injury caused to plaintiff by defendant's breach of duty." To that end, compensatory damages may include not only out-of-pocket loss and other monetary harms, but also such injuries as "impairment of reputation. . ., personal humiliation, and mental anguish and suffering." Deterrence is also an important purpose of this system, but it operates through the mechanism of damages that are compensatory— damages grounded in determinations of plaintiffs' actual losses. Congress adopted this common-law system of recovery when it established liability for "constitutional torts." Consequently, "the basic purpose" of § 1983 damages is "to *compensate persons for injuries* that are caused by the deprivation of constitutional rights."

Respondent does not, and could not reasonably, contend that the separate instructions authorizing damages for violation of constitutional rights were equivalent to punitive damages instructions. In these separate instructions, the jury was authorized to find damages for constitutional violations without any finding of malice or ill will. Moreover, the jury instructions separately authorized punitive damages, and the District Court expressly labeled the "constitutional rights" damages compensatory. The instructions concerning damages for constitutional violations are thus impermissible unless they reasonably could be read as authorizing *compensatory* damages.

Carey v. Piphus represents a straightforward application of these principles. *Carey* involved a suit by a high school student suspended for

---

[9]   The purpose of punitive damages is to punish the defendant for his willful or malicious conduct and to deter others from similar behavior. In Smith v. Wade, 461 U.S. 30 (1983), the Court held that punitive damages may be available in a proper § 1983 case. As the punitive damages instructions used in this case explained, however, such damages are available only on a showing of the requisite intent. App. 94–95 (authorizing punitive damages for acts "maliciously, or wantonly, or oppressively done").

smoking marijuana; the student claimed that he was denied procedural due process because he was suspended without an opportunity to respond to the charges against him. The Court of Appeals for the Seventh Circuit held that even if the suspension was justified, the student could recover substantial compensatory damages simply because of the insufficient procedures used to suspend him from school. We reversed, and held that the student could recover compensatory damages only if he proved actual injury caused by the denial of his constitutional rights. We noted: "[r]ights, constitutional and otherwise, do not exist in a vacuum. Their purpose is to protect persons from injuries to particular interests. . . ." Where no injury was present, no "compensatory" damages could be awarded.

The instructions at issue here cannot be squared with *Carey,* or with the principles of tort damages on which *Carey* and § 1983 are grounded. The jurors in this case were told that, in determining how much was necessary to "compensate [respondent] for the deprivation" of his constitutional rights, they should place a money value on the "rights" themselves by considering such factors as the particular right's "importance . . . in our system of government," its role in American history, and its "significance . . . in the context of the activities" in which respondent was engaged. These factors focus, not on compensation for provable injury, but on the jury's subjective perception of the importance of constitutional rights as an abstract matter. *Carey* establishes that such an approach is impermissible. The constitutional right transgressed in *Carey*—the right to due process of law—is central to our system of ordered liberty. We nevertheless held that *no* compensatory damages could be awarded for violation of that right absent proof of actual injury. *Carey,* 435 U.S. at 264. *Carey* thus makes clear that the abstract value of a constitutional right may not form the basis for § 1983 damages.[11]

Respondent nevertheless argues that *Carey* does not control here, because in this case a *substantive* constitutional right—respondent's First Amendment right to academic freedom—was infringed. The argument misperceives our analysis in *Carey.* That case does not establish a two-tiered system of constitutional rights, with substantive rights afforded greater protection than "mere" procedural safeguards. We did acknowledge in *Carey* that "the elements and prerequisites for recovery of damages"

---

[11] We did approve an award of nominal damages for the deprivation of due process in *Carey.* Our discussion of that issue makes clear that nominal damages, and not damages based on some undefinable "value" of infringed rights, are the appropriate means of "vindicating" rights whose deprivation has not caused actual, provable injury:

Common-law courts traditionally have vindicated deprivations of certain 'absolute' rights that are not shown to have caused actual injury through the award of a nominal sum of money. By making the deprivation of such rights actionable for nominal damages without proof of actual injury, the law recognizes the importance to organized society that those rights be scrupulously observed; but at the same time, it remains true to the principle that substantial damages should be awarded only to compensate actual injury or, in the case of exemplary or punitive damages, to deter or punish malicious deprivations of rights.

might vary depending on the interests protected by the constitutional right at issue. But we emphasized that, whatever the constitutional basis for § 1983 liability, such damages must always be designed "to *compensate injuries* caused by the [constitutional] deprivation." That conclusion simply leaves no room for non-compensatory damages measured by the jury's perception of the abstract "importance" of a constitutional right.

Nor do we find such damages necessary to vindicate the constitutional rights that § 1983 protects. Section 1983 presupposes that damages that compensate for actual harm ordinarily suffice to deter constitutional violations. Moreover, damages based on the "value" of constitutional rights are an unwieldy tool for ensuring compliance with the Constitution. History and tradition do not afford any sound guidance concerning the precise value that juries should place on constitutional protections. Accordingly, were such damages available, juries would be free to award arbitrary amounts without any evidentiary basis, or to use their unbounded discretion to punish unpopular defendants. Such damages would be too uncertain to be of any great value to plaintiffs, and would inject caprice into determinations of damages in § 1983 cases. We therefore hold that damages based on the abstract "value" or "importance" of constitutional rights are not a permissible element of compensatory damages in such cases.

B

Respondent further argues that the challenged instructions authorized a form of "presumed" damages—a remedy that is both compensatory in nature and traditionally part of the range of tort law remedies. * * *

Presumed damages are a *substitute* for ordinary compensatory damages, not a *supplement* for an award that fully compensates the alleged injury. When a plaintiff seeks compensation for an injury that is likely to have occurred but difficult to establish, some form of presumed damages may possibly be appropriate. In those circumstances, presumed damages may roughly approximate the harm that the plaintiff suffered and thereby compensate for harms that may be impossible to measure. As we earlier explained, the instructions at issue in this case did not serve this purpose, but instead called on the jury to measure damages based on a subjective evaluation of the importance of particular constitutional values. Since such damages are wholly divorced from any compensatory purpose, they cannot be justified as presumed damages.[14] Moreover, no rough substitute for

---

[14] For the same reason, Nixon v. Herndon, 273 U.S. 536 (1927), and similar cases do not support the challenged instructions. In *Nixon,* the Court held that a plaintiff who was illegally prevented from voting in a state primary election suffered compensable injury. This holding did not rest on the "value" of the right to vote as an abstract matter; rather, the Court recognized that the plaintiff had suffered a particular injury—his inability to vote in a particular election—that might be compensated through substantial money damages.

compensatory damages was required in this case, since the jury was fully authorized to compensate respondent for both monetary and nonmonetary harms caused by petitioners' conduct. * * *

IV

The judgment of the Court of Appeals is reversed, and the case is remanded for further proceedings consistent with this opinion.

JUSTICE BRENNAN and JUSTICE STEVENS join the opinion of the Court and also join JUSTICE MARSHALL's opinion concurring in the judgment.

JUSTICE MARSHALL, with whom JUSTICE BRENNAN, JUSTICE BLACKMUN, and JUSTICE STEVENS join, concurring in the judgment.

I agree with the Court that this case must be remanded for a new trial on damages. Certain portions of the Court's opinion, however, can be read to suggest that damages in § 1983 cases are necessarily limited to "out-of-pocket loss," "other monetary harms," and "such injuries as 'impairment of reputation . . ., personal humiliation, and mental anguish and suffering.'" I do not understand the Court so to hold, and I write separately to emphasize that the violation of a constitutional right, in proper cases, may itself constitute a compensable injury. * * *

Following *Carey,* the courts of appeals have recognized that invasions of constitutional rights sometimes cause injuries that cannot be redressed by a wooden application of common-law damages rules. In Hobson v. Wilson, 737 F.2d 1, 57–63 (1984), *cert. denied,* 470 U.S. 1084 (1985), which the Court cites, plaintiffs claimed that defendant Federal Bureau of Investigation agents had invaded their First Amendment rights to assemble for peaceable political protest, to associate with others to engage in political expression, and to speak on public issues free of unreasonable government interference. The District Court found that the defendants had succeeded in diverting plaintiffs from, and impeding them in, their protest

---

Nixon followed a long line of cases, going back to Lord Holt's decision in Ashby v. White, 2 Ld.Raym. 938, 92 Eng.Rep. 126 (1703), authorizing substantial money damages as compensation for persons deprived of their right to vote in particular elections. Although these decisions sometimes speak of damages for the value of the right to vote, their analysis shows that they involve nothing more than an award of presumed damages for a nonmonetary harm that cannot easily be quantified:

> In the eyes of the law th[e] right [to vote] is so valuable that damages are presumed from the wrongful deprivation of it without evidence of actual loss of money, property, or any other valuable thing, and the amount of the damages is a question peculiarly appropriate for the determination of the jury, because each member of the jury has personal knowledge of the value of the right.

Ibid; See also Ashby v. White, *supra,* at 955, 92 Eng.Rep., at 137 (Holt, C.J.) ("As in an action for slanderous words, though a man does not lose a penny by reason of the speaking [of] them, yet he shall have an action"). The "value of the right" in the context of these decisions is the money value of the particular loss that the plaintiff suffered—a loss of which "each member of the jury has personal knowledge." It is *not* the value of the right to vote as a general, abstract matter, based on its role in our history or system of government. Thus, whatever the wisdom of these decisions in the context of the changing scope of compensatory damages over the course of this century, they do not support awards of noncompensatory damages such as those authorized in this case.

activities. The Court of Appeals for the District of Columbia Circuit held that injury to a First Amendment-protected interest could itself constitute compensable injury wholly apart from any "emotional distress, humiliation and personal indignity, emotional pain, embarrassment, fear, anxiety and anguish" suffered by plaintiffs. The court warned, however, that that injury could be compensated with substantial damages only to the extent that it was "reasonably quantifiable"; damages should not be based on "the so-called inherent value of the rights violated."

I believe that the *Hobson* court correctly stated the law. When a plaintiff is deprived, for example, of the opportunity to engage in a demonstration to express his political views, "[i]t is facile to suggest that no damage is done." Loss of such an opportunity constitutes loss of First Amendment rights " 'in their most pristine and classic form.' " There is no reason why such an injury should not be compensable in damages. At the same time, however, the award must be proportional to the actual loss sustained.

The instructions given the jury in this case were improper because they did not require the jury to focus on the loss actually sustained by respondent. * * *

The Court therefore properly remands for a new trial on damages. I do not understand the Court, however, to hold that deprivations of constitutional rights can never themselves constitute compensable injuries. Such a rule would be inconsistent with the logic of *Carey*, and would defeat the purpose of § 1983 by denying compensation for genuine injuries caused by the deprivation of constitutional rights.

NOTES

1.   What it means to compensate someone for an injury is at the heart of a contemporary debate over the use of the legal system to award damages, particularly in tort cases. The usual explanation for compensatory damages is that compensatory damages make the plaintiff whole. By awarding a sum of money that represents the economic value of the losses the plaintiff has suffered, the court restores the plaintiff to his or her rightful position.

When the plaintiff's losses are economic or pecuniary in nature, the concept of compensation as correcting or rectifying the wrong done makes sense intuitively. But what if the plaintiff's losses are not economic? Compensatory damages are traditionally divided into two categories: compensatory damages for pecuniary, or economic, losses and compensatory damages for nonpecuniary losses, such as emotional distress, pain and suffering, loss of consortium, and so on. Justice Marshall reads the majority's opinion to allow compensatory damages for the deprivation of constitutional rights, provided the jury's award is based on the actual injury the plaintiff suffered and not on the abstract value of the constitutional right. The majority opinion seems to endorse this view by citing Nixon with approval, and by referring to the common law practice of presuming damages when a person has been battered, assaulted or falsely imprisoned.

But what does it mean to say that "deprivations of constitutional rights can themselves constitute compensable injuries"? Doesn't the idea of compensation connote that the thing lost can be replaced by money, that an award of money will make the plaintiff whole? Does an award of money undo the harm when, as in Nixon, a person has lost the right to vote in a particular election? If money won't make the plaintiff whole, what is the point of awarding compensatory damages?

2.   Doubtless, if the practice of awarding damages for the violation of constitutional rights implies that rights and money are fungible—that rights are commodities that can be replaced with money—the practice is troubling. Because most people believe rights and dollars are incommensurable, the practice of offering payment in exchange for something priceless seems arbitrary or punitive at best, and demeaning to the victim at worst. See Margaret Jane Radin, *Contested Commodities* 184–187 (1996).

Perhaps the problem is that "making the plaintiff whole" does not capture the full purpose of compensatory damages. As an alternative, Professor Radin suggests a "noncommodified" view of the practice of compensation. In that view, an award of damages serves a different function:

> Requiring payment is a way both to bring the wrongdoer to recognize that she has done wrong and to make redress to the victim. Redress is not restitution or rectification. "Redress" instead means showing the victim that her rights are taken seriously. It is accomplished by affirming that some action is required to symbolize public respect for the existence of certain rights and public recognition of the transgressor's fault in failing to respect those rights. In this conception of compensation, neither the harm to the victim nor the victim's right not to be harmed is commensurable with money . . . even if, because of money's symbolic importance for us, large cash payments would be needed to symbolize a serious offense.

Id. at 188.

3.   A third way to explain the purpose of awarding compensatory damages is to focus on their deterrent effect. As the Supreme Court noted in a different context, while compensatory damages are not retributive in the sense that punitive damages are, "compensatory damages are quintessentially backward-looking. Compensatory damages may be intended less to sanction wrongdoers than to make victims whole, but they do so by a mechanism that affects the liabilities of defendants." Landgraf v. USI Film Products, 511 U.S. 244 (1994).

The idea that violations of rights can be deterred by requiring wrongdoers to compensate their victims is central to the law of damages. Yet, Professor Darryl Levinson has argued that where constitutional torts are concerned, the damages remedy does not deter governmental actors, who "respond to political incentives, not financial ones." Darryl Levinson, *Making Government Pay: Markets, Politics, and the Allocation of Constitutional Costs*, 67 U.Chi.L.Rev. 345, 420 (2000). For example, Professor Levinson argues that remedies like the exclusionary rule are more effective than compensatory damages for Fourth Amendment violations as in *Bivens*, because they "eliminate * * * political rewards by derailing convictions—and in a highly visible, politically salient manner."

NOTE ON NOMINAL DAMAGES

Nominal damages are a nominal or trivial sum of money (frequently one dollar) awarded to plaintiffs who have established a cause of action, but have not shown an injury for which compensatory damages can be awarded. Nominal damages are not available for every cause of action; some wrongs are not actionable unless actual injury can be proved. For example, actual injury is part of the plaintiff's prima facie case in negligence. There is, thus, no such thing as a nominal damage award in a negligence case; if the plaintiff fails to show an actual injury, she simply loses. E.g., Right v. Breen, 890 A.2d 1287 (Conn. 2006).

History has played an important role in determining whether nominal damages are available for a particular cause of action. But now, Professor McCormick has argued that except for negligence, slander, slander of title and perhaps fraud, "in practically all other actions for torts formerly remediable in 'case' the modern decisions seem to adopt the view that, in the absence of actual damage, the defendant's misconduct renders him liable to nominal damages." Certainly it is well-accepted that nominal damages are available in contract cases. McCormick, *Handbook on the Law of Damages, supra*, at 89.

At early common law, wrongs were actionable without any showing of injury because tort law and criminal law overlapped and shared a common purpose—sanctioning the defendant's conduct. Even if the plaintiff had not been injured, the peace had been broken. Nominal damage awards also served a purpose now served by declaratory judgment awards. By suing for nominal damages, a plaintiff could obtain a definitive adjudication of his rights before any harm occurred. This was particularly useful in disputes over property lines. By seeking nominal damages for trespass, a property owner could establish the property's boundaries and prevent others from acquiring prescriptive rights.

Nominal damages also allowed courts to provide at least some remedy to plaintiffs whose cases failed for a simple lack of proof. This can be particularly important if the case involves a fee shifting statute that awards attorney fees to the prevailing party. If the plaintiff tried to show actual damages but failed to persuade the jury, an award of nominal damages may still qualify the plaintiff as a prevailing party entitled to attorney's fees. Farrar v. Hobby, 506 U.S. 103 (1992). The plaintiff's relative lack of success, however, can be taken into account in setting the amount of the award very low. Rivera v. Horton, 7 F.Supp.2d 147 (N.D.N.Y.1998) (fee award of 66 cents to a plaintiff who recovered one dollar against correctional officers for excessive use of force). But the success can also take account of injunction relief obtain or the public purpose served by the litigation. *E.g.*, Brandau v. Kansas, 168 F.3d 1179 (10th Cir.), (fee award of $41,000 to a plaintiff who recovered nominal damages in a sexual harassment suit), *cert. denied*, 526 U.S. 1133 (1999).

Can nominal damages also serve as a "hook" for punitive damages? Where common law causes of action are concerned, most courts require a showing of actual damages before punitive damages can be awarded, although there are exceptions. *See* Nappe v. Anschelewitz, Barr, Ansell & Bonello, 97 N.J. 37, 477 A.2d 1224 (1984) (punitive damages may be assessed in an action for an intentional tort involving egregious conduct whether or not compensatory damages are awarded). Where constitutional rights are violated, on the other hand, it seems to be settled that punitive damages can be awarded without an award of compensatory damages. Searles v. Van Bebber, 251 F.3d 869, 880 (10th Cir.2001); Alexander v. Riga, 208 F.3d 419, 430 (3d Cir.2000). Where statutory violations are concerned, the courts are divided. *See, e.g.,* Louisiana ACORN Fair Housing, Inc. v. LeBlanc, 211 F.3d 298 (5th Cir.2000), *cert. denied*, 532 U.S. 904 (2001) (concluding, after reviewing the split in authority, that punitive damages cannot be awarded for a violation of the Fair Housing Act unless actual damages have been awarded).

In summary, the practical significance of nominal damage awards has always been thought to be limited to two sorts of cases: cases where the plaintiff is really after a sort of declaratory judgment, and cases where the plaintiff simply could not persuade the jury to award substantial damages.

NOTE ON MONETARY RELIEF IN LAW AND EQUITY

In the brief quotation at the beginning of this chapter, Professor McCormick describes one of the salient characteristics of the damage award: it is a legal, as opposed to an equitable remedy. As we have seen, the equity courts sought to give a claimant specific relief, by undoing the harm that occurred or preventing it from happening in the first place. By contrast, the law courts relied on a substitutionary remedy, offering to cure the injury by offering recompense in money.

However, it is not quite this simple. The law courts sometimes granted specific relief. Someone whose personal property had been taken, for example, could post a bond and get a writ of replevin from the law courts, which would instruct the person executing the writ to seize the property and return it. The writ of ejectment could give a landowner possession of his property. The writ of habeas corpus could release a party from confinement.

Conversely, equity courts sometimes awarded compensatory monetary relief. If a claimant sought specific performance of an obligation to pay money, and the legal remedy was inadequate, an equity court would order the money paid. Or, if an injunction had issued, and an additional award of money for past harm could dispose of the case completely, an equity court could order monetary relief under its "clean up jurisdiction."

In cases like these, whether the relief sought should be characterized as legal or equitable turns on how the court's order would be enforced. Equity courts ordered defendants, personally, to act, and enforced their orders by their contempt power. Law courts relied on separate administrative proceedings to enforce their judgments. Thus, if the defendant failed to pay a money judgment, the plaintiff had to initiate separate proceedings to enforce the judgment, garnishing the defendant's wages, or executing against her property, for example. Even writs were executed by a sheriff or another administrative officer, who took possession of the property or person in question from the defendant and restored it to the plaintiff.

Although only a few jurisdictions in the United States still maintain separate equity or chancery courts, there are reasons why it remains important to understand the circumstances under which equity courts would order "equitable monetary relief." One, discussed in some detail below, is that the right to a jury trial may turn on the characterization of the remedy. Another is Congress's penchant for authorizing courts to grant "appropriate equitable relief" when a statute has been violated. Then, whether courts of equity could award a particular remedy becomes a critical question.

Such an issue surfaced in the Supreme Court's opinion in Mertens v. Hewitt Associates, 508 U.S. 248 (1993). In *Mertens*, beneficiaries of a pension plan alleged that an actuary's wrongdoing caused their pension plan to be underfunded. They sued under a federal statute, the Employee Retirement Income Security Act (ERISA), which provides that a plan beneficiary may bring a civil action to enjoin any practice or "to obtain other appropriate equitable relief to redress such violations." 29 U.S.C. § 1132(a)(3).

The beneficiaries argued that equity courts routinely awarded compensatory monetary relief against nonfiduciaries who participated in a fiduciary breach; therefore, Congress must have intended to authorize monetary relief against nonfiduciaries when it empowered the courts to award "appropriate equitable relief."

While Justice Scalia, writing for the Court on a 5–4 vote, conceded that equity courts routinely awarded monetary damages in breach of trust cases, the Court majority held that the phrase "appropriate equitable relief" should be read more narrowly. In other sections of the statute, Congress had authorized courts to award "legal or equitable relief"; in § 502(a)(3), Congress authorized only equitable relief. Therefore, the Court reasoned, Congress must have intended to maintain a distinction between actions in which both legal and equitable remedies were to be available, and actions in which only equitable remedies were to be available. To allow damages, the prototypical legal remedy, in an action in which the statute authorized only equitable remedies would obliterate the distinction. Therefore, Justice Scalia wrote, in using the phrase "appropriate equitable relief" Congress must have intended to refer to "those categories of relief that were typically available in equity (such as injunction, mandamus, and restitution, but not compensatory damages)." 508 U.S. at 256.

Justice Scalia's understanding of equity practice and his interpretation of ERISA have been harshly criticized:

> The main damage to ERISA remedy law was done in the Court's decision in *Mertens*, which construed "appropriate equitable relief" in section 502(a)(3) to preclude monetary damages for consequential injury on the ground that such relief was not "typical" of pre-fusion equity. I have explained why this holding entails a triple error: (1) make-whole monetary relief always was and remains routine in trust and other fields of equity; (2) there is no support for the suggestion that Congress intended the "unlikely" step of reviving pre-fusion equity practice; and (3) the suggestion that what Congress intended by its language was a category of "typically equitable" remedies is not only without foundation in the text or legislative history, but has unraveled in the application as well.
>
> The blunder that invited these errors was Justice Scalia's confusion in *Mertens* about the distinction between equitable jurisdiction and equitable relief. He rightly noted that equity courts had jurisdiction in some circumstances to award money damages in common law cases. His mistake was to infer that since "money damages are . . . the classic form of legal relief," when equity courts awarded money damages they were always awarding legal relief. That point is flatly wrong. Equity courts also awarded damages (sometimes called surcharge) as equitable relief in cases that were exclusively equitable, above all in breach of trust cases.

John H. Langbein, *What ERISA Means by "Equitable": The Supreme Court's Trail of Error in* Russell, Mertens *and* Great-West, 103 Colum.L.Rev. 1317, 1364 (2003). *See also* Colleen P. Murphy, *Money as a "Specific" Remedy*, 58 Ala.L.Rev. 119 (2006); Tracy A. Thomas, *Justice Scalia Reinvents Restitution*, 36 Loy.L.A.L.Rev. 1063 (2003).

Another legal anomaly exists in the Supreme Court's jurisprudence of front pay and backpay awards in employment discrimination cases. Here, the Court has taken a fairly expansive view of the equitable power of a court to award monetary relief in order to make the plaintiff whole. It has held that the power to award "front pay"—an award of money to replace wages lost between the time when a judgment is entered and the time the plaintiff is reinstated or, if reinstatement is not possible, finds equivalent employment—is authorized as a form of "other equitable relief," and thus is not subject to the $300,000 cap that otherwise applies to compensatory damage awards in civil rights cases. Pollard v. E.I. du Pont de Nemours & Co., 532 U.S. 843 (2001). This was because historically, employment discrimination statutes like Title VII were interpreted to provide only for equitable relief, and so courts working out of notions of equity read this expansively to fit money into this category. However, Congress later passed a new law in the Civil Rights Act of 1991 making compensatory damages and punitive damages available in Title VII and age discrimination actions, and provides for a jury trial when those damages are sought. 42 U.S.C. §§ 1981a(a), (c).

NOTE ON THE RIGHT TO A JURY TRIAL

One of the most important consequences of characterizing a remedy as legal or equitable is that the characterization may determine whether there is a right to a jury trial. The Seventh Amendment preserves the right to a jury trial "[i]n suits at common law, where the value in controversy shall exceed twenty dollars." The right extends beyond the common law forms of action, however; the phrase "suits at common law" includes any suit in which legal, as opposed to equitable, rights are at issue. Parsons v. Bedford, 28 U.S. (3 Pet.) 433, 447 (1830). The right to a jury trial applies even to causes of action created by Congress, if the cause of action is analogous to a suit at common law. Feltner v. Columbia Pictures Television, Inc., 523 U.S. 340 (1998) (recognizing right to a jury trial in an action for statutory damages under the Copyright Act); Tull v. United States, 481 U.S. 412, 417 (1987) (civil penalties).

There are two questions to be considered in deciding whether there is a right to a jury trial under a particular statute: are the rights analogous to common law rights, and is the remedy sought legal or equitable in nature? Chauffeurs, Teamsters and Helpers, Local No. 391 v. Terry, 494 U.S. 558. Of the two questions, the nature of the remedy is the more important. Granfinanciera S.A. v. Nordberg, 492 U.S. 33 (1989).

To illustrate the Court's approach to the jury trial question, in Terry the question was whether employees suing their union for failing to represent them had a right to a jury trial. The right to representation was a creature of statute, specifically section 301 of the National Labor Relations Act, unknown at common law. The Court struggled in its search for an analogous action. Writing for a plurality, Justice Marshall noted that the duty of fair representation is a fiduciary duty, and that the action was somewhat analogous to an equitable action for breach of trust. Yet, to show that the union had failed in its duty to enforce the labor agreement, the employees would first need to show that the employer had breached it. Therefore, the action was a hybrid, part legal—breach of contract—and part equitable—breach of fiduciary duty—in nature. (Justice Stevens thought the action more comparable to a legal malpractice claim, the three dissenting Justices thought the similarity to the equitable trust action was dispositive, and Justice Brennan thought the analysis should focus exclusively on the nature of the remedy sought, which he thought was legal in this case.)

As for the character of the remedy, Justice Marshall—writing for a majority of the Court on this point—concluded that the remedy sought, back pay and benefits, was essentially equivalent to compensatory damages. Because compensatory damages represented the traditional form of relief offered in courts of law, either party could demand a jury trial. While monetary relief might be characterized as equitable where it is "restitutionary, such as in actions for disgorgement of improper profits," or where it is "incidental to or intertwined with injunctive relief," neither exception was applicable in Terry. Therefore, as the issues in the case were neither clearly equitable nor clearly legal, the legal character of the relief sought was controlling, and the plaintiffs had a right to a jury trial. See also City of Monterey v. Del Monte Dunes, Ltd., 526 U.S. 687, 710 (1999) (recognizing right to a jury trial in suits seeking compensation for a regulatory taking, because compensation is legal relief, which "differs from equitable restitution and other monetary remedies available in equity, for in determining just compensation, the question is what has the owner lost, not what has the taker gained").

NOTE ON ELECTION OF REMEDIES

When multiple remedies are possible, the doctrine of "election of remedies" may come into play. The traditional formulation of the doctrine had two parts: (1) a plaintiff who has two (or more) remedies concurrently available to her must choose between those remedies if they are inconsistent; and (2) once a plaintiff has clearly elected a remedy, he or she is bound by that choice.

This traditional formulation of the rule could work harsh results. For example, the doctrine of election of remedies could put a plaintiff whose property had been converted to a very difficult choice. He could try to retrieve the property by a writ of replevin, but, having elected his remedy, he might not then be allowed to sue for consequential damages for the loss of his property's use. Or, he could sue for damages, but if the defendant turned out to have no assets to satisfy the judgment, he might be unable to get his stolen property back, having elected damages as his remedy.

Such a result might have made sense in a legal system that placed a high value on precise pleadings intended to narrow the case to a single issue for trial. It seems ludicrous in the modern system of notice pleading, in which multiple causes of action and liberal amendment are commonplace. Thus, modern courts have sharply curtailed and simplified the election of remedies doctrine.

So far as the first prong of the election doctrine is concerned, modern courts have shifted the emphasis from whether the remedies are different in form to asking whether allowing both remedies will result in double recovery or overcompensation. The cases now recognize that there is no reason not to allow a plaintiff to recover the specific property taken and also to recover damages for loss of the property's use. On the other hand, if allowing two remedies would put the plaintiff in better than the rightful position, clearly a choice must be made.

The second prong of the traditional doctrine had to do with the timing of the choice. If a plaintiff indicated, by his pleadings or even by his actions, that he intended to pursue a particular remedy, he might be bound by that choice and precluded from pursuing an alternative, inconsistent remedy. This insistence that a plaintiff had to stick with his first choice of remedy also could work harshly, by forcing plaintiffs to commit themselves to a remedy long before all the facts were in, or by interpreting acts that were not intended as a choice of remedy as manifesting an election.

Again, the modern cases have substantially reinterpreted the rule, emphasizing that the timing of the plaintiff's choice is relevant only to the extent that the choice—or the failure to choose—may harm the defendant. This aspect of the doctrine of election of remedies is effectively a variation on the doctrine of estoppel. If the plaintiff indicates that he will pursue one remedy, and it would prejudice the defendant to allow the plaintiff to change his mind, the court may find that the plaintiff has elected his remedy. If the plaintiff has not chosen, and the defendant is prejudiced by the delay, the court may put plaintiff to the choice, or choose for him in a way that will minimize the harm. If there is no harm to the defendant, however, there is no reason not to allow the plaintiff to pursue as many remedies as he wishes, even adding new theories up to the time of trial, so long as the pleading rules allow it. Thus, a plaintiff may generally now combine different forms of remedy—legal and equitable, damages and restitution—so long as the combination does not result in double recovery or overcompensation.

B. ELEMENTS OF LOSS

Turning to compensatory damages, after the cause of action has been determined, one can begin to zero in on the elements of damages that may be recoverable. For starters, the client usually will have a very clear idea of what losses she wants to recoup. These factual losses and the client's desires are the beginning of identifying the available damages and working through discovery to prove and quantify the amounts.

The next step is to look to the case law to determine which of these losses are compensable, that is, which is a proper element of damages for the plaintiff's cause of action. Here, an important distinction has developed in the cases between two categories of damages—general damages and consequential damages. *General or direct damages* are defined as those damages which typically flow from the defendant's wrongful act as the primary loss. *Consequential or special damages,* by contrast, are damages that are secondary to the typical loss and are more specific to the particular plaintiff's circumstances. ("Special" damages is the more antiquated term, and now has a separate meaning under modern trial practice for damages that must be specified for the jury prior to trial.) For example, if the defendant were held liable for destroying the plaintiff's car, the general damages would be the value of the car: any time property is destroyed, its value is lost. If the plaintiff, however, lost his job because without a car he was late for work, damages to compensate him for the loss of his job would be recoverable only as consequential damages, if at all. That loss is peculiar to his particular circumstances; it does not "naturally" flow from the destruction of a car in most cases.

The law assumes that general damages will adequately compensate the plaintiff; after all, general damages evolved because those losses were the ones most frequently experienced. General damages, however, are not always an accurate measure of actual loss. In particular cases, general damages may undercompensate the plaintiff because the plaintiff has suffered losses peculiar to her own circumstances and which are not included in the general damages. Returning to the example, the plaintiff who has lost her job because her car was destroyed will be undercompensated if she is limited to recovering the market value of the car. Thus, for her the critical step will be to determine if the loss of her job is compensable as consequential damages.

Whether consequential damages are recoverable turns on the application of the doctrines of *foreseeability, certainty*, and *avoidable consequences*. The courts are suspicious of consequential damages which are secondary and atypical, and concerned that compensating for them might result in a windfall to the plaintiff beyond her rightful position. Thus, courts have developed rules limiting recovery of damages to those which are foreseeable, certain, and not avoidable.

Foreseeability: Compensatory damages must be foreseeable, which means that they are reasonably expected to be within the knowledge of the defendant. Dan B. Dobbs, *The Law of Remedies* § 3.3 (2d ed.1993); e.g., UCC § 2–715(2). The foreseeability requirement focuses on the defendant's imputed awareness of the potential consequences at stake. ("Consequential damages resulting from the seller's breach include, (a) any loss resulting from general or particular requirements and needs of which the seller at the time of contracting had reason to know * * * "). Conversely, damages are not foreseeable when they are too remote, too far removed from the defendant's knowledge or general or particularized knowledge of potential loss. General damages are foreseeable by definition, because they are naturally expected to flow from the defendant's act. It is consequential damages which often encounter the limitation and must be proven to have been foreseeable.

In contract, the role of foreseeability in awarding consequential damages begins with Hadley v. Baxendale, 156 Eng.Rep. 145 (1854), a fixture of the basic course in contracts. In *Hadley,* the defendant breached a contract to deliver a mill shaft to be repaired. The delay that resulted caused the mill owner to lose profits, because his mill was unable to operate without the shaft. Yet the court denied the mill owner recovery, because the loss of profits was unforeseeable:

> When two parties have made a contract which one of them has broken, the damages which the other party ought to receive in respect of such breach of contract should be such as may fairly and reasonably be considered either arising naturally, i.e.,

according to usual course of things, from such breach of contract itself, or such as may reasonably be supposed to have been in the contemplation of both parties, at the time they made the contract as the probable result of the breach of it. Now, if the special circumstances under which the contract was actually made were communicated by the plaintiffs to the defendants, and thus known to both parties, the damages resulting from the breach of such a contract, which they would reasonably contemplate, would be the amount of the injury which would ordinarily follow from a breach of contract under these special circumstances so known and communicated.

156 Eng.Rep. at 151.

The Restatement (Second) of Contracts § 351, states the settled rule:

(2) Loss may be foreseeable as a probable result of a breach because it follows from the breach

    (a) in the ordinary course of events

    (b) as a result of special circumstances, beyond the ordinary course of events, that the party in breach had reason to know.

(3) A court may limit damages for foreseeable loss by excluding recovery for loss of profits, by allowing recovery only for loss incurred in reliance, or otherwise, if it concludes that in the circumstances justice so requires in order to avoid disproportionate compensation

In torts, foreseeability is often a question first for the substantive law, often framed as an issue of proximate causation. Palsgraf v. Long Island Railroad Co., 248 N.Y. 339, 162 N.E. 99 (N.Y. 1928). The plaintiff must be foreseeable before the defendant owes her a duty. Some harm must be foreseeable before the defendant's behavior will be labeled negligent. If the injury that results was unforeseeable, the court may declare it too remote to be considered proximately caused by the defendant's conduct.

Once a cause of action in tort has been established, the general rule has been that if the type of harm the plaintiff suffered was foreseeable, the extent of the harm need not have been. The classic case is McCahill v. New York Transportation Co., 201 N.Y. 221, 94 N.E. 616 (1911), in which the plaintiff was so weakened by his preexisting alcoholism that he unexpectedly died from the relatively minor injuries the defendant caused. Because of the rule that "you take your plaintiff as you find him" (also known as the "eggshell" or "thin skull" plaintiff rule), the defendant was liable for the plaintiff's death, although the death was unforeseeable. Foreseeability can be an issue, however, when a plaintiff attempts to recover damages for an injury that is different in kind, not merely in extent, from the injury that gave rise to his cause of action.

Certainty: The plaintiff must also prove the amount of her losses with reasonable certainty. Restatement (Second) of Torts § 912. As the Restatement (Second) of Contracts § 352 provides damages can be recovered "only to the extent that the evidence affords a sufficient basis for estimating their amount in money with reasonable certainty."

The certainty requirement has two aspects. The first overlaps with the substantive law of causation. The plaintiff must show that it is reasonably certain (or probable) that she has suffered a loss because of the defendant's conduct. The second aspect is evidentiary. Once the fact of loss is established, she then must provide the jury with evidence from which the amount of her loss can be established with "reasonable certainty." Courts are wont to say that if the existence of a loss is clearly shown, the plaintiff must merely provide the jury with the best evidence reasonably available of the amount. So long as it is certain that the plaintiff has actually suffered a loss, the certainty rule simply requires her to provide some evidence from which the jury can make a reasonable, non-speculative estimate of the amount of her damages. Questions regarding certainty often come up in contracts cases regarding the lost profits of a new, untested business venture.

Not Avoidable: The plaintiff may not recover damages for any losses that could reasonably have been avoided. Restatement (Second) of Contracts § 350; UCC § 2–715(1) (consequential damages which "could not reasonably be avoided by cover or otherwise" may be recovered). This rule requires the plaintiff to mitigate her damages by taking reasonable steps to limit the harm she suffers. Restatement (Second) of Torts § 918. In contract, the usual effect of the avoidable consequences rule is to promote cover, to give plaintiffs the incentive to continue to pursue their presumably profitable enterprises by obtaining an equivalent performance from someone else. In tort, if for example, the defendant has wrongfully caused the plaintiff to lose her job, the plaintiff must make a reasonable effort to find other, similar work if she wishes to claim lost wages. If the plaintiff is physically injured, she will not recover damages for any aggravation of the injury that medical care reasonably available to her could have avoided. Although the avoidable consequences rule may often function to limit the plaintiff's recovery, it has a positive aspect as well. Any expenses incurred by the plaintiff in a reasonable attempt to mitigate her losses are recoverable as damages.

There is two other practical limitations on recovery for damages. The first is for *offsetting benefits*. If the defendant's conduct has caused harm to the plaintiff, but at the same time has conferred a benefit on the plaintiff, under appropriate circumstances the plaintiff's recovery must be reduced by the amount of the benefit she has received. Restatement (Second) of Torts § 920; Restatement (Second) of Contracts § 347, comment e. For example, if a doctor performs an unauthorized operation that actually improves the plaintiff's health, the amount of damages the plaintiff recovers from the doctor will be reduced by the amount of benefit conferred. *Id.* comment a, illustration 1.

The second practical limitation is the rule against *double recovery*. A plaintiff cannot recover damages for a future harm she has remedied with an injunction. Nor can he recover two measures representing the same factual loss. These would both duplicate the plaintiff's recovery and create a windfall in violation of the rightful position.

EVRA CORP. v. SWISS BANK CORP.

United States Court of Appeals, Seventh Circuit
673 F.2d 951 (1982), *cert. denied*, 459 U.S. 1017

POSNER, CIRCUIT JUDGE.

The question—one of first impression—in this diversity case is the extent of a bank's liability for failure to make a transfer of funds when requested by wire to do so. The essential facts are undisputed. In 1972 Hyman-Michaels Company, a large Chicago dealer in scrap metal, entered into a two-year contract to supply steel scrap to a Brazilian corporation. Hyman-Michaels chartered a ship, the Pandora, to carry the scrap to Brazil. The charter was for one year, with an option to extend the charter for a second year; specified a fixed daily rate of pay for the hire of the ship during both the initial and the option period, payable semi-monthly "in advance"; and provided that if payment was not made on time the Pandora's owner could cancel the charter. Payment was to be made by deposit to the owner's account in the Banque de Paris et des Pays-Bas (Suisse) in Geneva, Switzerland.

The usual method by which Hyman-Michaels, in Chicago, got the payments to the Banque de Paris in Geneva was to request the Continental Illinois National Bank and Trust Company of Chicago, where it had an account, to make a wire transfer of funds. Continental would debit Hyman-Michaels' account by the amount of the payment and then send a telex to its London office for retransmission to its correspondent bank in Geneva— Swiss Bank Corporation—asking Swiss Bank to deposit this amount in the Banque de Paris account of the Pandora's owner. The transaction was completed by the crediting of Swiss Bank's account at Continental by the same amount.

When Hyman-Michaels chartered the Pandora in June 1972, market charter rates were very low, and it was these rates that were fixed in the charter for its entire term-two years if Hyman-Michaels exercised its option. Shortly after the agreement was signed, however, charter rates began to climb and by October 1972 they were much higher than they had been in June. The Pandora's owners were eager to get out of the charter if they could. At the end of October they thought they had found a way, for the payment that was due in the Banque de Paris on October 26 had not arrived by October 30, and on that day the Pandora's owner notified Hyman-Michaels that it was canceling the charter because of the breach of the payment term. Hyman-Michaels had mailed a check for the October 26 installment to the Banque de Paris rather than use the wire-transfer method of payment. It had done this in order to have the use of its money for the period that it would take the check to clear, about two weeks. But the check had not been mailed in Chicago until October 25 and of course did not reach Geneva on the twenty-sixth.

When Hyman-Michaels received notification that the charter was being canceled it immediately wired payment to the Banque de Paris, but the Pandora's owner refused to accept it and insisted that the charter was indeed canceled. The matter was referred to arbitration in accordance with the charter. On December 5, 1972, the arbitration panel ruled in favor of Hyman-Michaels. The panel noted that previous arbitration panels had "shown varying degrees of latitude to Charterers":

> In all cases, a pattern of obligation on Owners' part to protest, complain, or warn of intended withdrawal was expressed as an essential prerequisite to withdrawal, in spite of the clear wording of the operative clause. No such advance notice was given by Owners of M/V Pandora.

One of the three members of the panel dissented; he thought the Pandora's owner was entitled to cancel.

Hyman-Michaels went back to making the charter payments by wire transfer. On the morning of April 25, 1973, it telephoned Continental Bank and requested it to transfer $27,000 to the Banque de Paris account of the Pandora's owner in payment for the charter hire period from April 27 to May 11, 1973. Since the charter provided for payment "in advance," this payment arguably was due by the close of business on April 26. The requested telex went out to Continental's London office on the afternoon of April 25, which was nighttime in England. Early the next morning a telex operator in Continental's London office dialed, as Continental's Chicago office had instructed him to do, Swiss Bank's general telex number, which rings in the bank's cable department. But that number was busy, and after trying unsuccessfully for an hour to engage it the Continental telex operator dialed another number, that of a machine in Swiss Bank's foreign exchange department which he had used in the past when the general number was engaged. We know this machine received the telexed message because it signaled the sending machine at both the beginning and end of the transmission that the telex was being received. Yet Swiss Bank failed to comply with the payment order, and no transfer of funds was made to the account of the Pandora's owner in the Banque de Paris.

No one knows exactly what went wrong. One possibility is that the receiving telex machine had simply run out of paper, in which event it would not print the message although it had received it. Another is that whoever took the message out of the machine after it was printed failed to deliver it to the banking department. Unlike the machine in the cable department that the Continental telex operator had originally tried to reach, the machines in the foreign exchange department were operated by junior foreign exchange dealers rather than by professional telex operators, although Swiss Bank knew that messages intended for other departments were sometimes diverted to the telex machines in the foreign exchange department.

At 8:30 a.m. the next day, April 27, Hyman-Michaels in Chicago received a telex from the Pandora's owner stating that the charter was canceled because payment for the April 27–May 11 charter period had not been made. Hyman-Michaels called over to Continental and told them to keep trying to effect payment through Swiss Bank even if the Pandora's owner rejected it. This instruction was confirmed in a letter to Continental dated April 28, in which Hyman-Michaels stated: "please instruct your London branch to advise their correspondents to persist in attempting to make this payment. This should be done even in the face of a rejection on the part of Banque de Paris to receive this payment. It is paramount that in order to strengthen our position in an arbitration that these funds continue to be readily available." Hyman-Michaels did not attempt to wire the money directly to the Banque de Paris as it had done on the occasion of its previous default. Days passed while the missing telex message was hunted unsuccessfully. Finally Swiss Bank suggested to Continental that it retransmit the telex message to the machine in the cable department and this was done on May 1. The next day Swiss Bank attempted to deposit the $27,000 in the account of the Pandora's owner at the Banque de Paris but the payment was refused.

Again the arbitrators were convened and rendered a decision. In it they ruled that Hyman-Michaels had been "blameless" up until the morning of April 27, when it first learned that the Banque de Paris had not received payment on April 26, but that "being faced with this situation," Hyman-Michaels had "failed to do everything in [its] power to remedy it. The action taken was immediate but did not prove to be adequate, in that [Continental] Bank and its correspondent required some 5–6 days to trace and effect the lost instruction to remit. [Hyman-Michaels] could have ordered an immediate duplicate payment—or even sent a Banker's check by hand or special messengers, so that the funds could have reached owner's Bank, not later than April 28th." By failing to do any of these things Hyman-Michaels had "created the opening" that the Pandora's owner was seeking in order to be able to cancel the charter. It had "acted imprudently." The arbitration panel concluded, reluctantly but unanimously, that this time the Pandora's owner was entitled to cancel the agreement. * * *

Hyman-Michaels then brought this diversity action against Swiss Bank, seeking to recover its expenses in the second arbitration proceeding plus the profits that it lost because of the cancellation of the charter. The contract by which Hyman-Michaels had agreed to ship scrap steel to Brazil had been terminated by the buyer in March 1973 and Hyman-Michaels had promptly subchartered the Pandora at market rates, which by April 1973 were double the rates fixed in the charter. Its lost profits are based on the difference between the charter and subcharter rates. * * *

The case was tried to a district judge without a jury. [The judge ruled that] under Illinois law [Swiss Bank] was liable to Hyman-Michaels for $2.1 million in damages. This figure was made up of about $16,000 in arbitration expenses and the rest in lost profits on the subcharter of the Pandora. * * *

When a bank fails to make a requested transfer of funds, this can cause two kinds of loss. First, the funds themselves or interest on them may be lost, and of course the fee paid for the transfer, having bought nothing, becomes a loss item. These are "direct" (sometimes called "general") damages. Hyman-Michaels is not seeking any direct damages in this case and apparently sustained none. It did not lose any part of the $27,000; although its account with Continental Bank was debited by this amount prematurely, it was not an interest-bearing account so Hyman-Michaels lost no interest; and Hyman-Michaels paid no fee either to Continental or to Swiss Bank for the aborted transfer. A second type of loss, which either the payor or the payee may suffer, is a dislocation in one's business triggered by the failure to pay. Swiss Bank's failure to transfer funds to the Banque de Paris when requested to do so by Continental Bank set off a chain reaction which resulted in an arbitration proceeding that was costly to Hyman-Michaels and in the cancellation of a highly profitable contract. It is those costs and lost profits—"consequential" or, as they are sometimes called, "special" damages—that Hyman-Michaels seeks in this lawsuit, and recovered below. It is conceded that if Hyman-Michaels was entitled to consequential damages, the district court measured them correctly. The only issue is whether it was entitled to consequential damages. * * *

The rule of *Hadley v. Baxendale*—that consequential damages will not be awarded unless the defendant was put on notice of the special circumstances giving rise to them—has been applied in many Illinois cases, and *Hadley* cited approvingly. In Siegel v. Western Union Tel. Co., 312 Ill.App. 86, 92B93, 37 N.E.2d 868, 871 (1941), the plaintiff had delivered $200 to Western Union with instructions to transmit it to a friend of the plaintiff's. The money was to be bet (legally) on a horse, but this was not disclosed in the instructions. Western Union misdirected the money order and it did not reach the friend until several hours after the race had taken place. The horse that the plaintiff had intended to bet on won and would have paid $1650 on the plaintiff's $200 bet if the bet had been placed. He sued Western Union for his $1450 lost profit, but the court held that under the rule of *Hadley v. Baxendale*, Western Union was not liable, because it "had no notice or knowledge of the purpose for which the money was being transmitted."

The present case is similar, though Swiss Bank knew more than Western Union knew in *Siegel;* it knew or should have known, from Continental Bank's previous telexes, that Hyman-Michaels was paying the Pandora Shipping Company for the hire of a motor vessel named Pandora. But it did not know when payment was due, what the terms of the charter were, or that they had turned out to be extremely favorable to Hyman-Michaels. And it did not know that Hyman-Michaels knew the Pandora's owner would try to cancel the charter, and probably would succeed, if Hyman-Michaels was ever again late in making payment, or that despite this peril Hyman-Michaels would not try to pay until the last possible moment and in the event of a delay in transmission would not do everything in its power to minimize the consequences of the delay. Electronic funds transfers are not so unusual as to automatically place a bank on notice of extraordinary consequences if such a transfer goes awry. Swiss Bank did not have enough information to infer that if it lost a $27,000 payment order it would face a liability in excess of $2 million. * * *

[W]e conclude . . . that Swiss Bank is not liable for the consequences of negligently failing to transfer Hyman-Michaels' funds to Banque de Paris; reason for such a holding is found in the animating principle of *Hadley v. Baxendale*, which is that the costs of the untoward consequence of a course of dealings should be borne by that party who was able to avert the consequence at least cost and failed to do so. In *Hadley* the untoward consequence was the shutting down of the mill. The carrier could have avoided it by delivering the engine shaft on time. But the mill owners, as the court noted, could have avoided it simply by having a spare shaft. Prudence required that they have a spare shaft anyway, since a replacement could not be obtained at once even if there was no undue delay in carting the broken shaft to and the replacement shaft from the manufacturer. The court refused to imply a duty on the part of the carrier to guarantee the mill owners against the consequences of their own lack of prudence, though of course if the parties had stipulated for such a guarantee the court would have enforced it. The notice requirement of *Hadley v. Baxendale* is designed to assure that such an improbable guarantee really is intended.

This case is much the same, though it arises in a tort rather than a contract setting. Hyman-Michaels showed a lack of prudence throughout. It was imprudent for it to mail in Chicago a letter that unless received the next day in Geneva would put Hyman-Michaels in breach of a contract that was very profitable to it and that the other party to the contract had every interest in canceling. It was imprudent thereafter for Hyman-Michaels, having narrowly avoided cancellation and having (in the words of its appeal brief in this court) been "put . . . on notice that the payment provision of the Charter would be strictly enforced thereafter," to wait till [sic] arguably the last day before payment was due to instruct its bank to transfer the necessary funds overseas. And it was imprudent in the last degree for Hyman-Michaels, when it received notice of cancellation on the last possible day payment was due, to fail to pull out all the stops to get payment to the Banque de Paris on that day, and instead to dither while Continental and Swiss Bank wasted five days looking for the lost telex message. Judging from the obvious reluctance with which the arbitration panel finally decided to allow the Pandora's owner to cancel the charter, it might have made all the difference if Hyman-Michaels had gotten payment to the Banque de Paris by April 27 or even by Monday, April 30, rather than allowed things to slide until May 2.

This is not to condone the sloppy handling of incoming telex messages in Swiss Bank's foreign department. But Hyman-Michaels is a sophisticated business enterprise. It knew or should have known that even the Swiss are not infallible; that messages sometimes get lost or delayed in transit among three banks, two of them located 5000 miles apart, even when all the banks are using reasonable care; and that therefore it should take its own precautions against the consequences—best known to itself—of a mishap that might not be due to anyone's negligence.

We are not the first to remark the affinity between the rule of *Hadley v. Baxendale* and the doctrine, which is one of tort as well as contract law and is a settled part of the common law of Illinois, of avoidable consequences. If you are hurt in an automobile accident and unreasonably fail to seek medical treatment, the injurer, even if negligent, will not be held liable for the aggravation of the injury due to your own unreasonable behavior after the accident. If in addition you failed to fasten your seat belt, you may be barred from collecting the tort damages that would have been prevented if you had done so. Hyman-Michaels' behavior in steering close to the wind prior to April 27 was like not fastening one's seat belt; its failure on April 27 to wire a duplicate payment immediately after disaster struck was like refusing to seek medical attention after a serious accident. The seat-belt cases show that the doctrine of avoidable consequences applies whether the tort victim acts imprudently before or after the tort is committed.

The rule of *Hadley v. Baxendale* links up with tort concepts in another way. The rule is sometimes stated in the form that only foreseeable damages are recoverable in a breach of contract action. So expressed, it corresponds to the tort principle that limits liability to the foreseeable consequence of the defendant's carelessness. The amount of care that a person ought to take is a function of the probability and magnitude of the harm that may occur if he does not take care. If he does not know what that probability and magnitude are, he cannot determine how much care to take. That would be Swiss Bank's dilemma if it were liable for consequential damages from failing to carry out payment orders in timely fashion. To estimate the extent of its probable liability in order to know how many and how elaborate fail-safe features to install in its telex rooms or how much insurance to buy against the inevitable failures, Swiss Bank would have to collect reams of information about firms that are not even its regular customers. It had no banking relationship with Hyman-Michaels. It did not know or have reason to know how at once precious and fragile Hyman-Michaels' contract with the Pandora's owner was. These were circumstances too remote from Swiss Bank's practical range of knowledge to have affected its decisions as to who should man the telex machines in the foreign department or whether it should have more intelligent machines or should install more machines in the cable department, any more than the falling of a platform scale because a conductor jostled a passenger who was carrying fireworks was a prospect that could have influenced the amount of care taken by the Long Island Railroad. See Palsgraf v. Long Island R.R., 248 N.Y. 339, 162 N.E. 99 (1928).

In short, Swiss Bank was not required in the absence of a contractual undertaking to take precautions or insure against a harm that it could not measure but that was known with precision to Hyman-Michaels, which could by the exercise of common prudence have averted it completely. As Chief Judge Cardozo (the author of *Palsgraf*) remarked in discussing the application of *Hadley v. Baxendale* to the liability of telegraph companies for errors in transmission, "The sender can protect himself by insurance in one form or another if the risk of nondelivery or error appears to be too great. . . . The company, if it takes out insurance for itself, can do no more than guess at the loss to be avoided." Kerr S.S. Co. v. Radio Corp. of America, 245 N.Y. 284, 291–92, 157 N.E. 140, 142 (1927). * * *

The legal principles that we have said are applicable to this case were not applied below. Although the district judge's opinion is not entirely clear, he apparently thought the rule of *Hadley v. Baxendale* inapplicable and the imprudence of Hyman-Michaels irrelevant. He did state that the damages to Hyman-Michaels were foreseeable because "a major international bank" should know that a failure to act promptly on a telexed request to transfer funds could cause substantial damage; but *Siegel* * * * make[s] clear that that kind of general foreseeability, which is present in virtually every case, does not justify an award of consequential damages.

* * * The undisputed facts, recited in this opinion, show as a matter of law that Hyman-Michaels is not entitled to recover consequential damages from Swiss Bank. * * *

NOTES

1.   Both tort and contract rely on foreseeability to limit liability for remote losses. In contract, foreseeability is defined by *Hadley v. Baxendale*: the party charged with liability must be on notice of the special circumstances giving rise to the loss. See also UCC § 2–715(2) ("Consequential damages resulting from the seller's breach include, (a) any loss resulting from general or particular requirements and needs of which the seller at the time of contracting had reason to know * * * "). In tort, foreseeability casts its net farther: so long as the type of harm that occurs is foreseeable, the extent of harm or the manner in which it occurs is irrelevant. A defendant whose negligence causes harm will be liable for all the consequences that follow, so long as the damage that occurs is of the same general sort, from the same physical forces as the harm that was foreseeable. *See, e.g.,* Petition of Kinsman Transit Co., 338 F.2d 708 (2d Cir.1964).

2.   Economic explanations of *Hadley v. Baxendale* usually focus on how the rule promotes efficiency by giving the party who has better information about what is at stake an incentive to share that information. Then, the parties can bargain over who will take precautions against that loss, and at what cost. Knowing what steps to take to avoid a loss, however, requires two sorts of information: information about the size of the loss, and information about how likely the loss is to occur. In most contract contexts, it makes sense to encourage the party in possession of information about the size of the loss to disclose, because few promisors are likely to disclose candidly the probability that they will fail to perform. *See* Benjamin E. Hermalin et al., *Contract Law* in A. Mitchell Polinsky & Steven Shavell, 1 *Handbook of Law and Economics* (2007).

DILLON v. EVANSTON HOSPITAL

Supreme Court of Illinois
771 N.E.2d 357 (Ill. 2002)

JUSTICE FREEMAN delivered the opinion of the court.

[The plaintiff brought a medical malpractice action against Dr. Sener, Evanston Hospital, and others. The trial court found that Dr. Sener negligently failed to completely remove a catheter that he had inserted in patient's vein as means to administer chemotherapy. The catheter migrated to plaintiff's heart.]

* * *

V. DAMAGES: INCREASED RISK OF FUTURE INJURY

Dr. Sener and the hospital next contend that the trial court erred in instructing the jury that it could award plaintiff damages for "[t]he increased risk of future injuries." * * *

There was evidence presented at trial establishing the proximate causal connection between the actions of Dr. Sener and the hospital and the catheter fragment becoming embedded in plaintiff's heart. On medical advice, plaintiff chose not to attempt removal of the fragment. All the expert witnesses but one believed that the risks of injury from an attempted removal of the fragment outweighed the risks that would exist if the catheter remained in the heart. The attendant risks of the catheter remaining were infection, perforation of the heart, arrhythmia, embolization, and further migration of the fragment. At the time of trial, plaintiff had not suffered from any of these conditions, although she did suffer from anxiety over the fragment's presence.

The evidence was that it was not reasonably certain that plaintiff would in the future suffer the injuries for which she was at risk due to the fragment's presence in her heart. Several physicians testified about the risk of infection, with the lowest estimated risk being close to zero and the highest being 20%. The risk of arrhythmia was less than 5%. The risks of perforation and migration were also small. The risk of embolization was low to nonexistent.

The jury instruction that addressed compensation for plaintiff's increased risks stated in relevant part:

> If you decide for the plaintiff on the question of liability, you must then fix the amount of money which will reasonably and fairly compensate her for any of the following elements of damages proved by the evidence to have resulted from the negligence of one or more of the defendants, taking into consideration the nature, extent, and duration of the injury:

> *The increased risk of future injuries.*

> The pain and suffering experienced and reasonably certain to be experienced in the future as a result of the injuries.

(Emphasis added.)

* * *

The jury awarded plaintiff $500,000 for her increased risk of future injuries. * * *

This court has historically rejected assessing damages for future injuries. This court has explained: "It would be plainly unjust to require a defendant to pay damages for results that may or may not ensue and that are merely problematical. To justify a recovery for future damages the law requires proof of a reasonable certainty that they will be endured in the future." [This position] represents the majority rule.

* * *

Not all jurisdictions follow the majority rule. For example, in Petriello v. Kalman, 215 Conn. 377, 576 A.2d 474 (1990), the Supreme Court of Connecticut provided an analysis that revealed the problems inherent with the majority approach. That court criticized the "all-or-nothing" approach as follows:

> "In essence, if a plaintiff can prove that there exists a 51 percent chance that his injury is permanent or that future injury will result, he may receive full compensation for that injury as if it were a certainty. If, however, the plaintiff establishes only a 49 percent chance of such a consequence, he may recover nothing for the risk to which he is presently exposed. Although this all or nothing view has been adopted by a majority of courts faced with the issue, the concept has been severely criticized by numerous commentators. By denying any compensation unless a plaintiff proves that a future consequence is more likely to occur than not, courts have created a system in which a significant number of persons receive compensation for future consequences that never occur and, conversely, a significant number of persons receive no compensation at all for consequences that later ensue from risks not rising to the level of probability. This system is inconsistent with the goal of compensating tort victims fairly for all the consequences of the injuries they have sustained, while avoiding, so far as possible, windfall awards for consequences that never happen."

Petriello, 215 Conn. at 393–94, 576 A.2d at 482–83.

* * * Our review of cases from other jurisdictions indicates a trend toward allowing compensation for increased risk of future injury as long as it can be shown to a reasonable degree of certainty that the defendant's wrongdoing created the increased risk.

* * *

[We] believe that the Connecticut court's approach to this issue better comports with this state's principle of single recovery. An entire claim arising from a single tort cannot be divided and be the subject of several actions, regardless of whether or not the plaintiff has recovered all that he or she might have recovered. This is true even as to prospective damages. There cannot be successive actions brought for a single tort as damages in the future are suffered, but the one action must embrace prospective as well as accrued damages. * * *

Also, this court has previously held in a different context:

"There is nothing novel about requiring health care professionals to compensate patients who are negligently injured while in their care. To the extent a plaintiff's chance of recovery or survival is lessened by the malpractice, he or she should be able to present evidence to a jury that the defendant's malpractice, to a reasonable degree of medical certainty, proximately caused the increased risk of harm or lost chance of recovery. We therefore reject the reasoning of cases which hold, as a matter of law, that plaintiffs may not recover for medical malpractice injuries if they are unable to prove that they would have enjoyed a greater than 50% chance of survival or recovery absent the alleged malpractice of the defendant. To hold otherwise would free health care providers from legal responsibility for even the grossest acts of negligence, as long as the patient upon whom the malpractice was performed already suffered an illness or injury that could be quantified by experts as affording that patient less than a 50% chance of recovering his or her health."

Holton v. Memorial Hospital, 679 N.E.2d 1202 (1997).

The theories of lost chance of recovery and increased risk of future injury have similar theoretical underpinnings. * * *

Accordingly, we hold simply that a plaintiff must be permitted to recover for all demonstrated injuries. The burden is on the plaintiff to prove that the defendant's negligence increased the plaintiff's risk of future injuries. A plaintiff can obtain compensation for a future injury that is not reasonably certain to occur, but the compensation would reflect the low probability of occurrence. * * * "The defendant's proper remedy lies in objecting to the excessiveness of the verdict in an appropriate case."

Having determined that this element of damages is compensable, we now consider whether the jury was properly instructed thereon. * * * [We] conclude that the instruction which the jury received on this element of damages did not adequately state the law. * * *

[The] instruction fails to instruct the jury on several important legal requirements, e.g., the increased risk must be based on evidence and not speculation, and, more importantly, the size of the award must reflect the probability of occurrence. * * * Accordingly, we reverse plaintiff's damages award for the increased risk of future injury, and remand the cause to the trial court for a new trial solely on that element of damages.

NOTE

As *Dillon* notes, courts have shown increasing acceptance of probabilistic recovery, particularly in medical malpractice cases. When doctors misdiagnose an illness and deny the plaintiff the opportunity to undergo treatment, many courts allow the plaintiff to recover damages even if the treatment she was denied is successful much less than half the time. *See* Alexander v. Scheid, 726 N.E.2d 272, 277 (Ind.2000) (physician who negligently failed to diagnose lung cancer liable for increased risk of harm); Roberts v. Ohio Permanente Medical Group, 76 Ohio St.3d 483, 668 N.E.2d 480 (1996) (delay in diagnosis of lung cancer deprived plaintiff of a less than 50% chance of survival, proportional recovery allowed); Delaney v. Cade, 255 Kan. 199, 873 P.2d 175, 177–78, 182 (Kan.1994) (allowing paraplegic plaintiff to recover where risk of spinal cord injury was increased five to ten percent by prolonged period of shock following car accident and prior to surgery).

MUNN v. SOUTHERN HEALTH PLAN, INC.

United States District Court
719 F.Supp. 525 (N.D. Miss. 1989), *aff'd*, 924 F.2d 568 (5th Cir.), *cert. denied*, 502 U.S. 900 (1991)

L.T. SENTER, JR., CHIEF UNITED STATES DISTRICT JUDGE.

This wrongful death case presents some of the most difficult questions which this court has ever been asked to resolve. The case arose from an automobile accident which the defendant admits resulted from her negligence in attempting to pass another vehicle in dense fog. The plaintiff's wife was severely injured as a result of the collision and died approximately two hours after the accident. The problem arises because the plaintiff and his wife, both adherents to the Jehovah's Witness faith, refused on religious grounds to allow the doctors who were treating Mrs. Munn to administer a blood transfusion which the defendant contends would have saved her life.

The defendant seeks summary judgment to the effect that if the jury should find, for whatever reason, that she is not liable for damages for Mrs. Munn's death, then the plaintiff is not entitled to recover for any prospective harm beyond the point of Mrs. Munn's death. Because the answer to this question depends, at least in part, upon the legal doctrine which is to be applied to the facts of this case, the court will begin by attempting to resolve that issue.

The defendant has raised three theories which she insists apply under the facts of this case to bar, at least in part, the plaintiff's recovery. These are contributory negligence, assumption of the risk, and the doctrine of avoidable consequences. Only the latter of these clearly applies to the facts of this case.

The doctrine of avoidable consequences, sometimes referred to as the duty of the plaintiff to mitigate damages, "functions as a negative rule, denying an injured person recovery of damages for any reasonably avoidable consequences of the injury." The basic rule is that the plaintiff may not recover from the defendant for injuries which flow from the defendant's wrongful conduct but which could have been avoided by the plaintiff's availing herself of reasonable measures to limit the harm. Simply stated, once the injury has occurred, the plaintiff may not stand idly by and allow her damages to accumulate when she could take reasonable steps to minimize them. The doctrine of avoidable consequences comes into play only after the defendant has committed the wrongful act, but at a time when the plaintiff still has an opportunity to avoid the consequences in whole or in part. * * *

The doctrine is often referred to as the plaintiff's duty to mitigate damages, but such reference lacks legal precision and can lead to confusion with other concepts in the law of damages. The doctrine of avoidable consequences should not be confused with the doctrine of contributory negligence. The latter focuses on issues of proximate causation of, and ultimate liability for, an accident, whereas the former focuses only on measurement of damages resulting from the injury-producing event.

The distinction noted above makes it clear that the present case is not one where the doctrine of contributory negligence should be applied. There has been no allegation that any action or inaction of Mrs. Munn was causally related to the accident which resulted in her injuries. * * *

The other theory raised by the defendant is that by refusing the transfusion, Mrs. Munn assumed the risk of her own death. The doctrine of assumption of the risk provides that a plaintiff who voluntarily assumes a risk of harm arising from the negligent or reckless conduct of the defendant cannot recover for such harm. * * * [T]he risk that is being assumed is the known risk that the defendant does not intend to act, or has already failed to act, in accordance with a duty imposed on him by law. "The result is that the defendant is relieved of all legal duty to the plaintiff; and being under no duty, he cannot be charged with negligence." Prosser [Handbook of the Law of Torts § 68 (4th ed. 1971)] at 440. In the instant case, by assuming the risk that she would die if she did not agree to a blood transfusion, Mrs. Munn did not relieve the defendant of any duty because the defendant had no duty in relation to the transfusion. * * *

In an earlier motion for summary judgment, the plaintiff raised two issues in relation to the defense based on the doctrine of avoidable consequences which were not addressed by the court in its order denying the motion. Those issues need to be addressed prior to trial and both are relevant to the issue currently before the court. First, the plaintiff contends that the egg-shell or thin skull rule should be applied in this case. The "rule" is actually an exception to the more general rule that a defendant is liable only for those consequences which were the reasonably foreseeable results of an anticipated action. As stated by Prosser, a "defendant is held liable when his negligence operates upon a concealed *physical* condition, such as pregnancy, or a latent disease, or susceptibility to disease, to produce consequences which he could not reasonably anticipate." Prosser, Handbook of the Law of Torts § 43, p. 261 (4th ed.1971) (emphasis added). The statement of the rule in the Restatement is much the same:

> The negligent actor is subject to liability for harm to another although a *physical condition* of the other which is neither known nor should be known to the actor makes the injury greater than that which the actor as a reasonable man should have foreseen as a probable result of his conduct.

Restatement (2d) Torts § 461. (Emphasis added.)

Every authority which this court can find which states the "eggshell skull rule" speaks only of physical conditions which pre-exist the injury for which compensation is sought and lead to unforeseeably severe results. The religious beliefs of the plaintiff simply are not covered by this rule.

The plaintiff also presses a first amendment argument. This argument is not fleshed out and relies entirely on cases where a state attempted to force a Jehovah's Witness to accept a blood transfusion. There is a clear distinction, however, between the overt attempt by a state actor to force an individual to take some action which her religion forbids her to take and the application of a universally applied tort doctrine which leaves the person "free to make [her] choice between the practice of [her] religion and the acceptance of treatment that may be contrary thereto." Martin v. Industrial Accident Commission, 304 P.2d 828, 831 (Cal.1956) (upholding denial of worker's comp. death benefits where death was found to be result of refusal of transfusion on religious grounds). An individual has a right under the first amendment to hold religious beliefs and live by them, but that does not mean that anyone who commits a tort against that individual must suffer the consequences of decisions made by the victim based upon those religious beliefs.

It has been argued that persons who refuse medical treatment on religious grounds should be exempted on first amendment grounds from the operation of the doctrine of avoidable consequences. Comment, Medical Care, Freedom of Religion, and Mitigation of Damages, 87 Yale L.J. 1466 (1978). The author contends that the application of this facially neutral doctrine to a tort victim who refuses medical treatment for religious reasons is a denial of a state benefit on religious grounds. The argument is basically that putting the tort victim to the choice of acting in violation of his religious beliefs or losing the right conferred by state law to obtain complete recovery for all harm which results from the wrongful conduct of another places an undue burden on the victim's free exercise rights. Cited in support of this argument are Sherbert v. Verner, 374 U.S. 398 (1963), and Wisconsin v. Yoder, 406 U.S. 205 (1972). *Sherbert* involved the denial of state unemployment benefits to a woman who refused on religious grounds to accept a job which required her to work on Saturday. The Court held that this was an impermissible burden on her free exercise rights. In *Yoder,* the Court held that a state mandatory school attendance law violated the free exercise rights of people of the Amish faith. Each of these cases involves direct state action. If an exception to the doctrine of avoidable consequences is made for those who refuse medical treatment on religious grounds, payment for the harm which could have been avoided will come from the pockets of the tortfeasor, not from the coffers of the state. To adopt an absolute rule which required one citizen to pay damages for the consequences of another's exercising her religious freedom would favor an establishment of religion in a way which seems constitutionally unsupportable. Additionally, the doctrine of avoidable consequences does not automatically bar the plaintiff from recovering the losses sustained after the refusal of medical treatment; it bars recovery of those losses only when the refusal is found to be unreasonable under all of the circumstances known to the tort victim at the time of the refusal. In what has come to be considered as the leading case on this point, the Connecticut Supreme Court upheld the lower court's decision to submit the question of the objective reasonableness of the plaintiff's refusal of medical treatment to the jury with the instruction that the jurors were to consider the fact that the refusal was based on religious belief as one of the circumstances. Lange v. Hoyt, 114 Conn. 590, 159 A. 575 (1932). The author of the comment also takes exception to this procedure, arguing that the jury is, in effect, being asked to pass upon the reasonableness of the plaintiff's religious belief. This indeed presents a problem. However, neither of the parties have adequately addressed this issue, so the court will delay any attempt to resolve it until the parties may be heard at the jury instruction conference after the evidence is in.

The court holds that the doctrine of avoidable consequences is the appropriate standard to be applied in this case and that its application does not violate the first amendment.

APPLICATION OF THE DOCTRINE OF AVOIDABLE CONSEQUENCES IN A WRONGFUL DEATH CASE

As stated earlier, the doctrine of avoidable consequences prevents the plaintiff from recovering for that part of her injury which could have been avoided by taking reasonable steps after the injury occurred.[2] How does this rule operate when the harm which the defendant contends was avoidable is death?

Neither party has presented the court with a single authority on this point, nor has exhaustive research turned up a single case where any court

---

[2] Several courts have expanded the doctrine to include measures which if taken prior to the injury would have lessened the severity of the injury. The most common example is the application of the doctrine in cases where the injury resulting from an auto accident was aggravated by the plaintiff's failure to use a seat belt.

has addressed the issues presented by this case. Simply stated, the question is: if the jury should find that the refusal of the blood transfusion was unreasonable and that Mrs. Munn would have lived had she taken the transfusion, then what damages may the plaintiff recover.

The defendant's argument is that if the jury makes this dual finding, then there is no wrongful death and the plaintiff's cause of action is under the survival statute. From a purely technical standpoint, this is a compelling argument. At common law, "if a tortfeasor killed a man, neither the victim's losses before his death nor the losses to his survivors caused by his death were compensable." Because the statutes which have been passed to abrogate this rule are in derogation of the common law, they must be strictly construed. If recovery is not expressly provided for in either the wrongful death or survival statute, then there can be no recovery for the losses suffered by either the survivors or the estate. Given this backdrop, if Mrs. Munn's refusal to accept the transfusion is seen as cutting off the defendant's liability for her death, then the plaintiff must fall back on the Mississippi Survival Statute, Miss.Code Ann. § 91–7–233 (1972).

Section 91–7–233 provides: Executors, administrators, and temporary administrators may commence and prosecute any personal action whatever, at law or in equity, which the testator or intestate might have commenced and prosecuted. Mrs. Munn could clearly have commenced an action against Ms. Algee to recover for the injuries she sustained as a result of Ms. Algee's wrongful conduct. Included in her recovery, if any, would have been prospective relief for the future effects of the injuries which were received in the accident, such as lost income, future pain and suffering, and future medical expenses. However, in the usual survival action, the calculation of these damages is based, not upon a mortality table, but upon the actual date of the tort victim's death. In survival actions, "damages must of course be based upon the known period of life, and no recovery may be had for any prospective loss of earnings, expenses, or suffering based upon any probable life expectancy of the deceased, such as would be appropriate if the deceased were prosecuting the case in his lifetime." McCormick, *Damages,* 337–38 (1935). This rule clearly applies where the death results from an intervening cause which is deemed sufficient to break the causal connection between the tort and the death; but it is not so clear that it applies in this case.

In the usual personal injury case, in addition to the action under the survival statute, the plaintiff, as the husband of the decedent, would have a claim for his own losses which were caused by the injury to his wife—i.e., loss of services, loss of consortium, etc. This claim could be brought "at common law without the aid of statute." However, once again, recovery could be had only for the losses incurred by the plaintiff during the time period between the commission of the tort and the death of Mrs. Munn, if the damages resulting from the death are not attributable to the defendant.

The plaintiff counters with the argument that a straightforward application of the doctrine of avoidable consequences would allow him, both on his own behalf and on behalf of the decedent's estate, to recover damages for any harm which could not have been avoided by allowing the transfusion. A perfunctory reading of the rule, as generally stated, supports this argument. Generally, it is said that the plaintiff may recover for the harm which resulted from the defendant's wrongful act and which could not have been avoided by the plaintiff's acting reasonably after the injury has occurred. The plaintiff alleges that his wife suffered severe physical injury, including a broken pelvis, broken ribs, a punctured and collapsed lung, and a severed artery, which would have resulted in long term disability, pain and suffering, and future medical expenses if she had survived. These consequences could not have been avoided by allowing the transfusion and, therefore, should be recoverable. On a purely emotional level, this argument is appealing; however, any attempt to ground such a holding on legal principles is thwarted by the stark reality that these consequences were never actually suffered by the plaintiff's decedent. This court can find no authority for allowing recovery of purely hypothetical losses.

The argument for recovery of damages for injuries to Mr. Munn which were actually suffered as a result of the death, at least to the extent that they would have occurred even if the plaintiff had taken the transfusion and survived, does not share this infirmity. Clearly, given the extent of the decedent's injuries, if she had lived, there would have been some loss of consortium and services to her husband and quite possibly lost earnings which under this argument ought now to be recoverable by her estate. There are serious problems with allowing recovery of damages for these elements of the loss. Whether the problem is addressed in terms of proximate cause or simply in terms of a public policy against allowing recovery from this defendant for consequences which the plaintiff could have avoided matters little. The doctrine of avoidable consequences operates to relieve the defendant of any legal obligation to pay damages for harm which the victim of her wrongful act could have avoided. The damages which the plaintiff seeks to recover did not occur as a result of the personal injuries suffered by the decedent but as a result of Mrs. Munn's death—a death for which the defendant has no legal obligation to pay damages if the jury should find that the death was avoidable and that the refusal of the transfusion was unreasonable.

CONCLUSION

The court holds that the doctrine of avoidable consequences is the appropriate standard to be applied in this case and that its application does not violate the plaintiff's first amendment rights. The court further holds that this question should be submitted to the jury through an appropriate instruction telling the jurors that they may consider the fact that it was based on religious belief. The court also holds that the plaintiff may not recover for purely hypothetical injuries which never occurred because of her death if the jury should find that the refusal of the transfusion was unreasonable and that the decedent would have survived had she taken the transfusion; nor may he recover for the harm actually suffered which resulted from his wife's death even though it would have been suffered to some extent even if she had taken the transfusion and lived.

NOTE

At trial, the jury in *Munn* was instructed,

In determining whether or not Elaine Munn's decision to refuse the blood transfusion was unreasonable, you may consider that the blood transfusions were medically recommended. But, you may also consider her religious beliefs and related teachings, together with the known risks of blood transfusions, if you find that to be a factor in her decision.

The jury awarded damages of $241.44 for Mr. Munn's medical expenses, $10,411 for Mrs. Munn's medical expenses, and $10,000 for Mrs. Munn's pain and suffering.

On appeal, the Fifth Circuit (2–1) affirmed. The trial court had erred by allowing the defendant to question Mr. Munn about religious beliefs and practices completely unrelated to medical treatment (such as the refusal of Jehovah's Witnesses to salute the flag or "do service to their country"). Nonetheless, the error was harmless, because the jury was clearly persuaded that Mrs. Munn's objectively unreasonable refusal of treatment caused her death, and because the amount of the jury's award was not, in the court's opinion, influenced by the improperly admitted evidence. Munn v. Algee, 924 F.2d 568 (5th Cir.), *cert. denied*, 502 U.S. 900 (1991).

The court did question the trial court's jury instruction on avoidable consequences, however: "[A] case-by-case approach to religiously motivated refusals to mitigate damages can involve weighing the reasonableness of religious beliefs and thus arguably violate the establishment clause." 924 F.2d at 574–75. Therefore, a purely objective approach—one that avoids any mention of religious beliefs—is preferable. As for the Munns' argument that ignoring religious beliefs entirely impermissibly burdens free exercise rights, "generally applicable rules imposing incidental burdens on particular religions do not violate the free exercise clause." *Id.*

C. MEASURING VALUE

The concept of value is central to the award of compensatory damages. Whatever area of substantive law is involved—contract or tort, constitutional or statutory—determining the plaintiff's loss in money is the first step in making the plaintiff whole. There are several alternative standards, however, by which value of an economic loss can be measured. These include market value, replacement value, repair cost, diminution in value, or sentimental value. Market value also has various permutations including depreciated value when the market itself, rather than the harm by the defendant, caused the decrease in value. Questions of measuring intangible loss like pain and suffering or emotional distress are discussed later in the chapter in conjunction with tort damages.

BARKING HOUND VILLAGE, LLC. V. MONYAK

Supreme Court of Georgia
787 S.E.2d 191 (2016)

THOMPSON, CHIEF JUSTICE.

The subject matter of this case is near and dear to the heart of many a Georgian in that it involves the untimely death of a beloved family pet and concerns the proper measure of damages available to the owners of an animal injured or killed through the negligence of others. Observing that pet dogs are considered personal property under Georgia law, but finding that not all dogs have an actual commercial or market value, the Court of Appeals held that where the actual market value of the animal is non-existent or nominal, the appropriate measure of damages would be the actual value of the dog to its owners. * * * The Court of Appeals concluded that the actual value of the animal could be demonstrated by reasonable veterinary and other expenses incurred by its owners in treating its injuries, as well as by other economic factors, but held that evidence of non-economic factors demonstrating the dog's intrinsic value to its owners would not be admissible.

* * * Because we find that . . . the damages recoverable by the owners of an animal negligently killed by another include both the animal's fair market value at the time of the loss plus interest, and, in addition, any medical and other expenses reasonably incurred in treating the animal, we affirm in part and reverse in part the Court of Appeals' decision.

The damages at issue in this case arise from the death of a mixed-breed dachshund owned by Robert and Elizabeth Monyak. In 2012, the Monyaks boarded Lola, their 8 1/2-year-old dachshund mix,[a] for ten days at a kennel owned by Barking Hound Village, LLC ("BHV") and managed by William Furman. Along with Lola, the Monyaks boarded their 13-year-old mixed-breed Labrador retriever, Callie, who had been prescribed an anti-inflammatory drug for arthritis pain—medication which the Monyaks gave to kennel personnel with directions that it be administered to Callie.

---

[a]   Evidence in the record showed that the Monyaks adopted Lola from a rescue center when she was about two years old, there was no purchase price for the dog, she was not a pure breed or a show dog, she had never generated any revenue, and that at the time she was boarded at the kennel, her market value to the public at large was non-existent or nominal.

Three days after picking up their dogs from BHV, Lola was diagnosed with acute renal failure. Despite receiving extensive veterinary care over a nine-month period, including kidney dialysis treatment, Lola died in March 2013.

The Monyaks sued BHV and Furman for damages alleging that while boarded at the kennel Lola was administered toxic doses of the medication prescribed for Callie, a much larger dog. The Monyaks asserted various claims of negligence against BHV and Furman, and sought compensatory damages, including over $67,000 in veterinary and other expenses incurred in treating Lola. In addition, alleging fraud and deceit on the part of the defendants, the Monyaks sought litigation expenses and punitive damages.[b] * * *

1.   The parties agree . . . that a pet dog has value and is considered the personal property of its owner. * * *

2.   * * * Generally, in a suit to recover damages to personal property it is a well-established principle that "a plaintiff cannot recover an amount of damages against a tortfeasor greater than the fair market value of the property prior to impairment." * * * However, over 120 years ago this Court decided that such a limitation was not appropriate in negligence cases involving the injury or death of an animal. * * * Instead, this Court determined that where an animal is negligently injured and subsequently dies as a result of those injuries, the proper measure of damages recoverable by the animal's owner includes not only the full market value of the animal at the time of the loss plus interest, but also expenses incurred by the owner in an effort to cure the animal. * * *

An important distinction recognized * * * is that while a cap on the recovery of loss of use damages exists for an injured animal, there is no such cap on the amount of damages recoverable with respect to actual expenditures associated with the animal's treatment and recovery. Thus, where the injured animal survives, its owner is entitled to receive loss of hire and diminution in market value *up to* the full market value of the animal in addition to the animal's reasonable medical costs and treatment; whereas, when the animal fails to recover, damages are limited to the market value of the animal plus interest, as well as the reasonable costs expended on its care and treatment. * * *

By ensuring that property owners whose animals are negligently injured by another are able to recoup reasonable expenses incurred in attempting to save the animal, this Court's decisions . . . are consistent

---

[b]   Here, the record includes evidence that the defendants became aware during the dog's boarding stay that Lola had wrongfully been administered Callie's medication and, instead of notifying the Monyaks and/or seeking prompt veterinary care for the dog, attempted to hide the error, thus allegedly exacerbating the harm to Lola. Also included is evidence of multiple prior incidents involving errors in the administration of medication to dogs at BHV and Furman's personal knowledge of prior incidents.

with the position taken by courts in a majority of states, including those which have adopted an actual value to the owner measure of damages to determine a pet dog's worth, see Strickland v. Medlen, 397 S.W.3d 184, 193, n.58 (Tex. 2013) (recognizing that "[w]hile actual value cannot include the owner's 'feelings,'. . . it can include a range of other factors [such as] purchase price, reasonable replacement costs . . . breeding potential . . . special training . . . veterinary expenses related to the negligent injury, and so on"), as well as those which have declined to do so, see Shera v. N.C. State Univ. Veterinary Teaching Hosp., 723 S.E.2d 352 (N.C.Ct.App. 2012) (awarding plaintiffs damages for the death of their 12-year old dog due to veterinary malpractice in the amount of $3,105.72, which amount included reimbursement for the cost of the dog's medical treatment plus the replacement cost for a similar dog). Similarly, under the Federal Tort Claims Act, a dog owner has been allowed to recover veterinary expenses incurred in trying to save the life of a mixed-breed dog despite its ultimate death. *See* Kaiser v. United States, 761 F. Supp. 150, 156 (D.D.C. 1991) (awarding $1,786 in incurred veterinary expenses for a mixed-breed pet dog shot by a United States Capitol police officer).

At the time this lawsuit was filed, the Monyaks' injured dog was still alive and the veterinary fees incurred were in the neighborhood of $10,000. The fact that the dog's treatment ultimately proved unsuccessful and the animal died nine months later should not prevent the Monyaks from seeking compensatory damages for the reasonable veterinary fees incurred in their attempt to save their pet. Rather, we conclude, . . . that the proper measure of damages recoverable by the Monyaks for the negligent injury and death of their dog includes both the dog's fair market value plus interest *and* any reasonable medical costs and other expenses they incurred in treating the animal for its injuries.

3.   While we are sympathetic to the concerns expressed by the parties and others regarding the difficulties in establishing the fair market value of a family pet,[5] this Court long ago stated that, "[t]he value of [a] dog may be proved, as that of any other property, by evidence that he was of a particular breed, and had certain qualities, and by witnesses who knew the market value of such animal, if any market value be shown." * * * Thus, in an action for damages arising from the allegedly tortious killing of a dog belonging to a 12-year-old boy, testimony was provided regarding the dog's breed and age, how the boy acquired the dog, how long he owned the animal

---

[5]   We note that amicus briefs have been filed in this case by numerous entities concerned with the care and treatment of animals both in this State and nationwide. These groups include the Georgia Veterinary Medical Association, American Veterinary Medical Association, American Kennel Club, Cat Fanciers' Association, Animal Health Institute, National Animal Interest Alliance, American Pet Products Association, American Animal Hospital Association, Pet Industry Joint Advisory Council and the Animal Legal Defense Fund. The primary issue addressed by amici, however, is whether the law in Georgia should allow for the recovery of damages based on a pet's sentimental value to its owner, a position properly rejected by the Court of Appeals in this case and not disputed by either party on appeal.

prior to its death, and activities the boy did with the dog. * * * Although the only evidence presented of the dog's value was the boy's testimony that the dog was worth $100, the jury returned a verdict for the plaintiff in the amount of $10 and the plaintiff appealed, arguing that the verdict was contrary to the evidence. Concluding that the jury was entitled to place a different value on the property than that testified to by the witnesses, the Court of Appeals held that the jurors were authorized to consider the dog's allegedly vicious character and other qualities to reach their own conclusions regarding the dog's value. * * *

Georgia law provides that direct testimony regarding market value is opinion evidence and a witness need not be an expert to testify as to an object's value so long as the witness has had an opportunity to form a reasoned opinion. * * * Indeed, "[m]arket value is a question peculiarly for the jury, and a jury is not required to accept even uncontradicted opinions as to market value." Instead, in determining the value of personal property in tort cases, jurors "have the right to consider the nature of the property involved, together with any other facts or circumstances properly within the knowledge of the jury which throws light upon the question, and by their verdict, may fix either a lower or higher value upon the property than that stated in the opinions and estimates of the witnesses." * * *

4. [W]e find no error in that court's determination that Georgia precedent does not allow for the recovery of damages based on the sentimental value of personal property to its owner. *See Monyak*, 331 Ga. App. at 815 ("[D]amages for the intrinsic value of the dog are not recoverable."). Instead, we agree with those courts which have held that the unique human-animal bond, while cherished, is beyond legal measure. *See Shera*, 723 S.E.2d at 357 ("[T]he sentimental bond between a human and his or her pet companion can neither be quantified in monetary terms or compensated for under our current law."); *Strickland*, 397 S.W.3d at 197–198 (refusing to permit non-economic damages rooted in relational attachment).

This does not mean, however, that all qualitative evidence regarding the plaintiffs' dog is inadmissible. . . . [We] see no reason why opinion evidence, both qualitative and quantitative, of an animal's particular attributes—e.g., breed, age, training, temperament, and use—should be any less admissible than similar evidence offered in describing the value of other types of personal property. * * * The key is ensuring that such evidence relates to the value of the dog in a fair market, not the value of the dog solely to its owner.

5. * * * [I]n addition to recovering the fair market value of their deceased dog plus interest, the Monyaks would be entitled to recover the reasonable veterinary and other expenses they reasonably incurred in trying to save her. Whether the veterinary costs and other expenses

incurred by a pet owner in obtaining treatment for an animal negligently injured by another are reasonable will depend on the facts of each case. As observed by the Massachusetts Appeals Court in a case involving tortious injury to a dog,

> [a]mong the factors to be considered are the type of animal involved, the severity of its injuries, the purchase and/or replacement price of the animal, its age and special traits or skills, its income-earning potential, whether it was maintained as part of the owner's household, the likelihood of success of the medical procedures employed, and whether the medical procedures involved are typical and customary to treat the injuries at issue.

Irwin v. Degtiarov, 8 N.E.3d 296, 301 (Mass. App. Ct. 2014).

Of course, determining the reasonableness of medical treatment and the reasonableness of its cost is a function for the factfinder and well within the capability of jurors who routinely are asked to ascertain the appropriate value of professional services in other types of cases. * * * The burden of establishing the reasonableness of any medical treatment provided in light of the animal's injuries, condition and prognosis, as well as the reasonableness of the cost of that treatment considering factors such as the nature of the services rendered, the time required to perform them, and all attending circumstances rests with the animal's owner. * * *

* * * Accordingly, we remand this case to the Court of Appeals for further proceedings consistent with this opinion.

NOTES

1.   Market value is typically defined as the amount that a willing buyer would pay and a willing seller would accept. Research into a phenomenon known as the "endowment effect" suggests that people often value an item they have just acquired much more than they would be willing to pay to acquire it. To the extent that some seek to justify legal rules by models relying on rational actors, the endowment effect suggests an irrationality at the core of our concepts of value. Professors Owen D. Jones and Sarah F. Brosnan posit a biological basis for this phenomenon in *Law, Biology, and Property: A New Theory of the Endowment Effect*, 49 Wm. & Mary L.Rev. 1935 (2008). Should the rightful position necessarily be defined by market value? *See* Katrina Wyman, *The Measure of Just Compensation*, 41 U.C. Davis L.Rev. 239 (2007) (challenging the idea that the goal in eminent domain cases should be to make plaintiffs subjectively indifferent to the taking).

2.   For other pet cases, see Burgess v. Shampooch Pet Industries, Inc., 131 P.3d 1248 (Kan.App.2006) (consistent with "common-sense jurisprudence" measure of damages for injured pet dog with no discernable market value is the cost of veterinary care and treatment); Anzalone v. Kragness, 826 N.E.2d 472, 477 (Ill. App. 2005) (value of a pet cat killed by a dog while boarding at a

hospital); Mitchell v. Heinrichs, 27 P.3d 309 (Alaska 2001) (may recover actual value of pet to owner rather than limited to fair market value; measured by costs of replacement or original costs). Some allow for additional recovery, like Rhode Island that allows evidence of "actual value to the owner," rejected in *Barking Hollow*, R.I.Gen.Laws § 4–23–1, and Tennessee that allows a pet owner to recover up to $5,000 for the loss of the pet's "society, companionship, love and affection." Tenn. Code Ann. § 44–17–403. Most courts do not allow owners to recover for their emotional distress, though that is changing. *See* Plotnik v. Meihaus, 208 Cal.App.4th 1590 (2012) (allowing emotional distress); Kondaurov. v. Kerdasha, 629 S.E.2d 181 (Va.2006) (no emotional distress recoverable); *see also* Victor Schwartz & Emily Laird, *Non-Economic Damages in Pet Litigation: The Serious Need to Preserve a Rational Rule*, 33 Pepperdine L.Rev. 227, 241–42 (2006) (arguing for limiting to cost of replacement, original cost, and investments such as immunization or training can factor into valuation of pet).

The following case presents the question of quantifying damages in a public context where a statute has circumscribed the measurement options.

OHIO V. DEPARTMENT OF THE INTERIOR

United States Court of Appeals, District of Columbia Circuit
880 F.2d 432 (D.C.Cir. (1989)

WALD, CHIEF JUDGE, and ROBINSON and MIKVA, CIRCUIT JUDGES.[1]

Petitioners are 10 states, three environmental organizations ("State and Environmental Petitioners"), a chemical industry trade association, a manufacturing company and a utility company ("Industry Petitioners"), who seek review of regulations promulgated by the Department of the Interior ("DOI" or "Interior") pursuant to § 301(c)(1)–(3) of the Comprehensive Environmental Response, Compensation and Liability Act of 1980 ("CERCLA" or the "Act"), as amended, 42 U.S.C. § 9651(c). The regulations govern the recovery of money damages from persons responsible for spills and leaks of oil and hazardous substances, to compensate for injuries such releases inflict on natural resources. Damages may be recovered by state and in some cases the federal governments, as trustees for those natural resources.

Petitioners challenge many aspects of those regulations. State and Environmental Petitioners raise ten issues, all of which essentially focus on the regulations' alleged undervaluation of the damages recoverable from parties responsible for hazardous materials spills that despoil natural resources. Industry Petitioners attack the regulations from a different

---

[1] Parts I, II, III, IV, VII, VIII, IX, X, XI and XII were authored by Judge Wald. Part XIII was authored by Judge Robinson. Parts V and VI were authored by Judge Mikva.

vantage point, claiming they will permit or encourage overstated damages. * * *

We hold that the regulation limiting damages recoverable by government trustees for harmed natural resources to 'the lesser of' (a) the cost of restoring or replacing the equivalent of an injured resource, or (b) the lost use value of the resource is directly contrary to the clearly expressed intent of Congress and is therefore invalid. We also hold that the regulation prescribing a hierarchy of methodologies by which the lost-use value of natural resources may be measured, which focuses exclusively on the market values for such resources when market values are available, is not a reasonable interpretation of the statute. * * *

I.　BACKGROUND

* * *

The relevant provisions of CERCLA * * * [provide] that responsible parties may be held liable for "damages for injury to, destruction of, or loss of natural resources, including the reasonable costs of assessing such injury, destruction, or loss resulting from such a release." 42 U.S.C. § 9607(a)(C). Liability is to "the United States Government and to any State for natural resources within the State or belonging to, managed by, controlled by, or appertaining to such State." * * *

Congress conferred on the President (who in turn delegated to Interior) the responsibility for promulgating regulations governing the assessment of damages for natural resource injuries resulting from releases of hazardous substances or oil, for the purposes of CERCLA and the Clean Water Act's § 311(f)(4)–(5) oil and hazardous substance natural resource damages provisions. * * * CERCLA as amended provides that any assessment performed in accordance with the prescribed procedure is entitled to a rebuttable presumption of accuracy in a proceeding to recover damages from a responsible party. * * *

II.　STANDARD OF REVIEW

In reviewing an agency's interpretation of a statute, we first determine "whether Congress has directly spoken to the precise question at issue." *Chevron U.S.A., Inc. v. Natural Resources Defense Council, Inc.*, 467 U.S. 837, 842 (1984). If so, then both Interior and this court "must give effect to the unambiguously expressed intent of Congress."

If, on the other hand, the statute is ambiguous or is silent on a particular issue, this court must assume that Congress implicitly delegated to the agency the power to make policy choices that " 'represent [ ] a reasonable accommodation of conflicting policies that were committed to the agency's care by the statute.' " *Chevron*, 467 U.S. at 844–45. In that event, the court must defer to the agency's interpretation of the statute so long as it is reasonable and consistent with the statutory purpose. This is "Step Two" of *Chevron* analysis. * * *

III. THE "LESSER-OF" RULE

The most significant issue in this case concerns the validity of the regulation providing that damages for despoilment of natural resources shall be "the *lesser of*: restoration or replacement costs; or diminution of use values." 43 C.F.R. § 11.35(b)(2)(1987) (emphasis added).

State and Environmental Petitioners challenge Interior's "lesser of" rule, insisting that CERCLA requires damages to be at least sufficient to pay the cost in every case of restoring, replacing or acquiring the equivalent of the damaged resource (hereinafter referred to shorthandedly as "restoration"). Because in some—probably a majority of—cases lost-use-value will be lower than the cost of restoration, Interior's rule will result in damages award too small to pay for the costs of restoration. * * *

Although our resolution of the dispute submerges us in the minutiae of CERCLA text and legislative materials, we initially stress the enormous practical significance of the "lesser of" rule. A hypothetical example will illustrate the point: imagine a hazardous substance spill that kills a rookery of fur seals and destroys a habitat for seabirds at a sealife reserve. The lost use value of the seals and seabird habitat would be measured by the market value of the fur seals' pelts (which would be approximately $15 each) plus the selling price per acre of land comparable in value to that on which the spoiled bird habitat was located. Even if, as likely, that use value turns out to be far less than the cost of restoring the rookery and seabird habitat, it would nonetheless be the only measure of damages eligible for the presumption of recoverability under the Interior rule.

After examining the language and purpose of CERCLA, as well as its legislative history, we conclude that Interior's "lesser of" rule is directly contrary to the expressed intent of Congress.

A. The Contours of "The Precise Question at Issue"

Commencing our *Chevron* analysis, we must first decide exactly what "the precise question at issue" is in the present case. * * *

That question is not what measure of damages should apply in any or all cases which are brought under the Act. As to that larger question, Interior is obviously correct in asserting that Congress delegated to it a considerable measure of discretion in formulating a standard. The precise question here is a far more discrete one: whether DOI is entitled to treat use value and restoration cost as having equal presumptive legitimacy as a measure of damages.

Interior's "lesser of" rule operates on the premise that, as the cost of a restoration project goes up relative to the value of the injured resource, at some point it becomes wasteful to require responsible parties to pay the full cost of restoration. The logic behind the rule is the same logic that prevents an individual from paying $8,000 to repair a collision-damaged car that was worth only $5,000 before the collision. Just as a prudent individual would sell the damaged car for scrap and then spend $5,000 on a used car in similar condition, DOI's rule requires a polluter to pay a sum equal to the diminution in the use value of a resource whenever that sum is less than restoration cost. What is significant about Interior's rule is the point at which it deems restoration "inefficient." Interior chose to draw the line not at the point where restoration becomes practically impossible, nor at the point where the cost of restoration becomes grossly disproportionate to the use value of the resource, but rather at the point where restoration cost exceeds—by any amount, however small—the use value of the resource. Thus, while we agree with DOI that CERCLA permits it to establish a rule exempting responsible parties *in some cases* from having to pay the full cost of restoration of natural resources, we also agree with Petitioners that it does not permit Interior to draw the line on an automatic "which costs less" basis. * * *

B.   Text and Structure of CERCLA * * *

1.   Section 107(f)(1) and the Measure of Damages

The strongest linguistic evidence of Congress' intent to establish a distinct preference for restoration costs as the measure of damages is contained in § 107(f)(1) of CERCLA. That section states that natural resource damages recovered by a government trustee are "for use only to restore, replace, or acquire the equivalent of such natural resources." 42 U.S.C. § 9607(f)(1). It goes on to state: "The measure of damages in any action under [§ 107(a)(C)] shall not be limited by the sums which can be used to restore or replace such resources."

a.   Limitation on Uses of Recovered Damages

By mandating the use of all damages to restore the injured resources, Congress underscored in § 107(f)(1) its paramount restorative purpose for imposing damages at all. It would be odd indeed for a Congress so insistent that all damages be spent on restoration to allow a "lesser" measure of damages than the cost of restoration in the majority of cases. Only two possible inferences about congressional intent could explain the anomaly: Either Congress intended trustees to commence restoration projects only to abandon them for lack of funds, or Congress expected taxpayers to pick up the rest of the tab. The first theory is contrary to Congress' intent to effect a "make-whole" remedy of complete restoration, and the second is contrary to a basic purpose of the CERCLA natural resource damage provisions—that polluters bear the costs of their polluting activities. It is far more logical to presume that Congress intended responsible parties to be liable for damages in an amount sufficient to accomplish its restorative aims. Interior's rule, on the other hand, assumes that Congress purposely formulated a statutory scheme that would doom to failure its goals of restoration in a majority of cases.

In this connection, it should be noted that Interior makes no claim that a "use value" measure will provide enough money to pay for ANY of the three uses to which all damages must be assigned: restoration, replacement *or acquisition of an equivalent resource*. Nor could Interior make such a claim, because its "lesser of" rule not only calculates use value quite differently from restoration or replacement cost but it also fails to link measurement of use value in any way to the cost of acquiring an equivalent resource. For example, Interior could not possibly maintain that recovering $15 per pelt for the fur seals killed by a hazardous substance release would enable the purchase of an "equivalent" number of fur seals.

b.   The "Shall Not Be Limited by" Language

The same section of CERCLA that mandates the expenditures of all damages on restoration (again a shorthand reference to all three listed uses of damages) provides that the measure of damages "shall not be limited by" restoration costs. § 107(f)(1), 42 U.S.C. § 9607(f)(1). This provision obviously reflects Congress' apparent concern that its restorative purpose for imposing damages not be construed as making restoration cost a damages ceiling. But the explicit command that damages "shall not be limited by" restoration costs also carries in it an implicit assumption that restoration cost will serve as the basic measure of damages in many if not most CERCLA cases. It would be markedly inconsistent with the restorative thrust of the whole section to limit restoration-based damages, as Interior's rule does, to a minuscule number of cases where restoration is cheaper than paying for lost use. * * *

C.   Legislative History of CERCLA

The text and structure of CERCLA indicate clearly to us that Congress intended restoration costs to be the basic measure of recovery for harm to natural resources. We next examine the legislative history of CERCLA to ascertain if there are any countervailing indications to our conclusion. * * *

CERCLA's legislative history * * * shows that Congress soundly rejected the two basic premises underlying Interior's "lesser of" rule—first, that the common-law measure of damages is appropriate in the natural resource context, and second, that it is economically inefficient to restore a resource whose use value is less than the cost of restoration. * * *

Accepting for the sake of argument the contention that the "lesser of" rule reflects the common law,[37] support for the proposition that Congress

---

[37] We note in passing that the "lesser of" standard does not apply in all non-CERCLA contexts. *See, e.g.,* Denoyer v. Lamb, 22 Ohio App.3d 136, 490 N.E.2d 615, 618–19 (1984) (restoration cost is proper measure where property is used for a residence or for recreation, so long as restoration cost is not "grossly disproportionate" to diminution in market value); Heninger v.

adopted common-law damage standards wholesale into CERCLA is slim to nonexistent. * * * The legislative history illustrates* * * that a motivating force behind the CERCLA natural resource damage provisions was Congress' dissatisfaction with the common law. Indeed, one wonders why Congress would have passed a new damage provision at all if it were content with the common law. * * *

Alternatively, Interior justifies the "lesser of" rule as being economically efficient. Under DOI's economic efficiency view, making restoration cost the measure of damages would be a waste of money whenever restoration would cost more than the use value of the resource. Its explanation of the proposed rules included the following statement:

> [I]f use value is higher than the cost of restoration or replacement, then it would be more rational for society to be compensated for the cost to restore or replace the lost resource than to be compensated for the lost use. Conversely, if restoration or replacement costs are higher than the value of uses foregone, it is rational for society to compensate individuals for their lost uses rather than the cost to restore or replace the injured natural resource.

50 Fed.Reg. at 52,141. See also 51 Fed.Reg. at 27,704 ("lesser of" rule "promotes a rational allocation of society's assets").

This is nothing more or less than cost-benefit analysis: Interior's rule attempts to optimize social welfare by restoring an injured resource only when the diminution in the resource's value to society is greater in magnitude than the cost of restoring it. And, acknowledgedly, Congress did intend CERCLA's natural resource provisions to operate efficiently. For one thing, the Act requires that the assessment of damages and the restoration of injured resources take place as cost-effectively as possible. Moreover, as we have indicated, there is some suggestion in the legislative history that Congress intended recovery not to encompass restoration cost where restoration is infeasible or where its cost is grossly disproportionate to use value.

The fatal flaw of Interior's approach, however, is that it assumes that natural resources are fungible goods, just like any other, and that the value to society generated by a particular resource can be accurately measured in every case—assumptions that Congress apparently rejected. As the foregoing examination of CERCLA's text, structure and legislative history illustrates, Congress saw restoration as the presumptively correct remedy for injury to natural resources. To say that Congress placed a thumb on the

---

Dunn, 101 Cal.App.3d 858, 162 Cal.Rptr. 104, 106–09 (1980) (restoration cost is proper measure where owner has a personal reason for restoring land to its original condition, so long as restoration cost is not unreasonably disproportionate to diminution in market value); Restatement (Second) of Torts section 929, comment b (1977).

scales in favor of restoration is not to say that it forswore the goal of efficiency. "Efficiency," standing alone, simply means that the chosen policy will dictate the result that achieves the greatest value to society. Whether the particular choice is efficient depends on *how the various alternatives are valued*. Our reading of CERCLA does not attribute to Congress an irrational dislike of "efficiency"; rather, it suggests that Congress was skeptical of the ability of human beings to measure the true "value" of a natural resource. Indeed, even the common law recognizes that restoration is the proper remedy for injury to property where measurement of damages by some other method will fail to compensate fully for the injury.[41] Congress' refusal to view use value and restoration cost as having equal presumptive legitimacy merely recognizes that natural resources have value that is not readily measured by traditional means. Congress delegated to Interior the job of deciding at what point the presumption of restoration falls away, but its repeated emphasis on the primacy of restoration rejected the underlying premise of Interior's rule, which is that restoration is wasteful if its cost exceeds—by even the slightest amount—the diminution in use value of the injured resource.

* * *

VI. THE HIERARCHY OF ASSESSMENT METHODS

The regulations establish a rigid hierarchy of permissible methods for determining "use values," limiting recovery to the price commanded by the resource on the open market, unless the trustee finds that "the market for the resource is not reasonably competitive." If the trustee makes such a finding, it may "appraise" the market value in accordance with the relevant sections of the "Uniform Appraisal Standards for Federal Land Acquisition." Only when neither the market value nor the appraisal method is "appropriate" can other methods of determining use value be employed.

Environmental petitioners maintain that Interior's emphasis on market value is an unreasonable interpretation of the statute, under the so-called "second prong" of Chevron U.S.A., Inc. v. Natural Resources Defense Council, Inc., 467 U.S. 837, 845 (1984), and we agree. While it is not irrational to look to market price as *one* factor in determining the use value of a resource, it is unreasonable to view market price as the *exclusive* factor, or even the predominant one. From the bald eagle to the blue whale and snail darter, natural resources have values that are not fully captured

---

[41] *See, e.g.*, Trinity Church v. John Hancock Mut. Life Ins. Co., 399 Mass. 43, 502 N.E.2d 532, 536 (1987) (restoration cost is proper measure where diminution in market value is unsatisfactory or unavailable as a measure of damages, as in the case of structural damage to a church); Weld County Bd. of Com'rs v. Slovek, 723 P.2d 1309, 1316–17 (Colo.1986) (court may, in its discretion, award restoration cost where award of diminution in market value would not adequately compensate owner for some personal reason, provided that restoration cost is not "wholly unreasonable" in relation to diminution in value); see also supra note 37.

by the market system. * * * Courts have long stressed that market prices are not to be used as surrogates for value "when the market value has been too difficult to find, or when its application would result in manifest injustice to owner or public." We find that DOI erred by establishing "a strong presumption in favor of market price and appraisal methodologies."

We are not satisfied that the problem is solved by the provision * * * permitting nonmarket methodologies to be used when the market for the resource is not "reasonably competitive." There are many resources whose components may be traded in "reasonably competitive" markets, but whose total use values are not fully reflected in the prices they command in those markets. Interior itself provides ample proof of the inadequacy of the "reasonably competitive market" caveat. For example, DOI has noted that "the hierarchy established * * * " would dictate a use value for fur seals of $15 per seal, corresponding to the market price for the seal's pelt. Another example of DOI's erroneous equation of market price with use value is its insistence that the sum of the fees charged by the government for the use of a resource, say, for admission to a national park, constitutes "the value to the public of recreational or other public uses of the resource," because "these fees are what the government has determined to represent the value of the natural resource and represent an offer by a willing seller." This is quite obviously and totally fallacious; there is no necessary connection between the total value to the public of a park and the fees charged as admission, which typically are set not to maximize profits but rather to encourage the public to visit the park. In fact, the decision to set entrance fees far below what the traffic would bear is evidence of Congress's strong conviction that parks are priceless national treasures and that access to them ought to be as wide as possible, and not, as DOI would have it, a sign that parks are really not so valuable after all. * * *

On remand, DOI should consider a rule that would permit trustees to derive use values for natural resources by summing up all reliably calculated use values, however measured, so long as the trustee does not double count. Market valuation can of course serve as one factor to be considered, but by itself it will necessarily be incomplete.

* * *

XIII.   CONTINGENT VALUATION

* * * DOI's natural resource damage assessment regulations define "use value" as

> the value to the public of recreational or other public uses of the resource, as measured by changes in consumer surplus, any fees or other payments collectable by the government or Indian tribe for a private party's use of the natural resource, and any economic

rent accruing to a private party because the government or Indian tribe does not charge a fee or price for the use of the resource.

The regulations provide several approaches to use valuation. When the injured resource is traded in a market, the lost use value is the diminution in market price. When that is not precisely the case, but similar resources are traded in a market, an appraisal technique may be utilized to determine damages. When, however, neither of these two situations obtains, nonmarketed resource methodologies are available. One of these is "contingent valuation" (CV), the subject of controversy here.

The CV process "includes all techniques that set up hypothetical markets to elicit an individual's economic valuation of a natural resource." CV involves a series of interviews with individuals for the purpose of ascertaining the values they respectively attach to particular changes in particular resources. Among the several formats available to an interviewer in developing the hypothetical scenario embodied in a CV survey are direct questioning, by which the interviewer learns how much the interviewee is willing to pay for the resource; bidding formats, for example, the interviewee is asked whether he or she would pay a given amount for a resource and, depending upon the response, the bid is set higher or lower until a final price is derived; and a "take or leave it" format, in which the interviewee decides whether or not he or she is willing to pay a designated amount of money for the resource. CV methodology thus enables ascertainment of individually-expressed values for different levels of quality of resources, and dollar values of individuals' changes in well-being. * * *

Industry Petitioners point out that at common law there can be no recovery for speculative injuries, and they contend that CV methodology is at odds with that principle. CV methodology, they say, is rife with speculation, amounting to no more than ordinary public opinion polling.

We have already noted our disagreement with the proposition that the strictures of the common law apply to CERCLA. That much of Industry Petitioners' argument to the contrary thus fades away. CERCLA does, however, require utilization of the "best available procedures" for determinations of damages flowing from destruction of or injury to natural resources, and Industry Petitioners insist that CV methodology is too flawed to qualify as such. In their eyes, the CV process is imprecise, is untested, and has a built-in bias and a propensity to produce overestimation. * * *

Industry Petitioners urge * * * that even assuming that questions are artfully drafted and carefully circumscribed, there is such a high degree of variation in size of the groups surveyed, and such a concomitant fluctuation in aggregations of damages, that CV methodology cannot be considered a "best available procedure."[86] We think this attack on CV methodology is insufficient in a facial challenge to invalidate CV as an available assessment technique. The extent of damage to natural resources from releases of oil and hazardous substances varies greatly, and though the impact may be widespread and severe, it is in the mission of CERCLA to assess the public loss.[87] Certainly nothing in CV methodology itself shapes the injury inflicted by an environmental disaster, or influences identification of the population affected thereby. The argument of Industry Petitioners strikes at CERCLA, not CV's implementation, and can appropriately be considered only by Congress.

Similarly, we find wanting Industry Petitioners' protest that CV does not rise to the status of a "best available procedure" because willingness-to-pay—a factor prominent in CV methodology—can lead to overestimates by survey respondents. The premise of this argument is that respondents do not actually pay money, and likely will overstate their willingness-to-pay. One study relied upon by Industry Petitioners hypothesizes that respondents may "respond in ways that are more indicative of what they would like to see done than how they would behave in an actual market," and also observes that the converse is possible. The simple and obvious safeguard against overstatement, however, is more sophisticated questioning. Even as matters now stand, the risk of overestimation has not been shown to produce such egregious results as to justify judicial overruling of DOI's careful estimate of the caliber of worth of CV methodology.

Industry Petitioners also challenge the use of CV AFTER an oil leak or a hazardous waste release has occurred. They fear that application of CV methodology in those circumstances is fraught with a significant bias leading to overvaluation of the damaged resources. As a practical matter, it would be prohibitively expensive, if not physically impossible, to solicit individual valuations of each and every natural resource, or even a sizeable number thereof, in order to avoid any upward bias in the event that the resource is later damaged. Moreover, in light of CERCLA's preference for restoration, it would be a terrible waste of time and energy to conduct broadscale valuation interviewing beforehand. While, depending on whether interviewing occurs before or after damage, the results may differ

---

[86] Industry Petitioners cite a study estimating the combined option and existence values to Texas residents of whooping cranes at $109,000,000 (13.9 million Texas residents × $7.13). The estimate rested upon responses to a survey eliciting the amount an individual would pay for a permit to visit the National Wildlife Refuge where the whooping crane winters. Had the survey been nationwide in scope, the estimate would have been $1.58 billion. Brief for Industry Petitioners at 14 n. 24 (referring to J. Stoll & L. Johnson, Concepts of Value, Nonmarket Valuation, and the Case of the Whooping Crane (Natural Resources Working Paper Series, National Resource Workgroup, Dep't of Agricultural Economics, Texas A & M Univ.) (1984) at 23–24).

[87] Thus, in the whooping crane scenario referred to by industry petitioners the intent of CERCLA would be realized, not contravened, by a more expansive survey and a correspondingly higher assessment of damages if people beyond the borders of Texas were affected.

somewhat, that alone does not reduce CV methodology to something less than a "best available procedure." We have no cause to overturn DOI's considered judgment that CV methodology, when properly applied, can be structured so as to eliminate undue upward biases.

We sustain DOI in its conclusion that CV methodology is a "best available procedure." As such, its conclusion in the Natural Resource Damage Assessment regulations was entirely proper. * * *

NOTES

1.   The Department of the Interior issued new regulations in response to *Ohio*. The new regulations eliminate the "lesser of" rule and the hierarchy of assessment methods criticized in the case, and continue the use of contingent valuation methods. The new regulations state that the damage assessment includes the cost of "restoration, rehabilitation, replacement, and/or acquisition of the equivalent of the injured natural resource," and provide the official charged with assessment with a wide choice of methods, all focused on restoration. 43 C.F.R. § 11.82 et seq.

If contingent valuation methods were introduced in court, could they pass the *Daubert* test for admissibility of scientific evidence? *See* Sameer H. Doshi, *Making the Sale on Contingent Valuation*, 21 Tul.Envtl.L.J. 295 (2008). For further discussion of contingent valuation, see Richard T. Carson, *Contingent Valuation: A Comprehensive Bibliography and History* (2012).

2.   The same concept of the "lesser-of" rule exists in contract. Peevyhouse v. Garland Coal & Mining Company, 382 P.2d 109 (Okla.1962), is a classic example. Garland Coal leased the Peevyhouses' land for a strip-mining operation. When Garland Coal returned the land, they failed to perform remedial and restorative work the lease had specifically required at the demand of the Peevyhouses. The remedial work would have cost $29,000 to perform, but market value of the land was reduced only $300 by the failure to do the work. At trial, the jury awarded the Peevyhouses $5,000 in damages.

The Supreme Court of Oklahoma reversed:

> We * * * hold that where, in a coal mining lease, lessee agrees to perform certain remedial work on the premises concerned at the end of the lease period, and thereafter the contract is fully performed by both parties except that the remedial work is not done, the measure of damages in an action by lessor against lessee for damages for breach of contract is ordinarily the reasonable cost of performance of the work; however, where the contract provision breached was merely incidental to the main purpose in view, and where the economic benefit which would result to lessor by full performance of the work is grossly disproportionate to the cost of performance, the damages which lessor may recover are limited to the diminution in value resulting to the premises because of the non-performance. * * *

Under the most liberal view of the evidence herein, the diminution in value resulting to the premises because of non-performance of the remedial work was $300.00. * * * We are of the opinion that the judgment of the trial court for plaintiffs should be, and it is hereby, modified and reduced to the sum of $300.00, and as so modified it is affirmed.

382 P.2d at 114. For a thorough history of the case, see Judith L. Maute, Peevyhouse v. Garland Coal & Mining Co. *Revisited: The Ballad of Willie and Lucille*, 89 Nw.U.L.Rev. 1341 (1995).

On the other hand, in Groves v. John Wunder Co., 286 N.W. 235, 236 (Minn. 1939), a contractor leased the plaintiff's land for a gravel quarry, agreeing to grade the land evenly after removing the gravel. The contractor did not do the grading, and the plaintiff sued. The evidence showed that the cost of the grading would be $60,000, while the total value of the plaintiff's property would be only $12,160 even after the grading was done. Nonetheless, the court found that the proper measure of damages was the cost of performance. Any other rule "handsomely rewards bad faith and deliberate breach of contract."

Which is the better result? Would it matter whether the land were a family farm, or property held by a developer speculating on property values? Consider Judge Posner's assessment of the result in *Groves*:

Because the value of the plaintiff's land had fallen, the breach of contract did not actually impose any loss on him, and the only proper remedy for a harmless breach is nominal damages. The effect of the award of damages was to shift from the owner of the land to the contractor a part of the risk of the fall in land values caused by the Depression. One expects the risk of a fall of the value of land to be borne by the owner of the land rather than by a contractor.

Youngs v. Old Ben Coal Co., 243 F.3d 387, 392 (7th Cir.2001).

The argument that awarding the cost of restoration will result in economic waste is challenged in Alan Schwartz & Robert E. Scott, *Market Damages, Efficient Contracting and the Economic Waste Fallacy*, 108 Colum.L.Rev. 1610 (2008), and in Juanda Lowder Daniel & Kevin S. Marshall, *Avoiding Economic Waste in Contract Damages: Myths, Misunderstanding, and Malcontent*, 85 Neb.L.Rev. 875 (2007).

D. TORT DAMAGES

In tort, awards of compensatory damages typically include both pecuniary and nonpecuniary damages. *Pecuniary* or economic damages are for the economic losses suffered by the plaintiff like property, wages, medical costs, and other expenses. *Nonpecuniary* or non-economic damages are for intangible losses like pain and suffering, emotional distress, loss of society, and enjoyment of life. The availability of compensatory damages in torts also makes the plaintiff eligible for punitive damages, if the requirements for that additional punishment are also satisfied. See Chapter 6.

1. ELEMENTS OF LOSS

Broadly speaking, tort cases can be divided into cases involving harm to the person, and cases involving harm to real or personal property. The Restatement (Second) of Torts has helpfully tried to itemize the types of damages to expect in each case; but these are not limitations, only examples. For tort cases involving personal harm, compensatory damages typically include damages for:

(1) Past and future bodily harm and emotional distress;

(2) Lost earnings and loss of earning capacity;

(3) Reasonable past and future medical and other expenses; and

(4) Harm to property or business.

Restatement (Second) of Torts § 924 (1977).

In cases involving harm to property, damages include compensation for

(1) the difference between the property's pre-and post-tort market value, or the cost of repairing the harm; and

(2) where real property is harmed, the occupant's discomfort and annoyance.

Restatement (Second) of Torts §§ 928, 929 (1977).

All of these elements of loss and more are combined in the case that follows, which provides you an overview of compensatory damages in tort.

AYERS V. JACKSON TOWNSHIP

Supreme Court of New Jersey
525 A.2d 287 (1987)

STEIN, JUSTICE.

In this case we consider the application of the New Jersey Tort Claims Act (the Act), N.J.S.A. 59:1–1 to 12–3, to the claims asserted by 339 residents of Jackson Township against that municipality.

The litigation involves claims for damages sustained because plaintiffs' well water was contaminated by toxic pollutants leaching into the Cohansey Aquifer from a landfill established and operated by Jackson Township. After an extensive trial, the jury found that the township had created a "nuisance" and a "dangerous condition" by virtue of its operation of the landfill, that its conduct was "palpably unreasonable,"—a prerequisite to recovery under N.J.S.A. 59:4–2—and that it was the proximate cause of the contamination of plaintiffs' water supply. The jury verdict resulted in an aggregate judgment of $15,854,392.78, to be divided among the plaintiffs in varying amounts. The jury returned individual awards for each of the plaintiffs that varied in accordance with such factors as proximity to the landfill, duration and extent of the exposure to contaminants, and the age of the claimant.

The verdict provided compensation for three distinct claims of injury: $2,056,480 was awarded for emotional distress caused by the knowledge that they had ingested water contaminated by toxic chemicals for up to six years; $5,396,940 was awarded for the deterioration of their quality of life during the twenty months when they were deprived of running water; and $8,204,500 was awarded to cover the future cost of annual medical surveillance that plaintiffs' expert testified would be necessary because of plaintiffs' increased susceptibility to cancer and other diseases. * * *

I

* * * A substantial number—more than 150—of the plaintiffs gave testimony with respect to damages, describing in detail the impairment of their quality of life during the period that they were without running water, and the emotional distress they suffered. With regard to the emotional distress claims, the plaintiffs' testimony detailed their emotional reactions to the chemical contamination of their wells and the deprivation of their water supply, as well as their fears for the health of their family members. Expert psychological testimony was offered to document plaintiffs' claims that they had sustained compensable psychological damage as a result of the contamination of their wells.

We now consider each of the plaintiffs' damage claims in the context of the evidence adduced at trial and the legal principles that should inform our application of the Tort Claims Act.

QUALITY OF LIFE

[The court described how, for nearly two years, the plaintiffs' water was provided in 40 gallon, 100 pound barrels, the inconvenience that entailed, and the inevitable discomfort and tension the lack of running water produced among household members.]

The trial court charged the jury that plaintiffs' claim for "quality of life" encompassed "inconveniences, aggravation, and unnecessary expenditure of time and effort related to the use of the water hauled to their homes, as well as to other disruption in their lives, including disharmony in the family unit." The aggregate jury verdict on this claim was $5,396,940. This represented an average award of slightly over $16,000 for each plaintiff; thus, a family unit consisting of four plaintiffs received an average award of approximately $64,000.

* * *

[D]efendant argues that this segment of the verdict is barred by the New Jersey Tort Claims Act, which provides:

> No damages shall be awarded against a public entity or public employee for pain and suffering resulting from any injury; provided, however, that this limitation on the recovery of damages for pain and suffering shall not apply in cases of permanent loss of a bodily function, permanent disfigurement or dismemberment where the medical treatment expenses are in excess of $1,000.00.

Defendant contends that the legislative intent in restricting damages for "pain and suffering" was to encompass claims for all "non-objective" injuries, unless the statutory threshold of severity of injury or expense of treatment is met. The township asserts that the inconvenience, aggravation, effort and disruption of the family unit that resulted from the loss of plaintiff's water supply was but a form of "pain and suffering" and therefore uncompensable under the Act.

The Appellate Division rejected the township's contention, concluding that there was a clear distinction between

> the subjectively measured damages for pain and suffering, which are not compensable by the Tort Claims Act, and those which objectively affect quality of life by causing an interference with the use of one's land through inconvenience and the disruption of daily activities.

We agree with the Appellate Division's conclusion. The Tort Claims Act's ban against recovery of damages for "pain and suffering resulting from any injury" is intended to apply to the intangible, subjective feelings of discomfort that are associated with personal injuries. It was not intended to bar claims for inconvenience associated with the invasion of a property interest. * * * [T]he interest invaded here, the right to obtain potable running water from plaintiffs' own wells, is qualitatively different from "pain and suffering" related to a personal injury.

As the Appellate Division acknowledged, plaintiffs' claim for quality of life damages is derived from the law of nuisance. It has long been recognized that damages for inconvenience, annoyance, and discomfort are recoverable in a nuisance action. The Restatement (Second) of Torts section 929 (1977) sets out three distinct categories of compensation with respect to invasions of an interest in land:

(a) the difference between the value of the land before the harm and the value after the harm, or at [plaintiff's] election in an appropriate case, the cost of restoration that has been or may be reasonably incurred;

(b) the loss of use of the land, and

(c)   discomfort and annoyance to him as occupant.

While the first two of these components constitute damages for the interference with plaintiff's use and enjoyment of his land, the third category compensates the plaintiff for his personal losses flowing directly from such an invasion. As such, damages for inconvenience, discomfort, and annoyance constitute "distinct grounds of compensation for which in ordinary cases the person in possession is entitled to recover in addition to the harm to his proprietary interests." Restatement Second of Torts section 929 comment e (1977).

Accordingly, we conclude that the quality of life damages represent compensation for losses associated with damage to property, and agree with the Appellate Division that they do not constitute pain and suffering under the Tort Claims Act. We therefore sustain the judgment for quality of life damages.

EMOTIONAL DISTRESS

The jury verdict awarded plaintiffs damages for emotional distress in the aggregate amount of $2,056,480. The individual verdicts ranged from $40 to $14,000.

Many of the plaintiffs testified about their emotional reactions to the knowledge that their well-water was contaminated. * * * [T]he consistent thrust of the testimony offered by numerous witnesses was that they suffered anxiety, stress, fear, and depression, and that these feelings were directly and causally related to the knowledge that they and members of their family had ingested and been exposed to contaminated water for a substantial time period. * * *

[T]he township contended that the jury verdict for emotional distress constituted damages for "pain and suffering resulting from any injury," recovery for which is expressly barred by the Tort Claims Act. The Appellate Division, without deciding the issue of the sufficiency of plaintiffs' proofs, agreed that the verdict for emotional distress was barred by the Act:

> We cannot conceive how plaintiffs' concern that their exposure to toxic wastes might have precipitated a serious illness can be characterized as anything other than pain and suffering. It is a measure of their entirely subjective responses to a situation which, though threatening, never materialized into objective manifestations of injury. Under the circumstances, we conclude that although damages for these intangible harms might be recoverable from a non-governmental entity, as consequential to a nuisance, the language of N.J.S.A. 59:9B2(d), barring damages from a public entity "for pain and suffering resulting from any injury," clearly precludes recovery herein.

* * *

[W]e reject plaintiffs' assertion that the Tort Claims Act's limitation against recovery for "pain and suffering resulting from any injury" does not apply to claims based on emotional distress. * * *

Addressing first plaintiffs' contention that emotional distress is not an "injury" as that term is used in the Tort Claims Act, we observe that the Act broadly defines injury to include

> death, injury to a person, damage to or loss of property or any other injury that a person may suffer that would be actionable if inflicted by a private person.

The statutory definition is expansive and unqualified and clearly accommodates "emotional distress" as an injury "that a person may suffer that would be actionable if inflicted by a private person." The term "injury" is also used in N.J.S.A. 59:4–2, which defines the scope of public entity liability. Plainly, if emotional distress did not constitute an injury under this section, plaintiffs could not have asserted a cause of action for emotional distress under the Act. We discern no basis in the legislative history or in the statutory scheme of the Act for assigning a more restrictive meaning to the term "injury" as used in N.J.S.A. 59:9–2(d), the section that limits liability for pain and suffering, than that accorded to the same word in the section of the Act that imposes liability on a public entity. Accordingly, we hold that claims for emotional distress are encompassed by the term "injury" in N.J.S.A. 59:9–2(d).

The term "pain and suffering" is not defined in the Act. The Comment to N.J.S.A. 59:9–2 describes the limitation on damages for pain and suffering as reflecting "the policy judgment that in view of the economic burdens presently facing public entities a claimant should not be reimbursed for non-objective types of damages, such as pain and suffering, except in aggravated circumstances * * * ." We are in full accord with the conclusion of the Appellate Division that the subjective symptoms of depression, stress, health concerns, and anxiety described by the plaintiffs and their expert witness constitute "pain and suffering resulting from any injury" as that phrase is used in N.J.S.A. 59:9–2(d). * * *

CLAIMS FOR ENHANCED RISK AND MEDICAL SURVEILLANCE

No claims were asserted by plaintiffs seeking recovery for specific illnesses caused by their exposure to chemicals. Rather, they claim damages for the enhanced risk of future illness attributable to such exposure. They also seek to recover the expenses of annual medical examinations to monitor their physical health and detect symptoms of disease at the earliest possible opportunity.

Before trial, the trial court granted defendant's motion for summary judgment dismissing the enhanced risk claim. * * *

With regard to the claims for medical surveillance expenses, the trial court denied defendant's summary judgment motion, and the jury verdict included damages of $8,204,500 for medical surveillance. * * *

1

Our evaluation of the enhanced risk and medical surveillance claims requires that we focus on a critical issue in the management of toxic tort litigation: at what stage in the evolution of a toxic injury should tort law intercede by requiring the responsible party to pay damages?

[The court first concludes that any plaintiffs who do incur cancer at a later date will be able to sue the Township. The statute of limitations will not have run, because under New Jersey's discovery rule, the cause of action does not accrue until the victim is aware of the injury. Neither will the state's single controversy rule bar plaintiffs from suing. Usually, the single controversy rule would require the plaintiffs to raise all their claims—property claims and personal injury claims—in the same proceeding. According to the Court, however, the single controversy rule, "cannot sensibly be applied to a toxic-tort claim filed when disease is manifested years after the exposure, merely because the same plaintiff sued previously to recover for property damage or other injuries. In such a case, the rule is literally inapplicable since, as noted, the second cause of action does not accrue until the disease is manifested; hence, it could not have been joined with the earlier claims."] * * *

2

Much of the same evidence was material to both the enhanced risk and medical surveillance claims. Dr. Joseph Highland, a toxicologist * * * testified concerning the health hazards posed by the chemicals and the exposure levels at which adverse health effects had been experimentally observed. * * *

Dr. Highland testified that the Legler area residents, because of their exposure to toxic chemicals, had an increased risk of cancer; that unborn children and infants were more susceptible to the disease because of their immature biological defense systems; and that the extent of the risk was variable with the degree of exposure to the chemicals. Dr. Highland testified that he could not quantify the extent of the enhanced risk of cancer because of the lack of scientific information concerning the effect of the interaction of the various chemicals to which plaintiffs were exposed. However, the jury could reasonably have inferred from his testimony that the risk, although unquantified, was medically significant. * * *

Dr. Highland also testified that the exposure to chemicals had already caused actual physical injury to plaintiffs through its adverse effects on the genetic material within their cells.

Dr. Susan Daum, a physician * * * specializing in the diagnosis and treatment of diseases induced by toxic substances, testified that plaintiffs required a program of regular medical surveillance. Acknowledging her reliance on the report of Dr. Highland, Dr. Daum stated that plaintiffs' exposure to chemicals had produced "a reasonable likelihood that they have now or will develop health consequences from this exposure." * * *

Although both the enhanced risk and medical surveillance claims are based on Dr. Highland's testimony, supplemented by Dr. Daum's testimony in the case of the surveillance claim, these claims seek redress for the invasion of distinct and different interests. The enhanced risk claim seeks a damage award, not because of any expenditure of funds, but because plaintiffs contend that the unquantified injury to their health and life expectancy should be presently compensable, even though no evidence of disease is manifest. Defendant does not dispute the causal relationship between the plaintiffs' exposure to toxic chemicals and the plaintiffs' increased risk of diseases, but contends that the probability that plaintiffs will actually become ill from their exposure to chemicals is too remote to warrant compensation under principles of tort law.

By contrast, the claim for medical surveillance does not seek compensation for an unquantifiable injury, but rather seeks specific monetary damages measured by the cost of periodic medical examinations. The invasion for which redress is sought is the fact that plaintiffs have been advised to spend money for medical tests, a cost they would not have incurred absent their exposure to toxic chemicals. Defendant contends that the claim for medical surveillance damages cannot be sustained, as a matter of law, if the plaintiffs' enhanced risk of injury is not sufficiently probable to be compensable. In our view, however, recognition of the medical surveillance claim is not necessarily dependent on recognition of the enhanced risk claim.

3

The trial court declined to submit to the jury the issue of defendant's liability for the plaintiffs' increased risk of contracting cancer, kidney or liver damage, or other diseases associated with the chemicals that had migrated from the landfill to their wells. If the issue had not been withheld, the jury could have concluded from the evidence that most or all of the plaintiffs had a significantly but unquantifiably enhanced risk of the identified diseases, and that such enhanced risk was attributable to defendant's conduct. * * *

[N]either the trial court nor the Appellate Division challenged the contention that the enhanced risk of disease was a tortiously-inflicted injury, but both concluded that the proof quantifying the likelihood of disease was insufficient to submit the issue to the jury. As the Appellate Division observed:

While it is true that damages are recoverable for the prospective consequences of a tortious injury, it must be demonstrated that the apprehended consequences are reasonably probable. * * *

Our disposition of this difficult and important issue requires that we choose between two alternatives, each having a potential for imposing unfair and undesirable consequences on the affected interests. A holding that recognizes a cause of action for unquantified enhanced risk claims exposes the tort system, and the public it serves, to the task of litigating vast numbers of claims for compensation based on threats of injuries that may never occur. It imposes on judges and juries the burden of assessing damages for the risk of potential disease, without clear guidelines to determine what level of compensation may be appropriate. It would undoubtedly increase already escalating insurance rates. It is clear that the recognition of an "enhanced risk" cause of action, particularly when the risk is unquantified, would generate substantial litigation that would be difficult to manage and resolve.

Our dissenting colleague, arguing in favor of recognizing a cause of action based on an unquantified claim of enhanced risk, points out that "courts have not allowed the difficulty of quantifying injury to prevent them from offering compensation for assault, trespass, emotional distress, invasion of privacy or damage to reputation." Although lawsuits grounded in one or more of these causes of action may involve claims for damages that are difficult to quantify, such damages are awarded on the basis of events that have occurred and can be proved at the time of trial. In contrast, the compensability of the enhanced risk claim depends upon the likelihood of an event that has not yet occurred and may never occur—the contracting of one or more diseases the risk of which has been enhanced by defendant's conduct. It is the highly contingent and speculative quality of an unquantified claim based on enhanced risk that renders it novel and difficult to manage and resolve. If such claims were to be litigated, juries would be asked to award damages for the enhanced risk of a disease that may never be contracted, without the benefit of expert testimony sufficient to establish the likelihood that the contingent event will ever occur.

On the other hand, denial of the enhanced-risk cause of action may mean that some of these plaintiffs will be unable to obtain compensation for their injury. Despite the collateral estoppel effect of the jury's finding that defendant's wrongful conduct caused the contamination of plaintiffs' wells, those who contract diseases in the future because of their exposure to chemicals in their well water may be unable to prove a causal relationship between such exposure and their disease. * * * Dismissal of the enhanced risk claims may effectively preclude any recovery for injuries caused by exposure to chemicals in plaintiffs' wells because of the difficulty of proving that injuries manifested in the future were not the product of intervening events or causes. * * *

In deciding between recognition or nonrecognition of plaintiffs' enhanced-risk claim, we feel constrained to choose the alternative that most closely reflects the legislative purpose in enacting the Tort Claims Act. We are conscious of the admonition that in construing the Act courts should "exercise restraint in the acceptance of novel causes of action against public entities." In our view, the speculative nature of an unquantified enhanced risk claim, the difficulties inherent in adjudicating such claims, and the policies underlying the Tort Claims Act argue persuasively against the recognition of this cause of action. Accordingly, we decline to recognize plaintiffs' cause of action for the unquantified enhanced risk of disease, and affirm the judgment of the Appellate Division dismissing such claims. We need not and do not decide whether a claim based on enhanced risk of disease that is supported by testimony demonstrating that the onset of the disease is reasonably probable could be maintained under the Tort Claims Act.

4

The claim for medical surveillance expenses stands on a different footing from the claim based on enhanced risk. It seeks to recover the cost of periodic medical examinations intended to monitor plaintiffs' health and facilitate early diagnosis and treatment of disease caused by plaintiffs' exposure to toxic chemicals. At trial, competent medical testimony was offered to prove that a program of regular medical testing and evaluation was reasonably necessary and consistent with contemporary scientific principles applied by physicians experienced in the diagnosis and treatment of chemically-induced injuries.

The Appellate Division's rejection of the medical surveillance claim is rooted in the premise that even if medical experts testify convincingly that medical surveillance is necessary, the claim for compensation for these costs must fall, as a matter of law, if the risk of injury is not quantified, or, if quantified, is not reasonably probable. This analysis assumes that the reasonableness of medical intervention, and, therefore, its compensability, depends solely on the sufficiency of proof that the occurrence of the disease is probable. We think this formulation unduly impedes the ability of courts to recognize that medical science may necessarily and properly intervene where there is a significant but unquantified risk of serious disease.

This point is well-illustrated by the hypothetical case discussed in the opinion of the Court of Appeals in Friends for All Children v. Lockheed Aircraft Corp., 746 F.2d 816 (D.C.Cir.1984):

> Jones is knocked down by a motorbike when Smith is riding through a red light. Jones lands on his head with some force. Understandably shaken, Jones enters a hospital where doctors recommend that he undergo a battery of tests to determine whether he has suffered any internal head injuries. The tests

prove negative, but Jones sues Smith solely for what turns out to be the substantial cost of the diagnostic examinations.

From our example, it is clear that even in the absence of physical injury Jones ought to be able to recover the cost for the various diagnostic examinations proximately caused by Smith's negligent action. A cause of action allowing recovery for the expense of diagnostic examinations recommended by competent physicians will, in theory, deter misconduct, whether it be negligent motorbike riding or negligent aircraft manufacture. The cause of action also accords with commonly shared intuitions of normative justice which underlie the common law of tort. The motorbike rider, through his negligence, caused the plaintiff, in the opinion of medical experts, to need specific medical services—a cost that is neither inconsequential nor of a kind the community generally accepts as part of the wear and tear of daily life. Under these principles of tort law, the motorbike should pay. * * *

Compensation for reasonable and necessary medical expenses is consistent with well-accepted legal principles. It is also consistent with the important public health interest in fostering access to medical testing for individuals whose exposure to toxic chemicals creates an enhanced risk of disease. The value of early diagnosis and treatment for cancer patients is well-documented. * * *

Accordingly, we hold that the cost of medical surveillance is a compensable item of damages where the proofs demonstrate, through reliable expert testimony predicated upon the significance and extent of exposure to chemicals, the toxicity of the chemicals, the seriousness of the diseases for which individuals are at risk, the relative increase in the chance of onset of disease in those exposed, and the value of early diagnosis, that such surveillance to monitor the effect of exposure to toxic chemicals is reasonable and necessary. In our view, this holding is thoroughly consistent with our rejection of plaintiffs' claim for damages based on their enhanced risk of injury. That claim seeks damages for the impairment of plaintiffs' health, without proof of its likelihood, extent, or monetary value. In contrast, the medical surveillance claim seeks reimbursement for the specific dollar costs of periodic examinations that are medically necessary notwithstanding the fact that the extent of plaintiffs' impaired health is unquantified.

We find that the proofs in this case were sufficient to support the trial court's decision to submit the medical surveillance issue to the jury, and were sufficient to support the jury's verdict.

5

The medical surveillance issue was tried as if it were a conventional claim for compensatory damages susceptible to a jury verdict in a lump sum. The jury was so instructed by the trial court, and neither plaintiffs' nor defendant's request to charge on this issue sought a different instruction.

In the Appellate Division, defendant argued for the first time that a lump-sum damage award for medical surveillance was inappropriate. Defendant contended that if the court were to uphold all or any part of the medical surveillance award, it should "create an actuarially-sound fund, to which the plaintiffs may apply in the future for the cost of medical surveillance upon proof that those costs are not otherwise compensable * * * or after deduction of the amounts so reimbursed," and should leave to the trial court, on remand, the task of establishing "details of the creation and supervision of such a fund." * * *

In our view, the use of a court-supervised fund to administer medical-surveillance payments in mass exposure cases, particularly for claims under the Tort Claims Act, is a highly appropriate exercise of the Court's equitable powers. Such a mechanism offers significant advantages over a lump-sum verdict. For Tort Claims Act cases, it provides a method for offsetting a defendant's liability by payments from collateral sources. Although the parties in this case sharply dispute the availability of insurance coverage for surveillance-type costs, a fund could provide a convenient method for establishing credits in the event insurance benefits were available for some, if not all, of the plaintiffs.

In addition, a fund would serve to limit the liability of defendants to the amount of expenses actually incurred. A lump-sum verdict attempts to estimate future expenses, but cannot predict the amounts that actually will be expended for medical purposes. Although conventional damage awards do not restrict plaintiffs in the use of money paid as compensatory damages, mass-exposure toxic-tort cases involve public interests not present in conventional tort litigation. The public health interest is served by a fund mechanism that encourages regular medical monitoring for victims of toxic exposure. Where public entities are defendants, a limitation of liability to amounts actually expended for medical surveillance tends to reduce insurance costs and taxes, objectives consistent with the legislature's admonition to avoid recognition of novel causes of action. * * *

In litigation involving public-entity defendants, we conclude that the use of a fund to administer medical-surveillance damages should be the general rule, in the absence of factors that render it impractical or inappropriate.

However, we decline to upset the jury verdict awarding medical-surveillance damages in this case. Such a result would be unfair to these plaintiffs, since the medical-surveillance issue was tried conventionally, and neither party requested the trial court to withhold from the jury the power to return a lump-sum verdict for each plaintiff in order that relief by way of a fund could be provided. * * *

HANDLER, J., concurring in part and dissenting in part.

* * * The essence of the claim for damages here is the reality of the physical injury caused by the wrongful exposure to toxic chemicals and the increased peril of cancer and other serious diseases that the residents have incurred. * * *

The Court cannot, and does not, dispute or denigrate the expert testimony presented at trial "that the exposure to chemicals had already caused actual physical injury to plaintiffs through its adverse effects on the genetic material within their cells" and that plaintiffs' exposure to chemicals had produced "a reasonable likelihood that they have now and will develop health consequences from this exposure." Dr. Joseph Highland gave uncontested testimony that plaintiffs had already suffered physical injury from the damage to their cellular and genetic material caused by the chemicals to which they were exposed. These chemicals are mutagenic agents: they destroy parts of the genetic material of cells they contact. This destruction may affect only the function of a few cells or it may lead to the failure of major organs. It may make the cells likely starting points for cancer, and it may lead to mutations in the victims' children.

The majority recognizes that plaintiffs have suffered injury. It is self-evident that exposure to highly toxic chemicals is the "infliction of . . . harm," "an invasion of a legally protected interest." Nevertheless, the majority concludes that plaintiffs' injury cannot be redressed. Its reasons for treating their claims different from other injury claims are an unsupported fear of "vast numbers of claims" and a belief that no "clear guidelines [exist] to determine what level of compensation may be appropriate."

These reasons are an evasion of the challenge posed by tortious injury that carries with it an enhanced risk of even greater injury, and the need to provide fair compensation for innocent victims suffering this form of injury. The Court postponed a similar determination in Evers v. Dollinger, 95 N.J. 399 (1984). There a woman brought suit claiming that her doctor's negligent diagnosis and treatment enhanced the risk that her cancer would recur. While her appeal of the trial court's judgment was pending, she suffered a recurrence of the cancer. The majority decided that it need not decide whether enhanced risk, standing alone, is an actionable element. Nevertheless, the Court held that because the disease had recurred, plaintiff would be allowed to recover damages for enhanced risk.

Allowing recovery for enhanced risk in Evers where the plaintiff suffered subsequent harm cannot be reconciled with the denial of recovery for enhanced risk in the present case. The majority professes to deny compensation because it cannot "measure" or "quantify" the enhanced risk of future injury. The fact that the plaintiffs in the present case have not-yet-suffered extreme symptoms is no justification for denying recovery. As in *Evers v. Dollinger*, "[t]he Court is . . . troubled by a seeming inability to quantify the risk of future cancer. But, adding the incurrence of future harm as a requirement for the recovery for such increased risk does not resolve the dilemma since the risk still remains unquantified." *Id.* at 421, (Handler, J., concurring). When the Court allowed recovery for enhanced risk in *Evers*, it did not in the slightest way insist that the risk be quantified.

The majority reasons that plaintiffs' claim is not cognizable in part because the risk of future disease does not rise to the level of "reasonable probability." Yet the court concedes that the plaintiffs have proven that they have a "significantly . . . enhanced risk" of contracting serious diseases. It nowhere explains why a risk that generates the "reasonable probability" of future injury can be compensated while one that "significantly enhances" the likelihood of future injury cannot. * * *

The courts have not allowed the difficulty of quantifying injury to prevent them from offering compensation for assault, trespass, emotional distress, invasion of privacy, or damage to reputation. * * * Where new forms of injury have been put before the courts, the courts have developed procedures, standards, and formulas for determining appropriate compensation. This perception was expressed in Capron, *Tort Liability in Genetic Counseling*, 79 Colum.L.Rev. 618, 649 (1979):

> [T]he collective wisdom of the community on the proper redress for a particular harm, informed by experience, common sense, and a desire to be fair to the parties, seems an acceptable way of arriving at a damage verdict and probably one that is preferable to a more scientific (and sterile) process that excludes nonquantifiable elements to achieve an aura of objectivity and precision.

The plaintiffs' claim of an unquantified enhanced risk should not be characterized as "depend[ing] upon the likelihood of an event that has not yet occurred and may never occur." The injury involved is an actual event: exposure to toxic chemicals. The tortious contamination, moreover, is an event that has surely occurred; it is not a speculative or remote possible happening. Among the consequences of this unconsented-to invasion are genetic damage and a tangible risk of a major disease, a peril that is real even though it cannot be precisely measured or weighed. The peril, moreover, is unquestionably greater than that experienced by persons not similarly exposed to toxic chemicals. The toxic injury and claim for damages are not attributable only to some possible future event. Like claims based on the doctrines of trespass, assault, invasion of privacy, or defamation, the damages suffered are not solely actual consequential damages, but also the disvalue of being subjected to an intrinsically harmful event. The risk of dreadful disease resulting from toxic exposure and contamination is more frightening and palpable than any deficits we may feel or imagine from many other wrongful transgressions. * * *

In deciding whether to recognize plaintiffs' claims, the majority focuses on the problem of sovereign defendants in tort suits involving the unquantified nature of certain injuries. The majority, however, fails to note the long-term benefits lost when compensation is not allowed for injuries caused. Compensation serves to deter negligent behavior. We disserve this policy in this case, where the defendant municipality has engaged not simply in negligent conduct, but in "palpably unreasonable" conduct causing real and serious injury to its residents. * * *

"A tortfeasor should not be allowed to escape responsibility for causing an increased risk that would not have existed but for his negligence simply because of the statistical uncertainty of the risk." * * *

The majority speaks of the speculative nature of compensating claims of enhanced risk as if such would be an anomaly in the logical and orderly work of tort law compensation. The truth is to the contrary. There are relatively few injuries that can be easily or logically quantified. It is not merely the relatively new tort claims like "pain and suffering" and "emotional distress" that are difficult to quantify. What is the logical method of evaluation for compensating a claim of trespass on land, the battery of unconsented-to surgery, a violation of personal privacy, or an insult to character? When a jury awards $50,000 for an accident that led to the loss of a limb, how is that $50,000 a logical quantification of that injury?

The severe limitation of damages imposed by the Court in this case is inadequate and unfair. No person in her right mind would trade places with any one of these plaintiffs. Does this not suggest that a person would have to be paid a considerable sum of money, more than that permitted here by the Court, before tolerating the injuries suffered by these plaintiffs? Why should not a jury be permitted to make this determination? * * *

NOTES

1. *Itemizing the Damages.* The plaintiff's rightful position provides the starting point in determining what elements of damages are recoverable. To get started simply ask: What items of loss must be replaced to restore the plaintiff to her rightful position? In cases involving economic harm, a sort of balance sheet can be employed:

> In determining the measure of recovery, aside from harm to body, emotions or reputation, a balance sheet is in effect set up by the court in which are stated the items of assets and liabilities that have been affected by the tort, (a) before the tort and (b) as they appear at the

time of trial. In this are put on one side such assets of the injured person as have been affected by the tort, including his capacity to make profitable use of his time, and on the other side, the same assets at the time of the trial and any existing or prospective liabilities imposed upon him as a result of the tort. The difference, to the extent that it results from the tort, constitutes the theoretical measure of recovery.

Restatement (Second) of Torts § 906 comment a. While nonpecuniary harms are not susceptible of such precise measurement, the theory remains the same: restore the plaintiff to the pre-tort position.

2. *Collateral Source Rule.* If the plaintiffs in *Ayers* have health insurance that will pay for the costs of medical monitoring, should the award of damages for medical monitoring be reduced? No, according to the collateral source rule. The collateral source rule provides that "[p]ayments made to or benefits conferred on the injured party from other sources are not credited against the tortfeasor's liability, although they cover all or part of the harm for which the tortfeasor is liable." In other words, the amount of the plaintiffs' recovery is not reduced even though the plaintiffs may be compensated for the same loss again through their insurance, or by some other collateral source.

When an injured plaintiff is compensated by a collateral source for injuries the defendant caused, the stage is set for a conflict between two of the purposes of compensatory damages. If the plaintiff is allowed to keep the benefit from the collateral source and to recover again from the defendant, the plaintiff has a windfall. To the extent that compensatory damages are supposed to "make the plaintiff whole," the rule that collateral sources are ignored puts the plaintiff in better than his rightful position.

On the other hand, consider the effect on deterrence if benefits from a collateral source reduce the defendant's obligation to pay. If compensatory damages are intended to deter defendants by making them bear the full cost of the harm they cause, letting them off the hook in cases where the plaintiff was wise enough to insure, or fortunate enough to have friends to help out financially, would result in under-deterrence. Further, given the expense of litigation, compensatory damages don't really make the plaintiff whole anyway, and why should the defendant benefit from the insurance premiums the plaintiff wisely invested? After all, people should have an incentive to buy insurance, and a rule that deprived them of its benefits would discourage its purchase. *See* Helfend v. Southern California Rapid Transit District, 2 Cal.3d 1, 15, 84 Cal.Rptr. 173, 465 P.2d 61 (1970). Finally, many plaintiffs will not be overcompensated, because their insurance policies will have subrogation clauses that allow the insurer to recapture any benefits for which the plaintiff later receives compensation. So, double recovery is less common than the statement of the rule would suggest.

Eliminating the collateral source rule is high on the agenda of the current movement for tort reform. Legislation limiting the application of the rule has been enacted in at least thirty states. Some sixteen have enacted legislation eliminating or modifying the collateral source rule in all civil actions. Other states have been more selective, eliminating it in actions against public entities (Pennsylvania), construction defect cases (Alaska) or in medical malpractice actions (fifteen states). Interestingly, most of these statutes acknowledge the policy of encouraging potential plaintiffs to insure either by excluding collateral sources for which the plaintiff has paid premiums, or by offsetting the cost of some or all of the premiums paid to the collateral source. Like most tort reform statutes, these provisions have been challenged, sometimes successfully, on constitutional grounds. See Thompson v. KFB Insurance Co., 850 P.2d 773 (Kan.1993) (statute eliminating rule only where damages exceed $150,000 violates equal protection and due process); but see Marsh v. Green, 782 So.2d 223 (Ala.2000) (statute making evidence of collateral benefits admissible is constitutional); Germantown Savings Bank v. City of Philadelphia, 512 A.2d 756 (Pa.1986), aff'd 535 A.2d 1052 (Pa. 1988) (statute abrogating collateral source rule in actions against political subdivisions is constitutional).

　　　3.　　*Managing the Damage Award.* Tort damages have traditionally been awarded in a lump sum for past, present and future losses. The Ayers court suggests that were it not for the unfairness of changing the rules at such a late date in the litigation, it would abandon this practice. Instead of awarding a lump sum for medical surveillance, the court would create a fund against which the plaintiffs could make claims as they incur costs.

　　　The idea of a judicially administered fund for medical monitoring costs has turned out to be an attractive solution to the problem of uncertainty. For example, in Metro-North Commuter Railroad Co. v. Buckley, 521 U.S. 424 (1997), the Court rejected awarding lump sum damages for medical monitoring, but specifically reserved the question of whether a trust fund for medical monitoring expenses would have been an appropriate remedy.

　　　Tort reformers have found the notion of replacing lump sum awards with judgments that are paid out periodically, over time, to be attractive. That way, the defendant maintains control over the award, and gains the benefit of any expenses that, for one reason or another, do not eventuate. In return, the plaintiff gains a measure of security. If expenses exceed what might have been predicted, there is some protection, and the plaintiff is saved the burden of investing the award against future need. On the other hand, such paternalism may be unjustified, and it is not clear how periodically paid judgments are to accommodate the plaintiff's lawyer's fee, given that contingency fees predominate in personal injury litigation. Nonetheless, some tort reform statutes specifically provide for periodic payment of judgments. For an attempt to work out the problems periodic payment of judgments raises, see the Model Periodic Payment of Judgments Act.

　　　Ayers does not present very complicated problems in managing a damage award, compared to cases that may involve thousands or tens of thousands of claims, like asbestos, DES, or Agent Orange litigation. The problems in *Ayers* are sensitive primarily because a public entity is the defendant, and the public fisc can be jealously guarded.

THORN v. MERCY MEMORIAL HOSPITAL CORP.

Court of Appeals of Michigan
281 Mich. App. 644 (2008)

TALBOT, J.

In this wrongful death action, plaintiff appeals by leave granted the trial court's order granting defendants' motions to strike plaintiff's claim of economic damages for the loss of household services. We reverse and remand.

I.   BACKGROUND

Plaintiff, the personal representative of the estate of Laurie Ann Greene, deceased, contends that the medical malpractice committed by defendants Mercy Memorial Hospital Corporation (MMHC), Blessing B. Nwosu, M.D., S. Ahadi, M.D., P.C., Kianoush Khaghany, M.D., and Tanvir Iqbal Qureshi, M.D., resulted in the decedent's bleeding to death from the site of a Caesarean section. Plaintiff sought to recover damages pursuant to the wrongful death act (WDA), MCL 600.2922, including the economic value of household services the decedent had provided to her minor children. To develop an estimate of the replacement cost for these household services, plaintiff retained Dr. Nitin Parajpne as an expert in the field of economics. Parajpne opined that the cost to replace the services lost to the decedent's children was $1.45 million.

Defendants filed motions seeking to preclude plaintiff's claim for economic damages for the loss of household services and to exclude testimony by plaintiff's expert. Defendants argued that the language of MCL 600.2922(6) does not specifically list loss of services as a recoverable element of damages. Alternatively, defendants contend that plaintiff's claim for loss of services is merely a factor included in the damages for loss of society and companionship and is, therefore, noneconomic in nature and subject to the damages cap of MCL 600.1483.

Plaintiff responded that the language of MCL 600.2922(6) does not require a claim for damages to fit one of the categories of losses specifically enumerated in the statute. Rather, the statutory language, when considered fully and in context, demonstrates that the types of damages listed are intended to be examples and not limitations on recovery. In addition, plaintiff asserted that damages for loss of services are quantifiable and, therefore, should not be construed as being commensurate with the noneconomic compensation available for the more esoteric damages incurred for loss of society and companionship. Consequently, plaintiff argues that any such damages are not subject to the caps set forth under MCL 600.1483. Citing earlier versions of the WDA, plaintiff noted that the statute has historically permitted recovery for loss of services as a "pecuniary" injury even though the statute did not allow for the recovery of damages for loss of society and companionship until its amendment in 1971. Plaintiff also points to the language of M Civ JI 45.02, which specifically includes "loss of service" as a compensable damage, in addition to those items listed in MCL 600.2922(6).

The trial court granted defendants' motions on the basis of its interpretation of the language of MCL 600.2922(6). The trial court read the term "including" within the statute's language to be one of limitation, restricting recovery to only the categories of damages explicitly delineated. However, the trial court ruled that the jury could consider loss of services as noneconomic damages within the context of loss of society and companionship.

* * *

III. ARGUMENTS

A. Statutory Language

Defendants initially contend that the wording of MCL 600.2922(6) precludes the consideration of damages for loss of services in a wrongful death action. * * *

> (6) In every action under this section, the court or jury may award damages as the court or jury shall consider fair and equitable, under all the circumstances including reasonable medical, hospital, funeral, and burial expenses for which the estate is liable; reasonable compensation for the pain and suffering, while conscious, undergone by the deceased during the period intervening between the time of the injury and death; and damages for the loss of financial support and the loss of the society and companionship of the deceased.

Defendants contend that "including" is a term of limitation and that the list of damages provided following that term is inclusive and restrictive. In contrast, plaintiff asserts that the term "including" demonstrates the intent of the Legislature to provide a nonexhaustive list of examples of the types of damages recoverable under the WDA. * * *

The word "including" is directly preceded in the statutory subsection by the following language: "In every action under this section, the court or jury *may award damages* as the court or jury *shall consider fair and equitable, under all the circumstances. . . .*" (Emphasis added.) When viewed in context, rather than as a solitary term, the word "including" indicates an intent by the Legislature to permit the award of any type of damages, economic and noneconomic, deemed justified by the facts of the particular case. As such, the term "including" should be construed as merely providing specific examples of the types of damages available, and not an exhaustive list. To view the term in the limiting manner urged by defendants would result in an internal contradiction. Interpreted in the manner suggested by defendants, the statutory language would mandate both the award of damages "consider[ed] fair and equitable, under all the circumstances" while simultaneously limiting a plaintiff's recovery only to those items specified in the list following the term "including." * * *

In contrast to the caselaw relied on by defendants, we note that our Supreme Court has issued numerous rulings expressing an expansive interpretation of the damages available under the WDA. By way of example, when interpreting the survivor benefits provisions of the no-fault act, MCL 500.3108, the Michigan Supreme Court found guidance in MCL 600.2922. Specifically, the Court stated, in relevant part:

Thus, it appears that the Legislature's use of the language "contributions of tangible things of economic value" in § 3108 indicates an intent that survivors' loss benefits should at least roughly correspond to economic loss damages recoverable under our wrongful death act. MCL 600.2922; MSA 27A.2922.

Under our wrongful death act, a survivor's recoverable *economic losses include,* at a minimum, *the loss of financial support* from the deceased *and the loss of services* that the survivor would have received from the deceased had he lived. . . .

To the extent that survivors' loss benefits are intended to be analogous to wrongful death act economic loss damages, it is important to keep in mind that wrongful death act damages focus upon the financial loss actually incurred by the survivors as a result of their decedent's death.

* * * The clear implication of these rulings is that when awarding damages in a wrongful death action based on medical malpractice there must be (a) an initial determination regarding the full extent of damages available to the plaintiff deemed "fair and equitable" and (b) a subsequent reduction or limitation of those damages on the basis of the applicability of MCL 600. 1483.

Historically * * * "the wrongful-death act is essentially a 'filter' through which the underlying claim may proceed." This is consistent with other statutory provisions pertaining to the WDA, such as MCL 600.2921, which states: "All actions and claims survive death."

This Court, in discussing the history of the WDA, recognized that it has been *unquestioned* that the wrongful death act *permits recovery for the loss of services and companionship.*" Citing the mandatory language of MCL 600.2922(1) contained at that time that "all actions for a wrongful death 'shall be brought only under this section,' " the * * * Court noted that this requirement necessitated the bringing of an action for "loss of services" under the WDA, and not as a separate action.

Defendants' position is also contrary to caselaw involving earlier versions of the WDA, which did not recognize loss of society and companionship but did permit recovery for loss of services as pecuniary damages. In addressing a parent's right to recover for the loss of a minor child, our Supreme Court held:

Only pecuniary damages can be recovered in such actions as this. Nothing can be given as solace or for bereavement suffered. . . . It is not indispensable that there should be proof of actual services of pecuniary value rendered to next of kin, nor that any witness should express an opinion as to the value of services that may have been or might be rendered. Where the deceased was a minor, and left a father who would have been entitled to his services had he lived, the law implies a pecuniary loss, for which compensation, under the statute, may be given.

Similarly, the Court interpreted the WDA and held, "The statute and Michigan case law interpreting it allow consideration of loss of services of a minor in determining pecuniary injury of a parent."[T]he Court recognized that "[t]he pecuniary value of a human life is a compound of many elements" and that "an individual member of a family has a value to others as part of a functioning social and economic unit." [T]his Court recognized, that "adult children may recover from the tort-feasor for the unlawful death of a parent where loss of love, companionship and guidance have been proven," and indicated:

It has been the law in Michigan for a number of years that in an action under the death act, as amended, for damages arising because of the death of the wife, the husband is entitled to recovery for the loss of her services. . . .

The same elements of pecuniary injury plus loss of services of the wife . . . were also submitted as proper to be considered by the jury as a loss to the husband in assessing damages.

Earlier, the Court addressed the scope of pecuniary damages available under the WDA and ruled, in relevant part:

Although, under the death act . . . recovery is limited to those persons entitled to support from decedent, recovery is not limited to the amount of support actually received. The amended act is at least as broad in protecting recovery on behalf of minor children as the original act. And in spite of the rule just stated, a husband is still entitled to recovery for loss of his wife's services, apart from any earning capacity which she may or may not have had.

As discussed earlier in this opinion, the evolution of the WDA demonstrates that the statute has consistently been found to recognize the availability of damages for loss of services and that the various amendments of the statute have served to expand, rather than limit, the damages available to litigants. * * *

Further, when viewed in the context of the statutory scheme for medical malpractice, defendants' position is logically inconsistent with MCL 600.1483(1), which increases the cap for noneconomic damages when a more serious or permanent and irreparable injury is incurred. Defendants assert that the most serious injury, which results in death, serves to restrict and prohibit claims that would be compensable had the individual survived. Common sense would dictate the opposite—the more egregious the injury, the greater the damages. Any other result would be contrary to the history of litigation in this area of the law, which sought to assure that wrongdoers would be held accountable to their victims. * * *

We find it inconceivable, as argued by defendants, that a child would be precluded from recovering damages for loss of services stemming from the parent-child relationship following the harsher and irreversible outcome of a parent's death, but that these same damages would be recoverable by a parent who is injured but survives. Such a position is inconsistent with the stated purpose of the WDA, MCL 600.2921, to assure that "[a]ll actions and claims survive death," and contrary to the language of MCL 600.2922(1). The statutory language leads to the inescapable conclusion that the intervention of death neither limits nor precludes the type of damages that could have been recovered by the person had the person survived the injury. The cost of replacement services is a well-recognized component of damages that is recoverable by a person injured because of medical malpractice. Consequently, because the claim survives a decedent's death, a claim for loss of services must also be available in an action for wrongful death. In light of the statutory language and the cases cited earlier in this opinion there is no valid argument that a claim for loss of services is precluded by statutory language. * * *

B.   Loss of Society and Companionship

Unwilling to rely solely on a statutory language argument, defendants also assert an alternative, and seemingly contradictory, position. Defendants contend that damages for loss of services are available but fall strictly under the umbrella of loss of society and companionship. Defendants argue that loss of society and companionship is defined in the same manner, and encompasses the same criteria or elements, as loss of consortium and, as such, is noneconomic in nature and, therefore, subject to the damages cap of MCL 600. 1483. Defendants' characterization is inaccurate and oversimplifies these terms or concepts.

While loss of society and companionship and loss of consortium share certain components and have often been erroneously used interchangeably, defendants are incorrect in asserting that the terms are equivalent in meaning. Loss of consortium is typically construed to encompass two aspects of the marital relationship—the loss of support and the loss of society. " 'Loss of consortium technically means the loss of conjugal fellowship. However, it is legally recognized as including loss of society, companionship, service, and all other incidents of the marriage relationship.' " Although loss of consortium includes loss of services and loss of society as components, that does not make the concepts interchangeable or determine whether they are economic or noneconomic in nature.

In distinguishing between a claim for loss of consortium and a claim for loss of society under the WDA, " 'courts have consistently treated loss of consortium not as an item of damages, but as an independent cause of action. . . .' " Loss of consortium constitutes a broader or more encompassing claim focused on allowing recovery for the loss incurred for a family member's own relationship with the injured individual and is specifically precluded under the WDA. This Court recognized the distinctions between an action for loss of consortium and a claim for loss of society and companionship stating, "Such damages are not the same as common-law loss of consortium damages, which is why loss of consortium damages are not treated the same as loss of society and companionship damages allocated in a wrongful death action." Rather, the dispositive issue is whether loss of services damages constitute an economic or noneconomic loss.

Because an action under the WDA "grounded in medical malpractice is a medical malpractice action in which the plaintiff is allowed to collect damages related to the death of the decedent," to determine whether loss of services comprises an economic or noneconomic element of damages, we look to MCL 600.1483 to discern the nature and character of the damages available to plaintiff. MCL 600.1483(2) mandates that "[i]n awarding damages in an action alleging medical malpractice, the trier of fact shall itemize damages into damages for economic loss and damages for noneconomic loss." Our Supreme Court has already determined that WDA cases arising from medical malpractice permit a plaintiff to receive "damages awarded . . . for loss of society and companionship" and that these damages are "clearly noneconomic." MCL 600.1483(3) defines "noneconomic loss" as "damages or loss due to pain, suffering, inconvenience, physical impairment, physical disfigurement, or other noneconomic loss." However, there is no commensurate provision defining the types of damages encompassed by MCL 600.1483 for economic loss. * * *

While MCL 600.1483 fails to define what factors comprise an economic loss or fully delineate the components of a noneconomic loss, other sections of the Revised Judicature Act, MCL 600.101 et seq., pertaining to product liability actions resulting from injury or death provide guidance. The Legislature, in MCL 600.2945, specifically defined those items:

> (c) "Economic loss" means objectively verifiable pecuniary damages arising from medical expenses or medical care, rehabilitation services, custodial care, loss of wages, loss of future earnings, burial costs, loss of use of property, costs of repair or replacement of property, costs of obtaining substitute domestic services, loss of employment, or other objectively verifiable monetary losses.

> (f) "Noneconomic loss" means any type of pain, suffering, inconvenience, physical impairment, disfigurement, mental anguish, emotional distress, loss of society and companionship, loss of consortium, injury to reputation, humiliation, or other nonpecuniary damages.

We note that the definition of "economic loss" is consistent with prior versions of the WDA, which focused on pecuniary damages. The definition of noneconomic loss under this statutory provision parallels the historical progression of the WDA, which initially precluded recovery for nonpecuniary damages, such as loss of society and companionship, grief, and mental anguish. The definition in MCL 600.2945(f) is also consistent with the definition of noneconomic loss in MCL 600.1483(3).

Although the damages recoverable under the WDA are determined by the underlying action, it is nonsensical to construe the nature or character of those damages as being variable depending on the theory of liability. What comprises an economic loss in a medical malpractice action must be the same as what constitutes an economic loss under a different theory of tort liability. To find otherwise would be not only confusing, but also would lead to inconsistent and inequitable results when an injury is fatal. * * *

Clearly, this Court has recognized not only the availability of damages for loss of services, but also acknowledged these damages as economic and separate and distinguishable from compensation for loss of society or companionship.

IV. Conclusion

We conclude that the statutory language of MCL 600.2922(6) does not preclude plaintiff's claim for damages for loss of services. Further, we reject defendants' assertion that loss of services is merely a component of a claim for loss of society and companionship or the equivalent of a claim for loss of consortium. As a result, plaintiff's claim for loss of services comprises a claim for economic damages, which is not subject to the damages cap of MCL 600.1483.

Reversed and remanded for further proceedings consistent with this opinion.

NOTES

1. *The Plaintiff's Cause of Action: Survival and Wrongful Death Actions.* At English common law, actions for personal injury and other injuries to other personal interests terminated if either of the parties to the action died. (Causes of action based on property rights—like breach of contract—survived.) Further, there was no independent cause of action for causing a person's death.

Then, in 1846 Parliament enacted Lord Campbell's Act, 9 & 10 Vic., c. 93, which established a cause of action against one who wrongfully caused another's death for the benefit of those dependent on the decedent for support. Following this lead, every state now has a statutory remedy for wrongful death. See Stuart M. Speiser et al., *Recovery for Wrongful Death and Injury* (3d ed.1992).

2. *The Elements of Damages in Wrongful Death and Survival Actions.* The elements of damages in a survival action or a wrongful death action are fixed by statute. Survival statutes allow for an action to recover the damages on behalf of the decedent himself for his own injuries, which is said to "survive" after the death. *E.g.,* Ohio Rev. Code § 2305.21. The wrongful death action is then brought on behalf of the family members for their own losses resulting from the death. Here is a statutory example from Ohio. Ohio is unusual in awarding mental anguish for the grief.

OHIO REVISED CODE § 21215. ACTION FOR WRONGFUL DEATH

2125.02 Parties—damages.

(A)(1)   Except as provided in this division, a civil action for wrongful death shall be brought in the name of the personal representative of the decedent for the exclusive benefit of the surviving spouse, the children, and the parents of the decedent, all of whom are rebuttably presumed to have suffered damages by reason of the wrongful death, and for the exclusive benefit of the other next of kin of the decedent. A parent who abandoned a minor child who is the decedent shall not receive a benefit in a civil action for wrongful death brought under this division.

> (2)   The jury . . . may award damages . . . as it determines are proportioned to the injury and loss resulting to the beneficiaries . . . and may award the reasonable funeral and burial expenses incurred as a result of the wrongful death. . . .

> (3)(a)   The date of the decedent's death fixes . . . the status of all beneficiaries of the civil action for wrongful death for purposes of determining the damages suffered by them and the amount of damages to be awarded. * * *

(B)   Compensatory damages may be awarded in a civil action for wrongful death and may include damages for the following:

(1)   Loss of support from the reasonably expected earning capacity of the decedent;

(2)   Loss of services of the decedent;

(3)   Loss of the society of the decedent, including loss of companionship, consortium, care, assistance, attention, protection, advice, guidance, counsel, instruction, training, and education, suffered by the surviving spouse, dependent children, parents, or next of kin of the decedent;

(4)   Loss of prospective inheritance to the decedent's heirs at law at the time of the decedent's death;

(5)   The mental anguish incurred by the surviving spouse, dependent children, parents, or next of kin of the decedent.

Where the defendant's wrong caused the plaintiff's death, the survival statute and the wrongful death statute may overlap. Then, generally the survival action seeks recover of damages sustained by the decedent before the death, and the wrongful death action seeks damages sustained by the family after the death. For example, both the individual and the family might seek lost wages, where the family was dependent on the person's wages. The lost wages up until the time of death would be recovered in the survival action; the lost wages after the death recovered in the wrongful death action. (Procedurally, many states allow both actions to be prosecuted at the same time by the decedent's personal representative.)

3.   *Hedonic Damages:* Only five or six states allow recovery of damages for "loss of life"—sometimes known as hedonic damages—in a wrongful death action. *See* Eric A. Posner & Cass R. Sunstein, *Dollars and Death*, 72 U.Chi.L.Rev. 537, 545 (2005) (listing Arkansas, Connecticut, Hawai'i, New Hampshire and New Mexico); *see also* Choctaw Maid Farms, Inc. v. Hailey, 822 So.2d 911 (Miss.2002) (hedonic damages are recoverable in wrongful death action even where death is instantaneous). Damages for harm to the plaintiff's quality of life or lost enjoyment of life are less controversial in personal injury cases. It seems to be generally settled that general damages can include compensation for loss of the ability to participate in or to enjoy the ordinary activities of life. *See, e.g.,* Ogden v. J.M. Steel Erecting, Inc., 31 P.3d 806, 813 (Ariz.App.2001) (damages for loss of enjoyment of life "compensate the individual not only for the subjective knowledge that one can no longer enjoy all of life's pursuits, but also for the objective loss of the ability to engage in these activities").

Of course, without an award of damages for the lost value of life, damages in cases where the decedent has no dependents or has limited earning capacity—elders, homemakers or children for example—will be minimal. *See, e.g.,* McGowan v. Estate of Wright, 524 So.2d 308 (Miss.1988) (upholding a jury verdict that awarded only funeral expenses to the estranged spouse of a man who was instantly killed in a car accident). Consider:

[The loss to the victim in a wrongful death case] consists of the utility or satisfaction that the victim would have derived, net of any disutility, over the remaining course of his life. * * * [This] type of loss cannot, strictly speaking, be compensated. No award of damages will restore a dead person to the state of happiness he would have enjoyed but for his death. This is not a compelling argument against awarding damages, provided the purpose of tort damages is deterrent rather than compensatory. The threat of having to pay heavy damages will reduce the incidence of tortious conduct, and so increase social welfare, even though the payment of damages in a case where the victim dies will not compensate him.

Richard A. Posner, *Tort Law: Cases and Economic Analysis* 121–22 (1982).

On the other hand, does awarding damages for the value of a life commodify life in a way that is fundamentally offensive?

Many people believe that a human life is uniquely precious and therefore cannot be given a monetary valuation. See, for example, Frank Ackerman and Lisa Heinzerling, *Priceless: On Knowing the Price of Everything and the Value of Nothing* 61 (New Press 2004) ("Putting a price on human life . . . is clearly unacceptable to virtually all religions and moral philosophies."). Calculating the value of a human life demeans the victim of the wrong rather than vindicating his memory.

Dollars and Death, at 553.

2. MEASURING TORT DAMAGES

Elements of tort damages that are economic in character—medical expenses, lost earnings, harm to property, and so on—are generally measured the same way we have seen, by looking at value and alternative measurements. There are additional mathematical and legal issues raised with estimating future losses, as future lost wages or future medical expenses. But the biggest difference with measuring tort damages is difficulty of measuring intangible nonpecuniary losses like pain and suffering, emotional distress, or quality of life.

Very little law exists on the proper measurement of nonpecuniary losses, except to say that the amount of the award is in the fact-finder's discretion. Because the loss is intangible and subjective, the plaintiff's testimony as to the discomfort, annoyance, and so on that the injury has caused is central. Family and friends may also testify, corroborating the testimony. The testimony then provides a factual basis for a dollar amount to be assessed, looking at how severe or mild a loss might be.

The courts then have the ability on their own or at the defendant's request to reduce for prejudice the amount the jury awards for that nonpecuniary loss. One key approach is to compare the award to the range of awards in similar cases of similar harm. If it is found excessive, the court then uses *remittitur* to award a new trial unless the plaintiff accepts the reduced amount. When the verdict is thought inadequate, and the defendant is offered the choice of accepting a larger verdict or a new trial, it is called *additur*. Both remittitur and additur threaten the right of the parties to a jury trial, because the risk and expense of a new trial coerce the party into accepting the judge's opinion on damages over the jury's. Remittitur, however, was known at common law in 1791, and because the Seventh Amendment guarantees only the right to jury as it existed at common law, the United States Supreme Court has found it constitutional. Additur, however, was unknown at common law, and so in the federal system it has been held unconstitutional. Dimick v. Schiedt, 293 U.S. 474 (1935). It is still available, though, in many state court systems. *E.g.,* Right v. Breen, 890 A.2d 1287 (Conn. 2006).

TULLIS v. TOWNLEY ENGINEERING & MANUFACTURING CO.

United States Court of Appeals, Seventh Circuit, 2001
243 F.3d 1058

FLAUM, CHIEF JUDGE.

[William Tullis sued his employer for retaliatory discharge, alleging that he was fired for pursuing a workers compensation claim after injuring his back. At trial, he prevailed, recovering $80,185.58 in nonpecuniary damages. The Court of Appeals found that there was sufficient evidence to support the jury verdict in his favor on liability.]

* * *

B. COMPENSATORY DAMAGES

Townley contends that the $80,185.68 nonpecuniary damages jury award for "mental anguish and inconvenience" was the product of passion and prejudice and so it requests a new trial or reduction of the damages through remittitur. Townley is concerned about the massive and excessive size of the jury award. The district court reviewed Townley's request for a new trial based upon the nonpecuniary damage award and determined that the award should be upheld. We review the district court's refusal to grant a new trial on the basis that the damages the jury awarded were excessive for an abuse of discretion.

When we review a compensatory damages award, we employ the following three-part test: (1) whether the award is monstrously excessive; (2) whether there is no rational connection between the award and the evidence; and (3) whether the award is roughly comparable to awards made in similar cases. Townley argues that the jury award for $80,185.68 fails all three prongs of this test.

Specifically, Townley claims that the award is monstrously excessive because it is based exclusively upon Tullis' own testimony. No physician or other professional testified that Tullis suffered psychologically from Townley's conduct nor did Tullis or a family member, friend, or other lay witness testify to his emotional injury. * * * Townley asserts that Tullis' testimony was not very detailed and thus does not support the award. Further, Townley notes that Tullis did not claim that he suffered from periodic depression, fits of anger, or other physical symptoms. According to Townley, all of this combined displays that Tullis' award for mental anguish and inconvenience was monstrously excessive.

Townley also maintains that the award is not rationally related to the evidence and that Tullis did not make a specific request with regard to compensatory damages; rather he asked the jury to "do what's fair." Townley argues that the problem is that the evidence does not support the amount awarded. For instance, in Avitia v. Metropolitan Club of Chicago, Inc., 49 F.3d 1219, 1229–30 (7th Cir.1995), the court found damages for $21,000 because of emotional distress were excessive, even though the plaintiff in that case cried as a result of being discharged from a job that he had been at for 13 years and experienced such distress several years after he had been fired. Tullis, according to Townley, has provided far less compelling evidence regarding the intensity and duration of his emotional distress. Similarly, in Fleming v. County of Kane, 898 F.2d 553, 561–62 (7th Cir.1990), the Court found a $40,000 award, which had been reduced to this figure from the jury's amount of $80,000 by the trial court, was proper. The plaintiff in Fleming had been discharged for his whistle-blowing activities. Fleming testified to feelings of embarrassment, humiliation, certain depression, serious headaches, and sleeplessness. His wife and fellow department employees supported his testimony concerning his physical and emotional condition. Once again, Townley asserts that Tullis did not provide nearly the same type of evidence as was presented in Fleming, yet he received a substantially greater award, and these cases suggest that Tullis' nonpecuniary damage award is not rationally related to the evidence that he presented.

Finally, Townley advances that the jury award is not comparable to awards in similar cases. As previously discussed, the award in this case is larger than in *Avitia*, 49 F.3d at 1230 ($10,500 award after remittitur), and *Fleming*, 898 F.2d at 561–62 ($40,000 award). While it may be true that in Kasper v. Saint Mary of Nazareth Hosp., 135 F.3d 1170, 1174 (7th Cir.1998), a compensatory damage award for a retaliatory discharge claim in the amount of $150,000 was upheld, this was because the award was not challenged. Similarly, in *Jackson*, 40 F.3d at 245 n. 5, a case involving a retaliatory discharge claim under the Illinois Workers' Compensation Act, the parties agreed to compensatory damages in the amount of $75,000. Finally, in Peeler v. Village of Kingston Mines, 862 F.2d 135 (7th Cir.1988), the court addressed a $50,000 award for emotional distress based upon a retaliatory discharge claim. In that case, the evidence presented relayed "[p]oignant scenes of distress and abysmal poverty," while the plaintiff was unemployed. There, the plaintiff was evicted from his house, forced to live in a truck for three days, depended in part on charity to feed his family, used rags to diaper his child, friends donated clothes for his five children, could not afford a doctor when his children were sick, and suffered health problems. Townley argues that Tullis' experience does not rise nearly to this level and thus $80,185.68 is simply not warranted.

* * *

Although Townley characterizes Tullis' testimony regarding his emotional distress and inconvenience as relatively meager and scant, the jury obviously did not perceive it this way considering the award they granted Tullis. An award for nonpecuniary loss can be supported, in certain circumstances, solely by a plaintiff's testimony about his or her emotional distress. The jury was able to observe Tullis when he was testifying and they apparently found his testimony to be sincere and sufficient to convince them that he merited the award they gave him.

The jury, as seen by the amount they awarded Tullis, which some may even characterize as exceedingly generous, must have not believed that Tullis needed to show that he sought the help of psychologists or friends for his emotional distress or that he was required to provide more detail about either his emotional distress or the inconvenience that he experienced. Tullis' testimony did reveal he felt "low" and "degraded" when he was laid off and "back-stabbed" when the company opposed his unemployment claim. He also said that he was without work for nine to ten months, and this affected his personal life, including that he had to borrow money from family and friends and he had his lights and phone shut off. The jury could have determined that these were not minor events. The jury also may have taken into account that his family life was disrupted in that he was not able to buy his children new schools clothes, pay his child support, or take his children out dining and shopping. Tullis also did find a new job, but it was as a trucker, which required him to be away from home, and he even said that Townley "was a very convenient place for [him] to work at because it was close to the house. It was five minutes from the house." The jury may very well have found that these types of changes were significant to Tullis' family situation. Because it is within the jury's domain to assess the credibility of witnesses, specifically in this case the testimony of Tullis, we cannot find that the award was monstrously excessive or not rationally connected to the evidence. Further, since we have determined that the verdict was supported by the evidence, then necessarily it was not a result of passion and prejudice.

Thus, our remaining task is to examine "whether the award is out of line with other awards in similar cases." Townley cites *Avitia* and *Fleming* as cases that are roughly comparable and resulted in damage awards that were not nearly as substantial as the award in this case. *Avitia*, however, involved emotional distress only and not inconvenience. Similarly, in *Fleming* the damages concerned emotional distress, and unlike in this case, we affirmed the trial court's determination that a remittitur, reducing the damages to $40,000, was appropriate. More recently, we affirmed without much commentary, a $50,000 compensatory award (presumably for emotional distress) for retaliatory discharge brought under the Illinois Workers' Compensation Act. The most troubling case presented by Townley with regard to the issue is *Peeler*, 862 F.2d at 139, in which rather egregious facts led to the affirmation of a $50,000 compensatory award for the plaintiff. One must remember that this jury award is from 1988 and the current dollar value of this award is greater than $50,000; it is worth approximately $70,000 in 1999. The *Peeler* award is roughly comparable to Tullis' compensatory damage award, if one takes into account the jury's right to make awards based upon its view of a witness's demeanor and credibility. We cannot conclude that $80,185.68 is not roughly comparable to the small number of similar cases (albeit in most instances distinguishable) that we have discussed. Therefore, we affirm the district court's decision not to grant a new trial or remittitur on the issue of the $80,185.68 compensatory damage award.

NOTES

1. How else can the plaintiff's attorney introduce evidence of the intangible losses? Appellate courts have allowed lawyers a free hand in presenting demonstrative evidence to influence the jury's award. Some plaintiffs' lawyers place great stock in "day-in-the-life" films that show how the plaintiff's daily activities have been affected by the injury. The use of these films can raise a number of discovery and evidentiary issues. For example, must the opposing party be allowed to attend the filming or have access to all unused footage? *See, e.g.,* Cisarik v. Palos Community Hospital, 579 N.E.2d 873 (Ill. 1991) (no). What evidentiary standards must be met for a film to be admissible? *See* Jones v. City of Los Angeles, 20 Cal.App.4th 436, 24 Cal.Rptr.2d 528 (1993) (standard is the same as that for authentication of a writing; the proponent must show that the videotape accurately portrays what it purports to portray, for example by offering testimony by a person who was present at the filming).

As for jury arguments, appeals to the jury's sympathy and attempts to arouse the jury's passion and prejudice are impermissible. Beyond this vague restriction, the controversy has focused on two very specific types of jury argument. One of these is known as the Golden Rule argument. In a Golden Rule argument, counsel asks the jury to place itself in the shoes of the plaintiff, or defendant, and to ask, were I him, how much would I demand as compensation, or were I sued, how much would I think it fair for me to pay? Golden Rule arguments are generally not permitted.

Opinion is divided as to the other traditional argument, the per diem argument. In a per diem argument, counsel suggests a specific amount of compensation for each day, or hour, or minute that the plaintiff will suffer, and then demonstrates to the jury what the award should be by multiplying that amount by the plaintiff's life expectancy in days, hours, or minutes. With this calculation, a small amount can rapidly inflate into an astronomical award. Some jurisdictions permit the per diem argument, provided that the jury is instructed that the figures used are not evidence, but are simply offered by way of argument and illustration. Other jurisdictions do not allow it, because the technique gives a misleading impression of precision.

For examination of the way in which juries evaluate nonpecuniary loss, *see* Ronen Avraham, *Putting a Price on Pain-and-Suffering Damages: A Critique of the Current Approaches and a Preliminary Proposal for Change*, 100 Nw.U.L.Rev. 87 (2006); Nicole L. Mott, Valerie P. Hans & Lindsay Solomon, *What's Half a Lung Worth? Civil Jurors' Accounts of Their Award Decision Making*, 24 L. & Hum.Behav. 401 (2000); Roselle L. Wissler, Patricia F. Kuehn & Michael J. Saks, *Instructing Jurors on General Damages in Personal Injury Cases: Problems and Possibilities*, 6 Psych.Pub.Pol'y & L. 712 (2000).

2.   Does the indeterminacy associated with measuring nonpecuniary loss undermine the goals of tort law?

> The paramount contemporary efficiency based goals of tort law contemplate that the costs of accidents be allocated to the most suitable actors and enterprises whose activities and products generate them, thereby spreading the costs of accidents to the consumers of the products and services. * * * The attainment of [these] economic goals hinges on the integrity and soundness of the process of valuing victims' losses. Loss allocation and spreading are undermined by the incommensurability of pain and money. The deterrence-incentive-based goals depend on a rational foundation that individuals and enterprises can summon in making their cost-benefit analyses so as to optimize the expenditure of resources on loss avoidance. Deterrence and incentive goals of tort law are corrupted when the assessment of damages is arbitrary and lacks any objective referent.

Joseph H. King, *Pain and Suffering, Noneconomic Damages, and the Goals of Tort Law*, 57 S.M.U.L.Rev. 163, 209 (2004). Does the problem have a constitutional dimension? Paul DeCamp, *Beyond State Farm: Due Process Constraints on Noneconomic Compensation Damages*, 27 Harv. J.L. & Pub. Pol'y 231 (2003) (arguing due process may limit nonpecuniary damage awards, as it does punitive damage awards).

ARPIN V. UNITED STATES

United States Court of Appeals
521 F.3d 769 (7th Cir. 2008)

POSNER, CIRCUIT JUDGE.

The plaintiff's husband was a patient at the Belleville Family Practice Clinic, in southern Illinois. The clinic is jointly operated by the U.S. Air Force and St. Louis University, the defendants in this suit for wrongful death arising from alleged medical malpractice. * * * After a three-day bench trial, the district judge found the defendants jointly and severally liable and awarded the plaintiff damages in excess of $8 million, consisting of some $500,000 for medical care and lost wages, $750,000 for pain and suffering, and $7 million for loss of consortium by her and the couple's four children. The appeals challenge both the finding of liability and the amount of damages awarded for loss of consortium.

[The plaintiff's husband fell at work, injuring his hip. Because the pain worsened overnight, he went to a hospital, where the injury treated with painkillers. The pain continued to worsen, so the plaintiff took her husband to the defendants' family practice clinic. According to the appellate court, the evidence supported the trial court's determination that the defendants' doctors negligently diagnosed his hip pain as a muscle strain, rather than recognizing that it was a symptom of a serious infection. Had the infection been properly diagnosed, it would have been easily treated with antibiotics. Two days later, plaintiff's husband was admitted to a hospital with symptoms of septic shock and multiple organ failure. He died two weeks later.]

* * *

So both defendants were liable for Arpin's death, and the liability was joint and several; we now consider whether the judge's award of $7 million in damages for loss of consortium was so excessive as to "shock the judicial conscience," which is the test under Illinois law. The awarding of damages, such as for pain and suffering and loss of consortium, that do not merely replace a financial loss has been criticized, especially in medical malpractice cases because of concern with the high and rising costs of health care. Damages awards in malpractice cases drive up liability insurance premiums and, what may be the greater cost, promote "defensive medicine" that costs a lot but may do patients little good. Daniel P. Kessler & Mark B. McClellan, "Do Doctors Practice Defensive Medicine?," 111 Q.J. Econ. 353 (1998). A reaction has set in that includes the recent passage of an Illinois law capping noneconomic damages in malpractice cases at $1 million for hospitals and hospital affiliates and $500,000 for physicians and other health-care professionals, 735 ILCS 5/2–1706.5(a)(1), (2), though the law was passed too recently to be applicable to this case and a judge has ruled that it violates the Illinois constitution. LeBron v. Gottlieb Memorial Hospital, 2007 WL 3390918 (Ill.Cir.Ct. Nov. 13, 2007).

It used to be thought that noneconomic losses were arbitrary because incommensurable with any dollar valuation. That is not true. People are constantly trading off hazards to life and limb against money; consider combat pay and re-enlistment bonuses in the army. Even when the tradeoff is between two nonmonetary values, such as danger and convenience (as when one crosses a street against the lights because one is in a hurry, or drives in excess of the speed limit), it may be possible to express the tradeoff in monetary terms, for example by estimating, on the basis of hourly wage rates, the value of the time saving. And if we know both the probability of a fatal accident and the benefit that a person would demand to bear it we can estimate a value of life and use that value to calculate damages in wrongful death cases. See W. Kip Viscusi and Joseph E. Aldy, "The Value of a Statistical Life: A Critical Review of Market Estimates Throughout the World," 27 J. Risk & Uncertainty 5 (2003). Suppose a person would demand $7 to assume a one in one million chance of being killed. Then we would estimate the value of his life at $7 million. Not that he would sell his life for that (or for any) amount of money, but that if the risk could be eliminated at any cost under $7 he would be better off. Suppose it could be eliminated by the potential injurer at a cost of only $5. Then we would want him to do so and the prospect of a $7 million judgment if he failed to would give him the proper incentive.

Loss of life is a real loss even when it has no financial dimension (the decedent might have had no income). So is the loss of the companionship ("consortium") of a loved one. The problem is the lack of a formula for calculating appropriate damages for loss of consortium. The plaintiff's lawyer presented a good deal of evidence of the close and loving relationship between Mr. Arpin and his wife and children, but did not attempt—how could he?—to connect the evidence to the specific figures that he requested in his closing argument. He requested $5 million for Arpin's widow and $1 million for each of the children; the judge awarded $4 million to her and $750,000 to each child. All the judge said in explanation of his award of these amounts was that "it is difficult to put a value on something that is priceless. Mrs. Arpin is far more dependent on her husband than are her children. Her children have suffered the loss of a father that is great and the devastation to this family is immeasurable."

When a federal judge is the trier of fact, he, unlike a jury, is required to explain the grounds of his decision. Fed.R.Civ.P. 52(a). "This means, when the issue is the amount of damages, that the judge must indicate the reasoning process that connects the evidence to the conclusion." Jutzi-Johnson v. United States, 263 F.3d 753, 758 (7th Cir.2001). One cannot but sympathize with the inability of the district judge in this case to say more than he did in justification of the damages that he assessed for loss of consortium. But the figures were plucked out of the air, and that procedure cannot be squared with the duty of reasoned, articulate adjudication imposed by Rule 52(a).

The judge should have considered awards in similar cases, both in Illinois and elsewhere. * * *

Courts may be able to derive guidance for calculating damages for loss of consortium from the approach that the Supreme Court has taken in recent years to the related question of assessing the constitutionality of punitive damages. The Court has ruled that such damages are presumptively limited to a single-digits multiple of the compensatory damages, and perhaps to no more than four times those damages. State Farm Mutual Automobile Ins. Co. v. Campbell, 538 U.S. 408, 424–25 (2003). The first step in taking a ratio approach to calculating damages for loss of consortium would be to examine the average ratio in wrongful-death cases in which the award of such damages was upheld on appeal. The next step would be to consider any special factors that might warrant a departure from the average in the case at hand. Suppose the average ratio is 1:5—that in the average case, the damages awarded for loss of consortium are 20 percent of the damages awarded to compensate for the other losses resulting from the victim's death. The amount might then be adjusted upward or downward on the basis of the number of the decedent's children, whether they were minors or adults, and the closeness of the relationship between the decedent and his spouse and children. In the present case the first and third factors would favor an upward adjustment, and the second a downward adjustment because all of Arpin's children were adults when he died.

We suspect that such an analysis would lead to the conclusion that the award in this case was excessive, but it is not our place to undertake the analysis. It is a task for the trial judge in the first instance, though we cannot sustain the award of damages for loss of consortium on the meager analysis in the judge's opinion; it does not satisfy the requirements of Rule 52(a). We have suggested (without meaning to prescribe) an approach that would enable him to satisfy them.

We affirm the joint and several liability of the defendants. and the award of damages other than for loss of consortium. With regard to those damages we vacate the judgment and remand the case for further proceedings consistent with this opinion.

NOTES

1.   Loss of consortium is a separate cause of action brought by a person whose spouse has suffered debilitating injuries. The action protects the interest in intimate relationships. Elements of damages typically include loss of the spouse's society and comfort, physical and emotional support, physical

intimacy and diminished social activity. Loss of consortium is a derivative action. Defenses that are good against the physically injured person's case will also defeat the spouse's action for loss of consortium.

A controversial issue is whether relationships other than marriage deserve protection. Generally, courts have denied loss of consortium recovery to unmarried cohabitants whose partners suffer injuries that affect the relationship. Dan B. Dobbs, *Law of Remedies* § 8.1(5)(2d ed.1993); *but see* Cal. Code Civ.Pro. § 377.60 (permitting claims related to wrongful death by persons who have filed declaration of domestic partnership).

2.   Elsewhere, Judge Posner has advocated the same approach to understanding the monetary value of avoiding pain and suffering:

> Awarding any amount of damages for pain and suffering has long been criticized as requiring the trier of fact to monetize a loss that is incommensurable with any monetary measure. We do not agree with the criticism. Pain and suffering are perceived as costs, in the sense of adversities that one would pay to be spared, by the people who experience them. Unless tortfeasors are made to bear these costs, the cost of being adjudged careless will fall and so there will be more accidents and therefore more pain and suffering. The problem of figuring out how to value pain and suffering is acute, however. Various solutions, none wholly satisfactory, have been suggested, such as asking the trier of fact, whether jurors or judge, to imagine how much they would pay to avoid the kind of pain and suffering that the victim of the defendant's negligence experienced or how much they would demand to experience it willingly; or to estimate how much it would cost the victim (if he survived) to obtain counseling or therapy to minimize the pain and suffering, or how much they would demand to assume the risk of the pain and suffering that the victim experienced. If they said they would demand $1,000 to assume a .01 risk of such a misfortune, this would imply that the victim should receive an award of $100,000, as that is the judgment that, if anticipated, would have induced the defendant to spend up to $1,000 to prevent. Talk is cheap, though; and maybe a better approach would be to present the jury with evidence of how potential victims themselves evaluate such risks, an approach that has been used to infer the value of life from people's behavior in using safety devices such as automobile seatbelts or in demanding risk premiums to work at hazardous jobs.

Jutzi-Johnson v. United States, 263 F.3d 753, 758–759 (7th Cir.2001).

Administrative agencies often rely on the idea that the "value of a statistical life" can be derived from people's behavior when they must place a value on avoiding injury in order to justify regulations. By reasoning backward from the willingness of people to invest in safety devices that might save a life, a figure for the value of life can be calculated. Similarly, a figure can be calculated by examining the premium people are paid for engaging in risky occupations.

3.   There are two components to the problem of measuring damages for nonpecuniary loss. One component is accuracy. How can we be sure that the amount of damages awarded bears any real relationship to the loss? Contingent valuation techniques and statistical calculations of the value of a life attempt to address that problem.

The second component is consistency. Even if there is a general agreement that plaintiffs deserve compensation for nonpecuniary harms, is there any way to be sure that similarly injured plaintiffs receive similar awards?

The Seventh Circuit's solution is to compare awards in similar cases. Not all courts agree. For example, the California Court of Appeal rejected O.J. Simpson's argument that an $8.5 million award to Ron Goldman's parents for Ron's wrongful death was excessive:

> Simpson's argument on appeal essentially comes down to this: the largest award his counsel could find in California reported cases for the loss of comfort and society in the wrongful death of an adult child was $2 million. This method of attacking a verdict was disapproved by our Supreme Court in Bertero v. National General Corp., 13 Cal.3d 43, 65, footnote 12, where it said,
>
> > " * * * The vast variety of and disparity between awards in other cases demonstrate that injuries can seldom be measured on the same scale. The measure of damages suffered is a factual question and as such is a subject particularly within the province of the trier of fact. For a reviewing court to upset a jury's factual determination on the basis of what other juries awarded to other plaintiffs for other injuries in other cases based upon different evidence would constitute a serious invasion into the realm of factfinding. Thus, we adhere to the previously announced and historically honored standard of reversing as excessive only those judgments which the entire record, when viewed most favorably to the judgment, indicates were rendered as the result of passion and prejudice on the part of the jurors."

Rufo v. Simpson, 103 Cal.Rptr.2d 492, 522 (2001). *See also* Epping v. Commonwealth Edison Co., 734 N.E.2d 916 (2000) (clear weight of authority in Illinois rejects comparing awards to determine excessiveness); JoEllen Lind, *The End of Trial on Damages? Intangible Losses and Comparability Review*, 51 Buffalo L.Rev. 251 (2003). For an example of the problem, see the disagreement between the majority and the dissent in Jutzi-Johnson v. United States, 263 F.3d 753 (7th Cir.2001), over whether suffocation by hanging is comparable to drowning for purposes of comparing awards.

4.   Judge Posner suggests not simply comparing the size of the awards, but comparing the ratio between the wrongful death award and the award for loss of consortium. This very unusual approach to nonpecuniary

reasonableness is modeled on the Supreme Court's approach to punitive damages, which we will examine in Chapter 6.

NOTE ON TORT REFORM AND LIMITATION OF DAMAGES

As Judge Posner mentions in *Arpin*, nonpecuniary damages are a popular target for tort reform. Thirty-two states limit the recovery of pain and suffering damages by statute. States may cap recovery in all cases, or just for a particular defendant like the government or a hospital. For example, pain and suffering awards in medical malpractice cases are capped in 22 states, with the caps ranging from $250,000 in California to $1 million for especially severe injuries in Florida.

Federal statutes can involve caps as well. The Civil Rights Act of 1991, for example, gives victims of intentional discrimination a right to compensatory damages, including nonpecuniary damages, but limits the amount of the award according to the size of the employer's enterprise, in order to protect defendants with fewer assets from huge liability. 42 U.S.C. § 1981a.

Is it appropriate to undercompensate plaintiffs in order to avoid tapping the defendant's wallet too deeply and essentially balancing the hardships as we do in equity? In Ferdon ex rel. Petrucelli v. Wisconsin Patients Compensation Fund, 701 N.W.2d 440 (Wis.2005), the Wisconsin Supreme Court partially invalidated the state's cap on pain and suffering damages in medical malpractice cases. While leaving intact an earlier decision holding the cap constitutional in wrongful death cases, the court found the cap unconstitutional as applied to claims for personal injury. Noting that the cap's effect was felt most harshly by young, severely injured plaintiffs, whose awards were potentially large because their life expectancy was so long, and that the cap applied to each occurrence of medical malpractice, limiting the entire family's recovery, the court observed:

> The legislature enjoys wide latitude in economic regulation. But when the legislature shifts the economic burden of medical malpractice from insurance companies and negligent health care providers to a small group of vulnerable, injured patients, the legislative action does not appear rational. Limiting a patient's recovery on the basis of youth or how many family members he or she has does not appear to be germane to any objective of the law.

701 N.W.2d at 446. The Wisconsin court went on to find that the cap was not rationally related to any of the legislature's stated objectives—fair compensation, lowering malpractice premiums, keeping the state insurance fund solvent, reducing health care costs or ensuring quality health care. *See also* Catherine M. Sharkey, *Unintended Consequences of Medical Malpractice Damages Caps,* 80 N.Y.U.L.Rev. 391 (2005); Elizabeth Stewart Poisson, *Comments Addressing the Impropriety of Statutory Caps on Pain and Suffering Awards in the Medical Liability System,* 82 N.C.L.Rev. 759 (2004).

Other courts have disagreed:

Despite this court's concerns about the wisdom of depriving a few badly injured plaintiffs of full recovery, the cap is also constitutionally reasonable. Rather than cap all damages, like the cap struck down in Condemarin v. University Hospital, 775 P.2d 348 (Utah 1989), the limitation on recoverable damages in this case is narrowly tailored, by limiting quality of life damages alone. While Judd notes that Utah has not seen large damage awards in significant numbers, this position ignores at least one important factor. Although quality of life damages are very real, they are also less susceptible to quantification than purely economic damages. * * * The difficulty of predicting quality of life damages must be considered by insurers when setting rates and planning reserves. At least in some measure, then, predicting and controlling future costs can result in lower insurance rates. Taken as one of a number of measures enacted to help control health care costs, the cap on quality of life damages is thus a reasonable approach.

Judd v. Drezga, 103 P.3d 135, 141 (Utah 2004) (upholding cap's reduction of jury award from $1.25 million to $250,000).

Caps have been attacked on other constitutional grounds as well. State constitutional guarantees of the right to a jury trial, of open access to courts, and of a right to a remedy have all been invoked in challenges to caps, sometimes successfully, more often not. See Ferndon ex rel. Petrucelli v. Wisconsin Patients Compensation Fund, 284 Wis.2d 573, 701 N.W.2d 440, 459 n.12 (2005) (collecting cases). Courts, however, have not always had the last word. Often, legislatures have responded by modifying the cap, see, e.g., Fl.Stat. § 766.118; in Texas and Louisiana, the state constitutions were amended to authorize caps after the courts had struck them down. See Texas Const. Art. 3 § 66; Louisiana Const. Art. XII § 10(C).

WALKER V. RITCHIE
Ontario Court of Appeal, 2005
[2005] W.D.F.L. 2682, 197 O.A.C. 81

[Stephanie Walker was 17 years old and in Grade 12. Her car struck the rear end of a trailer as the defendant, Ritchie, tried to maneuver his tractor-trailer into a narrow driveway off a two-lane country road at night. As a result of the crash, Stephanie sustained catastrophic, permanent injuries, leaving her with residual paralysis and irreversible cognitive deficits. The trial court found that as a result of her injuries, Stephanie would be unable ever to work in a competitive job. The court found Ritchie and his employer liable, and awarded Stephanie $4,959,901 (Canadian) in damages.]

* * *

E. DAMAGES ISSUES

Of the total damages award of approximately $4.9 million, the appellants challenge $1,140,679.00. That challenge relates only to certain components of the award for pecuniary damages. In particular, the appellants argue that the trial judge erred in:

1) assuming that Stephanie would have attended university;

2) applying earning statistics for all university graduates;

* * *

1) The University Assumption

The trial judge was alert to the principles of law applicable to the assessment of non-pecuniary losses, including loss of future income. He recognized that the assessment of future income loss is, by its nature, somewhat speculative, particularly in predicting a future career for an adolescent who has not yet set her long-term education goals or embarked on a specific career path. In acknowledging these difficulties, the trial judge cited Graham v. Rourke (1990), 75 O.R. (2d) 622 (Ont. C.A.), at 634, which establishes that a plaintiff is not required to prove her future income loss on a balance of probabilities but rather to prove "a real and substantial risk of future pecuniary loss". Stephanie was accordingly not required to show that, but for the accident, she would have achieved a university education and therefore lost the earning capacity of a university graduate. Rather, the onus was on her to establish a real and substantial risk that she lost the earning capacity available to a person with that education.

As found by the trial judge, Stephanie was injured at a time when her post-secondary course was undecided. In those circumstances, the trial judge was required to ask himself if Stephanie had established a real and substantial risk that she lost the benefits of a university education.

To set a basis for Stephanie's loss of income, the trial judge considered Stephanie in the context of her familial and educational background. He dismissed the possibility that Stephanie would have stopped her education after grade twelve. Such a discontinuance of her education would have been inconsistent with her accomplishments to the date of the accident, inconsistent with her motivation to achieve, and inconsistent with the expectations of her parents and the accomplishments of her siblings.

If Stephanie had continued her education, the evidence established that she could have chosen from among a number of options: returning to high school to obtain [sufficient credits for admission to a Canadian university;] entering community college to pursue a career such as that of her younger sister; entering community college and then transferring to university; pursuing a soccer scholarship at a U.S. university; or entering university, when she was able to do so, as a mature student. All these options were open to Stephanie.

In choosing among these options, there were many unknowns, but the known factors were Stephanie's tenacity, significant academic potential, established athletic accomplishments, and a supportive family who expected her to continue her education. In deciding among the possible options, the trial judge had the benefit of evidence from Stephanie's family and her experienced high school guidance counselor. He decided that Stephanie's most reasonable and substantial possible option was the attainment of a university education.

* * *

Had Stephanie pursued a university education, as an average university graduate she would have expected, as a starting point, a salary of $57,190.00 annually, with an average annual salary over her lifetime of $65,769.00.

After setting a base annual earnings loss, a trial judge must refine the award by properly considering the potential negative and positive contingencies. Examples of negative contingencies that impede the production of income are job loss, forced retirement, disability prior to normal retirement age, and the possibility that a plaintiff may, after all, have pursued a different path. At least to some extent, however, these negative contingencies are offset by employer- or government-provided benefits programs. Factors that might improve the plaintiff's potential income (i.e. positive contingencies), include promotion, labour productivity increases, and continuing employment after normal retirement age. To some greater or lesser extent, negative contingencies and positive contingencies may be found to offset each other.

* * *

Looking at those contingencies, the trial judge recognized that Stephanie might not have gone to university, but instead pursued a community college education, an education that statistically would have resulted in lower average earnings. To reflect that contingency, he deducted 10% from Stephanie's award for loss of future income. As well, the trial judge made a further deduction from the award to reflect that, with her post-accident limitations, Stephanie might earn income in the future. He found such employment would likely be part-time clerical work in a supportive environment at or near the minimum wage. He quantified the appropriate deduction at $100,000 on evidence that Stephanie's future employment would be limited to about one-third of normal working hours and would not likely extend beyond age 60.

There was ample evidence to support the trial judge's conclusion that Stephanie might well, after some delay, have proceeded through university. There was also evidence to support the adjustments made by the trial judge by way of deductions for contingencies. Accordingly, this ground of appeal cannot succeed.

2) Earnings Statistics

The appellants argue that the trial judge erred in assessing Stephanie's income loss on the basis of gender-neutral earnings statistics. * * * They submit that the trial judge erred in basing his award on statistics for all university graduates, as opposed to statistics for all female university graduates. * * *

On the first ground, the trial judge discussed the legal principles. He considered Tucker (Public Trustee of) v. Asleson, [1991] B.C.J. No. 954 (B.C. S.C.), where Finch J. applied the average university earnings of male graduates to an eight year-old girl who suffered serious brain injury. In doing so, he found that "no educational or vocational opportunities were excluded to her", although he subsequently applied a significant deduction for negative contingencies. In Terracciano (Guardian ad litem of) v. Etheridge, [1997] B.C.J. No. 1051 (B.C. S.C.) at para. 80, Saunders J. queried the applicability of average female earnings statistics, which he noted, "have hidden in them serious discounts for lower and sporadic participation in the labour market which are duplicated by many of the negative contingencies used by economists to massage the numbers downward". Finally, the trial judge considered Gray v. Macklin, [2000] O.J. No. 4603 (Ont. S.C.J.), where evidence was called about the diminishing differential in men's and women's earnings. In Gray, the trial judge commented at para. 197 on historical wage inequities and the need for the court to "ensure as much as possible that the appropriate weight is given to societal trends in the labour market in order that the future loss of income properly reflects future circumstances." In that case, the trial judge also discounted the award by a total of 30% for negative contingencies.

* * *

As in the other authorities that have considered this issue, the trial judge decided damages on the evidence before him. On the first objection, while damages awards are compensatory in nature and cannot be calculated in a manner that overcompensates a particular individual, a court must be equally cognizant of the fact that gender-based earnings statistics are grounded in retrospective historical data that may no longer accurately project the income a person would achieve in the future.

In this case, the trial judge cannot be said to have erred in applying gender-neutral earnings tables to Stephanie's income loss. He did so on the basis of the evidence before him, which he accepted. In doing so, he noted that at least two of Stephanie's potential options—teaching and kinetics—were areas where pay equity had been achieved. Further, he noted at para.

135 that female earnings tables were based on historical data and might be inappropriate "where the court is attempting to make a forecast stretching many years into the future".

* * *

In this case, as in most, an individual approach is required to the assessment of future loss of income. The trial judge applied an individual approach to his assessment of Stephanie's loss of income. He chose to apply gender-neutral statistics. We see no error in his decision to do so or in his application of those statistics.

* * *

NOTES

1. While *Walker* is a Canadian case, its approach to the problem of earning capacity is typical of U.S. courts. If the plaintiff has a history of earnings on which to rely, that earning history provides a benchmark for evaluating future earning capacity. *See, e.g.,* Pretre v. United States, 531 F.Supp. 931 (E.D.Mo.1981) (auto plant worker).

On the other hand, where the plaintiff is young or unemployed, the court may have to rely on guesswork about the plaintiff's future plans and ambitions. As *Walker* points out, the determination is highly individualized. For example, in Snow v. Villacci, 754 A.2d 360 (Me. 2000), the plaintiff was injured in a car accident. His injuries limited his ability to participate in a two-year training program at a stock brokerage, which he alleged would have led to a position as a financial consultant. Because he did not do well in the rest of the training program, he was offered a less lucrative position in the brokerage. Although he had not earned any income at either job at the time of the accident, the plaintiff claimed damages for "loss of an earning opportunity."

Snow could not make out a traditional claim for loss of earning capacity, because he had no ongoing impairment that limited his ability to earn income. Nonetheless, the Supreme Court of Maine permitted the claim to proceed:

> Although we recognize that proof of this type of loss may be more complex than proof of other traditional losses, we are confident that trial judges will exercise appropriate discretion in excluding evidence that is nothing more than mere hope or speculation. Accordingly, recovery may be had for the loss of an earning opportunity if the claimant proves, by a preponderance of the evidence, that: (1) the opportunity was real and not merely a hoped-for prospect; (2) the opportunity was available not just to the public in general but to the plaintiff specifically; (3) the plaintiff was positioned to take advantage of the opportunity; (4) the income from the opportunity was measurable and demonstrable; and (5) the wrongdoer's negligence was a proximate cause of the plaintiff's inability to pursue the opportunity.

754 A.2d at 365. What was it that persuaded the *Walker* court that Stephanie would have successfully completed her university education?

2.   *Walker* is one of a series of Canadian cases attempting to come to grips with the fact that according to employment statistics, a woman is likely to earn much less money than a man. Presented with the same argument, albeit thirty years ago, an American court had a different response:

> I am constrained to agree with the defense that the present value of prospective earnings, female wages, before taxes must be used. However sympathetic this Court may be to equality in employment, it must look to the reality of the situation and not be controlled by its own convictions. One does not need expert testimony to conclude that there is inequality in the average earnings of the sexes. There is no criterion to help us predict when this unwarranted condition will be remedied and as a consequence I feel compelled to adopt the defendant's position.

Caron v. United States, 410 F.Supp. 378 (D.R.I.1975).

On the related issue of using race-based earning tables, at least two federal decisions line up with *Walker*. United States v. Serawop, 505 F.3d 1112 (10th Cir.2007) (affirming trial court's order for a race-and gender-neutral recalculation of lost income after expert provided a report that reduced estimated damages on the basis that the victim was Native American); Wheeler Tarpeh-Doe v. United States, 771 F.Supp. 427 (D.D.C.1991) (refusing to use race-based wage-earnings predictions), rev'd on other grounds, 28 F.3d 120 (D.C.Cir.1994). Are the issues different for race and gender? For a thorough discussion, see Martha Chamallas & Jennifer B. Wriggins, *The Measure of Tort Injury: Race, Gender, and Tort Law* (2010); Martha Chamallas, *Civil Rights in Ordinary Tort Cases: Race, Gender, and the Calculation of Economic Loss*, 38 Loy.L.A.L.Rev. 1435 (2005); Jennifer B. Wriggins, *Damages In Tort Litigation: Thoughts on Race and Remedies*, 1865–2007, 27 Rev.Litig. 37 (2007) (analysis of how black and white plaintiffs historically were treated unequally by the tort compensation system).

3.   Tort victims who do not work outside the home have presented particular problems in calculating earning capacity. Two points are clear. The award for earning capacity is an award for just that—capacity—and does not require an established employment record if the plaintiff can meet the burden of showing that a return to work was likely, but for the injury. Second, compensation for the value of replacement services for the victim's household work is commonplace. Martha Chamallas, *The September 11th Victim Compensation Fund: Rethinking the Damages Element in Injury Law*, 71 Tenn.L.Rev. 51, 73 (2003).

4.   Determining a plaintiff's life expectancy in a personal injury case makes similar demands on the court's clairvoyance. For example, in McMillan v. City of New York, 253 F.R.D. 247 (E.D.N.Y.2008), an African American was paralyzed in a ferry crash and required life-long care. The defendants

introduced actuarial evidence to show that African Americans with spinal cord injuries have a shorter life expectancy than similarly injured persons of other races.

Judge Jack Weinstein rejected the use of race-based data to determine life expectancy. Race, Judge Weinstein observed, is a social construct, not a biological category. Moreover, in a society with hundreds of years of racial mixing, assigning individuals to single racial categories to predict their life-span is arbitrary:

> In the United States, there has been "racial mixing" among "Whites," "Africans," "Native Americans," and individuals of other "racial" and "ethnic" backgrounds for more than three and a half centuries. * * * Statistical reliance on "race" leads to such questions as whether [the plaintiff in *Plessy v. Ferguson*, who was apparently 7/8 "white" and 1/8 "black"] would have been categorized today as "African-American" for life expectancy purposes. In a more recent example, "racially" characterizing for statistical purposes in a negligence lawsuit the current [President], born of a "White" American mother and an "African" citizen of Kenya, would be considered absurd by most Americans. See Colm Tóibín, James Baldwin & Barack Obama, N.Y. Rev. of Books, Oct. 23, 2008, at 18 ("When Obama was a child, he wrote, 'my father . . . was black as pitch, my mother white as milk.' "). Reliance on "race"-based statistics in estimating life expectancy of individuals for purposes of calculating damages is not scientifically acceptable in our current heterogeneous population.

Citing studies showing that socio-economic status—not race—accounts for most variation in life expectancy among groups, Judge Weinstein concluded that to use race-based statistics to determine plaintiff's life expectancy would deny the plaintiff both equal protection and substantive due process:

A. *Equal Protection*

> Chamallas notes, "when experts rely on race or gender-based statistics to calculate tort damages, we tend not to notice the discrimination and to accept it as natural and unproblematic." *Civil Rights in Ordinary Tort Cases*, *supra*, 38 Loy. L.A. L.Rev. at 1442. "Racial" classifications of individuals are "suspect categories," meaning that state action in reliance on "race"-based statistics triggers strict scrutiny. Judicial reliance on "racial" classifications constitutes state action. *See also* Martha Chamallas, *Questioning the Use of Race-Specific and Gender-Specific Economic Data in Tort Litigation: A Constitutional Argument*, 63 Fordham L.Rev. 73, 106 (1994). ("By conceding the relevance of race-based or gender-based data through its admission into evidence . . . the judge necessarily leads the jury to believe that gender and race are legally permissible factors and thus cannot be said to be neutral on the issue."). Equal protection in this context demands that the claimant not be subjected

to a disadvantageous life expectancy estimate solely on the basis of a "racial" classification.

B. *Due Process*

There is a right—in effect a property right—to compensation in cases of negligently caused damage to the person under state and federal law. *See* Martinez v. State of California, 444 U.S. 277, 282 (1980) ("[a]rguably" a tort cause of action created by a State constitutes "a species of 'property' protected by the Due Process Clause" and there is a federal "interest in protecting the individual citizen from state action that is wholly arbitrary or irrational").

By allowing use of "race"-based statistics at trial, a court would be creating arbitrary and irrational state action. * * * Were the court to apply an ill-founded assumption, automatically burdening on "racial" grounds a class of litigants who seek compensation, there would be a denial of due process.

253 F.R.D. at 255–256. *See* Debra Sydnor & Shirlethia Franklin, *Calculating the Damages: Race and Socio-Economic Status*, 26 Med. Malpractice L. & Strategy 3 (2009).

According to actuarial tables, women have a longer life-expectancy than men. If a man were to argue that the use of life-expectancy tables that distinguish between men and women violates his rights, would he have a good claim?

3. ALTERNATIVE COMPENSATION SYSTEMS

Most tort damages in reality are decided by settlement. Over 95 percent of all cases settle rather than go to trial. Settlements, however, are conducted "in the shadow of the law" with the law and doctrinal requirements guiding the lawyers' decisions as to when and what to settle for. With the growing prevalence of alternative dispute resolution systems of mediation and structured negotiation, the law of tort remedies has been adapted to deal with unusual mass harms. Generally, the tort system with or without the class action device works sufficiently to redress mass or public harm.

However, every once and a while, there is a very visible mass disaster in the United States that galvanizes the public and elected officials, and triggers a different approach to resolving the remedial claims. This has occurred only a handful of times in the last thirty years with disasters such as 9/11 and BP. When these types of unprecedented disasters have occurred, public officials have occasionally adopted out-of-the-box approaches to compensating the victims. But these alternative remedies require political consensus in order to avoid criticism and ensure the effectiveness of the attempted solution.

Kenneth R. Feinberg, *Unconventional Reponses to Unique Catastrophes*, 45 Akron L.Rev. 575, 576 (2012). Indeed while some, like the system created after September 11th have been held up as ideals, others, like the BP Oil Spill system, have been criticized as creating injustices outside the protection of the courts. These systems, however, provide an ability to be flexible with the rules of tort compensation, acting more like equity to balance hardships between plaintiffs and defendants and factoring in the public interest. While they have been applied to cases of national scope, the basic principles lend themselves to settlement in any case of multiple plaintiffs by creative lawyers looking to solve problems for their clients.

PETER H. SCHUCK, THE ROLE OF JUDGES IN SETTLING COMPLEX CASES: THE AGENT ORANGE EXAMPLE
53 U.Chi.L.Rev. 337, 341–48 (1986)

I.

On May 7, 1984, Chief Judge Jack B. Weinstein of the Eastern District of New York, flanked by his special masters, announced that the Agent Orange class action had been settled only a few hours earlier, just before jury selection was to begin. The settlement of that action, which was then probably the largest single personal injury litigation in history, created a fund that now totals about $200 million and increases by over $40,000 each day. Approximately 250,000 individual and group claims have been lodged against this fund, and in May of 1985 the court established the framework for the complicated administrative apparatus that is to resolve and administer those claims. * * *

The class was defined to include some 2.4 million American veterans exposed to Agent Orange during the war in Vietnam, the wives and children (born and unborn) of those veterans, and exposed Vietnam veterans from Australia and New Zealand. The seven defendants (pared down from an original twenty-four) were the chemical companies that manufactured Agent Orange.

* * * From the moment that Judge Weinstein replaced Judge Pratt on October 21, 1983, the goal of settlement was uppermost in his mind. He believed that toxic tort cases like Agent Orange, involving mass exposures and causal relationships that are extremely difficult and costly to prove, could not be litigated properly or at an acceptable social cost under traditional rules. Absent settlement, he predicted a one-year trial with results that would remain inconclusive for years to come. Although he harbored genuine doubts about the veterans' evidence on causation, he deeply sympathized with their plight. In open court and in his written opinions, he denounced the "injustices" they suffered, believed that "[t]hey and their families should receive recognition, medical treatment and financial support," and shared the now-conventional view that the

American people had failed to discharge "the nation's obligations to Vietnam veterans and their families." The prospect of having either to direct a verdict for the chemical companies or to reverse a jury verdict in favor of the veterans could not have been an appealing one. Unquestionably, he was prepared to do his duty if necessary, but a negotiated settlement offered the far more attractive possibility: everyone would gain something, soon, and at an acceptable social cost. * * *

In February 1984, Weinstein requested and obtained permission to retain, at the defendants' expense, an unnamed consultant to develop a settlement strategy and plan. That consultant was later revealed to be Ken Feinberg, a lawyer whom Weinstein knew and trusted. Feinberg was not only knowledgeable about toxic tort litigation, but also had a reputation as an effective mover, shaker, and conciliator. By mid-March, he had prepared a settlement plan. It stated no dollar amount but contained three sections: an analysis of the elements for determining the aggregate settlement amount, especially the various sources of uncertainty and the likely number and nature of claims; a discussion of alternative criteria for allocating any liability among the chemical companies; and a discussion of alternative criteria for distributing any settlement fund to claimants. This document, which the judge made available to the lawyers, occasioned considerable disagreement but succeeded in setting the terms for the negotiations that followed.

On April 10, less than three weeks before trial, Weinstein appointed three special masters for settlement. Feinberg and David I. Shapiro, a prominent class action expert and skillful negotiator, would work with the lawyers. Leonard Garment, a Washington political insider, would explore what resources the government might contribute to a settlement. Feinberg and Shapiro immediately identified three major obstacles to settlement: the parties were more than a quarter of a billion dollars apart; each side was deeply divided internally over whether and on what terms to settle (and in defendants' case, how to allocate liability); and the government was manifestly unwilling to contribute toward a settlement fund or even to participate in settlement negotiations.

The judge and special masters decided to convene an around-the-clock negotiating marathon at the courthouse during the weekend before the trial. The lawyers were ordered to appear on Saturday morning, May 5, with their "toothbrushes and full negotiating authority." On that morning, while preliminary jury selection work was proceeding in another room, Weinstein met with the lawyers and gave them a "pep talk" about settlement. Then the special masters undertook a grueling two-day course of shuttle diplomacy, holding separate meetings with each side interspersed with private conferences with Judge Weinstein. On several occasions, the judge met privately with each side.

Several features of the discussion were particularly salient in generating the settlement agreement. First, the court did not permit the two sides to meet face-to-face until the very end, after the terms of the deal had been defined. This strategy preserved the court's control over the negotiations and prevented them from fragmenting. In particular, it stymied the plaintiffs' lawyers in their last-ditch effort to improve on the deal by settling with five of the defendants and isolating Monsanto and Diamond Shamrock, the two companies they thought most vulnerable to liability and punitive damages.

Second, the masters attempted to break log-jams in the negotiations by helping the lawyers to predict the consequences of the various approaches under consideration, and by proposing alternative solutions. * * *

Third, when especially difficult issues arose that threatened to derail the settlement, the parties agreed to be bound by the judge's decision. The most important example of the judge acting as arbitrator involved perhaps the most difficult question facing the defendants—how to allocate liability among themselves. * * *

Fourth, the judge and his special masters, while being careful not to be duplicitous, did emphasize different things to each side. In their discussions with plaintiffs' lawyers, they stressed the weakness of the evidence on causation, the novelty of many questions of law in the case, the consequent risk of reversal on appeal of a favorable verdict, the prospect that they might lose everything if they rejected settlement, and the enormous costs of continued litigation. To the defendants' lawyers, they stressed the presumed pro-plaintiff sympathies of Brooklyn juries, the reputational damage that protracted litigation and unfavorable publicity would cause their clients, and the high costs of the trial and of the inevitable appeals.

Fifth, a common theme in all discussions was the pervasive uncertainty that surrounded the law, the facts, the duration and ultimate outcome of the litigation, and the damages likely to be awarded. By almost all accounts, it was this uncertainty that proved to be the decisive inducement to settlement. On one count, however, Judge Weinstein left little doubt in the lawyers' minds: the court, having crafted and taken responsibility for the settlement, was in a position to make it stick.

Sixth, the imminence and ineluctability of trial "concentrated the minds" of the lawyers as nothing else could have done. This deadline imparted to their deliberations an urgency and a seriousness that swept aside objections that might have undermined negotiations in less compelling circumstances. The lawyers' growing physical and mental exhaustion during that weekend of feverish intensity abetted the conciliatory effect. As one plaintiff's lawyer later complained in his challenge to the validity of the settlement, "the Judge wore us all down with that tactic."

Seventh, the judge and special masters displayed a degree of skill, sophistication, imagination, and artistry in fashioning the settlement that almost all the participants viewed as highly unusual. But even this would not have availed had Judge Weinstein not inspired an extraordinary measure of respect, even awe, in the lawyers, and had the special masters not been viewed as enjoying the authority to speak and make commitments for him.

Eighth, the settlement was negotiated without any agreement (or even any serious discussion) of how the settlement fund would be distributed among the claimants, and without reliable information as to the number of claims that would be filed. The first, of course, was of great interest to the plaintiffs and a matter of indifference to the defendants. The second, however, was significant to both sides. It is not at all certain that settlement could have been reached had the parties been required to resolve these issues in advance. The problem was not simply that preparation of a distribution plan required an immense amount of analysis. A protracted process of political compromise and education was also needed to gain support for the plan, a process whose results even now remain doubtful and perhaps legally vulnerable.

Ninth, the lawyers on the PMC [plaintiffs' management committee] at the time of the settlement possessed very different personalities, ideologies, and incentives than those of the group of lawyers that had launched the case and carried it through its first five years. These differences likely affected the lawyers' disposition to settle. The veterans' passionate desire for vindication at trial, quite apart from their wish for compensation, had strongly driven their chosen lawyer, Victor Yannacone, during the earlier stages of the litigation. Yet the PMC's deliberations concerning the settlement were strongly influenced by lawyers who had only the most attenuated relationship to the veterans. And under the terms of an internal fee-sharing agreement, these lawyers would be secured financially by even a "low" settlement.

Finally, the court was prepared to allocate substantial resources to the quest for a settlement. Judge Weinstein devoted a great deal of his own time to thinking through and implementing a settlement strategy. His three special masters for settlement commanded high compensation and worked long hours. Their billings to the court totaled hundreds of thousands of dollars, even excluding the massive amount of work they later invested in connection with the distribution plan.

––––––––––

The settlement reached in the Agent Orange case was for $180 million, although, as the article indicates, the fund increased as interest accrued.

The distribution plan called for nearly $150 million to be distributed through a payment program that distributed death and disability benefits to individual veterans and family members like an insurance policy but without requiring proof of causation or otherwise adhering to traditional tort principles. Another portion, roughly $45 million, was to be turned over to a class assistance foundation benefitting both veterans and family members.

On appeal, the Second Circuit upheld the plan to distribute funds to individual disabled veterans and families of deceased veterans without requiring a particularized showing of individual causation. In re Agent Orange Litigation, 818 F.2d 179 (2d Cir.1987), *cert. denied*, 487 U.S. 1234 (1988). The court did find it was improper, however, to devote $45 million to the class assistance foundation. Because there would be no assurance that the foundation's self-governing and self-perpetuating board of directors would possess the independent, disinterested judgment required to allocate the funds fairly, the appellate court held that the district court must either directly supervise the class assistance programs, or add the money to the fund for distribution. For a more detailed description and analysis of the Agent Orange litigation, see Peter H. Schuck, *Agent Orange on Trial: Mass Toxic Disasters in the Courts* (1986); Philip Jones Griffiths, *Agent Orange: "Collateral Damage" in Viet Nam* (2003).

THE 9/11 VICTIMS COMPENSATION FUND

Another example of an alternative compensation system is the 9/11 Victims Compensation Fund. Again, the mastermind was the Special Master from the Agent Orange case, Kenneth Feinberg. Indeed, Feinberg has become the king of designing and administering such compensation systems including those for the Virginia Tech shooting, Wall Street bail out, and the BP Oil Spill. *See* Tracy A. Thomas, *Remedies for Big Disasters: The BP Oil Spill and the Quest for Complete Justice*, 45 Akron L.Rev. 567, 568 (2012)

When Congress responded to the horrifying events of September 11, 2001, it did so by creating a compensation scheme modeled on tort damages. Rather than, for example, establishing a benefits system for victims of 9/11, or providing a fixed payment to those who were affected, Congress established a fund to be distributed to victims according to the loss each victim suffered. In the face of this unprecedented national tragedy, Congress opted for traditional compensation.

The story of the September 11th Victim Compensation Fund has been told by Ken Feinberg in a remarkable book, *What is Life Worth: The Unprecedented Effort to Compensate the Victims of 9/11* (2005). Although the fund operated as an alternative to compensation through the tort system, the stories the special master has to tell and the choices he (and Congress made) put an important, human face on the concept of compensation.

Feinberg initially argued that it would be unwise to attempt to replicate the fund's success in other areas, and that it "should remain limited to the unique circumstances that gave it birth." Feinberg, *What is Life Worth* at 181. At the same time, by all accounts the fund was extraordinarily successful:

> Nearly every family of an individual killed in the September 11th attacks chose to participate in the Fund. To the extent that participation is a measure of success, the Fund was extraordinarily successful. What factors contributed to this success? In our view, there are five major factors that resulted in this overwhelming acceptance of the Fund as a means of compensation. First, the alternative of litigation presented both uncertainty and delay. Second, the Fund took extraordinary steps to assure that families could obtain detailed information about their likely recovery from the Fund. Third, the Fund took a proactive approach—personally contacting each claimant, ensuring that claimants were able to obtain and present the best information in support of the claim; assisting claimants to obtain helpful information; explaining to claimants information that would assist the Fund in maximizing the computation of economic loss and resolving uncertainties in favor of the claimant. Fourth, the Fund offered in-person informal meetings along with hearings so that claimants could "have their day in court" and explain the magnitude of their loss and their views about the way in which the Fund should treat their particular situation. Fifth, the Fund offered certainty without significant delay, allowing families the option of a type of "closure." * * * Claimants had a personal stake and involvement in the process. Had the Fund opted to curtail access or failed to offer explanations of the manner in which the Fund would treat each individual's situation, some portion of claimants would likely have been sufficiently uncomfortable or uncertain to commit to the Fund.

Kenneth R. Feinberg, 1 Final Report of the Special Master for the September 11th Victim Compensation Fund of 2001, at 1–2.

Feinberg encountered same of the same limitations with the compensation fund as with traditional tort damages.

> Claimant after claimant referred to the disconnect between a life lost and the inadequacy of mere compensation: "Whatever award we receive will obviously never come close to the worth of our son. To be perfectly honest, this whole matter of victims' compensation is ghoulish and repulsive. We are in a no-win situation. Whatever we receive is not enough. The only way we win is if you had some magical power to bring [him] back."

Kenneth R. Feinberg, *What is Life Worth?* 141 (2005).

The September 11th Victim Compensation Fund used male work-life expectancy and income growth rate tables to calculate the presumed awards for economic loss for both male and female victims; even though women often earn less in the marketplace as pay equity cases and laws show. Would this gender-neutral approach be promising for all tort cases? *See* Martha Chamallas, *The September 11th Victim Compensation Fund: Rethinking the Damages Element in Injury Law*, 71 Tenn.L.Rev. 51 (2003); Martha F. Davis, *Valuing Women: A Case Study*, 23 Women's Rts.L.Rep. 219 (2002).

The legislation creating the 9/11 Fund defined noneconomic loss broadly, including pain and suffering, disfigurement, loss of enjoyment of life, loss of consortium and more. Air Transportation Safety and System Stabilization Act, Pub.L. 107–42, Sept. 22, 2001, 115 Stat. 237. The fund's final regulations, however, provided for a presumptive award of $250,000 in survival damages for the pre-death pain and suffering of victims, and $100,000 for the spouse and for each dependent. 28 CFR § 104.44. Similarly, the Special Master established noneconomic awards of $250,000 as presumed compensation for the pain and suffering each victim experienced before their deaths. 28 CFR § 104.44. What purpose does an award of noneconomic damages to the deceased serve in that context? *See* Chamallas, *supra,* 71 Tenn.L.Rev. at 76–77 (2003) (lump sum award "treats victims more like heroes than like tort victims * * * [and is] akin to a memorial").

The legislation also mandated that the Fund "reduce the amount of compensation * * * by the amount of the collateral source compensation the claimant has received or is entitled to receive" as a result of the terrorist attacks. According to the Fund's Final Report, "the deduction of collateral source payments from awards proved to be one of the Fund's most contentious issues." Final Report, at 43. The Special Master developed detailed regulations intended to ensure that savings—as distinguished from forms of insurance—were not deducted, that benefits were valued conservatively so that awards would be maximized, and that victim contributions, like premiums, were fully taken into account. *See* Kenneth S. Abraham & Kyle D. Logue, *The Genie and the Bottle: Collateral Sources Under the September 11th Victim Compensation Fund,* 53 DePaul L.Rev. 591 (2003); Stephan Landsman, *A Chance to be Heard: Thoughts About Schedules, Caps, and Collateral Source Deductions in the September 11th Victim Compensation Fund*, 53 DePaul L.Rev. 393 (2003).

Feinberg has applied the basic methodology to other compensation funds, most notably the BP Oil Spill cleanup fund. As he notes, "[m]ass disasters sometimes require creative remedies. The tort system may not provide the best means of compensation in unusual situations. . . ." Feinberg, *Unconventional Reponses*, at 575. He does still insist on the exceptional use of this approach, limiting it to unusual cases where it is likely to be of particular use apart from the tort system. *Id.*

E.　CONTRACT DAMAGES

In contract cases, the loss of the value of the defendant's performance is the measure of general damages; other items of loss are considered consequential damages. Unlike tort damages, contract damages do not generally include nonpecuniary damages like emotional distress; unless the breach of contract is also a tort or injury. In addition, contracts may provide for their own types or measures of damages through liquidated damages clauses agreed to by the parties. And finally, commercial contracts between buyers and sellers have their own special remedies under the Uniform Commercial Code (UCC), though these rules closely mirror the common-law development, but worded in plain language designed to help business owners.

Another difference in contract is that the plaintiff's rightful position is measured by the expectancy interest. According to the Restatement (Second) of Contracts § 344, judicial remedies serve to protect the expectation, reliance, or restitutionary interest of the promisee. (The alternative of restitution is discussed in Chapter 7). The "expectation interest," is the party's "interest in having the benefit of his bargain by being put in as good a position as he would have been in had the contract been performed." His "reliance interest" is "his interest in being reimbursed for loss caused by reliance on the contract by being put in as good a position as he would have been in had the contract not been made." Often, the reliance and expectation interests frequently overlap, where the party has lost what was expected under the contract. Lon Fuller & William Perdue, *The Reliance Interest in Contract Damages*, 46 Yale L.J. 52 (1936). But where the expectancy under the contract was greater, as when the plaintiff has made a good deal, the rightful position includes awarding the full benefit of the benefit or advantage expected.

The Restatement (Second) of Contracts § 347 provides that the expectation interest is measured by:

(a) the loss in the value to him of the other party's performance caused by its failure or deficiency, plus

(b) any other loss, including incidental or consequential loss, caused by the breach, less

(c) any cost or other loss that he has avoided by not having to perform.

Defining the rightful position in contract as expectancy may encourage breach under some circumstances. This concept of the "efficient breach" governs economic theories of contract damages. Judge Posner explains:

> [I]n some cases a party is tempted to break his contract simply because his profit from breach would exceed his profit from completing performance. He will do so if the profit would also exceed the expected profit to the other party from completion of the contract, and hence the damages from breach. So in this case awarding damages will not deter a breach of contract. It should not. It is an efficient breach. Suppose I sign a contract to deliver

100,000 custom-ground widgets at 10¢ apiece to A for use in his boiler factory. After I have delivered 10,000, B comes to me, explains that he desperately needs 25,000 custom-ground widgets at once since otherwise he will be forced to close his pianola factory at great cost, and offers me 15¢ apiece for them. I sell him the widgets and as a result do not complete timely delivery to A, causing him to lose $1,000 in profits. Having obtained an additional profit of $1,250 on the sale to B, I am better off even after reimbursing A for his loss, and B is also better off. The breach is therefore Pareto superior. True, had I refused to sell to B he could have gone to A and negotiated an assignment to him of part of A's contract with me. But this would have introduced an additional step, with additional transaction costs—and high ones, because it would be a bilateral-monopoly negotiation.

Could not the danger of deterring efficient breaches of contract be eliminated simply by redefining the legal concept of breach of contract so that only inefficient terminations counted as breaches? No. Remember that an important function of contracts is to assign risks to superior risk bearers. If the risk materializes, the party to whom it was assigned must pay. It is no more relevant that he could not have prevented the risk from occurring at a reasonable, perhaps at any, cost than that an insurance company could not have prevented the fire that destroyed the building it insured. The breach of contract corresponds to the occurrence of the event that is insured against.

Let us consider the case in which the expectation loss—that is, the loss of the expected profit of the contract—exceeds the reliance loss, that is, the expense that the victim of the breach incurred in performing his side of the contract. Seller agrees to sell a machine for $100,000, delivery to be made in six months. The day after the contract is signed he defaults, realizing that he would lose $5,000 at the contract price. The buyer's reliance loss— the costs he has irretrievably incurred as a result of the contract— is zero, but it would cost him, let's assume, $112,000 to obtain a substitute machine. So $12,000 is his expectation loss. Why should he be allowed to insist on a measure of damages that gives him more (by $12,000) than he has actually lost? Because awarding the reliance loss would encourage inefficient breaches. The net gain to the buyer from contractual performance, $12,000, would have exceeded by $7,000 the net loss to the seller, so if we make the buyer's net expected gain the cost of breach to the seller we discourage an inefficient breach.

Richard A. Posner, *Economic Analysis of Law* (9th ed. 2014) § 4.10, at 131–32. For a basic treatment of economic analysis, see A. Mitchell Polinsky, *An Introduction to Law and Economics* (4th ed.2011).

Of course, not all breaches are efficient. Some breaches are opportunistic; that is to say, some parties breach because they can get away with it. The potential for opportunistic breach arises because contract damage rules sometimes undercompensate the victim of a breach. Some argue that opportunistic breaches are appropriate for restitutionary recovery. (See Chapter 7). Although economic explanations of the contract remedy have gained wide acceptance, see Restatement (Second) of Contracts § 344, they are not without their detractors. *See, e.g.,* Marco J. Jimenez, *The Value of a Promise: A Utilitarian Approach to Contract Law Remedies,* 56 U.C.L.A.L.Rev. 59 (2008); Ian R. Macneil, *Efficient Breach of Contract: Circles in the Sky,* 68 Va.L.Rev. 947 (1982).

GREAT AMERICAN MUSIC MACHINE, INC. V. MID-SOUTH RECORD PRESSING CO.

United States District Court
393 F.Supp. 877 (M.D.Tenn. 1975)

MORTON, DISTRICT JUDGE.

This suit is brought by plaintiffs Great American Music Machine, Inc. (GrAMM), a Colorado corporation, and Ralph Harrison, a citizen and resident of Colorado, against Mid-South Record Pressing Company, a division of GRT Corporation, with its principal place of business in Davidson County, Tennessee. The complaint seeks monetary damages, based upon breach of contract and implied warranty in connection with some record albums which plaintiffs allege were defectively pressed by Mid-South. The defendant counterclaims on its open account with the plaintiff corporation in the stipulated amount of thirteen thousand and twenty-five dollars and thirty-nine cents ($13,025.39). Jurisdiction of this court is properly invoked under 28 U.S.C. § 1332.

FINDINGS OF FACT

In August of 1971, plaintiff Harrison and several of his close friends and business associates formed "Crossroads Limited Partnership," the predecessor to plaintiff corporation. The partnership was formed for the purpose of promoting and exploiting the musical talents of Harrison as a songwriter and singer, although he was then unknown in the entertainment field and had never performed professionally. The business plan of the partnership was to finance the production of a master tape for an album by Ralph Harrison, convert the partnership into a corporation, produce and promote the album and Harrison as an artist, and raise additional capital through a public offering of the stock of the corporation.

GrAMM was incorporated by the Crossroads venture in March of 1972, and all the rights of Crossroads were merged into the new corporation.

In the fall of 1971, Harrison went to New York City to produce the master tape for an album featuring himself as the singing artist. The production cost of the master tape was thirty-one thousand and eighty-eight dollars ($31,088.00). The title of the album was to be "Free Spirit Movin'."

In early February of 1972, Harrison and an investor in the venture came to Nashville, Tennessee, to contract for the pressing and packaging of the record album. On behalf of GrAMM, they contracted orally with the defendant, Mid-South Record Pressing Company, for the pressing of forty thousand (40,000) record albums, at a cost of thirteen thousand and twenty-five dollars and thirty-nine cents ($13,025.39). GrAMM received assurances that the records would be of high quality. Although there was some dispute in the testimony at trial, it appears to the satisfaction of this court that there was some discussion with Janet Tabor, manager of defendant company, concerning the overall business plan of GrAMM. It is the finding of this court that GrAMM's plan to offer stock to the public in June of 1972 was mentioned in this discussion.

Under the terms of the oral agreement between the parties, Mid-South was to mail directly to members of ESA, a national sorority, some thirty-two thousand (32,000) copies of the album. (One of Harrison's songs on the record had been adopted by ESA as its theme song.) GrAMM supplied the postage in advance for this mailing. To be enclosed with the albums sent to ESA members was a letter requesting that five dollars ($5.00) be remitted to GrAMM, of which one dollar ($1.00) would be donated to a certain service project of the sorority. The bulk of the remaining 8,000 albums was to be sent to Gambit Records, a Nashville company with whom GrAMM had contracted for nationwide distribution. By mid-February of 1972, a test pressing of good quality had been approved by GrAMM, and Mid-South commenced production of the album. Though there was some dispute in the testimony at trial, the court finds that the contemplated delivery date was the first week of April, 1972.

On April 3, 1972, GrAMM received a shipment of the records at its office in Denver, Colorado. At that time it was discovered by Harrison and others that the records were defective in that they were warped, pitted and blistered, producing excessive surface noises when played. GrAMM immediately sent two representatives to Nashville on April 4, 1972, to investigate the situation. Upon arrival, the GrAMM representatives learned that some eight thousand (8,000) of the records had already been shipped to ESA members; roughly four thousand (4,000) records had been delivered to Gambit, from which an undetermined number had been sent to distributors and disc jockeys around the country.

The court finds as a matter of fact that the first pressing of the record by Mid-South was for the most part commercially unacceptable. Witnesses for both the plaintiff and the defendant testified as to this fact. Gordon Close, one of the GrAMM representatives sent to Nashville in early April, and Janet Tabor of Mid-South both agreed that the larger part of the records still on hand at Mid-South were unusable and that the entire lot should be scrapped and new records pressed. To be included in the new pressing were replacements for the defective albums which had already been shipped out. * * *

Although GrAMM did not complain of the quality of the second pressing nor reject the second batch of albums, it has refused to pay its open account with Mid-South. The amount due on the account is $13,025.39.

In relation to the contemplated stock offering by GrAMM, plaintiff introduced evidence at trial attempting to show that Mr. Mike McBride of Equidyne, Inc., a brokerage firm in Salt Lake City, Utah, had agreed to a firm underwriting of five hundred thousand dollars ($500,000.00) worth of GrAMM securities. * * *

From the evidence developed at trial with regard to the underwriting offer, it is difficult for this court to ascertain exactly why the underwriting did not go through. * * *

CONCLUSIONS OF LAW

The court finds that the defendant company breached implied warranties of merchantability and fitness for a particular purpose, T.C.A. § 47–2–314 and § 47–2–315, in the first pressing of the record albums. Defendant also breached its express contractual agreement to produce records of high quality. * * *

The court finds as a matter of law that plaintiff justifiably rejected the entire first pressing of the record albums as nonconforming goods. T.C.A. § 47–2–602. This rejection included the 12,000 records which had already been shipped out to ESA members and Gambit. Plaintiff notified the defendant of the defects as soon as it became aware of them, on the day it received initial shipment. The defective records had only negligible value as scrap, and defendant made no request that they be returned to it. The cost of retrieving the records already distributed would have greatly exceeded their value as scrap. Any revenue from the records that were shipped to ESA members appears to have been from the second "replacement" batch of records.

With regard to the second pressing of the record albums, the court finds that plaintiff GrAMM is liable on its open account with defendant in the amount of $13,025.39. Plaintiff's liability is predicated upon the fact that it accepted the repressed records and under T.C.A. § 47–2–607 must pay at the contract rate for goods accepted by it. The fact that plaintiff accepted the second batch of records does not, however, in any way preclude its suit for damages occasioned by the defective pressing of the first batch of records. The delivery of the second batch of records did not constitute a cure within the meaning of T.C.A. § 47–2–508, as the damage had already occurred and the time set for performance had expired.

Having previously determined that defendant Mid-South breached express and implied warranties, we now turn to the question of damages. Plaintiff GrAMM has elected to sue for breach of contract, rather than suing in tort for negligence. The damages recoverable for a breach of contract " . . . are limited to those reasonably within the contemplation of the defendant when the contract was made, while in a tort action a much broader measure of damages is applied." Prosser, Handbook on the Law of Torts, p. 613.

The standard measure of damages under the Uniform Commercial Code, as adopted in Tennessee, is not particularly helpful under the facts of this case. Under T.C.A. § 47–2–714(2):

> The measure of damages for breach of warranty is the difference at the time and place of acceptance between the value of the goods accepted and the value they would have had if they had been as warranted. . . .

In the instant case, no credible evidence was proffered to the court to reflect the difference between the value that the records would have had if they had been perfectly pressed the first time and delivered on time, as warranted, and the value of the repressed records which were delivered late, after some of the defective records had already been distributed.

Fortunately, the drafters of the Code anticipated such unique factual circumstances and added the following provision to § 47–2–714(2):

> . . . unless special circumstances show proximate damages of a different amount.

Additionally, T.C.A. § 47–2–714(3) provides:

> In a proper case any incidental and consequential damages under the next section may also be recovered.

T.C.A. § 47–2–715 explains what may be included as incidental and consequential damages:

> (1) Incidental damages resulting from the seller's breach include expenses reasonably incurred in inspection, receipt, transportation and care and custody of goods rightfully rejected, any commercially reasonable charge, expenses or commissions in connection with effecting cover and *any other reasonable expense incident to the delay or other breach.*

Incidental and consequential damages

(2) Consequential damages resulting from the seller's breach include

(a) any loss resulting from general or particular requirements and needs of which the seller at the time of contracting had reason to know and which could not reasonably be prevented by cover or otherwise; and

(b) injury to person or property proximately resulting from any breach of warranty. (emphasis added)

According to Comment 4 to the above-quoted section:

The burden of proving the extent of loss incurred by way of consequential damage is on the buyer, but the section on liberal administration of remedies rejects any doctrine of certainty which requires almost mathematical precision in the proof of loss. *Loss may be determined in any manner which is reasonable under the circumstances.* (emphasis added)

With regard to certainty of proof required on damage questions generally, Tennessee law provides:

. . . there is a clear distinction between the measure of proof necessary to establish the fact that plaintiff had sustained some damage, and the measure of proof necessary to enable the jury to fix the amount. The rule which precludes the recovery of uncertain damages applies to such damages as are not the certain result of the wrong, not to those damages which are definitely attributable to the wrong and only uncertain in respect of their amount.

Acuff v. Vinsant, 443 S.W.2d 669, 674 (Tenn.App.1969).

The question of allowable damages in this case is made more difficult by the speculative nature of the business venture undertaken by GrAMM. It is undisputed that Harrison had not demonstrated that his talents as a songwriter and artist had any appreciable market value prior to the production of the record, "Free Spirit Movin'." The proof clearly indicates the extremely hazardous nature of an undertaking to produce a "hit" record and create a "star" in the entertainment world.

Plaintiff GrAMM contends that the defective first pressing and resultant delay and confusion virtually destroyed the market for the "Free Spirit Movin'" album, and that Mid-South's breach also caused the failure of the firm underwriting of $500,000 by Equidyne. Plaintiff concedes that it is impossible to project with reasonable certainty what the future profits of the new corporation might have been. Instead, plaintiff asks for (1) the cost of laying the ground work for the manufacture and distribution of the album, including production costs of the record, plus advertising and promotional costs; (2) the cost of keeping the corporation going as a business entity from the date of the breach until the date that plaintiff finally had a successful public offering and began producing music for commercial use; (3) the capital lost from the projected underwriting which failed to materialize, less that realized from a subsequent stock offering; and (4) expenses allegedly incurred following the breach in an attempt by GrAMM to rehabilitate the record, including: advertising expenses, promotional salaries, telephone costs, office supplies, payroll taxes, and salaries of management personnel and secretaries.

As previously noted, while the amount of damages may be approximated, the fact of damage attributable to the wrong must be proven with reasonable certainty. The court rejects the first two elements of damages propounded by the plaintiff, for the reason that the plaintiff did not prove to the court's satisfaction that there was ever any appreciable market for the record, nor that any such market was destroyed.

With regard to the existence of any market for the record, it is noteworthy that 32,000 of the 40,000 records pressed were to be shipped to ESA members as a promotional gimmick, with the request that $5.00 be remitted. The ESA members were, of course, under no legal obligation to pay the requested price for this unordered merchandise. 39 U.S.C. § 3010. There was no proof as to what percentage of the ESA members was likely to send in the requested price.

It was shown at trial that the usual practice among unknown artists in the record industry is to first put out a "single" record, as this is less expensive than an album. In this manner, the marketability of the artist can be tested prior to the production of an album. Ralph Harrison had never produced a single record, nor even performed professionally, prior to the production of the "Free Spirit Movin' " album. Therefore, the court must necessarily rely on the proof at trial with regard to the marketability potential of "Free Spirit Movin'."

James Fogelsong, President of Dot Records and an expert in the music field, testified that the lyrics and artist's performance in "Free Spirit Movin' " were not exceptional in any way; that its production was ordinary or worse; and that the musical instruments in the album "were not in time." Paul Perry, a disc jockey for a popular Nashville radio station, testified that he was impressed with the jacket of the album, but not with the ingredients of the record. He testified that he found no fault with the pressing of the album, and that the ingredients on the record couldn't measure up to the programming standards of his station in any event. He further testified that, in his opinion, the album "would not have had any major marketization," even with an initial pressing of highest quality.

Plaintiff offered no credible expert witnesses to refute the testimony of Fogelsong and Perry. No market survey or other reliable evidence with regard to market potential was introduced by plaintiff. Based upon the proof, the court concludes that no appreciable market existed for the "Free Spirit Movin'" album.

Although GrAMM proved the amount of its investment and the cost of operating its business during the period in question, it offered no convincing proof that, with an initial pressing of high quality, it would in all probability have sold a sufficient number of records to recoup its investment. "Ordinarily, damages are said to be speculative when the probability that a circumstance will exist as an element for compensation becomes conjectural." 25 C.J.S. § 2. In the absence of credible proof that the album had a probability of success, the court cannot speculate that this would have been the case. In fact, the proof at trial convinced the court that the album had a far greater chance of failure than of success. * * *

The law is well settled that the injured party is not to be put in a better position by a recovery of damages for breach of contract than he would have been in if there had been full performance. 25 C.J.S. Damages § 3. In this case, to grant plaintiff its entire investment in the album as damages for the breach by defendant would in all probability be to put GrAMM in a far better financial position than it would have been in had there been no breach. This the court will not do. It does not appear that plaintiff would have recouped the investment even if there had been no breach.

The court also rejects plaintiff's damages claim with regard to the failure of the $500,000.00 firm stock underwriting to materialize. First, the proof was not sufficiently clear as to why the underwriting did not go through. In absence of such satisfactory proof, the court cannot hold defendant liable for the failure.

Secondly, the court finds that such damages are too remote to have reasonably been within the contemplation of the parties at the time the contract was made. Although it appears from the proof that some mention was made of the stock offering in the conversation between GrAMM and Mid-South representatives, it does not appear that it was discussed in such detail that defendant would have had any idea that it might be held liable for the failure of the underwriting. As noted by the court in Baker v. Riverside Church of God, 453 S.W.2d 801 (Tenn.1970), in quoting from Squire et al. v. Western Union Telegraph Co., 98 Mass. 232 (1867):

> A rule of damages which should embrace within its scope all the consequences which might be shown to have resulted from a failure or omission to perform a stipulated duty or service would be a serious hindrance to the operations of commerce and to the transaction of the common business life. The effect would often be to impose a liability wholly disproportionate to the nature of the act or service which a party had bound himself to perform and to the compensation paid and received therefore.

453 S.W.2d 801, 810.

In the case currently before the court, plaintiff asks damages in excess of $200,000 for breach of a $13,000 contract. The breach of the contract has not been satisfactorily proven to be the cause of the alleged loss. Certainly, these damages may not be allowed.

Under the circumstances peculiar to this case, the court finds the best measure of allowable damages to be the expenses reasonably incurred by GrAMM in its efforts to rehabilitate the record following the breach.

The court concludes that the following elements may be included in the expenses of rehabilitating the record:

> (1) salaries and travel expenses of GrAMM representatives sent to Nashville to negotiate the re-pressing of the record album and act as GrAMM's quality control agents;

> (2) salaries of other GrAMM employees for the period in which they were actively engaged in the rehabilitation of the record;

> (3) extra mailing and handling costs attributable to the defective first pressing;

> (4) reasonable telephone costs;

> (5) advertising and promotional expenses reasonably incurred by GrAMM in rehabilitating the record; and

> (6) a reasonable amount for office supplies and various other miscellaneous expenses.

* * *

NOTES

1. *Measuring Contract Damages.* Because nonpecuniary losses are rarely recoverable in contract cases, the primary problem in measuring the damages lies in supplying the values necessary to fill in the relevant general damages formula, and in establishing the amount of whatever special damages have been incurred with reasonable certainty. *See, e.g.,* John Y. Gotanda, *Recovering Lost Profits in International Disputes*, 36 Geo.J. Int'l L. (2004) (describing use of the discounted cash flow method for determining the value of lost profits).

2. *Certainty.* Damages can be recovered for a particular element of loss "only to the extent that the evidence affords a sufficient basis for estimating their amount in money with reasonable certainty." Restatement (Second) of Contracts § 352. For example, in Evergreen Amusement Corp. v. Milstead, 112 A.2d 901 (Md.1955), a contractor breached an agreement to clear and grade a site for a drive-in movie theater. The property owner sued, seeking damages measured by the profits he lost because the theater's opening was delayed. The court denied recovery of this element of damages.

The requirement that the amount of the plaintiff's losses be shown with sufficient certainty has always posed particular problems for plaintiffs involved in new or entrepreneurial ventures, as GrAMM. In fact, lost profits from a new business have sometimes been considered presumptively uncertain and unrecoverable. This blanket rule is supported by the notion that while an established business can use its past earning records to show lost profits with reasonable certainty, a new business has no track record and thus cannot provide any non-speculative basis for calculating damages. Gotanda, supra.

However, as economic forecasting has become more sophisticated—and as courts have become more comfortable with economic experts—the presumptive rule regarding new businesses has declined, and what was an absolute rule has become a rule of evidence, in most jurisdictions. With regard to losses suffered by a new business, as with any other loss, the plaintiff must simply provide evidence from which the jury may estimate the amount with reasonable certainty, and without speculation.

CHARLES J. GOETZ & ROBERT E. SCOTT, MEASURING SELLERS' DAMAGES: THE LOST PROFITS PUZZLE
31 Stanford L.Rev. 323, 323–27 (1979)

A buyer repudiates a fixed-price contract to purchase goods, and the seller sues for damages. How should a court measure the seller's loss? The answer seems simple: The seller should be awarded damages sufficient to place it in the same economic position it would have enjoyed had the buyer performed the contract. But the seductive conceptual simplicity of the compensation principle disguises substantial practical problems in measuring seller's damages.

Contract law has traditionally minimized measurement difficulties by basing damages in most cases on the difference between the contract price and market value of the repudiated goods. The common law courts generally limited the seller to such market damages whenever the seller had a resale market for the contract goods. These courts assumed that combining this damage award with proceeds from a resale would give the seller the profits that performance would have earned it. * * *

But as the Uniform Commercial Code damages scheme supplanted the common law, the notion was advanced that the common law rule erroneously used the contract-market formula to measure loss in several circumstances in which the compensation principle demanded that the seller recover by direct proof the profit lost because of the breach. * * *

The "lost-volume seller" is the second category where market damages are frequently believed to measure true losses inadequately. Market resales do not replace or substitute for the breached contract when such resales would have been made even if the buyer had not breached. The seller may contend that, while it did in fact resell the contract goods, the other buyer would have purchased anyway. Therefore, if the breaching buyer had fully performed the contract, the seller would have realized two profits from two sales. Since selling the goods to the second buyer produced only one profit for the seller, the breaching party ought to pay over the other profit in order to put the seller in the position it would have achieved had the buyer performed. Conventional analysis has assumed that whenever the seller is able to supply all available buyers at the prevailing price, its damages are presumptively equal to the entire expected profit lost on the breached contract. * * *

Parties to a contract have the power to limit liability expressly in the agreement, or to alter the measure of damages the common law would impose. *See* UCC § 2–719(2). The power, however, is not unlimited. For example, the UCC provides:

> Consequential damages may be limited or excluded unless the limitation or exclusion is unconscionable. Limitation of consequential damages for injury to the person in the case of consumer goods is prima facie unconscionable but limitation of damages where the loss is commercial is not.

UCC § 2–719(3).

Contracting parties may limit exposure to damages in the event of breach in a liquidated damages clause. A liquidated damages clause sets a specific amount of damages that will be recoverable in the event of a breach. Not all liquidated damages clauses are enforceable, however:

> Damages for breach by either party may be liquidated in the agreement but only at an amount that is reasonable in the light of the anticipated or actual loss caused by the breach and the difficulties of proof of loss. A term fixing unreasonably large liquidated damages is unenforceable on grounds of public policy as a penalty.

Restatement (Second) of Contracts § 356.

GARDEN RIDGE V. ADVANCE INTERNATIONAL

Court of Appeals of Texas
403 S.W.3d 432 (Tex. App. 2013)

TRACY CHRISTOPHER, JUSTICE.

Appellant Garden Ridge, L.P. sued Advance International, Inc. and Herbert A. Feinberg for breach of contract and a declaratory judgment that Garden Ridge had complied with its contracts with Advance. Advance counterclaimed for breach of contract. The jury found in favor of Advance. Although Garden Ridge accepted two shipments of inflatable snowmen from Advance, Garden Ridge refused to pay anything for either shipment, claiming that one shipment was nonconforming. Garden Ridge based its refusal to pay on chargeback provisions outlined in the parties' contracts. Advance argued that the chargeback provisions are unenforceable penalties.

* * * We conclude that the chargeback provisions as applied in this case are unenforceable as a matter of law as penalties. * * *

I. FACTUAL AND PROCEDURAL BACKGROUND

Garden Ridge is a Houston-based chain of housewares and home décor stores. Advance International, a company owned by Feinberg, is one of Garden Ridge's vendors. In 2009, Advance sent Garden Ridge quote sheets for lighted inflatable holiday snowmen, which included a color photo of each item and described its cost, weight, dimensions, and packaging. The two snowmen on the quote sheets each wore a scarf, held a broom that stated "Merry Christmas" on it, and waved; one stood eight feet tall, and the other stood nine feet tall. We refer to this snowman as "waving snowman." Advance then sent two sample snowmen[1] to Garden Ridge; one of the samples did not match its quote sheet. The sample eight-foot snowman wore a Santa-type hat and held a "Merry Christmas" banner. We refer to this snowman as "banner snowman."

Garden Ridge sent Advance two purchase orders, one for approximately 950 nine-foot waving snowmen (PO '721), and the other for approximately 3,500 eight-foot waving snowmen (PO '743), based on the quote sheets. Garden Ridge planned to sell each nine-foot waving snowman for $59.99, and each eight-foot waving snowman for $39.00. Garden Ridge planned to mark down the eight-foot waving snowmen to $20.00 each during its one-day Thanksgiving Shop-a-Thon sale, and it prepared and had printed an advertising circular promoting this special price and picturing the eight-foot waving snowman.

Five days before Thanksgiving, Garden Ridge realized that the eight-foot snowmen that Advance sent were not waving snowmen, but instead were banner snowmen. The nine-foot snowmen that Advance sent were waving snowmen. Garden Ridge decided to honor the $20.00 Shop-a-Thon price on the nine-foot waving snowmen. There were no customer complaints, and both the eight-foot banner snowmen and the nine-foot waving snowmen sold well.

The parties' contracts consist of the purchase orders, the vendor cover letter, and the vendor compliance manual. Based on liquidated-damages provisions outlined in the vendor compliance manual, Garden Ridge assessed chargebacks against Advance for its alleged noncompliance violations. For Advance's "purchase order" violation—by sending the eight-foot banner snowman instead of the waving snowman, Garden Ridge charged back to Advance the entire merchandise cost plus the cost of freight on PO '743 as a "unauthorized substitution" chargeback, which totaled $49,176.00. In addition to paying nothing for the eight-foot banner snowmen, Garden Ridge paid nothing for the nine-foot waving snowman despite the fact that those snowmen complied with PO '721. Garden Ridge charged back to Advance the entire merchandise cost plus the cost of freight on the nine-foot waving snowmen as a "merchant initiated" chargeback, which totaled $29,178.00. Additionally, from September through November 2009, Garden Ridge assessed another $13,241.84 in noncompliance chargebacks to Advance on other merchandise for "ticketing/packing" violations involving not marking cartons sequentially or otherwise mislabeling them, and for "purchase order" violations involving short or incomplete orders.

Advance demanded payment for its snowmen and other items and staged protests at Garden Ridge's headquarters. Thereafter, Garden Ridge sued Advance for breach of contract and a declaratory judgment that Garden Ridge had complied with the contracts. Advance counterclaimed for breach of contract and asserted that Garden Ridge's claims were barred because the chargeback provisions are unenforceable as penalties. Garden Ridge defended against Advance's counterclaim by asserting that Advance breached the contracts first. *[Procedural Posture]*

At trial, Garden Ridge's divisional merchandise manager/vice president Linda Troy admitted that Garden Ridge made approximately $113,000 in profit on the snowmen it received from Advance, and further testified that Garden Ridge made all the money it would have made if the snowmen were delivered exactly as ordered. One of Garden Ridge's buyers, Sheria Cole, admitted she did not know of any dollar amount that Garden Ridge was harmed by the snowmen shipment and that Garden Ridge had less-than-zero receipt cost for the snowmen. Cole also testified that she was unaware of anyone at Garden Ridge having done any actual-harm calculations from the unauthorized substitution of the eight-foot banner snowmen or any calculations to determine whether Garden Ridge's chargebacks were reasonably proportional to any actual harm it suffered. Garden Ridge acknowledges that it did not argue any amount of actual damages other than zero and that the record reflects no actual damages resulting from Advance's noncompliance violations. * * *

II. ANALYSIS

* * *

1. Do the Chargeback Provisions at Issue Assess Liquidated Damages or Penalties?

The parties agree that this case is governed by the Uniform Commercial Code, as adopted by Texas, which applies to transactions involving goods. The parties agree that section 2.718(a) of the UCC, on liquidation of damages, governs the enforceability of the chargeback provisions in this case. Section 2.718(a) provides:

(a) Damages for breach by either party may be liquidated in the agreement but only at an amount which is reasonable in the light of the anticipated or actual harm caused by the breach, the difficulties of proof of loss, and the inconvenience or non-feasibility of otherwise obtaining an adequate remedy. A term fixing unreasonably large liquidated damages is void as a penalty.

* * * But what the parties do not agree on is the proper analysis by which courts determine the legal question of whether a liquidated-damages provision is unenforceable as a penalty.

a. Determining whether a liquidated-damages provision constitutes a penalty

Whether a contractual provision is an enforceable liquidated-damages provision or an unenforceable penalty is a question of law for courts to decide. The party asserting that a liquidated-damages clause is a penalty provision bears the burden of pleading and proof.

"Liquidated damages" ordinarily refers to an acceptable measure of damages that parties stipulate in advance will be assessed in the event of a contract breach. "The common law and the Uniform Commercial Code have long recognized a distinction between liquidated damages and penalties." Section 2.718(a) codified the common-law distinction between liquidated damages and penalties as part of Texas' adoption of the UCC's article on sales.

In *Phillips v. Phillips,* the Texas Supreme Court restated the common-law test for determining whether to enforce a liquidated-damages provision. "In order to enforce a liquidated damages clause, the court must find: (1) that the harm caused by the breach is incapable or difficult of estimation, and (2) that the amount of liquidated damages called for is a reasonable forecast of just compensation." The *Phillips* court explained that one way a party can "show that a liquidated damages provision is unreasonable" is by showing that "the actual damages incurred were much less than the amount contracted for," which requires the party "to prove what those actual damages were." Thus, in such a case, "factual issues must be resolved before the legal question can be decided." * * *

The common-law test as described in *Phillips* closely tracks the language of section 2.718(a) of the UCC. The code allows damages to be liquidated "only at an amount which is reasonable in the light of the anticipated or actual harm caused by the breach, the difficulties of proof of loss, and the inconvenience or non-feasibility of otherwise obtaining an adequate remedy." It further states: "A term fixing unreasonably large liquidated damages is void as a penalty." The first clause of section

2.718(a)—"reasonable in the light of the anticipated or actual harm caused by the breach"—correlates to "reasonable forecast of just compensation," from the common-law test. The second and third clauses of section 2.718(a)—"the difficulties of proof of loss, and the inconvenience or non-feasibility of otherwise obtaining an adequate remedy"—correlate to "that the harm caused by the breach is incapable or difficult of estimation," from the common-law test. Further, the sentence that "[a] term fixing unreasonably large liquidated damages is void as a penalty" under section 2.718(a) correlates to "a liquidated damages provision is unreasonable because the actual damages incurred were much less than the amount contracted for." We therefore conclude that the common-law test as described in *Phillips* and the UCC test as outlined in 2.718(a) reflect the same essential factors and the same type of reasonableness test. Thus, common-law case law continues to inform our analysis here.

b.   Do actual damages matter?

Garden Ridge argues that the test is conducted entirely on an *ex ante* basis. That is, if, at the time the contract is formed, actual damages are difficult to estimate and the amount specified in the contract is a reasonable forecast of just compensation, a liquidated-damages term is enforceable. Garden Ridge contends that the test contains no *ex post* actual-harm assessment to determine reasonableness. Thus, according to Garden Ridge, Advance could only show that the chargeback provisions were unenforceable as penalties if, *ex ante,* actual damages are easy to estimate or the liquidated damages are based on an unreasonable forecast. Garden Ridge asserts that Advance did not meet its burden because Garden Ridge's CFO, Bill Uhrig, testified that the chargeback schedule was created because actual damages from noncompliance violations are difficult to calculate, and that the schedule was based on computations and estimations by Garden Ridge's executive and purchasing staff.

This court . . . has recognized that actual harm factors into the test to determine whether a liquidated-damages provision is an enforceable penalty. "The test for determining whether a provision is valid and enforceable as liquidated damages is (1) if the damages for the prospective breach of the contract are difficult to measure; and (2) the stipulated damages are a reasonable estimate of actual damages." Further, we stated:

In order to meet this burden, the party asserting the defense is required to prove the amount of the other parties' actual damages, if any, to show that the liquidated damages are not an approximation of the stipulated sum. If the liquidated damages are shown to be disproportionate to the actual damages, then the liquidated damages must be declared a penalty. . . .

Most importantly, the UCC reasonableness test explicitly refers to actual harm, providing that one way a liquidated-damages provision can be invalidated is where the stipulated amount proves unreasonable in light of "the anticipated or *actual* harm caused by the breach." In addition, the UCC expressly provides that "[a] term fixing unreasonably large liquidated damages is void as a penalty." In order to determine whether a term fixes unreasonably large liquidated damages, it follows that courts would need to consider what actual harm, if any, was caused by the breach and then compare it to the stipulated amount of liquidated damages.

Thus, both the common law and the UCC allow for courts to determine the reasonableness of a liquidated-damages clause by considering whether the defendant has shown that the stipulated amount was "unreasonably large" compared to the actual damages.

c.   Comparing the amount of the chargebacks to Garden Ridge's actual damages

* * * We conclude Advance met its burden to show that the chargeback amounts constituted a disproportionate estimation of Garden Ridge's actual damages; therefore, the chargeback provisions are void as penalties under the UCC.

Advance elicited evidence from Garden Ridge employees Troy and Cole sufficient to prove that Garden Ridge suffered no actual damages as a result of Advance's substitution of the eight-foot banner snowmen. The trial court also determined that Garden Ridge suffered no actual damages from any of Advance's noncompliance violations when the court directed a verdict against Garden Ridge on its breach-of-contract claim; Garden Ridge does not challenge that ruling. And Garden Ridge itself acknowledges it argued no amount of actual damages other than zero and the record shows that Garden Ridge suffered no actual damages resulting from Advance's noncompliance violations.

Thus, Advance has shown that the chargebacks assessed by Garden Ridge for Advance's "unauthorized substitution" and "merchant initiated" noncompliance violations—100% of the invoiced merchandise cost plus freight for the eight-foot banner snowmen and the nine-foot waving snowmen, for a total of $79,457.00—were unreasonably large when compared to Garden Ridge's actual damages of zero. Advance also has shown that the additional chargebacks assessed by Garden Ridge for Advance's "short or incomplete order," "carton markings," and "cartons not numbered correctly" noncompliance violations on other merchandise— totaling approximately $13,000—were unreasonably large when compared to Garden Ridge's actual damages of zero. Therefore, as a matter of law, we conclude that, under these circumstances, the chargeback amounts were unreasonable, and that the chargeback provisions are unenforceable as penalties under the UCC because they fixed unreasonably large liquidated damages.

d.   Whether the amount of the chargebacks is reasonable in light of Garden Ridge's anticipated harm

Even if the concurring opinion is correct that Advance also had to prove the stipulated damages were unreasonable in light of the anticipated harm in order for us to conclude that the chargeback provisions are unreasonable under section 2.718(a), we conclude that Advance has done so in this case. * * * Advance has shown that the stipulated amounts are unreasonable in light of the *actual* harm—zero—suffered by Garden Ridge. Further, Advance has shown that the stipulated amounts are unreasonable in light of the harm *anticipated* by Garden Ridge.

Here, according to the challenged liquidated-damages provisions, Garden Ridge anticipated at the time of contract that an unauthorized substitution of any type would result in harm of 100% of the cost of the merchandise, plus freight. In fact, Garden Ridge's buyer Cole testified that Garden Ridge had the discretion to assess the full 100% chargeback, even if the only deviation in the snowmen had been green versus red buttons. Cole further testified that she was not aware of any instance where Garden Ridge had decided not to issue a chargeback because there was "no harm, no foul" or where Garden Ridge had exercised its discretion to not charge back "fully" for an unauthorized substitution. Garden Ridge's CFO Uhrig agreed that a button-color substitution would constitute noncompliance, for which Garden Ridge could charge back the full 100% of merchandise cost. In other words, no matter what the degree of substitution, and no matter whether the substitution is even anticipated to result in any harm, Garden Ridge's unauthorized-substitution rule provides that Garden Ridge keeps the merchandise without paying the vendor anything and makes the vendor cover the freight.

Even though, according to Uhrig, Garden Ridge is "very good at estimating our costs," he admitted that at the time it was developing the chargeback schedule Garden Ridge did not perform any actual studies on what costs it would incur due to vendor noncompliance. Further, Uhrig could not explain any specifics on how Garden Ridge "figure[d] out what the costs are and what would be appropriate charge-backs." Cole also testified that she was not aware of Garden Ridge having performed any analysis as to whether the 100% chargeback amount reasonably approximates the anticipated harm that Garden Ridge would suffer from an unauthorized substitution. Despite this lack of detail regarding the 100% chargeback amount for anticipated harm from vendor violations, Uhrig testified that "on average" charging back 100% somehow reflected Garden Ridge's costs for unauthorized substitutions. Uhrig further indicated that Garden Ridge's chargebacks communicate to vendors, "Don't do this"; and Garden Ridge's CEO, Tim Kibarian, agreed that chargebacks are the "penalty" if its vendors do not follow its rules.

We therefore conclude that Advance has proven that Garden Ridge's liquidated-damages provisions do not reasonably reflect Garden Ridge's anticipated harm for an unauthorized substitution, where the challenged provisions allowed Garden Ridge to charge back 100% of merchandise cost plus freight for any unauthorized substitution, no matter how slight and no matter if Garden Ridge even anticipated incurring any harm.

Accordingly, having overruled all of Garden Ridge's issues, we affirm the trial court's judgment.

Appendix A

KEM THOMPSON FROST, JUSTICE, concurring.

* * * By allowing a breaching party to show that a liquidated-damages provision is unreasonable based only upon a comparison between the amount of the stipulated damages and the amount of the actual damages incurred, the majority exposes liquidated-damages provisions in sale-of-goods contracts to a legal standard that may bar enforcement of many such provisions based upon a hindsight analysis that the Texas Legislature never intended. * * *

Under the legal standard the majority adopts today, parties breaching sale-of-goods contracts may avoid enforcement of liquidated-damages provisions based upon a hindsight analysis. This approach not only contravenes the statutory text but also undermines important freedom-of-contract values that are a cornerstone of Texas jurisprudence.

Texas has a fundamental public policy in favor of a broad freedom of contract. Liquidated-damages provisions in commercial transactions benefit both sides by providing certainty and predictability. By including Section 2–718(a) in Texas's version of the Uniform Commercial Code, the Texas Legislature recognized the utility of liquidated-damages clauses and parties' willingness and desire to choose this remedy in transactions involving the sale of goods. The Legislature also recognized that in certain situations, liquidated-damages provisions should not be enforceable, and the Legislature crafted a specific legal standard for making this determination.

When a buyer and a seller agree to a liquidated-damages provision, both parties have a potential upside and a potential downside. The idea is that, even though the non-breaching party's expectation damages may be far greater than the amount specified in the liquidated-damages clause, the non-breaching party's recovery is capped at the amount of specified liquidated damages. Under freedom-of-contract principles, courts must honor the parties' agreement unless the stipulated amount is shown to be unreasonable under Section 2.718(a). Under this standard, as discussed above, the party asserting that the provision is void as a penalty must prove that the stipulated amount is unreasonable based both on the harm anticipated at the time of contracting and the actual harm caused by the breach. At the time of contracting, unknown factors often make estimation and calculation of potential damages uncertain. This uncertainty at the time of contracting is often what makes the determination of liquidated damages difficult. Hindsight has a way of making estimations that were reasonable at the time seem unreasonable after a breach. By the time a breach has occurred and the dispute has come to court, the costs and valuations are often easier to estimate and, with hindsight, honest estimates made at the inception of the contract might prove to be too high or too low. This is part of the risk of doing business that parties embrace when agreeing to a liquidated-damages provision. In evaluating these provisions, courts should not lose sight of important principles of freedom of contract and must uphold the sanctity of contract unless the liquidated-damages provision is shown to be a penalty under the standard articulated by the Legislature in Section 2.718(a).

With the legal standard adopted by the majority today, the court fails to honor the Legislature's intent of providing leeway for the parties to have stipulated to an amount of liquidated damages that was reasonable under conditions prevailing at the time of contracting but that ends up not measuring damages in a completely accurate manner in a particular case. Enforcing liquidated-damages provisions when they accurately gauge actual damages and not enforcing them when they do not deprives the non-breaching party of the remedy it bargained to receive, contrary to Section 2.718(a).

NOTE

In determining whether a liquidated damages clause is enforceable, should the court consider actual damages that would be too uncertain or remote to be recoverable as compensatory damages? *See* Gregory Scott Crespi, *Measuring "Actual Harm" for the Purpose of Determining the Enforceability of Liquidated Damages Clauses*, 41 Hous.L.Rev. 1579 (2005).

F. ADJUSTMENTS TO THE DAMAGE AWARD

1. PREJUDGMENT INTEREST

KANSAS V. COLORADO
Supreme Court of the United States
533 U.S. 1 (2001)

JUSTICE STEVENS delivered the opinion of the Court.

The Arkansas River rises in the mountains of Colorado just east of the Continental Divide, descends for about 280 miles to the Kansas border, then flows through that State, Oklahoma, and Arkansas and empties into the Mississippi River. On May 20, 1901, Kansas first invoked this Court's original jurisdiction to seek a remedy for Colorado's diversion of water from the Arkansas River. In opinions written during the past century, we have described the history and the importance of the river. For present purposes it suffices to note that two of those cases led to the negotiation of the Arkansas River Compact (Compact), an agreement between Kansas and Colorado that in turn was approved by Congress in 1949. The case before us today involves a claim by Kansas for damages based on Colorado's violations of that Compact.

* * *

[The Court-appointed Special Master determined that groundwater well pumping in Colorado had materially depleted the river's waters, violating the Compact.]

[T]he Special Master recommends that damages be measured by Kansas' losses, rather than Colorado's profits, attributable to Compact violations after 1950; that the damages be paid in money rather than water; and that the damages should include prejudgment interest from 1969 to the date of judgment. Colorado has filed four objections to the report. It contends (1) that the recommended award of damages would violate the Eleventh Amendment to the United States Constitution; (2) that the damages award should not include prejudgment interest; (3) that the amount of interest awarded is excessive; and (4) that the Special Master improperly credited flawed expert testimony, with the result that Kansas' crop production losses were improperly calculated. On the other hand, Kansas has filed an objection submitting that prejudgment interest should be paid from 1950, rather than 1969. The United States, which intervened because of its interest in the operation of flood control projects in Colorado, submits that both States' objections should be overruled.

I

[The Court rejected Colorado's argument that because damages were measured by the losses Kansas farmers incurred, the suit was barred by the Eleventh Amendment. The Eleventh Amendment does not bar suits by one state seeking damages from another state, so long as the state suing is more than a nominal party merely forwarding its citizens' claims to avoid the Eleventh Amendment. Enforcing a water compact is in the public interest whatever damage measure might ultimately apply, and Kansas was in full control of the litigation throughout.]

* * *

II

Colorado next excepts to the Special Master's conclusion that the damages award should include prejudgment interest despite the fact that Kansas' claim is unliquidated.[2] At one point in time, the fact that the claim was unliquidated would have been of substantial importance. As a general matter, early common-law cases drew a distinction between liquidated and unliquidated claims and refused to allow interest on the latter. This rule seems to have rested upon a belief that there was something inherently unfair about requiring debtors to pay interest when they were unable to halt its accrual by handing over to their creditors a fixed and unassailable amount.

This common-law distinction has long since lost its hold on the legal imagination. Beginning in the early part of the last century, numerous courts and commentators have rejected the distinction for failing to acknowledge the compensatory nature of interest awards. This Court allied itself with the evolving consensus in 1933, when we expressed the opinion that the distinction between cases of liquidated and unliquidated damages "is not a sound one." The analysis supporting that conclusion gave no doubt as to our reasoning: "Whether the case is of the one class or the other, the injured party has suffered a loss which may be regarded as not fully compensated if he is confined to the amount found to be recoverable as of the time of breach and nothing is added for the delay in obtaining the award of damages." Our cases since 1933 have consistently acknowledged that a monetary award does not fully compensate for an injury unless it includes an interest component.

Relying on our cases, the Special Master "concluded that the unliquidated nature of Kansas' money damages does not, in and of itself, bar an award of prejudgment interest." In reaching that conclusion, the Special Master was fully cognizant of both the displaced common-law rule

---

[2] Though final damages have not yet been calculated, the importance of this issue is illustrated by breaking down the damages claimed by Kansas. Of $62,369,173 in damages so claimed, $9,218,305 represents direct and indirect losses in actual dollars when the damage occurred. Of the remaining $53,150,868, about $12 million constitutes an adjustment for inflation (a type of interest that Colorado concedes is appropriate) while the remaining amount (approximately $41 million) represents additional interest intended to compensate for lost investment opportunities. Third Report of Special Master 87–88 (hereinafter Third Report). The magnitude of prejudgment interest ultimately awarded in this case will, of course, turn on the date from which interest accrues. See Part III–B, infra.

and the subsequent doctrinal evolution. In addition, he gave careful consideration to equitable considerations that might mitigate against an award of interest, concluding that "considerations of fairness," supported the award of at least some prejudgment interest in this case.

We find no fault in the Special Master's analysis of either our prior cases or the equities of this matter. While we will deal with the amount of prejudgment interest below, to answer Colorado's second objection it is sufficient to conclude that the Special Master was correct in determining that the unliquidated nature of the damages does not preclude an award of prejudgment interest.

Colorado's second exception is overruled.

III

Colorado's third exception takes issue with both the rate of interest adopted by the Special Master and the date from which he recommended that interest begin to accrue. As to the second of these two concerns, Colorado submits that, if any prejudgment interest is to be awarded, it should begin to accrue in 1985 (when Kansas filed its complaint in this action), rather than in 1969 (when, the Special Master concluded, Colorado knew or should have known that it was violating the Compact).

On the other hand, Kansas has entered an exception, arguing that the accrual of interest should begin in 1950. We first address the rate question, then the timing issue.

Λ

The Special Master credited the testimony of Kansas' three experts who calculated the interest rates that they thought necessary to provide full compensation for the damages caused by Colorado's violations of the Compact in the years since 1950. As a result of inflation and changing market conditions those rates varied from year to year. In their calculation of the damages suffered by Kansas farmers, the experts used the interest rates that were applicable to individuals in the relevant years rather than the (lower) rates available to States.

Colorado argues that the lower rates should have been used because it is the State, rather than the individual farmers, that is maintaining the action and will receive any award of damages. But if, as we have already decided, see Part I, supra, it is permissible for the State to measure a portion of its damages by losses suffered by individual farmers, it necessarily follows that the courts are free to utilize whatever interest rate will most accurately measure those losses. The money in question in this portion of the damages award is revenue that would—but for Colorado's actions—have been earned by individual farmers. Thus, the Special Master correctly concluded that the economic consequences of Colorado's breach could best be remedied by an interest award that mirrors the cost of any additional borrowing the farmers may have been forced to undertake in order to compensate for lost revenue.

B

Although the Special Master rejected Colorado's submission that there is a categorical bar to the award of prejudgment interest on unliquidated claims, he concluded that such interest should not "be awarded according to [any] rigid theory of compensation for money withheld," but rather should respond to " 'considerations of fairness.' " Kansas argues that our decisions * * * have effectively foreclosed the equities-balancing approach that the Special Master adopted. There is some merit to Kansas' position. See [City of Milwaukee v. National Gypsum Co., 515 U.S. 189, 193, 115 S.Ct. 2091 (1995)] (affirming a decision of the Court of Appeals that had read our cases as "disapproving of a 'balancing of the equities' as a method of deciding whether to allow prejudgment interest").

However, despite the clear direction indicated by some of our earlier opinions, we cannot say that by 1949 our case law had developed sufficiently to put Colorado on notice that, upon a violation of the Compact, we would automatically award prejudgment interest from the time of injury. Given the state of the law at that time, Colorado may well have believed that we would balance the equities in order to achieve a just and equitable remedy, rather than automatically imposing prejudgment interest in order to achieve full compensation. While we are confident that, when it signed the Compact, Colorado was on notice that it might be subject to prejudgment interest if such interest was necessary to fashion an equitable remedy, we are unable to conclude with sufficient certainty that Colorado was on notice that such interest would be imposed as a matter of course. We, therefore, believe that the Special Master acted properly in carefully analyzing the facts of the case and in only awarding as much prejudgment interest as was required by a balancing of the equities.

We also agree with the Special Master that the equities in this case do not support an award of prejudgment interest from the date of the first violation of the Compact, but rather favor an award beginning on a later date. In reaching this conclusion, the Special Master appropriately considered several factors. In particular, he relied on the fact that in the early years after the Compact was signed, no one had any thought that the pact was being violated. In addition, he considered the long interval that passed between the original injuries and these proceedings, as well as the dramatic impact of compounding interest over many years.

In its exception, Kansas argues that the Special Master's reasoning would be appropriate if damages were being awarded as a form of punishment, but does not justify a refusal to provide full compensation to an injured party. Moreover, Kansas argues, a rule that rewards ignorance might discourage diligence in making sure that there is full compliance with the terms of the Compact. Kansas' argument is consistent with a "rigid theory of compensation for money withheld," but, for the reasons discussed above, we are persuaded that the Special Master correctly declined to adopt such a theory. The equitable considerations identified by the Special Master fully justify his view that in this case it would be inappropriate to award prejudgment interest for any years before either party was aware of the excessive pumping in Colorado.

In its third exception, Colorado argues that, if prejudgment interest is to be awarded at all, the equities are best balanced by limiting such interest to the time after the complaint was filed, rather than the time after which Colorado knew or should have known that it was violating the Compact. Specifically, Colorado suggests that prejudgment interest should begin to accrue in 1985 rather than 1969. The choice between the two dates is surely debatable; it is a matter over which reasonable people can—and do—disagree. After examining the equities for ourselves, however, a majority of the Court has decided that the later date is the more appropriate.[5]

When we overruled Colorado's objections to the Special Master's first report, we held that Kansas was not guilty of inexcusable delay in failing to complain more promptly about post-Compact well pumping. In saying that the delay was not inexcusable, we recognized that the nature and extent of Colorado's violations continued to be unclear even in the years after which it became obvious that the Compact was being violated. That conclusion is something of a two-edged sword, however. While Kansas' delay was understandable given the amorphous nature of its claims, there is no doubt that the interests of both States would have been served if the claim had been advanced promptly after its basis became known. Once it became obvious that a violation of the Compact had occurred, it was equally clear that the proceedings necessary to evaluate the significance of the violations would be complex and protracted. Despite the diligence of the parties and the Special Master, over 15 years have elapsed since the complaint was filed. Given the uncertainty over the scope of damages that prevailed during the period between 1968 and 1985 and the fact that it was uniquely in Kansas' power to begin the process by which those damages would be quantified, Colorado's request that we deny prejudgment interest for that period is reasonable.

For these reasons, we overrule Kansas' exception. We also overrule Colorado's third exception insofar as it challenges the interest rates

---

[5] Justice O'Connor, Justice Scalia, and Justice Thomas would not allow any prejudgment interest. Justice Kennedy and Chief Justice [Rehnquist] are of the opinion that prejudgment interest should run from the date of the filing of the complaint. Justice Souter, Justice Ginsburg, Justice Breyer, and the author of this opinion agree with the Special Master's view that interest should run from the time when Colorado knew or should have known that it was violating the Compact. In order to produce a majority for a judgment, the four Justices who agree with the Special Master have voted to endorse the position expressed in the text.

recommended by the Special Master, but we sustain that objection insofar as it challenges the award of interest for the years prior to 1985.

[The Court's discussion of Colorado's objection to the method by which crop losses were determined is omitted.]

JUSTICE O'CONNOR, with whom JUSTICE SCALIA and JUSTICE THOMAS join, concurring in part and dissenting in part.

* * * We are dealing with an interstate compact apportioning the flow of a river between two States. A compact is a contract. It represents a bargained-for exchange between its signatories and "remains a legal document that must be construed and applied in accordance with its terms." It is a fundamental tenet of contract law that parties to a contract are deemed to have contracted with reference to principles of law existing at the time the contract was made. The basic question before the Court is thus one of "the fair intendment of the contract itself." Specifically, the question is whether, at the time the Compact was negotiated and approved, Colorado and Kansas could fairly be said to have intended, or at least to have expected or assumed, that Colorado might be exposing itself to liability for prejudgment interest in the event of the Compact's breach.

I fail to see how Colorado and Kansas could have contemplated that prejudgment interest would be awarded. * * * To be sure, we had by then, along with other courts, criticized the common law rule that prejudgment interest was recoverable on claims for liquidated, but not for unliquidated, damages. But in the absence of a statute providing for such interest, many courts, including our own, still denied and would continue to deny prejudgment interest on claims for unliquidated and unascertainable damages in a great many, and probably most, circumstances.

* * * [U]ntil 1987, we had never even suggested that monetary damages could be recovered from a State as a remedy for its violation of an interstate compact apportioning the flow of an interstate stream. * * * How, then, can one say that, at the time the Compact was negotiated and approved, its signatories could fairly be said to have intended, or at least could reasonably be said to have expected or assumed, that Kansas might recover prejudgment interest on damages caused by Colorado's breach? * * * As both the Compact itself and the parties' post-Compact course of dealing make clear, the "fair intendment" of the Compact very probably was simply for the in-kind recovery of water as a remedy for its breach. * * *

The Court ignores all of this in awarding prejudgment interest to Kansas, seizing instead upon the compensatory rationale behind the criticism of the common law rule and awards of prejudgment interest on unliquidated claims for damages in general. I do not dispute that awards of interest are compensatory in nature or that, as a general matter, "a monetary award does not fully compensate for an injury unless it includes an interest component." But, as the Court itself recognizes, our precedents make clear that, at least today and in the absence of a governing statute, awards of prejudgment interest on unliquidated claims for damages are governed not by any "rigid theory of compensation for money withheld," but rather by "considerations of fairness." This is especially so where, as here, we are dealing with suits by one governmental body against another.

There is nothing fair about awarding prejudgment interest as a remedy for the Compact's breach when all available evidence suggests that the signatories to the Compact neither intended nor contemplated such an unconventional remedy. * * *

NOTES

1. In a subsequent appeal, Kansas argued that prejudgment interest should have been awarded from 1985 until the date of the judgment on the entire award. The Special Master disagreed, and calculated interest only on damages that accrued after 1985. The Court upheld the Special Master:

> After all, says Kansas, "[p]rejudgment interest serves to compensate for the loss of use of money due as damages . . . thereby achieving full compensation for the injury those damages are intended to redress." Why then, asks Kansas, calculate post 1985 interest on only some of the damages then due? * * * Kansas' argument would make good sense in an ordinary case. But the question here is not about the ordinary case * * * . [L]ike the Special Master, we did not seek to provide compensation for all lost investment opportunities; rather, we sought to weigh the equities.

Kansas v. Colorado, 543 U.S. 86, 96 (2004).

2. As the *Kansas* Court recognizes, an award of prejudgment interest is necessary to ensure that the plaintiff is fully compensated, given the inevitable delay between injury and recovery:

> If justice were immediate, there would never be an award of prejudgment interest. The injured party would receive an enforceable judgment immediately, with no loss in value from the time value of money. Because justice often takes many years to achieve, interest is added to the original judgment to ensure that compensation is complete.

Michael S. Knoll, *Primer on Prejudgment Interest,* 75 Tex.L.Rev. 293, 294 (1996). Depending on the length of the delay, the amount at stake can be considerable. In Cayuga Indian Nation of New York v. Pataki, 165 F.Supp.2d 266 (N.D.N.Y.2001), for example, the court awarded a tribe that had been deprived of its land for 204 years $211,000,326.80 in prejudgment interest. And that was after balancing the hardships and reducing the award by 60%! On appeal, however, the claim was found to be barred by laches. Cayuga Indian

Nation of New York v. Pataki, 413 F.3d 266 (2d Cir.2005), *cert. denied*, 547 U.S. 1128 (2006).

3.   Prejudgment interest was originally limited to cases in which the damages were liquidated, or at least ascertainable before judgment by reference to market values. Once the compensatory nature of prejudgment interest is recognized, the distinction between liquidated and unliquidated claims becomes difficult to defend. Nonetheless, some courts adhere to it. *See, e.g.,* Ventura v. Titan Sports, Inc. 65 F.3d 725 (8th Cir.1995) (under Minnesota law, prejudgment interest is available only for claims that are liquidated or readily ascertainable by reference to objective market values); Coho Resources v. McCarthy, 829 So.2d 1 (Miss.2002) (no prejudgment interest where principal amount has not been fixed prior to judgment).

4.   Generally speaking, prejudgment interest is not available for noneconomic losses. As one student commentator explained. Note, *Interest as Damages in California*, 5 U.C.L.A.L.Rev. 262, 264 (1958). Some jurisdictions give the judge or the jury broad discretion to award prejudgment interest in cases in which prejudgment interest would not have been available at common law. *See, e.g.,* Cal.Civ.Code § 3288 (jury has discretion to award prejudgment interest in cases "not arising from contract and in every case of oppression, fraud or malice").

5.   At common law, prejudgment interest has always been simple interest at the legal rate. The legal rate of interest is typically set by statute. Courts of equity would sometimes award compound interest where there was a breach of a fiduciary duty involving misuse of trust funds, or a failure to invest trust funds. See Restatement (Second) of Trusts § 207(2).

6.   The policy of promoting settlements also comes into play in thinking about prejudgment interest. Without an award of prejudgment interest, the defendant has an incentive to drag out the proceedings while having use of the amount in dispute. So, some jurisdictions have expanded the availability of prejudgment interest in order to promote settlement. See Cal.Civ.Code § 3291 (if plaintiff makes a statutory offer of settlement that the defendant refuses, and plaintiff's recovery at trial exceeds his demand, plaintiff may claim interest on the judgment at 10% from the time of the offer).

7.   Almost all jurisdictions have statutes calling for the award of post-judgment interest when there is a delay between the entry of a judgment and its satisfaction. *See, e.g.,* Cal.Code Civ.Pro. § 685.010 (interest accrues at a rate of 10% per year on the amount of an unsatisfied money judgment).

2. DISCOUNTING TO PRESENT VALUE

JONES & LAUGHLIN STEEL CORPORATION V. PFEIFER
Supreme Court of the United States
462 U.S. 523 (1983)

JUSTICE STEVENS delivered the opinion of the Court.

Respondent was injured in the course of his employment as a loading helper on a coal barge. As his employer, petitioner was required to compensate him for his injury under § 4 of the Longshoremen's and Harbor Workers' Compensation Act (the Act). We granted certiorari * * * to consider whether the Court of Appeals correctly upheld the trial court's computation of respondent's damages.

* * *

I

* * *

The District Court's calculation of damages was predicated on a few undisputed facts. At the time of his injury respondent was earning an annual wage of $26,065. He had a remaining work expectancy of 12 ½ years. On the date of trial (October 1, 1980), respondent had received compensation payments of $33,079,14. If he had obtained light work and earned the legal minimum hourly wage from July 1, 1979 until his 65th birthday, he would have earned $66,350.

The District Court arrived at its final award by taking 12 ½ years of earnings at respondent's wage at the time of injury ($325,312.50), subtracting his projected hypothetical earnings at the minimum wage ($66,352) and the compensation payments he had received under § 4 ($33,079.14), and adding $50,000 for pain and suffering. The court did not increase the award to take inflation into account, and it did not discount the award to reflect the present value of the future stream of income. The Court instead decided to follow a decision of the Supreme Court of Pennsylvania, which had held "as a matter of law that future inflation shall be presumed equal to future interest rates with these factors offsetting." Kaczkowski v. Bolubasz, 491 Pa. 561, 583, 421 A.2d 1027, 1038–1039 (1980). Thus, although the District Court did not dispute that respondent could be expected to receive regular cost-of-living wage increases from the date of his injury until his presumed date of retirement, the Court refused to include such increases in its calculation, explaining that they would provide respondent "a double consideration for inflation." For comparable reasons, the Court disregarded changes in the legal minimum wage in computing the amount of mitigation attributable to respondent's ability to perform light work.

* * *

The Damages Issue

The District Court found that respondent was permanently disabled as a result of petitioner's negligence. He therefore was entitled to an award of damages to compensate him for his probable pecuniary loss over the duration of his career, reduced to its present value. It is useful at the outset to review the way in which damages should be measured in a hypothetical inflation-free economy. We shall then consider how price inflation alters the analysis. Finally, we shall decide whether the District Court committed reversible error in this case.

In calculating damages, it is assumed that if the injured party had not been disabled, he would have continued to work, and to receive wages at periodic intervals until retirement, disability, or death. An award for impaired earning capacity is intended to compensate the worker for the diminution in that stream of income. The award could in theory take the form of periodic payments, but in this country it has traditionally taken the form of a lump sum, paid at the conclusion of the litigation. The appropriate lump sum cannot be computed without first examining the stream of income it purports to replace.

* * *

Each annual installment in the lost stream comprises several elements. The most significant is, of course, the actual wage. In addition, the worker may have enjoyed certain fringe benefits, which should be included in an ideal evaluation of the worker's loss but are frequently excluded for simplicity's sake. On the other hand, the injured worker's lost wages would have been diminished by state and federal income taxes. Since the damages award is tax-free, the relevant stream is ideally of after-tax wages and benefits. See Norfolk & Western R. Co. v. Liepelt, 444 U.S. 490 (1980). Moreover, workers often incur unreimbursed costs, such as transportation to work and uniforms, that the injured worker will not incur. These costs should also be deducted in estimating the lost stream.

In this case the parties appear to have agreed to simplify the litigation, and to presume that in each installment all the elements in the stream would offset each other, except for gross wages. However, in attempting to estimate even such a stylized stream of annual installments of gross wages, a trier of fact faces a complex task. The most obvious and most appropriate place to begin is with the worker's annual wage at the time of injury. Yet the "estimate of loss from lessened earnings capacity in the future need not be based solely upon the wages which the plaintiff was earning at the time of his injury." C. McCormick, Damages § 86 (1935). Even in an inflation-free economy—that is to say one in which the prices of consumer goods remain stable—a worker's wages tend to "inflate." This "real" wage inflation reflects a number of factors, some linked to the specific individual and some linked to broader societal forces.

With the passage of time, an individual worker often becomes more valuable to his employer. His personal work experiences increase his hourly contributions to firm profits. To reflect that heightened value, he will often receive "seniority" or "experience" raises, "merit" raises, or even promotions. Although it may be difficult to prove when, and whether, a particular injured worker might have received such wage increases, they may be reliably demonstrated for some workers.

Furthermore, the wages of workers as a class may increase over time. Through more efficient interaction among labor, capital, and technology, industrial productivity may increase, and workers' wages may enjoy a share of that growth. Such productivity increases—reflected in real increase in the gross national product per worker-hour—have been a permanent feature of the national economy since the conclusion of World War II. Moreover, through collective bargaining, workers may be able to negotiate increases in their "share" of revenues, at the cost of reducing shareholders' rate of return on their investments. Either of these forces could affect the lost stream of income in an inflation-free economy. In this case, the plaintiff's proffered evidence on predictable wage growth may have reflected the influence of either or both of these two factors.

To summarize, the first stage in calculating an appropriate award for lost earnings involves an estimate of what the lost stream of income would have been. The stream may be approximated as a series of after-tax payments, one in each year of the worker's expected remaining career. In estimating what those payments would have been in an inflation-free economy, the trier of fact may begin with the worker's annual wage at the time of injury. If sufficient proof is offered, the trier of fact may increase that figure to reflect the appropriate influence of individualized factors (such as foreseeable promotions) and societal factors (such as foreseeable productivity growth within the worker's industry).

Of course, even in an inflation-free economy the award of damages to replace the lost stream of income cannot be computed simply by totaling up the sum of the periodic payments. For the damages award is paid in a lump sum at the conclusion of the litigation, and when it—or even a part of it— is invested, it will earn additional money. It has been settled since our decision in Chesapeake & Ohio R. Co. v. Kelly, 241 U.S. 485 (1916) that "in all cases where it is reasonable to suppose that interest may safely be earned upon the amount that is awarded, the ascertained future benefits ought to be discounted in the making up of the award."

The discount rate should be based on the rate of interest that would be earned on "the best and safest investments." Once it is assumed that the injured worker would definitely have worked for a specific term of years, he is entitled to a risk-free stream of future income to replace his lost wages; therefore, the discount rate should not reflect the market's premium for investors who are willing to accept some risk of default. Moreover, since under *Liepelt*, supra, the lost stream of income should be estimated in after-tax terms, the discount rate should also represent the after-tax rate of return to the injured worker.

Thus, although the notion of a damage award representing the present value of a lost stream of earnings in an inflation-free economy rests on some fairly sophisticated economic concepts, the two elements that determine its calculation can be stated fairly easily. They are: (1) the amount that the employee would have earned during each year that he could have been expected to work after the injury; and (2) the appropriate discount rate, reflecting the safest available investment. The trier of fact should apply the discount rate to each of the estimated installments in the lost stream of income, and then add up the discounted installments to determine the total award.

II

Unfortunately for triers of fact, ours is not an inflation-free economy. Inflation has been a permanent fixture in our economy for many decades, and there can be no doubt that it ideally should affect both stages of the calculation described in the previous section. The difficult problem is how it can do so in the practical context of civil litigation under [the Longshoreman's Act].

The first stage of the calculation requires an estimate of the shape of the lost stream of future income. For many workers, including respondent, a contractual "cost-of-living adjustment" automatically increases wages each year by the percentage change during the previous year in the consumer price index calculated by the Bureau of Labor Statistics. Such a contract provides a basis for taking into account an additional societal factor—price inflation—in estimating the worker's lost future earnings.

The second stage of the calculation requires the selection of an appropriate discount rate. Price inflation—or more precisely, anticipated price inflation—certainly affects market rates of return. If a lender knows that his loan is to be repaid a year later with dollars that are less valuable than those he has advanced, he will charge an interest rate that is high enough both to compensate him for the temporary use of the loan proceeds and also to make up for their shrinkage in value.

At one time many courts incorporated inflation into only one stage of the calculation of the award for lost earnings. In estimating the lost stream of future earnings, they accepted evidence of both individual and societal factors that would tend to lead to wage increases even in an inflation-free economy, but required the plaintiff to prove that those factors were not influenced by predictions of future price inflation. No increase was allowed for price inflation, on the theory that such predictions were unreliably speculative. In discounting the estimated lost stream of future income to present value, however, they applied the market interest rate.

The effect of these holdings was to deny the plaintiff the benefit of the impact of inflation on his future earnings, while giving the defendant the benefit of inflation's impact on the interest rate that is used to discount those earnings to present value. Although the plaintiff in such a situation could invest the proceeds of the litigation at an "inflated" rate of interest, the stream of income that he received provided him with only enough dollars to maintain his existing nominal income; it did not provide him with a stream comparable to what his lost wages would have been in an inflationary economy. This inequity was assumed to have been minimal because of the relatively low rates of inflation.

In recent years, of course, inflation rates have not remained low. There is now a consensus among courts that the prior inequity can no longer be tolerated. There is no consensus at all, however, regarding what form an appropriate response should take.

Our sister common law nations generally continue to adhere to the position that inflation is too speculative to be considered in estimating the lost stream of future earnings; they have sought to counteract the danger of systematically undercompensating plaintiffs by applying a discount rate that is below the current market rate. Nevertheless, they have each chosen different rates, applying slightly different economic theories. In England, Lord Diplock has suggested that it would be appropriate to allow for future inflation "in a rough and ready way" by discounting at a rate of 4¾%. He accepted that rate as roughly equivalent to the rates available "[i]n times of stable currency." The Supreme Court of Canada has recommended discounting at a rate of seven percent, a rate equal to market rates on long-term investments minus a government expert's prediction of the long-term rate of price inflation. And in Australia, the High Court has adopted a 2% rate, on the theory that it represents a good approximation of the long-term "real interest rate."

In this country, some courts have taken the same "real interest rate" approach as Australia. They have endorsed the economic theory suggesting that market interest rates include two components—an estimate of anticipated inflation, and a desired "real" rate of return on investment—and that the latter component is essentially constant over time. They have concluded that the inflationary increase in the estimated lost stream of future earnings will therefore be perfectly "offset" by all but the "real" component of the market interest rate.

Still other courts have preferred to continue relying on market interest rates. To avoid undercompensation, they have shown at least tentative willingness to permit evidence of what future price inflation will be in estimating the lost stream of future income.

Finally, some courts have applied a number of techniques that have loosely been termed "total offset" methods. What these methods have in common is that they presume that the ideal discount rate—the after-tax market interest rate on a safe investment—is (to a legally tolerable degree of precision) completely offset by certain elements in the ideal computation of the estimated lost stream of future income. They all assume that the effects of future price inflation on wages are part of what offsets the market interest rate. The methods differ, however, in their assumptions regarding which if any other elements in the first stage of the damages calculation contribute to the offset.

The litigants and the amici in this case urge us to select one of the many rules that have been proposed and establish it for all time as the exclusive method in all federal trials for calculating an award for lost earnings in an inflationary economy. We are not persuaded, however, that such an approach is warranted. For our review of the foregoing cases leads us to draw three conclusions. First, by its very nature the calculation of an award for lost earnings must be a rough approximation. Because the lost stream can never be predicted with complete confidence, any lump sum represents only a "rough and ready" effort to put the plaintiff in the position he would have been in had he not been injured. Second, sustained price inflation can make the award substantially less precise. Inflation's current magnitude and unpredictability create a substantial risk that the damage award will prove to have little relation to the lost wages it purports to replace. Third, the question of lost earnings can arise in many different contexts. In some sectors of the economy, it is far easier to assemble evidence of an individual's most likely career path than in others.

These conclusions all counsel hesitation. Having surveyed the multitude of options available, we will do no more than is necessary to resolve the case before us. We limit our attention to suits under * * * the Act, noting that Congress has provided generally for an award of damages but has not given specific guidance regarding how they are to be calculated. Within that narrow context, we shall define the general boundaries within which a particular award will be considered legally acceptable.

III

* * * In calculating an award for a longshoreman's lost earnings caused by the negligence of a vessel, the discount rate should be chosen on the basis of the factors that are used to estimate the lost stream of future earnings. If the trier of fact relies on a specific forecast of the future rate of price inflation, and if the estimated lost stream of future earnings is calculated to include price inflation along with individual factors and other societal factors, then the proper discount rate would be the after-tax

market interest rate. But since specific forecasts of future price inflation remain too unreliable to be useful in many cases, it will normally be a costly and ultimately unproductive waste of longshoremen's resources to make such forecasts the centerpiece of litigation under [the Act]. As Judge Newman has warned, "The average accident trial should not be converted into a graduate seminar on economic forecasting." For that reason, both plaintiffs and trial courts should be discouraged from pursuing that approach.

On the other hand, if forecasts of future price inflation are not used, it is necessary to choose an appropriate below-market discount rate. As long as inflation continues, one must ask how much should be "offset" against the market rate. Once again, that amount should be chosen on the basis of the same factors that are used to estimate the lost stream of future earnings. If full account is taken of the individual and societal factors (excepting price inflation) that can be expected to have resulted in wage increases, then all that should be set off against the market interest rate is an estimate of future price inflation. This would result in one of the "real interest rate" approaches described above. Although we find the economic evidence distinctly inconclusive regarding an essential premise of those approaches, we do not believe a trial court adopting such an approach in a suit under § 5(b) should be reversed if it adopts a rate between one and three percent and explains its choice.[30]

* * *

As a result, the judgment below must be set aside. In performing its damages calculation, the trial court applied the theory of *Kaczkowski*, supra, as a mandatory federal rule of decision, even though the petitioner had insisted that if compensation was to be awarded, it "must be reduced to its present worth." Moreover, this approach seems to have colored the trial court's evaluation of the relevant evidence. At one point, the court noted that respondent had offered a computation of his estimated wages from the date of the accident until his presumed date of retirement, including projected cost-of-living adjustments. It stated, "We do not disagree with these projections, but feel they are inappropriate in view of the holding in *Kaczkowski*." Later in its opinion, however, the court declared, "We do not believe that there was sufficient evidence to establish a basis for estimating increased future productivity for the plaintiff, and therefore we will not inject such a factor in this award."

On remand, the decision on whether to reopen the record should be left to the sound discretion of the trial court. It bears mention that the present record already gives reason to believe a fair award may be more confidently expected in this case than in many. The employment practices in the

---

[30] The key premise is that the real interest rate is stable over time. It is obviously not perfectly stable, but whether it is even relatively stable is hotly disputed among economists. * * *

longshoring industry appear relatively stable and predictable. The parties seem to have had no difficulty in arriving at the period of respondent's future work expectancy, or in predicting the character of the work that he would have been performing during that entire period if he had not been injured. Moreover, the record discloses that respondent's wages were determined by a collective bargaining agreement that explicitly provided for "cost of living" increases, and that recent company history also included a "general" increase and a "job class increment increase." Although the trial court deemed the latter increases irrelevant during its first review because it felt legally compelled to assume they would offset any real interest rate, further study of them on remand will allow the court to determine whether that assumption should be made in this case.

IV

We do not suggest that the trial judge should embark on a search for "delusive exactness." It is perfectly obvious that the most detailed inquiry can at best produce an approximate result. And one cannot ignore the fact that in many instances the award for impaired earning capacity may be overshadowed by a highly impressionistic award for pain and suffering. But we are satisfied that whatever rate the District Court may choose to discount the estimated stream of future earnings, it must make a deliberate choice, rather than assuming that it is bound by a rule of state law.

The judgment of the Court of Appeals is vacated and the case is remanded for further proceedings consistent with this opinion.

NOTES

1.   The Court points out in a footnote that the arithmetic of discounting is simple if present value tables are used. Present value tables state the present value of $1 for any period at any discount rate. The present value of any sum is simply that sum multiplied by the present value of $1. *See* Stuart M. Speiser et al., *Recovery for Wrongful Death and Injury* (3d ed.1992). For the more mathematically inclined, the present value of $1 due in n periods, where the rate of interest is i, is $1/(1 + i)^n$. As the table below shows, the choice of a discount rate can affect the plaintiff's award dramatically:

PRESENT VALUE OF FUTURE RECEIPTS OF $25,000 A YEAR,
FOR VARIOUS PERIODS AND DISCOUNT RATES

Discount Rate

Period	2%	5%	10%	12%
10 years	$224,565	$193,043	$153,615	$141,255
20 years	408,785	311,555	212,840	186,735
30 years	501,603	384,313	235,673	201,138

Richard A. Posner, *Economic Analysis of Law* § 6.11 at 226 (9th ed.2014).

2.   The court notes three approaches to accounting for inflation: increasing the award to account for inflation and then discounting by the market rate of interest, partially offsetting inflation against interest and discounting by the real rate of interest, and totally offsetting inflation and interest. Each approach has its adherents. *See, e.g.,* Calva-Cerqueira v. United States, 281 F.Supp.2d 279 (D.D.C.2003) (because some expenses increase faster than inflation, proper approach is to calculate the likely escalation of expenses and then discount to present value using an after tax market rate); Nesmith v. Texaco, 727 F.2d 497 (5th Cir.1984) (proper approach is to exclude evidence of price inflation and discount by a below-market rate); Kaczkowski v. Bolubasz, 491 Pa. 561, 421 A.2d 1027 (1980) (total offset). *See* David Faigman et al., 1 *Modern Scientific Evidence* §§ 9.70–9.78 (2015-16 ed.).

NOTE ON TAXATION OF DAMAGE AWARDS

In Commissioner of Internal Revenue v. Banks, 543 U.S. 426 (2005), the Supreme Court addressed the question of "whether the portion of a money judgment or settlement paid to a plaintiff's attorney under a contingent-fee agreement is income to the plaintiff under the Internal Revenue Code, 26 U.S.C. § 1 et seq." It held that as a general rule, "when a litigant's recovery constitutes income, the litigant's income includes the portion of the recovery paid to the attorney as a contingent fee." Generally speaking, how a damage award is characterized for tax purposes depends on what the award replaces. Thus, Banks's award, which replaced taxable wages, had to be included in his gross taxable income.

Generally speaking, damages are taxable to the plaintiff as income. However, damages received for "personal physical injuries or physical sickness," can be excluded from gross income even when they replace otherwise taxable income. Section 104(a)(2) of the Internal Revenue Code, as amended in 1996 provides the details. See Conference Committee Report, Small Business Act of 1996, CCH Standard Federal Tax Reporter, Vol. 2, § 1.104–1, 6660.137 (1996). "Emotional distress shall not be treated as a physical injury or physical sickness," except for the "amount paid for medical care attributable to emotional distress," which is exempt. Punitive damages are taxable.

Thus, as the Court in Jones & Laughlin Steel Corp. v. Pfeifer, 462 U.S. 523, 534 (1983), "Since the damages award is tax-free, the relevant stream is ideally of after-tax wages and benefits." Despite this, most courts do not consider taxes when calculating lost earning capacity. The traditional rule has been that lost earning capacity is based on gross earnings, because evidence as to future tax rates and the plaintiff's future tax status is too speculative. In Norfolk & Western Railway v. Liepelt, 444 U.S. 490 (1980), the Supreme Court challenged the traditional rule, and held that in a wrongful death case arising under the Federal Employers' Liability Act (where federal and not state law controls), damages for lost support should be based on net earnings after taxes, to avoid overcompensation. Since *Norfolk,* a few states have followed the Supreme Court's lead. *See, e.g.,* Slater v. Skyhawk Transportation, Inc., 77 F.Supp.2d 580 (D.N.J.1999) (New Jersey bases damages on net earnings). Most, however, continue to exclude evidence that the plaintiff's wages would have been taxed. *E.g.,* Estevez v. United States, 72 F.Supp.2d 205 (S.D.N.Y.1999) (applying New York law).

If the jury is not going to hear evidence about the taxes the plaintiff is avoiding, should the jury at least be instructed that the award itself is not taxable, so they won't assume the award will be taxed and inflate it? Again, although Norfolk held it was error to refuse to instruct the jury that their award would not be taxed, most courts refuse to do so. *See* Stover v. Lakeland Square Owners Association, 434 N.W.2d 866 (Iowa 1989) (citing cases). Although *Norfolk* has had some impact, *see, e.g.,* Bussell v. DeWalt Products Corp., 105 N.J. 223, 519 A.2d 1379 (1987), most courts continue to believe that an instruction that awards are not taxable is unnecessary and unwise.

The consensus seems to be that prejudgment or postjudgment interest is not excludable from gross income, and is therefore taxed. In three circuits, courts of appeals have concluded that prejudgment interest on a personal injury award is not received "on account of" personal injury, and therefore is not excludable from gross income. *See* Rozpad v. Commissioner, 154 F.3d 1 (1st Cir.1998) (prejudgment interest award under Rhode Island law); Brabson v. United States, 73 F.3d 1040 (10th Cir.) (prejudgment interest award under Colorado law), *cert. denied,* 519 U.S. 1039 (1996); Kovacs v. Commissioner, 25 F.3d 1048 (6th Cir.1993) (prejudgment interest award under Michigan law), *cert. denied,* 513 U.S. 963 (1994). In each of these cases, the determination that prejudgment interest was not "damages on account of personal injury" turned on the fact that at common law, prejudgment interest was not recoverable in personal injury cases where the amount of damages was unliquidated. Therefore, the award of prejudgment interest in a personal injury case was seen as attributable to the defendant's delay, rather than "on account of" the personal injuries.

G. COLLECTING MONEY JUDGMENTS

Winning your lawsuit on the liability and remedial grounds may not be the end of the case.

You win the big one: a $5 million judgment. With it comes rave reviews from clients, colleagues, friends, and relatives. You have the judgment framed and hang it on your wall.

But wait a second. "Where's the money?" the managing partner asks. The real world rears its ugly head. It dawns on you that the defendant isn't going to stroll into your office with a certified check for five million bucks.

You close your door, take the judgment off your wall, and replace it with the certificate you got for coaching your daughter's little league team. You stop taking phone calls and start looking for the rules on collecting judgments.

James J. Brown, *Collecting a Judgment*, 13 Litigation 31 (Fall 1986).

"Civil money judgments are not self-executing. When a plaintiff obtains a judgment, the court does not order the defendant to pay; it merely issues an authoritative declaration that the defendant owes the plaintiff a debt in the amount of the judgment." Stephen G. Gilles, *The Judgment-Proof Society*, 63 Wash. & Lee L.Rev. 603, 617 (2006). Many defendants will pay the judgment owed. But others will not, or cannot. Bankruptcy or the "judgment-proof" defendant with no money or assets is always a practical concern with actually collecting the money owed.

When defendants refuse to pay or unable to pay, there are additional auxiliary collection remedies provided by state law to assist the plaintiff in getting the money. The procedural intricacies of collection remedies differ greatly by state as laid out in detailed state statutes and local rules. In federal district court, the available remedies for securing satisfaction of the judgment follow the law of the state in which the district court is held. Fed.R.Civ.Proc. 64. For now, we identify broadly the major types of actions that are available to collect on the judgment.

Execution: Execution is a remedy by which the judgment is executed by attaching it to the defendant's property, which is then sold by the sheriff to satisfy the judgment. *E.g.* Ohio Rev. Code § 2329, Execution Against Property; Fed.R.Civ.Proc. 69(a). The plaintiff's lawyer registers the judgment in the court where the defendant owns property in order to record the judgment lien and then seeks the writ of execution. Discovery is available to aid in identifying property for the execution. Fed.R.Civ.Proc. 69(a)(2). Once obtained, the writ of execution is then given to the sheriff who levies against the property by physically seizing it, auctions it, and applies the sale proceeds to the judgment and collection expenses. Real property can be attached, and in many states, so can personal property. The property includes all property of the defendant, not just that subject to the lawsuit. There are, however, many exemptions to execution. For example, exempt property typically includes a person's home, pension savings, one car, and more than 25% of income wages. While the law demands payment of money judgments, it also wants to ensure that debtors remain self-supporting and are not impoverished.

Turnover Statutes: Turnover statutes are *in person* injunctions to a defendant to turn over non-exempt property that is not otherwise easily reachable through execution. *E.g.,* Texas Civ. Prac. & Remedies Code § 31.0002. It can be useful to reach valuable intangible property like securities and intellectual property. For example, the family of Ron Goldman obtained the intangible rights of O.J. Simpson in a book, *If I Did It*, in which the former pro football star explained how he hypothetically might have committed the slayings of Goldman and Nicole Brown, Simpson's ex-wife. While Simpson was acquitted of the murders, he was found liable in the subsequent civil trial for the wrongful death of Goldman, a waiter who had come to Brown's house to return a pair of glasses. The Goldman family was awarded a judgment of $33.5 million in 1997, but has been unable to collect much of the award from Simpson because his major assets, his Florida home and pensions from his football and movie careers, are not subject to levy for the satisfaction of civil court judgments. Jennifer Kay, *Goldmans Get Rights to Simpson Book*, AP, June 15, 2007. *See also* Goldman v. Simpson, 160 Cal.App.4th 255 (2008) (renewing judgment against O.J. Simpson for an additional ten years).

Garnishment: Garnishment is an action filed against a third-party who owes money to the defendant. Typically, such third parties are banks and employers. The garnishment action directs the employer, for example, to pay a certain portion of the defendant's wages directly to the plaintiff in satisfaction of the judgment. Usually only a percentage of the garnishee's debt to the debtor may be used at any one time to satisfy the creditor. *E.g.,* Consumer Credit Protection Act, 15 U.S.C. §§ 1673 (limiting garnishment to 25% of take home pay, unless garnishment is for support of a spouse or child where 60% limitation applies.

Attachment: Many states allow for attachment or other action to freeze a defendant's assets prior to and during the pendency of the litigation to prevent dissipation of properties and monies potentially needed to satisfy an adverse judgment. *E.g.,* Ohio Rev. Code § 2715.01, Attachment. Such state statutes must provide for the minimum requirements of due process with notice and a hearing. Connecticut v. Doehr, 501 U.S. 1 (1991). However the Supreme Court has held that federal courts do not have such power prejudgment to issue a preliminary injunction freezing assets and prohibiting transfers in an action for money damages (only if there is an equitable right or interest). Grupo Mexicano de Desarrollo, S.A. v. Alliance Bond Fund, Inc. 527 U.S. 308 (1999). Prejudgment seizure is a powerful tool because it shifts the strategic balance of subsequent litigation: time and delay now becomes the creditor's friend. A defendant who needs the seized property before the termination of the lawsuit, which could be lengthy, may settle on terms worse than otherwise would result through litigation or negotiation.

CHAPTER 6

PUNITIVE DAMAGES

■ ■ ■

Punishment is a familiar concept under criminal law, where defendants are imprisoned or fined for illegal conduct deemed unacceptable by society. Punishment is also available under the civil law primarily through the remedy of punitive damages, which are monetary penalties designed to punish the defendant and deter the defendant and others from similar conduct in the future. Punitives are awarded on top of compensatory damages where the defendant has shown malicious intent or a conscious disregard of the probability of harm to others. This chapter explores the contours of punitive damages: why they are awarded, when they are awarded, and how the proper amount of punishment is determined.

A. THE PURPOSE OF PUNITIVE DAMAGES

The theories of criminal punishment are evident in the rationales underlying punitive damages. In criminal law, judges punish defendants for retribution as "just desserts" for committing morally reprehensible acts; to deter the defendant and others from committing such violations in the future; to protect society by incarcerating the offender; and to rehabilitate the defendant to lead a socially beneficial life. Similarly, as the Supreme Court explains in the case of *Exxon Shipping Co. v. Baker* (p. 478), "the consensus today is that punitives are aimed not at compensation but principally at retribution and deterring harmful conduct." *See* Mark Geistfeld, *Punitive Damages, Retribution, and Due Process*, 81 S.Cal.L.Rev. 263 (2008) (justifying punitive damages as retribution or "vindictive" damages); Dan Markel, *Retributive Damages: A Theory of Punitive Damages as Intermediate Sanction*, 94 Cornell L.Rev. 2 (2009) (providing a normative account of the theory of punitive damages as retribution); Anthony Sebok, *Punitive Damages: From Myth to Theory*, 92 Iowa L.Rev. 957 (2007) (urging a return to the theoretical emphasis on the retributive element of punitive damages in rectifying a private wrong); Benjamin C. Zipursky, *A Theory of Punitive Damages*, 84 Tex.L.Rev. 105 (2005) (grounding punitive damages in a theory of civil recourse and right of plaintiff to be punitive in response to a wrong); *but see* Jill Wieber Lens, *Justice Holmes's Bad Man and the Depleted Purposes of Punitive Damages*, 101 Ky.L.J. 789 (2012–13) (arguing that *Exxon Shipping* diminished the traditional morality roots of punishment goals by theorizing based on the economically motivated actor). Alternative theories have also been advanced, such as using punitive damages as societal damages or to advance the greater public good. *See* Christopher J. Robinette, *Peace: A Public Purpose for Punitive Damages?* 2 Charleston L.Rev. 327 (2008); Catherine M. Sharkey, *Punitive Damages as Societal Damages*, 113 Yale L.J. 347 (2003). The underlying theory for punitive damages is critical to many ongoing debates about these damages: whether they should be awarded at all or whether the criminal law will suffice; what the proper measure of relief is given the underlying goal; and, whether there are or should be limitations upon awards.

Sometimes, it may be difficult to distinguish between sanctions that are punitive to the defendant and those that are remedial in the sense that they return a plaintiff to his rightful position or further a public policy such as safety or preventing fraud. Frequently, a sanction serves both purposes. David Yellen & Carl V. Mayer, *Coordinating Sanctions for Corporate Misconduct: Civil or Criminal Punishment?*, 29 Am.Crim.L.Rev. 961 (1992) (discussing examples from government contracting). Treble damages are a good example. Treble damages are monetary remedies awarded in the amount of three times the proven damage to the plaintiff. Often these are automatically provided by statute; for example, the antitrust statute, 15 U.S.C. § 15, provides that successful plaintiffs can recover their damages plus treble damages. Treble damages serve multiple purposes, as they work to punish the defendant and also further remedial goals of facilitating the plaintiff's litigation where the damage award is small and the governmental burden would be larger in pursuing the case. The U.S. Supreme Court recognized in PacifiCare Health Systems, Inc. v. Book, 538 U.S. 401(2003), that treble damages can be construed as either punitive or compensatory, depending upon the context:

> Our cases have placed different statutory treble-damages provisions on different points along the spectrum between purely compensatory and strictly punitive awards. Thus, in Vermont Agency of Natural Resources v. United States ex rel. Stevens, 529 U.S. 765, 784 (2000), we characterized the treble-damages provision of the False Claims Act, 31 U.S.C. §§ 3729–3733, as "essentially punitive in nature." In Brunswick Corp. v. Pueblo Bowl-O-Mat, Inc., 429 U.S. 477, 485 (1977), on the other hand, we explained that the treble-damages provision of § 4 of the Clayton Act, 15 U.S.C. § 15, "is in essence a remedial provision." Likewise in American Soc. of Mechanical Engineers, Inc. v. Hydrolevel Corp., 456 U.S. 556, 575 (1982), we noted that "the antitrust private action [which allows for treble damages] was created primarily as *a remedy* for the victims of antitrust violations." And earlier this Term, in Cook County v. United States ex rel. Chandler, 538 U.S. 119, 130 we stated that "it is important to realize that treble damages have a compensatory side, serving remedial purposes in addition to punitive objectives." Indeed, we

have repeatedly acknowledged that the treble-damages provision contained in RICO itself is remedial in nature. In Agency Holding Corp. v. Malley-Duff & Associates, Inc., 483 U.S. 143, 151 (1987), we stated that "[b]oth RICO and the Clayton Act are designed *to remedy* economic injury by providing for the recovery of treble damages, costs, and attorney's fees." And in Shearson/American Express Inc. v. McMahon, 482 U.S. 220, 241(1987) we took note of the "remedial function" of RICO's treble-damages provision.

Given this ambiguity as to the nature of treble damages, the Court rejected the assertion that arbitration was not compelled in the case because treble damages under RICO were punitive and prohibited by the parties' arbitration agreements which precluded the arbitrator from awarding "punitive or exemplary damages." *PacifiCare*, 538 U.S. at 406.

The Supreme Court addressed this question again in the patent context in Halo Electronics, Inc. v. Pulse Electronics, 579 U.S. ___, 136 S.Ct. 1923 (2016). The patent act provides that courts "may increase the damages up to three times the amount found or assessed." 35 U.S.C. § 284. As originally enacted in 1793, treble damages were mandatory; then as of 1836 they became discretionary as "vindictive or punitive" damages to punish the malicious, egregious, and willful conduct of an infringer. Chief Justice Roberts noted that some cases had suggested these enhanced damages had a compensatory purpose as well, but held that "[s]uch statements, however, were not for the ages," as their concerns with compensation were addressed by fee-shifting statutes. The problem in *Halo Electronics* was that the Federal Circuit had created a strict standard for awarding treble damages, which contradicted the discretionary command of the statute. While "discretion is not whim," Roberts said, as he had several times before, it cannot be so restrained as to be practically unavailable.

The question of whether a sanction is punitive or compensatory also arises in cases of civil penalties where the question is whether the penalty is inherently criminal-like such that it runs afoul of criminal constitutional protections like the Double Jeopardy Clause or Excessive Fines Clause of the Eighth Amendment. *See* United States v. Bajakajian, 524 U.S. 321 (1998) (forfeiture of total amount not reported to customs inspectors was grossly excessive criminal penalty under the Excessive Fines Clause); Hudson v. United States, 522 U.S. 93 (1997) (administrative banking fines and occupational debarment were civil sanctions to which Double Jeopardy Clause did not apply). As for the Excessive Fines Clause and punitive damages, the Supreme Court has rejected the argument that punitive damages are "fines" that should be subject to the Eighth Amendment's prohibition of excessively disproportionate fines. Browning-Ferris Industries of Vermont, Inc. v. Kelco Disposal, Inc., 492 U.S. 257 (1989). Instead, as we shall see in part C of this chapter, the Court evaluates excessiveness and disproportionality of punitives under the guise of due process. *See* Colleen P. Murphy, *Comparison to Criminal Sanctions in the Constitutional Review of Punitive Damages*, 41 San Diego L.Rev. 1443 (2004) (questioning the legitimacy of the Court's parallel proportionality review for criminal fines and punitive damages). Professor Tracy Thomas argues that proportionality analysis, while seeming to be an objective calculus, is instead a subjective inquiry that disfavors punitives. *Proportionality and the Supreme Court's Jurisprudence of Remedies*, 59 Hastings L.J. 73 (2007).

B. PUNITIVE DAMAGES AT COMMON LAW

Claims for and awards of punitive damages exhibit aspects of both tort and criminal law. Punitive or exemplary damages "are not compensation for injury. Instead, they are private fines levied by civil juries to punish reprehensible conduct and to deter its future occurrence." Gertz v. Robert Welch, Inc., 418 U.S. 323, 350 (1974). The Restatement (Second) of Torts § 908 provides a similar definition:

> (1) Punitive damages are damages, other than compensatory or nominal damages, awarded against a person to punish him for his outrageous conduct and to deter him and others like him from similar conduct in the future.

> (2) Punitive damages may be awarded for conduct that is outrageous, because of the defendant's evil motive or his reckless indifference to the rights of others. In assessing punitive damages, the trier of fact can properly consider the character of the defendant's act, the nature and extent of the harm to the plaintiff that the defendant caused or intended to cause and the wealth of the defendant.

Many of the recurring issues raised by punitive damages reflect the unsure marriage of tort and criminal law that generated this remedy. If the remedy is a punishment of the defendant, should the trial procedures and the plaintiff's burden of proof differ from the civil law? Since the punitive award is generally thought to be over and above what the plaintiff receives to be made whole, what facts or conduct concerning the defendant are relevant to determining the amount of damages to be awarded? Is it appropriate for the successful plaintiff to retain all of a punitive award or should some or all of it pass to the government or to some organization devoted to countering the sort of injurious conduct in which the defendant engaged? In a mass tort, are multiple punitive awards against the same defendant for the same course of conduct fair to either the defendant or to a late-arriving plaintiff who finds the defendant insolvent? Is there any practical and realistic mechanism to address this problem? *See* Bert I. Huang, *Surprisingly Punitive Damages*, 100 Va.L.Rev. 1027 (2014) (suggesting procedural solution to the problem of redundant awards).

Until the middle of the last century, punitive damages were generally restricted to intentional and dignitary torts. Michael L. Rustad, *Happy No More: Federalism Derailed by the Court that Would be King of Punitive Damages*, 64 Md.L.Rev. 461 (2005). Since then, there has been a growth of punitive damage awards in other areas:

Contracts. The black letter rule for 200 years has been that punitive damages are not available for breach of contract. Restatement (First) of Contracts § 342 (1932). The reasoning developed in modern times is based on the theory of efficient breach and the conclusion that in many cases, it is "uneconomical to induce completion of performance of a contract after it has been broken" by the threat of punitive damages. Richard A. Posner, *Economic Analysis of Law* § 410 at 129 (9th ed.2014). Beginning in the 1960s, courts permitted the award of punitive damages for bad faith breach of insurance contract, and such awards are now allowed in a majority of jurisdictions. *E.g.,* Giampappa v. American Family Mutual Insurance Co., 64 P.3d 230 (Colo.2003). It is now the general rule that punitive damages are available when the conduct constituting the breach of contract is also an independent tort. Restatement (Second) of Contracts § 355 (1979); William S. Dodge, *The Case for Punitive Damages in Contracts*, 48 Duke L.J. 629 (1999). Indeed, it appears that punitive damages are now awarded more frequently, and in higher amounts, in cases involving contract-related torts (e.g., tortious interference with contract, fraud, employment discrimination) than in tort cases not involving contractual relationships. *See* U.S. Department of Justice, Bureau of Justice Statistics, "Civil Bench and Jury Trials in State Courts," 6–7 (2005).

Products Liability. Prior to 1976, there were very few punitive damage awards in product liability cases. There was limited comment on this, but since punishment was traditionally associated with willful or intentional acts, it may have appeared anomalous to the courts to punish a defendant for negligence or for tortious conduct for which he was strictly liable. In addition, in Roginsky v. Richardson-Merrell, Inc., 378 F.2d 832 (2d Cir.1967), Judge Friendly raised three other problems as he struck down a punitive damage award: (1) the inequity of punishing shareholders for the misdeeds of low-level employees; (2) the possibility that the defendant would be insured against punitive damage liability; and (3) the risk of excessive punishment through repeated punitive awards involving a single defective product. In 1976, Professor David G. Owen published his massive and seminal article, *Punitive Damages in Products Liability Litigation*, 74 Mich.L.Rev. 1257 (1976), arguing in favor of punitive damages in appropriate products liability cases. Such cases are no longer unusual. *E.g.,* Grimshaw v. Ford Motor Co., 119 Cal.App.3d 757 (1981) (reproduced *infra*).

Mass Torts. The first mass tort action in which punitive damages issues arose was brought in 1961 to challenge the sale of an allegedly defective anti-cholesterol drug. Such cases are now common and raise the issue of multiple punitive damage claims. *E.g.*, Dunn v. HOVIC, 1 F.3d 1371 (3d Cir. en banc), *cert. denied*, 510 U.S. 1031 (1993) (asbestos manufacturer).

GRIMSHAW V. FORD MOTOR CO.

California Court of Appeal, Fourth District
119 Cal.App.3d 757 (1981)

TAMURA, ACTING PRESIDING JUSTICE.

A 1972 Ford Pinto hatchback automobile unexpectedly stalled on a freeway, erupting into flames when it was rear ended by a car proceeding in the same direction. Mrs. Lilly Gray, the driver of the Pinto, suffered fatal burns and 13-year-old Richard Grimshaw, a passenger in the Pinto, suffered severe and permanently disfiguring burns on his face and entire body. Grimshaw and the heirs of Mrs. Gray (Grays) sued Ford Motor Company and others. Following a six-month jury trial, verdicts were returned in favor of plaintiffs against Ford Motor Company. Grimshaw was awarded $2,516,000 compensatory damages and $125 million punitive damages; * * * On Ford's motion for a new trial, Grimshaw was required to remit all but $3½ million of the punitive award as a condition of denial of the motion.

Ford appeals from the judgment and from an order denying its motion for a judgment notwithstanding the verdict as to punitive damages. Grimshaw appeals from the order granting the conditional new trial and from the amended judgment entered pursuant to the order. * * *

FACTS

* * *

The Accident

At the moment of impact, the Pinto caught fire and its interior was engulfed in flames. According to plaintiffs' expert, the impact of the Galaxie had driven the Pinto's gas tank forward and caused it to be punctured by the flange or one of the bolts on the differential housing so that fuel sprayed from the punctured tank and entered the passenger compartment through gaps resulting from the separation of the rear wheel well sections from the floor pan. By the time the Pinto came to rest after the collision, both occupants had sustained serious burns. When they emerged from the vehicle, their clothing was almost completely burned off. Mrs. Gray died a few days later of congestive heart failure as a result of the burns. Grimshaw managed to survive but only through heroic medical measures. He has undergone numerous and extensive surgeries and skin grafts and must undergo additional surgeries over the next 10 years. He lost portions of several fingers on his left hand and portions of his left ear, while his face required many skin grafts from various portions of his body. * * *

Design of the Pinto Fuel System

In 1968, Ford began designing a new subcompact automobile which ultimately became the Pinto. Mr. Iacocca, then a Ford Vice President, conceived the project and was its moving force. Ford's objective was to build a car at or below 2,000 pounds to sell for no more than $2,000. * * *

It was then the preferred practice in Europe and Japan to locate the gas tank over the rear axle in subcompacts because a small vehicle has less "crush space" between the rear axle and the bumper than larger cars. The Pinto's styling, however, required the tank to be placed behind the rear axle leaving only 9 or 10 inches of "crush space"—far less than in any other American automobile or Ford overseas subcompact. In addition, the Pinto was designed so that its bumper was little more than a chrome strip, less substantial than the bumper of any other American car produced then or later. The Pinto's rear structure also lacked reinforcing members known as "hat sections" (2 longitudinal side members) and horizontal cross-members running between them such as were found in cars of larger unitized construction and in all automobiles produced by Ford's overseas operations. The absence of the reinforcing members rendered the Pinto less crush resistant than other vehicles. Finally, the differential housing selected for the Pinto had an exposed flange and a line of exposed bolt heads. These protrusions were sufficient to puncture a gas tank driven forward against the differential upon rear impact. * * *

Crash Tests

During the development of the Pinto, prototypes were built and tested. Some were "mechanical prototypes" which duplicated mechanical features of the design but not its appearance while others, referred to as "engineering prototypes," were true duplicates of the design car. These prototypes as well as two production Pintos were crash tested by Ford to determine, among other things, the integrity of the fuel system in rear-end accidents. Ford also conducted the tests to see if the Pinto as designed would meet a proposed federal regulation requiring all automobiles manufactured in 1972 to be able to withstand a 20-mile-per-hour fixed barrier impact without significant fuel spillage and all automobiles manufactured after January 1, 1973, to withstand a 30-mile-per-hour fixed barrier impact without significant fuel spillage.

The crash tests revealed that the Pinto's fuel system as designed could not meet the 20-mile-per-hour proposed standard. * * *

The Cost to Remedy Design Deficiencies

When a prototype failed the fuel system integrity test, the standard of care for engineers in the industry was to redesign and retest it. The vulnerability of the production Pinto's fuel tank at speeds of 20 and 30-miles-per-hour fixed barrier tests could have been remedied by inexpensive "fixes," but Ford produced and sold the Pinto to the public without doing anything to remedy the defects. Design changes that would have enhanced the integrity of the fuel tank system at relatively little cost per car included the following: Longitudinal side members and cross members at $2.40 and $1.80, respectively; a single shock absorbent "flak suit" to protect the tank at $4; a tank within a tank and placement of the tank over the axle at $5.08 to.$5.79; a nylon bladder within the tank at $5.25 to $8; placement of the tank over the axle surrounded with a protective barrier at a cost of $9.95 per car; substitution of a rear axle with a smooth differential housing at a cost of $2.10; imposition of a protective shield between the differential housing and the tank at $2.35; improvement and reenforcement of the bumper at $2.60; addition of eight inches of crush space a cost of $6.40. Equipping the car with a reinforced rear structure, smooth axle, improved bumper and additional crush space at a total cost of $15.30 would have made the fuel tank safe in a 34 to 38-mile-per-hour rear end collision by a vehicle the size of the Ford Galaxie. If, in addition to the foregoing, a bladder or tank within a tank were used or if the tank were protected with a shield, it would have been safe in a 40 to 45-mile-per-hour rear impact. If the tank had been located over the rear axle, it would have been safe in a rear impact at 50 miles per hour or more.

FORD'S APPEAL

* * *

II

Other Evidentiary Rulings

Ford contends that the court erroneously admitted irrelevant documentary evidence highly prejudicial to Ford. We find the contention to be without merit. * * *

Exhibit No. 125:

Exhibit No. 125 was a report presented at a Ford production review meeting in April 1971, recommending action to be taken in anticipation of the promulgation of federal standards on fuel system integrity. The report recommended, inter alia, deferral from 1974 to 1976 of the adoption of "flak suits" or "bladders" in all Ford cars, including the Pinto, in order to realize a savings of $20.9 million. The report stated that the cost of the flak suit or bladder would be $4 to $8 per car. The meeting at which the report was presented was chaired by Vice President Harold MacDonald and attended by Vice President Robert Alexander and occurred sometime before the 1972 Pinto was placed on the market. A reasonable inference may be drawn from the evidence that despite management's knowledge that the Pinto's fuel system could be made safe at a cost of but $4 to $8 per car, it decided to defer corrective measures to save money and enhance profits. The evidence was thus highly relevant and properly received.

Ford's contention appears to be addressed not so much to the admissibility of exhibit No. 125 but to the use which Grimshaw's counsel made of it in his argument to the jury. Ford complains that while exhibit No. 125 recommended "that $100 million be spent," Grimshaw's counsel argued that the report showed $100 million would be saved and urged the jury to award that sum as punitive damages. It is not clear that exhibit No. 125 recommended that "$100 million be spent"; it states that over the period 1973 to 1976 the cost estimates to meet the federal standards would be $100 million. Nor is the record clear that Grimshaw's counsel was referring to exhibit No. 125 when he urged the jury to award punitive damages in the sum of $100 million. In any event, Ford failed to object to counsel's argument as a misstatement of the evidence.

* * *

VI

Punitive Damages

Ford contends that it was entitled to a judgment notwithstanding the verdict on the issue of punitive damages on two grounds: First, punitive damages are statutorily and constitutionally impermissible in a design defect case. Second, there was no evidentiary support for a finding of malice or of corporate responsibility for malice. In any event, Ford maintains that the punitive damage award must be reversed because of erroneous instructions and excessiveness of the award.

(1) "Malice" Under Civil Code Section 3294:

The concept of punitive damages is rooted in the English common law and is a settled principle of the common law of this country. (Owen, Punitive Damages in Products Liability Litigation, 74 Mich.L.Rev. 1258 (hereafter Owen); Mallor & Roberts, Punitive Damages, Towards A Principled Approach, 31 Hastings L.J. 639 (hereafter Mallor & Roberts); Note, Exemplary Damages in the Law of Torts, 70 Harv.L.Rev. 517.) The doctrine was a part of the common law of this state long before the Civil Code was adopted. When our laws were codified in 1872, the doctrine was incorporated in Civil Code section 3294, which at the time of trial read: "In an action for the breach of an obligation not arising from contract, where the defendant has been guilty of oppression, fraud, or malice, express or implied, the plaintiff, in addition to the actual damages, may recover damages for the sake of example and by way of punishing the defendant."

Ford argues that "malice" as used in section 3294 and as interpreted by our Supreme Court in Davis v. Hearst, 160 Cal. 143, 116 P. 530, requires *animus malus* or evil motive—an intention to injure the person harmed— and that the term is therefore conceptually incompatible with an unintentional tort such as the manufacture and marketing of a defectively designed product. This contention runs counter to our decisional law. As this court recently noted, numerous California cases after *Davis v. Hearst,* have interpreted the term "malice" as used in section 3294 to include, not only a malicious intention to injure the specific person harmed, but conduct evincing "a conscious disregard of the probability that the actor's conduct will result in injury to others."

In Taylor v. Superior Court, 24 Cal.3d 890, 157 Cal.Rptr. 693, 598 P.2d 854, our high court's most recent pronouncement on the subject of punitive damages, the court observed that the availability of punitive damages has not been limited to cases in which there is an actual intent to harm plaintiff or others. The court concurred with the *Searle* (G.D. Searle & Co. v. Superior Court, 49 Cal.App.3d 22, 122 Cal.Rptr. 218) court's suggestion that conscious disregard of the safety of others is an appropriate description of the *animus malus* required by Civil Code section 3294, adding: "In order to justify an award of punitive damages on this basis, the plaintiff must establish that the defendant was aware of the probable dangerous consequences of his conduct, and that he wilfully and deliberately failed to avoid those consequences." * * *

The interpretation of the word "malice" as used in section 3294 to encompass conduct evincing callous and conscious disregard of public safety by those who manufacture and market mass produced articles is consonant with and furthers the objectives of punitive damages. The primary purposes of punitive damages are punishment and deterrence of like conduct by the wrongdoer and others. In the traditional noncommercial intentional tort, compensatory damages alone may serve as an effective deterrent against future wrongful conduct but in commerce-related torts, the manufacturer may find it more profitable to treat compensatory damages as a part of the cost of doing business rather than to remedy the defect. (Owen, supra p. 1291; Note, Mass Liability and Punitive Damages Overkill, 30 Hastings L.J. 1797, 1802.) Deterrence of such "objectionable corporate policies" serves one of the principal purposes of Civil Code section 3294. Governmental safety standards and the criminal law have failed to provide adequate consumer protection against the manufacture and distribution of defective products. Punitive damages thus remain as the most effective remedy for consumer protection against defectively designed mass produced articles. They provide a motive for private individuals to enforce rules of law and enable them to recoup the expenses of doing so which can be considerable and not otherwise recoverable.

We find no statutory impediments to the application of Civil Code section 3294 to a strict products liability case based on design defect. * * *

(2) Constitutional Attacks on Civil Code Section 3294

[Ford's] contention that the potential liability for punitive damages in other cases for the same design defect renders the imposition of such damages violative of Ford's due process rights also lacks merit. Followed to its logical conclusion, it would mean that punitive damages could never be assessed against a manufacturer of a mass produced article. No authorities are cited for such a proposition; indeed, as we have seen, the cases are to the contrary. We recognize the fact that multiplicity of awards may present a problem, but the mere possibility of a future award in a different case is not a ground for setting aside the award in this case, particularly as reduced by the trial judge. If Ford should be confronted with the possibility of an award in another case for the same conduct, it may raise the issue in that case. We add, moreover, that there is no necessary unfairness should the plaintiff in this case be rewarded to a greater extent than later plaintiffs. As Professor Owen has said in response to such a charge of unfairness: "This conception ignores the enormous diligence, imagination, and financial outlay required of initial plaintiffs to uncover and to prove the flagrant misconduct of a product manufacturer. In fact, subsequent plaintiffs will often ride to favorable verdicts and settlements on the coattails of the firstcomers." That observation fits the instant case. * * *

(3) Sufficiency of the Evidence to Support the Finding of Malice and Corporate Responsibility

Ford contends that its motion for judgment notwithstanding the verdict should have been granted because the evidence was insufficient to support a finding of malice or corporate responsibility for such malice. The record fails to support the contention. * * * There was ample evidence to support a finding of malice and Ford's responsibility for malice.

Through the results of the crash tests Ford knew that the Pinto's fuel tank and rear structure would expose consumers to serious injury or death in a 20 to 30 mile-per-hour collision. There was evidence that Ford could have corrected the hazardous design defects at minimal cost but decided to defer correction of the shortcomings by engaging in a cost-benefit analysis balancing human lives and limbs against corporate profits. Ford's institutional mentality was shown to be one of callous indifference to public safety. There was substantial evidence that Ford's conduct constituted "conscious disregard" of the probability of injury to members of the consuming public.

Ford's argument that there can be no liability for punitive damages because there was no evidence of corporate ratification of malicious misconduct is equally without merit. California follows the Restatement rule that punitive damages can be awarded against a principal because of an action of an agent if, but only if, " '(a) the principal authorized the doing and the manner of the act, or (b) the agent was unfit and the principal was reckless in employing him, or (c) the agent was employed in a managerial capacity and was acting in the scope of employment, or (d) the principal or a managerial agent of the principal ratified or approved the act.' " The present case comes within one or both of the categories described in subdivisions (c) and (d).

There is substantial evidence that management was aware of the crash tests showing the vulnerability of the Pinto's fuel tank to rupture at low speed rear impacts with consequent significant risk of injury or death of the occupants by fire. There was testimony from several sources that the test results were forwarded up the chain of command * * * . It may be inferred from the testimony * * * that * * * two engineers had approached management about redesigning the Pinto or that, being aware of management's attitude, they decided to do nothing. In either case the decision not to take corrective action was made by persons exercising managerial authority. Whether an employee acts in a "managerial capacity" does not necessarily depend on his "level" in the corporate hierarchy. As the *Egan* court said: " 'Defendant should not be allowed to insulate itself from liability by giving an employee a nonmanagerial title and relegating to him crucial policy decisions.' "

* * *

(6) Amount of Punitive Damage Award

Ford's final contention is that the amount of punitive damages awarded, even as reduced by the trial court, was so excessive that a new trial on that issue must be granted. Ford argues that its conduct was less reprehensible than those for which punitive damages have been awarded in California in the past; that the $3½ million award is many times over the highest award for such damages ever upheld in California; and that the award exceeds maximum civil penalties that may be enforced under federal or state statutes against a manufacturer for marketing a defective automobile. We are unpersuaded.

In determining whether an award of punitive damages is excessive, comparison of the amount awarded with other awards in other cases is not a valid consideration. * * * In deciding whether an award is excessive as a matter of law or was so grossly disproportionate as to raise the presumption that it was the product of passion or prejudice, the following factors should be weighed: The degree of reprehensibility of defendant's conduct, the wealth of the defendant, the amount of compensatory damages, and an amount which would serve as a deterrent effect on like conduct by defendant and others who may be so inclined. Applying the foregoing criteria to the instant case, the punitive damage award as reduced by the trial court was well within reason.[20]

---

[20] A quantitative formula whereby the amount of punitive damages can be determined in a given case with mathematical certainty is manifestly impossible as well as undesirable. (Mallor & Roberts, *supra*, 31 Hastings L.J. 639, 666–667, 670.) The authors advocate abandonment of the rule that a reasonable relationship must exist between punitive damages and actual damages. They suggest that courts balance society's interest against defendant's interest by focusing on the following factors: Severity of threatened harm; degree of reprehensibility of defendant's conduct, profitability of the conduct, wealth of defendant, amount of compensatory damages (whether it was high in relation to injury), cost of litigation, potential criminal sanctions and other civil actions against defendant based on same conduct. In the present case, the amount of the award as reduced

In assessing the propriety of a punitive damage award, as in assessing the propriety of any other judicial ruling based upon factual determinations, the evidence must be viewed in the light most favorable to the judgment. Viewing the record thusly in the instant case, the conduct of Ford's management was reprehensible in the extreme. It exhibited a conscious and callous disregard of public safety in order to maximize corporate profits. Ford's self-evaluation of its conduct is based on a review of the evidence most favorable to it instead of on the basis of the evidence most favorable to the judgment. Unlike malicious conduct directed toward a single specific individual, Ford's tortious conduct endangered the lives of thousands of Pinto purchasers. Weighed against the factor of reprehensibility, the punitive damage award as reduced by the trial judge was not excessive.

Nor was the reduced award excessive taking into account defendant's wealth and the size of the compensatory award. Ford's net worth was 7.7 billion dollars and its income after taxes for 1976 was over 983 million dollars. The punitive award was approximately .005% of Ford's net worth and approximately .03% of its 1976 net income. The ratio of the punitive damages to compensatory damages was approximately 1.4 to one. Significantly, Ford does not quarrel with the amount of the compensatory award to Grimshaw.

Nor was the size of the award excessive in light of its deterrent purpose. An award which is so small that it can be simply written off as a part of the cost of doing business would have no deterrent effect. An award which affects the company's pricing of its product and thereby affects its competitive advantage would serve as a deterrent. The award in question was far from excessive as a deterrent against future wrongful conduct by Ford and others.

Ford complains that the punitive award is far greater than the maximum penalty that may be imposed under California or federal law prohibiting the sale of defective automobiles or other products. For example, Ford notes that California statutes provide a maximum fine of only $50 for the first offense and $100 for a second offense for a dealer who sells an automobile that fails to conform to federal safety laws or is not equipped with required lights or brakes; that a manufacturer who sells brake fluid in this state failing to meet statutory standards is subject to a maximum of only $50; and that the maximum penalty that may be imposed under federal law for violation of automobile safety standards is $1,000 per vehicle up to a maximum of $800,000 for any related series of offenses. It is precisely because monetary penalties under government regulations prescribing business standards or the criminal law are so inadequate and ineffective as deterrents against a manufacturer and distributor of mass

---

by the judge was reasonable under the suggested factors, including the factor of any other potential liability, civil or criminal.

produced defective products that punitive damages must be of sufficient amount to discourage such practices. Instead of showing that the punitive damage award was excessive, the comparison between the award and the maximum penalties under state and federal statutes and regulations governing automotive safety demonstrates the propriety of the amount of punitive damages awarded.

GRIMSHAW'S APPEAL

Grimshaw has appealed from the order conditionally granting Ford a new trial on the issue of punitive damages and from the amended judgment entered pursuant to that order.

Grimshaw contends that the new trial order is erroneous because (1) the punitive damages awarded by the jury were not excessive as a matter of law, (2) the specification of reasons was inadequate; and (3) the court abused its discretion in cutting the award so drastically. For reasons to be stated, we have concluded that the contentions lack merit.

The court prefaced its specification of reasons with a recitation of the judicially established guidelines[16] for determining whether a punitive award is excessive. The court then observed that there was evidence in the record (referring to Exhibit 125) which might provide a possible rational basis for the 125 million dollar jury verdict which would dispel any presumption of passion or prejudice, adding, however, that the court was not suggesting that the amount was warranted "or that the jury did utilize Exhibit 125, or any other exhibits, and if they did, that they were justified in so doing." The court then noted, based on the fact that Ford's net worth was 7.7 billion and its profits during the last quarter of the year referred to in the financial statement introduced into evidence were more than twice the punitive award, that the award was not disproportionate to Ford's net assets or to its profit generating capacity. The court noted, however, that the amount of the punitive award was 44 times the compensatory award, the court stated that while it did not consider that ratio alone to be controlling because aggravating circumstances may justify a ratio as high as the one represented by the jury verdict, it reasoned that the ratio coupled with the amount by which the punitive exceeded the compensatory damages (over 122 million dollars) rendered the jury's punitive award excessive as a matter of law.

Grimshaw contends that the court erred in determining that the ratio of punitive to compensatory damages rendered the punitive excessive as a matter of law. The trial court, however, did not base its decision solely on the ratio of punitive to compensatory. It took into account the ratio, the

---

[16] The court stated that "the principles by which the propriety of the amount of punitive damages awarded will be judged are threefold: (1) Is the sum so large as to raise a presumption that the award was the result of passion and prejudice and therefore excessive as a matter of law; (2) Does the award bear a reasonable relationship to the net assets of the defendant; and (3) Does the award bear a reasonable relationship to the compensatory damages awarded."

"aggravating circumstances" (the degree of reprehensibility), the wealth of the defendant and its profit generating capacity, the magnitude of the punitive award, including the amount by which it exceeded the compensatory. Those were proper considerations for determining whether the award was excessive as a matter of law. When a trial court grants a new trial for excessive damages, either conditionally or outright, a presumption of correctness attaches to the order and it will not be reversed unless it plainly appears that the judge abused his discretion. In the case at bench, we find no abuse of discretion. * * *

Finally, Grimshaw contends the court abused its discretion in reducing the award to $3½ million as a condition of its new trial order and urges this court to restore the jury award or at least require a remittitur of substantially less than that required by the trial court. * * *

Here, the judge, exercising his independent judgment on the evidence, determined that a punitive award of $3½ million was "fair and reasonable." Evidence pertaining to Ford's conduct, its wealth and the savings it realized in deferring design modifications in the Pinto's fuel system might have persuaded a different fact finder that a larger award should have been allowed to stand. Our role, however, is limited to determining whether the trial judge's action constituted a manifest and unmistakable abuse of discretion. Here, the judge referred to the evidence bearing on those factors in his new trial order and obviously weighed it in deciding what was a "fair and reasonable" award. We cannot say that the judge abused the discretion vested in him by Code of Civil Procedure section 662.5 or that there is "no substantial basis in the record" for the reasons given for the order. Finally, while the trial judge may not have taken into account Ford's potential liability for punitive damages in other cases involving the same tortious conduct in reducing the award, it is a factor we may consider in passing on the request to increase the award. Considering such potential liability, we find the amount as reduced by the trial judge to be reasonable and just. * * *

NOTES

1.   Exhibit 125, the report by Ford engineers showing savings which would be realized by deferring design and safety changes, has been called "possibly the most remarkable document ever produced in an American lawsuit." Stuart Speiser, *Lawsuit* 357 (1980). The *Grimshaw* case has taken on mythical proportions showing how disturbed jurors are by common business practices that balance life and safety against monetary cost. Gray T. Schwartz, *The Myth of the Ford Pinto Case*, 43 Rutgers L.Rev. 1013 (1991).

2.   Whether insurance is available to cover punitive damage awards turns on a number of issues: the explicit language of the insurance contract; the implicit exceptions to the contract (e.g., one is not insured against intentional acts); the legal standard of liability in a case; and the common and

statutory law of insurance in the relevant jurisdiction. The law in different states varies greatly on these issues. *See* Tom Baker, *Reconsidering Insurance for Punitive Damages*, 1998 Wis.L.Rev. 101 (1998); Christopher Wilson, Lazenby *After* Hodges—*Insurability of Punitive Damages Awards in Tennessee: A Continuing Question of Public Policy*, 36 U.Mem.L.Rev. 463 (2006).

EXXON SHIPPING CO. V. BAKER
Supreme Court of the United States
554 U.S. 471 (2008)

JUSTICE SOUTER delivered the opinion of the Court.

* * *

I

On March 24, 1989, the supertanker *Exxon Valdez* grounded on Bligh Reef off the Alaskan coast, fracturing its hull and spilling millions of gallons of crude oil into Prince William Sound. The owner, petitioner Exxon Shipping Co. * * *, and its owner, petitioner Exxon Mobil Corp. * * * have settled state and federal claims for environmental damage, with payments exceeding $1 billion, and this action by respondent Baker and others, including commercial fishermen and native Alaskans, was brought for economic losses to individuals dependent on Prince William Sound for their livelihoods.

A

The tanker was over 900 feet long and was used by Exxon to carry crude oil from the end of the Trans-Alaska Pipeline in Valdez, Alaska, to the lower 48 States. On the night of the spill it was carrying 53 million gallons of crude oil, or over a million barrels. Its captain was one Joseph Hazelwood, who had completed a 28-day alcohol treatment program while employed by Exxon, as his superiors knew, but dropped out of a prescribed follow-up program and stopped going to Alcoholics Anonymous meetings. According to the District Court, "[t]here was evidence presented to the jury that after Hazelwood was released from [residential treatment], he drank in bars, parking lots, apartments, airports, airplanes, restaurants, hotels, at various ports, and aboard Exxon tankers." The jury also heard contested testimony that Hazelwood drank with Exxon officials and that members of the Exxon management knew of his relapse. Although Exxon had a clear policy prohibiting employees from serving onboard within four hours of consuming alcohol, Exxon presented no evidence that it monitored Hazelwood after his return to duty or considered giving him a shoreside assignment. Witnesses testified that before the *Valdez* left port on the night of the disaster, Hazelwood downed at least five double vodkas in the waterfront bars of Valdez, an intake of about 15 ounces of 80-proof alcohol, enough "that a non-alcoholic would have passed out."

The ship sailed at 9:12 p.m. on March 23, 1989, guided by a state-licensed pilot for the first leg out, through the Valdez Narrows. At 11:20 p.m., Hazelwood took active control and, owing to poor conditions in the outbound shipping lane, radioed the Coast Guard for permission to move east across the inbound lane to a less icy path. Under the conditions, this was a standard move, which the last outbound tanker had also taken, and the Coast Guard cleared the *Valdez* to cross the inbound lane. The tanker accordingly steered east toward clearer waters, but the move put it in the path of an underwater reef off Bligh Island, thus requiring a turn back west into the shipping lane around Busby Light, north of the reef.

Two minutes before the required turn, however, Hazelwood left the bridge and went down to his cabin in order, he said, to do paperwork. This decision was inexplicable. There was expert testimony that, even if their presence is not strictly necessary, captains simply do not quit the bridge during maneuvers like this, and no paperwork could have justified it. And in fact the evidence was that Hazelwood's presence was required, both because there should have been two officers on the bridge at all times and his departure left only one, and because he was the only person on the entire ship licensed to navigate this part of Prince William Sound. To make matters worse, before going below Hazelwood put the tanker on autopilot, speeding it up, making the turn trickier, and any mistake harder to correct.

As Hazelwood left, he instructed the remaining officer, third mate Joseph Cousins, to move the tanker back into the shipping lane once it came abeam of Busby Light. Cousins, unlicensed to navigate in those waters, was left alone with helmsman Robert Kagan, a nonofficer. For reasons that remain a mystery, they failed to make the turn at Busby Light, and a later emergency maneuver attempted by Cousins came too late. The tanker ran aground on Bligh Reef, tearing the hull open and spilling 11 million gallons of crude oil into Prince William Sound.

After Hazelwood returned to the bridge and reported the grounding to the Coast Guard, he tried but failed to rock the *Valdez* off the reef, a maneuver which could have spilled more oil and caused the ship to founder. The Coast Guard's nearly immediate response included a blood test of Hazelwood (the validity of which Exxon disputes) showing a blood-alcohol level of .061 eleven hours after the spill. Experts testified that to have this much alcohol in his bloodstream so long after the accident, Hazelwood at the time of the spill must have had a blood-alcohol level of around three times the legal limit for driving in most States.

In the aftermath of the disaster, Exxon spent around $2.1 billion in cleanup efforts. * * * Exxon pleaded guilty to violations of the Clean Water Act, the Refuse Act, and the Migratory Bird Treaty Act and agreed to pay a $150 million fine, later reduced to $25 million plus restitution of $100 million. A civil action by the United States and the State of Alaska for environmental harms ended with a consent decree for Exxon to pay at least

$900 million toward restoring natural resources, and it paid another $303 million in voluntary settlements with fishermen, property owners, and other private parties.

B

* * *

[T]he jury awarded $287 million in compensatory damages to the commercial fishermen. * * * The jury awarded $5,000 in punitive damages against Hazelwood and $5 billion against Exxon. * * * [T]he [Ninth] Circuit remanded twice for adjustments in light of this Court's due process cases before ultimately itself remitting the award to $2.5 billion.

* * *

IV

A

The modern Anglo-American doctrine of punitive damages dates back at least to 1763, when a pair of decisions by the Court of Common Pleas recognized the availability of damages "for more than the injury received." Wilkes v. Wood, Lofft 1, 18, 98 Eng.Rep. 489, 498 (1763). In *Wilkes,* one of the foundations of the Fourth Amendment, exemplary damages awarded against the Secretary of State, responsible for an unlawful search of John Wilkes's papers, were a spectacular £4,000. And in Huckle v. Money, 95 Eng.Rep. 768, 768–769 (K.B. 1763), the same judge who is recorded in *Wilkes* gave an opinion upholding a jury's award of 300 (against a government officer again) although "if the jury had been confined by their oath to consider the mere personal injury only, perhaps [£20] damages would have been thought damages sufficient."

Awarding damages beyond the compensatory was not, however, a wholly novel idea even then, legal codes from ancient times through the Middle Ages having called for multiple damages for certain especially harmful acts. *See, e.g.,* Code of Hammurabi § 8 (R. Harper ed. 1904) (tenfold penalty for stealing the goat of a freed man); Statute of Gloucester, 1278, 6 Edw. I, ch. 5, 1 Stat. at Large 66 (treble damages for waste). But punitive damages were a common law innovation untethered to strict numerical multipliers, and the doctrine promptly crossed the Atlantic, to become widely accepted in American courts by the middle of the 19th century.

B

Early common law cases offered various rationales for punitive-damages awards, which were then generally dubbed "exemplary," implying that these verdicts were justified as punishment for extraordinary wrongdoing, as in Wilkes's case. Sometimes, though, the extraordinary element emphasized was the damages award itself, the punishment being "for example's sake," Tullidge v. Wade, 3 Wils. 18, 19, 95 Eng.Rep. 909 (K.B. 1769) "to deter from any such proceeding for the future." See also Coryell at 77 (instructing the jury "to give damages for *example's* sake, to prevent such offences in [the] future").

A third historical justification * * * was the need "to compensate for intangible injuries, compensation which was not otherwise available under the narrow conception of compensatory damages prevalent at the time." Cooper Industries, Inc. v. Leatherman Tool Group, Inc., 532 U.S. 424, 437–438, n. 11 (2001). But see Sebok, What Did Punitive Damages Do? 78 Chi.-Kent L.Rev. 163, 204 (2003) (arguing that "punitive damages have never served the compensatory function attributed to them by the Court in *Cooper*"). As the century progressed, and "the types of compensatory damages available to plaintiffs . . . broadened," the consequence was that American courts tended to speak of punitive damages as separate and distinct from compensatory damages.

Regardless of the alternative rationales over the years, the consensus today is that punitives are aimed not at compensation but principally at retribution and deterring harmful conduct. This consensus informs the doctrine in most modern American jurisdictions, where juries are customarily instructed on twin goals of punitive awards. *See, e.g.,* * * * N. Y. Pattern Jury Instr., Civil, No. 2:278 (2007) ("The purpose of punitive damages is not to compensate the plaintiff but to punish the defendant . . . and thereby to discourage the defendant . . . from acting in a similar way in the future"). The prevailing rule in American courts also limits punitive damages to cases of what the Court in *Day* spoke of as "enormity," where a defendant's conduct is "outrageous," 4 Restatement § 908(2), owing to "gross negligence," "willful, wanton, and reckless indifference for the rights of others," or behavior even more deplorable, 1 Schlueter § 9.3(A).

Under the umbrellas of punishment and its aim of deterrence, degrees of relative blameworthiness are apparent. Reckless conduct is not intentional or malicious, nor is it necessarily callous toward the risk of harming others, as opposed to unheedful of it. *See, e.g.,* 2 Restatement § 500, Comment *a*, pp. 587–588 (1964) ("Recklessness may consist of either of two different types of conduct. In one the actor knows, or has reason to know . . . of facts which create a high degree of risk of . . . harm to another, and deliberately proceeds to act, or to fail to act, in conscious disregard of, or indifference to, that risk. In the other the actor has such knowledge, or reason to know, of the facts, but does not realize or appreciate the high degree of risk involved, although a reasonable man in his position would do so"). Action taken or omitted in order to augment profit represents an enhanced degree of punishable culpability, as of course does willful or malicious action, taken with a purpose to injure. * * *

Regardless of culpability, however, heavier punitive awards have been thought to be justifiable when wrongdoing is hard to detect (increasing chances of getting away with it), or when the value of injury and the corresponding compensatory award are small (providing low incentives to sue), 4 Restatement § 908, Comment *c*, p. 465 ("Thus an award of nominal damages . . . is enough to support a further award of punitive damages, when a tort, . . . is committed for an outrageous purpose, but no significant harm has resulted"). And, with a broadly analogous object, some regulatory schemes provide by statute for multiple recovery in order to induce private litigation to supplement official enforcement that might fall short if unaided.

C

State regulation of punitive damages varies. A few States award them rarely, or not at all. Nebraska bars punitive damages entirely, on state constitutional grounds. Four others permit punitive damages only when authorized by statute: Louisiana, Massachusetts, and Washington as a matter of common law, and New Hampshire by statute codifying common law tradition. Michigan courts recognize only exemplary damages supportable as compensatory, rather than truly punitive, while Connecticut courts have limited what they call punitive recovery to the "expenses of bringing the legal action, including attorney's fees, less taxable costs."

As for procedure, in most American jurisdictions the amount of the punitive award is generally determined by a jury in the first instance, and that "determination is then reviewed by trial and appellate courts to ensure that it is reasonable." Pacific Mut. Life Ins. Co. v. Haslip, 499 U.S. 1, 15 (1991); *see also* Honda Motor Co. v. Oberg, 512 U.S. 415, 421–426 (1994). Many States have gone further by imposing statutory limits on punitive awards, in the form of absolute monetary caps, *see, e.g.,* Va. Code Ann. § 8.01–38.1 ($350,000 cap), a maximum ratio of punitive to compensatory damages, *see, e.g.,* Ohio Rev. Code Ann. § 2315.21(D)(2)(a) (2:1 ratio in most tort cases), or, frequently, some combination of the two, *see, e.g.,* Alaska Stat. § 09.17.020(f) (2006) (greater of 3:1 ratio or $500,000 in most actions). The States that rely on a multiplier have adopted a variety of ratios, ranging from 5:1 to 1:1.

Despite these limitations, punitive damages overall are higher and more frequent in the United States than they are anywhere else. * * * And some legal systems not only decline to recognize punitive damages themselves but refuse to enforce foreign punitive judgments as contrary to public policy. *See, e.g.,* Gotanda, *Charting Developments Concerning Punitive Damages: Is the Tide Changing?* 45 Colum. J. Transnat'l L. 507 (2007) (noting refusals to enforce judgments by Japanese, Italian, and German courts, positing that such refusals may be on the decline, but concluding, "American parties should not anticipate smooth sailing when seeking to have a domestic punitive damages award recognized and enforced in other countries").

D

American punitive damages have been the target of audible criticism in recent decades, *see, e.g.,* Note, *Developments, The Paths of Civil Litigation,* 113 Harv.L.Rev. 1783, 1784–1788 (2000) (surveying criticism), but the most recent studies tend to undercut much of it. A survey of the literature reveals that discretion to award punitive damages has not mass-produced runaway awards, and although some studies show the dollar amounts of punitive-damages awards growing over time, even in real terms, by most accounts the median ratio of punitive to compensatory awards has remained less than 1:1. Nor do the data substantiate a marked increase in the percentage of cases with punitive awards over the past several decades. The figures thus show an overall restraint and suggest that in many instances a high ratio of punitive to compensatory damages is substantially greater than necessary to punish or deter.

The real problem, it seems, is the stark unpredictability of punitive awards. Courts of law are concerned with fairness as consistency, and evidence that the median ratio of punitive to compensatory awards falls within a reasonable zone, or that punitive awards are infrequent, fails to tell us whether the spread between high and low individual awards is acceptable. The available data suggest it is not. A recent comprehensive study of punitive damages awarded by juries in state civil trials found a median ratio of punitive to compensatory awards of just 0.62:1, but a mean ratio of 2.90:1 and a standard deviation of 13.81. Even to those of us unsophisticated in statistics, the thrust of these figures is clear: the spread is great, and the outlier cases subject defendants to punitive damages that dwarf the corresponding compensatories. The distribution of awards is narrower, but still remarkable, among punitive damages assessed by judges: the median ratio is 0.66:1, the mean ratio is 1.60:1, and the standard deviation is 4.54. Other studies of some of the same data show that fully 14% of punitive awards in 2001 were greater than four times the compensatory damages, with 18% of punitives in the 1990s more than trebling the compensatory damages, see Ostrom, Rottman, & Goerdt, A Step Above Anecdote: A Profile of the Civil Jury in the 1990s, 79 Judicature 233, 240 (1996). And a study of "financial injury" cases using a different data set found that 34% of the punitive awards were greater than three times the corresponding compensatory damages.

Starting with the premise of a punitive-damages regime, these ranges of variation might be acceptable or even desirable if they resulted from judges' and juries' refining their judgments to reach a generally accepted optimal level of penalty and deterrence in cases involving a wide range of circumstances, while producing fairly consistent results in cases with similar facts. Cf. TXO Production Corp. v. Alliance Resources Corp., 509 U.S. 443, 457–458 (1993) (plurality opinion). But anecdotal evidence suggests that nothing of that sort is going on. One of our own leading cases on punitive damages, with a $4 million verdict by an Alabama jury, noted that a second Alabama case with strikingly similar facts produced "a comparable amount of compensatory damages" but "no punitive damages at all." See *Gore*, 517 U.S. at 565, n. 8. As the Supreme Court of Alabama candidly explained, "the disparity between the two jury verdicts . . . [w]as a reflection of the inherent uncertainty of the trial process." BMW of North America, Inc. v. Gore, 646 So.2d 619, 626 (1994). We are aware of no scholarly work pointing to consistency across punitive awards in cases involving similar claims and circumstances.

E

The Court's response to outlier punitive damages awards has thus far been confined by claims at the constitutional level * * * .

Today's enquiry differs from due process review because the case arises under federal maritime jurisdiction, and we are reviewing a jury award for conformity with maritime law, rather than the outer limit allowed by due process; we are examining the verdict in the exercise of federal maritime common law authority, which precedes and should obviate any application of the constitutional standard. Our due process cases, on the contrary, have all involved awards subject in the first instance to state law. *See, e.g., State Farm* (fraud and intentional infliction of emotional distress under Utah law); *Gore* (fraud under Alabama law); *TXO* (plurality opinion) (slander of title under West Virginia law); *Haslip* (fraud under Alabama law). These, as state-law cases, could provide no occasion to consider a "common-law standard of excessiveness," *Browning-Ferris Industries*, and the only matter of federal law within our appellate authority was the constitutional due process issue.

Our review of punitive damages today, then, considers not their intersection with the Constitution, but the desirability of regulating them as a common law remedy for which responsibility lies with this Court as a source of judge-made law in the absence of statute. Whatever may be the constitutional significance of the unpredictability of high punitive awards, this feature of happenstance is in tension with the function of the awards as punitive, just because of the implication of unfairness that an eccentrically high punitive verdict carries in a system whose commonly held notion of law rests on a sense of fairness in dealing with one another. Thus, a penalty should be reasonably predictable in its severity, so that even Justice Holmes's "bad man" can look ahead with some ability to know what the stakes are in choosing one course of action or another. See The Path of the Law, 10 Harv.L.Rev. 457, 459 (1897). And when the bad mans counterparts turn up from time to time, the penalty scheme they face ought to threaten them with a fair probability of suffering in like degree when they wreak like damage. Cf. Koon v. United States, 518 U.S. 81, 113 (1996) (noting the need "to reduce unjustified disparities" in criminal sentencing "and so reach toward the evenhandedness and neutrality that are the distinguishing marks of any principled system of justice"). The common sense of justice would surely bar penalties that reasonable people would think excessive for the harm caused in the circumstances.

F

1

With that aim ourselves, we have three basic approaches to consider, one verbal and two quantitative. As mentioned before, a number of state courts have settled on criteria for judicial review of punitive-damages awards that go well beyond traditional "shock the conscience" or "passion and prejudice" tests. Maryland, for example, has set forth a nonexclusive list of nine review factors under state common law that include "degree of heinousness," "the deterrence value of [the award]," and "[w]hether [the punitive award] bears a reasonable relationship to the compensatory damages awarded." Alabama has seven general criteria, such as "actual or likely harm [from the defendants conduct]," "degree of reprehensibility," and "[i]f the wrongful conduct was profitable to the defendant." * * *

These judicial review criteria are brought to bear after juries render verdicts under instructions offering, at best, guidance no more specific for reaching an appropriate penalty. In Maryland, for example, which allows punitive damages for intentional torts and conduct characterized by "actual malice," juries may be instructed that

"An award for punitive damages should be:

"(1) In an amount that will deter the defendant and others from similar conduct.

"(2) Proportionate to the wrongfulness of the defendant's conduct and the defendant's ability to pay.

"(3) But not designed to bankrupt or financially destroy a defendant."

Md. Pattern Jury Instr., Civil, No. 10:13 (4th ed. 2007).

In Alabama, juries are instructed to fix an amount after considering "the character and degree of the wrong as shown by the evidence in the case, and the necessity of preventing similar wrongs." 1 Ala. Pattern Jury Instr., Civil, No. § 23.21 (Supp. 2007).

These examples leave us skeptical that verbal formulations, superimposed on general jury instructions, are the best insurance against unpredictable outliers. Instructions can go just so far in promoting systemic consistency when awards are not tied to specifically proven items of damage (the cost of medical treatment, say), and although judges in the States that take this approach may well produce just results by dint of valiant effort, our experience with attempts to produce consistency in the analogous business of criminal sentencing leaves us doubtful that anything but a quantified approach will work. A glance at the experience there will explain our skepticism.

The points of similarity are obvious. "[P]unitive damages advance the interests of punishment and deterrence, which are also among the interests advanced by the criminal law." *Browning-Ferris Industries*, 492 U.S., at 275. See also 1977 Restatement § 908, Comment *a,* at 464 (purposes of punitive damages are "the same" as "that of a fine imposed after a conviction of a crime"); 18 U.S.C. § 3553(a)(2) (requiring sentencing courts to consider, inter alia, "the need for the sentence imposed . . . to provide just punishment for the offense" and "to afford adequate deterrence to criminal conduct"); United States Sentencing Commission, Guidelines Manual § 1A1.1, comment. (Nov. 2007).

It is instructive, then, that in the last quarter century federal sentencing rejected an "indeterminate" system, with relatively unguided discretion to sentence within a wide range, under which "similarly situated offenders were sentenced [to], and did actually serve, widely disparate sentences." Instead it became a system of detailed guidelines tied to exactly quantified sentencing results, under the authority of the Sentencing Reform Act of 1984, 18 U.S.C. § 3551 et seq.

The importance of this for us is that in the old federal sentencing system of general standards the cohort of even the most seasoned judicial penalty-givers defied consistency. Judges and defendants alike were "[l]eft at large, wandering in deserts of uncharted discretion," M. Frankel, Criminal Sentences: Law Without Order 7–8 (1973), which is very much the position of those imposing punitive damages today, be they judges or juries, except that they lack even a statutory maximum; their only restraint beyond a core sense of fairness is the due process limit. This federal criminal law development, with its many state parallels, strongly suggests that as long "as there are no punitive-damages guidelines, corresponding to the federal and state sentencing guidelines, it is inevitable that the specific amount of punitive damages awarded whether by a judge or by a jury will be arbitrary."

2

This is why our better judgment is that eliminating unpredictable outlying punitive awards by more rigorous standards than the constitutional limit will probably have to take the form adopted in those States that have looked to the criminal-law pattern of quantified limits. One option would be to follow the States that set a hard dollar cap on punitive damages, a course that arguably would come closest to the criminal law, rather like setting a maximum term of years. The trouble is, though, that there is no "standard" tort or contract injury, making it difficult to settle upon a particular dollar figure as appropriate across the board. And of course a judicial selection of a dollar cap would carry a serious drawback; a legislature can pick a figure, index it for inflation, and revisit its provision whenever there seems to be a need for further tinkering, but a court cannot say when an issue will show up on the docket again. *See, e.g.,* Jones & Laughlin Steel Corp. v. Pfeifer, 462 U.S. 523, 546–547 (1983) (declining to adopt a fixed formula to account for inflation in discounting future wages to present value, in light of the unpredictability of inflation rates and variation among lost-earnings cases).

The more promising alternative is to leave the effects of inflation to the jury or judge who assesses the value of actual loss, by pegging punitive to compensatory damages using a ratio or maximum multiple. *See, e.g.,* 2 ALI Enterprise Responsibility for Personal Injury: Reporters' Study 258 (1991) (hereinafter ALI Reporters' Study) ("[T]he compensatory award in a successful case should be the starting point in calculating the punitive award"); ABA, Report of Special Comm. on Punitive Damages, Section of Litigation, Punitive Damages: A Constructive Examination 64–66 (1986) (recommending a presumptive punitive-to-compensatory damages ratio). As the earlier canvass of state experience showed, this is the model many States have adopted, and Congress has passed analogous legislation from time to time, as for example in providing treble damages in antitrust, racketeering, patent, and trademark actions, see 15 U.S.C. §§ 15, 1117; 18 U.S.C. § 1964(c); 35 U.S.C. § 284. And of course the potential relevance of the ratio between compensatory and punitive damages is indisputable, being a central feature in our due process analysis. *See, e.g., State Farm; Gore.*

Still, some will murmur that this smacks too much of policy and too little of principle. But the answer rests on the fact that we are acting here in the position of a common law court of last review, faced with a perceived defect in a common law remedy. Traditionally, courts have accepted primary responsibility for reviewing punitive damages and thus for their evolution, and if, in the absence of legislation, judicially derived standards leave the door open to outlier punitive-damages awards, it is hard to see how the judiciary can wash its hands of a problem it created, simply by calling quantified standards legislative. See *State Farm* (Ginsburg, J., dissenting) ("In a legislative scheme or a state high court's design to cap punitive damages, the handiwork in setting single-digit and 1-to-1 benchmarks could hardly be questioned"); 2 ALI Reporters' Study 257 (recommending adoption of ratio, "probably legislatively, although possibly judicially").

History certainly is no support for the notion that judges cannot use numbers. The 21-year period in the rule against perpetuities was a judicial innovation, *see, e.g.,* Cadell v. Palmer, 1 Clark & Finnelly 372, 6 Eng.Rep. 956, 963 (H.L.1833), and so were exact limitations periods for civil actions, sometimes borrowing from statutes, but often without any statutory account to draw on. For more examples, see 1 W. Blackstone, Commentaries on the Laws of England 451 (1765) (listing other common law age cut-offs with no apparent statutory basis). And of course, adopting an admiralty-law ratio is no less judicial than picking one as an outer limit of constitutionality for punitive awards. *See State Farm.*

Although the legal landscape is well populated with examples of ratios and multipliers expressing policies of retribution and deterrence, most of them suffer from features that stand in the way of borrowing them as paradigms of reasonable limitations suited for application to this case. While a slim majority of the States with a ratio have adopted 3:1, others see fit to apply a lower one, *see, e.g.,* Colo. Rev. Stat. Ann. § 13–21–102(1)(a) (2007) (1:1); Ohio Rev. Code Ann. § 2315.21(D)(2)(a) (2:1), and a few have gone higher, *see, e.g.,* Mo. Ann. Stat. § 510.265(1) (5:1). Judgments may differ about the weight to be given to the slight majority of 3:1 States, but one feature of the 3:1 schemes dissuades us from selecting it here. With a few statutory exceptions, generally for intentional infliction of physical injury or other harm, *see, e.g,* Ala. Code § 6–11–21(j); Ark. Code Ann. § 16–55–208(b), the States with 3:1 ratios apply them across the board (as do other States using different fixed multipliers). That is, the upper limit is not directed to cases like this one, where the tortious action was worse than negligent but less than malicious, exposing the tortfeasor to certain regulatory sanctions and inevitable damage actions; the 3:1 ratio in these States also applies to awards in quite different cases involving some of the most egregious conduct, including malicious behavior and dangerous activity carried on for the purpose of increasing a tortfeasors financial gain. We confront, instead, a case of reckless action, profitless to the tortfeasor, resulting in substantial recovery for substantial injury. Thus, a legislative judgment that 3:1 is a reasonable limit overall is not a judgment that 3:1 is a reasonable limit in this particular type of case.

For somewhat different reasons, the pertinence of the 2:1 ratio adopted by treble-damages statutes (offering compensatory damages plus a bounty of double that amount) is open to question. Federal treble-damages statutes govern areas far afield from maritime concerns (not to mention each other); the relevance of the governing rules in patent or trademark cases, say, is doubtful at best. And in some instances, we know that the considerations that went into making a rule have no application here. We know, for example, that Congress devised the treble damages remedy for private antitrust actions with an eye to supplementing official enforcement by inducing private litigation, which might otherwise have been too rare if nothing but compensatory damages were available at the end of the day. That concern has no traction here, in this case of staggering damage inevitably provoking governmental enforcers to indict and any number of private parties to sue. To take another example, although 18 U.S.C. § 3571(d) provides for a criminal penalty of up to twice a crime victim's loss, this penalty is an alternative to other specific fine amounts which courts may impose at their option, see §§ 3571(a)–(c), a fact that makes us wary of reading too much into Congress's choice of ratio in one provision. State environmental treble-damages schemes offer little more support: for one thing, insofar as some appear to punish even negligence, while others target only willful conduct, some undershoot and others may overshoot the target here. For another, while some States have chosen treble damages, others punish environmental harms at other multiples. *See, e.g.*, N.H. Rev. Stat. Ann. § 146–A:10 (damages of one-and-a-half times the harm caused to private property by oil discharge); Minn. Stat. Ann. § 115A.99 (2005) (civil penalty of 2 to 5 times the costs of removing unlawful solid waste). All in all, the legislative signposts do not point the way clearly to 2:1 as a sound indication of a reasonable limit.

3

There is better evidence of an accepted limit of reasonable civil penalty, however, in several studies mentioned before, showing the median ratio of punitive to compensatory verdicts, reflecting what juries and judges have considered reasonable across many hundreds of punitive awards. We think it is fair to assume that the greater share of the verdicts studied in these comprehensive collections reflect reasonable judgments about the economic penalties appropriate in their particular cases.

These studies cover cases of the most as well as the least blameworthy conduct triggering punitive liability, from malice and avarice, down to recklessness, and even gross negligence in some jurisdictions. The data put the median ratio for the entire gamut of circumstances at less than 1:1, meaning that the compensatory award exceeds the punitive award in most cases. In a well-functioning system, we would expect that awards at the median or lower would roughly express jurors' sense of reasonable penalties in cases with no earmarks of exceptional blameworthiness within the punishable spectrum (cases like this one, without intentional or malicious conduct, and without behavior driven primarily by desire for gain, for example) and cases (again like this one) without the modest economic harm or odds of detection that have opened the door to higher awards. It also seems fair to suppose that most of the unpredictable outlier cases that call the fairness of the system into question are above the median; in theory a factfinder's deliberation could go awry to produce a very low ratio, but we have no basis to assume that such a case would be more than a sport, and the cases with serious constitutional issues coming to us have naturally been on the high side, *see, e.g., State Farm* (ratio of 145:1); *Gore* (ratio of 500:1). On these assumptions, a median ratio of punitive to compensatory damages of about 0.65:1 probably marks the line near which cases like this one largely should be grouped. Accordingly, given the need to protect against the possibility (and the disruptive cost to the legal system) of awards that are unpredictable and unnecessary, either for deterrence or for measured retribution, we consider that a 1:1 ratio, which is above the median award, is a fair upper limit in such maritime cases.

[handwritten margin note: 1:1 ratio is fair although above avg.]

The provision of the CWA respecting daily fines confirms our judgment that anything greater would be excessive here and in cases of this type. Congress set criminal penalties of up to $25,000 per day for negligent violations of pollution restrictions, and up to $50,000 per day for knowing ones. 33 U.S.C. §§ 1319(c)(1), (2). Discretion to double the penalty for knowing action compares to discretion to double the civil liability on conduct going beyond negligence and meriting punitive treatment. And our explanation of the constitutional upper limit confirms that the 1:1 ratio is not too low. In *State Farm*, we said that a single-digit maximum is appropriate in all but the most exceptional of cases, and "[w]hen compensatory damages are substantial, then a lesser ratio, perhaps only equal to compensatory damages, can reach the outermost limit of the due process guarantee."

V

Applying this standard to the present case, we take for granted the District Court's calculation of the total relevant compensatory damages at $507.5 million. A punitive-to-compensatory ratio of 1:1 thus yields maximum punitive damages in that amount.

JUSTICE ALITO took no part in the consideration or decision of this case.

JUSTICE SCALIA, with whom JUSTICE THOMAS joins, concurring.

I join the opinion of the Court, including the portions that refer to constitutional limits that prior opinions have imposed upon punitive damages. While I agree with the argumentation based upon those prior holdings, I continue to believe the holdings were in error. See State Farm Mut. Automobile Ins. Co. v. Campbell, 538 U.S. 408, 429 (2003) (Scalia, J., dissenting).

JUSTICE STEVENS, concurring in part and dissenting in part.

* * * [B]oth caps and ratios of the sort the Court relies upon in its discussion are typically imposed by legislatures, not courts. Although the Court offers a great deal of evidence that States have acted in various ways to limit punitive damages, it is telling that the Court fails to identify a single state *court* that has imposed a precise ratio, as the Court does today, under its common-law authority. State legislatures have done so, of course; and indeed Congress would encounter no obstacle to doing the same as a matter of federal law. But Congress is far better situated than is this Court to assess the empirical data, and to balance competing policy interests, before making such a choice.

The Court concedes that although "American punitive damages have been the target of audible criticism in recent decades," "most recent studies tend to undercut much of [that criticism]." It further acknowledges that "[a] survey of the literature reveals that discretion to award punitive damages has not mass-produced runaway awards." The Court concludes that the real problem is large *outlier* awards, and the data seem to bear this out. But the Court never explains why abuse-of-discretion review is not the precise antidote to the unfairness inherent in such excessive awards. * * *

On an abuse-of-discretion standard, I am persuaded that a reviewing court should not invalidate this award. In light of Exxon's decision to permit a lapsed alcoholic to command a supertanker carrying tens of millions of gallons of crude oil through the treacherous waters of Prince William Sound, thereby endangering all of the individuals who depended upon the sound for their livelihoods, the jury could reasonably have given expression to its "moral condemnation" of Exxon's conduct in the form of this award.

JUSTICE GINSBURG, concurring in part and dissenting in part.

* * * The 1:1 ratio is good for this case, the Court believes, because Exxon's conduct ranked on the low end of the blameworthiness scale: Exxon was not seeking "to augment profit," nor did it act "with a purpose to injure." What ratio will the Court set for defendants who acted maliciously or in pursuit of financial gain? Should the magnitude of the risk increase the ratio and, if so, by how much? Horrendous as the spill from the *Valdez* was, millions of gallons more might have spilled as a result of Captain Hazelwood's attempt to rock the boat off the reef; cf. TXO Production Corp. v. Alliance Resources Corp., 509 U.S. 443, 460–462 (1993) (plurality opinion) (using potential loss to plaintiff as a guide in determining whether jury verdict was excessive). In the end, is the Court holding only that 1:1 is the maritime-law ceiling, or is it also signaling that any ratio higher than 1:1 will be held to exceed "the constitutional outer limit"? On next opportunity, will the Court rule, definitively, that 1:1 is the ceiling due process requires in all of the States, and for all federal claims? * * *

Is it how 1:1 for all cases

JUSTICE BREYER, concurring in part and dissenting in part.

* * * Like the Court, I believe there is a need, grounded in the rule of law itself, to assure that punitive damages are awarded according to meaningful standards that will provide notice of how harshly certain acts will be punished and that will help to assure the uniform treatment of similarly situated persons. Legal standards, however, can secure these objectives without the rigidity that an absolute fixed numerical ratio demands. In setting forth constitutional due process limits on the size of punitive damages awards, for example, we said that "*few* awards exceeding a single-digit ratio between punitive and compensatory damages, to a significant degree, will satisfy due process." State Farm Mut. Automobile Ins. Co. v. Campbell, 538 U.S. 408, 425 (2003) (emphasis added). We thus foresaw exceptions to the numerical constraint.

In my view, a limited exception to the Court's 1:1 ratio is warranted here. As the facts set forth in Part I of the Court's opinion make clear, this was no mine-run case of reckless behavior. The jury could reasonably have believed that Exxon knowingly allowed a relapsed alcoholic repeatedly to pilot a vessel filled with millions of gallons of oil through waters that provided the livelihood for the many plaintiffs in this case. Given that conduct, it was only a matter of time before a crash and spill like this occurred. And as Justice Ginsburg points out, the damage easily could have been much worse.

NOTES

1.   After the Supreme Court's decision, the parties finally settled the nineteen-year-old case for $383.4 million. *Exxon Mobil Agrees to Partial Settlement: $383 Million in Punitives for Valdez Spill*, Legal News, BNA (Sept. 16, 2008). This reduced amount subtracted payments previously made to corporate plaintiffs who settled early in the case in exchange for not executing on compensatory damages and ceding back to Exxon any punitive damages they might later be awarded. Each remaining plaintiff was to receive approximately $11,000 in punitive damages, adding to the $15,000 awarded for compensatory damages. At the same time, Exxon reported its greatest corporate profits ever. Jad Mouawad, *Exxon's Profit Jumped to a Record in a Quarter*, N.Y. Times, Oct. 31, 2008, at B3 (setting record for most profitable American corporation).

2.   The punitive award—even as reduced by the Supreme Court to $507.7 million—is still about the third largest award ever upheld. *See* Hilao v. Estate of Marcos, 103 F.3d 767 (9th Cir.1996) ($1.2 billion against estate of Ferdinand Marcos for human rights violations in the Philippines); Motorola Credit Corp. v. Uzan, 509 F.3d 74 (2d Cir.2007) ($1 billion against Turkish corporations and one of the world's richest families for fraudulent financial scheme); Time Warner Entertainment v. Six Flags Over Georgia, 563 S.E.2d 178 (Ga. 2002), *cert. denied,* 538 U.S. 977 (2003) ($257 million for dishonest business conduct for parent company's preference of own financial interest as against limited partnership).

3.   *Ratio*: The Supreme Court holds that the 3:1 is generally an appropriate ratio for punitive damages, but that the 1:1 ratio between compensatory and punitive damages is appropriate for "this particular type of case." What type of case is that? Do Justices Ginsburg and Breyer agree?

4.   *Vicarious Liability*: The Supreme Court was evenly divided on whether the Exxon Corporation could be held vicariously liable for the actions of its managerial employee, the alcoholic captain. (Only 8 Justices considered the case as Justice Alito recused himself because of his ownership of Exxon stock.) This left standing a lower court decision affirming the jury instruction that permitted the jury to assign vicarious liability based on the involvement of an employee acting in a managerial capacity. In re Exxon Valdez, 270 F.3d 1215, 1233–36 (9th Cir. 2001) (*Valdez I*). Given what we know about vicarious liability from *Grimshaw* and the *Restatement*, should Exxon be liable here? In Kolstad v. American Dental Association, 527 U.S. 526, 545–46 (1999), the

Supreme Court rejected the managerial scope of employment rule for imposing liability for punitive damages upon an employer for a discriminatory employment decision by a manager that was contrary to the employer's policies and good faith efforts to comply with Title VII's prohibition of workplace sex discrimination.

5.   The Court's concern with the unpredictability of punitive damages was shown by one study to be unfounded. *See* Theodore Eisenberg, Michael Heise, Martin T. Wells, *Variability of Punitive Damages: An Empirical Assessment of the U.S. Supreme Court's Decision in* Exxon Shipping v. Baker, 166 J. Inst'l & Theor. Econ. 5 (2010). Instead, the study showed that the perceived problems of a high mean and standard deviation of punitive damages was attributed to the variation in *compensatory* awards. The authors concluded that the Court's 1:1 ratio was not statistically supportable and could contribute to an inability to tailor punitive awards as necessary.

6.   *Exxon Shipping* may not be "just a little boat case." Jill Wieber Lyons, *Justice Holmes's Bad Man and the Depleted Purposes of Punitive Damages*, 101 Ky.L.J. 789 (2012–13). Several courts have found that it has much broader application to questions of punitive damages at common law beyond maritime cases. Hayduk v. City of Johnstown, 580 F.Supp.2d 429 (W.D.Pa.2008), *aff'd other grounds*, 386 Fed.Appx. 55 (3d. Cir. 2010), *cert. denied*, 562 U.S. 1183 (2011); Clausen v. Icicle Seafoods, Inc., 272 P.3d 827, 838 (Wash. 2012) (Johnson, J., dissenting) (noting the potential broad application of *Exxon*). Scholars seem to agree. *See* Joni Hersch & W. Kip Viscusi, *Punitive Damages by Numbers:* Exxon Shipping Co. v. Baker, 18 Sup.Ct. Econ. Rev. 259, 259 (2010) (recognizing "potential implications for other types of cases as well."); Victor E. Schwartz et al., *The Supreme Court's Common Law Approach to Excessive Punitive Damage Awards: A Guide for the Development of State Law*, 60 S.C. L.Rev. 881, 882 (2009) (questioning whether "the high court's powerful reasoning" will influence state courts struggling to cabin outlier punitive damage verdicts?"). It seemed clear that the Supreme Court did not intend its holding to apply to review under due process, *see* Myers v. Central Florida Investments, Inc., 592 F.3d 1201, 1222 (11th Cir.2010), but at least one court has extended the case to that constitutional inquiry. Guidance Endodontics, L.L.C. v. Dentsply Int'l, Inc., 791 F.Supp.2d 1026 (D.N.Mex.2011).

NOTES ON TORT REFORM

As the Court notes in *Exxon Shipping*, many states have legislatively limited punitive damages. There has been an active public debate in recent decades as to whether there has been a substantial growth of punitive damage awards and whether the large size and uneven imposition of punitive awards support the "reform" of punitive damages. Critics raise multiple challenges to the awards: (1) the contradiction of "civil" punishment; (2) inadequate procedural protections; (3) runaway juries; (4) unpredictability; and (5) windfalls to plaintiffs and plaintiffs' lawyers. Doug Rendleman, *Common Law Punitive Damages: Something for Everyone?*, 7 Univ. St.Thomas L.J. 1 (2009).

A large amount of empirical material, including studies of the size and frequency of punitive awards, an examination of the effect of punitive awards on settlement behavior, and an examination of the relation of punitive awards to business decisions and economic outcomes is found in *Special Issue: The Future of Punitive Damages*, 1998 Wis.L.Rev. 1. For some of the recent empirical work questioning whether punitive damages are in fact a problem, see Theodore Eisenberg, et al., *Juries, Judges and Punitive Damages: Empirical Analysis Using the Civil Justice Survey of State Courts*, 1992, 1996, and 2001, 3 J.Emp.Leg.Stud. 263 (2006) (concluding that the level of punitive damages has not increased over time, the awards of punitives are infrequent and awarded in only 2.4% of cases tried, and that 24% of awards were under $10,000 and 60% under $100,000); Martin T. Wells & Theodore Eisenberg, *The Significant Association Between Punitive and Compensatory Damages in Blockbuster Cases: A Methodological Primer*, 3 J.Emp.Leg.Stud. 169 (2006) (showing a strong, statistically significant relation between punitive and compensatory awards contrary to conventional assertions); Theodore Eisenberg, *Variability of Punitive Damages*, *supra* (attributing variability of punitive damages award to disparity in compensatory damages).

With some statutory exceptions, no punitive damages are allowed in Nebraska, New Hampshire, and Washington. Kansas limits punitive damage awards in professional liability actions to 25% of the annual gross income of the defendant or $5 million; any award is divided equally between the plaintiff and a state fund. Missouri, Mo.Rev.Stat. § 537.675(2), Oregon, Or.Rev.Stat. § 18.540(1), and Utah, Utah Code Ann. § 78B-8-201(3), also have statutes requiring payment of a portion of a punitive damage award to the state. Some of these legislative efforts to address windfalls to successful plaintiffs have had a mixed reception in the courts. In Kirk v. Denver Publishing Co., 818 P.2d 262 (Colo.1991), the Colorado Supreme Court held that a state statute that directed one-third of the exemplary damages collected by a plaintiff be paid to the state general fund was an unconstitutional taking of the plaintiff's property, i.e., his judgment against the defendant. But in Hoskins v. Business Men's Assurance, 79 S.W.3d 901 (Mo.2002), the Missouri Supreme Court upheld a statute allowing the state to assert a 50% lien on any final judgment for punitive damages. It rejected claims that this was an excessive fine prohibited under the Excessive Fines Clause of the Eighth Amendment, or the Takings Clause or the Due Process Clause because the state's award was entirely derivative of a final judgment.

There are other ways to avoid windfall to one plaintiff. Illinois gives the trial court discretion to apportion a punitive damage award between the plaintiff, her attorney, and the Illinois Department of Rehabilitation Services. 735 Ill.Comp.Stat. 5/2–1207 (1997). The Ohio Supreme Court ordered sua sponte the diversion of the bulk of a $30 million punitive damage award (less $10 million awarded to the plaintiff and the contractual attorney's fees) to a cancer research fund, to be named after the decedent and to be established at a cancer hospital at the Ohio State University. Dardinger v. Anthem Blue Cross & Blue Shield, 781 N.E.2d 121 (Ohio 2002). Lawyers and courts are thus recasting punitive damages as "curative damages" used to cure a problem by directing funds to charitable organizations. Molly McDonough, *Handing Down Help: In Ohio, "Curative Damages" Are Embraced by Tort Plaintiffs and the Supreme Court*, 91 ABA J.24 (Oct. 2005). Another way for the legislature to address this issue would be to tax the awards at a high rate. *See* James Serven, *The Taxation of Punitive Damages: Horton Lays an Egg?*, 72 Den.U.L.Rev. 215 (1995) (discussing federal taxation of punitive damage awards).

A number of states have adopted procedural mechanisms in an effort to attain more clearly defensible results in punitive damage cases. In an asbestos case with the possibility of multiple punitive damage awards against the defendant, the Florida Supreme Court bifurcated the issue of the amount of punitive damages from the trial of other issues. Thus, the defendant can put previous punitive damage awards before the jury and build a record for a due process argument on the cumulative effect of the awards with a reduced risk. W.R. Grace & Co. v. Waters, 638 So.2d 502 (Fla.1994). Several states have adopted statutes requiring a stricter standard of proof for punitive damages and at least eight states have adopted a requirement that trial courts explain their refusal to disturb a jury award of punitive damages. See Transportation Insurance Co. v. Moriel, 879 S.W.2d 10 (Tex.1994). *See also Developments— The Paths of Civil Litigation: Problems and Proposals in Punitive Damages Reform*, 113 Harv.L.Rev. 1783 (2000). And other states place a cap on the defendant's bond posted during the appeal of a punitive damages award. Doug Rendleman, *A Cap on the Defendant's Appeal Bond? Punitive Damages Tort Reform*, 39 Akron L.Rev. 1089 (2006).

The most common legislative reform of punitive damages has been to limit the total measure of recovery, often at three times the compensatory damages awarded. These damages caps, seen also in statutory limitations on non-economic compensatory damages, have been challenged under numerous state constitutional grounds arguing that caps deny plaintiffs their right to a fair remedy for their injuries. Most state courts have upheld punitive damages caps. *See* Arbino v. Johnson & Johnson, 880 N.E.2d 420 (Ohio 2007); Rhyne v. K-Mart Corp., 594 S.E.2d 1 ((N.C. 2004); Evans v. State, 56 P.3d 1046 (Alaska 2002); DeMendoza v. Huffman (Or. 2002). But a few courts have declared them unconstitutional. See Lewellen v. Franklin, 2014 WL 4425202 (Mo. 2014) (violated right to trial by jury); Bayer CropScience LP v. Schafer, 385 S.W.3d 822 (Ark. 2011) (violated prohibition on limiting recovery for injury).

NOTE ON ECONOMICS AND DETERRENCE

The courts' main rationale for upholding limitations and statutory caps on punitive damages is because of the unpredictability and unfairness to the defendant. Professor Andrew Popper, however, challenges this conventional wisdom, and argues that making punitives easily calculable through a ratio removes all deterrent value and renders them innocuous. Andrew F. Popper, *Capping Incentives, Capping Innovation, Courting Disaster: The Gulf Oil Spill and Arbitrary Limits on Civil Liability*, 60 DePaul L.Rev. 975, 994–98 (2011). He uses the example of the disaster of the BP Gulf Oil spill as a context to revisit the economic problems with limiting punitive damages:

Limiting liability by establishing an arbitrary cap on civil damages is bad public policy. Caps are antithetical to the interests of consumers and at odds with the national interest in creating incentives for better and safer products. * * *

While most of tort reform is predicated on the importance of open-market functions and accountability for those who engage in misconduct, when it comes to capping liability for certain privileged industries, open market theory vanishes. Instead of the normal pressures of competition ensuring accountability for wrongdoing, industry protection becomes the norm. * * *

The deterrent effect will have to be compromised for the greater good, or so goes the argument. The truth is, the greater good is compromised; victims are undercompensated, deterrence is greatly lessened, and those who engage in misconduct are rewarded. There is a simple truth with capped damages: They lessen the likelihood of optimal safety and efficiency. * * *

The loss of deterrence is a real and dramatic consequence of a cap on damages across the board. * * *

Damages imposed for wrongdoing, particularly those that cannot be predicted in advance and passed along to consumers, are the deterrent force in the civil justice system. Writing about punitive damages more than a quarter century ago, the Colorado Supreme Court noted the obvious: "If punitive damages are predictably certain, they become just another item in the cost of doing business, much like other production costs, and thereby induce a reluctance on the part of the manufacturer to sacrifice profit by removing a correctible defect."

The arbitrary limitation of punitive damages to the harm suffered by the plaintiff 'undermines deterrence because the sanction is then limited to a predictable amount of money." This fact alone allows for profit-maximizing behavior without the risk and critical disciplining effect of unplanned exposure to liability. The risk of unplanned exposure provides a market force of great consequence. It forces actors to consider the possibility of harm and injury associated with product or service failure. It pushes companies to optimize safety, within reasonable limits. This pressure is absent with a cap on liability.

C. CONSTITUTIONAL LIMITATIONS ON PUNITIVE DAMAGES

The U.S. Supreme Court has joined in the refrain about the excessiveness of some punitive damage awards. In a series of relatively recent cases, the Court has crafted a judicial inquiry to assess when punitive damages are so grossly excessive as to violate the Constitution's due process guarantee against arbitrary state action. Many have criticized the Court's venture into punitive damages review, arguing that constitutional analysis should not extend to this type of judicial tort reform. A. Benjamin Spencer, *Due Process and Punitive Damages: The Error of Federal Excessiveness Jurisprudence*, 79 S.Cal.L.Rev. 1085 (2006) (arguing that the excessiveness review is defective because it conflicts with important rules of constitutional construction and goes beyond the procedural protections demanded by due process); Benjamin C. Zipursky, *A Theory of Punitive Damages*, 84 Tex.L.Rev. 105 (2005) (contending that the Court's heightened constitutional scrutiny of punitive damages is inappropriate where a private plaintiff is exercising her right to be punitive rather than where the state is imposing punishment); Kevin S. Marshall & Patrick Fitzgerald, *Punitive Damages and the Supreme Court's Reasonable Relationship Test: Ignoring the Economics of Deterrence*, 19 St. John's J. Legal Comment. 237 (2005) (arguing that Supreme Court rulings that limit punitive damages to an award "reasonably related" to actual damages eliminates the economic foundations of deterrence); *but see* Mark Geistfeld, *Constitutional Tort Reform*, 38 Loy.L.A.L.Rev. 1093 (2005) (endorsing the Court's expanded substantive due process review to limit tort damages).

STATE FARM MUTUAL AUTOMOBILE INSURANCE CO. V. CAMPBELL

Supreme Court of the United States
538 U.S. 408 (2003)

JUSTICE KENNEDY delivered the opinion of the Court.

We address once again the measure of punishment, by means of punitive damages, a State may impose upon a defendant in a civil case. The question is whether, in the circumstances we shall recount, an award of $145 million in punitive damages, where full compensatory damages are $1 million, is excessive and in violation of the Due Process Clause of the Fourteenth Amendment to the Constitution of the United States.

I

In 1981, Curtis Campbell (Campbell) was driving with his wife, Inez Preece Campbell, in Cache County, Utah. He decided to pass six vans traveling ahead of them on a two-lane highway. Todd Ospital was driving a small car approaching from the opposite direction. To avoid a head-on collision with Campbell, who by then was driving on the wrong side of the highway and toward oncoming traffic, Ospital swerved onto the shoulder, lost control of his automobile, and collided with a vehicle driven by Robert G. Slusher. Ospital was killed, and Slusher was rendered permanently disabled. The Campbells escaped unscathed.

In the ensuing wrongful death and tort action, Campbell insisted he was not at fault. Early investigations did support differing conclusions as to who caused the accident, but "a consensus was reached early on by the investigators and witnesses that Mr. Campbell's unsafe pass had indeed caused the crash." Campbell's insurance company, petitioner State Farm Mutual Automobile Insurance Company, nonetheless decided to contest liability and declined offers by Slusher and Ospital's estate to settle the claims for the policy limit of $50,000 ($25,000 per claimant). State Farm also ignored the advice of one of its own investigators and took the case to trial, assuring the Campbells that "their assets were safe, that they had no liability for the accident, that State Farm would represent their interests, and that they did not need to procure separate counsel." To the contrary, a jury determined that Campbell was 100 percent at fault, and a judgment was returned for $185,849, far more than the amount offered in settlement.

At first State Farm refused to cover the $135,849 in excess liability. Its counsel made this clear to the Campbells: " 'You may want to put for sale signs on your property to get things moving.' " Nor was State Farm willing to post a supersedeas bond to allow Campbell to appeal the judgment against him. Campbell obtained his own counsel to appeal the verdict. During the pendency of the appeal, in late 1984, Slusher, Ospital, and the Campbells reached an agreement whereby Slusher and Ospital agreed not to seek satisfaction of their claims against the Campbells. In exchange the Campbells agreed to pursue a bad faith action against State Farm and to be represented by Slusher's and Ospital's attorneys. The Campbells also agreed that Slusher and Ospital would have a right to play a part in all major decisions concerning the bad faith action. No settlement could be concluded without Slusher's and Ospital's approval, and Slusher and Ospital would receive 90 percent of any verdict against State Farm.

In 1989, the Utah Supreme Court denied Campbell's appeal in the wrongful death and tort actions. State Farm then paid the entire judgment, including the amounts in excess of the policy limits. The Campbells nonetheless filed a complaint against State Farm alleging bad faith, fraud, and intentional infliction of emotional distress. * * * At State Farm's request the trial court bifurcated the trial into two phases conducted before different juries. In the first phase the jury determined that State Farm's decision not to settle was unreasonable because there was a substantial likelihood of an excess verdict.

Before the second phase of the action against State Farm we decided BMW of North America, Inc. v. Gore, 517 U.S. 559 (1996), and refused to sustain a $2 million punitive damages award which accompanied a verdict of only $4,000 in compensatory damages. Based on that decision, State Farm * * * moved for the exclusion of evidence of dissimilar out-of-state conduct. The trial court denied State Farm's motion.

The second phase addressed State Farm's liability for fraud and intentional infliction of emotional distress, as well as compensatory and punitive damages. The Utah Supreme Court aptly characterized this phase of the trial:

> "State Farm argued during phase II that its decision to take the case to trial was an 'honest mistake' that did not warrant punitive damages. In contrast, the Campbells introduced evidence that State Farm's decision to take the case to trial was a result of a national scheme to meet corporate fiscal goals by capping payouts on claims company wide. This scheme was referred to as State Farm's 'Performance, Planning and Review,' or PP & R, policy. To prove the existence of this scheme, the trial court allowed the Campbells to introduce extensive expert testimony regarding fraudulent practices by State Farm in its nation-wide operations. Although State Farm moved prior to phase II of the trial for the exclusion of such evidence and continued to object to it at trial, the trial court ruled that such evidence was admissible to determine whether State Farm's conduct in the Campbell case was indeed intentional and sufficiently egregious to warrant punitive damages."

Evidence pertaining to the PP & R policy concerned State Farm's business practices for over 20 years in numerous States. Most of these practices bore no relation to third-party automobile insurance claims, the type of claim underlying the Campbells' complaint against the company. The jury awarded the Campbells $2.6 million in compensatory damages and $145 million in punitive damages, which the trial court reduced to $1 million and $25 million respectively. Both parties appealed.

The Utah Supreme Court sought to apply the three guideposts we identified in *Gore* and it reinstated the $145 million punitive damages award. Relying in large part on the extensive evidence concerning the PP & R policy, the court concluded State Farm's conduct was reprehensible. The court also relied upon State Farm's "massive wealth" and on testimony indicating that "State Farm's actions, because of their clandestine nature, will be punished at most in one out of every 50,000 cases as a matter of statistical probability," and concluded that the ratio between punitive and compensatory damages was not unwarranted. Finally, the court noted that the punitive damages award was not excessive when compared to various civil and criminal penalties State Farm could have faced, including $10,000 for each act of fraud, the suspension of its license to conduct business in Utah, the disgorgement of profits, and imprisonment. We granted certiorari.

II

We recognized in Cooper Industries, Inc. v. Leatherman Tool Group, Inc., 532 U.S. 424 (2001), that in our judicial system compensatory and punitive damages, although usually awarded at the same time by the same decisionmaker, serve different purposes. Compensatory damages "are intended to redress the concrete loss that the plaintiff has suffered by reason of the defendant's wrongful conduct." By contrast, punitive damages serve a broader function; they are aimed at deterrence and retribution. * * *

While States possess discretion over the imposition of punitive damages, it is well established that there are procedural and substantive constitutional limitations on these awards. The Due Process Clause of the Fourteenth Amendment prohibits the imposition of grossly excessive or arbitrary punishments on a tortfeasor. * * * To the extent an award is grossly excessive, it furthers no legitimate purpose and constitutes an arbitrary deprivation of property. * * *

Although these awards serve the same purposes as criminal penalties, defendants subjected to punitive damages in civil cases have not been accorded the protections applicable in a criminal proceeding. This increases our concerns over the imprecise manner in which punitive damages systems are administered. We have admonished that "[p]unitive damages pose an acute danger of arbitrary deprivation of property. Jury instructions typically leave the jury with wide discretion in choosing amounts, and the presentation of evidence of a defendant's net worth creates the potential that juries will use their verdicts to express biases against big businesses, particularly those without strong local presences." * * * Our concerns are heightened when the decisionmaker is presented, as we shall discuss, with evidence that has little bearing as to the amount of punitive damages that should be awarded. Vague instructions, or those that merely inform the jury to avoid "passion or prejudice," do little to aid the decisionmaker in its task of assigning appropriate weight to evidence that is relevant and evidence that is tangential or only inflammatory.

In light of these concerns, in *Gore* we instructed courts reviewing punitive damages to consider three guideposts: (1) the degree of reprehensibility of the defendant's misconduct; (2) the disparity between the actual or potential harm suffered by the plaintiff and the punitive damages award; and (3) the difference between the punitive damages awarded by the jury and the civil penalties authorized or imposed in comparable cases. We reiterated the importance of these three guideposts in *Cooper Industries* and mandated appellate courts to conduct *de novo* review of a trial court's application of them to the jury's award. Exacting appellate review ensures that an award of punitive damages is based upon an "application of law, rather than a decisionmaker's caprice."

III

Under the principles outlined in *BMW of North America, Inc. v. Gore,* this case is neither close nor difficult. It was error to reinstate the jury's $145 million punitive damages award. We address each guidepost of *Gore* in some detail.

A

"[T]he most important indicium of the reasonableness of a punitive damages award is the degree of reprehensibility of the defendant's conduct." *Gore.* We have instructed courts to determine the reprehensibility of a defendant by considering whether: the harm caused was physical as opposed to economic; the tortious conduct evinced an indifference to or a reckless disregard of the health or safety of others; the target of the conduct had financial vulnerability; the conduct involved repeated actions or was an isolated incident; and the harm was the result of intentional malice, trickery, or deceit, or mere accident. The existence of any one of these factors weighing in favor of a plaintiff may not be sufficient to sustain a punitive damages award; and the absence of all of them renders any award suspect. It should be presumed a plaintiff has been made whole for his injuries by compensatory damages, so punitive damages should only be awarded if the defendant's culpability, after having paid compensatory damages, is so reprehensible as to warrant the imposition of further sanctions to achieve punishment or deterrence.

Applying these factors in the instant case, we must acknowledge that State Farm's handling of the claims against the Campbells merits no praise. The trial court found that State Farm's employees altered the company's records to make Campbell appear less culpable. State Farm disregarded the overwhelming likelihood of liability and the near-certain probability that, by taking the case to trial, a judgment in excess of the policy limits would be awarded. State Farm amplified the harm by at first assuring the Campbells their assets would be safe from any verdict and by later telling them, postjudgment, to put a for-sale sign on their house. While we do not suggest there was error in awarding punitive damages based upon State Farm's conduct toward the Campbells, a more modest punishment for this reprehensible conduct could have satisfied the State's legitimate objectives, and the Utah courts should have gone no further.

This case, instead, was used as a platform to expose, and punish, the perceived deficiencies of State Farm's operations throughout the country. The Utah Supreme Court's opinion makes explicit that State Farm was being condemned for its nationwide policies rather than for the conduct direct toward the Campbells. ("[T]he Campbells introduced evidence that State Farm's decision to take the case to trial was a result of a national scheme to meet corporate fiscal goals by capping payouts on claims company wide"). This was, as well, an explicit rationale of the trial court's decision in approving the award, though reduced from $145 million to $25 million. * * *

A State cannot punish a defendant for conduct that may have been lawful where it occurred. *Gore* * * * . Nor, as a general rule, does a State have a legitimate concern in imposing punitive damages to punish a defendant for unlawful acts committed outside of the State's jurisdiction.

Any proper adjudication of conduct that occurred outside Utah to other persons would require their inclusion, and, to those parties, the Utah courts, in the usual case, would need to apply the laws of their relevant jurisdiction. Phillips Petroleum Co. v. Shutts, 472 U.S. 797, 821–822 (1985).

Here, the Campbells do not dispute that much of the out-of-state conduct was lawful where it occurred. They argue, however, that such evidence was not the primary basis for the punitive damages award and was relevant to the extent it demonstrated, in a general sense, State Farm's motive against its insured. * * * This argument misses the mark. Lawful out-of-state conduct may be probative when it demonstrates the deliberateness and culpability of the defendant's action in the State where it is tortious, but that conduct must have a nexus to the specific harm suffered by the plaintiff. A jury must be instructed, furthermore, that it may not use evidence of out-of-state conduct to punish a defendant for action that was lawful in the jurisdiction where it occurred. * * * A basic principle of federalism is that each State may make its own reasoned judgment about what conduct is permitted or proscribed within its borders, and each State alone can determine what measure of punishment, if any, to impose on a defendant who acts within its jurisdiction. * * *

For a more fundamental reason, however, the Utah courts erred in relying upon this and other evidence: The courts awarded punitive damages to punish and deter conduct that bore no relation to the Campbells' harm. A defendant's dissimilar acts, independent from the acts upon which liability was premised, may not serve as the basis for punitive damages. A defendant should be punished for the conduct that harmed the plaintiff, not for being an unsavory individual or business. Due process does not permit courts, in the calculation of punitive damages, to adjudicate the merits of other parties' hypothetical claims against a defendant under the guise of the reprehensibility analysis, but we have no doubt the Utah Supreme Court did that here. ("Even if the harm to the Campbells can be appropriately characterized as minimal, the trial court's assessment of the situation is on target: 'The harm is minor to the individual but massive in the aggregate'"). Punishment on these bases creates the possibility of multiple punitive damages awards for the same conduct; for in the usual case nonparties are not bound by the judgment some other plaintiff obtains. *Gore* (Breyer, J., concurring) ("Larger damages might also 'double count' by including in the punitive damages award some of the compensatory, or punitive, damages that subsequent plaintiffs would also recover").

The same reasons lead us to conclude the Utah Supreme Court's decision cannot be justified on the grounds that State Farm was a recidivist. Although "[o]ur holdings that a recidivist may be punished more severely than a first offender recognize that repeated misconduct is more reprehensible than an individual instance of malfeasance," in the context of civil actions courts must ensure the conduct in question replicates the prior transgressions.

The Campbells have identified scant evidence of repeated misconduct of the sort that injured them. Nor does our review of the Utah courts' decisions convince us that State Farm was only punished for its actions toward the Campbells. Although evidence of other acts need not be identical to have relevance in the calculation of punitive damages, the Utah court erred here because evidence pertaining to claims that had nothing to do with a third-party lawsuit was introduced at length. Other evidence concerning reprehensibility was even more tangential. For example, the Utah Supreme Court criticized State Farm's investigation into the personal life of one of its employees and, in a broader approach, the manner in which State Farm's policies corrupted its employees. The Campbells attempt to justify the courts' reliance upon this unrelated testimony on the theory that each dollar of profit made by underpaying a third-party claimant is the same as a dollar made by underpaying a first-party one. * * * [T]his argument is unconvincing. The reprehensibility guidepost does not permit courts to expand the scope of the case so that a defendant may be punished for any malfeasance, which in this case extended for a 20-year period. In this case, because the Campbells have shown no conduct by State Farm similar to that which harmed them, the conduct that harmed them is the only conduct relevant to the reprehensibility analysis.

B

Turning to the second *Gore* guidepost, we have been reluctant to identify concrete constitutional limits on the ratio between harm, or potential harm, to the plaintiff and the punitive damages award. ("[W]e have consistently rejected the notion that the constitutional line is marked by a simple mathematical formula, even one that compares actual *and potential* damages to the punitive award"). We decline again to impose a bright-line ratio which a punitive damages award cannot exceed. Our jurisprudence and the principles it has now established demonstrate, however, that, in practice, few awards exceeding a single-digit ratio between punitive and compensatory damages, to a significant degree, will satisfy due process. In [Pacific Mutual Life Insurance Co. v. Haslip, 499 U.S. 1 (1991)] in upholding a punitive damages award, we concluded that an award of more than four times the amount of compensatory damages might be close to the line of constitutional impropriety. We cited that 4-to-1 ratio again in *Gore*. The Court further referenced a long legislative history, dating back over 700 years and going forward to today, providing for sanctions of double, treble, or quadruple damages to deter and punish. While these ratios are not binding, they are instructive. They demonstrate what should be obvious: Single-digit multipliers are more likely to comport with due process, while still achieving the State's goals of deterrence and retribution, than awards with ratios in range of 500 to 1, or, in this case, of 145 to 1.

Nonetheless, because there are no rigid benchmarks that a punitive damages award may not surpass, ratios greater than those we have previously upheld may comport with due process where "a particularly egregious act has resulted in only a small amount of economic damages." See also [*Gore*] (positing that a higher ratio *might* be necessary where "the injury is hard to detect or the monetary value of noneconomic harm might have been difficult to determine"). The converse is also true, however. When compensatory damages are substantial, then a lesser ratio, perhaps only equal to compensatory damages, can reach the outermost limit of the due process guarantee. The precise award in any case, of course, must be based upon the facts and circumstances of the defendant's conduct and the harm to the plaintiff.

In sum, courts must ensure that the measure of punishment is both reasonable and proportionate to the amount of harm to the plaintiff and to the general damages recovered. In the context of this case, we have no doubt that there is a presumption against an award that has a 145-to-1 ratio. The compensatory award in this case was substantial; the Campbells were awarded $1 million for a year and a half of emotional distress. This was complete compensation. The harm arose from a transaction in the economic realm, not from some physical assault or trauma; there were no physical injuries; and State Farm paid the excess verdict before the complaint was filed, so the Campbells suffered only minor economic injuries for the 18-month period in which State Farm refused to resolve the claim against them. The compensatory damages for the injury suffered here, moreover, likely were based on a component which was duplicated in the punitive award. Much of the distress was caused by the outrage and humiliation the Campbells suffered at the actions of their insurer; and it is a major role of punitive damages to condemn such conduct. Compensatory damages, however, already contain this punitive element. See Restatement (Second) of Torts § 908, Comment *c,* p. 466 (1977) ("In many cases in which compensatory damages include an amount for emotional distress, such as humiliation or indignation aroused by the defendant's act, there is no clear line of demarcation between punishment and compensation and a verdict for a specified amount frequently includes elements of both").

* * *

The remaining premises for the Utah Supreme Court's decision bear no relation to the award's reasonableness or proportionality to the harm. They are, rather, arguments that seek to defend a departure from well-established constraints on punitive damages. While States enjoy considerable discretion in deducing when punitive damages are warranted, each award must comport with the principles set forth in *Gore.* Here the argument that State Farm will be punished in only the rare case, coupled with reference to its assets (which, of course, are what other insured parties in Utah and other States must rely upon for payment of claims) had little to do with the actual harm sustained by the Campbells. The wealth of a defendant cannot justify an otherwise unconstitutional punitive damages award. *Gore* ("The fact that BMW is a large corporation rather than an impecunious individual does not diminish its entitlement to fair notice of the demands that the several States impose on the conduct of its business"); *see also id.,* at 591 (Breyer, J., concurring) ("[Wealth] provides an open-ended basis for inflating awards when the defendant is wealthy. . . . That does not make its use unlawful or inappropriate; it simply means that this factor cannot make up for the failure of other factors, such as 'reprehensibility,' to constrain significantly an award that purports to punish a defendant's conduct"). The principles set forth in *Gore* must be implemented with care, to ensure both reasonableness and proportionality.

C

The third guidepost in *Gore* is the disparity between the punitive damages award and the "civil penalties authorized or imposed in comparable cases." We note that, in the past, we have also looked to criminal penalties that could be imposed. The existence of a criminal penalty does have bearing on the seriousness with which a State views the wrongful action. When used to determine the dollar amount of the award, however, the criminal penalty has less utility. Great care must be taken to avoid use of the civil process to assess criminal penalties that can be imposed only after the heightened protections of a criminal trial have been observed, including, of course, its higher standards of proof. Punitive damages are not a substitute for the criminal process, and the remote possibility of a criminal sanction does not automatically sustain a punitive damages award.

Here, we need not dwell long on this guidepost. The most relevant civil sanction under Utah state law for the wrong done to the Campbells appears to be a $10,000 fine for an act of fraud, an amount dwarfed by the $145 million punitive damages award. The Supreme Court of Utah speculated about the loss of State Farm's business license, the disgorgement of profits, and possible imprisonment, but here again its references were to the broad fraudulent scheme drawn from evidence of out-of-state and dissimilar conduct. This analysis was insufficient to justify the award.

IV

An application of the *Gore* guideposts to the facts of this case, especially in light of the substantial compensatory damages awarded (a portion of which contained a punitive element), likely would justify a punitive damages award at or near the amount of compensatory damages. The punitive award of $145 million, therefore, was neither reasonable nor proportionate to the wrong committed, and it was an irrational and arbitrary deprivation of the property of the defendant. The proper calculation of punitive damages under the principles we have discussed should be resolved, in the first instance, by the Utah courts. * * *

JUSTICE SCALIA, dissenting.

I adhere to the view expressed in my dissenting opinion in BMW of North America, Inc. v. Gore, 517 U.S. 559, 598–99 (1996), that the Due Process Clause provides no substantive protections against "excessive" or "unreasonable" awards of punitive damages. I am also of the view that the punitive damages jurisprudence which has sprung forth from *BMW v. Gore* is insusceptible of principled application; accordingly, I do not feel justified in giving the case stare decisis effect. I would affirm the judgment of the Utah Supreme Court.

JUSTICE THOMAS, dissenting.

I would affirm the judgment below because "I continue to believe that the Constitution does not constrain the size of punitive damages awards." Accordingly, I respectfully dissent.

JUSTICE GINSBURG, dissenting.

Not long ago, this Court was hesitant to impose a federal check on state-court judgments awarding punitive damages. It was not until 1996, in BMW of North America, Inc. v. Gore, 517 U.S. 559(1996), that the Court, for the first time, invalidated a state-court punitive damages assessment as unreasonably large. If our activity in this domain is now "well-established," it takes place on ground not long held.

In *Gore,* I stated why I resisted the Court's foray into punitive damages "territory traditionally within the States' domain." * * *

The large size of the award upheld by the Utah Supreme Court in this case indicates why damage-capping legislation may be altogether fitting and proper. Neither the amount of the award nor the trial record, however, justifies this Court's substitution of its judgment for that of Utah's competent decisionmakers. In this regard, I count it significant that, on the key criterion "reprehensibility," there is a good deal more to the story than the Court's abbreviated account tells.

Ample evidence allowed the jury to find that State Farm's treatment of the Campbells typified its "Performance, Planning and Review" (PP & R) program; implemented by top management in 1979, the program had "the explicit objective of using the claims-adjustment process as a profit center." "[T]he Campbells presented considerable evidence," the trial court noted, documenting "that the PP & R program . . . has functioned, and continues to function, as an unlawful scheme . . . to deny benefits owed consumers by paying out less than fair value in order to meet preset, arbitrary payout targets designed to enhance corporate profits." That policy, the trial court observed, was encompassing in scope; it "applied equally to the handling of both third-party and first-party claims." * * *

Regarding liability for verdicts in excess of policy limits, the trial court referred to a State Farm document titled the "Excess Liability Handbook"; written before the Campbell accident, the handbook instructed adjusters to pad files with "self-serving" documents, and to leave critical items out of files, for example, evaluations of the insured's exposure. Divisional superintendent Bill Brown used the handbook to train Utah employees. While overseeing the Campbell case, Brown ordered adjuster Summers to change the portions of his report indicating that Mr. Campbell was likely at fault and that the settlement cost was correspondingly high. The Campbells' case, according to expert testimony the trial court recited, "was a classic example of State Farm's application of the improper practices taught in the Excess Liability Handbook."

The trial court further determined that the jury could find State Farm's policy "deliberately crafted" to prey on consumers who would be unlikely to defend themselves. In this regard, the trial court noted the testimony of several former State Farm employees affirming that they were trained to target "the weakest of the herd"—"the elderly, the poor, and other consumers who are least knowledgeable about their rights and thus most vulnerable to trickery or deceit, or who have little money and hence have no real alternative but to accept an inadequate offer to settle a claim at much less than fair value."

The Campbells themselves could be placed within the "weakest of the herd" category. The couple appeared economically vulnerable and emotionally fragile. At the time of State Farm's wrongful conduct, "Mr. Campbell had residuary effects from a stroke and Parkinson's disease."

NOTES

1.   On remand, the Utah Supreme Court did not completely take the hint at the end of Justice Kennedy's opinion that applying the *Gore* factors to the *State Farm* facts, "likely would justify a punitive damages award at or near the amount of compensatory damages," that is, about $1 million. Reviewing the evidence in light of the guidance the U.S. Supreme Court gave in its opinion, the Utah Supreme Court concluded that a punitive award of just over $9 million was appropriate. The Utah court focused on the reprehensibility of the insurer's conduct as well as the need to observe the single digit ratio Justice Kennedy prescribed. Campbell v. State Farm Mutual Automobile Insurance Co., 98 P.3d 409 (Utah), *cert. denied*, 543 U.S. 874 (2004). *But see* Walker v. Farmers Insurance Exchange, 153 Cal.App.4th 965, 63 Cal.Rptr.3d 507 (2007) (*State Farm's* 9:1 ratio not binding and a 1:1 ratio of punitive to compensatory damages was more appropriate in the case because fewer reprehensible factors were present).

2.   The three guideposts to constitutional punitive damages were first articulated by the Court in BMW of North America, Inc. v. Gore, 517 U.S. 559 (1996). In *Gore*, a wealthy doctor who purchased a BMW discovered that the company had fraudulently failed to disclose that the new car had been

repainted. Dr. Gore discovered the fraud when he took the car to Mr. Slick at Slick Finish for detailing and finishing. Under state consumer law, such disclosure was not required. The diminution in market value to the car was $4,000, and the Alabama jury originally awarded him $4 million in punitive damages. That amount was reduced to $2 million on appeal as the court found that it was inappropriate to compute punitive damages by multiplying the number of repainted cars sold nationally (approximately 1000) by $4,000 or the amount of economic harm per consumer. (It did not explain where $2 million came from). After reversal by the Supreme Court, the state court remitted the amount of punitives to $50,000. After *State Farm*, is this punitive award to Dr. Gore justified? Before *Gore*, the Supreme Court had decided TXO Production Corp. v. Alliance Resources Corp., 509 U.S. 443 (1993), which upheld a ten million dollar punitive damages award, 526 times the amount of compensatory damages, finding that the jury could have rationally considered the potential harm that might have occurred from the defendant's conduct.

3.   In *State Farm*, the Court did not address the role of the more extensive list of factors it had approved a few years before in Pacific Mutual Life Insurance Co. v. Haslip, 499 U.S. 1 (1991). In particular, the Court said little in *State Farm* of the importance of the financial position of the defendant or the profitability to the defendant of the wrongful conduct. Justice Kennedy briefly observed, "The wealth of a defendant cannot justify an otherwise unconstitutional punitive damages award." Should these wealth factors play a role in deciding how much punishment is constitutional? *See* Jane Mallor & Barry S. Roberts, *Punitive Damages: On the Path to a Principled Approach?* 50 Hastings L.J. 1001 (1999).

The California Supreme Court concluded that some consideration of the defendant's financial condition would still be relevant to satisfying the state's legitimate objectives, even as it recognized that wealth cannot substitute for *State Farm's* guideposts in limiting awards. Simon v. San Paolo U.S. Holding Co., 35 Cal.4th 1159, 113 P.3d 63, 29 Cal.Rptr.3d 379 (2005) (reducing $1.7 million punitive damage award to $50,000). In a companion case, the California Supreme Court affirmed the right of the state to protect the public from harmful corporate policies and practices; nevertheless, the court refused to measure punitive damages by the disgorgement of all profits due to the wrongful conduct. Johnson v. Ford Motor Co., 35 Cal.4th 1191, 113 P.3d 82, 29 Cal.Rptr.3d 401 (2005) (remanding for reconsideration the appellate court's reduction of punitive damages from $10 million to $53,000 based upon a compensatory award of $17,000). *See* Keith N. Hylton, *A Theory of Wealth and Punitive Damages,* 17 Widener L.J. 927 (2008) (arguing that wealth will tend to be a relevant factor when optimal deterrence requires elimination of the defendant's gain); Kathleen S. Kizer, *California's Punitive Damages Law: Continuing to Punish and Deter Despite* State Farm v. Campbell, 57 Hastings L.J. 827 (2006).

Should the defendant's *lack* of wealth impact the judgment? In Engle v. Liggett Group, Inc., 945 So.2d 1246 (Fla. 2006), *cert. denied*, 552 U.S. 941 (2007), the Florida Supreme Court invalidated a $145 billion punitive damages award to the class of smokers concluding, without analysis, that it would "result in an unlawful crippling" of the defendant tobacco companies. The court's main basis for overturning the award was the inability to assess the reasonableness of the ratio because compensatory damages had only been determined for 3 of the class plaintiffs in the amount of $12.7 million.

4.   The requirement that state trial and appellate courts review the amount of punitive damage awards was established in Honda Motor Co., Ltd. v. Oberg, 512 U.S. 415 (1994). In that case, the Supreme Court found that the practice under the Oregon Constitution of allowing the courts to vacate a judgment only when there was no evidence to support the jury decision, but not permitting review for excessive awards, was not consistent with due process standards.

5.   A court reduces an excessive jury award by the historical procedure of *remittitur*. Under remittitur, the judge offers the plaintiff a choice between accepting the reduced award or conducting a new trial. While this satisfies the Seventh Amendment right to jury trial because of the plaintiff's choice of trial, "[i]n issuing a remittitur, a judge effectively redetermines, in final form, the amount of damages that a plaintiff will receive." Sarah M.R. Cravens, *The Brief Demise of Remittitur: The Role of Judges in Shaping Remedies Law*, 42 Loy.L.A. L.Rev. 247 (2008). If the trial court reduces the award for lack of evidence, the appellate court reviews for an abuse of discretion; if the reduction is based on constitutional excessiveness the appellate review is de novo. Cooper Indus., Inc. V. Leatherman Tool Group, Inc. 532 U.S. 424 (2001); Cortez v. Trans Union, LLC, 617 F.3d 688 (3d Cir. 2010). The Supreme Court has held that the opposite procedure of additur (the judicial increase of the award) is not permitted by the Seventh Amendment in federal court, though it is available in some state courts. Dimick v. Schiedt, 293 U.S. 474 (1935).

6.   The Supreme Court elaborated upon the question presented in *State Farm* as to when conduct outside of the case might appropriately be the basis for a punitive damages award. In Philip Morris USA v. Williams, 549 U.S. 346 (2007), the Court reversed an award of $79.5 million in punitives, roughly a ratio of 100-to-1 with the $821,000 in compensatory damages, for the company's conduct in leading the plaintiff's deceased husband to believe it was safe to smoke. The Court held that it was an unconstitutional taking of the defendant's property without due process for a jury to base a punitive award upon its desire to punish the defendant for harming non-parties. In *Williams*, the jury calculated punitive damages, in part, upon the number of other people similar to the plaintiff in the state who had suffered physical harm or death of family members because of the tobacco company's fraud. The evidence did not suffer from the *State Farm* problem because it was the exact same conduct at issue in the case. The Court held that the jury instruction should have excluded these other possible harms to nonparties from factoring into the punishment. *See* Thomas B. Colby, *Clearing the Smoke from* Philip Morris v. Williams: *The Past, Present, and Future of Punitive Damages,* 118 Yale L.J. 392 (2008) (supporting the Court's return to a theory of punitive damages for only private, and not public, wrongs). However, the Court noted that evidence of harm to

others is permitted to assess the reprehensibility of the defendant's conduct. As Justice Stevens observed in his dissent, "This nuance eludes me." *See also Symposium on* Philip Morris v. Williams, 2 Charleston L.Rev. 287–519 (2008).

On remand, the Oregon Supreme Court boldly affirmed its prior decision leaving in place the $79.5 million punitive damages award. Williams v. Philip Morris, Inc., 176 P.3d 1255 (2008), *cert. dismissed as improvidently granted*, 556 U.S. 178 (2009); *see* Catherine M. Sharkey, *Federal Incursions and State Defiance: Punitive Damages in the Wake of* Philip Morris v. Williams, 46 Willamette L.Rev. 449 (2010) (discussing *Williams* as an example of state court defiance of the federalization of punitive damages law).

7.   Does Justice Kennedy's opinion in *State Farm* suggest that a similar 3:1 ratio should be imposed on non-pecuniary damages? *See* Michael Rustad, *The Uncert-Worthiness of the Court's Unmaking of Punitive Damages,* 2 Charleston L.Rev. 459 (2008) (predicting that the Court will extend its punitive damages jurisprudence to curtail the award of non-economic damages); Paul DeCamp, *Beyond* State Farm*: Due Process Constraints on Noneconomic Compensatory Damages*, 27 Harv. J.L. & Pub. Policy 231 (2003) (arguing for similar due process review of non-economic damages, but rejecting the *State Farm* criteria in favor of a standard of review comparing the award with the range of prior decisions in similar cases).

MATHIAS V. ACCOR ECONOMY LODGING, INC.

United States Court of Appeals
347 F.3d 672 (7th Cir. 2003)

POSNER, CIRCUIT JUDGE.

The plaintiffs brought this diversity suit governed by Illinois law against affiliated entities that own and operate the "Motel 6" chain of hotels and motels. One of these hotels (now a "Red Roof Inn," though still owned by the defendant) is in downtown Chicago. The plaintiffs, a brother and sister, were guests there and were bitten by bedbugs, which are making a comeback in the U.S. as a consequence of more conservative use of pesticides. The plaintiffs claim that in allowing guests to be attacked by bedbugs in a motel that charges upwards of $100 a day for a room and would not like to be mistaken for a flophouse, the defendant was guilty of "willful and wanton conduct" and thus under Illinois law is liable for punitive as well as compensatory damages. The jury agreed and awarded each plaintiff $186,000 in punitive damages though only $5,000 in compensatory damages. The defendant appeals, complaining primarily about the punitive-damages award. * * *

The defendant argues that at worst it is guilty of simple negligence, and if this is right the plaintiffs were not entitled by Illinois law to any award of punitive damages. It also complains that the award was excessive-indeed that any award in excess of $20,000 to each plaintiff would deprive the defendant of its property without due process of law. The first complaint has no possible merit, as the evidence of gross negligence, indeed of recklessness in the strong sense of an unjustifiable failure to avoid a *known* risk was amply shown. In 1998, EcoLab, the extermination service that the motel used, discovered bedbugs in several rooms in the motel and recommended that it be hired to spray every room, for which it would charge the motel only $500; the motel refused. The next year, bedbugs were again discovered in a room but EcoLab was asked to spray just that room. The motel tried to negotiate "a building sweep [by EcoLab] free of charge," but, not surprisingly, the negotiation failed. By the spring of 2000, the motel's manager "started noticing that there were refunds being given by my desk clerks and reports coming back from the guests that there were ticks in the rooms and bugs in the rooms that were biting." She looked in some of the rooms and discovered bedbugs. The defendant asks us to disregard her testimony as that of a disgruntled ex-employee, but of course her credibility was for the jury, not the defendant, to determine.

Further incidents of guests being bitten by insects and demanding and receiving refunds led the manager to recommend to her superior in the company that the motel be closed while every room was sprayed, but this was refused. This superior, a district manager, was a management-level employee of the defendant, and his knowledge of the risk and failure to take effective steps either to eliminate it or to warn the motel's guests are imputed to his employer for purposes of determining whether the employer should be liable for punitive damages. The employer's liability for compensatory damages is of course automatic on the basis of the principle of respondeat superior, since the district manager was acting within the scope of his employment.

The infestation continued and began to reach farcical proportions, as when a guest, after complaining of having been bitten repeatedly by insects while asleep in his room in the hotel, was moved to another room only to discover insects there; and within 18 minutes of being moved to a third room he discovered insects in that room as well and had to be moved still again. (Odd that at that point he didn't flee the motel.) By July, the motel's management was acknowledging to EcoLab that there was a "major problem with bed bugs" and that all that was being done about it was "chasing them from room to room." Desk clerks were instructed to call the "bedbugs" "ticks," apparently on the theory that customers would be less alarmed, though in fact ticks are more dangerous than bedbugs because they spread Lyme Disease and Rocky Mountain Spotted Fever. Rooms that the motel had placed on "Do not rent, bugs in room" status nevertheless were rented.

It was in November that the plaintiffs checked into the motel. They were given Room 504, even though the motel had classified the room as "DO NOT RENT UNTIL TREATED," and it had not been treated. Indeed, that night 190 of the hotel's 191 rooms were occupied, even though a number of them had been placed on the same don't-rent status as Room 504. One of the defendant's motions in limine that the judge denied was to exclude evidence concerning all other rooms—a good example of the frivolous character of the motions and of the defendant's pertinacious defense of them on appeal.

Although bedbug bites are not as serious as the bites of some other insects, they are painful and unsightly. Motel 6 could not have rented any rooms at the prices it charged had it informed guests that the risk of being bitten by bedbugs was appreciable. Its failure either to warn guests or to take effective measures to eliminate the bedbugs amounted to fraud and probably to battery as well, as in the famous case of Garratt v. Dailey, 279 P.2d 1091, 1093–94 (Wash. 1955), appeal after remand, 304 P.2d 681 (Wash. 1956), which held that the defendant would be guilty of battery if he knew with substantial certainty that when he moved a chair the plaintiff would try to sit down where the chair had been and would land on the floor instead. There was, in short, sufficient evidence of "willful and wanton conduct" within the meaning that the Illinois courts assign to the term to permit an award of punitive damages in this case.

But in what amount? In arguing that $20,000 was the maximum amount of punitive damages that a jury could constitutionally have awarded each plaintiff, the defendant points to the U.S. Supreme Court's recent statement that "few awards [of punitive damages] exceeding a single-digit ratio between punitive and compensatory damages, to a significant degree, will satisfy due process." State Farm Mutual Automobile Ins. Co. v. Campbell, 538 U.S. 408 (2003). The Court went on to suggest that "four times the amount of compensatory damages might be close to the line of constitutional impropriety." Hence the defendant's proposed ceiling in this case of $20,000, four times the compensatory damages awarded to each plaintiff. The ratio of punitive to compensatory damages determined by the jury was, in contrast, 37.2 to 1.

The Supreme Court did not, however, lay down a 4-to-1 or single-digit-ratio rule—it said merely that "there is a presumption against an award that has a 145-to-1 ratio," State Farm, 123 S.Ct. at 1524—and it would be unreasonable to do so. We must consider why punitive damages are awarded and why the Court has decided that due process requires that such awards be limited. The second question is easier to answer than the first. The term "punitive damages" implies punishment, and a standard principle of penal theory is that "the punishment should fit the crime" in the sense of being proportional to the wrongfulness of the defendant's action, though the principle is modified when the probability of detection is very low (a familiar example is the heavy fines for littering) or the crime is potentially lucrative (as in the case of trafficking in illegal drugs). Hence, with these qualifications, which in fact will figure in our analysis of this case, punitive damages should be proportional to the wrongfulness of the defendant's actions.

Another penal precept is that a defendant should have reasonable notice of the sanction for unlawful acts, so that he can make a rational determination of how to act; and so there have to be reasonably clear standards for determining the amount of punitive damages for particular wrongs. And a third precept, the core of the Aristotelian notion of corrective justice, and more broadly of the principle of the rule of law, is that sanctions should be based on the wrong done rather than on the status of the defendant; a person is punished for what he does, not for who he is, even if the who is a huge corporation.

What follows from these principles, however, is that punitive damages should be admeasured by standards or rules rather than in a completely ad hoc manner, and this does not tell us what the maximum ratio of punitive to compensatory damages should be in a particular case. To determine that, we have to consider why punitive damages are awarded in the first place.

England's common law courts first confirmed their authority to award punitive damages in the eighteenth century, see Dorsey D. Ellis, Jr., "Fairness and Efficiency in the Law of Punitive Damages," 56 S.Cal.L.Rev. 1, 12–20 (1982), at a time when the institutional structure of criminal law enforcement was primitive and it made sense to leave certain minor crimes to be dealt with by the civil law. And still today one function of punitive-damages awards is to relieve the pressures on an overloaded system of criminal justice by providing a civil alternative to criminal prosecution of minor crimes. An example is deliberately spitting in a person's face, a criminal assault but because minor readily deterrable by the levying of what amounts to a civil fine through a suit for damages for the tort of battery. Compensatory damages would not do the trick in such a case, and this for three reasons: because they are difficult to determine in the case of acts that inflict largely dignitary harms; because in the spitting case they would be too slight to give the victim an incentive to sue, and he might decide instead to respond with violence—and an age-old purpose of the law of torts is to provide a substitute for violent retaliation against wrongful injury—and because to limit the plaintiff to compensatory damages would enable the defendant to commit the offensive act with impunity provided that he was willing to pay, and again there would be a danger that his act would incite a breach of the peace by his victim.

When punitive damages are sought for billion-dollar oil spills and other huge economic injuries, the considerations that we have just canvassed fade. As the Court emphasized in *Campbell,* the fact that the plaintiffs in that case had been awarded very substantial compensatory damages—$1 million for a dispute over insurance coverage—greatly reduced the need for giving them a huge award of punitive damages ($145 million) as well in order to provide an effective remedy. Our case is closer to the spitting case. The defendant's behavior was outrageous but the compensable harm done was slight and at the same time difficult to quantify because a large element of it was emotional. And the defendant may well have profited from its misconduct because by concealing the infestation it was able to keep renting rooms. Refunds were frequent but may have cost less than the cost of closing the hotel for a thorough fumigation. The hotel's attempt to pass off the bedbugs as ticks, which some guests might ignorantly have thought less unhealthful, may have postponed the instituting of litigation to rectify the hotel's misconduct. The award of punitive damages in this case thus serves the additional purpose of limiting the defendant's ability to profit from its fraud by escaping detection and (private) prosecution. If a tortfeasor is "caught" only half the time he commits torts, then when he is caught he should be punished twice as heavily in order to make up for the times he gets away.

Finally, if the total stakes in the case were capped at $50,000 (2 x [$5,000 + $20,000]), the plaintiffs might well have had difficulty financing this lawsuit. It is here that the defendant's aggregate net worth of $1.6 billion becomes relevant. A defendant's wealth is not a sufficient basis for awarding punitive damages. *State Farm*; *Gore* (concurring opinion); Zazu Designs v. L'Oreal, S.A., 979 F.2d 499, 508–09 (7th Cir.1992). That would be discriminatory and would violate the rule of law, as we explained earlier, by making punishment depend on status rather than conduct. Where wealth in the sense of resources enters is in enabling the defendant to mount an extremely aggressive defense against suits such as this and by doing so to make litigating against it very costly, which in turn may make it difficult for the plaintiffs to find a lawyer willing to handle their case, involving as it does only modest stakes, for the usual 33–40 percent contingent fee.

In other words, the defendant is investing in developing a reputation intended to deter plaintiffs. It is difficult otherwise to explain the great stubbornness with which it has defended this case, making a host of frivolous evidentiary arguments despite the very modest stakes even when the punitive damages awarded by the jury are included.

As a detail (the parties having made nothing of the point), we note that "net worth" is not the correct measure of a corporation's resources. It is an accounting artifact that reflects the allocation of ownership between equity and debt claimants. A firm financed largely by equity investors has a large "net worth" (= the value of the equity claims), while the identical firm financed largely by debt may have only a small net worth because accountants treat debt as a liability.

All things considered, we cannot say that the award of punitive damages was excessive, albeit the precise number chosen by the jury was arbitrary. It is probably not a coincidence that $5,000 + $186,000 =

$191,000/191 = \$1,000$: i.e., \$1,000 per room in the hotel. But as there are no punitive-damages guidelines, corresponding to the federal and state sentencing guidelines, it is inevitable that the specific amount of punitive damages awarded whether by a judge or by a jury will be arbitrary. (Which is perhaps why the plaintiffs' lawyer did not suggest a number to the jury.) The judicial function is to police a range, not a point. See *Gore*; TXO Production Corp. v. Alliance Resources Corp., 509 U.S. 443, 458 (1993) (plurality opinion).

But it would have been helpful had the parties presented evidence concerning the regulatory or criminal penalties to which the defendant exposed itself by deliberately exposing its customers to a substantial risk of being bitten by bedbugs. That is an inquiry recommended by the Supreme Court. But we do not think its omission invalidates the award. We can take judicial notice that deliberate exposure of hotel guests to the health risks created by insect infestations exposes the hotel's owner to sanctions under Illinois and Chicago law that in the aggregate are comparable in severity to the punitive damage award in this case.

"A person who causes bodily harm to or endangers the bodily safety of an individual by any means, commits reckless conduct if he performs recklessly the acts which cause the harm or endanger safety, whether they otherwise are lawful or unlawful." 720 ILCS 5/12–5(a). This is a misdemeanor, punishable by up to a year's imprisonment or a fine of \$2,500, or both. (For the application of the reckless-conduct criminal statute to corporate officials, see Illinois v. Chicago Magnet Wire Corp., 534 N.E.2d 962, 963 (Ill. 1989).) Of course a corporation cannot be sent to prison, and \$2,500 is obviously much less than the \$186,000 awarded to each plaintiff in this case as punitive damages. But this is just the beginning. Other guests of the hotel were endangered besides these two plaintiffs. And, what is much more important, a Chicago hotel that permits unsanitary conditions to exist is subject to revocation of its license, without which it cannot operate. Chi. Munic. Code §§ 4–4–280, 4–208–020, 050, 060, 110. We are sure that the defendant would prefer to pay the punitive damages assessed in this case than to lose its license.

NOTES

1.   For further insight into *Mathias*, see Colleen P. Murphy, *The "Bedbug" Case and* State Farm v. Campbell, 9 Roger Williams U.L.Rev. 579 (2004) (comparing the approaches of Justice Kennedy and Judge Posner).

2.   Some courts have adhered to the single digit ratio. *E.g.,* Eden Electrical, Ltd. v. Amana Co., 370 F.3d 824 (8th Cir.2004) (affirming district court's reduction of punitive damages from \$17 million to \$10 million), *cert. denied*, 543 U.S. 1150(2005); Lauren R. Goldman & Nickholai G. Levin, State Farm *at Three: Lower Courts' Application of the Ratio Guidepost*, 2 N.Y.U.J.L & Bus. 509 (2006) (concluding that *State Farm* has altered the landscape of

punitive damages litigation in a wide variety of cases). Others have found exceptions to the rule. *E.g.,* Saunders v. Branch Banking & Trust Co., 526 F.3d 142 (4th Cir.2008) (upholding punitive damages with 80:1 ratio, $80,000 punitives/$1,000 statutory damages under Fair Credit Reporting Act because of need for meaningful deterrent in case of trivial compensatory damages and reprehensibility of bank preying on financially vulnerable car loan customer); Kemp v. American Telephone & Telegraph Co., 393 F.3d 1354 (11th Cir.2004) (upholding punitive award of $250,000 for mere $115 in compensatory damages to plaintiff's grandson who rang up telephone charges for playing a 900 number "Let's Make a Deal" game that violated state gambling laws); Timm v. Progressive Steel Treating, Inc., 137 F.3d 1008 (7th Cir.1998) (upholding punitive damages in a sex discrimination suit with no compensatory damages where jury may have thought employee quit to take a higher paying job); Alexandra B. Klass, *Punitive Damages and Valuing Harm*, 92 Minn.L.Rev. 83 (2007) (arguing that courts should depart from a single-digit ratio where harm is "undervalued" as when compensatory damages are small or difficult to determine).

CHAPTER 7

RESTITUTION

■ ■ ■

A. INTRODUCTION

Restitution is the third of the big three remedies, joining damages and injunctions. It is based on defendant's profit or *unjust enrichment*. As a remedy, it seeks to return the *defendant* to its *rightful position* by requiring the *disgorgement* of all of the *unjust gain*. "Despite its importance, restitution is a relatively neglected and underdeveloped part of the law. In the mental map of most lawyers, restitution consists largely of blank spaces with undefined borders and only scattered patches of familiar ground." Douglas Laycock, *The Scope and Significance of Restitution*, 67 Tex.L.Rev. 1277, 1277 (1989).

Restitution developed in both law and equity; thus there are different mechanisms and different measures seen in what otherwise would be the unified remedy of restitution. "Restitution arose to avoid unjust results in specific cases—as a series of innovations to fill gaps in the rest of the law." Laycock, *Restitution*, at 1277. Courts tend to adhere to anachronistic rules and jargon when adjudicating restitution, unlike the modern practice in the context of damages and injunctions. This presents some challenges when reading the restitution cases. The revised Restatement (Third) of Restitution and Unjust Enrichment redone in 2011 tries to organize this morass into understandable principles, but it is still limited by the rules applied by the courts and the many inconsistencies.

Despite this seeming complexity, at its core, restitution is simply a remedy for defendant's profit. It is a viable remedial option for the plaintiff who doesn't need a future order and believes the wrong is better measured by the defendant's gain than her loss. The remedy of restitution is almost self-evident to practitioners and clients; but attorneys must learn to frame their claims using the applicable standards of the courts.

RESTATEMENT (THIRD) OF RESTITUTION (2011)

§ 1. Restitution and Unjust Enrichment

A person who is unjustly enriched at the expense of another is subject to liability in restitution.

Comment:

a. Liability in restitution. Liability in restitution derives from the receipt of a benefit whose retention without payment would result in the unjust enrichment of the defendant at the expense of the claimant. While the paradigm case of unjust enrichment is one in which the benefit on one side of the transaction corresponds to an observable loss on the other, the consecrated formula "at the expense of another" can also mean "in violation of the other's legally protected rights," without the need to show that the claimant has suffered a loss.

The usual consequence of a liability in restitution is that the defendant must restore the benefit in question or its traceable product, or else pay money in the amount necessary to eliminate unjust enrichment.

The identification of unjust enrichment as an independent basis of liability in common-law legal systems-comparable in this respect to a liability in contract or tort-was the central achievement of the 1937 Restatement of Restitution. That conception of the subject is carried forward here. The use of the word "restitution" to describe the cause of action as well as the remedy is likewise inherited from the original Restatement, despite the problems this usage creates. There are cases in which the essence of a plaintiffs right and remedy is the reversal of a transfer, and thus a literal "restitution," without regard to whether the defendant has been enriched by the transfer in question. Conversely, there are cases in which the remedy for unjust enrichment gives the plaintiff something-typically, the defendant's wrongful gain that the plaintiff did not previously possess.

Such is the inherent flexibility of the concept of unjust enrichment that almost every instance of a recognized liability in restitution might be referred to the broad rule of the present section. The same flexibility means that the concept of unjust enrichment will not, by itself, yield a reliable indication of the nature and scope of the liability imposed by this part of our legal system. It is by no means obvious, as a theoretical matter, how "unjust enrichment" should best be defined; whether it constitutes a rule of decision, a unifying theme, or some thing in between; or what role the principle would ideally play in our legal system. Such questions preoccupy much academic writing on the subject. This Restatement has been written on the assumption that the law of restitution and unjust enrichment can be usefully described without insisting on answers to any of them.

Academic attention to restitution and unjust enrichment has increased sharply. Domestically, at least part of the impetus for the renewed interest in the field is the appearance of the American Law Institute's Restatement (Third) of Restitution and Unjust Enrichment. See Doug Rendleman, *Restating Restitution: The Restatement Process and Its Critics*, 65 Wash. & Lee L.Rev. 933 (2008); Andrew Kull, *Restitution and Reform*, 32 So.Ill.U.L.J. 83–92 (2007); and Chaim Saiman, *Restating Restitution: A Case of Contemporary Common Law Conceptualism*, 52 Vill.L Rev. 487 (2007) (arguing that the Restatement has more in common with the high formalism of the nineteenth century than with contemporary modes of private law discourse). The interest in restitution is international in scope. *See, e.g.,* Peter Birks, *Unjust Enrichment* (2d rev.ed.2005) (Great Britain); Chaim Saiman, *Restitution in America: Why the U.S. Refuses to Join the Global Restitution Party*, 28 Oxford J.Leg.Stud. 99 (2008); I.M. Jackman, *The Varieties of Restitution* (1998) (Australia); Ross B. Grantham & Charles E.F. Rickett, *Enrichment and Restitution in New Zealand* (2000).

Another reason for the apparent revival of the law of unjust enrichment and restitution is a sense that unjust enrichment may be today's "new frontier" in the development of the common law. As Professor Rendleman has explained, where the limits of tort and contract have been reached, characterizing a case as involving unjust enrichment and requiring a restitutionary remedy can open the court's eyes to new possibilities. Doug Rendleman, *Common Law Restitution in the Mississippi Tobacco Settlement: Did the Smoke Get in Their Eyes?* 33 Ga.L.Rev. 847, 848–49 (1999). In this way, restitution has been explored as a solution to problems ranging from reparations for slavery to crime to employment discrimination to destructive products to human rights. *See, e.g.,* In re African-American Slave Descendants Litigation, 471 F.3d 754, 760 (7th Cir.2006), *cert. denied*, 552 U.S. 941 (2007) (denying suit on grounds of standing and statute of limitations); Tracy A. Thomas, *Bailouts, Bonuses, and the Return of Unjust Gains*, 87 Wash. U. L. Rev. 437 (2009) (discussing possible restitution remedies for redressing corporate misuse of government bailout funds); Candace S. Kovacic-Fleisher, *Restitution in Public Concern Cases*, 36 Loy.L.A.L.Rev. 901 (2003); Anthony J. Sebok, *Two Concepts of Injustice in Restitution for Slavery*, 84 B.U.L.Rev. 1405 (2004).

Analytically, the blackletter rules of restitution focus on three key inquiries: liability, procedure, and remedy.

1. *Liability*: By now, the Restatement's characterization of restitution as constituting—along with torts and contracts—the third main branch of civil liability has gained wide acceptance. Yet, while torts and contracts are mainstays of the first year curriculum, it usually falls to the remedies course to cover the substantive law of restitution.

The classic case establishing restitution at English common law is Moses v. Macferlan, 2 Burr. 1005, 1012, 97 Eng.Rep. 676, 681 (K.B.1760). In this case, Lord Mansfield explained that the obligation to make restitution comes into being when "the defendant, upon the circumstances of the case, is obliged by the ties of natural justice and equity to refund the money." The Restatement (Third) of Restitution attempts to avoid this problem by defining unjust enrichment in terms of legal, rather than moral obligations:

> The concern of restitution is not, in fact, with unjust enrichment in any such broad sense, but with a narrower set of circumstances giving rise to what might more appropriately be called *unjustified enrichment*. Compared to the open-ended implications of the term "unjust enrichment," instances of unjustified enrichment are both predictable and objectively determined, because the justification in question is not moral but legal. Unjustified enrichment is enrichment that lacks an adequate legal basis; it results from a transaction that the law treats as ineffective to work a conclusive alteration in ownership rights. Broadly speaking, an ineffective transaction for these purposes is one that is *nonconsensual*. Such a transaction may occur when the claimant's consent to the transaction is impaired for some reason. . . ; or when the claimant confers unrequested benefits without obtaining the recipient's agreement to pay for them . . . ; or when an attempted contractual exchange miscarries after partial performance . . . ; or when the defendant acquires benefits by wrongful interference with the claimant's rights [or] [a] residual set of cases, in which benefits are conferred on the recipient by a third party (rather than by the claimant). . . .

Restatement (Third) of Restitution, § 1 comment *b*.

The main limitation is that "there is no liability in restitution for an unrequested benefit voluntarily conferred." *Id.* § 2(3). A valid gift is not a source of unjust enrichment, unless it is a gift induced by mistake, fraud, or undue influence. *Id.* As Judge Posner colorfully explained:

> If while you are sitting on your porch sipping Margaritas a trio of itinerant musicians serenades you with mandolin, lute, and hautboy, you have no obligation, in the absence of a contract, to pay them for their performance no matter how much you enjoyed it; and likewise if they were gardeners whom you had hired and

on a break from their gardening they took up their musical instruments to serenade you.

Indiana Lumbermens Mut. Ins. Co. v. Reinsurance Results, Inc., 513 F.3d 652 (7th Cir. 2008) (Posner, J.). It is not simply the receipt of a benefit, but the unjust or unjustified retention of that benefit, that forms the basis of liability.

2. *Procedure.* The original Restatement of Restitution grouped the many historical restitution writs into two main procedures, quasi-contract and constructive trust, corresponding to the two kinds of actions that lawyers then used most frequently to bring claims based on a theory of unjust enrichment. Quasi-contract claims were closely associated with the common law form restitution and constructive trust was the main restitution device developed in courts of equity. However, there are more restitution forms of action than these two. Other restitutionary remedies at law include quantum meruit, rescission, and replevin; courts of equity also had the equitable lien and accounting for profits. In addition, actions for third-party reimbursement like subrogation, contribution, and indemnification sound in restitution.

The importance of selecting the proper restitutionary procedural mechanism is that each historic device comes with its own rules for application and own default measurement. Thus, for example, constructive trust often requires fraud and prior actual ownership of the property by plaintiff, and measures the disgorgement by the appreciated measure of profits. In addition, the equitable devices permit tracing, allowing the plaintiff to trace monies through various conversions and possession in order to recover.

3. *Remedy.* As with tort and contract remedies, the concept of rightful position is critical to understanding restitutionary remedies. Instead of aiming at the plaintiff's rightful position, however, restitution aims at the defendant's. Disgorgement is the key concept. By making the defendant disgorge the benefits she cannot justly retain, the law of restitution returns the defendant to the position she should, "in equity and good conscience," have occupied. Measuring the defendant's gain uses the same measures of value that are used with damages, such as market value, replacement, repair, and use value.

As we will see in the following cases, plaintiffs will generally elect restitution in three types of cases: (1) when unjust enrichment is the only source of liability; (2) when they prefers to measure recovery by defendant's gain, either because it exceeds plaintiff's loss or because it is easier to measure; and (3) when they prefers specific restitution, either because defendant is insolvent, because the thing plaintiff lost has changed in value, or because plaintiff values the thing he lost for nonmarket reasons. Laycock, *Restitution, supra.*

B. LIABILITY FOR RESTITUTION

The word "restitution" is used to connote both the liability and the remedy, unlike the case in tort where for example, the liability is negligence and the remedy is damages. When a plaintiff seeks the remedy of restitution, it must frame its claim of liability as one for "restitution" or unjust enrichment. Liability in restitution can be based on an independent wrong or a mistaken transfer of a benefit. Where there is an existing wrong that independently violates another tort or contract law, then the wrongfulness of the conduct is established, and the question is merely whether the plaintiff can elect to choose to sue in restitution for the larger recovery of defendant's gain. But restitution also establishes liability for unjust enrichment on lesser conduct than an independent wrong. Restitution is an alternative basis of liability apart from existing contract and tort, and thus it can establish liability for the unjust enrichment when no other liability exists.

Three patterns of "unjust" behavior tend to be repeated in the cases. In the first, the plaintiff has conferred a benefit on the defendant that the defendant did not request. In the second pattern, the plaintiff has conferred a benefit on the defendant at the defendant's request—perhaps pursuant to a contract—and, rather than attempting to enforce the contract, the plaintiff prefers to seek the return of his performance or its value. In the third pattern, the defendant has acquired a benefit tortiously or by other wrongdoing.

The main limitations on liability are that blackletter rules provide that a volunteer cannot recover for the benefit she gifts. These questions, often involved in family disputes, provide one of the ripe grounds for expanded use of the liability theory of unjust enrichment, as the next case shows.

LEWIS v. LEWIS
Supreme Court of Colorado
189 P.3d 1134 (2008)

JUSTICE MARTINEZ delivered the Opinion of the Court.

The trial court found that the defendants were unjustly enriched when they failed to compensate the plaintiff for her contribution to a home that was sold for a significant profit. * * *

We hold that claims of unjust enrichment by close family members or confidants should be evaluated by considering the mutual purpose of the parties. To determine unjust enrichment in situations involving a failed gift or failed contract between close family members and confidants, trial courts must determine whether there existed a mutual purpose between the parties. If such a purpose did exist and one party profited from a significant deviation from this mutual purpose, that party is unjustly enriched.

Applying this standard to the present case, we find support in the record for the trial court's determination that the plaintiff's in-laws purchased the home so that their son and daughter-in-law could have the benefits of home ownership. As a consequence, we find that the trial court did not abuse its discretion when it determined that the defendants in the case were unjustly enriched.

I.   FACTS AND PROCEDURAL HISTORY

Cassandra Lewis asserts that her ex-in-laws were unjustly enriched through the sale of the house where Cassandra and her husband Sammy lived from June 1986 to September 2000. On September 6, 1984, Cassandra and Sammy Lewis were married. Over the next two years, the couple lived with Sammy's parents, Frank and Lucy Lewis. After the birth of their daughter in February 1986, Cassandra and Sammy began looking for a place of their own to either rent or purchase. One house they considered was at 403 Division Avenue in Platteville, but on the advice of Frank Lewis, they decided against purchasing it because it needed too much work. Although Frank Lewis discouraged Cassandra and Sammy from buying the property, he and Lucy Lewis surreptitiously purchased the home on May 20, 1986. When Cassandra and Sammy found out that the Lewises bought the house, the Lewises told them that they meant the purchase to be a surprise gift for Cassandra and Sammy.

Frank Lewis purchased the house for a sale price of $29,500. He made a $5,000 down payment and executed a mortgage to the seller for the balance. The mortgage was calculated over twenty years with monthly payments of principal plus interest of $236.43. Cassandra and Sammy made the monthly mortgage payments, paying $236.46 directly to the Lewises. The Lewises then paid that same amount to the mortgage holder. At trial, Cassandra testified that the Lewises told her "that they put down $5,000 as a gift on the house as a surprise for us." The trial court made a factual finding that the Lewises proposed this arrangement to "ensure that the payments were made because [the Lewises] were concerned that Sammy had a drinking problem and that payments might not otherwise be made on time." The court further found that Cassandra and Sammy faithfully made all the payments for the fourteen years they occupied the house prior to their separation.

In addition to paying the Lewises the mortgage amount due each month, Cassandra and Sammy were named the insureds on the homeowner's insurance policy. The trial court found that Cassandra and Sammy paid the full cost of insuring the house. The trial court also found that when the property suffered a loss, such as hail damage, the insurance benefits were paid directly to Cassandra and Sammy. Cassandra and Sammy paid the real estate taxes, utilities, and all maintenance costs. Each of these bills were mailed directly to Cassandra and Sammy. Likewise, Cassandra and Sammy paid each bill directly to the party owed.

Further, Cassandra and Sammy presented themselves as owners of the property. The trial court made a finding of fact that when hearings were held to determine whether Platteville would put in a new sewer line, Cassandra and Sammy attended the hearings and spoke as the property's owners. They also undertook various improvements to the property. Over the fourteen years in which Cassandra and Sammy lived in the house, they added carpet, vinyl flooring for the kitchen and bathroom, tiled the laundry room, painted the interior and exterior of the house "a couple of times," removed old wallpaper and put up new wallpaper, replaced light fixtures, vanities, and mirrors, and added ceiling fans in three rooms.

As for the exterior of the house, the trial court found that Cassandra and Sammy first put in a rock driveway and later replaced it with concrete. They put up a chain link fence, installed a satellite dish, and built an above-ground swimming pool. In addition, Cassandra and Sammy cleared space for and installed a basketball court on the property. They also laid new sod.

The trial court made a specific factual finding that at no point did Cassandra and Sammy seek the approval of the Lewises when they undertook these improvements. No evidence was presented and the trial court did not find that the Lewises contributed financially to any of these improvements, aside from some early cleanup work before the house was habitable.

After the birth of their second child in 1992, Cassandra and Sammy began looking for a larger home. The trial court found that during this time, the Lewises told Cassandra and Sammy "that they should not sell the property but should instead rent it out and use the rental income to pay for the new home." Cassandra and Sammy decided to build an addition to the house. The record indicates and the trial court found that the Lewises did not hire the contractor, nor sign the construction contract; rather, Cassandra and Sammy did.

Throughout the fourteen years, the parties made several comments concerning property ownership. Besides putting the title in their name because of Sammy's drinking problem, the trial court found that the Lewises assured Cassandra "that the house was hers and she could live there as long as she wanted." Some years later, Frank Lewis was asked by his six-year-old granddaughter, "Grandpa, when is this going to be our house?" Frank Lewis claimed to have responded that it was her house, as long as her parents paid the rent. Frank Lewis testified that he told Cassandra the same thing. Cassandra disputed this claim.

The trial court made a factual finding that at one point during the fourteen years in which Cassandra and Sammy occupied the residence, "Frank Lewis went to the County to try to change the title out of his and Lucy Lewis' names and into [Cassandra] and Sammy's." However, when he was told by county officials that he must first refinance the property to put it in Cassandra and Sammy's names, he did not follow through on the title change. Frank Lewis testified that he decided to sell the house to Cassandra and Sammy, presumably for the remaining balance plus the $5,000 down payment, but that sale never occurred.

Frank Lewis further testified that he told Sammy he could purchase the house if he paid back the $5,000 down payment and refinanced the loan to assume the remaining balance owed. Both Lucy and Frank Lewis conceded that while Sammy was aware of this option, Cassandra was never told that the house could be purchased by repaying the down payment.

After sixteen years of marriage and fourteen years living at the Platteville residence, Cassandra, along with her two daughters moved out in September 2000. Less than two months later, on November 22, 2000, the Lewises sold the house to an unrelated buyer for $122,000. The net proceeds from the sale of the house were $108,879.86. Cassandra and Sammy's marriage dissolution was finalized on April 20, 2002. The dissolution did not include reference to the house, and Cassandra received no compensation from the sale.

Cassandra filed suit against the Lewises claiming ownership of the Platteville home. At trial, Cassandra argued that the Lewises gave Cassandra and Sammy the house as a gift and that the court should enforce the gift and give Cassandra and Sammy the house. In the alternative, Cassandra asserted that the court should enforce the parties' mutual desire that the property be sold to Cassandra and Sammy upon payment of the remaining balance of the note and reimbursement for the down payment. However, because Cassandra was unaware of the option to purchase the house before it was sold to the unrelated party, she asserted that the only way to enforce the mutual purpose of the parties and to prevent the unjust enrichment of the Lewises was to place her in the shoes of the seller at the time of the house was sold. Under this theory, she would be entitled to the Lewises net proceeds of $108,879.86 minus the $5,000 down payment.

The Lewises' main argument against Cassandra's ownership claim was that they were renting the property to Cassandra and Sammy for the fourteen years in question. During that time, however, the Lewises neither raised the rent from the original $236.43 nor reported the monthly payments as income. Further, the Lewises did not pay for the refurbishment and updating that is customary when owning rental property. In addition, the Lewises did not claim rental property deductions on their tax returns for any of the fourteen years.

Following the presentation of evidence, the trial court made its ruling from the bench. "ORDERED that judgment enter in favor of Plaintiff and against Defendants in the amount of $17,345.37. Plaintiff is also awarded costs."

On the minute order, the court noted that this amount was the difference between the original sale price of the house, $29,500, and the amount owed on the mortgage at the time of the sale, $12,154.63. Cassandra's costs came to $1,411.20.

Cassandra appealed, and the Lewises cross-appealed. Cassandra claimed that the trial court erred when it failed to find in her favor for the entire sale price, minus the existing mortgage and down payment. The Lewises countered that the trial court's partial finding for Cassandra was unsupported by the facts and unreasonable under the applicable law. Upon review, the court of appeals vacated the trial court's judgment. * * *

On remand, the trial court made extensive factual findings from the trial record and supporting documents. It explained that its first ruling, awarding Cassandra $17,345.37, was wrong. It then entered a new, different ruling in Cassandra's favor, and explained the legal basis for the new decision.

Among the court's factual findings were the following. The court ruled that Cassandra failed to prove that the house was a gift to her and Sammy from the Lewises. However, the trial court concluded that there was an oral agreement between the parties that allowed Cassandra and Sammy to acquire legal title to the property if they refinanced the loan balance and reimbursed the Lewises for the $5,000 down payment. The trial court further found that in making its first ruling it believed that "although only [Sammy] had actual knowledge of the agreement, [Cassandra] had 'constructive knowledge' of it by her being married to [the Lewises'] son."

In support of its finding that Cassandra and Sammy had the option to purchase the house, the trial court found that the Lewises "had an identical agreement with another son" regarding a different piece of property, adjacent to 403 Division Avenue in Platteville. The court noted that evidence presented at trial "revealed that the other son purchased that property by paying the down payment and paying off the indebtedness," at which point the Lewises conveyed the property to him. The trial court concluded that the Lewises offered the same agreement to Cassandra and Sammy.

After stating its factual findings, the trial court changed its ruling. It stated, "The court concludes that it was in error in its award of damages." The court then awarded Cassandra $103,879.86. This amount was the sale price, $122,000, minus the remaining balance on the note, $12,154.63, and the $5,000 down payment. * * *

As a consequence of the Lewises' quick sale of the property, the trial court found that Cassandra was prevented from acquiring the value in the property. Instead, the court concluded that they merely "paid rent and performed maintenance and improvements at their own expense." Conversely, the Lewises "profited from [Cassandra and Sammy]'s efforts in the form of the increased value they received when [they] sold the property." Consequently, the Lewises unfairly benefited from the sale, causing the trial court to conclude that "if it weren't for the special trust relied upon by [Cassandra and Sammy] because of the familial relationship, the agreement would have been reduced to writing or [Cassandra and Sammy] would have chosen to purchase another property instead of continuing to 'rent' from [the Lewises]."

The trial court cited two legal bases for its decision that Cassandra was due the profits from the sale of the house. First, the trial court concluded that Cassandra should recover on a theory of resulting trust. Second, the court determined that Cassandra should recover on a theory of unjust enrichment.

The Lewises appealed Cassandra's award of $103,879.86. The court of appeals held that Cassandra could not recover under resulting trust because there was no express trust, nor did the Lewises intend that a third-party vendor convey the property. Furthermore, the court of appeals found that the Lewises were not unjustly enriched when they sold the property * * * finding that Cassandra and Sammy's failure to take advantage of their purchase option before the Lewises sold the property made them mere tenants, without standing to claim an ownership right or an equity loss. As a consequence, the court of appeals concluded that the enrichment of the Lewises by the contribution of Cassandra and Sammy to the property was not unjust.

To analyze whether the trial court abused its discretion, we reexamine the third prong of unjust enrichment and apply it to the specific circumstance presented here. In so doing, we find that claims of unjust enrichment by close family members or confidants require that the trial court employ a particularized legal standard to evaluate the parties' commonality of purpose. When an enriched party deviates significantly from this mutual purpose, resulting in his enrichment at the expense of the close family member or confidant, he has been unjustly enriched.

* * *

III. UNJUST ENRICHMENT BETWEEN CLOSE FAMILY MEMBERS OR CONFIDANTS

A person is unjustly enriched when he benefits as a result of an unfair detriment to another. The proper remedy upon a finding of unjust enrichment is to restore the harmed party "to the position he formerly occupied either by the return of something which he formerly had or by the receipt of its monetary equivalent." Restatement of Restitution § 1 cmt. a (1937).

The claim of unjust enrichment is a judicially-created remedy designed to undo the benefit to one party that comes at the unfair detriment of another. Unjust enrichment is based on principles commonly associated with restitution. "When restitution is the primary basis of a claim, as opposed to a remedy for bargains gone awry, it invokes what has been called a 'contract implied in law.' " As such, it is an equitable remedy and does not depend on any contract, oral or written.

We have previously determined that a party claiming unjust enrichment must prove that (1) the defendant received a benefit (2) at the plaintiff's expense (3) under circumstances that would make it unjust for the defendant to retain the benefit without commensurate compensation. We do not question the determination that the Lewises were conferred a benefit at Cassandra's expense. Instead, we turn our attention to the third prong consideration of whether the enrichment was unjust, which creates difficult questions for trial courts. We have not previously addressed this third prong in circumstances similar to the case before us now. * * *

The case before us presents the difficult but not altogether uncommon circumstance of a failed gift or failed contract between close family members or confidants, resulting in a claim of unjust enrichment. By considering the factual basis, the court may better understand the parties' intentions when they entered into the agreement. However, claims of unjust enrichment arising from the implicit assumptions inherent in an arrangement between close family members or confidants bear little similarity to the circumstance for which we required malfeasance. * * * In the circumstance of a failed gift or contract between close family members or confidants, the claim arises from the close relationship, the mutual purpose, and the often ill-defined agreement of the parties. Thus, we do not apply the requirement of malfeasance from *DCB* to the third prong of the test for unjust enrichment to these types of factual circumstances. Instead, claims involving close family members or confidants are a consequence of a significant deviation from the mutual purpose. Thus, we find the need for a particularized third prong analysis for such circumstances.

Claims arising between close family members or confidants, where one party reasonably relies on the assertions of another in absence of a written document stems from a confidential relationship between the parties. Such a relationship exists when one party justifiably reposes confidence in another such that the parties drop their guard and assume that each side is acting fairly. A confidential relationship between dealing parties may "impel or induce one party to relax the care and vigilance one would and should ordinarily exercise in dealing with a stranger." Further, a confidential relationship may serve as indication of fiduciary status.

Further, in various familial legal circumstances, we have found that the parties' mutuality of purpose in agreeing to the gift or making the agreement is informative in determining whether one party has been unjustly enriched.

Borrowing from this diverse jurisprudence, we find that the unifying element is the commonality of purpose of the parties. In addition, in other factual circumstances we have looked to the intentions, expectations, and behavior of the parties to determine whether recovery in unjust enrichment is appropriate. Consequently, we hold that the parties' actions expressing mutual purpose should govern the third prong of unjust enrichment when trial courts consider situations involving failed gifts or failed contracts between close family members or confidants. In such cases, malfeasance is not necessary to make a claim of unjust enrichment. Instead, we conclude that when close family members or confidants act with a mutual purpose, unjust enrichment occurs when one party benefits from an action that is a significant deviation from that mutual purpose.

Courts considering the third prong of an unjust enrichment claim arising from a confidential relationship should look to the factual support establishing the mutuality of purpose of both the giving and receiving parties. This includes a determination by the trial court of whether both parties' actions indicate that each party possessed the same or similar purpose. In particular, the trial court should consider whether either party acted in furtherance of or detrimentally relied on the gift or agreement. Finally, the court should consider the length of time that the parties acted in furtherance of this misunderstanding. In the event that the parties intended the same outcome or the parties' mutual purpose is easily discernable, the trial court should seek by its equity determination to fulfill this failed mutual purpose when one party benefits from acting in significant deviation with this mutual purpose.

IV. Unjust Enrichment in the Present Case

Here, the trial court determined that a confidential relationship existed between Cassandra and the Lewises. The trial court stated that "[Cassandra] and her husband reasonably relied upon the confidential relationship between the parties in not requiring that the agreement be in writing." Further, in its order on remand, the trial court stated that "if it weren't for the special trust relied upon by [Cassandra] and Sammy because of the familial relationship, the agreement would have been reduced to writing or [Cassandra] and Sammy would have chosen to purchase another property instead of continuing to 'rent' from the [Lewises]." We find no basis in the record to dispute this finding. The record supports the conclusion that Cassandra and Sammy reasonably relied on the close relationship they had with the Lewises. Thus, we find persuasive the trial court's determination that the parties' relationship was confidential, which required that the parties deal fairly with one another.

Because there is no question that the Lewises were enriched by the contributions of Cassandra and Sammy, we turn to the third prong of the analysis, namely whether the Lewises were unjustly enriched when they sold the Platteville property, despite the existence of confidential relationship indicating that the parties' mutual intent was that Cassandra and Sammy have the benefits of home ownership. We find that while the trial court did not express the particularized third prong analysis as we do today, it understood that to reach a finding of unjust enrichment, there must be a deviation from a mutual purpose, and it correctly applied that analysis in ruling for Cassandra.

Specifically, we find that the trial court correctly determined that, in light of the confidential relationship, both parties intended that Cassandra and Sammy obtain full and complete possession of the property. The trial court made factual findings demonstrating that by initially purchasing the Platteville home and encouraging Cassandra and Sammy to live there like owners, the Lewises intended that Cassandra and Sammy enjoy the benefits of home ownership. Further, we find support in the record for the trial court's determination that Cassandra and Sammy acted as though they owned or would own the property, while the Lewises did nothing to counter this perception. For instance, the trial court found that each month Cassandra and Sammy provided a check to the Lewises in the amount of the mortgage. Moreover, the record supports the trial court's conclusion that when routine maintenance was necessary, Cassandra and Sammy performed it themselves or paid others to complete the work. Additionally, the trial court determined that when the house proved too small for their growing family, Cassandra and Sammy constructed an addition to the house. The trial court also found it noteworthy, as do we, that Cassandra and Sammy paid the property taxes on the property, and that the Lewises did not declare the rental property on their income taxes.

These factual findings support the trial court's determination that the parties' mutual purpose in acquiring the home was that Cassandra and Sammy enjoy the benefits of home ownership. The trial court's findings also indicate that Cassandra and Sammy's actions in maintaining and improving the property at their own expense demonstrated this mutual intent. Furthermore, the Lewises presented no evidence and the trial court found no support in the record for the Lewises' claim that Cassandra and Sammy were merely renters. In fact, the trial court found, with adequate support in the record, that the Lewises failed to make any substantive attempt to clarify their ownership claim over the fourteen years in which the parties relied on these assumptions.

In sum, we find support for the trial court's conclusion that the Lewises intended to give Cassandra and Sammy the benefits of home ownership, not reap those benefits for themselves. Consequently, when they sold the house without providing Cassandra the opportunity to assume ownership, the Lewises were unjustly enriched as a result of acting in significant deviation from the parties' mutual purpose. Thus, the trial court applied the correct legal analysis and acted within its discretion in finding that the Lewises were unjustly enriched when the Lewises deviated significantly from the mutual purpose indicated by the parties' actions over the previous fourteen years.

V. CONCLUSION

We hold that the trial court acted within its discretion when it determined that the Lewises were unjustly enriched by the sale of the Platteville house. We therefore overturn the decision of the court of appeals and order that the court of appeals reinstate the trial court's ruling in Cassandra's favor for $103,879.86.

JUSTICE EID, dissenting.

The majority's opinion permits Cassandra to recover the full value of the home owned by the Lewises under a claim of unjust enrichment. In order to reach this result, the majority devises a theory of recovery that enforces the "mutual purpose of the parties." The major flaw with the majority's theory is that it bears no resemblance to the unjust enrichment cause of action. I could not find a single reported case in this jurisdiction (or any other, for that matter) that recognized a "mutual purpose of the parties" theory of unjust enrichment. That is because unjust enrichment is not focused on the intent of the parties, as the majority seems to believe, but rather on the benefit conferred, if any, by the plaintiff that is unjustly retained by the defendant. The consequence of the majority's interpretation is that it awards full benefit of the bargain damages—that is, the value of the home—to Cassandra, even though no bargain ever existed. Because I believe the majority's opinion reflects a fundamental misunderstanding of the law of unjust enrichment, I respectfully dissent.

In order to prevail on a claim for unjust enrichment, the plaintiff must show that she conferred a benefit on the defendant "under circumstances that would make it unjust for defendant *to retain the benefit without paying.*" Thus, the centerpiece of an unjust enrichment claim is the benefit that has been unjustly retained. Here, the majority makes virtually no attempt to determine whether Cassandra has conferred a benefit on the Lewises, and if so, what that benefit might be; nor does it attempt to quantify that benefit in order to determine what the Lewises may have unjustly "retain[ed] . . . without paying." In other words, it makes no attempt to apply the elements of unjust enrichment as they have been traditionally understood in this and other jurisdictions.

Instead, the majority forges a new cause of action for "a failed gift or failed contract between close family members or confidants." According to the majority, this new cause of action, as applied to Cassandra, is based on the facts that (1) the parties had an agreement (i.e., a "mutual purpose") to convey the benefits of home ownership to Cassandra and Sammy, (2) the Lewises breached (i.e., "deviated significantly from") that agreement, and (3) Cassandra suffered damages as a result of the breach. But these are the elements of a claim for breach of contract, not unjust enrichment. The consequence of the majority's flawed analysis is that Cassandra is awarded contract damages where no contract existed.

The trial court calculated damages by subtracting the remaining mortgage and the Lewises' $5,000 down payment from the sale price of the home. In other words, the court placed Cassandra in the position she would have been in had there been a contract to transfer ownership of the home to her, including awarding her full expectation damages such as the increase in value of the home due to market conditions. But because she does not have such a contract claim, the trial court erred by awarding contract damages, and the majority errs by applying contract principles, under the guise of unjust enrichment, to uphold the trial court's award.

The majority comes up with its "mutual purpose of the parties" cause of action by "[b]orrowing from . . . diverse jurisprudence," including trust and family law. Yet it ignores precedent precisely on point in the field of unjust enrichment. For example, in Salzman v. Bachrach, 996 P.2d 1263 (Colo.2000), we examined an unjust enrichment claim strikingly similar to Cassandra's. In that case, plaintiff and defendant "agreed to build a home together" to serve as their residence. Plaintiff designed the home and paid almost $170,000 of the construction costs. Soon after they moved into the home, plaintiff quitclaimed his interest in the home to defendant, ostensibly so that she could obtain a favorable mortgage on the home and for the tax advantages. After a little more than a year of living together in the home, defendant changed the locks and essentially evicted plaintiff. Plaintiff brought an unjust enrichment claim against defendant.

In analyzing plaintiff's claim, we did not seek, as the majority does today, to discern a "mutual agreement of the parties," even though there was evidence that they had some sort of an agreement with regard to how the expenses would be shared. Instead, we focused on whether plaintiff had conferred a benefit on defendant that was unjustly retained. We concluded that he had. Specifically, we found that he paid "nearly $170,000" toward construction costs of the home and expended considerable effort in "designing the home and managing the project." On remand, we instructed the trial court to "determine the exact worth of [plaintiff's] contribution [to building the home] to date, and the reasonable rental value for the periods [defendant] lived in the house." In other words, we found that the proper measure of damages would be the net benefit unjustly retained by the defendant—that is, the "exact worth of [plaintiff's] contribution" to the home, less the "reasonable rental value" he would have paid to live there.

Applying *Salzman's* analysis (that is, the elements of unjust enrichment) to the facts of this case, the trial court should have determined what net benefit, if any, Cassandra conferred on the Lewises. For example, over the fourteen years of living in the home, Cassandra and Sammy paid $236 per month to the Lewises to cover the mortgage payment; paid the real estate taxes; paid the costs of maintaining the home, including homeowner's insurance; and paid for various improvements to the home. These are costs that Cassandra and Sammy paid that benefited the

Lewises. On the other hand, Cassandra and Sammy received a place to live for fourteen years at far below market cost. As in *Salzman,* I would instruct the trial court to calculate the net benefit that Cassandra conferred on the Lewises, if any—that is, the benefit she conferred on the Lewises minus the rent she would have paid at market value. This calculation will necessarily require the trial court to determine what portion of the benefit should be attributed to Cassandra, as opposed to Sammy.[3]

Plainly, the effect of today's decision is to untether unjust enrichment from its central focus on the benefit conferred by the plaintiff on the defendant. The majority attempts to gloss over this fundamental shift in unjust enrichment law by stating that "the Lewises intended to give Cassandra and Sammy the benefits of home ownership, not reap those benefits for themselves," the implication being that one of those benefits is the ability to sell a home for profit. However, it is irrelevant whether the Lewises intended to convey the benefits of home ownership, or any other benefits, to Cassandra. This is because, as discussed above, the centerpiece of unjust enrichment is the value of the benefit conferred *by Cassandra on the Lewises,* not the other way around. Consequently, the majority's consideration of the benefit intended to be conferred *by the Lewises on Cassandra* turns this fundamental rule on its head.

OLWELL V. NYE & NISSEN

Supreme Court of Washington
173 P.2d 652 (Wash. 1946)

MALLERY, JUSTICE.

On May 6, 1940, plaintiff, E.L. Olwell, sold and transferred to the defendant corporation his one-half interest in Puget Sound Egg Packers, a Washington corporation having its principal place of business in Tacoma. By the terms of the agreement, the plaintiff was to retain full ownership in an "Eggsact" egg-washing machine, formerly used by Puget Sound Egg Packers. The defendant promised to make it available for delivery to the plaintiff on or before June 15, 1940. It appears that the plaintiff arranged for and had the machine stored in a space adjacent to the premises occupied by the defendant but not covered by its lease. Due to the scarcity of labor immediately after the outbreak of the war, defendant's treasurer, without the knowledge or consent of the plaintiff, ordered the egg washer taken out of storage. The machine was put into operation by defendant on May 31, 1941, and thereafter for a period of three years was used approximately one day a week in the regular course of the defendant's business. Plaintiff

---

[3]   The majority does not account for the fact that Cassandra and Sammy paid costs jointly. Even under its own analysis, and assuming *arguendo* that the Lewises did indeed intend "to give Cassandra and Sammy the benefits of home ownership," it follows that Cassandra must share any recovery with Sammy, the other beneficiary of the parties' "mutual purpose." In other words, even under the majority's analysis, Cassandra would not be entitled to recover the full sale price of the home

first discovered this use in January or February of 1945 when he happened to be at the plant on business and heard the machine operating. Thereupon plaintiff offered to sell the machine to defendant for $600 or half of its original cost in 1929. A counter offer of $50 was refused and approximately one month later this action was commenced to recover the reasonable value of defendant's use of the machine, and praying for $25 per month from the commencement of the unauthorized use until the time of trial. * * * The court entered judgment for plaintiff in the amount of $10 per week for the period of 156 weeks covered by the statute of limitations, or $1,560, and gave the plaintiff his costs.

The theory of the respondent was that the tort of conversion could be "waived" and suit brought in quasi-contract, upon a contract implied in law, to recover, as restitution, the profits which inured to appellant as a result of its wrongful use of the machine. With this the trial court agreed and in its findings of facts found that the use of the machine "resulted in a benefit to the users, in that said use saves the users approximately $1.43 per hour of use as against the expense which would be incurred were eggs to be washed by hand; that said machine was used by Puget Sound Egg Packers and defendant, on an average of one day per week from May of 1941, until February of 1945 at an average saving of $10.00 per each day of use."

In substance, the argument presented by the assignments of error is that the principle of unjust enrichment, or quasi-contract, is not of universal application, but is imposed only in exceptional cases because of special facts and circumstances and in favor of particular persons; that respondent had an adequate remedy in an action at law for replevin or claim and delivery; that any damages awarded to the plaintiff should be based upon the use or rental value of the machine and should bear some reasonable relation to its market value. * * *

It is uniformly held that in cases where the defendant *tortfeasor* has benefitted by his wrong, the plaintiff may elect to "waive the tort" and bring an action in assumpsit for restitution. Such an action arises out of a duty imposed by law devolving upon the defendant to repay an unjust and unmerited enrichment.

It is clear that the saving in labor cost which appellant derived from its use of respondent's machine constituted a benefit.

According to the Restatement of Restitution, § 1(b), p. 12,

"A person confers a benefit upon another if he gives to the other possession of or some other interest in money, land, chattels, or choses in action, performs services beneficial to or at the request of the other, satisfies a debt or a duty of the other, or in any way adds to the other's security or advantage. *He confers a benefit not only where he adds to the property of another, but also where he* saves the other from expense or loss. The word 'benefit', therefore denotes any form of advantage." (Italics ours)

It is also necessary to show that while appellant benefitted from its use of the egg-washing machine, respondent thereby incurred a loss. It is argued by appellant that since the machine was put into storage by respondent, who had no present use for it, and for a period of almost three years did not know that appellant was operating it and since it was not injured by its operation and the appellant never adversely claimed any title to it, nor contested respondent's right of repossession upon the latter's discovery of the wrongful operation, that the respondent was not damaged because he is as well off as if the machine had not been used by appellant.

The very essence of the nature of property is the right to its exclusive use. Without it, no beneficial right remains. However plausible, the appellant cannot be heard to say that his wrongful invasion of the respondent's property right to exclusive use is not a loss compensable in law. To hold otherwise would be subversive of all property rights since his use was admittedly wrongful and without claim of right. The theory of unjust enrichment is applicable in such a case.

We agree with appellant that respondent could have elected a "common garden variety of action," as he calls it, for the recovery of damages. It is also true that except where provided for by statute, punitive damages are not allowed, the basic measure for the recovery of damages in this state being compensation. If, then, respondent had been *limited* to redress *in tort* for damages, as appellant contends, the court below would be in error in refusing to make a finding as to the value of the machine. In such case the award of damages must bear a reasonable relation to the value of the property.

But respondent here had an election. He chose rather to waive his right of action *in tort* and to sue *in assumpsit* on the implied contract. Having so elected, he is entitled to the measure of restoration which accompanies the remedy.

> Actions for restitution have for their primary purpose taking from the defendant and restoring to the plaintiff something to which the plaintiff is entitled, or if this is not done, causing the defendant to pay the plaintiff an amount which will restore the plaintiff to the position in which he was before the defendant received the benefit. If the value of what was received and what was lost were always equal, there would be no substantial problem as to the amount of recovery, since actions of restitution are not punitive. In fact, however, the plaintiff frequently has lost more than the defendant has gained, and sometimes the defendant has gained more than the plaintiff has lost.

In such cases the measure of restitution is determined with reference to the tortiousness of the defendant's conduct or the negligence or other fault of one or both of the parties in creating the situation giving rise to the right to restitution. If the defendant was tortious in his acquisition of the benefit he is required to pay for what the other has lost although that is more than the recipient benefitted. *If he was consciously tortious in acquiring the benefit, he is also deprived of any profit derived from his subsequent dealing with it.* If he was no more at fault than the claimant, he is not required to pay for losses in excess of benefit received by him and he is permitted to retain gains which result from his dealing with the property.

Restatement of Restitution, pp. 595, 596.

Respondent may recover the profit derived by the appellant from the use of the machine.

[The court then held that the plaintiff could not recover more than he had prayed for in the complaint, and directed the trial court to reduce the judgment to $25.00 per month, or $900.]

NOTES

1.   *On liability.* As you may recall from contracts class, an implied-in-law contract is quite distinct from an implied-in-fact contract. A quasi-contract is an implied-in-law contract, a fiction, created by the court out of law as a vehicle for awarding restitutionary recovery. In contrast, an implied-in-fact contract is when the facts and the parties' behavior suggest that the recipient of a benefit implicitly promised to pay for it; this establishes an actual contract subject to all the usual contractual remedies of damages, specific performance, and modification.

2.   *On procedure.* "Assumpsit" was the common law form of action used to bring a quasi-contract claim. As you might remember from your civil procedure class, the forms of action were pleading devices. To bring a case in the law courts, the plaintiff had to fit it to one of the recognized forms, which were often highly technical. By "waiving" the tort form of action and suing in assumpsit, the plaintiff could base his claim on the benefit the defendant had received rather than on the loss caused by the tort.

Many jurisdictions have abandoned the forms of action in favor of modern rules of code or notice pleading under generalized "unjust enrichment." Under modern pleading, to bring a restitution case, or any other case, it is simply necessary to set forth the facts that entitle the plaintiff to relief. Yet, other jurisdictions continue to operate under the old technical forms of action, and understanding forms is helpful in reading the older cases.

3.   *The plaintiff's loss and the defendant's gain may be equal.* In such a case, "There [is] no substantial problem as to the amount of recovery, since actions of restitution are not punitive." Of course, if the plaintiff's loss and the

defendant's gain are equal, there is also no immediately apparent reason to sue in restitution. The plaintiff can sue in tort and recover the same amount. In such cases, there may be a conceptual difference between tort and restitution, but there is no practical difference in the amount recovered.

There may, however, be other practical consequences to the choice. Because of quasi-contract's distinct historical roots, some technical distinctions between tort and quasi-contract still exist. Thus, in some states, different rules with regard to the statute of limitations, survivorship, and sovereign immunity may apply depending on the plaintiff's choice of tort or quasi-contract. Practically, the defendant's gain may also be easier to prove with the evidence, thus making restitution the preferred remedial choice.

4.   Does allowing the election of recovery for defendant's profits in *Olwell* promote inefficiency? After all, the plaintiff had stored the egg machine in the closet and forgotten about it, while the defendant used it to provide food needed during war time. All the plaintiff lost was the opportunity to rent or sell the machine, as he could no longer use it himself after he sold the factory.

The law, however, supports efficiency through negotiated transactions; not opportunistic ones. Here is an explanation from the copyright context:

> It is true that if the infringer makes greater profits than the copyright owner lost, because the infringer is a more efficient producer than the owner or sells in a different market, the owner is allowed to capture the additional profit even though it does not represent a loss to him. It may seem wrong to penalize the infringer for his superior efficiency and give the owner a windfall. But it discourages infringement. By preventing infringers from obtaining any net profit it makes any would-be infringer negotiate directly with the owner of a copyright that he wants to use, rather than bypass the market by stealing the copyright and forcing the owner to seek compensation from the courts for his loss. Since the infringer's gain might exceed the owner's loss, especially as loss is measured by a court, limiting damages to that loss would not effectively deter this kind of forced exchange.

Taylor v. Meirick, 712 F.2d 1112 (7th Cir.1983).

The Restatement (Third) of Restitution § 39 explains the difference as one between an "efficient breach" and an "opportunistic" breach. An opportunistic breach is defined as deliberate and profitable. Is this a helpful distinction? Isn't this the very definition of an efficient breach too?

5.   *On measurement.* As *Olwell* begins to illustrate, there are multiple ways a court may choose to measure the defendant's gain. These include market value, profits, apportionment of profits, or cost savings. *See* Daniel Friedmann, *Restitution for Wrongs: The Measure of Recovery*, 79 Tex.L.Rev. 1879 (2001).

The *Olwell* court discussed the options of market value for either the rental or purchase of the machine, and then settled on the cost savings to the defendant. Despite *Olwell*'s assertions, restitution in quasi-contract for conversion has usually been measured by the value of the chattel. Restatement (Third) of Restitution and Unjust Enrichment § 51. Or why didn't the court measure the recovery by the percentage of the plant's profits proportionate to the increased production the machine made possible? Wouldn't that be a more accurate measure of the defendant's profits than the labor costs saved? Although the court did not explicitly consider the possibility, profits above the labor expenses saved are more directly attributable to the defendant's skill in marketing than to the egg-washing machine. After all, the defendant could have made those profits without infringing the plaintiff's rights simply by hiring more workers.

The classic hypothetical exploring the possible measures of disgorgement runs along these lines: If an artist steals paint, brushes and canvas and creates a masterpiece, can the victim of the theft recover the entire market value of the painting by way of restitution? The usual answer is no. The painting's value is largely the product of the artist's skill, not of the theft. Thus, at some point, it is inappropriate to measure restitution by profits, if the profits are primarily attributable to the defendant's skill and efforts, not to the wrongdoing. The plaintiff's recovery would be limited to the value of the stolen property.

Or, in a similar setting, a court might award an apportionment of profits. The leading case is Sheldon v. Metro-Goldwyn Pictures Corp., 309 U.S. 390 (1940). Metro-Goldwyn produced a movie that plagiarized the plaintiff's play. While Metro-Goldwyn was clearly liable to the plaintiff for the profits attributable to the infringement of plaintiff's copyright, the Court found it necessary to apportion the profits, because "[t]he testimony showed quite clearly that in the creation of profits from the exhibition of a motion picture, the talent and popularity of the 'motion picture stars' generally constitutes the main drawing power of the picture, and that this is especially true where the title of the picture is not identified with any well-known play or novel." 309 U.S. at 407. Therefore, the Court affirmed an award of twenty per cent of the net profits to the plaintiffs. Yet, in another case which we will discuss later in this chapter, the Supreme Court awarded all of the profits to the plaintiffs despite the defendant's creative contributions as a book author. Snepp v. United States, 444 U.S. 507 (1980).

Thus, as Professor Palmer has noted, there are "no easy formulas" to determine "whether, or the extent to which, the defendant's gain is the product not solely of the plaintiff's interest but also of contributions made by the defendant. * * * Instead, the court must resort to general considerations of fairness, taking into account the nature of the defendant's wrong, the relative extent of his contribution, and the feasibility of separating this from the contribution traceable to the plaintiff's interest." George E. Palmer, *Law of Restitution* § 2.12 at 161 (1978).

C. RESTITUTION REMEDIES

Once the basis for restitution is established by the existence of an unjust enrichment, the next analytical question is what restitution remedy is appropriate. The restitution remedy often provides both the procedural device for awarding restitution and the corresponding measure of recovery. Restitution developed in both law and equity; thus there are various specific remedial devices. In law, these were quasi-contract, quantum meruit, and rescission. In equity, the restitutionary devices were constructive trust, equitable lien, and accounting of profits. A few, rescission and accounting of profits, were available in both law and equity. There are also several restitutionary remedies designed for reconciling payments among multiple parties, including subrogation, indemnification, and contribution, commonly used today in insurance settings.

The first Restatement of Restitution tried to move away from these specific writs or choses in action to more generalized notions of restitution. It, however, maintained the two distinctions between legal restitution of quasi-contract and equitable restitution of constructive trust. Modern courts then moved further away from specific devices, adopting a unified restitution remedy for unjust enrichment. This developed was welcomed by attorneys and courts for eliminating archaic distinctions in restitution no longer relevant to a modern merged court and appreciating the core commonalities of all the procedures as one of restitution.

However, the U.S. Supreme Court revived the historic practice in a long series of cases of shockingly inconsistent cases interpreting the federal employee retirement and benefits statute, ERISA, which allows private actions for "equitable" but not legal relief. *See* Mertens v. Hewitt Associates, 508 U.S. 248 (1993); Great-West Life & Annuity Ins.Co. v. Knudson, 534 U.S. 204 (2002); Sereboff v. Mid Atlantic Medical Services, Inc., 547 U.S. 356 (2006); CIGNA Corp. v. Amara, 563 U.S. 421 (2011); US Airways, Inc. v. McCutchen, 569 U.S. ___, 133 S.Ct. 1537 (2013). All essentially involved insurance companies trying to seek repayment from their insureds who recovered damages from third parties. These cases delved into the minutia of long-forgotten causes of action and elements for recovery that had not been used for centuries, reaching crazily different results. Scholars argued that the Court got much of it wrong, both historically and as applied. *See* Tracy A. Thomas, *Justice Scalia Reinvents Restitution*, 36 Loyola L.Rev.L.A. 1063 (2003) (arguing that the Supreme Court incorrectly classified restitution and that equitable restitution is unrecognizable in the Court's decisions); John H. Langbein, *What ERISA Means by "Equitable": The Supreme Court's Trail of Error* in Russell, Mertens, *and* Great-West, 103 Colum. L. Rev. 1317, 1365 (2003); Colleen P. Murphy, *Misclassifying Monetary Restitution*, 55 S.M.U.L.Rev. 1577 (2002) (helpful discussion of the taxonomy of restitution). Attorneys and courts, however, are stuck with this evolving line of cases and tasked with the job of trying to make sense of it all.

MONTANILE V. BOARD OF TRUSTEES OF THE NATIONAL ELEVATOR INDUSTRY HEALTH BENEFIT PLAN

Supreme Court of the United States
577 U.S. ___, 136 S.Ct. 651 (2016)

JUSTICE THOMAS delivered the opinion of the Court.

When a third party injures a participant in an employee benefits plan under the Employee Retirement Income Security Act of 1974 (ERISA) the plan frequently pays covered medical expenses. The terms of these plans often include a subrogation clause requiring a participant to reimburse the plan if the participant later recovers money from the third party for his injuries. And under ERISA § 502(a)(3) plan fiduciaries can file civil suits "to obtain . . . appropriate equitable relief . . . to enforce . . . the terms of the plan."

In this case, we consider what happens when a participant obtains a settlement fund from a third party, but spends the whole settlement on nontraceable items (for instance, on services or consumable items like food). We evaluate in particular whether a plan fiduciary can sue under § 502(a)(3) to recover from the participant's remaining assets the medical expenses it paid on the participant's behalf. We hold that, when a participant dissipates the whole settlement on nontraceable items, the fiduciary cannot bring a suit to attach the participant's general assets under § 502(a)(3) because the suit is not one for "appropriate equitable relief." In this case, it is unclear whether the participant dissipated all of his settlement in this manner, so we remand for further proceedings.

I

Petitioner Robert Montanile was a participant in a health benefits plan governed by ERISA and administered by respondent, the Board of Trustees of the National Elevator Industry Health Benefit Plan. The plan must pay for certain medical expenses that beneficiaries or participants incur. The plan may demand reimbursement, however, when a participant recovers money from a third party for medical expenses. The plan states: "Amounts that have been recovered by a [participant] from another party are assets of the Plan . . . and are not distributable to any person or entity without the Plan's written release of its subrogation interest." The plan also provides that "any amounts" that a participant "recover[s] from another party by award, judgment, settlement or otherwise . . . will promptly be applied first to reimburse the Plan in full for benefits advanced by the Plan . . . and without reduction for attorneys' fees, costs, expenses or damages claimed by the covered person." * * *

In December 2008, a drunk driver ran through a stop sign and crashed into Montanile's vehicle. The accident severely injured Montanile, and the plan paid at least $121,044.02 for his initial medical care. Montanile signed a reimbursement agreement reaffirming his obligation to reimburse the plan from any recovery he obtained "as a result of any legal action or settlement or otherwise."

Thereafter, Montanile filed a negligence claim against the drunk driver and made a claim for uninsured motorist benefits under Montanile's car insurance. He obtained a $500,000 settlement. Montanile then paid his attorneys $200,000 and repaid about $60,000 that they had advanced him. Thus, about $240,000 remained of the settlement. Montanile's attorneys held most of that sum in a client trust account. This included enough money to satisfy Montanile's obligations to the plan.

The Board of Trustees sought reimbursement from Montanile on behalf of the plan, and Montanile's attorney argued that the plan was not entitled to any recovery. The parties attempted but failed to reach an agreement about reimbursement. After discussions broke down, Montanile's attorney informed the Board that he would distribute the remaining settlement funds to Montanile unless the Board objected within 14 days. The Board did not respond within that time, so Montanile's attorney gave Montanile the remainder of the funds.

Six months after negotiations ended, the Board sued Montanile in District Court under ERISA § 502(a)(3), seeking repayment of the $121,044.02 the plan had expended on his medical care. The Board asked the court to enforce an equitable lien upon any settlement funds or any property which are " 'in [Montanile's] actual or constructive possession.' " * * *

The District Court granted summary judgment to the Board. * * * The Court of Appeals for the Eleventh Circuit affirmed. It reasoned that a plan can always enforce an equitable lien once the lien attaches, and that dissipation of the specific fund to which the lien attached cannot destroy the underlying reimbursement obligation. The court therefore held that the plan can recover out of a participant's general assets when the participant dissipates the specifically identified fund. 593 Fed.Appx., at 908.

We granted certiorari to resolve a conflict among the Courts of Appeals over whether an ERISA fiduciary can enforce an equitable lien against a defendant's general assets under these circumstances. We hold that it cannot, and accordingly reverse the judgment of the Eleventh Circuit and remand for further proceedings.

II

A

As previously stated, § 502(a)(3) of ERISA authorizes plan fiduciaries like the Board of Trustees to bring civil suits "to obtain other appropriate equitable relief . . . to enforce . . . the terms of the plan." Our cases explain that the term "equitable relief" in § 502(a)(3) is limited to "those categories of relief that were *typically* available in equity" during the days of the divided bench (meaning, the period before 1938 when courts of law and equity were separate). Mertens v. Hewitt Associates, 508 U.S. 248, 256 (1993). Under this Court's precedents, whether the remedy a plaintiff seeks "is legal or equitable depends on [1] the basis for [the plaintiff's] claim and [(2)] the nature of the underlying remedies sought." Sereboff v. Mid Atlantic Medical Services, Inc., 547 U.S. 356, 363 (2006). Our precedents also prescribe a framework for resolving this inquiry. To determine how to characterize the basis of a plaintiff's claim and the nature of the remedies sought, we turn to standard treatises on equity, which establish the "basic contours" of what equitable relief was typically available in premerger equity courts. Great-West Life & Annuity Ins. Co. v. Knudson, 534 U.S. 204, 217 (2002).

We have employed this approach in three earlier cases where, as here, the plan fiduciary sought reimbursement for medical expenses after the plan beneficiary or participant recovered money from a third party. Under these precedents, the basis for the Board's claim is equitable. But our cases do not resolve whether the *remedy* the Board now seeks—enforcement of an equitable lien by agreement against the defendant's general assets—is equitable in nature.

First, in *Great-West,* we held that a plan with a claim for an equitable lien was—in the circumstances presented—seeking a legal rather than an equitable remedy. In that case, a plan sought to enforce an equitable lien by obtaining a money judgment from the defendants. The plan could not enforce the lien against the third-party settlement that the defendants had obtained because the defendants never actually possessed that fund; the fund went directly to the defendants' attorneys and to a restricted trust. We held that the plan sought a legal remedy, not an equitable one, even though the plan claimed that the money judgment was a form of restitution. We explained that restitution in equity typically involved enforcement of "a constructive trust or an equitable lien, where money or property identified as belonging in good conscience to the plaintiff could clearly be traced to particular funds or property in the defendant's possession." But the restitution sought in *Great-West* was legal—not equitable—because the specific funds to which the fiduciaries "claim[ed] an entitlement . . . [we]re not in [the defendants'] possession." Since both the basis for the claim and the particular remedy sought were not equitable, the plan could not sue under § 502(a)(3).

Next, in *Sereboff,* we held that both the basis for the claim and the remedy sought were equitable. The plan there sought reimbursement from beneficiaries who had retained their settlement fund in a separate account. We held that the basis for the plan's claim was equitable because the plan sought to enforce an equitable lien by agreement, a type of equitable lien created by an agreement to convey a particular fund to another party. The lien existed in *Sereboff* because of the beneficiaries' agreement with the plan to convey the proceeds of any third-party settlement. We explained that a claim to enforce such a lien is equitable because the plan "could rely on a familiar rul[e] of equity" to collect—specifically, the rule "that a contract to convey a specific object even before it is acquired will make the contractor a trustee as soon as he gets a title to the thing." The underlying remedies that the plan sought also were equitable, because the plan "sought specifically identifiable funds that were within the possession and control" of the beneficiaries—not recovery from the beneficiaries' "assets generally."

Finally, in *US Airways, Inc. v. McCutchen,* we reaffirmed our analysis in *Sereboff* and again concluded that a plan sought to enforce an equitable claim by seeking equitable remedies. As in *Sereboff,* "the basis for [the plan's] claim was equitable" because the plan's terms created an equitable lien by agreement on a third-party settlement. And, as in *Sereboff,* "[t]he nature of the recovery requested" by the plan "was equitable because [it] claimed specifically identifiable funds within the [beneficiaries'] control— that is, a portion of the settlement they had gotten."

Under these principles, the basis for the Board's claim here is equitable: The Board had an equitable lien by agreement that attached to Montanile's settlement fund when he obtained title to that fund. And the nature of the Board's underlying *remedy* would have been equitable had it immediately sued to enforce the lien against the settlement fund then in Montanile's possession. That does not resolve this case, however. Our prior cases do not address whether a plan is still seeking an equitable remedy when the defendant, who once possessed the settlement fund, has dissipated it all, and the plan then seeks to recover out of the defendant's general assets.

B

To resolve this issue, we turn to standard equity treatises. As we explain below, those treatises make clear that a plaintiff could ordinarily enforce an equitable lien only against specifically identified funds that remain in the defendant's possession or against traceable items that the defendant purchased with the funds (*e.g.,* identifiable property like a car). A defendant's expenditure of the entire identifiable fund on nontraceable items (like food or travel) destroys an equitable lien. The plaintiff then may have a personal claim against the defendant's general assets—but recovering out of those assets is a *legal* remedy, not an equitable one.

Equitable remedies "are, as a general rule, directed against some specific thing; they give or enforce a right to or over some particular thing . . . rather than a right to recover a sum of money generally out of the defendant's assets." 4 S. Symons, Pomeroy's Equity Jurisprudence § 1234, p. 694 (5th ed. 1941). Equitable liens thus are ordinarily enforceable only against a specifically identified fund because an equitable lien "is simply a right of a special nature *over* the thing . . . so that the very thing itself may be proceeded against in an equitable action." *[S]ee also* Restatement of Restitution § 215, Comment *a,* p. 866 (1936) (enforcement of equitable lien requires showing that the defendant "still holds the property or property which is in whole or in part its product"); 1 D. Dobbs, *Law of Remedies* § 1.4, p. 19 (2d ed. 1993). This general rule's application to equitable liens includes equitable liens by agreement, which depend on "the notion . . . that the contract creates some right or interest in or over specific property," and are enforceable only if "the decree of the court can lay hold of" that specific property. 4 Pomeroy § 1234, at 694–695.

If, instead of preserving the specific fund subject to the lien, the defendant dissipated the entire fund on nontraceable items, that complete dissipation eliminated the lien. Even though the defendant's conduct was wrongful, the plaintiff could not attach the defendant's general assets instead. Absent specific exceptions not relevant here, "where a person wrongfully dispose[d] of the property of another but the property cannot be traced into any product, the other . . . cannot enforce a constructive trust or lien *upon any part of the wrongdoer's property.*" The plaintiff had "merely a personal claim against the wrongdoer"—a quintessential action at law.

In sum, at equity, a plaintiff ordinarily could not enforce any type of equitable lien if the defendant once possessed a separate, identifiable fund to which the lien attached, but then dissipated it all. The plaintiff could not attach the defendant's general assets instead because those assets were not part of the specific thing to which the lien attached. This rule applied to equitable liens by agreement as well as other types of equitable liens.

III

The Board of Trustees nonetheless maintains that it can enforce its equitable lien against Montanile's general assets. We consider the Board's arguments in turn.

A

First, the Board argues that, while equity courts ordinarily required plaintiffs to trace a specific, identifiable fund in the defendant's possession to which the lien attached, there is an exception for equitable liens by agreement. The Board asserts that equitable liens by agreement require no such tracing, and can be enforced against a defendant's general assets. According to the Board, we recognized this exception in *Sereboff* by distinguishing between equitable restitution (where a lien attaches because the defendant misappropriated property from the plaintiff) and equitable liens by agreement.

The Board misreads *Sereboff,* which left untouched the rule that *all* types of equitable liens must be enforced against a specifically identified fund in the defendant's possession. The question we faced in *Sereboff* was whether plaintiffs seeking an equitable lien by agreement must "identify an asset they originally possessed, which was improperly acquired and converted into property the defendant held." We observed that such a requirement, although characteristic of restitutionary relief, does not "appl[y] to equitable liens by agreement or assignment." That is because the basic premise of an equitable lien by agreement is that, rather than physically taking the plaintiff's property, the defendant constructively possesses a fund to which the plaintiff is entitled. But the plaintiff must still identify a specific fund in the defendant's possession to enforce the lien. ("Having a lien upon the fund, as soon as it was identified they could follow it into the hands of the appellant").

B

Second, the Board contends that historical equity practice supports enforcement of its equitable lien against Montanile's general assets. The Board identifies three methods that equity courts purportedly employed to effectuate this principle: substitute money decrees, deficiency judgments, and the swollen assets doctrine. This argument also fails.

We have long rejected the argument that "equitable relief" under § 502(a)(3) means "whatever relief a court of equity is empowered to provide in the particular case at issue," including ancillary legal remedies. In "many situations . . . an equity court could establish purely legal rights and grant legal remedies which would otherwise be beyond the scope of its authority." But these legal remedies were not relief "typically available in equity," and interpreting them as such would eliminate any limit on the meaning of "equitable relief" and would "render the modifier superfluous." As we have explained—and as the Board conceded at oral argument—as a general rule, plaintiffs cannot enforce an equitable lien against a defendant's general assets. The Board contends that there is an exception if the defendant wrongfully dissipates the equitable lien to thwart its enforcement. But none of the Board's examples show that such relief was "typically available" in equity.

The specific methods by which equity courts might have awarded relief from a defendant's general assets only confirm that the Board seeks legal, not equitable, remedies. While equity courts sometimes awarded money decrees as a substitute for the value of the equitable lien, they were still legal remedies, because they were "wholly pecuniary and personal." 4 Pomeroy § 1234, at 694. The same is true with respect to deficiency judgments. Equity courts could award both of these remedies as part of their ancillary jurisdiction to award complete relief. But the treatises make clear that when equity courts did so, "the rights of the parties are strictly legal, and the final remedy granted is of the kind which might be conferred by a court of law." But legal remedies—even legal remedies that a court of equity could sometimes award—are not "equitable relief" under § 502(a)(3). See *Mertens.*

The swollen assets doctrine also does not establish that the relief the Board seeks is equitable. Under the Board's view of this doctrine, even if a defendant spends all of a specifically identified fund, the mere fact that the defendant wrongfully had assets that belonged to another increased the defendant's available assets, and justifies recovery from his general assets. But most equity courts and treatises rejected that theory. * * * To the extent that courts endorsed any version of the swollen assets theory, they adopted a more limited rule: that commingling a specifically identified fund—to which a lien attached—with a different fund of the defendant's did not destroy the lien. Instead, that commingling allowed the plaintiff to recover the amount of the lien from the entire pot of money. See Restatement § 209, at 844; Scott, The Right To Follow Money Wrongfully Mingled With Other Money, 27 Harv. L. Rev. 125, 125–126 (1913). Thus, even under the version of the swollen assets doctrine adopted by some courts, recovery out of Montanile's general assets—in the absence of commingling—would not have been "typically available" relief.

C

Finally, the Board argues that ERISA's objectives—of enforcing plan documents according to their terms and of protecting plan assets—would be best served by allowing plans to enforce equitable liens against a participant's general assets. The Board also contends that, unless plans can enforce reimbursement provisions against a defendant's general assets, plans will lack effective or cost-efficient remedies, and participants will dissipate any settlement as quickly as possible, before fiduciaries can sue.

We have rejected these arguments before, and do so again. "[V]ague notions of a statute's 'basic purpose' are . . . inadequate to overcome the words of its text regarding the *specific* issue under consideration." *Mertens.* Had Congress sought to prioritize the Board's policy arguments, it could have drafted § 502(a)(3) to mirror ERISA provisions governing civil actions. One of those provisions, for instance, allows participants and beneficiaries to bring civil actions "to enforce [their] rights under the terms of the plan" and does not limit them to equitable relief.

In any event, our interpretation of § 502(a)(3) promotes ERISA's purposes by "allocat[ing] liability for plan-related misdeeds in reasonable proportion to respective actors' power to control and prevent the misdeeds." *Mertens.* More than a decade has passed since we decided *Great-West,* and plans have developed safeguards against participants' and beneficiaries' efforts to evade reimbursement obligations. Plans that cover medical expenses know how much medical care that participants and beneficiaries require, and have the incentive to investigate and track expensive claims. Plan provisions—like the ones here—obligate participants and beneficiaries to notify the plan of legal process against third parties and to give the plan a right of subrogation.

The Board protests that tracking and participating in legal proceedings is hard and costly, and that settlements are often shrouded in secrecy. The facts of this case undercut that argument. The Board had sufficient notice of Montanile's settlement to have taken various steps to preserve those funds. Most notably, when negotiations broke down and Montanile's lawyer expressed his intent to disburse the remaining settlement funds to Montanile unless the plan objected within 14 days, the Board could have—but did not—object. Moreover, the Board could have filed suit immediately, rather than waiting half a year.

IV

Because the lower courts erroneously held that the plan could recover out of Montanile's general assets, they did not determine whether Montanile kept his settlement fund separate from his general assets or dissipated the entire fund on nontraceable assets. At oral argument, Montanile's counsel acknowledged "a genuine issue of . . . material fact on how much dissipation there was" and a lack of record evidence as to whether Montanile mixed the settlement fund with his general assets. A remand is necessary so that the District Court can make that determination.

* * *

We reverse the judgment of the Eleventh Circuit and remand the case for further proceedings consistent with this opinion.

JUSTICE GINSBURG, dissenting.

Montanile received a $500,000 settlement out of which he had pledged to reimburse his health benefit plan for expenditures on his behalf of at least $121,044.02. He can escape that reimbursement obligation, the Court decides, by spending the settlement funds rapidly on nontraceable items. What brings the Court to that bizarre conclusion? As developed in my dissenting opinion in *Great-West Life & Annuity Ins. Co. v. Knudson,* the Court erred profoundly in that case by reading the work product of a Congress sitting in 1974 as "unravel[ling] forty years of fusion of law and equity, solely by employing the benign sounding word 'equitable' when authorizing 'appropriate equitable relief.' " Langbein, What ERISA Means by "Equitable": The Supreme Court's Trail of Error in *Russell, Mertens,* and *Great-West,* 103 Colum. L. Rev. 1317, 1365 (2003). The Court has been persuasively counseled "to confess its error." I would not perpetuate *Great-West*'s mistake. * * *

NOTES

1. The moral of the story seems to be, as Justice Ginsburg says in dissent, that insured parties should quickly dissipate their funds to avoid having to reimburse their insurance company. Is the attorney's fourteen-day letter sufficient here? Or ethical? What about all the subsequent litigation (and costs) the client and/or attorney was subjected to as a result of this default? Or is it the insurance company's fault, as Justice Thomas suggests, for not adequately acting to protect its interest.

2. *Equitable Lien.* An equitable lien, like any lien, is a security interest in another's property; it gives the lien holder the right to foreclose on and sell the property and have the proceeds applied to his claim. It is a real lien, even though it is a created legally by the court as a remedy. As one of the equitable restitutionary remedy, it allows for tracing. If the proceeds of the sale exceed the claim, the excess belongs to the property owner (and his creditors). If the proceeds of the sale are insufficient to satisfy the claim, the lienholder may, at least in the case of an equitable lien, have a money judgment for the deficiency. This is the problem in *Montanile.* There is no property left to sell and so all that's left is a money judgment, which is a legal remedy.

The Restatement (Third) of Restitution and Unjust Enrichment provides for that equitable liens are available when "the claimant's assets or services are applied to enhance or preserve the value of particular property to which the recipient has legal title." § 56(1)(a). This represents the typical case for equitable liens, where for example as in Lewis, the daughter-in-law contributed money and remodeling services to enhance the property owned by her in-laws. *See also* Robinson v. Robinson, 429 N.E.2d 183 (Ill. App.Ct. 1981). But the Restatement goes on to say that an equitable lien is available whenever "the connection between unjust enrichment and the recipient's ownership of particular property makes it equitable that the claimant have recourse to the property for the satisfaction of the recipient's liability in restitution." Restatement (Third) of Restitution § 56(1)(b). In other words, anytime restitution is otherwise appropriate.

1. CONTRACT ALTERNATIVES

Restitution can be used as an alternative to contract in several ways. First, it can be used to fill in a legal gap where no contract exists, as in *Lewis,* or where there is a failed contract, as traditionally discussed in first-year contracts class. *E.g.,* Pyeatte v. Pyeatte, 661 P.2d 196 (Ariz. App.1982) (restitution available to recover for former wife's support of ex-husband's law school education and expectation of support for her education). Second, it can serve as an option for a plaintiff to elect, rather than proceeding under the contract. This is attractive to plaintiffs where they have entered a losing contract or where the defendant profited more by the breach than the plaintiff lost. Restitution in contract also includes the restitutionary remedy of rescission. Rescission allows the plaintiff to cancel the contract.

This can then allow the plaintiff out of a problematic contract or allow it to sue alternatively for unjust enrichment for the solicited benefit.

The Restatement (Second) of Contracts § 371 measures the restitution interest in contract by either "the reasonable value" to the defendant of what he received (in terms of what it would have cost him to obtain it from the claimant) or the increase in the value of the defendant's property.

HUTCHISON V. PYBURN

Court of Appeals of Tennessee
567 S.W.2d 762 (Tenn. 1977)

DROWOTA, JUDGE.

This is a case involving fraud in the sale of realty in which plaintiffs-vendees were awarded both rescission of the deed and punitive damages by the Chancery Court of Davidson County. Since the case is before us without a bill of exceptions, our recitation of the facts follows the allegations of plaintiffs-appellees and the findings of the Chancellor.

In January of 1973, plaintiffs William and Jo Lynn Hutchison purchased a house and lot from defendants Robert and Carol Pyburn for $24,000.00. Of this amount, $23,500.00 represented a loan from Home Federal Savings & Loan Association which was secured by a deed of trust. Defendant Jack Williams built the house and sold the property to the Pyburns, and his brother, defendant John Williams, was real estate agent for the Pyburns in the sale of the property to plaintiffs. In July of 1973, plaintiffs noticed seepage from their sewage disposal system, investigated, and discovered that their property had not been approved as a home site by the Metropolitan Board of Health because it lacked the requisite topsoil to sustain the septic tank and overflow field needed for sewage disposal. Further, the Metropolitan Department of Code Administration had been informed of the problem, and had issued a building permit to defendant Jack Williams only by mistake. Evidently defendant Pyburn had become aware of the sewage problem after purchasing the property from Williams and had prevailed on Williams to release him from his obligation to purchase it, whereupon Pyburn and Williams negotiated the sale to plaintiffs.

Plaintiffs brought suit, alleging that the defendants Pyburn and Williams knew of the property's condition and that there was no practical means of correcting it at the time of the sale. They charged that defendants' failure to inform them of the sewage problem amounted to fraud and deceit, and that the condition of the property represented a breach of the warranties contained in the deed. The Chancellor dismissed the case against defendant John Williams, but entered a decree in favor of plaintiffs against the Pyburns and Jack Williams. The decree allowed plaintiffs rescission of the contract, incidental damages in the form of expenses incurred in connection with the property, moving costs, and attorney's fees, from all of which was deducted the reasonable rental value of the property for the period of plaintiffs' occupancy. In addition to the sum due plaintiffs in incidental damages, which was set at $3,168.94, the Chancellor assessed $5,000.00 in punitive damages against the defendants and made a specific finding that defendants' misrepresentation was fraudulent. * * *

Defendants * * * assert that the trial court erred in awarding punitive damages for misrepresentations incident to a contract when rescission of the contract and deed was also decreed. * * *

In Tennessee it is established that courts of equity are empowered to award punitive damages. * * *

One objection raised to the award of punitive damages in this case is that it is inconsistent with rescission of the deed under the doctrine of election of remedies. That doctrine estops a plaintiff who has clearly chosen to pursue one of two inconsistent and irreconcilable remedies from later resorting to the other. The "essential element" here is "that the remedies be inconsistent." * * * There is no such inconsistency, however, between the remedy of rescission and an award of punitive damages. The latter * * * is designed to penalize and deter, and results from the nature of defendant's conduct rather than from the harm it causes. The character of punitive damages, then, is in no wise inconsistent with rescission and its concomitant remedies of restitution and incidental damages. The latter are all aimed at *redressing* the harm done the plaintiff and, while this means they may be considered inconsistent with a remedy such as compensatory damages, which also aims at redress but by a different method, they may not be so considered with respect to the *deterrent* sanction of punitive damages. Thus, plaintiffs' choice of rescission as a means of redress is not inconsistent with their request for punitive damages and does not estop them from making that request.

Similarly, punitive damages do not conflict with the theoretical aim of equitable rescission, which is to return the parties to the status in which they were prior to the transaction. That aim is simply one approach to redressing the wrong done to plaintiff, an approach that differs from that of compensatory damages, which are intended to redress the wrong by directly compensating the plaintiff for what he has lost. But again, punitive damages are not intended to redress the plaintiff's wrong, but to make an example of the defendant's conduct. Since they thus relate to considerations totally different from those of rescission, punitive damages neither frustrate rescission's redressing of plaintiff's wrong by return of the parties to the *status quo,* nor are they inconsistent with it.

Cases often announce the rule that there must be proof of "actual damages" before punitive damages may be awarded. The cases are unclear, however, as to the meaning of "actual damages" in this context. It has been logically suggested that the phrase should mean no more than that the plaintiff cannot get punitive damages without proving a valid cause of action, that is, without showing that he has been legally injured in some way, which is really a roundabout way of saying that there can be no cause of action for punitive damages alone. * * * That approach, applied broadly, would allow recovery of punitive damages if plaintiff, in addition to showing the requisite degree of bad conduct and intent by defendant, could merely prove his entitlement to injunctive relief or nominal damages. But we need not go so far here in construing "actual damages" not to mean strictly an award of compensatory damages. Returning to the case before us, we hold simply that plaintiffs' proof of their entitlement to rescission of the deed, refund of the purchase price, and incidental damages such as moving expenses, shows sufficient harm and loss to them to satisfy the "actual damages" prerequisite to recovery of punitive damages in Tennessee.

Finally, defendants point to a proposition which we agree is the general rule in Tennessee and elsewhere: punitive damages may not be recovered in an action for breach of contract. This case, however, is not one for breach of contract, for plaintiffs asked that the contract be made a nullity by rescission. Further, the pleadings and memorandum of the trial court indicate that the main thrust of the action is a claim of fraud and misrepresentation against all the defendants, although an additional claim of breach of warranty was asserted against the Pyburns, with whom plaintiffs were in privity. Thus, regardless of any overtones of contract that may appear in this suit, there also clearly exists here a cause of action against all defendants for the sort of tortious misconduct required as a basis for recovery of punitive damages * * * . For this reason, such a recovery cannot be defeated by the rule that punitive damages are unavailable in contract actions. * * *

NOTES

1. Although *Hutchison* speaks of rescission as an equitable remedy, rescission was not restricted to the equity courts. At law, rescission was available by an action in quasi-contract. Thus, in *Hutchison,* the plaintiff could have rescinded the contract by offering to return the property, and then sued in quasi-contract for the return of the purchase price. (One of the distinctions between legal and equitable rescission is that, at law, the plaintiff rescinded the contract by tendering restitution to the defendant and then suing. In the equity courts, tender was not required; the plaintiff sued, and the court rescinded the contract if the plaintiff prevailed.)

Depending on the case, there can be advantages to seeking equitable rescission. In a case like *Hutchison*, rescission, or cancellation, of the deed is the type of remedy that would not have been available at law. While the law courts effected restitution by entering a money judgment in the plaintiff's favor, the equity courts could order the defendant to return the specific property he had received. As a result, equitable rescission gave the plaintiff an advantage over the defendant's creditors, if the defendant was insolvent. Indeed, a court of equity could create a lien on the property in order to secure the plaintiff's entitlement to return of the purchase price and incidental damages.

2.   *On the substantive law.* Rescission of a contract is available for substantial breach of contract, mistake, fraud, duress, or coercion.

3.   Should punitive damages be recoverable in a restitution case? Courts are divided. *See, e.g.,* Madrid v. Marquez, 33 P.3d 683, 685 (N.M.App.2001) (while majority rule is that punitive damages are not permitted in equity, court follows the "modern trend" of allowing punitive damages in equity, without prerequisite of an award of compensatory damages); Dan B. Dobbs, *Law of Remedies* § 4.5(5) (2d ed.1993). Some see the doctrine of election of remedies as a bar; if you want punitives, you must sue for damages. Others deny recovery because punitive damages cannot be awarded without actual, compensatory damages or because punitive damages were not awarded in equity courts. *See* Alcorn County, Mississippi v. U.S. Interstate Supplies, Inc., 731 F.2d 1160 (5th Cir.1984). None of these reasons can really withstand critical scrutiny, and the trend is probably to allow punitive damages where fraud, oppression or malice is shown.

4.   *Reformation*: Rescission is often contrasted with reformation, especially on the bar exam. However, reformation is a little-used remedy in contrast to the prevalence of rescission. One important distinction is that the result of the two remedies is exactly opposite: rescission terminates the contract between the parties, while reformation restores it.

Reformation is a remedy that somewhat resembles a declaratory judgment in that it declares what a contract actually says. Reformation is available when a written document—typically a contract or conveyance—does not accurately reflect the parties' actual agreement. Suppose, for example, Superstar agrees to sell 100 signed jerseys to Sporting Goods Store for $10,000 and tells his attorney to draw papers to that effect. Superstar's attorney puts in a price of $1,000 by mistake and forwards the paper to Store, who signs it without being aware of the error.

To correct the error, Superstar could seek reformation. Once the terms of the parties' actual agreement were shown, the court would order the document reformed or corrected to reflect the parties' intentions accurately. Or the court could simply state the reformed terms of the document in its opinion, making it unnecessary to change the document physically. It is important to emphasize, however, that in a reformation action the court is not creating a new agreement, but rather simply changing the form of the agreement so that the original substance is correctly stated.

If all a reformation action achieves is correcting the documents to reflect the parties' actual intent, one might wonder why the parties need to resort to the court at all and whether there is any case or controversy for the court to resolve. Reformation is an important remedy in at least three circumstances. First, there may be an honest dispute over what terms the parties agreed to at the time. Second, if one of the parties is a corporation or a political body, the true controversy may lie not between the individuals who reached agreement but between one party and the corporate successors of the other. Third, fraud or misrepresentation may be involved, in recording the agreement or in trying to take unfair advantage of the improperly documented agreement.

EARTHINFO, INC. V. HYDROSPHERE RESOURCE CONSULTANTS, INC.

Supreme Court of Colorado
900 P.2d 113 (1995)

JUSTICE SCOTT delivered the Opinion of the Court.

In January 1990, Hydrosphere Resource Consultants, Inc. (Hydrosphere), filed this action against petitioner, EarthInfo, Inc. (EarthInfo), seeking to rescind the parties' software development contracts due to EarthInfo's failure to make royalty payments. The trial court determined that EarthInfo had breached its contracts with Hydrosphere, ordered the contracts rescinded, and ordered that EarthInfo repay to Hydrosphere all the net profits it realized as a result of its breach. The court of appeals affirmed the trial court. * * *

I

Between 1986 and 1988, Hydrosphere entered into several contracts with US West, Inc. (US West) * * * to develop a number of products that employ CD-ROM technology. The products were designed to exploit hydrological and meteorological information collected by government agencies and to make that information available to the general public through Hydrosphere. Under the Contracts, Hydrosphere was to develop the CD-ROM units and create the software that enables end-users to access the otherwise public information on line from the CD-ROM units.

The Contracts vested all rights of ownership, copyrights, and patents in the products to US West. Under the terms of the Contracts, Hydrosphere had an ongoing obligation to provide technical support to end-users of the products, and US West was to create user manuals, and package and market the products. US West was also to pay Hydrosphere a fixed hourly development fee as well as royalties, calculated as a percentage of net sales, for "inventive product ideas." Payments under the Contracts were made on a quarterly basis.

On February 10, 1989, US West assigned its interest in the Contracts to EarthInfo. * * * EarthInfo agreed to pay US West $60,432. EarthInfo also entered into a separate agreement with Hydrosphere in which it agreed to honor US West's obligations under the Contracts, including the continued payment of royalties on the products already developed by Hydrosphere. EarthInfo fulfilled its contractual obligations through June 30, 1990. Hydrosphere then claimed that sales of a new derivative product were subject to royalty payments; EarthInfo claimed that the Contracts did not address derivative products, and therefore objected to increasing its royalty obligation. On October 30, 1990, when the third-quarter royalty payments were due, EarthInfo informed Hydrosphere that it was withholding these payments and any further royalty payments pending clarification of the basis for the royalty payments. EarthInfo continued to make payments of the fixed hourly development fees. A total of $19,000 in fixed fees was paid to Hydrosphere after June 30, 1990. After strained negotiations, Hydrosphere notified EarthInfo by letter on December 12, 1990, that it was rescinding the Contracts.

On January 11, 1991, Hydrosphere filed a breach of contract action against EarthInfo * * * . [After trial], the trial court ruled that EarthInfo did not owe royalties on sales of the derivative product, but the court determined that EarthInfo had breached its Contracts with Hydrosphere when it unilaterally suspended royalty payments on the other products. In a subsequent hearing, both parties sought rescission of the Contracts and restitution as a remedy. The trial court found "the breach was substantial" and that "due to the nature of the contracts between the parties and the depth of their disputes, damages would be inadequate." The trial court determined that the appropriate remedy would be rescission. * * * [The court] set June 30, 1990, the date through which EarthInfo had paid royalties, as the date of rescission.

As restitution between the parties, the court ordered EarthInfo to return to Hydrosphere all tangible property developed under the Contracts. In addition, the court found that "since rescission is an equitable remedy the court has discretion in determining the appropriate relief for the parties," and ordered EarthInfo to return to Hydrosphere all property, promotional materials and proprietary information related to the Hydrodata products. In addition, the court held EarthInfo responsible in equity "for the repayment to Hydrosphere of the net profits realized by EarthInfo" from June 30, 1990, until the date of the order, totaling $265,204.91. The court found Hydrosphere "in equity responsible for the repayment to EarthInfo of amounts paid by EarthInfo" in acquiring the Hydrodata product line from US West, totaling $60,432, and in fixed hourly development fees paid by EarthInfo after June 30, 1990, in the amount of $19,000. The costs incurred by EarthInfo were deducted from the net profits, resulting in a judgment in favor of Hydrosphere in the amount of $185,772.91.

EarthInfo appealed * * * .

II

This case presents a question of first impression for this court: whether a party that breaches a contract can be required to disgorge to the non-breaching party any benefits received as a result of the breach. Because this issue has remained largely unexplored, the rules of application are neither settled nor uniform. The difficulty in resolving this issue stems from a subtle conflict between the law of restitution and the law of contracts. This conflict is well articulated in what has become a leading article on the disgorgement principle:

> It is a principle of the law of restitution that one should not gain by one's own wrong; it is a principle of the law of contracts that damages for breach should be based on the injured party's lost expectation. In many cases, the principles are mutually consistent. If, on breach, the injured party's lost expectation equals or exceeds the gain by the party in breach, then damages based on expectation strip the party in breach of all gain, and make the injured party whole. But if the injured party's lost expectation is less than the gain realized by the party in breach, then damages based on expectation do not strip the party in breach of all gain. This situation brings the two principles into conflict.

E. Allan Farnsworth, Your Loss or My Gain? The Dilemma of the Disgorgement Principle in Breach of Contract, 94 Yale L.J. 1339, 1341 (1985). According to Farnsworth, courts have been reluctant to award profits to a nonbreaching party in a breach of contract action, thus allowing the party in breach to keep part of the gain, since in effect "a 'mere' breach of contract is not a 'wrong.' " Many others, however, have suggested that if the gain realized by the party in breach exceeds the injured party's loss, the measure of damages should strip the party in breach of all gain. We adopt neither approach as a general rule, and hold instead that whether profits are awarded to a nonbreaching party shall be determined within the discretion of the trial court on a case by case basis.

A

Rescission of a contract may be granted if the facts show a substantial breach, that the injury caused by the breach is irreparable, and that damages are inadequate, difficult or impossible to assess. A contract can also be rescinded by the "mutual consent" or "actions" of the parties.

Here, the trial court found not only that EarthInfo's breach was substantial, but that "due to the nature of the contracts between the parties and the depth of their disputes, damages would be inadequate." The trial court also found that although the Contracts "contemplate an ongoing relationship" between the parties, "[i]t is unrealistic to assume that damages could be computed and awarded and that the parties could then resume that relationship in a productive manner." The trial court found further that both parties sought rescission of the Contracts. Thus, the trial court concluded that rescission was necessary.[7] Since evidence in the

---

[7] The trial court held: The court finds not only that the breach was substantial, but that due to the nature of the contracts between the parties and the depth of their disputes, damages would be inadequate. The contracts contemplate an ongoing relationship. It is unrealistic to assume that

record supports the trial court's findings, we conclude that rescission of the Contracts was warranted.

Rescission of a contract normally is accompanied by restitution on both sides. The contract is "being unmade, so restoration of benefits received under the contract seems to follow." Restitution measures the remedy by the defendant's gain and seeks to force disgorgement of that gain in order "to prevent the defendant's unjust enrichment." Restitution, which seeks to prevent unjust enrichment of the defendant, differs in principle from damages, which measure the remedy by the plaintiff's loss and seek to provide compensation for that loss. As a consequence, "in some cases the defendant gains more than the plaintiff loses, so that the two remedies may differ in practice as well as in principle."[9]

A party seeking to rescind a contract must return the opposite party to the status quo ante, or the position in which he or she was prior to entering into the contract. The rule of returning the parties to the status quo ante is equitable and it requires the use of practicality in the readjustment of the parties' rights. Since rescission is an equitable remedy, it is within the trial court's sound discretion to determine the method for accomplishing a return to the status quo ante based upon the facts as determined by the trier of fact. All uncertainties as to the amount of benefit are to be resolved against the party committing the material breach.

The main options for measurement of the benefit conferred on the breaching party are these:

(1) the increased assets in the hands of the defendant from the receipt of property;

(2) the market value of services or intangibles provided to the defendant, without regard to whether the defendant's assets were actually increased; that is, the amount which it would cost to obtain similar services, whether those services prove to be useful or not;

(3) the use value of any benefits received, as measured by (i) market indicators such as rental value or interest or (ii) actual gains to the defendant from using the benefits, such as the gains identified in item (5) below;

---

damages could be computed and awarded and that the parties could then resume that relationship in a productive manner. . . . Rescission is, therefore, an appropriate remedy. The court explained further that "[a] principal reason why a remedy limited to damages is inappropriate is that it would leave the products developed by Hydrosphere in the hands of a hostile and uncooperative EarthInfo, with the latter under a continuing duty to pay royalties, and also with an interest in promoting its own product line."

[9] In the event a defendant's gains in a transaction exceed the plaintiff's losses and the plaintiff recovers the defendant's gains as restitution, the plaintiff will receive a greater reward and will be better off than if he or she were awarded damages for the defendant's breach. Thus, the plaintiff's expectations are exceeded because recovery is not based on the loss in value to the plaintiff, but rather on the benefit to the breaching defendant.

(4) the gains realized by the defendant upon sale or transfer of an asset received from the plaintiff;

(5) collateral or secondary profits earned by the defendant by use of an asset received from the plaintiff, or, what is much the same thing, the savings effected by the use of the asset.

Dan B. Dobbs, Law of Remedies § 4.1(4) at 566–67 (footnote omitted). It is the fifth option, disgorgement of profits, which is principally at issue in this case.

No easy formulas exist for determining when restitution of profits realized by a party is permissible. Instead, the court must resort to general considerations of fairness, taking into account the nature of the defendant's wrong, the relative extent of his or her contribution, and the feasibility of separating this from the contribution traceable to the plaintiff's interest. 1 George E. Palmer, The Law of Restitution § 2.12 at 161 (1978) [hereinafter "Palmer"]. Thus, the more culpable the defendant's behavior, and the more direct the connection between the profits and the wrongdoing, the more likely that the plaintiff can recover all defendant's profits. *See, e.g.,* Douglas Laycock, *The Scope and Significance of Restitution*, 67 Tex.L.Rev. 1277, 1289 (1989). The trial court must ultimately decide whether the whole circumstances of a case point to the conclusion that the defendant's retention of any profit is unjust.

Generally, the mere breach of a contract will not make the defendant accountable for benefits thereby obtained, whether through dealings with a third person or otherwise. As noted by Dobbs § 4.1(4) at 566–67:

[t]o require a defendant to give up profits may operate with particular severity because at least some of the profits would almost always be attributable to the defendant's efforts or investment. So the profit recovery as a measure of restitution is extraordinary. In general, the defendant who is not a serious wrongdoer is held only to make restitution measured by actual gains in assets or in gains of services or intangibles which he [or she] in fact sought in the relevant transaction.

If, however, the defendant's wrongdoing is intentional or substantial, or there are no other means of measuring the wrongdoer's enrichment, recovery of profits may be granted. See generally George E. Palmer, Law of Restitution § 2.12 at 164–65.

B

The trial court determined that EarthInfo's breach of the Contracts was substantial, damages were difficult to assess, and the parties mutually consented to rescission. Thus, the trial court required EarthInfo to disgorge all the profits it realized as a result of the breach. The court returned to EarthInfo the consideration it agreed to pay for the Hydrodata product line and also allowed it to retain the profits it earned when it was making the royalty payments. The court held EarthInfo responsible, however, for the repayment to Hydrosphere of the net profits it realized from June 30, 1990 until the date of the order, determining that to be the most equitable treatment of the parties given the nature of the dispute. We agree that EarthInfo must be required to disgorge the profits it accrued as a result of its breach since its breach was conscious and substantial.

The trial court found that the Contracts between EarthInfo and Hydrosphere did not require EarthInfo to pay royalties on sales of the derivative product. EarthInfo was still required, however, to pay royalties on all other products under the written Contracts. The trial court determined that EarthInfo's repudiation of its long-standing royalty obligations to Hydrosphere was a substantial breach of the Hydrodata Contracts. The trial court's factual determinations are supported by the evidence and should not be disturbed on appeal absent a clear showing of abuse of discretion. The trial court's order represents a permissible exercise of its discretion.

Since the record supports the trial court's findings that EarthInfo consciously and substantially breached its Contracts with Hydrosphere, damages were difficult to assess, and the parties mutually agreed to rescission, retention of profits by EarthInfo would be an unjust enrichment. Accordingly, we find that the extraordinary remedy of restitution and disgorgement of profits is justified.

III

The remaining issue then is the determination of the profits to be returned to Hydrosphere. The petitioner contends that the trial court erred in failing to apportion the net profits in a way that reflected the relative contributions to those profits by the parties. We agree.

"Courts have recognized that some apportionment must be made between those profits attributable to the plaintiff's property and those earned by the defendant's efforts and investment, limiting the plaintiff to the profits fairly attributable to his share." "Even the wilful wrongdoer should not be made to give up that which is his [or her] own; the principle is disgorgement, not plunder." The defendant's personal efforts in contributing to profits must be taken into account, but are often difficult to measure. For example, if the defendant uses the plaintiff's machine in producing goods, which it packages, distributes and sells to retail customers, it may increase its profits, but we are not so sure that the increase has much if any connection with the plaintiff's machine. We can be sure, however, that the defendant's profits relate in part to the defendant's own investments, efforts, or enterprising attitude. [Dobbs § 4.5(3)] at 647.

Dobbs' example of profit-making complexity is similar to the profit-making in the case at hand. EarthInfo used Hydrosphere's software programming in five items produced, packaged, distributed, and sold by EarthInfo. EarthInfo's marketing, packaging and enhancement of the products presumably contributed to the earning of the net profits; that contribution should be accounted for and withheld from the disgorgement of those profits by Hydrosphere.

No single rule governing the burden of proving apportionment is adequate for all cases or all facets of a single case. Profit claims can be calculated first by identifying and deducting legitimate business expenses from gross income. The defendant usually has the best access to this information and may properly be required to prove such expenses. Second, gross income of the defendant is produced at least in part "by investment, enterprise, and management skill of the defendant," and the defendant should receive credit for its own efforts and investments. * * * The court must determine which part of the profit results from the defendant's own independent efforts and which part results from the benefits provided by the plaintiff. The court must seek to determine a fair apportionment that will result in a reasonable approximation or informed estimate of the relative contributions of the two parties. The allocation of the burden of establishing such approximation, and degree of specificity of proof required, may be affected by such factors as the seriousness of the defendant's wrongdoing and the extent to which the plaintiff's contribution was at risk in the profit making enterprise. Where the relative contributions of the two parties are inseparable or untraceable, there should be no recovery of profits by the plaintiff unless the defendant is a very serious wrongdoer. In the present case, considering the nature and extent of the breach as well as the other relevant factors, we hold that it is the burden of the plaintiff to establish facts sufficient to permit the trial court to determine the relative contributions of the parties so that profits can be fairly apportioned. * * *

The trial court made no findings with respect to the relative contributions of each party and whether they are inseparable. Thus, this case should be remanded to the trial court for further proceedings so that the court's order that EarthInfo disgorge its profits is limited to those profits attributable to Hydrosphere. Accordingly, we affirm in part, reverse in part, and return this case to the court of appeals with directions that it remand the case to the trial court for recalculation of wrongful profits attributable to Hydrosphere and entry of a new order of restitution.

NOTES

1. According to the Restatement (Second) of Contracts, the victim of a serious breach or repudiation of contract is entitled "to restitution for any benefit that he has conferred on the other party by way of part performance or

reliance." Restatement (Second) of Contracts § 373(a). The only exception is that there is no right to restitution if the victim has completely performed and the only obligation owing is the payment of a definite sum of money for the performance. *Id.* § 373(b). *EarthInfo* simply takes this principle to its logical extreme, by measuring the restitutionary recovery according to principles developed in restitution cases like *Olwell*.

2.   Restitutionary recovery is particularly valuable—and controversial—when a party finds itself in a losing contract. When enmeshed in a losing deal, there is a strong incentive for a party to find a way out, if that can be done without risking liability for damages. The question is whether the expectancy measure of damages should cap the restitution recovery. The classic case is Boomer v. Muir, 24 P.2d 570 (Cal.App. 1933). The subcontractor had performed the majority, but not all, of the work for constructing a dam when the defendant breached. Under the contract, he was owed only $20,000 more, but he had actually expended labor services worth $250,000 more. Because the suit was in quantum meruit after rescission based on the substantial breach, the court allowed the actual value of the services rendered rather than capping them at the contract's expectancy. The Restatement (Second) of Contracts § 371 doesn't answer the question as it measures the restitution interest by "the reasonable value to the other party of what he received in terms of what it would have cost him to obtain it from a person in the claimant's position." What it would have cost him is either the original contract price or what the actual costs turned out to be.

The question of restitution for the losing contract is controversial. On the one hand, if recovery is based on unjust enrichment, it seems only logical that the plaintiff should recover the full value of the benefits the defendant received. On the other hand, full restitutionary recovery effectively rewrites the parties' bargain, obliging the defendant to pay full value when he promised—with the plaintiff's consent—to pay less. It invites opportunism, giving the party who made a bad deal a tremendous incentive to induce a breach by the other party. It complicates reaching fair settlements, and is not a remedy either party to a contract would agree to in advance of a breach. Andrew Kull, *Restitution as a Remedy for Breach of Contract*, 67 S.C.L.Rev. 1465 (1994).

Professor Kull argues that the Restatement's position rests on a misunderstanding of rescission as a remedy for breach. Rescission, properly understood, is a remedy that simply unwinds an agreement that can no longer go forward, and it traditionally was available as a remedy only where the transaction was still capable of being unwound. The early cases thus limited rescission to cases in which: (1) the breach was substantial, tantamount to a repudiation of the contract, (2) the transaction could be fully unwound by returning the benefits received, *in specie*, and (3) the performance had not gone so far as to make unwinding the deal impracticable. Applying these in Boomer where the contract cannot be easily unwound by a return of benefits, restitution should not be available and the party limited to its expectancy.

3. *Earthinfo* raises again the question of distinctions between an efficient and an opportunistic breach. Recall that the Restatement (Third) of Restitution allows for an election of restitution over damages for breach of contract where the defendant's breach is "opportunistic" meaning deliberate and profitable. *Id.* § 39(2). *Earthinfo* is actually an easy case: the defendant's actions were deliberate and unexcused. It simply refused to pay. It did not act like a defendant in efficient breach by entering a contract with another party at a greater price, and thus breaching the first contract for a profit-maximizing reason. In the absence of any efficiency justification, the deliberate and wrongful nature is more apparent, thus supporting the election of restitution.

The Restatement (Third) of Restitution, however, goes on to say that a breach is "opportunistic" if "the promisee's right to recover damages for the breach affords inadequacy protection to the promisee's contractual entitlement." *Id.* § 39(2)(c). This is a formulation of the adequacy rule, requiring that a contracting party electing restitution show that damages are inadequate. Is this element satisfied in *Earthinfo*?

The commentators are divided about whether disgorgement is either widely available or appropriate as a remedy for breach of contract. Professor Palmer acknowledged that courts required disgorgement in a few cases—for example, when a seller in a land sale agreement breaches to sell to a third party at a higher price, or where an employee breaches by revealing trade secrets—but concluded that "the evidence points to the rejection of any general principle" that disgorgement is available as a remedy for breach of contract. George E. Palmer, *Law of Restitution* § 4.9(e) at 449 (1978). Professor Melvin Eisenberg, however, believes that the Restatement (Second) of Contracts' failure to recognize disgorgement as an interest protected by contract law was misguided. "[M]ore than a dozen appellate cases decided by various state appellate courts, the United States Supreme Court, the House of Lords, and the highest courts of other common law jurisdictions have awarded disgorgement in a contract setting." Melvin Eisenberg, *The Disgorgement Interest in Contract Law*, 105 Mich.L.Rev. 559, 565–566 (2006); *see also* E. Allan Farnsworth, *Your Loss or My Gain? The Dilemma of the Disgorgement Principle in Breach of Contract*, 94 Yale L.J. 1339 (1985) (arguing disgorgement should be available for "abuse of contract" leaving the plaintiff no way to obtain a reasonable substitute). Would this be such a case?

2. EQUITABLE RESTITUTION

Historically, English courts of equity also developed restitution remedies that allowed them to award money. The theories of such equitable restitution remedies were based on specific restoration: that the defendant held something specific belonging to the plaintiff that must be ordered returned. This fit without the general framework of courts of equity ordering the defendant to action.

The primary equitable restitution device is the constructive trust. The Restatement (Third) of Restitution defines the remedy and its operation:

§ 55. Constructive Trust

(1) If a defendant is unjustly enriched by the acquisition of title to identifiable property at the expense of the claimant or in violation of the claimant's rights, the defendant may be declared a constructive trustee, for the benefit of the claimant, of the property in question and its traceable product.

(2) The obligation of a constructive trustee is to surrender the constructive trust property to the claimant, on such conditions as the court may direct.

Comment:

a. *General principles and scope; relation to other sections.* The present section offers a paraphrase of Judge Cardozo's more eloquent statement:

> A constructive trust is the formula through which the conscience of equity finds expression. When property has been acquired in such circumstances that the holder of the legal title may not in good conscience retain the beneficial interest, equity converts him into a trustee.

Beatty v. Guggenheim Exploration Co., 122 N.E. 378, 380 (N.Y. 1919). * * *

Constructive trust is the principal device for vindicating equitable ownership against conflicting legal title; the rules by which equitable property rights are recognized are among the most predictable of equity jurisprudence. Because such rules are less familiar than they were in Cardozo's day, however, the present section employs a paraphrase. A transaction in which the defendant (i) has been unjustly enriched (ii) by acquiring legal title to specifically identifiable property (iii) at the expense of the claimant or in violation. This is the state of affairs, described by Cardozo, for which constructive trust is the standard remedy.

The decision to impose a constructive trust accordingly involves a sequence of inquiries that might be separately analyzed. The first step is to establish that the defendant is liable in restitution by one of the substantive provisions of this Restatement. The second is to show that the transaction that is the source of the liability is one in which the defendant acquired specifically identifiable property. If the property the claimant seeks to recover via constructive trust is a substitute for the property originally acquired by the defendant, its continued identification depends on the tracing rules of §§ 58 and 59. . . .

The preference that the constructive trust claimant acquires over general creditors of the defendant is usually the object of the remedy, not a reason to disallow it.

The modern significance of equitable restitution is that its specific restoration theory allows tracing of the money, which offers advantage in creditor and bankruptcy situations. As an equitable remedy, it may also be subject to certain equitable defenses like unclean hands and laches, which will be discussed in Chapter 8. A key question exists as to whether equitable restitution requires that a claimant prove the inadequacy of the legal remedy. *See* Caprice L. Roberts, *The Restitution Revival and the Ghosts of Equity*, 68 Wash. & Lee L. Rev. 1027 (2011) (criticizing the third Restatement of Restitution for maintaining the inadequacy rule and the hierarchy of legal restitution over equitable). As we have seen, this is the requirement for proceeding with an equitable remedy for injunctive relief; that the plaintiff must show the inadequacy of the legal remedy. While typically this rule operates in the election of an injunction over damages, the jurisdictional origin of the preference for legal remedies is broader. Thus, technically, the answer is probably yes, inadequacy must be shown; however, courts frequently ignore the requirement. *See* George E. Palmer, *Law of Restitution* § 1.6 at 36 (1978).

SNEPP V. UNITED STATES

Supreme Court of the United States
444 U.S. 507 (1980)

PER CURIAM.

* * *

I

Based on his experiences as a CIA agent, Snepp published a book about certain CIA activities in South Vietnam. Snepp published the account without submitting it to the Agency for prepublication review. As an express condition of his employment with the CIA in 1968, however, Snepp had executed an agreement promising that he would "not ... publish ... any information or material relating to the Agency, its activities or intelligence activities generally, either during or after the term of [his] employment ... without specific prior approval by the Agency." The promise was an integral part of Snepp's concurrent undertaking "not to disclose any classified information relating to the Agency without proper authorization." Thus, Snepp had pledged not to divulge *classified* information and not to publish *any* information without prepublication clearance. The Government brought this suit to enforce Snepp's agreement. It sought a declaration that Snepp had breached the contract, an injunction requiring Snepp to submit future writings for prepublication review, and an order imposing a constructive trust for the Government's benefit on all profits that Snepp might earn from publishing the book in violation of his fiduciary obligations to the Agency.

The District Court found that Snepp had "willfully, deliberately and surreptitiously breached his position of trust with the CIA and the [1968] secrecy agreement" by publishing his book without submitting it for prepublication review. The court also found that Snepp deliberately misled CIA officials into believing that he would submit the book for prepublication clearance. Finally, the court determined as a fact that publication of the book had "caused the United States irreparable harm and loss." The District Court therefore enjoined future breaches of Snepp's agreement and imposed a constructive trust on Snepp's profits.

The Court of Appeals accepted the findings of the District Court and agreed that Snepp had breached a valid contract. It specifically affirmed the finding that Snepp's failure to submit his manuscript for prepublication review had inflicted "irreparable harm" on intelligence activities vital to our national security. Thus, the court upheld the injunction against future violations of Snepp's prepublication obligation. The court, however, concluded that the record did not support imposition of a constructive trust. The conclusion rested on the court's perception that Snepp had a First Amendment right to publish unclassified information and the Government's concession—for the purposes of this litigation—that Snepp's book divulged no classified intelligence. In other words, the court thought that Snepp's fiduciary obligation extended only to preserving the confidentiality of classified material. It therefore limited recovery to nominal damages and to the possibility of punitive damages if the Government—in a jury trial—could prove tortious conduct. * * *

II

Snepp's employment with the CIA involved an extremely high degree of trust. In the opening sentence of the agreement that he signed, Snepp explicitly recognized that he was entering a trust relationship. The trust agreement specifically imposed the obligation not to publish *any* information relating to the Agency without submitting the information for clearance. Snepp stipulated at trial that—after undertaking this obligation—he had been "assigned to various positions of trust" and that he had been granted "frequent access to classified information, including information regarding intelligence sources and methods." Snepp published his book about CIA activities on the basis of this background and exposure. He deliberately and surreptitiously violated his obligation to submit all material for prepublication review. Thus, he exposed the classified information with which he had been entrusted to the risk of disclosure.

Whether Snepp violated his trust does not depend upon whether his book actually contained classified information. The Government does not deny—as a general principle—Snepp's right to publish unclassified information. Nor does it contend—at this stage of the litigation—that

Snepp's book contains classified material. The Government simply claims that, in light of the special trust reposed in him and the agreement that he signed, Snepp should have given the CIA an opportunity to determine whether the material he proposed to publish would compromise classified information or sources. Neither of the Government's concessions undercuts its claim that Snepp's failure to submit to prepublication review was a breach of his trust.

Both the District Court and the Court of Appeals found that a former intelligence agent's publication of unreviewed material relating to intelligence activities can be detrimental to vital national interests even if the published information is unclassified. When a former agent relies on his own judgment about what information is detrimental, he may reveal information that the CIA—with its broader understanding of what may expose classified information and confidential sources—could have identified as harmful. In addition to receiving intelligence from domestically based or controlled sources, the CIA obtains information from the intelligence services of friendly nations and from agents operating in foreign countries. The continued availability of these foreign sources depends upon the CIA's ability to guarantee the security of information that might compromise them and even endanger the personal safety of foreign agents.

Undisputed evidence in this case shows that a CIA agent's violation of his obligation to submit writings about the Agency for prepublication review impairs the CIA's ability to perform its statutory duties. Admiral Turner, Director of the CIA, testified without contradiction that Snepp's book and others like it have seriously impaired the effectiveness of American intelligence operations. He said:

> Over the last six to nine months, we have had a number of sources discontinue work with us. We have had more sources tell us that they are very nervous about continuing work with us. We have had very strong complaints from a number of foreign intelligence services with whom we conduct liaison, who have questioned whether they should continue exchanging information with us, for fear it will not remain secret. I cannot estimate to you how many potential sources or liaison arrangements have never germinated because people were unwilling to enter into business with us.

In view of this and other evidence in the record, both the District Court and the Court of Appeals recognized that Snepp's breach of his explicit obligation to submit his material—classified or not—for prepublication clearance has irreparably harmed the United States Government.

III

The decision of the Court of Appeals denies the Government the most appropriate remedy for Snepp's acknowledged wrong. Indeed, as a practical matter, the decision may well leave the Government with no reliable deterrent against similar breaches of security. No one disputes that the actual damages attributable to a publication such as Snepp's generally are unquantifiable. Nominal damages are a hollow alternative, certain to deter no one. The punitive damages recoverable after a jury trial are speculative and unusual. Even if recovered, they may bear no relation to either the Government's irreparable loss or Snepp's unjust gain.

The Government could not pursue the only remedy that the Court of Appeals left it without losing the benefit of the bargain it seeks to enforce. Proof of the tortious conduct necessary to sustain an award of punitive damages might force the Government to disclose some of the very confidences that Snepp promised to protect. The trial of such a suit, before a jury if the defendant so elects, would subject the CIA and its officials to probing discovery into the Agency's highly confidential affairs. Rarely would the Government run this risk. In a letter introduced at Snepp's trial, former CIA Director Colby noted the analogous problem in criminal cases. Existing law, he stated, "requires the revelation in open court of confirming or additional information of such a nature that the potential damage to the national security precludes prosecution." When the Government cannot secure its remedy without unacceptable risks, it has no remedy at all.

A constructive trust, on the other hand, protects both the Government and the former agent from unwarranted risks. This remedy is the natural and customary consequence of a breach of trust. It deals fairly with both parties by conforming relief to the dimensions of the wrong. If the agent secures prepublication clearance, he can publish with no fear of liability. If the agent publishes unreviewed material in violation of his fiduciary and contractual obligation, the trust remedy simply requires him to disgorge the benefits of his faithlessness. Since the remedy is swift and sure, it is tailored to deter those who would place sensitive information at risk. And since the remedy reaches only funds attributable to the breach, it cannot saddle the former agent with exemplary damages out of all proportion to his gain. The decision of the Court of Appeals would deprive the Government of this equitable and effective means of protecting intelligence that may contribute to national security. We therefore reverse the judgment of the Court of Appeals insofar as it refused to impose a constructive trust on Snepp's profits, and we remand the cases to the Court of Appeals for reinstatement of the full judgment of the District Court.

MR. JUSTICE STEVENS, with whom MR. JUSTICE BRENNAN and MR. JUSTICE MARSHALL join, dissenting.

In 1968, Frank W. Snepp signed an employment agreement with the CIA in which he agreed to submit to the Agency any information he intended to publish about it for prepublication review. The purpose of such an agreement, as the Fourth Circuit held, is not to give the CIA the power to censor its employees' critical speech, but rather to ensure that classified, nonpublic information is not disclosed without the Agency's permission.

In this case Snepp admittedly breached his duty to submit the manuscript of his book, *Decent Interval*, to the CIA for prepublication review. However, the Government has conceded that the book contains no classified, nonpublic material. Thus, by definition, the interest in confidentiality that Snepp's contract was designed to protect has not been compromised. Nevertheless, the Court today grants the Government unprecedented and drastic relief in the form of a constructive trust over the profits derived by Snepp from the sale of the book. Because that remedy is not authorized by any applicable law and because it is most inappropriate for the Court to dispose of this novel issue summarily on the Government's conditional cross-petition for certiorari, I respectfully dissent.

I

The rule of law the Court announces today is not supported by statute, by the contract, or by the common law. Although Congress has enacted a number of criminal statutes punishing the unauthorized dissemination of certain types of classified information, it has not seen fit to authorize the constructive trust remedy the Court creates today. Nor does either of the contracts Snepp signed with the Agency provide for any such remedy in the event of a breach. The Court's per curiam opinion seems to suggest that its result is supported by a blend of the law of trusts and the law of contracts. But neither of these branches of the common law supports the imposition of a constructive trust under the circumstances of this case.

Plainly this is not a typical trust situation in which a settlor has conveyed legal title to certain assets to a trustee for the use and benefit of designated beneficiaries. Rather, it is an employment relationship in which the employee possesses fiduciary obligations arising out of his duty of loyalty to his employer. One of those obligations, long recognized by the common law even in the absence of a written employment agreement, is the duty to protect confidential or "classified" information. If Snepp had breached that obligation, the common law would support the implication of a constructive trust upon the benefits derived from his misuse of confidential information.

But Snepp did not breach his duty to protect confidential information. Rather, he breached a contractual duty, imposed in aid of the basic duty to maintain confidentiality, to obtain prepublication clearance. In order to justify the imposition of a constructive trust, the majority attempts to equate this contractual duty with Snepp's duty not to disclose, labeling them both as "fiduciary." I find nothing in the common law to support such an approach. * * *

[E]ven assuming that Snepp's covenant to submit to prepublication review should be enforced, the constructive trust imposed by the Court is not an appropriate remedy. If an employee has used his employer's confidential information for his own personal profit, a constructive trust over those profits is obviously an appropriate remedy because the profits are the direct result of the breach. But Snepp admittedly did not use confidential information in his book; nor were the profits from his book in any sense a product of his failure to submit the book for prepublication review. For, even if Snepp had submitted the book to the Agency for prepublication review, the Government's censorship authority would surely have been limited to the excision of classified material. In this case, then, it would have been obliged to clear the book for publication in precisely the same form as it now stands. Thus, Snepp has not gained any profits as a result of his breach; the Government, rather than Snepp, will be unjustly enriched if he is required to disgorge profits attributable entirely to his own legitimate activity.

Despite the fact that Snepp has not caused the Government the type of harm that would ordinarily be remedied by the imposition of a constructive trust, the Court attempts to justify a constructive trust remedy on the ground that the Government has suffered *some* harm. The Court states that publication of "unreviewed material" by a former CIA agent "can be detrimental to vital national interests even if the published information is unclassified." * * * I do not believe, however, that the Agency has any authority to censor its employees' publication of unclassified information on the basis of its opinion that publication may be "detrimental to vital national interests" or otherwise "identified as harmful." * * *

The Court also relies to some extent on the Government's theory at trial that Snepp caused it harm by flouting his prepublication review obligation and thus making it appear that the CIA was powerless to prevent its agents from publishing any information they chose to publish, whether classified or not. * * *

In any event, to the extent that the Government seeks to punish Snepp for the generalized harm he has caused by failing to submit to prepublication review and to deter others from following in his footsteps, punitive damages is, as the Court of Appeals held, clearly the preferable remedy "since a constructive trust depends on the concept of unjust enrichment rather than deterrence and punishment." * * *

NOTES

1. A strikingly similar case happened again in 2016. Ex-Navy SEAL Mark Bissonnette published the book *No Easy Day* of his firsthand account of the raid that killed terrorist leader Osama bin Laden. To settle civil and criminal actions filed against him by the government, Bissonnette agreed to forfeit $6.8 million in all of his book royalties and speaking fees, and $180,000

in related consulting fees. He apologized for failing to clear the book with the Pentagon before it was published so officials could ensure that it did not include classified information, and blamed his lawyer for advising him that he did not need to do so. Christopher Drew, *Ex-SEAL Member Who Wrote Book on Bin Laden Raid Forfeits $6.8 Million*, N.Y.Times, Aug. 20, 2016.

2.   The courts of equity called their restitutionary remedy "constructive trust" building on their usual work of enforcing actual trusts. The equity courts got into the business of supervising trustees to ensure that they observed their fiduciary duties in the handling of funds and property entrusted to them.

Yet, it is important to recognize that the constructive trust and the express trust have little but the name in common. An express trust is a substantive (and potentially complex) legal arrangement. Establishing a trust creates property rights in the beneficiary, and imposes substantive duties on the trustee. A constructive trust is a mere fiction, "constructed" out of law. It is a remedy, not the basis for a legal right. Just as a quasi-contract is not a real contract, a constructive trust is not a real trust.

3.   Another option for measuring restitution here would have been an accounting for profits. One of the duties equity imposed upon real trustees was the duty to account to the beneficiary for the disposition of the trust's property. Equitable accounting drew on that analogy, allowing the beneficiary of a trust to hold the trustee to answer for the property entrusted to him; if the property was income-generating, the trustee could be held answerable for the profits through an accounting for profits. Dan B. Dobbs, *Law of Remedies* § 4.3(5) (2d ed.1993). From its origins in the law of trusts, the accounting for profits later became available as a remedy whenever a fiduciary profited wrongfully from his position, or whenever profit-generating property was acquired wrongfully and the legal remedy was inadequate, either because tracing was involved or because the accounts involved were so complex that the simple forms of accounting available at law were inadequate. Dale Oesterle, *Restitution and Reform*, 79 Mich.L.Rev. 336, 351 (1979). For example, accounting for profits became available as a remedy in cases of unfair competition, trademark infringement and copyright infringement, among others. Dan B. Dobbs, *Law of Remedies* § 4.3 (2d ed.1993).

As seen in the *Earthinfo* case, an accounting for profits would have segregated out profits from the book associated with Snepp's own work as an author or the marketing of the book, and required the disgorgement only of the illegally-gotten gains. Why didn't the Court do this? (Hint: deterrence). *See* Daniel Friedmann, *Restitution for Wrongs: The Measure of Recovery*, 79 Tex.L.Rev. 1879 (2001).

TORRES V. EASTLICK (IN RE NORTH AMERICAN COIN & CURRENCY, LTD.)

United States Court of Appeals, Ninth Circuit
767 F.2d 1573, *cert. denied*, 475 U.S. 1083 (1985)

CANBY, CIRCUIT JUDGE.

North American Coin and Currency, Ltd. (hereinafter NAC or debtor) was an Arizona corporation in the business of buying and selling precious metals. The appellants are former customers of NAC who placed orders with the company and paid for them during the week of September 13, 1982, immediately before NAC filed for voluntary reorganization under Chapter 11 of the Bankruptcy Code. They brought this class action against the Bankruptcy Trustee, seeking to recover their funds from the bankruptcy estate. They claim that the trustee holds the funds in constructive trust for them because the debtor obtained the money by fraud or misrepresentation. On cross-motions for summary judgment, the bankruptcy court found for the trustee. The district court affirmed. We have jurisdiction over the appeal pursuant to 28 U.S.C. § 1291, and we affirm. * * *

[After discovering that NAC was threatened with insolvency, several people affiliated with NAC ("the principals") decided that they should try to operate the company for one more week until a scheduled board of director's and shareholder's meeting. To keep the company operating, while protecting new customers in case the company did not survive, the principals placed all receipts from new transactions during the week before the shareholder's meeting in a new bank account, labeled "Special Trust Account." If the board of directors voted to keep the company going and the shareholders infused the necessary new capital, the trust account funds were to be used to fill the customers' precious metals orders. If the company failed, the principals anticipated that the customers would get their money back.]

* * * NAC filed a Chapter 11 petition for reorganization on September 23, 1982. The funds in the "Special Trust Account" remain intact. The plaintiffs now assert that the trustee for NAC holds those funds in constructive trust for them.

Property that is truly in trust is not "property of the [trustee's] estate" within the meaning of section 541 of the Bankruptcy Code, 11 U.S.C. § 541. Plaintiffs argue that the same result must follow for property that is subject to a constructive trust. They further contend that, because the existence and nature of the debtor's interests in property are determined by reference to state law, they are entitled to all of the funds in the Special Account if Arizona law would view those funds as subject to a constructive trust.

While we agree that any constructive trust that is given effect must be a creature of Arizona law, we cannot accept the proposition that the bankruptcy estate is automatically deprived of any funds that state law might find subject to a constructive trust. * * * A constructive trust is not the same kind of interest in property as a joint tenancy or a remainder. It is a remedy, flexibly fashioned in equity to provide relief where a balancing of interests in the context of a particular case seems to call for it. Moreover, in the case presented here it is an inchoate remedy; we are not dealing with property that a state court decree has in the past placed under a constructive trust. We necessarily act very cautiously in exercising such a relatively undefined equitable power in favor of one group of potential creditors at the expense of other creditors, for ratable distribution among all creditors is one of the strongest policies behind the bankruptcy laws.

While state law must be applied in a manner consistent with federal bankruptcy law, we do not suggest that it is irrelevant. Arizona law permits the imposition of a constructive trust "whenever title to property has been obtained through actual fraud, misrepresentation, concealment, undue influence, duress, or through any other means which render it unconscionable for the holder of legal title to retain and enjoy its beneficial interest."

In permitting the imposition of a constructive trust for actions amounting to actual fraud, Arizona law is not inconsistent with federal bankruptcy law. Bankruptcy trustees have been held to have no interest in property acquired by fraud of bankrupts, as against the rightful owners of the property. The principle underlying this rule is that the creditors should not benefit from fraud at the expense of those who have been defrauded. * * *

In Arizona, as elsewhere, "actual fraud" is characterized by a willful intent to deceive. The debtor commits fraud, even though he has made no affirmative false representations, if he commits himself to a transaction with no intention of carrying it out. An intention not to carry out the transaction—in other words, a fraudulent intent—may be inferred where the debtor conceals his insolvency knowing that his financial situation is so hopeless that he can never meet the obligation he has acquired. However, the debtor's mere failure to disclose his insolvency, without more, does not constitute a fraud entitling the creditor to rescind the transaction. If the debtor believes in good faith that he will be able to carry out the transaction, he lacks the deceptive intent necessary for a finding of fraud.

We conclude that the evidence on which the plaintiffs rely does not support an inference that NAC intended to defraud them. * * *

Plaintiffs' final contention is that, even if the circumstances do not amount to actual fraud, we should impose a constructive trust on the ground that plaintiffs' funds were obtained by "means which render it unconscionable for the holder of legal title to retain and enjoy its beneficial interest." For reasons of federal bankruptcy policy to which we have already referred, we are reluctant so to exercise a general equitable power in the circumstances here presented. We fully recognize that plaintiffs have sustained substantial losses as a result of the NAC bankruptcy. Plaintiffs, however, comprise only one of several comparable groups of creditors who sustained substantial losses. Plaintiffs happened to place their orders during the week of September 13, with the result that their funds were placed in a "trust" account (even though it was contemplated that the funds might later be removed to complete the transactions). Another group of customers placed their orders shortly before September 13, but sent in their purchase money during the week of September 13. Their funds were not placed in a special account, and they must look to the bankruptcy proceeding for their relief. Other customers both placed their orders and sent in their funds prior to September 13, but their orders had not been executed at the time of the bankruptcy. They, too, are treated as general creditors in the bankruptcy. We fail to discern the equitable principle that requires us to protect the plaintiffs' investments fully, at the expense of these other creditors. Indeed, the equities, as well as the principles underlying the bankruptcy laws, point in the other direction. * * *

NOTES

1. *On the substantive law.* Although the constructive trust is often used as a remedy for wrongdoing—fraud, breach of fiduciary duty, and the like—it is not limited to those situations. Unjust enrichment is all that is required. "If a defendant is unjustly enriched by the acquisition of title to identifiable property at the expense of the claimant or in violation of the claimant's rights, the defendant may be declared a constructive trustee, for the benefit of the claimant, of the property in question and its traceable product." Restatement (Third) of Restitution, Constructive Trust, §55. A constructive trust can be used to recover benefits conferred by mistake, Citizens Federal Bank v. Cardian Mortgage Corp., 122 B.R. 255 (Bankr.E.D.Va.1990) (Virginia law) (money credited to account by bookkeeping error), or simply to avoid unfairness, Carr v. Carr, 576 A.2d 872 (N.J. 1990) (constructive trust imposed over a portion of the decedent's estate in favor of the spouse who, because decedent died while their divorce was pending, had no claim under New Jersey statutes).

On the other hand, the fact that the defendant owes the plaintiff a debt is not, standing alone, sufficient to give rise to a constructive trust. If money were paid or property delivered to another under circumstances that merely gave rise to a debt, the fact that the defendant was insolvent would not make that debt specifically enforceable. Restatement (Third) of Restitution § 55, cmt. *f.* Thus, the plaintiffs in *North American Coin and Currency* failed because they could not show that the money had been obtained by fraud, and under Arizona law, without fraud, a constructive trust could not arise. They were left with a mere debt.

The Ninth Circuit attempted to clarify *North American Coin and Currency* in Mitsui Manufacturers Bank v. Unicom Computer Corp., 13 F.3d 321 (9th Cir.1994). Holding that under California law a constructive trust could arise when a debtor negligently detained another's property, the court commented: "[W]e reject the [view] that our opinion in *In re North Am. Coin & Currency, Ltd.* created an elaborate, multi-part test to determine whether and under what circumstances a constructive trust may be imposed on property of a debtor * * * . Our decision should not be read as saying more than what it actually says; viz., that while state law must be the starting point in determining whether a constructive trust may arise in a federal bankruptcy case, that law must be applied in a manner not inconsistent with federal bankruptcy law." Is that clear? *See* Andrew Kull, *Restitution in Bankruptcy: Reclamation and Constructive Trust,* 72 Am.Bankr.L.J. 265 (1998).

2. *On the remedy.* As discussed above, a constructive trust can be specifically enforced, at least when the property in question is unique or the defendant insolvent. Then, it results in an order, directed to the defendant, to turn the wrongfully acquired property over to the plaintiff. Because the constructive trust gives the plaintiff the subject property *in specie,* the plaintiff acquires an advantage over an insolvent defendant's other creditors. Thus, had a constructive trust been imposed in *North American Coin & Currency,* the account in question would simply have been turned over to the plaintiffs. Similarly, the constructive trust can allow a plaintiff to reach property that would otherwise be exempt from a money judgment under a homestead or other exemption.

Without the constructive trust, the account remains in the debtor's estate. The plaintiffs are free to pursue their claim by seeking a money judgment for the amounts they are owed, but that judgment will simply establish them as general creditors, entitled to a share of the debtor's assets.

In order to establish a constructive trust, according to the court, they must show that the money was acquired by fraud. Why should that be the case? If NAC still has the plaintiffs' money, shouldn't NAC return it?

On the other hand, why should the plaintiffs have an advantage over NAC's other creditors, even if they can show fraud? According to the court, property acquired by fraud never becomes part of the bankrupt's estate because, in a sense, it is never his property. Why, though, does the manner in which the property was acquired make a difference? The court says that creditors should not benefit from the debtor's fraud at the expense of the one who was defrauded. Should they benefit from the defendant's breach of contract at the expense of the plaintiff?

PROBLEM: *MOORE V. REGENTS OF THE UNIVERSITY OF CALIFORNIA*

John Moore suffered from hairy cell leukemia. As part of his treatment, a doctor at one of the University of California's hospitals removed Moore's spleen, which had swollen from its normal weight of a few ounces to more than fifteen pounds. Using various bioengineering techniques, the doctor and his research colleagues developed a cell line using Moore's spleen that has extraordinary research and therapeutic potential. It has already been patented and sold to biotech firms, and the cell line's worth is probably measured in the tens, if not hundreds of millions of dollars. Assuming that the doctor violated his fiduciary duty to disclose his research and economic interests before obtaining Moore's consent to the operation (see Moore v. Regents of University of California, 793 P.2d 479 (Cal. 1990), *cert. denied*, 499 U.S. 936 (1991)), what remedies may be available to Moore? For a similar story, see Rebecca Skloot, *The Immortal Life of Henrietta Lacks* (2010) (detailing story of physician taking a black woman's cancerous cells to develop cure for cancer earning him great profits, though the woman was not helped and died).

3.   TRACING

In seeking restitution, plaintiffs may have to trace the proceeds of the defendant's profit through various conversions and forms. One advantage of equitable restitutionary remedies is the ability to trace. Tracing is a composition of legal fictions and doctrines allowing courts to identify property that must be returned to the plaintiff. This has advantages in cases of fraudulent defendants and defendants will long lines of creditors awaiting repayment.

THE CORPORATION OF THE PRESIDENT OF THE CHURCH OF JESUS CHRIST OF LATTER-DAY SAINTS V. JOLLEY

Supreme Court of Utah
467 P.2d 984 (1970)

CROCKETT, CHIEF JUSTICE.

This appeal challenges a judgment and decree of the district court which impressed against the defendant Vickie C. Jolley a constructive trust upon two new automobiles, a 1968 Pontiac Firebird and a 1968 Chevrolet Corvette which had been given her by one LaMar Kay, who had purchased the cars with money embezzled from the plaintiff church. On appeal defendant makes two contentions: 1) that a constructive trust can be imposed only on a fiduciary or confidant and not upon a third person with respect to whom no such relationship exists; and 2) that even if such a constructive trust could be imposed it should extend only to the amount of funds which were identified as being embezzled from the plaintiff and traced into that property.

Where the evidence is in dispute it is surveyed in the light favorable to the trial court findings. The said LaMar Kay was an accountant employed by the plaintiff church. During 1967 and 1968, by the use of fictitious firm names and pretended payment of claims he was engaged in a scheme of embezzling funds. In April of 1968 he drew from a fictitious account in the name of "Barker and Clayton" in the Murray State Bank a check in the amount of $4,305.57 made payable to Peck and Shaw, automobile dealers, with which he paid $4,224.62 for the Pontiac Firebird in question.

In August, 1968, he drew another check on the same account in the amount of $3,000 with which he purchased a cashier's check payable to Capital Chevrolet; this check was then presented to the latter company as part payment for the 1968 Chevrolet Corvette which had a total purchase price of $5,008.87. The balance on this car was paid by $50 cash on August 26, 1968, and $1,958.87 on August 30, 1968. The latter two cash payments admittedly were not traced directly through the "Barker and Clayton" account of embezzled funds into the Corvette automobile. But the evidence does show that a few days before he made those cash payments on that automobile, LaMar Kay had drawn $2,700 in cash from that account.

Upon completion of the purchases as above stated, the titles to both of these automobiles were transferred to the defendant Vickie C. Jolley; and there is no evidence nor contention made that she gave any legal consideration for them. Inasmuch as she is not a bona fide purchaser for value, her defenses in raising the question as to her lack of knowledge of the source of the funds which purchased the automobiles, and her averment that a constructive trust can only be impressed upon the wrongdoing fiduciary or confidant are of no avail to her. Where one has stolen or embezzled the money or property of another, he obtains no title whatsoever. A constructive trust may be impressed upon it in his hands; and equity may continue the trust effective against any subsequent transferee, unless transferred to a bona fide purchaser and under circumstances where equity would require a different result. The evidence in this case justified the court in its conclusion that the defendant had no better title to these automobiles than LaMar Kay had, and that they were held in constructive trust for the benefit of the plaintiff.

As to the defendant's second contention: that the plaintiff is not entitled to recover an equitable portion of the Corvette represented by the $1,958.87 and $50 cash payments which were not traced directly to the embezzled funds, this is to be said: Such direct tracing of funds is not an indispensable requisite to the conclusion arrived at. In the nature of the function of determining facts it is essential that the court or jury have the prerogative of finding not only facts based upon direct evidence, but also those which may be established from the reasonable inferences that may be deduced therefrom. The circumstances here shown concerning the associations of the defendant with LaMar Kay, including the facts that she went with him on the occasion of the purchase of the automobile; and that a few days previous to making the payments in question he had withdrawn $2,700 from the embezzled funds account, provide a reasonable basis for the trial court to believe that it was paid for entirely by money embezzled from plaintiff.

Affirmed.

HENRIOD, JUSTICE (dissenting).

Without expressing any opinion as to the rest of the main opinion and its conclusion, I dissent from that portion which includes $50 and $1,958.87 cash, in any amount upon which a purported trust could be impressed. The main opinion's own language reflects the weakness of the decision with respect to those amounts, which is compounded by the obvious conjecture indulged by 'guessing' that such amounts must have been a part of a much greater withdrawal. * * *

NOTE

Jolley demonstrates another advantage of the equitable remedies for unjust enrichment. To prevent unjust enrichment, the equity courts would follow, or "trace," the wrongfully held property through changes both in form (from money to car) and in possession (from Kay to Jolley), so long as a bona fide purchase for value did not intervene. The benefits of tracing are obvious. If the property has changed forms, only by tracing can the plaintiff obtain a specific restitutionary remedy and the advantage over general creditors that goes with it. The same is true if the property has changed hands. Tracing allows a specific remedy against the new holder, as to whom there might otherwise be no remedy at all.

Moreover, in the right circumstances, following property into its product can turn a neat profit for the plaintiff. Suppose Kay had bought stock with the church's money, instead of buying the cars. The stock would then be the product of the embezzled funds, and the church would be able to assert a constructive trust over it, profiting from any appreciation in its value. The church would get a windfall, which would be justified by adverting to the maxim that a wrongdoer should not profit from his wrongdoing.

Thus, while a profit-based measure of recovery has been the exception rather than the rule where legal restitution is concerned, equity has always admitted the possibility through the constructive trust. Both the profit-based measure of damages, however, and the capture of profits through the constructive trust have been restricted to cases of conscious wrongdoing. If the defendant acquired the plaintiff's property innocently and exchanged it for more valuable property, a constructive trust would not be enforced over the acquired property. That is, if Jolley, not knowing the cars were bought with embezzled money, had exchanged the cars for stock, and the stock appreciated in value, the church could not enforce a constructive trust over the stock. The church, instead, would be limited to another equitable remedy of the equitable lien.

In some circumstances, as where the innocent recipient of property subject to a constructive trust has exchanged it for more valuable property, an equitable lien may be the only equitable remedy available to a plaintiff. In other cases, however, the plaintiff may actually prefer an equitable lien even though a constructive trust would also be available. For example, if Kay had used the embezzled funds to purchase stock and the stock's value had depreciated, should the church seek a constructive trust over the stock, an equitable lien against it, or a money judgment for the amount embezzled?

IN RE MUSHROOM TRANSPORTATION CO.

United States Bankruptcy Court, Eastern District of Pennsylvania
227 B.R. 244 (Bank.E.D. Pa. 1998)

BRUCE FOX, BANKRUPTCY JUDGE.

The chapter 7 trustee of the consolidated entities known as Mushroom Transportation, Jeoffrey L. Burtch, has brought suit against a number of defendants, [asserting] that [the] defendants received the proceeds of property stolen from the estate of Mushroom Transportation by former counsel to the debtor, Jonathan Ganz. Further, the trustee averred that these * * * defendants "knew or reasonably should have known that the monies received" by them from Mr. Ganz did not belong to him. His complaint sought * * * monetary relief in four separate counts: two in common law—conversion and constructive trust; and two statutory claims—turnover (under 11 U.S.C. § 542 or 543) and "unauthorized transfer" pursuant to 11 U.S.C. §§ 549, 550.

In their opposition to the trustee's claims, the four defendants asserted that they had lent money to Mr. Ganz, they had been properly repaid by him, and there was no evidence that he had repaid them with money stolen from Mushroom Transportation. Further, Fidelity argued at trial that if it had been repaid with stolen money, it neither knew nor should have known of this fact and so were entitled to be treated as a good faith transferee who received the property for fair value.

* * *

I.

* * *

A.

The four causes of action stated against the defendants have a common evidentiary element: each of them requires a showing that the proceeds of funds stolen from the now consolidated estate of Mushroom Transportation were paid to the defendants. That is, the plaintiff here cannot prevail unless he can establish that the proceeds of estate funds from the debtor were transferred by Mr. Ganz to the defendants. * * *

Here, of course, Mr. Ganz deposited the funds he stole from the Mushroom estate into his personal bank account with Fidelity Bank. These funds were then commingled with other deposits (both before and after the thefts) and used to pay a large number of individuals and entities. Many of the other deposits were derived from legitimate sources; some were derived from thefts from other bankruptcy estates.

Obviously, Mr. Ganz, by his embezzlement of Mushroom funds, converted property of the bankruptcy estates to his own use as a matter of Pennsylvania law. Pennsylvania law would apply in this adversary proceeding because the theft of funds arose from Pennsylvania corporations, occurred in Pennsylvania, and the misappropriated funds were deposited in Pennsylvania. Since the proceeding here does not involve competing creditor claims to bankruptcy estate property, there are no federal bankruptcy policies which suggest that state law should be preempted. Thus, the bankruptcy trustee, acting on behalf of the Mushroom estate, has a claim against Mr. Ganz due to his theft of property.

* * *

Under state law, the bankruptcy estates, acting through the bankruptcy trustee, had the right to claim that the funds stolen by Mr. Ganz were held in trust by the thief on their behalf. Such a claim would prefer them to other creditors of Mr. Ganz. That is, even if Mr. Ganz were insolvent, the bankruptcy trustee could validly assert under Pennsylvania law that he should be repaid first from all funds stolen by Mr. Ganz and still in his possession, because those funds as a matter of state law were held by Mr. Ganz in trust for the Mushroom estate. However, in order to prevail on any trust claim against Ganz, the bankruptcy trustee must "trace the proceeds received from the conversion and identify them as contained in some specific fund or property in possession [of the wrongdoer.]" If the stolen funds were no longer in the possession of Mr. Ganz when the bankruptcy trustee made demand for their return, no such recovery would be ordered and the bankruptcy trustee would hold but a general unsecured claim against Ganz for conversion.

Were a third party to receive the converted funds from Ganz with knowledge that they were converted (either actual or presumed knowledge) then the bankruptcy trustee could recover the converted property from the third party recipient on the common law claims of conversion or constructive trust.

The fact that Ganz deposited the stolen funds into a bank account does not preclude the imposition of a constructive trust being established. However, it is necessary that the stolen funds be traced into that particular account. Where improperly converted assets of a trust estate are traced into the fund for distribution, a preference has always been allowed on the theory that such assets have never become a part of those of the trustee but at all times have remained, whether in their original or substituted form, the property of the cestui que trust, and therefore the trustee's general creditors are not entitled to any share in their distribution.

The fact that Ganz commingled the stolen Mushroom funds by depositing other funds, derived from both legitimate and illegitimate sources, into this bank account does not by itself preclude the imposition of a trust. However, tracing the amount of stolen funds remaining in the account at any given time involves the application of a number of common law presumptions.

As a general rule, in tracing the origins of funds withdrawn from a bank account, Pennsylvania applies the rule established in Clayton's Case, 1 Merrival 572 (Ch. 1816), that the funds first deposited are the funds first withdrawn.

This principle has been modified by application of the presumptions articulated in English common law in In re Hallett's Estate [Knatchbull v. Hallett], 13 Ch.D. 696 (1879) when tracing funds which have been commingled by a tortfeasor into a bank account. There are two related presumptions derived from *Hallett's Estate* and accepted in Pennsylvania (and federal) common law. First, if the fiduciary (i.e., tortfeasor/depositor) has a choice of withdrawing either the proceeds of trust funds or legitimate funds, then the fiduciary will withdraw the legitimate funds. Second, once the proceeds of the trust (i.e., stolen funds) are spent by the fiduciary, new deposits made are not treated as replenishing the trust proceeds. Together, these two tracing presumptions are sometimes referred to as the "lowest intermediate balance" rule.

As summarized by the Third Circuit Court of Appeals:

> The lowest intermediate balance rule, a legal construct, allows trust beneficiaries to assume that trust funds are withdrawn last from a commingled account. Once trust money is removed, however, it is not replenished by subsequent deposits. Therefore, the lowest intermediate balance in a commingled account represents trust funds that have never been dissipated and which are reasonably identifiable.

* * *

Counsel for the trustee in this adversary proceeding assumed at the end of the trial that certain commingled bank account presumptions, which as a matter of equity were established to resolve disputes regarding claims to property held by a tortfeasor, were applicable to the instant litigation. That is, the tracing decisions cited above generally involved disputes over claims to funds remaining on deposit in bank accounts still in the possession of the tortfeasor, rather than to claims against innocent third parties who dealt with the tortfeasor. Here, the application of the intermediate balance rule in any claim by the trustee for a constructive trust against Mr. Ganz would result in a conclusion that he no longer held any funds in trust, since his account balance reached zero on October 10, 1989—years before this litigation commenced.

Nonetheless, if I accept plaintiff's position, arguendo, and apply commingled bank account tracing presumptions to this dispute, there remain two defects to his claims against these four defendants on the evidence presented.

First, the evidence does not support the bankruptcy trustee's argument that the defendants here received the proceeds of funds stolen from the Mushroom estate. Not only does the plaintiff overlook the intermediate balance rule, but he also ignores the principle accepted in Pennsylvania that when trust funds from various estates are commingled, there is a presumption that they are treated on a "first in, first out" basis. *See* Fischbach & Moore v. Philadelphia Nat. Bank, 134 Pa. Super. at 91; *see also* Empire State Surety Co. v. Carroll County:

> Where a trustee has mingled in a common fund the moneys of many separate cestuis que trustent and then made payments out of this common fund, the legal presumption is that the moneys were paid out in the order in which they were paid in, and the cestuis que trustent are equitably entitled to any allowable preference in the inverse order of the times of their respective payments into the fund.

194 F. at 605.

Recently, the Pennsylvania Superior Court was faced with competing claims of two fraud victims to the remaining funds in a bank account of a tortfeasor who had deposited funds wrongfully obtained from both victims. Certain withdrawals had been made leaving a balance insufficient to repay both claimants. The appellate court concluded that, under Pennsylvania law, the funds withdrawn were derived from the first victim only based upon the "first in, first out" presumption:

> In attempting to trace funds, the rule in Pennsylvania is "first in, first out." Pursuant to this rule, "the legal presumption is that the moneys were paid out in the order which they were paid in, and [the parties claiming ownership] are equitably entitled to any allowable preference in the inverse order of the times of their respective payments into the fund." * * *

Here, the government audit of Mr. Ganz's Fidelity account makes clear that, upon application of the intermediate balance rule along with the first in, first out principle for the proceeds of stolen funds, there were no Mushroom funds remaining in that account at the time of Mr. Ganz's challenged payments to these defendants. If any stolen funds were presumptively in the Fidelity account at the time the two challenged transfers were made, using the intermediate balance rule that legitimate funds were dispersed first, and then using the first in, first out principle regarding stolen funds, the proceeds of stolen funds on hand at the time of the two transfers could only have been derived from bankruptcy estates other than Mushroom; Mr. Ganz deposited the proceeds of those other thefts after he deposited the Mushroom proceeds, and the Mushroom proceeds would have been spent.

Accordingly, the defendants did not receive any of the proceeds of funds stolen from the Mushroom estate. Since these four defendants never received any estate property, the trustee has no right to recover any funds paid to them based upon the four theories he has asserted. Therefore, the defendants are entitled to judgment.

B.

Second, even if the trustee had proven that the defendants had received the proceeds of Mr. Ganz's theft from the Mushroom estates, plaintiff's claims founder on a second requirement: that any recovery be against third parties who were not bona fide transferees for value.

* * *

As explained recently by the Pennsylvania Superior Court:

A cause of action for money had and received entitles a party to relief where money is wrongfully diverted from its proper use and that money subsequently falls into the hands of a third person who has not given valuable consideration for it. . . . The cause of action fails, however, where the recipient of the money has given consideration in exchange for the funds and is unaware that the money was procured by fraudulent means.

Under the Restatement of Restitution, the cause of action is defined as follows:

A person who, non-tortiously and without notice that another has the beneficial ownership of it, acquires property which it would not have been wrongful for him to acquire with notice of the facts and of which he is not a purchaser for value is, upon discovery of the facts, under a duty to account to the other for the direct product of the subject matter and the value of the use to him, if any, and in addition, to

a) return the subject matter in specie, if he has it;

b) pay its value to him, if he has non-tortiously consumed it in beneficial use;

c) pay its value or what he received therefor at his election, if he has disposed of it.

Restatement of Restitution § 123

Therefore, had Fidelity Bank and the A-1 defendants received funds from Mr. Ganz which could be traced to the proceeds of funds stolen from the Mushroom estates, there is no evidence that these defendants were not bona fide purchasers for value under state law.

Further, under Pennsylvania law it is well established that a tortfeasor's payments to third parties in satisfaction of antecedent debts represent fair value for the payments received.

* * *

In this proceeding there was no evidence presented to demonstrate that the four defendants involved in the instant trial received any payments from Mr. Ganz for which fair consideration was not given, or that they knew or should have known that the funds used to pay them did not belong to Mr. Ganz. On the contrary, the evidence is unrebutted that the defendants had lent money either to Mr. Ganz or an entity for which he provided a guarantee, and that the challenged transfers were simply repayments of those earlier obligations. * * *

Based upon this evidence, I conclude that the defendants were good faith transferees for value. As such, the plaintiff is not entitled to any relief.

* * *

NOTES

1.   Another advantage of tracing is that it can allow a plaintiff to recover misappropriated money that has been commingled with other money. Tracing, however, may be difficult when the commingled account has been subject to multiple deposits and withdrawals. Courts have developed a number of tracing fictions to be used in such cases. The first of these, the rule in *Clayton's Case*, or first-in, first-out (FIFO), is basically an accounting principle. FIFO posits that withdrawals are made in the same order as deposits, so that the money first deposited is first withdrawn. Suppose Thief steals $100 from Owner, and deposits it in an account, to which he adds $100 of his own. He then withdraws $100, and spends it, leaving $100 in the account. Under FIFO, the $100 remaining in the account belongs to Thief. The first money deposited (Owner's) is presumed to have been the first money withdrawn.

2.   Whatever its merits as an accounting principle, FIFO has little to recommend it in restitution cases, if equity and the prevention of unjust enrichment are the goals. In cases involving the commingling of a claimant's and a wrongdoer's funds, it has largely been replaced by the rule in *Hallett's Estate* (Knatchbull v. Hallett, 13 Ch.Div. 356 (1879)). According to *Hallett's Estate,* the wrongdoer is presumed to spend his own money first, whatever the order of deposits. Thus, in the above example, Thief would be presumed to have spent his own money first, and the $100 remaining in the account would be presumed to be Owner's.

The rule in *Hallett's Estate* is qualified, however, by the *lowest intermediate balance* rule. Once all the wrongdoer's money has been withdrawn, subsequent withdrawals can only have been from the misappropriated funds. Even if the balance in the account later increases, the claimant's stake cannot exceed the lowest balance in the account between the time of the original deposit and the present. Subsequent deposits to the account are not treated as restoring the claimant's funds, unless there is specific evidence that they were so intended. Thus, to continue with the example, if Thief withdraws an additional $25 from the account, reducing the balance to $75, the $25 withdrawal must have been Owner's money, as Thief's money has all already been withdrawn. Even if the balance in the account later increases to $100 or more because of subsequent deposits, Owner's claim against the account is limited to $75, the lowest intermediate balance. (It is important to keep in mind, however, that tracing is only required when an equitable remedy is sought. Owner can only impose a constructive trust on $75 in the account. He can, of course, seek a money judgment to compensate him for the additional $25.)

Applying the lowest intermediate balance rule, however, can be complicated. *See, e.g.,* Republic Supply Co. v. Richfield Oil Co., 79 F.2d 375 (9th Cir.1935) (rule is to be applied not by looking at the precise order of deposits and withdrawals, but by the account's daily closing balance). Also, some courts have made it relatively easy to establish that subsequent deposits to an account were intended to restore the trust fund, in which case the lowest intermediate balance rule does not preclude recovery. *See, e.g.,* Mitchell v. Dunn, 294 P. 386 (Cal.1930).

3. Thieves are not necessarily wastrels. Suppose Thief's first withdrawal from the account is invested lucratively, rather than wasted. Should it then be presumed that he spent his own money first? In *In re: Oatway* (Hertslet v. Oatway [1903] 2 Ch.Div. 356), an English case that has been followed in many American jurisdictions, the court developed the "option rule." The option rule allows the claimant against a fund that has commingled trust funds and the wrongdoer's funds to choose whether to treat any particular withdrawal as his, so long as his money could be traced to the account at the time of the withdrawal, consistent with the lowest intermediate balance rule.

4. When funds belonging to more than one claimant are commingled in an account, the *averaging approach* can provide an attractive, though sometimes complicated, alternative to FIFO. Suppose Thief embezzles $100 from Owner One and $100 from Owner Two and deposits it all in one account. Then, Thief spends $100 from the account on stock, which has appreciated by the time of trial to a value of $150. Finally, Thief withdraws the remaining $100, and spends it. Under the FIFO approach, the stock (the first withdrawal) would be presumed to have been purchased with Owner One's money (the first deposit). Owner One would have a claim to the stock, and Owner Two (whose money remained in the account, according to the fiction) would have a money judgment against the presumably insolvent Thief. (The *Hallett's Estate* approach is irrelevant because there is no reason to presume that Thief would spend one claimant's money before another's.)

The *averaging,* or *pro rata,* approach attempts to treat all claimants equitably by giving each a proportionate claim against any withdrawal in an amount determined by the claimant's share in the account at the time the withdrawal was made. Thus, since Owner One and Owner Two each had a claim to half of the account at the time of the withdrawal, each would have a claim to half of the stock.

5.   Keep in mind that the tracing fictions are equitable devices, and their use may be limited to avoid harm to creditors. *See* Bank of Alex Brown v. Goldberg, 158 B.R. 188 (Bankr.E.D.Cal.1993) (creditor must show his property was specifically and directly exchanged for the property subject to the trust if defendant is insolvent, unless tracing will not harm other creditors), aff'd, 168 B.R. 382 (9th Cir.BAP 1994); Emily Sherwin, *Unjust Enrichment and Creditors,* 27 Rev.Litig. 141 (2007).

6.   The first Restatement of Restitution attempted to develop an approach to tracing that would simplify and rationalize the law by eliminating tracing fictions, but its approach proved to be difficult to apply in complex cases and was not well-received by the courts. *See* George E. Palmer, *Law of Restitution* § 2.17 at 208 (1978). The Restatement (Third) of Restitution and Unjust Enrichment § 59 returns to more familiar ground, largely following traditional tracing rules. Within the limits of the lowest intermediate balance rule, it endorses the "marshalling" or "option" approach of *In re Oatway,* allowing a claimant whose funds are commingled with a wrongdoer's to follow his funds into any traceable product of the commingled account. As between claimants whose funds are commingled, the rule in *Clayton's Case (FIFO)* is rejected in favor of the averaging approach, giving each claimant a share of the account or its traceable products in proportion to the claimant's stake.

7.   Courts have adapted many of the tracing fictions in implementing statutory forfeiture schemes. *See, e.g.,* United States v. Banco Cafetero Panama, 797 F.2d 1154 (2d Cir.1986) (using tracing fictions to determine if funds in an account are "proceeds" of a drug transaction.); United States v. All Funds, 832 F.Supp. 542 (E.D.N.Y.1993). *See also* 18 U.S.C. § 984 (abrogating the lowest intermediate balance rule in forfeiture cases).

A TRACING PROBLEM

Arielle is an accountant who keeps the books for several small businesses. On August 17, she embezzled $10,000 from Grady, one of her clients. She used $4,000 to make the last payment on her car loan, and deposited the remaining $6,000 in her personal checking account. On August 30, she wrote a check to her landlord, George Mazel, for $1,000. On September 1, she deposited $2,000 of her own money in the account. On September 15, she bought 30 shares of common stock in Notachance, Inc., for $100 a share, paying for it with money from the account. On September 19, she embezzled $8,000 from a second client, Brennan, and deposited it in the account. On October 1, she deposited $2,000 of her own money in the account. On October 3, she purchased 600 shares of common stock in Quikbux, Inc., for $10 a share.

Grady and Brennan have discovered Arielle's embezzling. Identify the remedies available to them. (Notachance, Inc. is currently selling for $50 a share; Quikbux is going for $20.)

CHAPTER 8

REMEDIAL DEFENSES: CONDUCT OF THE PLAINTIFF

■ ■ ■

In both equity and law there are traditional rules, principles, and maxims that focus on the behavior of the plaintiff and, when applicable, bar the plaintiff from obtaining relief. Ultimately all of the principles and rules that we examine in this chapter involve misconduct by the plaintiff, but the degree and type of misconduct varies and traditionally a number of different maxims or principles have been invoked by the courts to bar a plaintiff from obtaining relief. Stated in their boldest traditional form, these rules and principles bar the plaintiff from all relief; in some circumstances they are used to modify or adjust a remedy. Frequently law and equity expressed the same root idea in different terms and applied different tests to the plaintiff's behavior. The categories established by the various principles are frequently not well defined at the margin, so that one category shades imperceptibly into another. For instance, the proposition that in order to obtain relief one must come into a court with "clean hands" is a very broad proposition. It can include the stricture against misleading another party to his detriment, which is found in equitable estoppel, or the prohibition against delaying the commencement of an action while the defendant proceeds with the activity that the plaintiff complains of, which is part of laches. The principles which have been inherited from equity are typically more flexible and less distinct than those which are derived from law.

These principles barring relief based on the plaintiff's conduct are conceptualized in practice as defenses to the remedy. Remedial defenses are in addition to existing procedural defenses, like the statute of limitations, or liability defenses, such as contributory negligence in tort. The main remedial defenses are unclean hands, *in pari delicto*, estoppel, waiver, and laches. Three of these, unclean hands, estoppel, and laches, derive from equity, and as equitable defenses there is often the question of whether they equally apply to claims for legal damages. The courts have said sometimes yes, and sometimes no.

A. AN OVERVIEW OF DEFENSES

Here is a brief summary of each of the key remedial defenses:

Unclean hands: "He who comes into equity must come with clean hands" is a central maxim of equity with a direct effect on the plaintiff's ability to obtain relief: the court will not provide relief to one who does not come with clean hands. While the metaphor of the maxim is a powerful image, it is, of course, remarkably uninformative as to the legal principle involved. As the Seventh Circuit has noted, "Today, 'unclean hands' really just means that in equity as in law the plaintiff's fault, like the defendant's, is relevant to the question of what if any remedy the plaintiff is entitled to." Scheiber v. Dolby Laboratories, Inc., 293 F.3d 1014, 1021 (7th Cir.2002), *cert. denied*, 537 U.S. 1109 (2003). The "unclean hands" maxim could be reformulated to state that the courts will not grant relief to plaintiffs who have committed improper conduct with regard to the matter in litigation. But this reformulation of the maxim still leaves a central issue vague: what conduct might be considered "improper"? Moreover, it may too narrowly restrict the sweep of the maxim, which has been interpreted elastically when considering how closely the plaintiff's behavior must be connected to the matter in litigation.

In pari delicto: "*In pari delicto potior est conditio defendentis*"—in a case of equal or mutual fault, the position of the defending party is the better one—is the common law parallel to the clean hands doctrine. A plaintiff who is *in pari delicto* with the defendant will receive no relief from the court. *In pari delicto* carries a greater emphasis on equality of fault than does the unclean hands defense and involves a mutuality of wrongdoing. The Supreme Court explained that "[t]he defense is grounded on two premises: first, that the courts should not lend their good offices to mediating disputes among wrongdoers; and second, that denying judicial relief to an admitted wrongdoer is an effective means of deterring illegality." Bateman Eichler, Hill Richards, Inc. v. Berner, 472 U.S. 299 (1985).

Estoppel: The remedial defense of estoppel stops a plaintiff from taking inconsistent positions when the defendant has relied upon a prior position, to its detriment. The legal maxim provides that litigants "should not be permitted to 'blow hot and cold' with reference to the same transaction, or insist, at different times, on the truth of each of two conflicting allegations, according to the promptings of their private interests." T. Leigh Anenson, *The Triumph of Equity: Equitable Estoppel in Modern Litigation*, 27 Rev. Litig. 377, 384 (2008) (noting "Lord Kenyon's definition of equitable estoppel" that "stands the test of time"). To qualify for this defense, defendants must show plaintiff's inconsistent actions and its detrimental reliance upon that inconsistency.

Waiver: Waiver and estoppel often are pled together. Estoppel arose in equity while waiver developed in common law. Waiver is the voluntary and intentional abandonment of a known right by the plaintiff. It is distinct from estoppel in that waiver emphasizes intentional contact and does not require any change or reliance by the defendant to operate as an effective defense. "Estoppel is designed to prevent the actor from profiting by exploiting actions or inaction he has induced another to take: waiver on the other hand focuses on the conduct of the actor himself in disavowing a right." James F. Fischer, *Understanding Remedies* § 65.0 (3d.ed.2014).

Laches: Laches is a remedial defense for the plaintiff's unreasonable delay. An equitable doctrine, "laches if founded on the notion that equity aids the vigilant and not those who slumber on their rights." Pro-Football, Inc. v. Harjo, 415 F.3d 44 (D.C. Cir. 2005). It is often called equity's statute of limitations. However, laches is much broader than this. Statutes of limitations address delay only by designating the set period of time after events have occurred by which the lawsuit must be filed, typically one to three years after an alleged injury or breach. The basic rationale of statutes of limitation is that with the passage of time evidence becomes less reliable—memories fade, witnesses die, documents can no longer be found—and there is an interest in ensuring repose and finality even in potential disputes.

Laches is delay that occurs at any time, not just in the initial filing of the lawsuit. It is defined as delay by a plaintiff in asserting rights that is not excusable or reasonable and that works to the prejudice or injury of the defendant. Prejudice comes in a variety of forms; changing one's economic position based on the belief that there is no live controversy with the plaintiff and the routine destruction of documents through a corporate document retention policy are two common examples. Laches is a defense to equitable actions; some courts following the merger of law and equity will allow the laches defense in legal actions, but generally the defense is limited to equitable actions.

These defenses have important common threads. First, their successful invocation leads to the denial of relief to the plaintiff. Second, this result is not justified by the defendant's conduct, which may be reprehensible, but by the plaintiff's misconduct. Third, the basis on which the maxims are applied is often not the rights of the litigant to the case but the interests of the public and the protection of the integrity of the court. But it is an open question in many cases whether the decision of the court to accept one of these defenses and leave things as it found them clearly serves the interests of the public. Frequently the court has to rely on long-term arguments to the effect that its refusal to grant relief to plaintiffs who behave in an unacceptable manner will discourage others from such behavior in the future. Not only do these arguments look to the long-term impacts, they ignore the windfall that the defendant obtains. Ideally, the doctrine will be simultaneously just to the plaintiff, defendant and the public.

B. UNCLEAN HANDS

McKENNON V. NASHVILLE BANNER PUBLISHING CO.

Supreme Court of the United States
513 U.S. 352 (1995)

JUSTICE KENNEDY delivered the opinion of the Court.

The question before us is whether an employee discharged in violation of the Age Discrimination in Employment Act of 1967 is barred from all relief when, after her discharge, the employer discovers evidence of wrongdoing that, in any event, would have led to the employee's termination on lawful and legitimate grounds.

I

For some 30 years, petitioner Christine McKennon worked for respondent Nashville Banner Publishing Company. She was discharged, the Banner claimed, as part of a work force reduction plan necessitated by cost considerations. McKennon, who was 62 years old when she lost her job, thought another reason explained her dismissal: her age. She filed suit . . . alleging that her discharge violated the Age Discrimination in Employment Act of 1967.

McKennon sought a variety of legal and equitable remedies available under the ADEA, including backpay.

In preparation of the case, the Banner took McKennon's deposition. She testified that, during her final year of employment, she had copied several confidential documents bearing upon the company's financial condition. She had access to these records as secretary to the Banner's comptroller. McKennon took the copies home and showed them to her husband. Her motivation, she averred, was an apprehension she was about to be fired because of her age. When she became concerned about her job, she removed and copied the documents for "insurance" and "protection." A few days after these deposition disclosures, the Banner sent McKennon a letter declaring that removal and copying of the records was in violation of her job responsibilities and advising her (again) that she was terminated. The Banner's letter also recited that had it known of McKennon's misconduct it would have discharged her at once for that reason. * * *

II

We shall assume, as summary judgment procedures require us to assume, that the sole reason for McKennon's initial discharge was her age, a discharge violative of the ADEA. Our further premise is that the misconduct revealed by the deposition was so grave that McKennon's immediate discharge would have followed its disclosure in any event. * * *

The Court of Appeals considered McKennon's misconduct, in effect, to be supervening grounds for termination. That may be so, but it does not follow ... that the misconduct renders it "irrelevant whether or not [McKennon] was discriminated against." We conclude that a violation of the ADEA cannot be so altogether disregarded.

The ADEA, enacted in 1967 as part of an ongoing congressional effort to eradicate discrimination in the workplace, reflects a societal condemnation of invidious bias in employment decisions. * * * When confronted with a violation of the ADEA, a district court is authorized to afford relief by means of reinstatement, backpay, injunctive relief, declaratory judgment, and attorney's fees. In the case of a willful violation of the Act, the ADEA authorizes an award of liquidated damages equal to the backpay award. The Act also gives federal courts the discretion to "grant such legal or equitable relief as may be appropriate to effectuate the purposes of [the Act]."

Congress designed the remedial measures in these statutes to serve as a "spur or catalyst" to cause employers "to self-examine and to self-evaluate their employment practices and to endeavor to eliminate, so far as possible, the last vestiges" of discrimination. Deterrence is one object of these statutes. Compensation for injuries caused by the prohibited discrimination is another.

As we have said, the case comes to us on the express assumption that an unlawful motive was the sole basis for the firing. McKennon's misconduct was not discovered until after she had been fired. The employer could not have been motivated by knowledge it did not have and it cannot now claim that the employee was fired for the nondiscriminatory reason. Mixed motive cases are inapposite here, except to the important extent they underscore the necessity of determining the employer's motives in ordering the discharge, an essential element in determining whether the employer violated the federal antidiscrimination law.

Our inquiry is not at an end, however, for even though the employer has violated the Act, we must consider how the after-acquired evidence of the employee's wrongdoing bears on the specific remedy to be ordered. Equity's maxim that a suitor who engaged in his own reprehensible conduct in the course of the transaction at issue must be denied equitable relief because of unclean hands, a rule which in conventional formulation operated *in limine* to bar the suitor from invoking the aid of the equity court, 2 S. Symons, *Pomeroy's Equity Jurisprudence* § 397, pp. 90–92 (5th ed. 1941), has not been applied where Congress authorizes broad equitable relief to serve important national policies. We have rejected the unclean hands defense "where a private suit serves important public purposes." Perma Life Mufflers, Inc. v. International Parts Corp., 392 U.S. 134, 138

(1968) (Sherman and Clayton Antitrust Acts). That does not mean, however, the employee's own misconduct is irrelevant to all the remedies otherwise available under the statute. The statute controlling this case provides that "the court shall have jurisdiction to grant such legal or equitable relief as may be appropriate to effectuate the purposes of this chapter, including without limitation judgments compelling employment, reinstatement or promotion, or enforcing the liability for [amounts owing to a person as a result of a violation of this chapter]." In giving effect to the ADEA, we must recognize the duality between the legitimate interests of the employer and the important claims of the employee who invokes the national employment policy mandated by the Act. The employee's wrongdoing must be taken into account, we conclude, lest the employer's legitimate concerns be ignored. The ADEA, like Title VII, is not a general regulation of the workplace but a law which prohibits discrimination. The statute does not constrain employers from exercising significant other prerogatives and discretions in the course of the hiring, promoting, and discharging of their employees. In determining appropriate remedial action, the employee's wrongdoing becomes relevant not to punish the employee, or out of concern "for the relative moral worth of the parties," but to take due account of the lawful prerogatives of the employer in the usual course of its business and the corresponding equities that it has arising from the employee's wrongdoing.

The proper boundaries of remedial relief in the general class of cases where, after termination, it is discovered that the employee has engaged in wrongdoing must be addressed by the judicial system in the ordinary course of further decisions, for the factual permutations and the equitable considerations they raise will vary from case to case. We do conclude that here, and as a general rule in cases of this type, neither reinstatement nor front pay is an appropriate remedy. It would be both inequitable and pointless to order the reinstatement of someone the employer would have terminated, and will terminate, in any event and upon lawful grounds.

The proper measure of backpay presents a more difficult problem. Resolution of this question must give proper recognition to the fact that an ADEA violation has occurred which must be deterred and compensated without undue infringement upon the employer's rights and prerogatives. The object of compensation is to restore the employee to the position he or she would have been in absent the discrimination, but that principle is difficult to apply with precision where there is after-acquired evidence of wrongdoing that would have led to termination on legitimate grounds had the employer known about it. Once an employer learns about employee wrongdoing that would lead to a legitimate discharge, we cannot require the employer to ignore the information, even if it is acquired during the course of discovery in a suit against the employer and even if the information might have gone undiscovered absent the suit. The beginning point in the trial court's formulation of a remedy should be calculation of backpay from the date of the unlawful discharge to the date the new information was discovered. In determining the appropriate order for relief, the court can consider taking into further account extraordinary equitable circumstances that affect the legitimate interests of either party. An absolute rule barring any recovery of backpay, however, would undermine the ADEA's objective of forcing employers to consider and examine their motivations, and of penalizing them for employment decisions that spring from age discrimination.

Where an employer seeks to rely upon after-acquired evidence of wrongdoing, it must first establish that the wrongdoing was of such severity that the employee in fact would have been terminated on those grounds alone if the employer had known of it at the time of the discharge. The concern that employers might as a routine matter undertake extensive discovery into an employee's background or performance on the job to resist claims under the Act is not an insubstantial one, but we think the authority of the courts to award attorney's fees, mandated under the statute, 29 U.S.C. §§ 216(b), 626(b), and to invoke the appropriate provisions of the Federal Rules of Civil Procedure will deter most abuses.

NOTE

The Court says that it has rejected the unclean hands defense for certain claims with an important public purpose like the antitrust laws, citing *Perma Life Mufflers*. The Court has, however, recognized the analogous common-law defense of *in pari delicto* (in equal fault) in a limited context in public law causes like antitrust and securities. Bateman Eichler, Hill Richards, Inc. v. Berner, 472 U.S. 299 (1985) (*in pari delicto* defense may bar damages action only if plaintiff equally responsible for violations and preclusion of suit would not significantly interfere with enforcement of securities law and protection of the investing public); *accord* Pinter v. Dahl, 486 U.S. 622 (1988). *In pari delicto* requires a higher threshold of bad conduct by the plaintiff, that it be equal to or greater than the illegal conduct of the defendant and that it be related to the subject of the lawsuit. Unclean hands requires only some wrongdoing by the plaintiff, not necessarily worse than the defendant's wrongdoing and not necessarily related to the claim.

C. LACHES

PRO-FOOTBALL, INC. V. HARJO

United States Court of Appealst
565 F.3d 880 (D.C. Cir. 2009), *cert. denied*, 558 U.S. 1025 (2009)

TATEL, CIRCUIT JUDGE.

At bottom, this case concerns whether various trademarks related to the Washington Redskins football team disparage Native Americans within the meaning of the Lanham Trademark Act, § 2, 15 U.S.C.

§ 1052(a). But that question has since been overshadowed by the defense of laches, the basis on which the district court first entered judgment for the Redskins six years ago. We reversed that decision, finding that the district court had misapplied the law of laches to the particular facts of the case. Pro-Football, Inc. v. Harjo (Harjo II), 415 F.3d 44, 50 (D.C.Cir.2005). On remand, the district court reconsidered the evidence in light of our instructions and again ruled for the team. Pro-Football, Inc. v. Harjo (Harjo III), 567 F.Supp.2d 46, 62 (D.D.C.2008). Now appealing that decision, the Native Americans who originally petitioned for cancellation of the mark argue only that the district court improperly assessed evidence of prejudice in applying laches to the facts at issue. Limited to that question, we see no error and affirm.

I

Because previous opinions have already described the background of this case at length, we provide only the essentials. Appellants, seven Native Americans, filed a 1992 action before the Patent and Trademark Office seeking cancelation of six Redskins trademarks that were, they argued, impermissibly disparaging towards members of their ethnic group. Pro-Football, the Redskins' corporate entity and the owner of the marks, argued to the Trademark Trial and Appeal Board that its long-standing use of the name, combined with petitioners' delay in bringing the case, called for application of laches, an equitable defense that applies where there is "(1) lack of diligence by the party against whom the defense is asserted, and (2) prejudice to the party asserting the defense." The TTAB disagreed, observing that petitioners asserted an interest in preventing "a substantial segment of the population" from being held up "to public ridicule," and that insofar as that interest reached "beyond the personal interest being asserted by the present petitioners," laches was inappropriate. Harjo v. Pro Football Inc., 30 U.S.P.Q.2d 1828, 1831 (TTAB 1994). Finding on the merits that the marks were indeed disparaging, the TTAB cancelled them, see Harjo v. Pro-Football Inc., 50 U.S.P.Q.2d 1705, 1749 (TTAB 1999), depriving Pro-Football of the ability to pursue infringers.

Pro-Football then exercised its option to dispute this holding by means of a civil action in the United States District Court for the District of Columbia. The district court sided with Pro-Football on the laches issue, holding that the 25-year delay between the mark's first registration in 1967 and the TTAB filing in 1992 indeed required dismissal of the action. We reversed. "[L]aches," we said, "attaches only to parties who have unjustifiably delayed," and the period of unjustifiable delay cannot start before a party reaches the age of majority. The youngest petitioner, Mateo Romero, was only a year old in 1967. Because the correct inquiry would have assessed his delay and the consequent prejudice to Pro-Football only from the day of his eighteenth birthday in December 1984, we remanded the record to the district court to consider, in the first instance, the defense of laches with respect to Romero.

On remand in this case, the district court again found the defense of laches persuasive. It held that the seven-year, nine-month "Romero Delay Period" evinced a lack of diligence on Romero's part, and following our instructions to consider both trial and economic prejudice, it found that that delay harmed Pro-Football. Now appealing from that decision, Romero challenges neither the applicability of laches *vel non* nor the district court's finding of unreasonable delay. We thus confine our review to the only question Romero does raise: whether the district court properly found trial and economic prejudice sufficient to support a defense of laches.

II

* * * Reviewing the district court's analysis of prejudice in light of its considerable discretion, we see no reason to reverse. The district court carefully followed our instruction to assess both trial and economic prejudice arising from the Romero Delay Period, finding both. Romero now challenges those determinations, and while his arguments are not without merit, the errors alleged cannot overcome our deferential standard of review.

The district court relied primarily on two factors in finding trial prejudice: (1) the death of former Redskins president Edward Bennett Williams during the Romero Delay Period; and (2) the delay period's general contribution to the time lapse from the date of registration. * * * According to the district court, both factors limited Pro-Football's ability to marshal evidence supporting its mark: Williams had met with Native American leaders close to the time of registration to discuss their views, while the nearly eight years of further delay made it more difficult to obtain any other contemporaneous evidence of public attitudes towards the mark. Romero mainly argues that this "lost evidence" would have had minimal value. He believes that Williams' testimony would have reflected only a narrow set of views on the disparaging nature of the Redskins marks, and that any possibility that 1967 attitudes could have been better surveyed at the time of an earlier suit is outweighed by other overwhelming evidence of disparagement. We needn't cast doubt on Romero's view of the evidence to hold that there was no abuse of discretion. The lost evidence of contemporaneous public opinion is surely not entirely irrelevant, and weighing the prejudice resulting from its loss falls well within the zone of the district court's discretion. In reviewing that assessment, we cannot assume that legally relevant evidence possibly available in an earlier action would have lacked persuasive content.

Nor can we fault the district court's evaluation of economic prejudice. Undisputed record evidence reveals a significant expansion of Redskins merchandising efforts and sizable investment in the mark during the Romero Delay Period. Romero believes this investment is irrelevant absent some evidence that Pro-Football would have acted otherwise—by, say, changing the Redskins name—if Romero had sued earlier. But the district court repeatedly rejected this argument * * * citing the holding in Bridgestone/Firestone Research, Inc. v. Automobile Club, 245 F.3d 1359, 1363 (Fed.Cir.2001), that "[e]conomic prejudice arises from investment in and development of the trademark, and the continued commercial use and economic promotion of a mark over a prolonged period adds weight to the evidence of prejudice." The court thus thought it sufficient that the team deployed investment capital toward a mark Romero waited too long to attack, whether or not the team could prove that it would necessarily have changed its name or employed a different investment strategy had Romero sued earlier.

This was no abuse of discretion. To be sure, a finding of prejudice requires at least some reliance on the absence of a lawsuit—if Pro-Football would have done exactly the same thing regardless of a more timely complaint, its laches defense devolves into claiming harm not from Romero's tardiness, but from Romero's success on the merits. But in contrast to the defense of estoppel—which requires evidence of specific reliance on a particular plaintiff's silence—laches requires only general evidence of prejudice, which may arise from mere proof of continued investment in the late-attacked mark alone. * * * We have thus described as sufficient "a reliance interest resulting from the defendant's continued development of good-will during th[e] period of delay," and treated evidence of continued investment as proof of prejudice sufficient to bar injunctive relief. * * * . Such continued investment was unquestionably present here. The district court thus acted well within our precedent—as well as the precedent of the Federal Circuit, which directly reviews TTAB decisions— in finding economic prejudice on the basis of investments made during the delay period. The lost value of these investments was sufficient evidence of prejudice for the district court to exercise its discretion to apply laches, even absent specific evidence that more productive investments would in fact have resulted from an earlier suit.

In so holding, we stress two factors. First, as the district court correctly noted, the amount of prejudice required in a given case varies with the length of the delay. "If only a short period of time elapses between accrual of the claim and suit, the magnitude of prejudice required before suit would be barred is great; if the delay is lengthy, a lesser showing of prejudice is required." This reflects the view that "equity aids the vigilant and not those who slumber on their rights," as well as the fact that evidence of prejudice is among the evidence that can be lost by delay. Eight years is a long time— a delay made only more unreasonable by Romero's acknowledged exposure to the various Redskins trademarks well before reaching the age of majority. The second point follows the first: because laches requires this equitable weighing of both the length of delay and the amount of prejudice, it leaves the district court very broad discretion to take account of the particular facts of particular cases. We have no basis for finding abuse of that discretion where, as here, the claim of error ultimately amounts to nothing more than a different take on hypothetical inquiries into what might have been.

[As a final issue, the court similarly held that laches barred the plaintiff's claim with respect to the "Redskinettes" trademark even though there was only 29 months of delay. The district court found the two marks intertwined, and the court of appeals agreed, holding "it is difficult to see how it could be inequitable to allow Romero to complain about the Redskins but equitable to allow his complaint about the Redskinettes, particularly because the Redskinettes name had been in use well before the date of registration."]

NOTE

A new set of (younger) Native American plaintiffs, presumably not barred by laches, then brought a separate sue to void the Redskins trademarks. The Trademark Office again canceled the registration, and the district court upheld that cancellation. Blackhorse v. Pro-Football, Inc., 112 F.Supp.3d 439 (E.D.Va. 2015). The team appealed to the Fourth Circuit, where it is now pending. Meanwhile, the House of Representatives introduced a bill to void all trademarks that disparage Native Americans, and members of Congress and the President appealed informally to the National Football League to cancel the mark. In December 2015, in a case denying the registration for a music band called "The Slants," the U.S. Court of Appeals for the Federal Circuit struck down the provision of the Lanham Act that allows cancellation for disparagement, finding it violated the First Amendment. In re Tam, 808 F.3d 1321 (Fed. Cir. 2015), *petition for cert. granted*, 2016 WL 1587871 (Sept. 29, 2016). The *Blackhorse* district court held to the contrary; that the trademark law did not violate the First Amendment. Even if the Redskins mark was ultimately cancelled, it would not prohibit the team from using it; rather, the lack of registration would only limit the team's ability to go after infringers, for example, in the lucrative merchandising market.

D. ESTOPPEL

PETRELLA V. METRO-GOLDWYN-MAYER, INC.

Supreme Court of the United States
572 U.S. __, 134 S.Ct. 1962 (2014)

JUSTICE GINSBURG delivered the opinion of the Court.

The Copyright Act provides that "[n]o civil action shall be maintained under the [Act] unless it is commenced within three years after the claim accrued." 17 U.S.C. § 507(b). This case presents the question whether the equitable defense of laches (unreasonable, prejudicial delay in commencing suit) may bar relief on a copyright infringement claim brought within

§ 507(b)'s three-year limitations period. Section 507(b), it is undisputed, bars relief of any kind for conduct occurring prior to the three-year limitations period. To the extent that an infringement suit seeks relief solely for conduct occurring within the limitations period, however, courts are not at liberty to jettison Congress' judgment on the timeliness of suit. Laches, we hold, cannot be invoked to preclude adjudication of a claim for damages brought within the three-year window. As to equitable relief, in extraordinary circumstances, laches may bar at the very threshold the particular relief requested by the plaintiff. And a plaintiff's delay can always be brought to bear at the remedial stage, in determining appropriate injunctive relief, and in assessing the "profits of the infringer . . . attributable to the infringement." § 504(b).

Petitioner Paula Petrella, in her suit for copyright infringement, sought no relief for conduct occurring outside § 507(b)'s three-year limitations period. Nevertheless, the courts below held that laches barred her suit in its entirety, without regard to the currency of the conduct of which Petrella complains. That position, we hold, is contrary to § 507(b) and this Court's precedent on the province of laches. * * *

II

A

The allegedly infringing work in this case is the critically acclaimed motion picture Raging Bull, based on the life of boxing champion Jake LaMotta. After retiring from the ring, LaMotta worked with his longtime friend, Frank Petrella, to tell the story of the boxer's career. Their venture resulted in three copyrighted works: two screenplays, one registered in 1963, the other in 1973, and a book, registered in 1970. This case centers on the screenplay registered in 1963. The registration identified Frank Petrella as sole author, but also stated that the screenplay was written "in collaboration with"

In 1976, Frank Petrella and LaMotta assigned their rights in the three works, including renewal rights, to Chartoff-Winkler Productions, Inc. Two years later, respondent United Artists Corporation, a subsidiary of respondent Metro-Goldwyn-Mayer, Inc. (collectively, MGM), acquired the motion picture rights to the book and both screenplays, rights stated by the parties to be "exclusiv[e] and forever, including all periods of copyright and renewals and extensions thereof." *Id.* In 1980, MGM released, and registered a copyright in, the film Raging Bull, directed by Martin Scorsese and starring Robert De Niro, who won a Best Actor Academy Award for his portrayal of LaMotta. MGM continues to market the film, and has converted it into formats unimagined in 1980, including DVD and Blu-ray.

Frank Petrella died in 1981, during the initial terms of the copyrights in the screenplays and book. As this Court's decision in Stewart confirmed,

Frank Petrella's renewal rights reverted to his heirs, who could renew the copyrights unburdened by any assignment previously made by the author.

Paula Petrella (Petrella) is Frank Petrella's daughter. Learning of this Court's decision in Stewart, Petrella engaged an attorney who, in 1991, renewed the copyright in the 1963 screenplay. Because the copyrights in the 1973 screenplay and the 1970 book were not timely renewed, the infringement claims in this case rest exclusively on the screenplay registered in 1963. Petrella is now sole owner of the copyright in that work.

In 1998, seven years after filing for renewal of the copyright in the 1963 screenplay, Petrella's attorney informed MGM that Petrella had obtained the copyright to that screenplay. Exploitation of any derivative work, including Raging Bull, the attorney asserted, infringed on the copyright now vested in Petrella. During the next two years, counsel for Petrella and MGM exchanged letters in which MGM denied the validity of the infringement claims, and Petrella repeatedly threatened to take legal action.

B

Some nine years later, on January 6, 2009, Petrella filed a copyright infringement suit in the United States District Court for the Central District of California. She alleged that MGM violated and continued to violate her copyright in the 1963 screenplay by using, producing, and distributing Raging Bull, a work she described as derivative of the 1963 screenplay. Petrella's complaint sought monetary and injunctive relief. Because the statute of limitations for copyright claims requires commencement of suit "within three years after the claim accrued," § 507(b), Petrella sought relief only for acts of infringement occurring on or after January 6, 2006. No relief, she recognizes, can be awarded for infringing acts prior to that date.

MGM moved for summary judgment on several grounds, among them, the equitable doctrine of laches. Petrella's 18-year delay, from the 1991 renewal of the copyright on which she relied, until 2009, when she commenced suit, MGM maintained, was unreasonable and prejudicial to MGM.

The District Court . . . held, laches barred Petrella's complaint. Petrella had unreasonably delayed suit by not filing until 2009, the court concluded, and further determined that MGM was prejudiced by the delay. In particular, the court stated, MGM had shown "expectations-based prejudice," because the company had "made significant investments in exploiting the film"; in addition, the court accepted that MGM would encounter "evidentiary prejudice," because Frank Petrella had died and LaMotta, then aged 88, appeared to have sustained a loss of memory.

The U.S. Court of Appeals for the Ninth Circuit affirmed the laches-based dismissal. * * * "[T]he true cause of Petrella's delay," the court suggested, "was, as [Petrella] admits, that 'the film hadn't made money' [in years she deferred suit]." Agreeing with the District Court, the Ninth Circuit determined that MGM had established expectations-based prejudice: the company had made a large investment in Raging Bull, believing it had complete ownership and control of the film.

III

We consider first whether, as the Ninth Circuit held, laches may be invoked as a bar to Petrella's pursuit of legal remedies under 17 U.S.C. § 504(b). The Ninth Circuit erred, we hold, in failing to recognize that the copyright statute of limitations, § 507(b), itself takes account of delay. As earlier observed, a successful plaintiff can gain retrospective relief only three years back from the time of suit. No recovery may be had for infringement in earlier years. Profits made in those years remain the defendant's to keep. Brought to bear here, § 507(b) directs that MGM's returns on its investment in Raging Bull in years outside the three-year window (years before 2006) cannot be reached by Petrella. * * *

Last, but hardly least, laches is a defense developed by courts of equity; its principal application was, and remains, to claims of an equitable cast for which the Legislature has provided no fixed time limitation. See 1 D. Dobbs, Law of Remedies § 2.4(4), p. 104 (2d ed. 1993) ("laches . . . may have originated in equity because no statute of limitations applied, . . . suggest[ing] that laches should be limited to cases in which no statute of limitations applies"). Both before and after the merger of law and equity in 1938, this Court has cautioned against invoking laches to bar legal relief.

Because we adhere to the position that, in face of a statute of limitations enacted by Congress, laches cannot be invoked to bar legal relief, the dissent thinks we "plac[e] insufficient weight upon the rules and practice of modern litigation." True, there has been, since 1938, only "one form of action—the civil action." Fed. Rule Civ. Proc. 2. But "the substantive and remedial principles [applicable] prior to the advent of the federal rules [have] not changed." * * * Yet tellingly, the dissent has come up with no case in which this Court has approved the application of laches to bar a claim for damages brought within the time allowed by a federal statute of limitations. There is nothing at all "differen[t]," about copyright cases in this regard.

IV

We turn now to MGM's principal arguments regarding the contemporary scope of the laches defense, all of them embraced by the dissent.

A

Laches is listed among affirmative defenses, along with, but discrete from, the statute of limitations, in Federal Rule of Civil Procedure 8(c).

Accordingly, MGM maintains, the plea is "available . . . in every civil action" to bar all forms of relief.

The expansive role for laches MGM envisions careens away from understandings, past and present, of the essentially gap-filling, not legislation-overriding, office of laches. Nothing in this Court's precedent suggests a doctrine of such sweep. Quite the contrary, we have never applied laches to bar in their entirety claims for discrete wrongs occurring within a federally prescribed limitations period. Inviting individual judges to set a time limit other than the one Congress prescribed, we note, would tug against the uniformity Congress sought to achieve when it enacted § 507(b). * * *

B

MGM observes that equitable tolling "is read into every federal statute of limitation," and asks why laches should not be treated similarly. Tolling, which lengthens the time for commencing a civil action in appropriate circumstances, applies when there is a statute of limitations; it is, in effect, a rule of interpretation tied to that limit. Laches, in contrast, originally served as a guide when no statute of limitations controlled the claim; it can scarcely be described as a rule for interpreting a statutory prescription. That is so here, because the statute, § 507(b), makes the starting trigger an infringing act committed three years back from the commencement of suit, while laches, as conceived by the Ninth Circuit and advanced by MGM, makes the presumptive trigger the defendant's *initial* infringing act.

C

MGM insists that the defense of laches must be available to prevent a copyright owner from sitting still, doing nothing, waiting to see what the outcome of an alleged infringer's investment will be. In this case, MGM stresses, "[Petrella] conceded that she waited to file because 'the film was deeply in debt and in the red and would probably never recoup.'" The Ninth Circuit similarly faulted Petrella for waiting to sue until the film Raging Bull "made money."

It is hardly incumbent on copyright owners, however, to challenge each and every actionable infringement. And there is nothing untoward about waiting to see whether an infringer's exploitation undercuts the value of the copyrighted work, has no effect on the original work, or even complements it. Fan sites prompted by a book or film, for example, may benefit the copyright owner. Even if an infringement is harmful, the harm may be too small to justify the cost of litigation.

If the rule were, as MGM urges, "sue soon, or forever hold your peace," copyright owners would have to mount a federal case fast to stop seemingly innocuous infringements, lest those infringements eventually grow in magnitude. Section 507(b)'s three-year limitations period, however, coupled to the separate-accrual rule, avoids such litigation profusion. It allows a copyright owner to defer suit until she can estimate whether litigation is worth the candle. She will miss out on damages for periods prior to the three-year look-back, but her right to prospective injunctive relief should, in most cases, remain unaltered.

D

MGM points to the danger that evidence needed or useful to defend against liability will be lost during a copyright owner's inaction. Recall, however, that Congress provided for reversionary renewal rights exercisable by an author's heirs, rights that can be exercised, at the earliest for pre-1978 copyrights, 28 years after a work was written and copyrighted. At that time, the author, and perhaps other witnesses to the creation of the work, will be dead. Congress must have been aware that the passage of time and the author's death could cause a loss or dilution of evidence. Congress chose, nonetheless, to give the author's family "a second chance to obtain fair remuneration."

Moreover, a copyright plaintiff bears the burden of proving infringement. Any hindrance caused by the unavailability of evidence, therefore, is at least as likely to affect plaintiffs as it is to disadvantage defendants. That is so in cases of the kind Petrella is pursuing, for a deceased author most probably would have supported his heir's claim. * * *

E

Finally, when a copyright owner engages in intentionally misleading representations concerning his abstention from suit, and the alleged infringer detrimentally relies on the copyright owner's deception, the doctrine of estoppel may bar the copyright owner's claims completely, eliminating all potential remedies. The test for estoppel is more exacting than the test for laches, and the two defenses are differently oriented. The gravamen of estoppel, a defense long recognized as available in actions at law, is misleading and consequent loss. Delay may be involved, but is not an element of the defense. For laches, timeliness is the essential element. In contrast to laches, urged by MGM entirely to override the statute of limitations Congress prescribed, estoppel does not undermine Congress' prescription, for it rests on misleading, whether engaged in early on, or later in time.

Stating that the Ninth Circuit "ha[d] taken a wrong turn in its formulation and application of laches in copyright cases," Judge Fletcher called for fresh consideration of the issue. "A recognition of the distinction between . . . estoppel and laches," he suggested, "would be a good place to start." We agree.

V

The courts below summarily disposed of Petrella's case based on laches, preventing adjudication of any of her claims on the merits and foreclosing the possibility of any form of relief. That disposition, we have explained, was erroneous. Congress' time provisions secured to authors a copyright term of long duration, and a right to sue for infringement occurring no more than three years back from the time of suit. That regime leaves "little place" for a doctrine that would further limit the timeliness of a copyright owner's suit. See 1 Dobbs § 2.6(1), at 152. In extraordinary circumstances, however, the consequences of a delay in commencing suit may be of sufficient magnitude to warrant, at the very outset of the litigation, curtailment of the relief equitably awardable.

Chirco v. Crosswinds Communities, Inc., 474 F.3d 227 (C.A.6 2007), is illustrative. In that case, the defendants were alleged to have used without permission, in planning and building a housing development, the plaintiffs' copyrighted architectural design. Long aware of the defendants' project, the plaintiffs took no steps to halt the housing development until more than 168 units were built, 109 of which were occupied. Although the action was filed within § 507(b)'s three-year statute of limitations, the District Court granted summary judgment to the defendants, dismissing the entire case on grounds of laches. The trial court's rejection of the entire suit could not stand, the Court of Appeals explained, for it was not within the Judiciary's ken to debate the wisdom of § 507(b)'s three-year look-back prescription. Nevertheless, the Court of Appeals affirmed the District Court's judgment to this extent: The plaintiffs, even if they might succeed in proving infringement of their copyrighted design, would not be entitled to an order mandating destruction of the housing project. That relief would be inequitable, the Sixth Circuit held, for two reasons: the plaintiffs knew of the defendants' construction plans before the defendants broke ground, yet failed to take readily available measures to stop the project; and the requested relief would "work an unjust hardship" upon the defendants and innocent third parties. *See also* New Era Publications Int'l v. Henry Holt & Co., 873 F.2d 576, 584–585 (C.A.2 1989) (despite awareness since 1986 that book containing allegedly infringing material would be published in the United States, copyright owner did not seek a restraining order until 1988, after the book had been printed, packed, and shipped; as injunctive relief "would [have] result[ed] in the total destruction of the work," the court "relegat[ed plaintiff] to its damages remedy").

In sum, the courts below erred in treating laches as a complete bar to Petrella's copyright infringement suit. The action was commenced within the bounds of § 507(b), the Act's time-to-sue prescription, and does not present extraordinary circumstances of the kind involved in Chirco and New Era. Petrella notified MGM of her copyright claims before MGM invested millions of dollars in creating a new edition of Raging Bull. And the equitable relief Petrella seeks—e.g., disgorgement of unjust gains and an injunction against future infringement—would not result in "total destruction" of the film, or anything close to it. MGM released Raging Bull more than three decades ago and has marketed it continuously since then.

Allowing Petrella's suit to go forward will put at risk only a fraction of the income MGM has earned during that period and will work no unjust hardship on innocent third parties, such as consumers who have purchased copies of Raging Bull. Cf. Chirco, 474 F.3d, at 235–236 (destruction remedy would have ousted families from recently purchased homes). The circumstances here may or may not (we need not decide) warrant limiting relief at the remedial stage, but they are not sufficiently extraordinary to justify threshold dismissal.

Should Petrella ultimately prevail on the merits, the District Court, in determining appropriate injunctive relief and assessing profits, may take account of her delay in commencing suit. In doing so, however, that court should closely examine MGM's alleged reliance on Petrella's delay. This examination should take account of MGM's early knowledge of Petrella's claims, the protection MGM might have achieved through pursuit of a declaratory judgment action, the extent to which MGM's investment was protected by the separate-accrual rule, the court's authority to order injunctive relief "on such terms as it may deem reasonable," § 502(a), and any other considerations that would justify adjusting injunctive relief or profits. * * * *See also* Tr. of Oral Arg. 23 (Government observation that, in fashioning equitable remedies, court has considerable leeway; it could, for example, allow MGM to continue using Raging Bull as a derivative work upon payment of a reasonable royalty to Petrella). Whatever adjustments may be in order in awarding injunctive relief, and in accounting for MGM's gains and profits, on the facts thus far presented, there is no evident basis for immunizing MGM's present and future uses of the copyrighted work, free from any obligation to pay royalties.

JUSTICE BREYER, with whom THE CHIEF JUSTICE, and JUSTICE KENNEDY join, dissenting.

Legal systems contain doctrines that help courts avoid the unfairness that might arise were legal rules to apply strictly to every case no matter how unusual the circumstances. "[T]he nature of the equitable," Aristotle long ago observed, is "a correction of law where it is defective owing to its universality." *Nicomachean Ethics* 99 (D. Ross transl. L. Brown ed. 2009). Laches is one such equitable doctrine. It applies in those extraordinary cases where the plaintiff "unreasonably delays in filing a suit," and, as a result, causes "unjust hardship" to the defendant. Its purpose is to avoid "inequity." * * *

Today's decision disables federal courts from addressing that inequity. I respectfully dissent. * * *

A 20-year delay in bringing suit could easily prove inequitable. * * * Cases that present these kinds of delays are not imaginary. One can easily find examples from the lower courts where plaintiffs have brought claims years after they accrued and where delay-related inequity resulted. * * *

Consider, too, the present case. The petitioner claims the MGM film Raging Bull violated a copyright originally owned by her father, which she inherited and then renewed in 1991. She waited 18 years after renewing the copyright, until 2009, to bring suit. During those 18 years, MGM spent millions of dollars developing different editions of, and marketing, the film. MGM also entered into numerous licensing agreements, some of which allowed television networks to broadcast the film through 2015. Meanwhile, three key witness died or became unavailable, making it more difficult for MGM to prove that it did not infringe the petitioner's copyright (either because the 1963 screenplay was in fact derived from a different book, the rights to which MGM owned under a nonchallenged license, or because MGM held a license to the screenplay under a 1976 agreement that it signed with Jake LaMotta, who coauthored the screenplay with the petitioner's father.

[I]n permitting laches to apply to copyright claims seeking equitable relief but not to those seeking legal relief, the majority places insufficient weight upon the rules and practice of modern litigation. Since 1938, Congress and the Federal Rules have replaced what would once have been actions "at law" and actions "in equity" with the "civil action." Fed. Rule Civ. Proc. 2. A federal civil action is subject to both equitable and legal defenses. Fed. Rule Civ. Proc. 8(c)(1). Accordingly, since 1938, federal courts have frequently allowed defendants to assert what were formerly equitable defenses—including laches—in what were formerly legal actions. Why should copyright be treated differently? Indeed, the majority concedes that "restitutional remedies" like "profits" (which are often claimed in copyright cases) defy clear classification as "equitable" or "legal." Why should lower courts have to make these uneasy and unnatural distinctions?

[T]he majority believes it can prevent the inequities that laches seeks to avoid through the use of a different doctrine, namely equitable estoppel. I doubt that is so. As the majority recognizes, "the two defenses are differently oriented." The "gravamen" of estoppel is a misleading representation by the plaintiff that the defendant relies on to his detriment. The gravamen of laches is the plaintiff's unreasonable delay, and the consequent prejudice to the defendant. Where due to the passage of time, evidence favorable to the defense has disappeared or the defendant has continued to invest in a derivative work, what misleading representation by the plaintiff is there to estop?

In sum, as the majority says, the doctrine of laches may occupy only a "little place" in a regime based upon statutes of limitations. But that place is an important one.

NOTE

As the attorney for MGM on remand, how would you follow the Supreme Court's advice and make the case that Petrella should be barred from relief because of equitable estoppel? What are Petrella's inconsistent actions? Has she waived her claims? *See* Petrella v. MGM, 584 Fed.Appx. 653 (9th Cir. 2014) (making estoppel claims with respect to facts rather than factors of equitable estoppel defense).

CHAPTER 9

ATTORNEY'S FEES

■ ■ ■

Court-awarded attorney's fees are an important aspect of many types of litigation. In these cases, the fees are awarded as a remedy to the prevailing party to compensate her for having to fund the litigation in the case. Yet, these cases are the exception to the rule; the normal rule in the U.S. is that each party pays its own fees.

Where fees are available, compiling, negotiating, and litigating a fee request can take perhaps as much as a tenth of the time spent on the case, or more if fee issues are hotly disputed. Working on a fee application is a time for retrospection. It forces the attorneys and the judge to think back on a train of events that often goes back years. Since the application should document how each block of hours was used, the process makes one recall events that were so intense when they happened that one would have never believed that they could be forgotten. Moreover, it is now the prevailing attorney who is on trial: did she use her time prudently or could she have conducted the case in a more cost-effective manner? Perhaps it is these elements, as much as the amounts of money involved that makes the fee application so hotly contested in some cases; the case in chief is over, but the attorneys fight on, reviewing their own behavior in the suit.

Attorney's fees are important for reasons beyond the time and money involved. Just as the availability of damages tends to encourage or discourage particular conduct by would-be plaintiffs and defendants, the possible award of fees affects, and is intended to affect, the behavior of the litigants and their attorneys. Fees can prompt litigation which could not be paid for otherwise or fund the expansion of a private firm or public interest group after a successful suit. The availability of fees for supervising compliance with a decree can radically enlarge the plaintiff's role in decree administration and enforcement. At the same time, the availability of fees to a prevailing defendant, or even the threat of such fees, can discourage suits altogether or prompt plaintiffs to delete from complaints less promising causes of action.

A. THE AMERICAN RULE

The basic "American Rule" regarding attorney's fees has long been that each side pays its own unless the parties have agreed otherwise in advance by contract, or unless a court is authorized by a statute or by a recognized equitable exception to shift payment of the fees to the opposing party.

Arcambel v. Wiseman, 3 U.S. (3 Dall.) 306 (1796), is recognized as the judicial source of the American Rule. In contrast, under the "English Rule," prevailing parties recover fees as a matter of course from the losing party. The English Rule is followed in most common law countries and in Europe. *See* Robert G. Bone, *The Economics of Civil Procedure* 158–86 (2003) (considering whether the U.S. should adopt the English rule); Charles E. Hyde & Philip L. Williams, *Necessary Costs and Expenditure Incentives Under the English Rule,* 22 Int'l L. & Econ. 133 (2002) (under English rule, the sum awarded to winning party is actually based upon the amount the court finds was "necessary" for the attainment of justice); Virginia G. Maurer, Robert E. Thomas & Pamela A. DeBooth, *Attorney Fee Arrangements: The U.S. and Western European Perspectives*, 19 Nw. J. Int'l L. & Bus. 272 (1999). Japan is one of the very few other major industrial countries in the world to have adopted the American Rule. *See* Kojima & Taniguchi, *Access to Justice in Japan: Japanese National Report on Access to Justice*, 1 Access to Justice 689, 705 (1978) (significant exception of fee shifting in favor of prevailing tort plaintiffs). Alaska is an example of the rare state where the English Rule has been adopted in a modified form—prevailing parties are partially compensated for productive work performed by their attorneys. Susanne Di Pietro & Teresa W. Carns, *Alaska's English Rule: Attorney's Fee Shifting in Civil Cases*, 13 Alaska L. Rev. 33 (1996).

The Supreme Court of the United States has offered several reasons for its adherence to the American Rule. These include: 1) to avoid discouraging the poor from bringing a meritorious lawsuit because of the possibility of having to pay the other side's fees; 2) not penalizing any party merely for bringing a suit; and 3) not imposing a great burden on judicial administration due to the inherent difficulty in computing fees. *See, e.g.,* Fleischmann Distilling Corp. v. Maier Brewing Co., 386 U.S. 714 (1967); Oelrichs v. Spain, 82 U.S. (15 Wall.) 211 (1872). Thus, "[i]n combination with the contingent fee, the American Rule has opened the courthouse door to individuals who would have lacked either adequate resources or ability to tolerate (let alone diversify) risk to bring a lawsuit." Stephen B. Burbank & Linda J. Silberman, *Civil Procedure Reform in Comparative Context: The United States of America*, 45 Am. J. Comp. L. 675, 691–92 (1997). On the other hand, because application of the American Rule means that a vindicated party usually pays its own fees, critics note that it fails to restore the parties to their rightful positions by making prevailing parties whole. *E.g.,* Walter Olson & David Bernstein, *Loser-Pays: Where Next?,* 55 Md.L.Rev. 1161 (1996) (contending that more legislatures should experiment with the English Rule). Combined with that other unique American device, the contingency fee, the American Rule almost certainly contributes to the increased quantity and cost of litigation in the United States as compared to other industrialized countries. Robert A. Kagan, *Adversarial Legalism: The American Way of Law* (2001). *See also* Herbert

M. Kritzer, *Risks, Reputations and Rewards: Contingency Fee Legal Practice in the United States* (2004) (using empirical data to assess to what degree the contingency fee contributes to litigiousness in the United States).

Perhaps because there are situations where the American Rule appears to be unfair, the courts have created and applied certain exceptions to the rule, and thereby have allowed some parties to obtain fees. These equitable exceptions include:

(1) *Bad Faith*—where fees are awarded because the losing party has brought the suit in bad faith, vexatiously or for oppressive reasons, *see, e.g.,* Kansas City Southern Ry. Co. v. Guardian Trust Co., 281 U.S. 1 (1930), or as sanctions against counsel or a party for bad faith or behavior during the litigation process. F.R.Civ.P. 11; *e.g.,* Chambers v. NASCO, Inc., 501 U.S. 32(1991); Willy v. Coastal Corp., 503 U.S. 131(1992).

(2) *Contempt*—where fees are awarded against a party who willfully disobeys a court order which leads to additional legal expenses for the prevailing party, *see, e.g.,* Trustees v. Greenough, 105 U.S. (15 Otto) 527 (1881); and

(3) *Common Fund*—where fees are awarded to a party who preserves or generates a common fund for a class of plaintiffs. *See* Charles Silver, *A Restitutionary Theory of Attorneys' Fees in Class Actions*, 76 Cornell L.Rev. 656 (1991).

In Alyeska Pipeline Service Co. v. Wilderness Society, 421 U.S. 240 (1975), the Supreme Court held that it must wait for Congress to create additional federal exceptions to the American Rule. Therefore, the Court rejected an opportunity to establish a new exception for federal courts, the "private attorney general" theory, which would shift fees in cases where private citizens brought suits benefiting society as a whole. The Court held that Congress had made specific and explicit provisions for the allowance of attorney's fees under selected statutes granting or protecting various federal rights.

The Supreme Court's interpretation of the American Rule in *Alyeska* is a limit on federal courts only; state courts have more freedom to create new equitable exceptions. Thus in Serrano v. Priest, 20 Cal.3d 25, 141 Cal.Rptr. 315, 569 P.2d 1303 (1977), the California Supreme Court adopted the private attorney general theory soon after *Alyeska* rejected it. *But see* Lloyd C. Anderson, *Equitable Power to Award Attorney's Fees: The Seductive Appeal of "Benefit,"* 48 S.D.L.Rev. 217 (2003) (contending that the private attorney general theory exceeds the equitable power of state courts).

BOEING CO. v. VAN GEMERT
Supreme Court of the United States
444 U.S. 472 (1980)

JUSTICE POWELL delivered the opinion of the Court.

The question presented in this class action is whether a proportionate share of the fees awarded to lawyers who represented the successful class may be assessed against the unclaimed portion of the fund created by a judgment.

I

In March 1966, The Boeing Co. called for the redemption of certain convertible debentures. * * *

Van Gemert and several other nonconverting debenture holders brought a class action against Boeing in the United States District Court for the Southern District of New York. They claimed that Boeing had violated federal securities statutes as well as the law of New York by failing to give them reasonably adequate notice of the redemption. As damages, they sought the difference between the amount for which their debentures could be redeemed and the value of the shares into which the debentures could have been converted. * * *

On the second remand, the District Court entered the judgment now at issue. The court first established the amount of Boeing's liability to the class as a whole. It provided that respondents, "in behalf of all members of the plaintiff class, . . . shall recover as their damages . . . the principal sum of $3,289,359 together with [prejudgment] interest. . . ." The court then fixed the amount that each member of the class could recover on a principal amount of $100 in debentures. Each individual recovery was to carry its proportionate share of the total amount allowed for attorney's fees, expenses, and disbursements.[2] That share, the court declared, "shall bear the same ratio to all such fees, expenses and disbursements as such class member's recovery shall bear to the total recovery" awarded the class. Finally, the court ordered Boeing to deposit the amount of the judgment into escrow at a commercial bank,[3] and it appointed a Special Master to administer the judgment and pass on the validity of individual claims. * * *

Boeing appealed only one provision of the judgment. It claimed that attorney's fees could not be awarded from the unclaimed portion of the judgment fund for at least two reasons. First, the equitable doctrine that allows the assessment of attorney's fees against a common fund created by

---

[2]   The class lawyers have requested fees totaling about $2 million.

[3]   Interest on the principal sum of $3,289,359 from the conversion deadline to the date of judgment amounted to $2,459,647, bringing the judgment to $5,749,006. With income earned on investments and other additions, the fund now totals over $7 million.

the lawyers' efforts was inapposite because the money in the judgment fund would not benefit those class members who failed to claim it. Second, because Boeing had a colorable claim for the return of the unclaimed money, awarding attorney's fees from those funds might violate the American rule against shifting fees to the losing party. Therefore, Boeing contended, the District Court should award attorney's fees from only the portion of the fund actually claimed by class members.

II

Since the decisions in Trustees v. Greenough, 105 U.S. 527 (1882), and Central Railroad & Banking Co. v. Pettus, 113 U.S. 116 (1885), this Court has recognized consistently that a litigant or a lawyer who recovers a common fund for the benefit of persons other than himself or his client is entitled to a reasonable attorney's fee from the fund as a whole. * * * The common-fund doctrine reflects the traditional practice in courts of equity and it stands as a well-recognized exception to the general principle that requires every litigant to bear his own attorney's fees. The doctrine rests on the perception that persons who obtain the benefit of a lawsuit without contributing to its cost are unjustly enriched at the successful litigant's expense. Jurisdiction over the fund involved in the litigation allows a court to prevent this inequity by assessing attorney's fees against the entire fund, thus spreading fees proportionately among those benefited by the suit.

In *Alyeska Pipeline Service Co. v. Wilderness Society,* we noted the features that distinguished our common-fund cases from cases where the shifting of fees was inappropriate. First, the classes of persons benefited by the lawsuits "were small in number and easily identifiable." Second, "[t]he benefits could be traced with some accuracy . . . ." Finally, "there was reason for confidence that the costs [of litigation] could indeed be shifted with some exactitude to those benefiting." Those characteristics are not present where litigants simply vindicate a general social grievance. On the other hand, the criteria are satisfied when each member of a certified class has an undisputed and mathematically ascertainable claim to part of a lump-sum judgment recovered on his behalf. Once the class representatives have established the defendant's liability and the total amount of damages, members of the class can obtain their share of the recovery simply by proving their individual claims against the judgment fund. This benefit devolves with certainty upon the identifiable persons whom the court has certified as members of the class. Although the full value of the benefit to each absentee member cannot be determined until he presents his claim, a fee awarded against the entire judgment fund will shift the costs of litigation to each absentee in the exact proportion that the value of his claim bears to the total recovery. * * *

In this case, the named respondents have recovered a determinate fund for the benefit of every member of the class whom they represent.

Boeing did not appeal the judgment awarding the class a sum certain. Nor does Boeing contend that any class member was uninjured by the company's failure adequately to inform him of his conversion rights. Thus, the damage to each class member is simply the difference between the redemption price of his debentures and the value of the common stock into which they could have been converted. To claim their logically ascertainable shares of the judgment fund, absentee class members need prove only their membership in the injured class. Their right to share the harvest of the lawsuit upon proof of their identity, whether or not they exercise it, is a benefit in the fund created by the efforts of the class representatives and their counsel. Unless absentees contribute to the payment of attorney's fees incurred on their behalves, they will pay nothing for the creation of the fund and their representatives may bear additional costs. The judgment entered by the District Court and affirmed by the Court of Appeals rectifies this inequity by requiring every member of the class to share attorney's fees to the same extent that he can share the recovery. Since the benefits of the class recovery have been "traced with some accuracy" and the costs of recovery have been "shifted with some exactitude to those benefiting," we conclude that the attorney's fee award in this case is a proper application of the common-fund doctrine.

III

The common-fund doctrine, as applied in this case, is entirely consistent with the American rule against taxing the losing party with the victor's attorney's fees. See *Alyeska*. The District Court's judgment assesses attorney's fees against a fund awarded to the prevailing class. Since there was no appeal from the judgment that quantified Boeing's liability Boeing presently has no interest in any part of the fund. The members of the class, whether or not they assert their rights, are at least the equitable owners of their respective shares in the recovery. Any right that Boeing may establish to the return of money eventually unclaimed is contingent on the failure of absentee class members to exercise their present rights of possession. Although Boeing itself cannot be obliged to pay fees awarded to the class lawyers, its latent claim against unclaimed money in the judgment fund may not defeat each class member's equitable obligation to share the expenses of litigation.

B. FEE-SHIFTING STATUTES

Congress responded to *Alyeska* and its refusal to create more equitable exceptions for awarding attorney's fees by creating a plethora of targeted fee shifting statutes, including: Civil Rights Attorney's Fees Awards Act of 1976, 42 U.S.C. § 1988, Toxic Substance Control Act, 15 U.S.C. § 2619, Truth in Lending Act, 15 U.S.C. § 1640, and many more. Nearly two hundred federal statutes now authorize courts to award attorney's fees in particular circumstances. *See* Mary F. Derfner & Arthur D. Wolf, *Court Awarded Attorney Fees* at chs. 29–43 (2003). The bulk of attorney's fees litigation at the Supreme Court level now consists of interpreting congressional intent in these statutes.

Congress authorizes the award of fees for a variety of reasons. First, Congress may wish to encourage citizens to bring actions against the government to ensure compliance with congressional directives. Many environmental and civil rights fee awards provisions are designed to foster citizen oversight of government. *E.g.,* Clean Air Act, 42 U.S.C. § 7604(a)(2)(d). Second, Congress sometimes encourages citizens to bring enforcement actions against other private parties because, even though government enforces the law, private attorneys general have the resources, information, or interest needed to get the job done or because the rights involved are sufficiently important that private persons should not have to wait upon government action. *E.g.,* Clayton Act, 15 U.S.C. § 15, False Claims Act, 31 U.S.C. § 3730, Clean Air Act, 42 U.S.C. § 7604(a)(1). Third, Congress may want to make justice more accessible to those who are not rich. *E.g.,* Equal Access to Justice Act, 5 U.S.C. § 504, 28 U.S.C. § 2412. Fourth, Congress may want to deter and punish those who abuse the judicial process. *E.g.,* 28 U.S.C. § 1927; *cf.* F.R.Civ.P. 11, 16(f), 26(g), 37(a)(4), 56(g).

Congress has not applied these purposes uniformly. Sometimes statutes that would seem to fit within the pattern of those under which fees are awarded do not authorize fees. It must also be emphasized that statutes that authorize fees do not necessarily allow them for all actions brought under the statute. For instance, fees may be unavailable to certain successful parties. Because there are differences between the fee provisions under many of these statutes, caution must be used in carrying results under one statute over to a case under another. It is necessary to check the specific language, legislative history, and interpretation of each fee provision. It is also important to plead clearly entitlement to relief on the merits under statutes that provide for an award of fees and to request attorney's fees as a specific item in the prayer for relief.

It is generally the prevailing plaintiff who can recover her attorney's fees under fee-shifting statutes. Despite the fact that most statutes textually refer to "prevailing parties," the usual rule is that the prevailing *defendant* does not get fees unless the case is "frivolous, unreasonable, or without foundation." Christiansburg Garment Co. v. EEOC, 434 U.S. 412 (1978); *see* Harold J. Krent, *Explaining One-Way Fee Shifting*, 79 Va.L.Rev. 2039 (1993). The Supreme Court, however, distinguished attorney's fees under the Copyright Act, endorsing two-way fee shifting for copyright in the following case.

FOGERTY v. FANTASY, INC.

Supreme Court of the United States
510 U.S. 517 (1994)

CHIEF JUSTICE REHNQUIST delivered the opinion of the Court.

The Copyright Act of 1976, 17 U.S.C. § 505, provides in relevant part that in any copyright infringement action "the court may . . . award a reasonable attorney's fee to the prevailing party as part of the costs." The question presented in this case is what standards should inform a court's decision to award attorney's fees to a prevailing defendant in a copyright infringement action—a question that has produced conflicting views in the Courts of Appeals.

Petitioner John Fogerty is a successful musician, who, in the late 1960's, was the lead singer and songwriter of a popular music group known as "Creedence Clearwater Revival." [2] In 1970, he wrote a song entitled "Run Through the Jungle" and sold the exclusive publishing rights to predecessors-in-interest of respondent Fantasy, Inc., who later obtained the copyright by assignment. The music group disbanded in 1972 and Fogerty subsequently published under another recording label. In 1985, he published and registered a copyright to a song entitled "The Old Man Down the Road," which was released on an album distributed by Warner Brothers Records, Inc. Respondent Fantasy, Inc., sued Fogerty, Warner Brothers, and affiliated companies in District Court, alleging that "The Old Man Down the Road" was merely "Run Through the Jungle" with new words. The copyright infringement claim went to trial and a jury returned a verdict in favor of Fogerty.

After his successful defense of the action, Fogerty moved for reasonable attorney's fees pursuant to 17 U.S.C. § 505. The District Court denied the motion, finding that Fantasy's infringement suit was not brought frivolously or in bad faith as required by Circuit precedent for an award of attorney's fees to a successful defendant. The Court of Appeals affirmed, and declined to abandon the existing Ninth Circuit standard for awarding attorney's fees which treats successful plaintiffs and successful defendants differently. Under that standard, commonly termed the "dual" standard, prevailing plaintiffs are generally awarded attorney's fees as a matter of course, while prevailing defendants must show that the original suit was frivolous or brought in bad faith. In contrast, some Courts of Appeals follow the so-called "evenhanded" approach in which no distinction is made between prevailing plaintiffs and prevailing defendants. * * *

Respondent advances three arguments in support of the dual standard followed by the Court of Appeals for the Ninth Circuit in this case. First, it

---

[2]   Creedence Clearwater Revival (CCR), recently inducted into the Rock and Roll Hall of Fame, has been recognized as one of the greatest American rock and roll groups of all time. With Fogerty as its leader, CCR developed a distinctive style of music, dubbed "swamp rock" by the media due to its southern country and blues feel.

contends that the language of § 505, when read in the light of our decisions construing similar fee-shifting language, supports the rule. Second, it asserts that treating prevailing plaintiffs and defendants differently comports with the "objectives" and "equitable considerations" underlying the Copyright Act as a whole. Finally, respondent contends that the legislative history of § 505 indicates that Congress ratified the dual standard which it claims was "uniformly" followed by the lower courts under identical language in the 1909 Copyright Act. We address each of these arguments in turn.

Fantasy's content.

The statutory language—"the court may also award a reasonable attorney's fee to the prevailing party as part of the costs"—gives no hint that successful plaintiffs are to be treated differently from successful defendants. But respondent contends that our decision in Christiansburg Garment Co. v. EEOC, 434 U.S. 412 (1978), in which we construed virtually identical language, supports a differentiation in treatment between plaintiffs and defendants.

Christiansburg construed the language of Title VII of the Civil Rights Act of 1964, which in relevant part provided that the court, "in its discretion, may allow the prevailing party . . . a reasonable attorney's fee as part of the costs. . . . " 42 U.S.C. § 2000e–5(k). We had earlier held, interpreting the cognate provision of Title II of that Act, 42 U.S.C. § 2000a–3(b), that a prevailing plaintiff "should ordinarily recover an attorney's fee unless some special circumstances would render such an award unjust." Newman v. Piggie Park Enterprises, Inc., 390 U.S. 400, 402 (1968). This decision was based on what we found to be the important policy objectives of the Civil Rights statutes, and the intent of Congress to achieve such objectives through the use of plaintiffs as " 'private attorney[s] general.' " In *Christiansburg,* we determined that the same policy considerations were not at work in the case of a prevailing civil rights defendant. We noted that a Title VII plaintiff, like a Title II plaintiff in *Piggie Park,* is "the chosen instrument of Congress to vindicate 'a policy that Congress considered of the highest priority.' " We also relied on the admittedly sparse legislative history to indicate that different standards were to be applied to successful plaintiffs than to successful defendants.

Respondent points to our language in Flight Attendants v. Zipes, 491 U.S. 754, 758, n. 2 (1989), that "fee-shifting statutes' similar language is a 'strong indication' that they are to be interpreted alike." But here we think this normal indication is overborne by the factors relied upon in our *Christiansburg* opinion that are absent in the case of the Copyright Act. The legislative history of § 505 provides no support for treating prevailing plaintiffs and defendants differently with respect to the recovery of attorney's fees. The attorney's fees provision of § 505 of the 1976 Act was carried forward *verbatim* from the 1909 Act with very little discussion. The relevant House Report provides simply: "Under section 505 the awarding of costs and attorney's fees are left to the court's discretion, and the section also makes clear that neither costs nor attorney's fees can be awarded to or against the United States." * * *

The goals and objectives of the two Acts are likewise not completely similar. Oftentimes, in the civil rights context, impecunious "private attorney general" plaintiffs can ill afford to litigate their claims against defendants with more resources. Congress sought to redress this balance in part, and to provide incentives for the bringing of meritorious lawsuits, by treating successful plaintiffs more favorably than successful defendants in terms of the award of attorney's fees. The primary objective of the Copyright Act is to encourage the production of original literary, artistic, and musical expression for the good of the public. In the copyright context, it has been noted that "[e]ntities which sue for copyright infringement as plaintiffs can run the gamut from corporate behemoths to starving artists; the same is true of prospective copyright infringement defendants." * * *

Respondent next argues that the policies and objectives of § 505 and of the Copyright Act in general are best served by the "dual approach" to the award of attorney's fees. The most common reason advanced in support of the dual approach is that, by awarding attorney's fees to prevailing plaintiffs as a matter of course, it encourages litigation of meritorious claims of copyright infringement. * * * We think the argument is flawed because it expresses a one-sided view of the purposes of the Copyright Act. While it is true that *one* of the goals of the Copyright Act is to discourage infringement, it is by no means the *only* goal of that Act. In the first place, it is by no means always the case that the plaintiff in an infringement action is the only holder of a copyright; often times, defendants hold copyrights too, as exemplified in the case at hand. * * *

More importantly, the policies served by the Copyright Act are more complex, more measured, than simply maximizing the number of meritorious suits for copyright infringement. The Constitution grants to Congress the power "To promote the Progress of Science and useful Arts, by securing for limited Times to Authors and Inventors the exclusive Right to their respective Writings and Discoveries." U.S. Const., Art. I, § 8, cl. 8. We have often recognized the monopoly privileges that Congress has authorized, while "intended to motivate the creative activity of authors and inventors by the provision of a special reward," are limited in nature and must ultimately serve the public good. * * * Because copyright law ultimately serves the purpose of enriching the general public through access to creative works, it is peculiarly important that the boundaries of copyright law be demarcated as clearly as possible. To that end, defendants who seek to advance a variety of meritorious copyright defenses should be encouraged to litigate them to the same extent that plaintiffs are encouraged to litigate meritorious claims of infringement. In the case before us, the successful defense of "The Old Man Down the Road" increased public exposure to a musical work that could, as a result, lead to further creative pieces. Thus a successful defense of a copyright infringement action may further the policies of the Copyright Act every bit as much as a successful prosecution of an infringement claim by the holder of a copyright.

Respondent finally urges that the legislative history supports the dual standard, relying on the principle of ratification. Respondent surveys the great number of lower court cases interpreting the identical provision in the 1909 Act, 17 U.S.C. § 116 (1976 ed.), and asserts that "it was firmly established" that prevailing defendants should be awarded attorney's fees only where the plaintiff's claim was frivolous or brought with a vexatious purpose. Furthermore, respondent claims that Congress was aware of this construction of former § 116. * * *

Our review of the prior case law itself leads us to conclude that there was no settled "dual standard" interpretation of former § 116 about which Congress could have been aware. We note initially that at least one reported case stated no reason in awarding attorney's fees to successful defendants. More importantly, while it appears that the majority of lower courts exercised their discretion in awarding attorney's fees to prevailing defendants based on a finding of frivolousness or bad faith, not all courts expressly described the test in those terms. In fact, only one pre-1976 case expressly endorsed a dual standard. * * * This is hardly the sort of uniform construction that Congress might have endorsed.

* * * We now turn to petitioner's argument that § 505 was intended to adopt the "British Rule." Petitioner argues that, consistent with the neutral language of § 505, both prevailing plaintiffs and defendants should be awarded attorney's fees as a matter of course, absent exceptional circumstances. For two reasons we reject this argument for the British Rule.

First, just as the plain language of § 505 supports petitioner's claim for disapproving the dual standard, it cuts against him in arguing for the British Rule. The statute says that "the court may also award a reasonable attorney's fee to the prevailing party as part of the costs." The word "may" clearly connotes discretion. The automatic awarding of attorney's fees to the prevailing party would pretermit the exercise of that discretion.

Second, we are mindful that Congress legislates against the strong background of the American Rule. Unlike Britain where counsel fees are regularly awarded to the prevailing party, it is the general rule in this country that unless Congress provides otherwise, parties are to bear their own attorney's fees. Alyeska Pipeline Service Co. v. Wilderness Society, 421 U.S. 240, 247–262 (1975); Flight Attendants v. Zipes, 491 U.S., at 758. While § 505 is one situation in which Congress has modified the American Rule to allow an award of attorney's fees in the court's discretion, we find it impossible to believe that Congress, without more, intended to adopt the

British Rule. Such a bold departure from traditional practice would have surely drawn more explicit statutory language and legislative comment. * * *

Thus we reject both the "dual standard" adopted by several of the Courts of Appeals and petitioner's claim that § 505 enacted the British Rule for automatic recovery of attorney's fees by the prevailing party. Prevailing plaintiffs and prevailing defendants are to be treated alike, but attorney's fees are to be awarded to prevailing parties only as a matter of the court's discretion. "There is no precise rule or formula for making these determinations," but instead equitable discretion should be exercised "in light of the considerations we have identified." Hensley v. Eckerhart, 461 U.S. 424, 436–437 (1983).[19] Because the Court of Appeals erroneously held petitioner, the prevailing defendant, to a more stringent standard than that applicable to a prevailing plaintiff, its judgment is reversed, and the case is remanded for further proceedings consistent with this opinion.

NOTES

1. The Supreme Court elaborated on the point made in footnote 19 as to what factors should guide the court's discretion in deciding to award attorney's fees to a prevailing party in a copyright case. In *Kirtsaeng v. John Wiley & Sons, Inc*, the Court reversed a case denying fees to a defendant based on the dispositive factor of the objective reasonableness of the losing party's arguments. 579 U.S. ___, 136 S.Ct. 1979 (2016). The Court instructed that the objective reasonableness of arguments is only one factor for consideration, and it may not operate as a presumption. Other factors might include litigation misconduct or deterrence of either repeated infringement or overaggressive assertions. The *Kirtsaeng* defendant successfully defended against a lawsuit for copyright infringement brought by a publisher challenging his resale of books bought in Thailand, in a case that went all the way to the Supreme Court on the merits of the case and the first-sale doctrine. Kirtsaeng v. John Wiley & Sons, Inc., 133 S.Ct. 1351 (2013). As a prevailing defendant, he then sought attorney's fees of $2 million, which the lower courts denied.

2. A statute may change the operable standard for when fees are awarded. For example, the Patent Act provides that fees may be awarded to prevailing parties in "exceptional cases." 35 U.S.C. § 285. The Supreme Court struck down the Federal Circuit's interpretation of exceptional as meaning only the rare case of misconduct or where the case is brought in bad faith. Octane Fitness LLC, v. ICON Health & Fitness, Inc., 572 U.S. ___, 134 S.Ct.

---

[19] Some courts following the evenhanded standard have suggested several nonexclusive factors to guide courts' discretion. * * * These factors include "frivolousness, motivation, objective unreasonableness (both in the factual and in the legal components of the case) and the need in particular circumstances to advance considerations of compensation and deterrence." Lieb v. Topstone Industries, Inc., 788 F.2d 151, 156 (1986). We agree that such factors may be used to guide courts' discretion, so long as such factors are faithful to the purposes of the Copyright Act and are applied to prevailing plaintiffs and defendants in an evenhanded manner.

1749 (2014). Instead, it said that "an 'exceptional' case is simply one that stands out from others with respect to the substantive strength of a party's litigating position (considering both the governing law and the facts of the case) or the unreasonable manner in which the case was litigated." *Id.* at 1756. In the first nine months after the decision, the number of petitions for fees significantly increased and the number of awards granted doubled (from 20–42%). Hannah Jiam, Note, *Fee-Shifting and* Octane Fitness: *An Empirical Approach to Understanding "Exceptional,"* 30 Berkeley Tech.L.J. 611 (2015).

3.   Does the Eleventh Amendment bar the award of attorney's fees against the states? Hutto v. Finney, 437 U.S. 678 (1978), in a divided opinion held that an award may be made against a state under section 1988 because Congress may qualify the Eleventh Amendment in implementing the Fourteenth Amendment and the fees are awarded as an element of costs, which have long been awarded against the states. In Missouri v. Jenkins (*Jenkins I*), 491 U.S. 274 (1989), the Supreme Court reaffirmed that the Eleventh Amendment has no application to an award of attorney's fees which is ancillary to a grant of prospective relief against a State.

C. MEASURING FEES

Once a court has decided that fees should be awarded in a particular case, it must determine what is a "reasonable" fee under the pertinent statute. Courts now generally adopt the "lodestar" formulation, which entails multiplying compensable hours by an hourly rate, discussed in the following case. Unless, of course, the applicable statute provides otherwise. *See, e.g.,* Prison Litigation Reform Act, 42 U.S.C. § 1997e (limiting attorney hourly rate in prison cases to 150% of the maximum hourly rate paid to appointed counsel in the particular district court).

PERDUE V. KENNY A.

Supreme Court of the United States
559 U.S. 542 (2010)

JUSTICE ALITO delivered the opinion of the Court.

This case presents the question whether the calculation of an attorney's fee, under federal fee-shifting statutes, based on the "lodestar," *i.e.,* the number of hours worked multiplied by the prevailing hourly rates, may be increased due to superior performance and results. We have stated in previous cases that such an increase is permitted in extraordinary circumstances, and we reaffirm that rule. But as we have also said in prior cases, there is a strong presumption that the lodestar is sufficient; factors subsumed in the lodestar calculation cannot be used as a ground for increasing an award above the lodestar; and a party seeking fees has the burden of identifying a factor that the lodestar does not adequately take into account and proving with specificity that an enhanced fee is justified. Because the District Court did not apply these standards, we reverse the decision below and remand for further proceedings consistent with this opinion.

I

A

Respondents * * * are children in the Georgia foster-care system and their next friends. They filed this class action on behalf of 3,000 children in foster care. * * * Claiming that deficiencies in the foster-care system in two counties near Atlanta violated their federal and state constitutional and statutory rights, respondents sought injunctive and declaratory relief, as well as attorney's fees and expenses.

The United States District Court for the Northern District of Georgia eventually referred the case to mediation, where the parties entered into a consent decree, which the District Court approved. The consent decree resolved all pending issues other than the fees that respondents' attorneys were entitled to receive under 42 U.S.C. § 1988.

B

Respondents submitted a request for more than $14 million in attorney's fees. Half of that amount was based on their calculation of the lodestar—roughly 30,000 hours multiplied by hourly rates of $200 to $495 for attorneys and $75 to $150 for non attorneys. In support of their fee request, respondents submitted affidavits asserting that these rates were within the range of prevailing market rates for legal services in the relevant market.

The other half of the amount that respondents sought represented a fee enhancement for superior work and results. Affidavits submitted in support of this request claimed that the lodestar amount "would be generally insufficient to induce lawyers of comparable skill, judgment, professional representation and experience" to litigate this case. Petitioners objected to the fee request, contending that some of the proposed hourly rates were too high, that the hours claimed were excessive, and that the enhancement would duplicate factors that were reflected in the lodestar amount.

The District Court awarded fees of approximately $10.5 million. * * * The District Court found that the hourly rates proposed by respondents were "fair and reasonable," but that some of the entries on counsel's billing records were vague and that the hours claimed for many of the billing categories were excessive. The court therefore cut the non-travel hours by 15% and halved the hourly rate for travel hours. This resulted in a lodestar calculation of approximately $6 million.

The court then enhanced this award by 75%, concluding that the lodestar calculation did not take into account "(1) the fact that class counsel were required to advance case expenses of $1.7 million over a three-year period with no on[-]going reimbursement, (2) the fact that class counsel were not paid on an on-going basis as the work was being performed, and (3) the fact that class counsel's ability to recover a fee and expense reimbursement were completely contingent on the outcome of the case." The court stated that respondents' attorneys had exhibited "a higher degree of skill, commitment, dedication, and professionalism . . . than the Court has seen displayed by the attorneys in any other case during its 27 years on the bench." The court also commented that the results obtained were " 'extraordinary' " and added that "[a]fter 58 years as a practicing attorney and federal judge, the Court is unaware of any other case in which a plaintiff class has achieved such a favorable result on such a comprehensive scale." The enhancement resulted in an additional $4.5 million fee award.

Relying on prior Circuit precedent, a panel of the Eleventh Circuit affirmed. 532 F.3d 1209 (2008). * * * The Eleventh Circuit denied rehearing en banc over the dissent of three judges. See 547 F.3d 1319 (2008).

II

The general rule in our legal system is that each party must pay its own attorney's fees and expenses, see Hensley v. Eckerhart, 461 U.S. 424, 429 (1983), but Congress enacted 42 U.S.C. § 1988 in order to ensure that federal rights are adequately enforced. Section 1988 provides that a prevailing party in certain civil rights actions may recover "a reasonable attorney's fee as part of the costs." Unfortunately, the statute does not explain what Congress meant by a "reasonable" fee, and therefore the task of identifying an appropriate methodology for determining a "reasonable" fee was left for the courts.

One possible method was set out in Johnson v. Georgia Highway Express, Inc., 488 F.2d 714, 717–719 (C.A.5 1974), which listed 12 factors that a court should consider in determining a reasonable fee.[4] This method, however, "gave very little actual guidance to district courts. Setting attorney's fees by reference to a series of sometimes subjective factors placed unlimited discretion in trial judges and produced disparate results."

An alternative, the lodestar approach, was pioneered by the Third Circuit and "achieved dominance in the federal courts" after our decision

---

[4]   These factors were: "(1) the time and labor required; (2) the novelty and difficulty of the questions; (3) the skill requisite to perform the legal service properly; (4) the preclusion of employment by the attorney due to the acceptance of the case; (5) the customary fee; (6) whether the fee is fixed or contingent; (7) time limitations imposed by the client or the circumstances; (8) the amount involved and the results obtained; (9) the experience, reputation, and ability of the attorneys; (10) the 'undesirability' of the case; (11) the nature and length of the professional relationship with the client; and (12) awards in similar cases." Hensley v. Eckerhart, 461 U.S. 424, 430 n.3 (1983).

in *Hensley.* Gisbrecht v. Barnhart, 535 U.S. 789, 801 (2002). "Since that time, '[t]he "lodestar" figure has, as its name suggests, become the guiding light of our fee-shifting jurisprudence.' " * * *

Although the lodestar method is not perfect, it has several important virtues. First, in accordance with our understanding of the aim of fee-shifting statutes, the lodestar looks to "the prevailing market rates in the relevant community." Blum v. Stenson, 465 U.S. 886, 895 (1984). Developed after the practice of hourly billing had become widespread the lodestar method produces an award that *roughly* approximates the fee that the prevailing attorney would have received if he or she had been representing a paying client who was billed by the hour in a comparable case. Second, the lodestar method is readily administrable, and unlike the *Johnson* approach, the lodestar calculation is "objective," and thus cabins the discretion of trial judges, permits meaningful judicial review, and produces reasonably predictable results.

III

Our prior decisions concerning the federal fee-shifting statutes have established six important rules that lead to our decision in this case.

First, a "reasonable" fee is a fee that is sufficient to induce a capable attorney to undertake the representation of a meritorious civil rights case. Section 1988's aim is to enforce the covered civil rights statutes, not to provide "a form of economic relief to improve the financial lot of attorneys."

Second, the lodestar method yields a fee that is presumptively sufficient to achieve this objective. Indeed, we have said that the presumption is a "strong" one.

Third, although we have never sustained an enhancement of a lodestar amount for performance, we have repeatedly said that enhancements may be awarded in "rare" and "exceptional" circumstances.

Fourth, we have noted that "the lodestar figure includes most, if not all, of the relevant factors constituting a 'reasonable' attorney's fee," and have held that an enhancement may not be awarded based on a factor that is subsumed in the lodestar calculation. We have thus held that the novelty and complexity of a case generally may not be used as a ground for an enhancement because these factors "presumably [are] fully reflected in the number of billable hours recorded by counsel." We have also held that the quality of an attorney's performance generally should not be used to adjust the lodestar "[b]ecause considerations concerning the quality of a prevailing party's counsel's representation normally are reflected in the reasonable hourly rate."

Fifth, the burden of proving that an enhancement is necessary must be borne by the fee applicant.

Finally, a fee applicant seeking an enhancement must produce "specific evidence" that supports the award. This requirement is essential if the lodestar method is to realize one of its chief virtues, *i.e.,* providing a calculation that is objective and capable of being reviewed on appeal.

IV

A

In light of what we have said in prior cases, we reject any contention that a fee determined by the lodestar method may not be enhanced in any situation. The lodestar method was never intended to be conclusive in all circumstances. Instead, there is a "strong presumption" that the lodestar figure is reasonable, but that presumption may be overcome in those rare circumstances in which the lodestar does not adequately take into account a factor that may properly be considered in determining a reasonable fee.

B

In this case, we are asked to decide whether either the quality of an attorney's performance or the results obtained are factors that may properly provide a basis for an enhancement. We treat these two factors as one. When a plaintiff's attorney achieves results that are more favorable than would have been predicted based on the governing law and the available evidence, the outcome may be attributable to superior performance and commitment of resources by plaintiff's counsel. Or the outcome may result from inferior performance by defense counsel, unanticipated defense concessions, unexpectedly favorable rulings by the court, an unexpectedly sympathetic jury, or simple luck. Since none of these latter causes can justify an enhanced award, superior results are relevant only to the extent it can be shown that they are the result of superior attorney performance. Thus, we need only consider whether superior attorney performance can justify an enhancement. And in light of the principles derived from our prior cases, we inquire whether there are circumstances in which superior attorney performance is not adequately taken into account in the lodestar calculation. We conclude that there are a few such circumstances but that these circumstances are indeed "rare" and "exceptional," and require specific evidence that the lodestar fee would not have been "adequate to attract competent counsel."

First, an enhancement may be appropriate where the method used in determining the hourly rate employed in the lodestar calculation does not adequately measure the attorney's true market value, as demonstrated in part during the litigation. This may occur if the hourly rate is determined by a formula that takes into account only a single factor (such as years since admission to the bar) or perhaps only a few similar factors. In such a case, an enhancement may be appropriate so that an attorney is compensated at the rate that the attorney would receive in cases not governed by the federal fee-shifting statutes. But in order to provide a calculation that is objective and reviewable, the trial judge should adjust the attorney's hourly rate in accordance with specific proof linking the attorney's ability to a prevailing market rate.

Second, an enhancement may be appropriate if the attorney's performance includes an extraordinary outlay of expenses and the litigation is exceptionally protracted. As Judge Carnes noted below, when an attorney agrees to represent a civil rights plaintiff who cannot afford to pay the attorney, the attorney presumably understands that no reimbursement is likely to be received until the successful resolution of the case, and therefore enhancements to compensate for delay in reimbursement for expenses must be reserved for unusual cases. In such exceptional cases, however, an enhancement may be allowed, but the amount of the enhancement must be calculated using a method that is reasonable, objective, and capable of being reviewed on appeal, such as by applying a standard rate of interest to the qualifying outlays of expenses.

Third, there may be extraordinary circumstances in which an attorney's performance involves exceptional delay in the payment of fees. An attorney who expects to be compensated under § 1988 presumably understands that payment of fees will generally not come until the end of the case, if at all. Compensation for this delay is generally made "either by basing the award on current rates or by adjusting the fee based on historical rates to reflect its present value." But we do not rule out the possibility that an enhancement may be appropriate where an attorney assumes these costs in the face of unanticipated delay, particularly where the delay is unjustifiably caused by the defense. In such a case, however, the enhancement should be calculated by applying a method similar to that described above in connection with exceptional delay in obtaining reimbursement for expenses.

We reject the suggestion that it is appropriate to grant performance enhancements on the ground that departures from hourly billing are becoming more common. As we have noted, the lodestar was adopted in part because it provides a rough approximation of general billing practices, and accordingly, if hourly billing becomes unusual, an alternative to the lodestar method may have to be found. However, neither respondents nor their *amici* contend that that day has arrived. Nor have they shown that permitting the award of enhancements on top of the lodestar figure corresponds to prevailing practice in the general run of cases.

We are told that, under an increasingly popular arrangement, attorneys are paid at a reduced hourly rate but receive a bonus if certain specified results are obtained, and this practice is analogized to the award of an enhancement such as the one in this case. The analogy, however, is flawed. An attorney who agrees, at the outset of the representation, to a *reduced hourly rate* in exchange for the opportunity to earn a performance bonus is in a position far different from an attorney in a § 1988 case who is compensated at the *full prevailing rate* and then seeks a performance enhancement in addition to the lodestar amount after the litigation has concluded. Reliance on these comparisons for the purposes of administering enhancements, therefore, is not appropriate.

V

In the present case, the District Court did not provide proper justification for the large enhancement that it awarded. The court increased the lodestar award by 75% but, as far as the court's opinion reveals, this figure appears to have been essentially arbitrary. Why, for example, did the court grant a 75% enhancement instead of the 100% increase that respondents sought? And why 75% rather than 50% or 25% or 10%?

The District Court commented that the enhancement was the "minimum enhancement of the lodestar necessary to reasonably compensate [respondents'] counsel." But the effect of the enhancement was to increase the top rate for the attorneys to more than $866 per hour, and the District Court did not point to anything in the record that shows that this is an appropriate figure for the relevant market.

The District Court pointed to the fact that respondents' counsel had to make extraordinary outlays for expenses and had to wait for reimbursement, but the court did not calculate the amount of the enhancement that is attributable to this factor. Similarly, the District Court noted that respondents' counsel did not receive fees on an ongoing basis while the case was pending, but the court did not sufficiently link this factor to proof in the record that the delay here was outside the normal range expected by attorneys who rely on § 1988 for the payment of their fees or quantify the disparity. Nor did the court provide a calculation of the cost to counsel of any extraordinary and unwarranted delay. And the court's reliance on the contingency of the outcome contravenes our holding in *Dague*.

Finally, insofar as the District Court relied on a comparison of the performance of counsel in this case with the performance of counsel in unnamed prior cases, the District Court did not employ a methodology that permitted meaningful appellate review. Needless to say, we do not question the sincerity of the District Court's observations, and we are in no position to assess their accuracy. But when a trial judge awards an enhancement on an impressionistic basis, a major purpose of the lodestar method— providing an objective and reviewable basis for fees—is undermined.

Determining a "reasonable attorney's fee" is a matter that is committed to the sound discretion of a trial judge, see 42 U.S.C. § 1988 (permitting court, "in its discretion," to award fees), but the judge's discretion is not unlimited. It is essential that the judge provide a reasonably specific explanation for all aspects of a fee determination, including any award of an enhancement. Unless such an explanation is given, adequate appellate review is not feasible, and without such review, widely disparate awards may be made, and awards may be influenced (or at least, may appear to be influenced) by a judge's subjective opinion regarding particular attorneys or the importance of the case. In addition, in future cases, defendants contemplating the possibility of settlement will have no way to estimate the likelihood of having to pay a potentially huge enhancement.

Section 1988 serves an important public purpose by making it possible for persons without means to bring suit to vindicate their rights. But unjustified enhancements that serve only to enrich attorneys are not consistent with the statute's aim. In many cases, attorney's fees awarded under § 1988 are not paid by the individuals responsible for the constitutional or statutory violations on which the judgment is based. Instead, the fees are paid in effect by state and local taxpayers, and because state and local governments have limited budgets, money that is used to pay attorney's fees is money that cannot be used for programs that provide vital public services.

For all these reasons, the judgment of the Court of Appeals is reversed, and the case is remanded for proceedings consistent with this opinion.

JUSTICE KENNEDY, concurring.

If one were to ask an attorney or a judge to name the significant cases of his or her career, it would be unsurprising to find the list includes a case then being argued or just decided. When immersed in a case, lawyers and judges find within it a fascination, an intricacy, an importance that transcends what the detached observer sees. So the pending or just completed case will often seem extraordinary to its participants. That is the dynamic of the adversary system, the system that so well serves the law.

NOTES

1. *Whose time is included within the "attorney" fee remedy and how is it calculated?* In Blum v. Stenson, 465 U.S. 886 (1984), the Supreme Court held that the appropriate hourly rate awarded under the Civil Rights Attorney's Fees Awards Act of 1976, 42 U.S.C. § 1988, should be based on prevailing market rates rather than rates commensurate with the actual cost of providing the service and that these rates should apply to all attorneys, whether they work for a private firm or a public interest group. In a similar vein, the Court has held that a "reasonable attorney's fee" may include separate compensation for paralegals, law clerks, and recent law graduates at prevailing market rates, where the practice in the relevant market is to bill for such work separately. Missouri v. Jenkins (*Jenkins I*), 491 U.S. 274 (1989).

In contrast to these decisions, the Supreme Court has consistently held that expert fees are not reimbursable under statutes allowing the recovery of "attorney's fees" or "costs," absent express legislative authority. For example, in Arlington Central School District Board of Education v. Murphy, 548 U.S. 291 (2006), the Court held that expenses incurred by parents for expert serving as an educational consultant in an Individuals with Disabilities Education Act case were not recoverable as "costs." *See also* Crawford Fitting Co. v. J.T. Gibbons, Inc., 482 U.S. 437 (1987) (rejecting fees charged by an expert witness to testify at trial); West Virginia University Hospitals, Inc. v. Casey, 499 U.S. 83 (1991) (rejecting fees of expert who helped attorney prepare for trial). The one big exception is the 42 U.S.C. § 1988(c) which does include such express language, and so for civil rights cases, expert fees are reimbursable as attorney fees.

2. *Contingency-Fee Cases*: Many attorneys bill on a contingency-fee basis, where allowed, rather than by an hourly rate. In City of Burlington v. Dague, 505 U.S. 557 (1992), the Supreme Court held that where these attorneys are entitled to reimbursement under a fee-shifting statute, it is not appropriate to enhance the lodestar based on a contingency rate. Instead, the court must identify a comparable hourly market rate for the attorney, even if she does not usually have one.

In Blanchard v. Bergeron, 489 U.S. 87 (1989), the Court was faced with whether an award of attorney's fees under section 1988 was limited to no more than the amount provided in the plaintiff's contingent-fee arrangement with the attorney. In this case, the 40% contingency contract would have yielded a $4,000 fee on a $10,000 recovery; the district court had calculated the reasonable fee to be $7,500 plus costs. The Court unanimously held that recovery for a reasonable attorney's fee was not limited by the contingency contract. The Court dismissed the defendant's concern that this would create a windfall to attorneys, finding that the lodestar formula was designed to result in reasonable awards. 489 U.S. at 93–96.

3. A court awarding a fee under state law need not follow the Supreme Court's interpretation of the federal attorney's fees statutes. *E.g.,* Schefke v. Reliable Collection Agency, Ltd., 32 P.3d 52 (Haw. 2001) (enhancements permitted despite *Dague*); Rendine v. Pantzer, 661 A.2d 1202 (N.J. 1995) (same); Softsolutions, Inc. v. Brigham Young University, 1 P.3d 1095 (Utah 2000) (despite *Blum*, fees for in-house counsel are limited to consideration actually paid, not market rate).

4. *Proportionality*: Attorney's fees also generally have to be proportionate to the relief obtained. In City of Riverside v. Rivera, 477 U.S. 561 (1986), the Supreme Court affirmed an attorney's fee award of $245,000 where the jury awarded only $33,350 in compensatory and punitive damages. The Court found the fees to be proportional to the overall magnitude of relief awarded, as there had been a significant injunction issued against the police in addition to the money awarded. *See also* Mercer v. Duke University, 401 F.3d 199 (4th Cir.2005) (upholding award of $350,000 in attorney's fees to female college football place kicker, who had prevailed in her Title IX discrimination action but obtained only $1 nominal damages, because the case decided an issue of first impression and served a significant public purpose for

female athletes everywhere); Farrar v. Hobby, 506 U.S. 103 (1992) (when no other relief except nominal damages is awarded, only reasonable fee may be no fee at all). Fees can also be awarded proportionally by segregating the frivolous and non-frivolous aspects of a case and awarding fees based only on the valid claims. Fox v. Vice, 563 U.S. 826 (2011).

5.   Percentage of recovery approaches for common-fund cases seem to be on the increase, perhaps because of the complexities and costs of the lodestar approach. Gascho v. Global Fitness Holdings, 2016 WL 2802473 (6th Cir. 2016); Laffitte v. Robert Halft Int'l Inc., 1 Cal.5th 480 (2016); In re Diet Drugs, 582 F.3d 524 (3d Cir. 2009); Goldberger v. Integrated Resources, Inc. 209 F.3d 43 (2d Cir. 2000). Sometimes the percentage of recovery approach, typically a benchmark of 25% with case-specific deviations, is easier. Sometimes it is used as a double-check on the lodestar, or the lodestar is used as a double-check on the percentage approach. Ultimately, the courts have cautioned that the fee must be based on the traditional factors of the time and labor expended by counsel; the magnitude and complexities of the litigation; the risk of litigation; the quality of representation; the requested fee in relation to the settlement; and public policy considerations, whether these are reflected in a hourly rate formula of the lodestar or a percentage. *Goldberger*, 209 F.3d at 50; In re Cabletron Systems Securities Litigation, 239 F.R.D. 30 (D.N.H. 2006); *Gascho, supra*; Judge Vaughn R. Walker & Ben Horwich, *The Ethical Imperative of a Lodestar Cross-Check: Judicial Misgivings about "Reasonable Percentage" Fees in Common Fund Cases*, 18 Geo. J. Legal Ethics 1453 (2005). There is also the question of whether a court may use its equitable discretion to opt for the common-fund percentage theory approach where an applicable statute provides for fee shifting. Haggart v. Woodley, 809 F.3d 1336 (Fed. Cir. 2016), *cert. denied*, 136 S.Ct. 2509 (2016).

APPENDIX: COUNTRY LODGE V. MILLER

■ ■ ■

Problem: Country Lodge v. Miller

This problem of a nuisance caused by an individual organic apple farmer provides a running problem that follows the key issues in the casebook. It stops at each juncture of a new key issue of Remedies to apply the legal standards to the same fact pattern.

1. Remedies in a Traditional Private Case

Miller owns an apple orchard where she recently built a plant to press and bottle apple cider. The cider press produces apple mash as waste. Last fall, in her first season of operation, she disposed of the waste by putting it into a pipe that empties into the Rural River. This cost her nothing while the cheapest alternative means of disposal would have cost $20,000 per year. The guests at the nearby, long-established Country Lodge disliked the sight of the apple mash in the water. As a result, Country Lodge lost $10,000 in profits that fall. In a suit Country Lodge brought against Miller, the judge found Miller's operation to be a nuisance, because her conduct was unreasonable and resulted in substantial harm to Country Lodge.

Consider the remedies that should be available to Country Lodge. Do not be constrained by what you think you know of the applicable precedent. What purpose does each remedy serve? Do you see any problem in achieving that purpose?

2. Remedies in a Public Law Case

How would your answer in *Country Lodge v. Miller* change if:

(a) Miller's pollution hurts people beyond Country Lodge?

(b) putting the apple mash in the river is not a common law nuisance but does violate a federal environmental statute?

(c) the violator of the statute is not Miller but rather a municipality that puts untreated municipal waste into the river?

(d) the court orders the municipality to build a sewage treatment plant and have it in operation in three years, but the city council does not appropriate the necessary funds?

(e) the city council appropriates the necessary funds, but makes them available on a schedule that would mean that the plant will not be operational for five years?

3. The Choice Between an Injunction and Damages

Country Lodge has requested an injunction: (a) requiring Miller to clean up the apple mash that washed ashore on its property last fall; and (b) prohibiting Miller from committing future nuisances. Miller urges the court to deny injunctive relief and instead give Country Lodge compensatory damages for both past and future harms. What should the court do?

So, for example, denying Country Lodge an injunction against future nuisances means that Miller may override Country Lodge's entitlement to be free from the nuisance by merely paying damages. Suppose that the court sets the damages at $10,000 annually, based upon an estimate of lost profits. Miller would obviously prefer this outcome to an injunction because it would cost her $20,000 annually to dispose of the waste without making a nuisance.

There are many reasons why Country Lodge may prefer an injunction. First, and most basically, Miller is taking Country Lodge's entitlement by paying compensation. In contrast, the Constitution's fifth and fourteenth amendments prohibit the taking of private property for *private* purposes, even if compensation is paid. Second, Country Lodge may believe that $10,000 annually underestimates its lost profits. Third, Country Lodge's owners may place a subjective value on a clean river that is not recoverable as damages.

Fourth, and finally, if Country Lodge gets an injunction, it might make a deal with Miller to trade the injunction for more than $10,000 annually. Miller would be better off paying any amount up to $20,000, and Country Lodge would be better taking any amount more than the value to it of a clean river. If that amount is less than $20,000, there is room for a deal. If a deal is made, the price that Miller will pay to Country Lodge will depend upon their respective negotiating skills and bargaining positions. Economists call the difference between what a seller (Country Lodge) and a buyer (Miller) each place on a right "gains from trade." Relegating Country Lodge to damages gives all of the gains from trade to Miller. Issuing an injunction gives Country Lodge some of these gains, if they make a deal. Country Lodge may think this only fair. On the other hand, Miller may view Country Lodge's demanding more than its subjective loss as extortion.

Miller has other reasons to prefer paying damages to an injunction. First, Miller may fail to get Country Lodge to agree to sell its entitlement. Second, Miller would be the target of what is, in essence, a mini-criminal statute aimed exclusively at her. Third, the court may draft an injunction that is quite broad, prohibiting her from otherwise legal activity. Fourth, should she happen to violate the injunction, Miller will have to pay Country Lodge's attorney's fees and will not have the option to have a jury, as she would in an ordinary civil suit for damages.

4. Defining the Rightful Position

Suppose the court found Miller liable because it is a private nuisance to put enough debris in the river to be visible.

(a) Country Lodge has asked for an injunction permanently barring Miller from placing any effluent into the river. Should the court grant such an injunction?

(b)   Would your answer change if the basis of liability was, instead of the common law of nuisance, a statute prohibiting placing effluent into a river without a permit?

(c)   Can the court include in the injunction an order for Miller to attend a two-hour course at the local community college on environmental values?

5.   The Threat of Harm

Should the court refuse to grant Country Lodge an injunction prohibiting future nuisances if:

(a)   Miller was just beginning to build her cider press and has not indicated how she will dispose of the apple mash?

(b)   Miller has put mash in the river, was found in violation, and then wrote Country Lodge a letter promising never again to put waste in the river?

(c)   Miller wrote such a letter and dismantled her cider press?

(d)   Miller made no promises but last fall's discharge of waste would not have caused any harm to Country Lodge except for unusual river conditions—conditions which occur only one year in a hundred?

6.   The Choice Between Legal and Equitable Remedies

(a)   Is Country Lodge barred from obtaining an injunction to prevent future water pollution because it might instead get a money judgment for compensatory damages?

(b)   Is Country Lodge barred from obtaining an injunction to require Miller to clean up the waste because it might get a money judgment for compensatory damages?

(c)   If Miller's pollution is a crime, could the prosecutor get an injunction against its repetition? Would it make a difference if the criminal penalty were a $50 fine or a $50,000 fine?

(d)   Suppose that Country Lodge contracts with Eco-cleaners, Inc., for removal of the apple mash from the river bank. The contract specifies that Eco-cleaners will reduce the concentration of apple mash on the bank to less than one part per ten thousand. After Eco-cleaners applies the usual clean-up techniques that it thought would do the job, the concentration is reduced, but still twice that specified in the contract. Eco-cleaners does not want to take any additional steps because the present concentration is neither visible nor attracts insects, and meeting the specifications would result in Eco-cleaners incurring a considerable loss on the contract. Country Lodge wants the contract carried out to the letter. Should Country Lodge's request for specific performance be granted by the court?

7.   Balancing the Equities

Recall that Miller set up her cider press to dump waste apple mash into the river in order to save $20,000 a year. Suppose that Country Lodge has satisfied all the prerequisites for injunctive relief. Miller asks the court to award damages rather than grant an injunction on the ground that the cost to her of complying is greater than the benefit that Country Lodge would derive from the injunction.

(a)   What result if the action is brought before the cider press is built (the action being ripe because Miller's intentions are clear)?

(b)   What result if compliance would cost Miller no more now than when she built the press and it generates sufficient profits to pay that cost?

(c)   What result if compliance would cost Miller not only $20,000 a year, but also an additional one-time expenditure of $50,000 to retrofit the cider press plant, which would have been unnecessary if she had built the press to avoid discharging effluent into the river in the first place? If these retrofit costs were $1,000,000? If these retrofit costs would put her out of business? Should the judge postpone the effective date of the injunctive relief by a month if doing so would reduce the retrofit cost from $50,000 to $5,000?

(d)   Should the court refuse to listen to Miller's claim of undue hardship if she had promised Country Lodge that there would be no nuisance? If she knew her planned conduct would be illegal?

(e)   Should the court be more likely to deny an injunction on the grounds of undue hardship if Country Lodge knew that Miller's operation would create a nuisance but did not try to prevent it before Miller began to build her cider press?

(f)   Should Miller be able to claim undue hardship if liability arises from her building the press on Country Lodge's land rather than creating a nuisance in the river? If liability arises from a contract to supply cider?

(g)   In deciding whether a hardship is undue, should the court consider the benefit to nonparties of stopping the pollution?

(h)   Should the court refuse to listen to Miller's claim of undue hardship if her liability arises from a constitutional prohibition instead of common law nuisance? From a statutory prohibition?

8.   Prophylactic Orders

Suppose that Country Lodge's rightful position is that Miller put into the river no more than 50 pounds of waste per week. Country Lodge asks that Miller be enjoined from putting any apple mash in the river on the grounds that it does not know how much is going into the river. Miller objects that she will then have to cart away not only the mash, at a cost of $20,000 per year, but also the water used to clean the cider press at an additional cost of $30,000 per year. Should the court grant Country Lodge's request?

9.   Drafting and Administering an Injunction

Assume that the trial court has found that Miller created a nuisance to Country Lodge by dumping too much of the unsightly apple mash waste into the Rural River. The court also finds that because Country Lodge does not have an adequate remedy at law, an injunction is the appropriate relief. According to the court, the test of a violation is whether apple mash is visible in the river as it flows past the Country Lodge property.

The following facts have been established at trial. Miller employs eighteen people. Miller and her employees usually dump apple mash into the river through a pipe leading from the apple press; occasionally they find it easier to use wheel barrows to dump excess apple mash into the river. During times of ordinary water flow, if Miller and her employees dump more than 50 pounds of apple mash per hour into the river, it is visible as the water passes by Country Lodge. However, the water flow varies greatly with the seasons and weather conditions, so there are times when just one pound of apple mash per hour is visible at Country Lodge and others when even 100 pounds per hour are not visible. There is equipment available at a cost of $28,000 that can meter the flow of apple mash through the pipe. In a prior case a few years ago, Miller was held in contempt of court for willfully violating an injunction, which was unrelated to water pollution.

(a) Who should draft the injunction? (b) What should be the precise terms of an injunction that would restore and protect Country Lodge's rightful position under these circumstances? (Try to draft the injunction). (c) How will the injunction be administered; in particular, how will the court know if Miller is violating the injunction?

10.   Determining Compliance with an Injunction

Suppose that the court prohibits Miller from dumping more than 500 pounds of apple mash waste into the river every week. In the alternative, suppose that the court permits Miller to dump apple mash into the river so long as it is not visible from the Country Lodge property. How can the court determine whether Miller is in compliance with either of these injunctions?

11.   Obtaining Release from an Injunction

For six months, Miller has obeyed the terms of a permanent injunction, which ordered her to conduct an expensive clean-up and banned any further dumping of apple mash waste in the river. Miller now seeks termination of the injunction. Country Lodge opposes the motion. What result? If the injunction is vacated and Country Lodge subsequently finds a small amount of apple mash in the river (but not as much as before the court issued the injunction originally), may the court sanction Miller for violating the injunction?

12.   Violating an Anticipated Order

In the early fall, the trial court denies an injunction against Miller discharging waste into the river. Country Lodge appeals. While the appeal is pending, Miller discharges waste into the river during the busy apple harvesting season. In the winter, the appellate court directs the trial court to grant the injunction. Is Miller in contempt?

13. Civil or Criminal Contempt

Miller is enjoined from putting anything in the river under a statute that prohibits discharges into the waters of the state without a permit. The court holds Miller in contempt for violating the order. Would it be improper for the court to sentence Miller to five days in prison after finding her guilty of contempt by clear and convincing evidence?

14. The Collateral Bar Rule

In the early fall, the trial court enjoins Miller from discharging waste into the river. Miller continues to discharge waste while she appeals. In the winter, the appellate court overturns the injunction. Is Miller guilty of criminal contempt for violating the injunction prior to the appellate court's action?

15. Injunctions That Coerce Persons Who Are Not Parties

Assume that a court has enjoined Miller to stop discharging apple mash.

(a) Would it be proper to enforce the injunction against Miller's employees, who are not parties, if they help her continue to discharge?

(b) Is Jones, who buys Miller's cider mill, bound by the injunction that the court issued against Miller?

(c) Suppose that the defendant is the Miller County Sewage District, a municipal corporation that operates a sewage treatment plant. Miller County's discharge into the river illegally contains toxic chemicals because some users of the sewage system flush them down the drain and the treatment plant presently has no way of removing them. The culprits are probably a small number of the many thousand factories and commercial buildings in the district. Their identity is, so far, unknown. The court decides not to enjoin all discharge from the treatment plant because this would make the county uninhabitable. Instead, it enjoins anyone from putting the toxic chemicals into the sewage system and warns that it will impose heavy sanctions on any person found to violate this order. Newspapers and radio and television stations prominently report the story and a copy of the injunction is mailed to every postal address in the district. Is the injunction binding against anyone other than Miller County?

16. Injunctions That Require the Cooperation of Public Officials

Suppose the court decides that the best of way to prevent nonparties from putting toxics in the sewage system is to make the Miller County Sewage District stop them.

(a) If the district has regulations forbidding such disposal but is not enforcing them, can the court compel it to enforce its regulations?

(b) If the state's highest court rules that the district lacks the authority, under state law, to promulgate the regulations and the state legislature refuses to grant the authority, can a federal court compel the district to promulgate the regulations, compel the state legislature to grant the district authority to promulgate the regulations, or itself promulgate regulations for the district?

17. Declaratory Judgment

Miller has operated her apple press for three years, disposing of the apple mash into the Rural River. Her downstream neighbor, Country Lodge, has complained to the newspaper about Miller's dumping, but has never approached Miller about it. Miller plans to enlarge her operation and to invest several thousand dollars in a new apple press that would discharge even more mash into the river.

If Miller sues Country Lodge, seeking a declaratory judgment that disposing of apple mash into the Rural River is not a nuisance and does not invade Country Lodge's rights as a downstream riparian owner, should the court rule on the dispute? Would your answer be different if:

(a) Country Lodge had never complained to anyone, and Miller were not contemplating a new press?

(b) Country Lodge has threatened Miller with suit each year, telling her that if she put apple mash in the river again it would get an injunction to stop her, but never following through on the threat?

On the original facts, if Country Lodge seeks a judgment declaring that the larger press and increased dumping will create a nuisance, should the court rule on that claim? Should the law be symmetrical, so that declaratory relief would be available to both or to neither?

18. The Damages Option

Suppose that when Miller began to build her facility, the owners of Country Lodge threatened to sue for an injunction prohibiting construction of the cider mill on the grounds that it might pollute the river. The owners of Country Lodge refrained from suing when Miller wrote them a letter that said:

I do not believe that my cider press will cause any negative environmental impact. Indeed, I share your belief that the river's integrity must be protected. If you allow construction to go forward, I will take whatever steps are reasonably necessary to protect the interest we all share in keeping our river pristine.

Using the five inquiries identified by Professor McCormick in the excerpt that follows, plan litigation strategies to maximize and minimize Country Lodge's damages. If Country Lodge is not successful in obtaining an injunction, but does prove that Miller is liable for the pollution, what damages should Country Lodge recover? If Country Lodge does obtain an injunction, should damages also be awarded?

19. Valuing the Plaintiff's Loss

Assume that the apple mash Miller dumped into Rural River was contaminated by pesticide. If someone had standing to sue for the harm done to the river as a natural resource, how would the damages be calculated?

20. Prejudgment Interest

The court has declared Miller's operation a nuisance and enjoined it. In addition, the court has awarded Country Lodge damages for: (1) the cost of restoring the riverfront to its original condition; (2) the profits Country Lodge lost; and (3) the Lodge owner's annoyance and discomfort. Should prejudgment interest be awarded on all or any part of the award.

21. Restitution for Benefits Conferred

Suppose that after Country Lodge threatened to sue Miller for polluting the river, Miller built settling ponds down river from her plant to clear the water. Because the ponds also remove silt from the river, the water flowing past Country Lodge now is even clearer and purer than it was before the apple mill began operation. For the first time in years, Country Lodge's guests are able to enjoy wading and swimming in the water. Can Miller recover in restitution for the benefit she has bestowed on Country Lodge? Can Miller recover in restitution from her property insurer, if the insurer would have been liable for any damages recovered by Country Lodge had the pollution been allowed to continue?

22. A Restitution Option?

During the first year of the cider mill's operation, Miller saved $20,000 by dumping her apple mash into the river instead of installing an alternative means of disposal. Country Lodge lost $10,000 as a result of the pollution. Assuming that Country Lodge can establish that dumping the apple mash was a nuisance, could Country Lodge seek restitution rather than tort damages? In the language of the case that follows, could Miller waive the tort of nuisance and sue Miller in assumpsit? If so, how would the award be measured?

23. Remedial Defenses: Plaintiff's Conduct

Country Lodge has sued, seeking to enjoin Miller from polluting the Rural River which flows from Miller's property past that of Country Lodge. Country Lodge also claims damages for loss of business, alleging that numerous customers have complained of the unsightly river in the fall when Miller discharges her apple mash. Miller first defends by claiming that Country Lodge has unclean hands since it, too, is discharging garbage into the river. Should Country Lodge be denied relief in the following circumstances:

a)   Country Lodge's discharges are only one-tenth the volume of Miller's?

b)   Miller, being upstream, is not directly affected by Country Lodge's discharges?

Would your answers be different if Country Lodge's discharges were a breeding ground for insects which harmed Miller's apples?

What if Miller had gone to Country Lodge before beginning the discharges, told Country Lodge what she planned to do, and Country Lodge said it had no objection to Miller discharging apple mash?

Assume Country Lodge's owner had read in the newspaper that Miller was about to install a big apple press and discharge mash into the river and that experience in a neighboring county showed that the discharge would be unsightly. If Country Lodge waited to sue until Miller starting discharging the apple mash, should that delay bar Country Lodge from obtaining relief? Should it matter whether the relief sought was damages or an injunction?

On the same set of facts, suppose the Environmental Protection Agency sued Miller for discharging apple mash without a permit; should EPA be barred from obtaining relief? Would it make a difference to your answer if Miller had applied to EPA for a discharge permit a year before but, despite a statutory requirement that EPA act on all permit applications within six months, EPA had failed to act because it considered other permit applications more important? What if EPA's Director of Water Pollution had erroneously, but in good faith, told Miller that she came within an exception to the statute and did not need a permit for her apple mash discharge?

24. Paying the Attorneys

Assume that Country Lodge prevails in its suit against Miller and wins a judgment for $8500 for lost profits. Country Lodge's attorney submits a bill for 28 hours of work at $100 per hour ($2800). If that bill is paid out of the judgment, has the law restored Country Lodge to its rightful position?

Now assume that Miller prevails because the court determines that she had a legal right to put biodegradable apple mash into the river. Miller's attorneys billed her $2000 to defend her in the suit Country Lodge brought. Should Country Lodge have to reimburse Miller for the cost of the defense?

INDEX

References are to Pages

ACCOUNTING FOR PROFITS
Generally, 521, 539, 569

ADDITUR
Generally, 396
Federal court, 509

ADMINISTRATIVE LAW
Remand as remedy, 38–40
Rightful position, 38–40
Ripeness, 306

ADMINISTRATOR
See also Receiver
Generally, 178–179

ALL WRITS ACT
Injunctions binding non violators, 360

ASSUMPSIT
See also Electing Restitution
Generally, 534–536

ATTORNEY'S FEES
Generally, 605–626
American rule, 605–610, 615
Bad faith, 607, 612, 615–616
Civil Rights Attorney's Fees Awards Act,
§ 1988, 610, 617–625
Common fund, 607–610, 626
Contempt, 257, 607
Contingency-fee cases, 625
Eleventh Amendment, 617
Equal Access to Justice Act, 611
Equitable exception, 607
Fee-Shifting Statutes, 610–616
Lodestar, 617–626
Measuring, 617–626
Percentage of recovery, 626
Prevailing parties, 325, 605, 607, 612–613,
615–626, 619
Private attorney general, 607, 614
Reasonable fee, 617, 619–621, 625–626

AVOIDABLE CONSEQUENCES
Generally, 332, 334, 340, 346–347, 349,
351–352

BALANCING THE EQUITIES
See also Injunctions; Preliminary
Injunctions
Generally, 33, 62, 79–97

BIVENS ACTION
Generally, 9–24, 325

CERTAINTY
Compensatory damages, 332, 334, 344–345
Contract damages, 316, 428–29, 431–32
Liquidated damages, 440–441
Preliminary Injunction, 159, 167
Specific performance, 128
Tort damages, 385, 420

CHANCELLOR
See also Equity
Generally, 27, 32, 94, 158

CIVIL CONTEMPT
See Contempt

CIVIL RIGHTS
See also *Bivens* Action
Attorney's fees, Section 1988, 610–611,
613–614, 619–620, 624–625
Declaratory judgment, 293
Education, 228
Elections and voting, 40–41, 321–322, 324
Employment discrimination, 37, 328
Enforcement, 89, 180
First Amendment, 25, 35–36, 73, 100, 103,
105, 108, 143, 161, 259–260, 268, 279,
282, 292, 318, 320, 322–323, 348
Housing discrimination, 244, 273–290
Injunctions, 8, 33, 60, 88
Irreparable Injury, 72
Nominal damages, 320, 625
Police misconduct, 42–47, 63, 66, 69–70,
180–182
Prison conditions, 4–5, 8, 21, 25, 48–60, 87,
197–198, 208, 231–233, 617
School desegregation, 5, 45, 85–88, 108–
127, 145, 174, 193, 209–217, 278
Section 1983 actions, 17, 19, 23–24, 43–44,
68, 161, 317–322
Tort reform, 406
Value of constitutional rights, 321

CLEAN UP JURISDICTION
Generally, 326

COLLATERAL BAR RULE
Generally, 259–268

COLLATERAL SOURCE RULE
Generally, 384–385

COLLECTION OF JUDGMENTS
Generally, 459–462
Attachment, 461
Execution, 460–461
Garnishment, 461
Turnover statutes, 461

COMMINGLED FUNDS
Tracing, 577–580, 582–584

CONSENT DECREE
Generally, 51, 61, 175, 187–192, 196,
220–221, 226, 231–233, 272,
274–175, 292, 618
Federal Consent Decree Fairness Act, 231
Interpretation and modification, 196–207
Successors in office, 221, 229–230

CONSTITUTIONAL TORTS
See *Bivens* Action; Civil Rights

CONSTRUCTIVE TRUSTS
See also Accounting for Profits;
Restitution; Unjust
Enrichment
Generally, 521, 539. 542, 544, 561–
576
Adequacy of legal remedy, 563
Bankruptcy, 570–571, 573, 577
Commingled funds, tracing, 582–583
Defined, 561–562
Express trusts distinguished, 569
Fraud, 521, 571–572
Tracing, 562–563, 574–584

CONTEMPT
See also Collateral Bar Rule
Generally, 3, 26–27, 128, 139, 171,
234–259, 261–264
Ability to comply, 243, 279
Attorney's fees, 257, 607
Civil and criminal, distinguished, 234, 239,
244, 255
Classification of, 234, 242–43, 256
Coercive civil, 234, 257
Compensatory, civil, 234, 256, 259
Criminal, 234–235, 239, 261
Elements of, 234
Fines, 218, 258
In personam, 242
Persons subject to, 145–146
Procedures, 258
Public officials, 269, 273–274, 277, 282–292
Purpose, 233–234
Specificity of order requirement, 171–172,
182, 233
Summary, 258

CONTRACTS
See also Damages; Liquidated
Damages; Restatement
(Second) of Contracts;
Specific Performance
Generally, 196, 302, 424, 433, 447,
536, 553, 563

Attorney's fees, 605
Avoidable consequences rule, 334
Bad faith breach, 467
Certainty, 334, 421
Consequential damages, 332, 428, 433
Construction contracts, 89, 560
Damages, 421–441
Declaratory judgment, 293
Efficient breach theory, 423–424
Emotional distress recovery, 421–422
Expectancy, 422, 430
Foreseeability, 332–333, 340, 342
Incidental damages, 427, 549–550
Lesser-of rule, 368
Losing contract, 560
Measure of damages, 352, 431
Mutuality of remedy, 129
Nominal damages, 325
Personal service, 78, 89, 128–129
Profit losses, 432–433
Punitive damages, 467, 477
Reliance damages, 422
Restitutionary recovery, 518, 522, 536,
548–560
Rightful position, 4, 315, 422
Uniform Commercial Code, 130–133, 332,
334, 342, 422, 427, 432–438

CONVERSION
Generally, 534, 538, 577–578

COPYRIGHT
Generally, 75, 132–133, 329, 595–598
Attorney's fees, 611–616
Injunctions, 75, 78
Remedial Defenses, 595–603
Restitution, 537–538
Statutory Damages, 329

COUNTRY LODGE V. MILLER
Problem, Appendix, 627–636

CRIMINAL CONTEMPT
See Contempt

CRIMINAL PROSECUTION
Injunction against, 313–314

DAMAGES
See also Economic Analysis of
Law; Personal Injury;
Prejudgment Interest
Generally, 315–462
Additur, 396, 509
Avoidable consequences, see that topic
Caps, 406–407
Collateral source rule, 384–385
Comparability review, 405
Compensatory damages, defined, 315–316,
323
Consequential damages, 331–334, 338, 342,
421, 427
See also Special Damages
Cost of repair, 353, 370
Earning capacity, 370, 394, 411–412, 459

Eggshell or thin-skull plaintiff, 333, 348
Emotional distress, see that topic
Foreseeability, see that topic
Future harm, 382
Gender discrimination, 412–413
General damages, 331–332, 338, 421, 431
Hedonic damages, 394
Incidental damages, 422, 427
Increased risk, 343, 345–346, 383
Jury argument, 399
Lesser-of rule, 360, 368
Liquidated damages, see Contracts, that
    topic
Loss of consortium, 323, 350–351, 390–392,
    401, 403–404, 421
Market value, see Value, that topic
Measurement, see that topic
Medical surveillance, 371, 374
Mitigation, duty of, see Avoidable
    Consequences
Nominal, see that topic
Non-pecuniary damages, 323, 368, 384,
    386, 392, 395–396, 400–401, 405–408,
    421–422, 431, 449, 510
    See also Emotional Distress; Loss of
        Consortium, this topic; Pain
        and Suffering, this topic
Offset, 334, 385, 454–456, 458
Pain and suffering, 323m 343, 352, 369,
    372–374, 387, 395, 400–401, 404, 406,
    421
Presumed, 321, 322n14
Property damage, 370, 375
Punitive Damages, see that topic
Purpose of, 319, 324
Race discrimination, 412–413
Redress, 10, 14, 25, 72, 324
Reliance, generally, 333, 422–423
Remittitur, 395–396, 399
Replacement cost, 355, 360, 362–363, 386
Restoration, 360–361
Section 1983, 319–320
Sentimental value, 353, 355n5, 356
Special damages, 331, 431
Survival, 350, 393–394, 421
    See also Wrongful Death
Wrongful death, see that topic

DECLARATORY JUDGMENT
    Generally, 218, 293–314
Adequacy rule, no requirement, 313
Actual controversy requirement, 294–306
Discretion, 306–312
Federal Declaratory Judgment Act, 294,
    308
Further relief, 294–295
Insurance cases, 303–304
Jury trial, 295
Nominal damages compared, 325–326
Reformation compared, 552
Ripeness, 306
Uniform Declaratory Judgment Act, 294

DEFENSES
See Estoppel; Laches; Unclean Hands;
    Waiver

DISCOUNT RATE
See Interest; Present Value

ECONOMIC ANALYSIS OF LAW
Balancing the equities, 168
Compensatory damages, 342, 395, 423
Efficiency, 84, 422–4223
Efficient breach, 422–423, 467
Inadequate remedy requirement, 168
Injunctions, 84
Nonpecuniary harm, 395
Preliminary Injunction, 165, 168

ECONOMIC HARM
    Generally, 323, 369, 383, 388, 391,
        478, 503
Loss of Services as, 386–392
Measuring, 353, 412, 420–421

ELECTIONS
See Civil Rights

ELECTION OF REMEDIES
Generally, 330–331, 550, 552

ELEVENTH AMENDMENT
    See also Immunity, Sovereign
Generally, 271–272, 278, 313, 442–443, 617

EMOTIONAL DISTRESS
    Generally, 21, 318–319, 323, 358,
        369–370, 373–374, 392, 458,
        594
Contract breach, 422
Fear of cancer, 371, 373, 382
Measuring, 395, 397–399
Wrongful death cases generally, 392–394

EMPLOYMENT
After-acquired evidence, 37
Back pay claims, 328–329
Damages for loss of, 392, 412
Discrimination, 5, 34–37, 40, 396, 519, 588
Specific performance, 128
Wrongful discharge, 396

ENVIRONMENTAL INJURY
CERCLA, 358–368
Endangered Species Act, 90–95, 149
Federal Water Pollution Control Act, 95
Injunction, statutorily mandated, 90–95
Oil spill, damages, 358–368
Restoration, 360–368

EQUITABLE LIENS
    See also Constructive Trusts;
        Restitution
Generally, 521, 539, 541–548, 577

EQUITABLE MONETARY RELIEF
Generally, 327

EQUITY
        See also Contempt; Injunctions;
           Laches; Unclean Hands
        Generally, 6, 17, 45, 58, 73, 96
Clean up doctrine, 326
Damages contrasted, 71, 139, 315, 330, 546
Equitable discretion, 27–29, 32, 153
Equitable monetary relief, 326–327, 449
Jurisdiction, 27–32, 71, 256, 327
Jury trial, 330
Maxims, 5, 71, 242, 576, 585–589
Merger of law and equity, 27, 72, 547
Rescission, 551–552
Restitution in equity, generally, 328, 517,
      520–521, 539, 542–546, 561–563, 569,
      576
        See also Accounting for Profits;
           Constructive Trusts; Equitable
           Liens

ESTOPPEL
        See also Equity
Generally, 28, 331, 586–587, 594–605

EXEMPLARY DAMAGES
See Punitive Damages

EXPECTANCY
See Contracts

FEDERAL RULES OF CIVIL
      PROCEDURE
Rule 2, 598, 603
Rule 8, 603
Rule 11, 249, 607, 611
Rule 23, 175
Rule 53, 174
Rule 60, 195, 199, 218–219
Rule 65, 141–144, 173, 182

FEDERALISM
        Generally, 25
Declaratory Relief, 313
Injunctions, 45–46, 100, 179, 182, 204,
      220–222, 226, 230, 270–271

FIRST AMENDMENT
See Civil Rights

FORESEEABILITY
        See also Hadley v. Baxendale
        Generally, 316, 332–334, 342
Pre-existing condition, eggshell skull, 333
Tort and contract rules compared, 342

FORFEITURE
Generally, 584

FRAUD
        Generally, 195
Punitive damages, 464, 467, 484, 507, 514
Restitution, 520, 549, 552–553, 572, 574

FULL FAITH AND CREDIT CLAUSE
Generally, 90

GARNISHMENT
Generally, 461

HADLEY V. BAXENDALE
Generally, 332, 338–342

HAMMURABI, CODE OF
Generally, 1, 480

IMMUNITY
        See also Eleventh Amendment
Legislative, 277–279, 282–284, 288
Official, 272–273, 292
Sovereign, 25, 271–272, 278, 537

IMPLIED CAUSES OF ACTION
Generally, 23–24

IN PARI DELICTO
        See also Unclean Hands
Generally, 585–586, 591

INADEQUATE REMEDY AT LAW
        See also Irreparable Harm;
           Irreparable Injury
        Generally, 62, 71–78, 88
Land contracts, 72
Multiplicity of suits, 72
Personal rights, 72
Rescission, 555, 561
Restitution, 561, 569
Specific Performance, 128, 134–135, 326

INCOME TAX
See Taxation of Damage Awards

INFLATION
        See also Present Value
Generally, 450–456, 458

INJUNCTIONS
Appeals from, 145–146
Balancing the equities, 79–128
Declaratory judgment compared, 293
Drafting, 170–175
Effect on third parties, 62, 78, 166
Efficient, 83–85
Enforcement, 233–293
        See also Contempt
Enforcement against government officials,
      233–293
Formulating and administering, 170–195
Inadequate Remedy at Law, see that topic
In personam, 27
Institutional reform, 176–187, 31–233
Jury trials, 28
Modification, 195–233
Mootness, 62, 64
Nature of, 27–32
Out of state activities, 90
Parties bound, 145
Practicality of enforcement, 89–90
Preliminary Injunctions, see that topic
Preventive, 33, 127, 270
Prohibitory, 250
Prophylactic injunctions, see that topic

Public interest, 33, 62, 74, 78, 86, 128, 151–152
Reparative injunctions, 33, 127, 270, 273
Rightful Position, see that topic
Ripeness, 62
School Desegregation, see Civil Rights, that topic
Scope, 3–4, 47, 55, 79, 111, 118–119, 174
Specific Performance, see that topic
Specificity of order, 172
Structural Injunctions, see that topic
Tax Injunction Act, 73, 314
Temporary restraining order, see that topic
Termination, 209–217, 231–232
Threat of harm, 62–71
Undue hardship, 79–82

INTEREST
Compound or simple, 444–446
Inflation and, 458
Legal or market rate, 449
Liquidated and unliquidated claims, 449
Nonpecuniary harm, 449
Postjudgment, 449
Prejudgment, 442–450

IRREPARABLE HARM
See also Equity; Inadequate
    Remedy at Law
Generally, 62–63, 68, 71–75, 78, 135,
    143, 151–52, 159, 162–163, 165,
    168
Restitution, 564–565

IRREPARABLE INJURY
See Irreparable Harm

JUDGMENTS
See also Collection of
    Judgments
Generally, 4
Enforcement, 90, 459–462
See also Contempt
Modification of, 195, 218–219, 229
Money judgments, 242
Periodic payment of, 385

JURY TRIAL
Generally, 327, 329–330, 396, 407,
    509
Contempt cases, 244–249, 254, 258–259
Damage awards, 509
Declaratory judgment, 295
Preliminary Injunction, 142

LACHES
See also Equity
Generally, 448, 585, 587, 591–599,
    602
Estoppel compared, 600
Statutes of limitation compared, 587, 596,
    598

LIQUIDATED DAMAGES
Generally, 133, 316, 422, 433–441, 443

LOST VOLUME SELLER
Generally, 432

MAGNA CARTA
Generally, 10

MEDIATORS
Generally, 178, 190, 245

MENTAL ANGUISH
See Emotional Distress

MENTAL DISTRESS
See Emotional Distress

MONEY JUDGMENTS
See Judgments

MONITORS
Generally, 172–179

MUTUALITY OF REMEDY
Generally, 129

NOMINAL DAMAGES
Generally, 317, 320n11, 325–326,
    369, 551, 566
Attorney's fees, 626–626
Declaratory judgments, compared, 326
Negligence, 325
Punitive damages, relation, 326, 466, 482

NUISANCE
Damages, 3, 372–373
Injunction, 3, 72, 82–83, 137
Problem, 627–635

OFFICIAL IMMUNITY
See Immunity

PATENT
Generally, 73–78, 99, 295–296, 465
Attorney's fees, 616
Declaratory judgment, 295, 302, 304
Injunctions, 73–78, 99, 145, 209

PERSONAL INJURY
See also Emotional Distress;
    Damages
Attorney's fees, 385
Avoidable consequences, 349
Damages, 394, 412, 415
Declaratory judgment, 309–310
Per diem arguments for, 400
Wrongful death, 350, 393

PRELIMINARY INJUNCTIONS
See also Federal Rule of Civil
    Procedure 65
Generally, 64, 89, 141, 144, 147, 164–
    165, 170, 173, 268
Appealability, 145
Balancing the hardships, 78, 151
Economic test, 165–169
Public interest, 153, 159–160
Security requirement, 143–144
Sliding scale test, 159, 168

Standards for issuance, 146, 151–152, 163
Status quo, preservation of, 146, 159
Temporary restraining order,
    distinguished, 141, 144

PRESENT VALUE
    Generally, 450–457
Discount rate, 4457–458
In contract cases, 134
In tort cases, 412

PRISON LITIGATION REFORM ACT
    Generally, 8, 25, 208, 231–233
Attorney's fees, 617
Injunctions limited by, 48, 59
Damages barred by, 21

PROBLEMS
Country Lodge v. Miller, 627–637
Moore v. Regents, 573
Tracing Problem, 584
Unauthorized Merchants, 164

PROHIBITION, WRIT OF
Injunction, compared, 139

PROPHYLACTIC INJUNCTION
    See also Injunctions
    Generally, 33, 41, 45, 60, 97, 100,
        107, 233, 270
Defined, 33, 97–100

PROPORTIONALITY
    Generally, 55, 323, 346, 435, 466,
        504, 512–513, 625
Attorney's fees, 626–626

PUBLIC LAW LITIGATION
Generally, v, 4–9, 12, 228, 254, 591

PUNITIVE DAMAGES
    Generally, 463–516
Actual damage requirement, 550
Civil rights cases, 328
Compared to compensatory damages, 317,
    319
Contract breach, 467
Defined, 466
Due process, 496–517
Empirical studies, 494
Excessive fines, 465
Eighth Amendment, 465, 494
History, 480
Insurance, 477–478
Malice defined, 471–472
Mass torts, 467
Measuring, 477
Nominal damages, sufficiency, 326
Products liability, 467
Purpose, 463–464, 466, 480–481
Ratio to actual damages, 477, 487–489, 515
Remittitur, 509
Restitution, 549, 552
Statutory reforms, 482, 495
Theories of punishment, 463

Treble damages, 464–465
Vicarious liability, 492
Wealth of defendant, 508

QUASI-CONTRACT
    See also Restitution
Generally, 521, 534, 536–537, 539, 551, 569

RECEIVERS
Generally, 28, 50, 177, 179–180, 270, 292

REFORMATION
Generally, 552

REMITTITUR
    Generally, 395–396, 399, 509
Punitive damages, 477, 509

REPLEVIN
Generally, 131, 326, 521, 534

RESCISSION
    See also Restitution
Generally, 521, 539, 548–552, 554–556, 560

RESTATEMENT OF RESTITUTION
    Generally, 518, 521, 539, 584
Section 1, 527, 534
Section 123, 581
Section 215, 544

RESTATEMENT (FIRST) OF
    CONTRACTS
Section 342, 467

RESTATEMENT (SECOND) OF
    CONFLICT OF LAWS
Section 102, 90

RESTATEMENT (SECOND) OF
    CONTRACTS
Section 342, 467
Section 344, 422, 424
Section 347, 335, 422
Section 350, 334
Section 351, 333
Section 352, 334, 431
Section 355, 467
Section 356, 433
Section 360, 128
Section 362, 128
Section 364, 128
Section 365, 128
Section 366, 89, 128
Section 371, 549, 560
Section 373, 560

RESTATEMENT (SECOND) OF TORTS
Section 461, 348
Section 906, 384
Section 908, 466, 481, 486, 504
Section 912, 334
Section 918, 334
Section 920, 335
Section 924, 370
Section 928, 370

Section 929, 363n37, 370, 372–373
Section 942, 78
Section 951, 78

RESTATEMENT (SECOND) OF TRUSTS
Section 207, 449

RESTATEMENT (THIRD) OF RESTITUTION
Generally, 517–520
Section 1, 518, 520
Section 39, 537, 561
Section 51, 538
Section 55, 562, 572
Section 56, 548
Section 59, 584

RESTITUTION
See also Constructive Trust; Equitable Lien; Quasi-Contract; Restatement of Restitution; Restatement (Third) of Restitution
Generally, 517–585
Apportionment of profits, 538
Assumpsit, 536
Choice principle, 520, 534
Constructive Trusts, see that topic
Contract breach, 548–561
Damages, compared, 330, 422
Defendant's profits, 517
Disgorgement, 517, 520
Equitable lien, see that topic
Equitable Restitution, 540, 561–574
Fraud, 520, 572
Gift principle, 520, 528
Liability for, 520, 522, 536
Losing contract, 560
Measurement, 536–538, 549, 561
Mistake, generally, 520, 522, 572
Opportunistic breach, 424, 537, 561
Procedures, 521
Punitive damages, 552
Rescission, see that topic
Quasi-contract, see that topic
Tracing, generally, 563, 574–585
Unjust Enrichment, 517–518, 520, 527–528
Waiving the tort, 534, 536

RIGHTFUL POSITION
See also Balancing the Equities
Generally, 2, 33, 37–38, 256
Contract claims, 422
Damages, 315, 323, 332, 335, 383, 422
Defendants', 2, 517, 521. See also Restitution
Injunctions, 33–60
Microsoft litigation, 60–61
Plaintiffs', 2, 33, 40, 230
Awarding less than, 62, 79–96
Awarding more than, 97–109

SEPARATION OF POWERS
Generally, 25, 95, 100, 232, 269–270

SEPTEMBER 11TH FUND
Generally, 412, 415, 419–421

SOVEREIGN IMMUNITY
See Eleventh Amendment; Immunity

SPECIAL MASTERS
Generally, 51, 174, 179–180, 416

SPECIFIC PERFORMANCE
See also Contract; Equity; Injunctions
Generally, 6, 28, 128–141

STANDING
Generally, 22, 66, 70

STATUTES OF LIMITATIONS
Generally, 537, 585, 597–599

STRUCTURAL INJUNCTION
See also Injunctions
Generally, 7–8, 33, 58, 60, 67, 292
Defined, 33, 58

SUBROGATION
Generally, 384, 521, 539–540, 547

TAXATION OF DAMAGE AWARDS
Generally, 458–459

TEMPORARY RESTRAINING ORDER
See also Federal Rule of Civil Procedure 65; Injunctions
Generally, 141–143, 161, 261
Appealability, 267
Ex parte orders, 143
Irreparable harm, 143
Notice requirements, 142

TORT REFORM
Collateral source rule, 384–385
Constitutionality, 495–496
Damage caps, 406–407
Medical malpractice, 406, 496
Periodic payment of judgments, 385
Punitive damages, 493–497

TORT
See Conversion, Constitutional Torts, Damages, Nuisance, Personal Injury, Trespass, Wrongful Death

TRACING
See Constructive Trust

TREBLE DAMAGES
See Punitive Damages, this topic

UNCLEAN HANDS
Generally, 28, 585–586, 588–591

UNJUST ENRICHMENT
See Restitution

VALUE
Generally, 3, 137, 323, 353–355
Constitutional right, 317, 320
Contingent valuation, 365
Diminution in, 82, 353–354, 360, 372
Economic waste, 369
Lesser of rule, 368
Market value, 132, 332, 353, 357, 360, 370
Measuring, 352–369
Repair cost, 353, 370
Replacement, 360
Sentimental value, 353
Use value, 360
Value to owner, 358

WAIVER
Generally, 585, 587

WRITS, JUDICIAL
Attachment, 461
Ejectment, 326
Execution, 460
Habeas Corpus, 139
Mandamus, 139
Prohibition, 139
Replevin, 326

WRONGFUL DEATH
Generally, 346, 386, 383–395

Jenna Thomas
(304) 993 - 7668